The Law of Sexual Offences in Scotland

Paul Harvey

Alan Turnbull
(The Rt. Hon. Lord Turnbull)

Bloomsbury Professional

LONDON • DUBLIN • EDINBURGH • NEW YORK • NEW DELHI • SYDNEY

BLOOMSBURY PROFESSIONAL

Bloomsbury Publishing Plc

50 Bedford Square, London, WC1B 3DP, UK
1385 Broadway, New York, 10018, USA
Bloomsbury Publishing Ireland Ltd
29 Earlsfort Terrace, Dublin 2, D02 AY28, Ireland

2

Reprinted 2025

British Library Cataloguing-in-Publication Data

A catalogue record for this book is available from the British Library.

ISBN: PB: 978-1-52652-802-5
Epdf: 978-1-52652-804-9
Epub: 978-1-52652-803-2

Typeset by Evolution Design & Digital Ltd (Kent)
Printed and bound in Great Britain by CPI Group (UK) Ltd, Croydon, CR0 4YY

MIX
Paper | Supporting responsible forestry
FSC® C013604

For product safety related questions, contact productsafety@bloomsbury.com

The Law of Sexual Offences in Scotland

Foreword

The prosecution of sexual cases in the High Court has significantly increased in recent years, constituting the vast majority of High Court trials. The number of cases under Sheriff Court solemn procedure is also significant. The legal landscape in which sexual offences are prosecuted has changed substantially in the past 15 years, starting with the Sexual Offences (Scotland) Act 2009, applicable from the end of 2010, which fundamentally changed the nature of sexual offences in this jurisdiction. This change in the substantive law has been accompanied by numerous changes procedurally and evidentially, whether in the form of legislation such as the Abusive Behaviour and Sexual Harm (Scotland) Act 2016; and the Witnesses (Criminal Evidence) (Scotland) Act 2019; by Practice Notes such as Practice Note No 1 of 2017; and No 1 of 2019; or following my report on Improving the Management of Sexual Offence Cases.

These measures have, in combination, resulted in a rapid and considerable increase in the use of commissions to take the evidence of vulnerable witnesses ahead of trial; with written questions for children, where appropriate; written directions for jurors; the introduction of detailed directions on rape myths, misconceptions and stereotypes; Ground Rules hearings with enhanced case management; and the adoption of trauma informed practice in the management of sexual offences.

Added to this, there has been a long overdue emphasis on the careful and proper application of the terms of the rape shield legislation contained in sections 274 and 275 of the Criminal Procedure (Scotland) Act 1995; and a major restatement of the law of corroboration in the case of *Lord Advocate's Reference No 1 of 2023*.

As the number of cases has risen, they have often become more serious and more complex. This pattern of growth, both as to volume and complexity, is likely to continue. Further change, legislative or otherwise, may be anticipated. Practice Note No 1 of 2017 has just been modernised and superseded by Practice Note No 1 of 2024; and further changes are ahead under the current Victims, Witnesses, and Justice Reform (Scotland) Bill.

Against that background the publication of this work by a retired senior judge with unparalleled experience in the criminal law, and an experienced practitioner, could not be more timely. The modern practitioner more than ever needs a pilot to steer them through the changing landscape, to help them keep abreast of developments, and to understand the philosophical foundations of the law. They are fortunate in having this invaluable work to rely on.

The Rt Hon Lady Dorrian
Lord Justice Clerk

Preface

Our aim in writing this book has been to provide a guide:

- (i) to all of the sexual offences currently prosecuted in the Scottish courts and not just those in the Sexual Offences (Scotland) Act 2009;
- (ii) to those offences that, though not strictly sexual offences, are more often committed against intimate partners, often at the same time as serious sexual offences;
- (iii) to the law of evidence as it applies to sexual offences cases;
- (iv) to the types of expert evidence most commonly seen in sexual offences cases;
- (v) to the investigation, prosecution and trial of sexual offences; and
- (vi) to sentencing in such cases.

In the fourth of these, we have been immensely fortunate to have the contributions of two highly regarded experts in their fields, Dr Deborah Wardle and Dr Nighean Stevenson, who kindly agreed to write Chapters 15 and 16, on medical evidence and on forensic-scientific evidence respectively. We would like to record our gratitude for their expert contributions and for the time they gave to writing them.

We are also grateful for the support we received from Paula O'Connell and Abby Somers at Bloomsbury Professional and to our copy editor, Chris Harrison, for his skill and patience in editing the initial manuscript.

A number of distinguished practitioners took time which they could little spare to read and comment on draft chapters. These were: Alan Cameron KC, Ashley Edwards KC, Isabella Ennis KC, Emma Forbes, Lisa Gillespie KC, Michael MacIntosh, Shona McJannett, Scott McKenzie, Dominic Scullion and the Lord Justice Clerk, Lady Dorrian. We are very grateful for the time they sacrificed and the comments they gave. Any errors remain our responsibility.

We have endeavoured throughout simply to state the law as we believe it to be. Where there are conflicting authorities on a subject, or simply an absence of judicial interpretation of particular statutory provisions, we have attempted to state what we think the correct position is. When we have done so, the views we have expressed are personal.

We have generally tried to state the law as at 30 August 2024 but have been able to accommodate some recent developments. These include the nine-judge decision in *Lord Advocate's References Nos 2 and 3* [2024] HCJAC 43, 30 October 2024, and the amendments which the Scottish Government intends to introduce to the Victims, Witnesses, Justice Reform (Scotland) Bill, presently before the Scottish Parliament, at Stage 2 of the Parliament's consideration of the Bill. All references to sections of the Bill are to the Bill as introduced. References to the Jury Manual and the Preliminary Hearings e-Bench Book are to the 29 July 2024 and 16 July 2024 editions respectively. References to Rook and Ward (*Rook and Ward on Sexual Offences and Practice*) are to the sixth edition, 2021, Sweet & Maxwell.

Our final and deepest thanks are to Dimana and Dorothy.

PH and ADT
Edinburgh
November 2024

Contents

Table of Statutes

[References are to paragraph number]

Table of Statutory Instruments

[References are to paragraph number]

Table of International and European Union Instruments

[*References are to paragraph number*]

Table of Cases

[*References are to paragraph number*]

I

J

K

L

M

Part I

Sexual Offences

Chapter 1

The Scottish courts and jurisdiction over sexual offences

INTRODUCTION

1.01 This chapter sets the jurisdiction of the Scottish courts to try sexual offences cases, that is, which courts have the power and authority to try such cases, and which people and places fall within those courts' jurisdiction. We consider first the three levels of jurisdiction within the Scottish criminal courts and which level of jurisdiction can try which types of sexual offences. We also note the changes to this system that will be introduced if the Victims, Witnesses, and Justice Reform (Scotland) Bill becomes law, and the Sexual Offences Court comes into existence. We then set out various aspects of the Scottish courts' jurisdiction to try sexual offences that take place in Scotland and, finally, the Scottish courts' jurisdiction to try sexual offences that take place outside Scotland.

THE CURRENT POSITION: THE THREE LEVELS OF JURISDICTION

1.02 If enacted, the Victims, Witnesses, and Justice Reform (Scotland) Bill currently before the Scottish Parliament will create a national Sexual Offences Court to try sexual offences. We summarise the current position in this section and the changes the court will bring in the following section.

1.03 Sexual offences are currently tried in the ordinary criminal courts, at the three levels of jurisdiction that exist in those courts: (i) at summary level (that is, either in the sheriff court, before a sheriff or summary sheriff sitting alone; or the Justice of the Peace (JP) Court, before a summary sheriff or one or more justices); (ii) before a sheriff and jury in the sheriff court; and (iii) in the High Court of Justiciary, before a judge of the High Court and a jury.[1] Compared with other jurisdictions,

[1] The first is known as 'summary proceedings' and the charges against the accused are contained in a complaint. The second two are known as 'solemn proceedings' and the charges are contained in an indictment. Summary proceedings are thus often referred to as 'proceedings on complaint', and solemn proceedings are often referred to as 'proceedings on indictment'.

there are few rules in Scotland as to which level of jurisdiction should try a case. The few that do exist create a relatively simple and workable system for the allocation of cases. We set out the three main rules that apply, in so far as they relate to sexual offences cases.

1.04 The first rule is that only the High Court of Justiciary can try rape cases. That was so when rape was a crime at common law, and remains now that rape is an offence under section 1 of the Sexual Offences (Scotland) Act 2009 ('the 2009 Act'). When proposing the legislation that ultimately became the 2009 Act, the Scottish Law Commission (SLC) proposed (and the Scottish Parliament agreed) that the new offence of rape of a young child, contrary to section 18 of the 2009 Act, should also be tried only in the High Court because it was a particular instance of rape.[2] The High Court's exclusive jurisdiction over rape at common law and rape under sections 1 and 18 of the 2009 Act is now enshrined in section 3(6) of the Criminal Procedure (Scotland) Act 1995.[3] These three sexual offences, rape at common law, rape under section 1 and rape of a young child under section 18, are now the only three sexual offences that are within the exclusive jurisdiction of the High Court.

1.05 There is no legal requirement for the offence of engaging in a course of abusive behaviour, contrary to section 1 of the Domestic Abuse (Scotland) Act 2018, to be prosecuted in the High Court if one of the incidents in the alleged course of abusive behaviour would amount to the crime of rape if it were in a separate charge (see *McKenzie v HM Advocate* 2024 JC 121) but as a matter of Crown policy, it generally will be. There is no requirement for attempted rapes to be prosecuted in the High Court, though particularly serious ones will be. By implication, any section 1 charge under the 2018 Act which includes, in effect, an allegation of attempted rape need not be prosecuted in the High Court.

1.06 The common law crime of indecent assault, where it involves the non-consensual penile penetration of a man's anus before 1 December 2010 (the date on which the 2009 Act entered into force), will also, as a matter of Crown policy, be prosecuted in the High Court. This preserves gender parity with common law rape as it existed before the 2009 Act (which could only be committed against a woman) and rape in the 2009 Act (which, for non-consensual oral or anal penetration with the penis, can be committed against a man or woman). This has the effect of ensuring that all forms of rape, whether committed against a man or a woman and whether committed before or after the entry into force of the 2009 Act, are prosecuted in the High Court.

1.07 The second rule is that, with certain exceptions (notably, for present purposes, common law rape),[4] all common law offences can be tried either on

2 Para 7.15 of its final report.

3 Which provides that it shall be lawful to indict in the sheriff court all crimes except these three offences, and murder, treason, and breach of duty by magistrates.

4 The other exceptions are murder, treason, breach of duty by magistrates (because all three crimes fall within the exclusive jurisdiction of the High Court), and deforcement of messengers.

indictment or summarily. This means that the few remaining common law sexual offences can be tried on indictment or summarily, depending on the seriousness of the conduct alleged.

1.08 The third rule is that all modern statutes which create a criminal offence specify that the offence: (i) may be tried only summarily; (ii) may be tried on indictment only; or (iii) may be tried either summarily or on indictment. None of the sexual offences contained in the principal sexual offences statutes are summary-only offences. A handful are indictable only, such as rape as above; sexual assault by penetration, contrary to section 2 of the 2009 Act; and sexual assault on a young child by penetration, contrary to section 19 of the 2009 Act. This means that most sexual offences in Scotland are triable both at summary level and on indictment.

1.09 To the extent that an accused might be alleged to have committed a summary offence at the same time as a serious sexual offence, section 292(6) of the Criminal Procedure (Scotland) Act 1995 provides that an offence that may be tried only summarily can instead be tried on an indictment, if it can be competently libelled as an additional or alternative charge on that indictment. It is common to see relatively minor charges on indictments in sexual offences cases because of the rule against leading evidence of a crime not libelled. For instance, if the Crown wishes to lead evidence that the accused gave the complainer drugs (or took drugs with her) before raping her, an appropriate charge under the Misuse of Drugs Act 1971 will have to appear on the indictment.[5]

1.10 Beyond these three main rules, the decision on whether a case will be prosecuted at summary, sheriff and jury, or High Court level is for the Crown. That decision, as with all decisions the Crown takes, must follow the Prosecution Code and the public-interest considerations set out in it. There are 13 such public-interest considerations in the code.[6] One of them is the powers of the court on conviction. As such, the likely sentence for the offence that the court will impose is one factor (though not the only or even paramount factor) that the Crown must consider in deciding at which level the case should be prosecuted. At summary level, the maximum sentence is 60 days' imprisonment in the JP Court or 12 months' imprisonment in the sheriff court. At sheriff-and-jury level, the maximum sentence

5 For the rules on such evidential charges, see Chapter 13 at **13.54**.

6 The 13 public interest considerations are: (i) the nature and gravity of the offence; (ii) the impact of the offence on the victim and other witnesses; (iii) the age, background and personal circumstances of the accused; (iv) the age and personal circumstances of the victim and other witnesses; (v) the attitude of the victim; (vi) the motive for the crime; (vii) the age of the offence; (viii) mitigating circumstances; (ix) the effect of prosecution on the accused; (x) the risk of further offending; (xi) the availability of a more appropriate civil remedy; (xii) the powers of the court; and (xiii) public concern. The Code also requires prosecutors to take account of legal considerations (whether the conduct is a crime, any legal impediments to prosecution, and compatibility with international law) and evidential considerations (whether there is sufficient admissible evidence that is credible and reliable). https://www.copfs.gov.uk/publications/prosecution-code/html/.

is five years' imprisonment.[7] At High Court level, the maximum sentence is life imprisonment. The Crown's assessment of the likely sentence is based principally on two considerations: (i) the seriousness of the offence (that is, the intrinsic seriousness of a particular offence and whether the offence is alleged to have been committed in a more or less serious way); and (ii) the accused's criminal record because having committed analogous offences will normally increase any sentence.

1.11 One of the reasons the Scottish system of three levels of jurisdiction generally works well is the power of the sheriff, in sheriff-and-jury cases, to remit a case for sentencing to the High Court if he or she considers that the sentencing power of five years' imprisonment is inadequate: section 195 of the 1995 Act. Under section 195, a sheriff in a sheriff-and-jury case can also remit a case to the High Court for sentencing if it appears that the criteria for the imposition of an order for lifelong restriction (OLR) are met, this being a sentence only the High Court can impose.[8] OLRs and the criteria for their imposition are considered in Chapter 20: Sentencing in sexual offences cases.

THE SEXUAL OFFENCES COURT

1.12 If the Victims, Witnesses, and Justice Reform (Scotland) Bill is enacted, it will create the Sexual Offences Court (SOC), a Scotland-wide court with the power to try any sexual offence which is triable on indictment. The Bill currently defines 'sexual offence' to cover every offence considered in this work, save for human trafficking cases with a sexual element, and obscene material, extreme pornography and indecent images offences. This includes offences under section 1 of the Domestic Abuse (Scotland) Act 2018 that have a substantial sexual element. Judges are to be appointed to the court by the Lord Justice General, and the court will have a president and vice president, who can be the Lord Justice General and Lord Justice Clerk or other judges of the court. Cases will be able to be transferred out of the ordinary courts to the SOC on the application of the prosecutor or joint application of the prosecutor and accused but it will also be possible for an accused to be cited to attend a diet of the SOC (that is, it appears, simply be indicted in the SOC by the Crown). There is similar provision for cases to be transferred out of the SOC to the High Court of Justiciary or sheriff court. The Bill also makes provision for the procedures of the 1995 Act to apply to the SOC as though the proceeding were taking place in the High Court of Justiciary, though it also makes specific amendments to the 1995 Act for proceedings in the SOC, most notably on the vulnerable witnesses provisions contained in Part 12 of the 1995 Act. These are considered in Chapter 17. The SOC will have the sentencing powers of the High Court of Justiciary.

7 With the power, when imposing an extended sentence, to impose a custodial term of five years and an extension period not exceeding five years: s 210A(6) of the 1995 Act. Extended sentences in sexual offences cases are considered in Chapter 20.

8 S 210F of the 1995 Act.

TERRITORIAL JURISDICTION

1.13 There are three principal bases for Scottish courts to exercise jurisdiction over persons accused of offences: (i) the offence has been committed within Scotland; (ii) the offence is a cross-border offence and the common law rules on jurisdiction apply to give the Scottish courts jurisdiction; and (iii) the offence has been committed outside Scotland and legislation expressly allows for the Scottish courts to try that particular offence when it is committed outside Scotland (extra-territorial jurisdiction). For the first two, the rules on jurisdiction are general, but we highlight particular considerations that apply to sexual offences. For the third, specific rules apply to sexual offences, which are a result of the progressive extension of the extra-territorial jurisdiction for sexual offences by the Westminster and Scottish Parliaments. We consider each of these three bases for jurisdiction below.

(i) Offences committed within Scotland

1.14 In most cases, the jurisdiction of the Scottish courts to try sexual offences will be uncontroversial. The majority of sexual offences are 'contact' offences (that is, offences involving physical contact between the accused and complainer), and it will be clear that the offence has been committed (or alleged to have been committed) at a particular place in Scotland. In those circumstances, the following rules on jurisdiction apply and they generally do so without controversy.

1.15 The High Court of Justiciary has jurisdiction over the whole of Scotland and, by section 3(2) of the 1995 Act, may sit at any place in Scotland. Sheriff courts have jurisdiction over offences committed within their sheriffdom.[9] Section 4(3) of the 1995 Act makes clear that where an offence is alleged to have been committed in one district in a sheriffdom it is competent (that is, lawful) to try that offence in a sheriff court in any other district in that sheriffdom.[10] Thus a sexual offence committed in Edinburgh (one district in the sheriffdom of Lothian and Borders) can be tried either in the Edinburgh Sheriff Court or in the sheriff courts in Jedburgh, Livingston and Selkirk (other districts in that sheriffdom).

1.16 For 'non-contact' sexual offences, that is, offences not involving physical contact, such as communicating indecently with someone, contrary to section 7 of the 2009 Act, in addition to the above rules, the time-honoured rule in *Lipsey v Mackintosh*[11] will apply: that offences committed by sending communications from one place to another may be tried in any court having jurisdiction over either place. The rules on proper specification of the place of a criminal offence in a complaint or indictment are set out in Chapter 13, but generally, in such cases the Crown

9 And all rivers, etc, in or adjoining that sheriffdom: s 4(1) of the 1995 Act.

10 There are six sheriffdoms: Glasgow & Strathkelvin; Grampian, Highland & Islands; Lothian & Borders; North Strathclyde; South Strathclyde; Dumfries & Galloway; and Tayside, Central & Fife.

11 (1913) 7 Adam 182.

will establish jurisdiction on the basis of the place the complainer has said he or she received the communications and the Crown enjoys an exceptional latitude in specifying that place.[12]

1.17 The situation often arises where a series of sexual offences are alleged to have been committed in different places, either against the same partner over a long period of time or against a series of ex-partners. For High Court prosecutions, this situation is addressed by the rule above that the High Court has jurisdiction over the whole of Scotland. For prosecutions in the JP and sheriff courts, this is addressed by sections 9(4) and 10 of the Criminal Procedure (Scotland) Act 1995. Section 9(4) provides that where several offences, which, if committed in one sheriff court district, could be tried together, are alleged to have been committed in different districts, the accused may be tried for all or any of the offences under one indictment or complaint in any one of those districts. Section 10 allows the Lord Advocate to determine which district a prosecution should take place in when a person is alleged to have committed a crime or crimes in more than one sheriff court district. This applies where: (i) a crime is committed partly in one sheriff court district and partly in another; (ii) crimes are connected but committed in different districts; or (iii) crimes have been committed in different districts in succession and, if committed in one district, could have been tried together.[13]

1.18 There are a number of other miscellaneous rules that supplement these principal rules on the exercise of territorial jurisdiction. Many are arcane and rarely applied at all, still less in sexual offences cases (such as the rules on jurisdiction over the territorial waters and over offshore installations on the continental shelf). We mention two that occasionally arise in sexual offences cases.

1.19 First, like any other offence, a sexual offence committed on an aircraft over Scotland is within Scotland's territorial jurisdiction. The same is true: (i) for an act committed on a British-controlled aircraft flying elsewhere, if that act would be an offence if the aircraft were over the United Kingdom; and (ii) for any foreign aircraft where its next landing is in the United Kingdom and the act would also be an offence in the country where it is registered: section 92 of the Civil Aviation Act 1982. This jurisdiction is occasionally exercised to try cases of mid-air sexual assault against passengers and cabin crews.

1.20 Second, allegations are occasionally made that a member of the Armed Forces or a civilian subject to service discipline has committed a sexual offence whilst in Scotland (though not in any greater proportion to other types of offences occasionally alleged against them or in any greater proportion to sexual offences

12 *K (M) v PF, Kilmarnock* [2021] SAC (Crim) 3.

13 The two provisions substantially overlap and the reason for having two such sections is unclear. To the extent that they are different, they are different in two ways. First, s 9(4) acts to establish jurisdiction; s 10 provides the Lord Advocate the authority to determine where the prosecution should take place. Second, while s 9 only applies to separate offences, s 10 applies to both separate offences and to a single crime committed partly in one sheriff court district and partly in another (sometimes referred to as a *crimen continuum* or continuing crime).

alleged against the general population). In such cases, the Scottish criminal courts enjoy concurrent jurisdiction with the service courts (the Court Martial or the Service Civilian Court).[14] It is for the procurator fiscal (or, in serious cases, Crown Counsel) to decide whether to exercise civilian jurisdiction, that is, to retain the case and prosecute the accused in the Scottish criminal courts rather than allow it to be prosecuted in the military courts. This decision is usually taken after the views and any representations of the accused's commanding officer have been obtained. Where the offence has affected the person or property of civilians, there is currently a presumption in favour of exercising civilian jurisdiction. Thus, in the majority of sexual offences cases, the prosecution will proceed in the Scottish criminal courts. In addition, serious sexual offences cases where both the accused and complainer are serving members of the Armed Forces are usually prosecuted in the Scottish criminal courts.[15]

(ii) Cross-border offences: the common-law rules on jurisdiction

1.21 The Westminster and Scottish Parliaments have legislated to allow the Scottish courts to try certain, specified sexual offences when those offences are alleged to have been committed outside Scotland, including in the rest of the UK, and we consider these rules on extra-territorial jurisdiction in the next section. However, this legislation does not apply to all sexual offences. There is thus a residue of sexual offences which might have a cross-border element (for instance, if either the accused or complainer is outside Scotland), but there is no express statutory provision allowing for them to be tried in the Scottish courts. Examples of such offences include (in cases where the complainer is over 18): coercing someone to look at a sexual image (section 6 of the 2009 Act); communicating indecently with someone (section 7 of the 2009 Act); and disclosing or threatening to disclose an intimate photograph or film (section 2 of the Abusive Behaviour and Sexual Harm (Scotland) Act 2016).

1.22 That does not mean that the Scottish courts have no jurisdiction over such offences. For such offences, the Scottish courts can – and often do – have jurisdiction on the basis of the common-law rules on jurisdiction that apply to cross-border offences. There are three bases for the Scottish courts to have jurisdiction over such offences. The first is if the material part of the offence is committed in Scotland: *Laird v HM Advocate*.[16] The second is where the practical effect of the offence is felt in Scotland: *Clements v HM Advocate*.[17] The third is where the offence is a

14 The Scottish courts under their ordinary powers of jurisdiction over offences committed in Scotland; the service courts by virtue of ss 50 and 51 of the Armed Forces Act 2006.

15 S 320B of the Armed Forces Act 2006 requires the Director of Service Prosecutions and the Lord Advocate to agree a protocol on the exercise of concurrent jurisdiction. This is currently the subject of a consultation process.

16 1985 JC 37.

17 1991 JC 62.

continuing crime (*crimen continuum*) which is committed partly outside Scotland and partly in Scotland: *Lauchlan v HM Advocate*.[18]

1.23 The most common applications of these rules are to the non-contact offences set out above and to charges brought under section 1 of the Domestic Abuse (Scotland) Act 2018, where the intention of the Scottish Government was that these common-law rules should apply to give the Scottish courts jurisdiction over the whole of a course of abusive behaviour when certain parts of it occur in Scotland and other parts in the rest of the United Kingdom: see **1.41** below.

1.24 When none of these three common-law rules apply, it is important to then consider whether there are any statutory rules which would give the Scottish courts extra-territorial jurisdiction. We set these rules out in the following section.

(iii) Statutory extra-territorial jurisdiction

1.25 The Scottish courts' extra-territorial jurisdiction over certain, specified sexual offences has been progressively extended by successive Acts of the Westminster and Scottish Parliaments. Different statutory rules apply depending on the date of the offence, and different rules apply to different offences. As such, the statutory rules require careful consideration in any case where extra-territorial jurisdiction might arise. The short point is that it should no longer be assumed that simply because a sexual offence takes place entirely outside Scotland, the Scottish courts have no jurisdiction to try it.

1.26 The rules are best understood by tracing their development from the 1990s (when extra-territorial jurisdiction over certain sexual offences was first established) to the present day, and we set out this evolution below. Before doing so, we make two preliminary remarks. First, sexual offences are not the only offences over which the Scottish courts exercise extra-territorial jurisdiction,[19] but they are the offences where the extra-territorial jurisdiction is at its widest. Second, Scotland is not unique in exercising extra-territorial jurisdiction: because the extra-territorial jurisdiction was first established through the enactment of UK-wide legislation in the mid-1990s, similar rules exist in the rest of the UK; indeed, the most recent changes have been enacted on UK-wide basis by the Domestic Abuse Act 2021, a Westminster statute.

[18] 2015 JC 75.

[19] For instance, s 11 of the 1995 Act gives the Scottish courts jurisdiction over offences such as murder, culpable homicide and assault when committed outside the United Kingdom by UK nationals or those habitually resident in Scotland.

The Criminal Law (Consolidation) (Scotland) Act 1995: sections 16A and 16B

1.27 The root of the extra-territorial jurisdiction over sexual offences lies in the Westminster Parliament's desire to clamp down on the growing phenomenon of child-sex tourism in the mid-1990s. This led first, to the UK-wide Sexual Offences (Conspiracy and Incitement) Act 1996, which made it an offence for any person in Scotland or elsewhere in the UK to conspire to commit, or to incite the commission of, certain sexual offences[20] abroad against children. For Scotland, this was achieved by inserting section 16A into the Criminal Law (Consolidation) (Scotland) Act 1995. This was followed in 1997 by the Sex Offenders Act 1997, which made it an offence for a British citizen or resident (or someone who has subsequently become a British citizen or resident) to commit certain sexual offences against children himself when outside the United Kingdom. For Scotland, this was achieved by inserting section 16B into the 1995 Act.[21] Both section 16A and section 16B contained a dual-criminality requirement, meaning the child-sex offence in question also needed to be an offence under the law of the country or territory where it was committed. On 4 September 1998 the law changed slightly on conspiracy. On that date, section 11A of the Criminal Procedure (Scotland) Act 1995 made it a general offence to conspire, in Scotland, to commit an offence outwith Scotland, meaning the references to conspiracy in section 16A were repealed on that date. That also had the effect that a conspiracy in Scotland to commit any sexual offence abroad (and not just a child-sex offence) could be prosecuted in the Scottish courts.

The Sexual Offences (Scotland) Act 2009: sections 54 and 55 as enacted

1.28 Sections 16A and 16B were repealed by the 2009 Act and replaced, respectively, by sections 54 and 55 of that Act. The effect was the same: to give the Scottish courts extra-territorial jurisdiction over sexual offences committed abroad against children or other vulnerable persons. There were two main differences. First, sections 54 and 55 removed the dual-criminality requirement for UK nationals but

20 The list is in s 16A(9) and covered the main contact sexual offences at that time which could be committed against boys and girls under 16. The provision entered into force on 1 October 1996.

21 In force from 1 September 1997 to 30 November 2010. The list of offences is in s 16B(7). It is the same as the list in s 16A(9) save for the addition of the offence of taking or distributing indecent images of children, contrary to s 52 of the Civic Government (Scotland) Act 1982, and, by s 16B(8) including conspiracy or incitement and aiding and abetting the offences. The list was updated on 7 October 2005 to include possession of indecent photographs of children (s 52A of the 1982 Act) and the offences created by the Protection of Children and Prevention of Sexual Offences (Scotland) Act 2005.

kept it for all other persons.[22] Second, sections 54 and 55 updated and expanded the list of sexual offences against children and other vulnerable persons that the Scottish courts could try if they were either incited from Scotland or committed by a UK national or resident outside the UK. Different lists applied to section 54 and 55.

1.29 For section 54, the section on inciting in Scotland the commission of offences outside the UK, the relevant offences were listed in Part 1 of Schedule 4 to the 2009 Act. These offences were:

- any offence under Part 1 of the 2009 Act (that is, sections 1-11 of the Act) against a person under 18;
- any offence under Part 4 of the 2009 Act (the specific offences against children in the Act);
- the sexual abuse-of-trust offences under Part 5 of the 2009 Act; and
- the continuing common law offence of indecent assault when committed against a person under 18.

1.30 For section 55, the section on a UK national or resident committing offences abroad, a longer list of offences were listed in Part 2 of the same schedule. These offences were:

- any offence under Part 1 of the 2009 Act (that is, sections 1-11 of the Act) against a person under 18;
- any offence under Part 4 of the 2009 Act (the specific offences against children in the Act);
- the sexual abuse-of-trust offences under Part 5 of the 2009 Act;
- the continuing common law offence of indecent assault when committed against a person under 18;
- the offences under section 52 and 52A of the Civic Government (Scotland) Act 1982 (taking and distribution of indecent images of children, and possession of indecent images of children);
- the offences under sections 9 to 12 of the Protection of Children and Prevention of Sexual Offences (Scotland) 2005 Act; and
- conspiracy, incitement to commit any of the above offences, and aiding and abetting all of the above offences, save for indecent assault.

1.31 The initial effect of sections 54 and 55 was that if any of the specified offences were incited by anyone in Scotland, or if a UK national or resident committed any of those offences outside the United Kingdom, the Scottish courts had jurisdiction

22 The policy objective being to implement Art 25(1)(d) and (4) of the Council of Europe Convention on the Protection of Children Against Sexual Exploitation and Sexual Abuse (the Lanzarote Convention), which obliges Contracting States to criminalise certain offences in the Convention, and, for the offences of sexual abuse, child prostitution, and pornographic offences against children to do so without a dual criminality requirement for the state's own nationals or habitual residents. The Scottish Government's policy memorandum on the introduction of the Bill is frank in stating the desire to go beyond just these offences and remove the dual-criminality requirement for all sexual offences committed abroad by UK nationals. Arguably, however, at the time of enactment, ss 54 and 55 failed to implement the similar requirement to remove the dual criminality requirement for habitual residents.

to try the person (subject, of course, to the dual-criminality requirement for non-UK nationals). Section 56 of the Act created a continuity provision, similar to that in section 53, to allow for conviction of certain of the offences listed in section 16B, where the court was satisfied that the conduct had taken place but not the time at which the conduct took place.

The changes made to the 2009 Act by the Abusive Behaviour and Sexual Harm (Scotland) Act 2016

1.32 The Abusive Behaviour and Sexual Harm (Scotland) Act 2016 made several changes to the extra-territorial provisions in the 2009 Act.

1.33 First, it made clear, in both sections 54 and 55, that the dual-criminality requirement also applied to those who were not UK nationals or residents at the time of the offence but who had become UK nationals or UK residents by the time of trial.[23]

1.34 Second, the 2016 Act extended section 54 so that the offence of incitement also applied to incitement, in Scotland, to commit sexual acts elsewhere in the United Kingdom (previously it had only applied to incitement, in Scotland, to commit sexual acts outside the United Kingdom).[24]

1.35 Third, in an often-looked and potentially far-reaching exercise, the 2016 Act inserted three provisions into the 2009 Act, sections 54A, B and C, to allow the prosecution in Scotland of certain sexual offences committed elsewhere in the United Kingdom. Section 54A(1) sets out the general principle that if a person does an act elsewhere in the United Kingdom which would, if it had been done in Scotland, constitute a listed offence, then the person commits an offence. The list of offences for section 54A is the same as the list of offences for section 55: those in Part 2 of Schedule 4 (see the list at **1.30** above)

1.36 The rest of section 54A and sections 54B and 54C set out the limits on this principle. Section 54A(2) creates a dual-criminality requirement for those who are not habitual residents of Scotland: to prosecute such a person in Scotland, the offence also has to be an offence under the law of the country where it took place (ie, in England and Wales or Northern Ireland). Given the substantial overlap between sexual offences in the different parts of the UK, this requirement will usually be met. Section 54B(2)(a) prevents double jeopardy by providing that prosecution is not competent if the person has been or is being prosecuted for the offence in the country where it took place.[25] Section 54B(2)(b) further limits prosecution to cases where: (i) before prosecution is initiated, the Scottish prosecutor has consulted the relevant

23 S 54(2) and (2A) and s 55(2A), (2B) and (8) as amended and inserted.

24 Subsection (1) as amended.

25 For this purpose, a person is not to be regarded as having been prosecuted if the prosecution was withdrawn in order to enable the prosecution of the person in Scotland: s 54B(3).

director of public prosecutions in England and Wales or Northern Ireland about the prosecution; and (ii) the person is being prosecuted, on the same indictment or complaint, in respect of any act in Scotland constituting a listed offence. Section 54C provides that the indictment or complaint need not specify which country in the United Kingdom the offence took place in, and, when it does not, specifies which directors of public prosecutions should be consulted.[26]

1.37 It will be seen that sections 54A-C, which first appear very general, are heavily circumscribed to a situation where a person is being prosecuted in Scotland for certain sexual offences and it is considered desirable to prosecute them at the same time for similar offences committed elsewhere in the United Kingdom (with an additional, but easily met, dual-criminality requirement for those who are not habitually resident in Scotland). It might also be thought that a single section in the Act stating this would have sufficed rather than the three sections which have been used to arrive at this point, not least when the purpose of section 54C is not entirely apparent. But the principal effect remains that two or more offences against children or other vulnerable persons can be prosecuted together in Scotland (and the doctrine of mutual corroboration can apply between them), when all of the offences have been committed in the United Kingdom and at least one of those offences has been committed in Scotland.

Changes to the 2009 Act made by the Domestic Abuse Act 2021

1.38 The final changes to the extra-territorial provisions in the 2009 Act were made by the Domestic Abuse Act 2021 (a Westminster statute) and entered into force on 29 June 2021. This significantly extended the Scottish courts' extra-territorial jurisdiction because it extended that extra-territorial jurisdiction to all offences committed under sections 1-4 of the 2009 Act (rape, sexual assault

26 The manner in which it does this is far from clear. S 54C(1) states that the indictment or complaint need not specify which country in the United Kingdom the offence took place in. S 54C(2)(a) provides that, in such a situation, the prosecution is not competent if the person has been or is being prosecuted elsewhere in the United Kingdom (a provision which appears simply to duplicate s 54B(2)(a)). S 54C(2)(b) provides that the prosecution is only competent if further conditions in s 54C(3) are met. The first is that if the indictment or complaint specifies that the conduct took place either: (i) in Scotland or in England and Wales; or (ii) in Scotland or in Northern Ireland, the prosecutor has consulted the relevant DPP. This appears to duplicate the general consultation requirement in s 54B(2)(b)(i) but not waive the requirement in s 54B(2)(b)(ii) for the offence to be prosecuted on the same indictment or complaint as an offence committed in Scotland. The second condition is that if the indictment or complaint specifies that the offence took place either in England and Wales or Northern Ireland but not Scotland, the prosecutor must have consulted both DPPs and the person must be being prosecuted, on the same indictment or complaint, for an act in Scotland constituting a listed offence. This appears to duplicate both the general consultation requirement in s 54B(2)(b)(i) and the requirement that the offence be prosecuted at the same time as an offence committed in Scotland in s 54B(2)(b)(ii). The third condition is that if neither of these conditions apply, the prosecutor has consulted both DPPs (again, appearing to duplicate s 54B(2)(b)(i) and appearing not to waive the requirement in s 54B(2)(b)(ii), otherwise the section creates the power to prosecute in Scotland a single offence without it being specified where in the UK the offence has been committed).

by penetration, sexual assault, and sexual coercion), not just offences committed against children. The Domestic Abuse Act 2021 did so by inserting section 54D into the 2009 Act. By section 54D, this extra-territorial jurisdiction applies when any of these offences have been committed outside the UK by a UK national or by a person habitually resident in Scotland. For habitual residents, a dual-criminality requirement applies. The effect is that the Scottish courts now have jurisdiction to try the most serious sexual offences committed by UK nationals or Scottish residents, wherever outside the UK they are committed and irrespective of the age of the victim.

1.39 Table 1.1 summarises the evolution of these extra-territorial provisions, from their introduction in the 1990s to the present day.

Table 1.1: Extra-territorial jurisdiction over sexual offences

Period	**Statute**	**Offences covered**	**Scope of the extra-territorial jurisdiction**	**Dual criminality requirement**
1 October 1996 – 30 November 2010	Section 16A of the Criminal Law (Consolidation) (Scotland) Act 1995	Conspiracy/ incitement to commit the principal child-sex offences then in force (For conspiracy, from 4 September 1998 all sexual offences under section 11A of the Criminal Procedure (Scotland) Act 1995)	Anywhere outside the UK	Yes: for both British citizens and residents
1 September 1997 - 30 November 2010	Section 16B of the Criminal Law (Consolidation) (Scotland) Act 1995	Committing the principal child-sex offences then in force	Anywhere outside the UK	Yes: for both British citizens and residents
1 December 2010 - 23 April 2017	Section 54 of the Sexual Offences (Scotland) Act 2009 (as initially enacted)	Incitement to commit any offences listed in Part 1 of Schedule 4 to the Sexual Offences (Scotland) Act 2009	Anywhere outside the UK	No for UK nationals; yes for all other persons

Period	Statute	Offences covered	Scope of the extra-territorial jurisdiction	Dual criminality requirement
1 December 2010 - present	Section 55 of the Sexual Offences (Scotland) Act 2009	Committing any of the offences listed in Part 2 of Schedule 4 to the Sexual Offences (Scotland) Act 2009	Anywhere outside the UK	No for UK nationals; yes for all other persons
24 April 2017 - present	Section 54 (as amended by the Abusive Behaviour and Sexual Harm (Scotland) Act 2016)	Incitement to commit any of the offences listed in Part 1 of Schedule 4 to the Sexual Offences (Scotland) Act 2009	Anywhere outside Scotland	No for UK nationals Yes for all other persons (including those who are not UK nationals or residents at the time of the offence and who have become UK nationals or residents by the time of trial)
24 April 2017 - present	Sections 54A-C (as inserted by the Abusive Behaviour and Sexual Harm (Scotland) Act 2016	Committing any of the offences listed in Part 2 of Schedule 4 to the Sexual Offences (Scotland) Act 2009 But the person must be prosecuted, on the same indictment or complaint, for a listed offence that has been committed in Scotland	Any other part of the United Kingdom	No for UK nationals and habitual residents of Scotland Yes for all other persons
29 June 2021 - present	Section 54D (as inserted by the Domestic Abuse Act 2021)	Committing any of the offences under sections 1-4 of the Sexual Offences (Scotland) Act 2009 (irrespective of the age of the victim)	Anywhere outside the UK	No for UK nationals or habitual residents of Scotland Yes for all other persons

Extra-territorial jurisdiction and other offences that may contain a substantial sexual element

1.40 Other statutes have extra-territorial provisions. The Human Trafficking and Exploitation (Scotland) Act 2015, which creates the offence of human trafficking, provides that a UK national, habitual resident, or body incorporated in the UK can commit that offence regardless of where the relevant action for the offence takes place: section 2(1) and (2) of the Act. Section 2(3) provides that any other person commits the offence if any part of the relevant action takes place in the United Kingdom or the relevant action is taken with a view to a person arriving in or entering into, departing from, or travelling within the United Kingdom. Section 2(1) and (2) thus create an extra-territorial jurisdiction for UK nationals, residents and organisations; section 2(3) is the application of the traditional rule on jurisdiction for cross-border offences to other persons.

1.41 Section 3(1) of the Domestic Abuse (Scotland) Act 2018 provides that the offence of engaging in a course of abusive behaviour towards a partner or ex-partner, can be constituted by a course of behaviour that occurs wholly or partly outside the United Kingdom. This is limited to UK nationals and those habitually resident in Scotland. There is no dual-criminality requirement for habitual residents, which is perhaps surprising given the reference to 'wholly … outside the United Kingdom' in section 3(1).[27] It was the Scottish Government's understanding during the passage of the 2018 Act that, where the behaviour occurs principally in Scotland and partly elsewhere in the United Kingdom, the Scottish courts would have jurisdiction based on the common-law principles regarding cross-border offences set out at **1.22** above,[28] and we respectfully agree with that assessment. It is the principal reason we have set out the common-law rules on cross-border offences in that paragraph.

1.42 Finally, Schedule 3 to the Domestic Abuse Act 2021 extended the Scottish courts' jurisdiction to cover the offences of stalking and assault when committed by a UK national or Scottish habitual resident outside the United Kingdom, removing the anomaly that a person might stalk, assault, and then commit a sexual offence against another outside the UK, but only the latter could be prosecuted in the Scottish

27 The extra-territorial jurisdiction was introduced at the Committee stage, purportedly to give effect to the Council of Europe Convention on preventing and combating violence against women and domestic violence (the Istanbul Convention). Article 44(3) of the Convention obliges states to remove the dual-criminality requirement for the offences contained in Arts 36–39 of the Convention. These articles do not cover controlling and abusive behaviour but do cover: sexual violence, including rape (Art 36); forced marriage (Art 37); FGM (Art 38); and forced abortion and sterilisation (Art 39). It may be that these offences could be contained in a libel for s 1 of the 2018 Act (though perhaps more for the Art 36 offences than the others). But it is possible (and indeed usual) for a s 1 libel not to contain these offences. In that sense, s 3 goes further than the Convention requires. In addition, the UK has entered a reservation to the Convention, reserving the right not to apply Art 44(3) to the offences listed in Art 36 when those offences have been committed by habitual residents who are not UK nationals.

28 Stage 2, second meeting on amendments, Michael Matheson MSP, 21 November 2017.

courts.[29] For assault, a dual-criminality requirement applies to both UK nationals and habitual residents. There is no dual-criminality requirement for stalking.

Table 1.2: Extra-territorial jurisdiction over other offences which may contain a substantial sexual element

Period	Statute	Offences covered	Scope of the extra-territorial jurisdiction	Dual criminality requirement
31 May 2016 - present	Section 2 of the Human Trafficking and Exploitation (Scotland) Act 2015	Offence of human trafficking, contrary to section 1 of the Human Trafficking and Exploitation (Scotland) Act 2015	For UK nationals, habitual residents, and corporate bodies, anywhere. For others, if the relevant action takes place in the UK or it is taken with a view to trafficking in or out of the UK	No
1 April 2019 - present	Section 1 of the Domestic Abuse (Scotland) Act 2018	Engaging in a course of abusive behaviour towards a partner or ex-partner	Outside Scotland (outside the UK by virtue of section 3; anywhere else in the UK by virtue of the common law rules on cross-border offences) Applies only to UK nationals and those habitually resident in Scotland	No
29 June 2021 - present	Section 11(2A) of the Criminal Procedure (Scotland) Act 1995 (as inserted by the Domestic Abuse Act 2021)	Assault	Outside the UK Applies only to UK nationals and those habitually resident in Scotland	Yes

29 For assault by amending s 11 of the Criminal Procedural (Scotland) Act 1995; for stalking, by inserting s 39A into the Criminal Justice and Licensing (Scotland) Act 2010. Both provisions entered into force on 29 June 2021.

Period	Statute	Offences covered	Scope of the extra-territorial jurisdiction	Dual criminality requirement
29 June - present	Section 39A of the Criminal Justice and Licensing (Scotland) Act 2010 (as inserted by the Domestic Abuse Act 2021)	Stalking	Outside the UK Applies only to UK nationals and those habitually resident in Scotland	No

Common statutory provisions on extra-territorial jurisdiction

1.43 Similar, though not always identical, statutory language is used to create extra-territorial jurisdiction for these sexual offences and offences with a substantial sexual element. In all cases, the statutes provide that any question over whether a dual-criminality requirement has been met is for the judge alone to decide. The statutes also provide, however, that the requirement is to be taken as satisfied unless, by service of a notice in advance of trial, it is challenged by the accused, setting out why it is said that it is not satisfied and requiring the prosecutor to prove that it is. The court can waive the need for prior service of a notice. If challenged, the matter would require to be considered by the judge after hearing evidence of the relevant foreign law from skilled witnesses.

1.44 There is a standard clause in all the statutes defining a 'UK national', with reference to the principal categories of British citizenship.[30] The term 'resident' is not defined in the legislation (Scottish or otherwise), nor does it appear to have been the subject of any sustained judicial consideration in any of the UK criminal appeal courts. It is suggested that no gloss on the term is necessary, and whether someone is resident is simply a question of fact, considering whether or not they are living in Scotland. Equally, habitually resident is not defined. The term is regularly used in private international law cases, such as family cases where the courts are often required to consider a child's place of habitual residence. In that context, the courts have consistently refused to further define the term, considering that this too is a

30 Should a dispute arise on whether an accused is a UK national, the standard work on immigration law, *MacDonald's Immigration Law & Practice* (10th edn, LexisNexis Butterworths 2021) at para 2.30, notes the complexity of this area of law and directs practitioners to *Fransman's British Nationality Law* (4th edn, Bloomsbury Professional 2023) and we do the same.

question of fact.[31] Though the Scottish Parliament did hear evidence on the question of any possible differences between the terms, with both 'resident' and 'habitual resident' being questions of fact, we see little practical significance in the shift toward using the latter term.

1.45 We also suggest that the terms UK national and resident (and their permutations) are all special capacities, that is, they are positions or states which the accused has and are necessary for the commission of the offence. As such, section 255 of the Criminal Procedure (Scotland) Act 1995 applies to these terms. This has two effects: first, the fact of being a UK national, resident, etc, must be libelled in the charge, and secondly, when it is, unless challenged, it will be held to be admitted. If ever these matters were challenged, they would in the majority of cases be proved by production of a birth certificate, housing records or the like.

1.46 A final common provision is that, for sheriff court matters, the accused may be tried in any sheriff court district in which he is apprehended or in custody, or in such district as the Lord Advocate may determine.

31 See, as recent authority, *F v M* 2021 SLT 1121, with full discussion of the relevant authorities at paras 4–6.

Chapter 2

The general provisions of the Sexual Offences (Scotland) Act 2009

INTRODUCTION

2.01 The 2009 Act contains three categories of offences: general offences in Part 1, offences against children in Part 4, and abuse-of-trust offences in Part 5. We consider these categories of offences in Chapters 3, 4 and 5 respectively. A key feature of the 2009 Act, though, is that it also contains a series of general provisions which apply across different offences. Foremost are the concepts of consent and reasonable belief, which are defined in Part 2, sections 12 to 16, of the Act. The Act also gives guidance on establishing an accused's purpose in committing an offence (where that is an element of the offence) in section 49 and a definition of what is 'sexual' in section 60. We consider each of these concepts in this chapter, with a particular focus on consent since it is arguably the cornerstone of the Act.

2.02 The Act also contains technical provisions on alternative verdicts and the continuity of law between the common law and the Act, and we set out these provisions in the second part of the chapter. The extra-territorial jurisdiction provisions in sections 54 to 56 are considered separately in Chapter 1. The protective principle, the key concept underpinning Parts 4 and 5 of the Act, is considered in Chapters 4 and 5.

FROM THE COMMON LAW TO THE SLC'S CONSENT MODEL

2.03 Until the passing of the 2009 Act, the commission of sexual offences within Scotland was largely governed by the common law.[1] When the 2009 Act came into force, it reflected the first occasion on which the Scottish Parliament had determined that a significant area of the common law of Scotland was to be comprehensively replaced by a statutory code. The bulk of the provisions came

1 From at least 1885, and the passage of the Criminal Law Amendment Act 1885, there were statutory offences concerning sexual conduct with children: see Chapter 12 on historical offences at **12.08** and following.

into force on 1 December 2010 but the commencement of section 52 of the 2009 Act, which abolished the common law crimes of rape, clandestine injury to women, lewd, indecent or libidinous practice or behaviour, and sodomy, was not triggered until 16 December 2013, along with section 53 which provided for transitional arrangements.[2]

2.04 An understanding of the policy considerations underpinning the 2009 Act can be informed by a brief reflection on the history of the common law in this area. From the first edition of Baron Hume's *Commentaries on the Law of Scotland Respecting Crimes,* published in 1797, the crime of rape had been defined as 'The knowledge of the woman's person … against her will, and by force.'[3] The use of force to obtain intercourse against the will of the woman was deemed an essential component of the crime.

2.05 The law as stated by Hume, and other writers of the time, was authoritatively confirmed by the majority decision of the court in the case of *HM Advocate v Sweenie* in 1858,[4] although it was recognised that the force necessary did not require to involve physical violence. For the following 144 years, students and practitioners were taught that rape was committed where a man had intercourse with a woman by force and against her will. The use of force was part of the *actus reus* of the crime. Consent was not part of the *actus reus* but was recognised as a defence. Every jury asked to adjudicate upon a charge of rape was given this definition of the crime.

2.06 There matters remained until the case of *Lord Advocate's Reference No 1 of 2001*.[5] In the majority decision of the seven-judge Bench, delivered on 22 March 2002, the case of *Sweenie* was overruled, and the court determined that the crime of rape was committed by a man having sexual intercourse with a woman, without her consent, where he knows that the woman is not consenting or is reckless as to whether she is consenting. As a consequence, and for the first time, the absence of consent became part of the *actus reus* of the crime of rape. The use of force no longer featured as an aspect of the *actus reus*, other than, if available, to evidence the absence of consent.

2.07 Two subsequent decisions of the High Court[6] were widely interpreted as suggesting that the decision in *Lord Advocate's Reference* had inadvertently created major problems for the Crown in proving the accused person's *mens rea*. As a consequence of those concerns (and an awareness of reviews in other jurisdictions) the Scottish Law Commission was invited to examine the law relating to rape and

2 See further at **2.134** below. Those common law offences still apply to offences committed before the entry into force of the Sexual Offences Act 2009 and are considered in Chapter 12 on historical offences.

3 All references to Hume are to the 1986 reprint of the 1844 edition. The passage appears in vol i, p 302 of that edition. The same text appears in all previous editions.

4 (1858) 3 Irv 109.

5 2002 SLT 466.

6 *McKearney v HM Advocate* 2004 JC 87 and *Cinci v HM Advocate* 2004 JC 103.

other sexual offences and the evidential requirements for proving such offences and to report.

2.08 Having issued its Discussion Paper in January 2006, and thereafter conducted a lengthy consultation process, the SLC produced its final report in December 2007. The core principle which underpinned the recommendations set out in the report was that respect had to be given to a person's sexual autonomy. The operation of this principle was seen as triggering three consequences: first, that a person's sexual autonomy is infringed upon when she participates in a sexual act which she has not freely chosen to participate in; second, that any such breach of a person's sexual autonomy is a wrong which the law should treat as a crime; and third, that where a person freely chooses to participate in sexual activity the law should not (subject to truly exceptional circumstances) prohibit that activity.

2.09 This principle and its associated consequences were reflected in the Draft Bill attached to the report, the terms of which were largely, although not entirely, replicated in the provisions of the 2009 Act as subsequently enacted.

2.10 The method selected to give effect to this principle was to propose that Scots law on sexual offences should be based on a consent model. In short, rather than consent being seen as a defence, absence of consent was to be seen as a constituent element of the sexual offence itself. Part 1 of the 2009 Act sets out, in sections 1 to 9, a series of offences each of which has the absence of consent and the absence of a reasonable belief as to consent as constituent elements.

CONSENT

2.11 For the offences created by the 2009 Act (other than those governed by the protective principle) absence of consent is part of the *actus reus* of the crime.

2.12 To understand properly the place and meaning of consent in the statutory framework, the offence of rape can be taken as an example. Section 1 of the Act provides that the *actus reus* of the crime consists of the intentional or reckless vaginal, anal or oral penile penetration by A without B consenting to that conduct. The use of the present participle indicates the need for consent to be given at the time of the sexual act and not at a point remote from it.[7] Person B's state of mind is therefore a crucial aspect of the *actus reus* and requires to be established as a fact. A particular state of mind is a fact, like any other, to be established either by direct evidence or by inference from other proven facts.

2.13 The absence of a specific definition of consent for the purposes of the common law crime of rape was identified by the SLC as a particular deficiency in the law as it then stood. Prior to the implementation of the 2009 Act, the only occasion on which the Appeal Court had considered the question of what definition of consent

7 *GW v HM Advocate* 2019 JC 109 at para 28.

should be given to a jury was in the case of a taxi driver charged with indecent assault on a passenger, where the jury asked the sheriff for guidance on the legal definition of consent – *Marr v HM Advocate*.[8] In response the sheriff explained that:

> 'the definition of consent is a common, straightforward definition of consent. It's the common English word given its normal meaning. And that I am afraid is it. Consent is consent.'

2.14 In rejecting the suggestion that the sheriff ought to have given a dictionary meaning of consent the Lord Justice Clerk (Ross) observed that:

> 'We recognise that the sheriff might have decided in the face of this request to use some synonym for consent and, for example, tell the jury that they must look for agreement, but we are not persuaded that it was necessary for her to do so. What was important was that she made it plain to the jury that the word 'consent' had no special meaning in law but required to be given its normal meaning.'

2.15 The SLC's view was that this left the law in an unsatisfactory state and therefore recommended that a statutory definition of consent should be provided. The approach favoured by the SLC, and adopted in the legislation, was to provide a general definition of consent and to supplement this by providing a non-exhaustive list of situations where consent is not present.

Section 12 of the 2009 Act

2.16 Section 12 gives the general definition of consent by providing:

> **'Meaning of 'consent' and related expressions**
>
> 'In parts 1 and 3 'consent' means free agreement (and related expressions are to be construed accordingly).'

2.17 Section 13(2) then provides a list of situations in which free agreement is absent. This is not intended as an exhaustive set of situations in which consent will be absent, but the effect of this section is that where the Crown establishes one of the factual situations specified that is sufficient to establish the lack of free agreement, and thus of consent.[9] The specified situations are:

> '(a) where the conduct occurs at a time when B is incapable because of the effects of alcohol or any other substance of consenting to it,
>
> (b) where B agrees or submits to the conduct because of violence used against B or any other person, or because of threats of violence made against B or any other person,

8 1996 SCCR 696.

9 *Winton v HM Advocate* 2016 SLT 393 at para 9.

(c) where B agrees or submits to the conduct because B is unlawfully detained by A,
(d) where B agrees or submits to the conduct because B is mistaken, as a result of deception by A, as to the nature or purpose of the conduct,
(e) where B agrees or submits to the conduct because A induces B to agree or submit to the conduct by impersonating a person known personally to B, or
(f) where the only expression or indication of agreement to the conduct is from someone other than B.'

2.18 In addition to these specific situations, section 14 of the Act provides that a person who is asleep or unconscious is incapable of consenting to any conduct. Section 15 further reinforces the principle of autonomy by providing statutory recognition for the understanding that consent to one type of conduct does not imply consent to any other conduct, that consent may be withdrawn at any stage, and that any conduct which takes place, or continues to take place, after consent has been withdrawn is conduct engaged in without consent. Finally, in this regard, section 17 makes specific provision for when mentally disordered persons lack the capacity to consent. We consider each of these concepts in turn.

Free agreement

2.19 As set out above, section 12 provides that, for the purposes of the statutory offences where absence of consent is a constituent element, 'consent' is defined as meaning free agreement. It is important to bear in mind that the provisions of sections 13, 14 and 17 are without prejudice to the generality of the section 12 definition. In order to understand the part which the absence of consent plays in the prosecution of sexual offences it is necessary to ask: what does consent as free agreement mean, and in what circumstances will consent of this sort be absent? The answer is not always straightforward.

2.20 In the paradigm case, the complainer's own evidence will be that she did not wish to have sexual activity with the accused and did not consent to doing so. If this evidence is accepted, that will be sufficient to establish the absence of consent as a fact. As a matter of principle, this will be so regardless of whether, or how, this absence of consent was communicated to the accused. What then remains is the question of whether the complainer's account of the commission of the offence has been corroborated.[10] In many of such cases the complainer will explain that her lack of consent was overcome by force, whereas the accused will explain that no force was used and the complainer was a willing participant. In this type of example, there is no difficulty in understanding what is meant by consent and the conflict between the Crown and the defence will be a stark one as to credibility.

10 *Lord Advocate's Reference No 1 of 2023* 2024 JC 140 at para 239.

2.21 Even here, however, the focus in evidence tends to be on the complainer's actions and words in order to resolve the clash of credibility between the two and to come to a conclusion as to what her state of mind actually was, and thus to reach a decision as to whether she was consenting or not. Accordingly, as the SLC predicted in recommending a consent-based model, the focus in many sexual offences trials has generally come to be on what the complainer did with the accused, rather than on what the accused did to the victim.[11]

2.22 By way of contrast, where sexual activity takes place in circumstances which are not associated with force or overt violence, the concept of consent may be less easy to pin down. In such circumstances a complainer's state of mind may be described in less clear terms and this may require an examination of what it means to consent to conduct.

2.23 The terminology used in section 12 is helpful in this respect. While the scope and concept of consent may not have been altered by the statutory definition, the concept of 'free agreement' is likely to assist a jury in understanding what sort of state of mind is being described in the definition. It carries with it more obviously the recognition that a person can 'agree' to participate in conduct without there being 'real' or 'valid' agreement. But it remains the case that the statute attempts to identify a state of affairs which can be elusive, which may not depend on the language used by the complainer and which will require the setting of boundaries by the court. For example, to what extent is the concept of consent to be viewed through a purely subjective prism and what type of factors may legitimately be taken account of in determining whether consent was truly and effectively given?

2.24 The situations specified in section 13(2) can help to illuminate what is meant by free agreement but as the list is not exhaustive, it is clear that there will be many other factual circumstances which may involve the question of whether consent was or was not present. In any such other circumstances, the question will be determined by addressing the general definition in section 12.[12] It is nevertheless helpful to begin by looking at each of the section 13(2) situations separately. In this exercise it should be kept in mind that the scope of the concept of consent has to date received only limited judicial analysis in Scotland. A little more consideration has been given to this concept by the courts of England and Wales where consent is also the subject of a statutory definition.

2.25 The relevant English legislation is the Sexual Offences Act 2003 and, for the purposes of consent, it has a similar but not identical structure to the 2009 Act. The structure which it provides is to set out a general definition of consent in section 74: that 'a person consents if he agrees by choice, and has the freedom and capacity to make that choice'. Rather than give examples of the absence of consent, the 2003 Act then sets out, in sections 75 and 76 respectively, some circumstances which

11 Report para 2.6 and 2.13.

12 As the SLC put it at para 2.54 'the general definition is not empty in content or devoid of application'.

raise a presumption of the absence of consent and two circumstances in which it will be conclusively presumed that consent is absent.[13] The section 74 definition of consent is sufficiently close to the general definition set out in section 12 of the 2009 Act to mean that cases which analyse the scope of that provision will be of value in understanding the meaning of free agreement. We therefore include the leading English authorities in our discussion of section 13 and, in the following sections, of the other circumstances in which a complainer's consent might be vitiated: the effect of other forms of pressure on free agreement, the effect of deception, and section 14 (the lack of capacity to consent when sleeping).

The section 13(2) situations

Section 13(2)(a) – Intoxication

2.26 Section 13(2)(a) provides that free agreement is absent:

> 'where the conduct occurs at a time when B is incapable because of the effects of alcohol or any other substance of consenting to it'.

2.27 This principle is a restatement of the common law position. There is no differentiation to be drawn here between the effects of alcohol or any other substance, and the principle applies regardless of how the state of intoxication came about. One distinction which does arise though is the important one of recognising the difference between a complainer who is incapable because of the effect of alcohol of consenting to sexual activity and a complainer who is asleep or unconscious as a consequence of intoxication. Capacity to consent should not be confused with consciousness, capacity may evaporate well before a complainer becomes unconscious.[14] Conversely, where a complainer is asleep or unconscious the provisions of section 14 become operative and the issue of consent may well be more straightforward.

2.28 Section 13(2)(a) thus contemplates the situation of a complainer who is intoxicated but likely to be mobile and capable of making some form of expression, or indication, of apparent interest in sexual activity. The value of this provision was seen by the SLC as including putting a person on notice as to the danger of engaging

13 In s 75: (a) using violence against the complainant or causing the complainant to fear that immediate violence would be used; (b) causing the complainant to fear that violence was being used, or that immediate violence would be used, against another person; (c) that the complainant was, and the defendant was not, unlawfully detained at the time of the relevant act; (d) that the complainant was asleep or otherwise unconscious at the time of the relevant act; (e) because of the complainant's physical disability, the complainant would not have been able at the time of the relevant act to communicate to the defendant whether the complainant consented; and (f) that any person had administered to or caused to be taken by the complainant, without the complainant's consent, a substance which, having regard to when it was administered or taken, was capable of causing or enabling the complainant to be stupefied or overpowered at the time of the relevant act. In s 76: (a) that the defendant intentionally deceived the complainant as to the nature or purpose of the relevant act; or (b) the defendant intentionally induced the complainant to consent to the relevant act by impersonating a person known personally to the complainant.

14 *R v Bree* [2007] EWCA Crim 804 at para 34.

in sexual activity with an intoxicated individual, regardless of what she may say or do.[15] It was also seen as helping to counter any social stereotype that people who are drunk, especially young women, are, by that very fact, consenting to sexual activity or are to blame for any unwanted sexual activity which occurs.[16]

2.29 Whilst these are undoubtedly important societal aspirations, the application of this provision may raise issues of difficulty. The statutory provision does not, for example, create the offence of having sexual intercourse with a drunken woman. A woman who has voluntarily consumed a large amount of alcohol may in fact still be capable of providing meaningful consent to sexual activity, individual tolerance to the effects of alcohol may vary widely. So when the absence of free agreement is based on the state of the complainer's intoxication, the focus will not be on the complainer's state of mind, in the sense of determining as a fact whether or not there was consent. The issue will be capacity to consent and the jury or court will be required to form a view as to the extent to which the complainer's level of intoxication impeded her ability to make a meaningful decision as to whether to engage in that particular sexual activity or not. If she lacked the capacity to consent, then the sexual conduct occurred without her consent.

2.30 No guidance is given in the statutory framework as to what level of intoxication constitutes incapacity to consent, and it is unlikely that a judge would feel able to offer any test to apply or advice as to how to decide this question.[17] It has been judicially observed that it is unrealistic to endeavour to create some kind of grid system which would enable the question to be answered by reference to a prescribed level of alcohol consumption, and that experience shows that different individuals have a greater or lesser capacity to cope with alcohol than others, and that the ability of a single individual may vary from day to day.[18]

2.31 Something more than a lack of inhibition would be necessary before the section 13(2)(a) example could be held to be established. Equally, something more than a lack of inhibition which leads to activity which is later regretted would be necessary. In each of two Scottish civil cases[19] in which damages were awarded for acts of rape which were held to have occurred when the complainer was incapable of consenting as a consequence of intoxication, the presiding judge and sheriff (as he then was) framed the essential issue by drawing on what had been said in the case of *R v Bree*:

> '… the essential distinction to be drawn is that between intoxication which, on the one hand, results in a lack of capacity to make free agreement, and that, on the other, which results merely in loss of inhibition such as to alter the choices

15 SLC report at para 2.62.

16 Ibid.

17 The Jury Manual suggested directions at p 118.15/133 provide no guidance and simply repeat the statutory provision, adding only that it makes no difference whether the complainer took the alcohol or drugs him/herself/themselves or was plied them by another.

18 *R v Bree* (n 14) para 35.

19 *C v G* 2018 SC 47 and *AR v Coxen* 2018 SLT (Sh Ct) 335.

which a person might otherwise make when sober, but being insufficient to deprive that person of the capacity to consent'.

2.32 The import of subsection 13(2)(a) was considered in the case of *Maqsood v HM Advocate*,[20] where the court explained that lack of consent might be established through the evidence of the complainer as to her state of intoxication, as supported by other evidence indicative of a sufficient level of intoxication.[21] It might also be established solely through evidence of the complainer's observed behaviour. The crucial question of whether a complainer who was intoxicated did or did not have the capacity to consent will depend on an overall assessment of the whole circumstances, including her observed conduct.

2.33 It is in the nature of cases of this sort that the complainer's evidence as to her state of mind and level of thinking may be confused or unreliable. She may well have an absence of recollection for part or all of the events. In such circumstances, she may not be able to provide an answer to the question of whether she consented or not, or may be in no position to reject a suggestion that she did consent. Factors such as these do not prevent a conclusion from being reached that free agreement was absent. In the case of *HM Advocate v I*[22] (a Crown appeal against the upholding of a no case to answer submission) the court held that evidence to the effect that the complainer was heavily intoxicated was sufficient to entitle the jury to infer that she was incapable of consenting to sexual activity, despite her having no recollection of what had happened. The court emphasised that issues of consent and capacity to consent should normally be left to the jury to determine. The same approach was taken in the case of *R v Tambedou*[23] where the accused was convicted of rape when the complainer accepted in evidence that she might, or could, have consented but could not remember having intercourse at all. There was no evidence of her having been unconscious. The court held that her evidence that she could not recall whether or not she gave consent was not, without more, sufficient to allow the judge to withdraw the case from the jury. The case turned on a consideration of all of the evidence and was described as 'a classic issue for a jury'. The jury's entitlement to infer lack of consent, in an appropriate case, where a complainer had not been asked whether she was consenting to the act of intercourse was reinforced in the case of *Cowan v HM Advocate*.[24]

2.34 Accordingly, it may be appropriate to conclude that a complainer is incapable of consenting even where she instigates the sexual activity or engages in it with apparent enthusiasm. In each individual case it will be for the jury to assess whether

20 2019 JC 45.

21 *Maqsood* is expressed in terms of incapacity requiring formal proof (that is corroboration). That now falls to be read in light of *Lord Advocate's Reference No 1 of 2023* 2024 JC 140, that the elements of the crime do not need to be separately corroborated.

22 2022 SCCR 1888.

23 [2014] EWCA Crim 954.

24 [2024] HCJAC 35.

it would be appropriate to characterise the complainer as having been incapable of consenting due to her state of intoxication.

2.35 In a case based on incapacity to consent through intoxication, a reasonable belief in consent may, if put into issue, be a live consideration.[25] However, the Crown will not be seen to have periled its case on incapacity (or in a section 14 case on sleeping)[26]. Even if the court or a jury is satisfied that the complainer retained the capacity to consent, it will be essential to determine whether she did or did not in fact consent to the act alleged.[27] We discuss reasonable belief in consent below at **2.107–2.117**.

2.36 Finally, in relation to intoxication, it should be noted that the Scottish Parliament did not accept the SLC's recommendation that persons could agree in advance to have sex in such an intoxicated state as to be incapable at that point of giving consent. Accordingly, and in keeping with the general interpretation of the legislation, there can be no advance consent.

Section 13(2)(b) – Submission in the face of threats or violence

2.37 Section 13(2)(b) provides that free agreement is absent:

> '… where B agrees or submits to the conduct because of violence used against B or any other person, or because of threats of violence made against B or any other person'.

2.38 The common law position was that submission in the face of violence or threats directed towards the complainer did not equate to consent.[28] The provisions of paragraph (b) go further by expressly stating that submission in the face of violence or threats made against someone else will not constitute free agreement. In addition, the violence does not have to have occurred at or around the time of the sexual conduct. It could have occurred in the past or be a threat to inflict it in the future.[29] The subsection also contemplates that the violence or threat may be issued by someone other than person A. In this situation, if A was unaware of the reason for person B's submission, he may have a reasonable belief in consent.[30] For example, if a person pays a prostitute for sexual activity but is unaware of the fact that she has been coerced by violence into prostitution by another, he might be able to rely on a defence of reasonable belief in consent, subject to satisfying the considerations mentioned in section 16 of the 2009 Act.

25 See *Nyiam v HM Advocate* 2021 SCCR 315 at para 8.

26 See *HM Advocate v Bilaal Afzal* [2019] HCJAC 37, *Van Der Schyff v HM Advocate* [2015] HCJAC 67 and *Cowan v HM Advocate* [2024] HCJAC 35 at paras 3 and 15.

27 *LW v HM Advocate* 2023 JC 184 at para 19.

28 See *Lord Advocate's Reference No 1 of 2001*, the opinion of Lord Justice General Cullen at para 11 and Hume i, 302 as quoted by the Lord Justice General at para 4 of his opinion.

29 SLC report paras 2.67 and 2.68.

30 Subject to s 16 considerations and the basis of the claimed absence of knowledge.

2.39 The example mentioned in paragraph (b) makes it plain that this form of submission is not to be equated with free agreement but tells us nothing more about how submission in other circumstances is to be viewed. There may well be other circumstances in which there is no consent even though the situation described in section 13(2)(b) is not present: see the section below on the effect of other forms of pressure on free agreement.

Section 13(2)(c) – Unlawful detention

2.40 The example given in this paragraph is that free agreement is absent:

> '… where B agrees or submits to the conduct because B is unlawfully detained by A'.

2.41 This is a good illustration of the fact that the section 13(2) provisions are not exhaustive as to where free agreement will be absent. They are not intended to be a comprehensive list, nor to define the scope of consent within the type of circumstance identified and they do not limit the scope of the section 12 general definition. This paragraph specifies detention by the individual engaging in the sexual conduct. However, free agreement could just as easily be absent where a person is unlawfully detained by one person and then submits to intercourse by one of his associates or an entirely unconnected individual.

Section 13(2)(d) – Deception as to nature or purpose

2.42 This paragraph of section 13(2) introduces consideration of the effect of deception in determining whether consent is or is not present. The scope of this example is limited. It provides that free agreement is absent where:

> '… B agrees or submits to the conduct because B is mistaken, as a result of deception by A, as to the nature or purpose of the conduct'.

2.43 As the SLC noted, there may be a degree of overlap between the distinct ideas of nature and purpose[31] but the type of deception envisaged in the example set out in this paragraph is likely to occur in the context of conduct agreed to as part of a medical procedure, or what is understood or represented to be a medical procedure. The case of *Baillie v HM Advocate*[32] concerned a doctor who pleaded guilty to 17 charges of indecent assault by engaging in sexual acts with female patients conducted under the guise of behaviour conducted as medical examinations, or for other clinical purposes. This lends support to the proposition that such deception as to nature or

31 Para 2.73.

32 2007 SCCR 26.

purpose negated consent at common law[33] but the issue was not the subject of judicial analysis in that case or in any other reported Scottish case.

2.44 The position in England and Wales, where judicial analysis has been brought to bear, is instructive because section 13(2)(d) is identical to the conclusive presumption against consent specified in section 76(2)(a) of the 2003 Act. The common law position in England and Wales was always that fraud as to the nature of the act done vitiated consent.[34] This was illustrated by what came to be referred to as the 'medical cases' such as *R v Flattery*[35] and *R v Williams*[36] in each of which the accused engaged in sexual intercourse having deceived the complainer as to the nature of the conduct. As it was explained in the subsequent case of *R v Linekar*,[37] the victim did not agree in those cases to sexual intercourse. In the former she agreed to a surgical procedure which she hoped would cure her fits, and in the latter, she agreed to physical manipulation which would provide her with extra air supply to improve her singing. The rationale for the conviction in each case was explained as being:

> '... it is the non-consent to sexual intercourse rather than the fraud of the doctor or choirmaster that makes the offence rape'.

2.45 For the purposes of the English common law the 'nature of the conduct' fell to be strictly construed as the actual sexual act itself. This is clear from the circumstances of *R v Clarence* where the accused kept his diagnosis of gonorrhoea from his wife, who would not have agreed to have intercourse with him had she known. He was charged with assault, but the analysis by the court made it clear that the deceit which he engaged in by suppressing the knowledge of his condition did not alter the fact that she had consented to intercourse.

2.46 The analysis undertaken in subsequent case law demonstrates that the section 76(2)(a) conclusive presumption was declaratory of the common law position. It is likely that the Scottish courts would follow that analysis should similar issues arise in this jurisdiction. The consequence would be that the deception specified in paragraph 13(2)(d) will continue to have very limited application. The impact of other types of deception may, however, fall to be examined in terms of the general section 12 definition of free agreement.

Section 13(2)(e) – Impersonation

2.47 The example set out in this paragraph provides that free agreement will be absent:

33 *Gordon, Criminal Law* at para 38.10 states that the common law courts recognised fraud as to nature but not fraud as to purpose but no mention is made of *Baillie* nor the English cases.

34 *R v Clarence* (1889) 22 QBD 23 per Stephen J at p 43.

35 (1887) 2 QBD 410.

36 [1923] 1 KB 340.

37 [1995] QB 250.

> 'where B agrees or submits to the conduct because A induces B to agree or submit to the conduct by impersonating a person known personally to B'.

2.48 The common law position in both Scotland and England and Wales was at least confused as to whether a man who obtained intercourse by impersonating a woman's husband committed rape[38] but legislation passed in 1885, which remained in force in Scotland until the implementation of the 2009 Act, declared that it was.[39] In England and Wales the legislation was deemed to be declaratory of the common law position. As a consequence, in the case of *R v Elbekkay*[40] the court felt able to approve of the trial judge's direction that it was rape to impersonate the complainer's partner as much as it would have been to impersonate her husband. However, since the common law position in Scotland (as explained in *William Fraser*) was that rape was not committed by impersonating a woman's husband the pre-2009 Act position here concerning impersonation of a partner remains unclear.

2.49 The section 13(2)(e) provision, however, is straightforward and extends the offence beyond the impersonation of a woman's husband. The offence is no longer limited by sex or marriage and the most obvious situation contemplated in the paragraph is the impersonation of person B's partner. Whilst the scope is clearly wider than this, no explanation is given as to 'what known personally to B' encompasses. A common sense approach would suggest a straightforward meaning. Sexual activity entered into as part of an encounter in which one party deceived the other by pretending to be, for example, a famous celebrity or sportsperson (assuming that the complainer did not know that individual personally) would not fall within the circumstances in which consent is deemed absent.

Section 13(2)(f) – agreement provided by someone other than person B

2.50 The final section 13(2) paragraph provides the example that free agreement will be absent:

> 'where the only expression or indication of agreement to the conduct is from a person other than B'.

2.51 This example appears to anticipate circumstances such as those present in the case of *DPP v Morgan*,[41] where three young men convicted of rape claimed that the victim's husband had informed them that she would be willing to consent to intercourse with them and that any apparent resistance on her part would be a mere pretence. The decision in the case concerned the issue of mistaken belief in consent, and the court held that a genuine belief in consent, even if based on

38 The case of *William Fraser* (1847) Ark. 280 held that it was not. *R v Barrow* LR 1 CCR 156 was to the same effect but the contrary view in the case of *R v Dee* (1884) 14 LR Ir 468 came to be preferred.

39 Criminal Law Consolidation (Scotland) Act 1995, s 7(3) which derived from the Criminal Law Amendment Act 1885, s 4.

40 [1995] Crim LR 163.

41 [1976] AC 182.

unreasonable grounds would constitute a defence to a charge of rape. The definition of rape in section 1 of the 2009 Act addresses this by providing that any belief in consent must be reasonable and section 16 focuses this further. At first blush, therefore, the paragraph (f) example might appear to be out of place. It might be thought that the absence of consent would be established by the victim's testimony and any such explanation as was advanced in *Morgan* could only go to reasonable belief. The real import of this example, however, is to underline that as a matter of law consent cannot be granted by someone other than person B. The consequence of this statement is that any explanation as to consent given to the accused by a third party will not be capable of providing the basis for a reasonable belief in consent.[42]

The effects of other forms of pressure on free agreement

2.52 The experience of the courts demonstrates that sexual activity may take place in a range of circumstances involving the application of pressure, or coercion, falling short of threats of violence. The cases discussed below show that apparent consent may not constitute free agreement where the complainer participates in circumstances short of conventionally understood threats. The application of pressure, or coercion, short of violence, may mean that apparent consent is not to be treated as 'real' consent or as free agreement. This is an application of the principle of autonomy which underpins the entire policy of the 2009 Act and which directs attention to the complainer's state of mind rather than just what she may have said or done. The lesson to be drawn is that free agreement involves a positive model of consent. Instead of questioning whether a complainer (usually female) took any steps to stop the particular sexual activity engaged in from happening, the focus ought to be on what the accused person did to achieve the woman's consent.

2.53 The cases discussed for this purpose are: *HM Advocate v SM*,[43] *Briggs v HM Advocate*,[44] *Anderson v HM Advocate*,[45] *R v Jheeta*[46] and *R v Ivor and others*.[47]

42 This proposition is supported by analogy with the statement in *HM Advocate v JW* 2020 SCCR 174 para 21 where the view of the first instance judge, as adopted by the Appeal Court, was that since as a matter of law a prior expression of willingness to engage in sexual activity could not constitute consent to a subsequent act of that kind, then it could not provide the basis for a 'reasonable' belief in consent either. This analysis excludes for example the position of an interpreter translating sign language for an individual incapable of speech: the difference is that B communicates her consent through the interpreter.

43 2019 JC 176.

44 2019 SCCR 323.

45 HCA/2021/501/XC.

46 [2008] 1 WLR 2582.

47 [2021] EWCA Crim 923.

HM Advocate v SM

2.54 The accused was charged with abduction, assault, and rape at common law of his then partner. Having assaulted her when they left a nightclub together, the accused drove the complainer to an isolated area where the sexual activity took place. The complainer's explanation was that she was worried by his behaviour and decided she needed to calm the situation down. She 'agreed to sleep with him' and accepted that she had started the sexual interaction between the two, explaining that she did so because she needed to defuse the situation and get home. As she stated: 'I consented not because I wanted sex … But just to calm him down'.

2.55 The case came before the Appeal Court on a Crown appeal against the trial judge's decision to uphold a submission of no case to answer. The trial judge agreed with the defence submission that the complainer's testimony did not amount to a description of rape. In allowing the appeal, the court held that it would be open to the jury to conclude that the complainer did not wish to have intercourse and acquiesced only by reason of very pressing circumstances brought about by the accused. The Lord Justice General stated:

> 'The issue is whether, taking the evidence of the complainer at its highest the jury could infer a lack of consent as a matter of fact.'[48]

2.56 The concept of consent was addressed by Lord Brodie (with whose analysis the other judges agreed) in the course of which he took account of the decision of the Court of Appeal of England and Wales in *R v Olugboja*[49] and the decision of the New Zealand Court of Appeal in *R v Daniels*.[50] He stated:

> 'I do not consider that it can be suggested that the law of Scotland as to what was meant by 'consent' in the context of the law of rape post Lord Advocate's Reference (No 1 of 2001) was any different from what was understood by consent by the courts in Olugboja and Daniels. As the sheriff said in Marr v HM Advocate, with the approval of the Appeal Court: 'Consent is consent.' Such a meaning is consistent with the definition of 'free agreement' which is now provided by sec 12 of the Sexual Offences (Scotland) Act 2009 (asp 9). In making their proposals which led to the enactment of the 2009 Act the Scottish Law Commission saw a need to provide a definition for consent but there is no suggestion that in what they described as defining the law that they were departing from what was understood to be meant by consent as a matter of the pre-existing common law. An agreement is not free if it only arises as a result of very pressing circumstances brought about by the acts of the other party, just as consent is not real if it is only the result of such circumstances.'

2.57 Lord Brodie observed elsewhere in his opinion that consent has no single 'normal meaning'. The point he was making was that there is a place on the spectrum

48 Para 9 quoting *Marr v HM Advocate* per Lord Justice Clerk Ross at p 699.
49 [1982] QB 320.
50 [1986] 2 NZLR 106.

of what might be called 'consent' where consent may not have been entirely vitiated but nevertheless acquiescence in sexual activity is so reluctant by reason of external circumstances that it does not amount to consent in any real sense.

Briggs v HM Advocate

2.58 In this case, the 17-year-old appellant was convicted on a charge of indecent assault of his 15-year-old cousin, which included penetrating her mouth with his penis and of rape. Evidence was also led in support of a docket that on various occasions when the complainer was aged between 4 and 15 years the appellant had engaged in similar sexual conduct with her, short of vaginal intercourse. On those occasions, the complainer often tried to resist in various ways, but the appellant would persist in the face of this and she would sometimes comply reluctantly in the face of his 'incessant attempts'.

2.59 Speaking of the events in the charge, the complainer described how she reacted to the appellant approaching her while she was in bed and touching her sexually. She used language which implied that she was not a willing participant, although she said nothing about this to the appellant. She explained that he then 'asked' her to suck his penis and she acceded to this request. An act of this sort consensually engaged in could not constitute indecent assault at common law (or rape under section 1 of the 2009 Act). On appeal, it was contended that the trial judge had erred in refusing to give effect to a motion of no case to answer. Whilst in the end the focus of the appeal came to be on the issue of the appellant's *mens rea* the court assessed both the evidence as to consent and the accused's understanding.

2.60 The court concluded that whilst it was possible to point to certain actions by the complainer which might have indicated that she was willing to participate in sexual activity with the appellant, there was sufficient when taken at its highest in her evidence about her body language to entitle the jury to conclude that she had been unwilling. The court also observed that the history of unwanted sexual advances by the appellant would have entitled the jury to consider whether any apparent consent was 'real' consent or simply acquiescence.

Anderson v HM Advocate

2.61 In this case, the question for the court was whether the evidence of the complainer entitled the jury to be satisfied that she was not consenting to the sexual acts, including rape, all of which were charged as contraventions of the 2009 Act. The sexual conduct occurred within the context of what was described as a coercive and controlling relationship. The complainer gave evidence that the accused had intercourse with her in a manner which was sore, but she did not ask him to stop. At paragraph 6 of the opinion the court stated:

> 'Whether or not there is free agreement is a matter for the jury to determine having regard to all of the circumstances. The evidence of the complainer has to be looked at as a whole.'

2.62 The court was satisfied there was sufficient evidence for the jury to conclude that the complainer was not consenting and explained its decision by stating:

> 'It was not necessary for her to articulate that lack of consent to the accused, although her evidence was that she moved and he knew it was sore for her. She made that plain on many occasions. Despite that, he carried on, although she did not want to have sexual intercourse which was painful. The relationship was a coercive and controlling one and the jury could infer that her acquiescence did not amount to free agreement.'

2.63 The import of the court's decision was that in the circumstances of the parties' relationship, acquiescence in painful intercourse was capable of constituting something less than free agreement.

2.64 Whilst none of these three cases involved direct threats or violence preceding the sexual acts, it may be said that the events in each took place in an intimidating atmosphere and where the complainer was influenced by fear or a sense of futility. They make it clear that there is no requirement for the Cown to prove that the complainer did or said something to demonstrate that she was not consenting, or that she otherwise communicated that absence of consent to the accused.

R v Jheeta

2.65 Other forms of pressure applied to a complainer which had the effect of persuading her to engage in sexual activity can also be capable of leading to a conclusion that consent was absent, as is evidenced by the decision in the case of *R v Jheeta*.

2.66 In that case, the complainer's boyfriend created an elaborate scheme designed to persuade her that she was in danger and that he could protect her and pretended to have involved the police on her behalf. When she tried to break off the relationship he sent her various text messages pretending to be coming from police officers informing her that her boyfriend had tried to kill himself, that she needed to take care of him, that she should sleep with him and that she would be liable to a fine if she did not. The Court of Appeal accepted that the accused had persuaded the complainer to have intercourse with him more frequently than she otherwise would have, and that the persuasion took the form of the pressures imposed upon her by the unpleasant scheme which he had fabricated. In these circumstances the complainer had not exercised a free choice or consented. The approach taken in this case was subsequently described as an example of the 'well-established approach to cases involving pressure or coercion short of violence'.[51]

51 *R (Monica) v DPP* [2019] QB 1019 at para 69.

R v Ivor and others

2.67 In this case, the four appellants were prosecuted for various offences arising out of a large drugs supply conspiracy in which their co-defendant, referred to as 'Smith', was the leading drugs conspirator. The complainant Miss 'X' was Smith's much younger partner and he obtained sexual satisfaction from watching her having sex with his friends, who included the four appellants. Whilst Miss X apparently consented to engaging in sexual activity with the appellants, the issues in the case included the question of whether that consent was genuine.

2.68 The evidence disclosed that Smith was known to be violent and engaged in coercive control over Miss X. Her evidence was that she acquiesced to his demands to have sex with his friends to stop him from getting angry and that the reality was that he was passing her around his friends like a sex doll. The prosecution case against each appellant was that they knew Smith well and, as was known to them, he was demonstrably a man of violence who sought to dominate. He ran his crime business with a rod of iron. They knew that there was a disparity of power in his relationship with Miss X and they were aware that before engaging in sexual activity with each of them she needed to drink a lot of alcohol and take drugs. None of them made any inquiry of her. Accordingly it should have been apparent to them that her ostensible consent was not real. On appeal the Court held that the trial judge had been right to leave the question of consent to the jury.[52]

2.69 The combined analysis in these five cases is capable of helping to inform what constitutes consent in terms of the general definition given in section 12 of the 2009 Act. It also demonstrates the importance of context. For example, and by way of contrast with the case of *Anderson*, if one partner in a happy and loving relationship found a particular form of sexual activity to be uncomfortable or painful but nevertheless agreed to participate to please their partner, it would seem unlikely that this state of mind could be described as anything other than free agreement.

2.70 The cases considered demonstrate the extent to which consent is dependent upon an assessment of the complainer's state of mind, and they make it clear that submission, or acquiescence, even without accompanying threats of violence, or any other form of threat, may constitute an absence of free agreement and entitle a jury to conclude that the activity occurred without the complainer's consent.

2.71 What has become clear is that context may acquire particular importance. It may be necessary to take account of the surrounding circumstances in which the conduct occurred so as to acknowledge the effects of any form of intimidation or similar pressure, any history of coercive conduct, any relevant power imbalance or other vulnerability. All of these considerations may apply to the issue of determining

52 In the preface to the 6th edition of Rook and Ward the authors describe this case as an example of an increasing approach towards leaving cases of psychological coercion rather than violence to juries. They suggest that the case illustrates how juries are correctly being left to decide whether apparent consent was in reality a genuine consent in situations where such an argument would not have seen the light of day only a few years previously.

the fact of a complainer's state of mind. Once the question of what constitutes consent is viewed in this manner, it becomes clear that what the complainer did, or the language used by her in describing what took place is not necessarily the determining feature (as it was not in *SM*). Even in the absence of a threat of, or actual violence, consent which is properly understood to be mere submission, or acquiescence, may not amount to consent in any real sense for common law purposes, or to free agreement if considering the statutory definition.

2.72 The matter does not end there of course; the accused's state of mind, or *mens rea* may remain to be determined separately. At this stage we remain solely concerned with the issue of consent and therefore with the *actus reus*.

The effect of deception on free agreement

2.73 The statutory provisions say nothing about the effect of deception on free agreement, other than in the very narrow circumstances relating to the impersonation of someone known to the complainer and in relation to the nature of the activity. There may be many other forms of deception which lead to sexual activity which would not have occurred but for that deceit. Certain very obvious examples of deception which would have no effect on the issue of consent can be identified. Lies about status or wealth which induce one party to enter into a sexual relationship would have no effect on the issue of consent. The same applies to lies about not being married, or about being committed to a relationship with the other sexual partner. A collection of cases decided in the English courts since the passing of the 2003 Act has provided a degree of clarity about the extent to which consent does or does not depend on the subjective view of the woman concerned and identifies the nature of acts of deception which will go to vitiate consent.

2.74 The cases concerned are *R (F) v DPP*,[53] *Assange v Swedish Prosecution Authority*,[54] *R v B*,[55] *R v Lawrence*,[56] *R v McNally*,[57] *R (Monica) v DPP*[58] and *R v Linekar*.[59]

2.75 The analysis brought to bear in these cases, all involving different forms of deception, affirmed that freedom of choice is crucial to the issue of consent and recognised that the general definition of consent in section 74 of the 2003 Act may have made a modest extension to the common law position. But any suggestion that Parliament had intended a sea change in the meaning of consent was firmly rejected (as it was in the Scottish case of *HM Advocate v SM*). The principle which can be identified is that deception, which is closely connected

53 [2014] QB 581.
54 [2011] EWHC 2849 (Admin).
55 [2007] 1 WLR 1567.
56 [2020] EWCA Crim 971.
57 [2014] QB 593.
58 [2019] QB 1019.
59 [1995] QB 250.

with the nature or purposes of the act, because it relates to sexual intercourse itself rather than the broad circumstances surrounding it, is capable of negating a complainer's consent.

2.76 In light of the authority of the various courts in which these decisions were reached, and the detailed analysis undertaken in each, it is likely that the principle identified would be applied in this jurisdiction and that if similar types of deception were engaged in within Scotland similar approaches would be taken by the Scottish courts. It may therefore be helpful to give a brief account of the guidance available.

2.77 A woman is entitled to insist that the man withdraws from within her before ejaculating as a condition of agreeing to intercourse. If, having pretended to agree to that condition, the man has no intention of so doing and ejaculates inside her the consent which the woman gave is vitiated – *R (F) v DPP*.

2.78 A woman is entitled to insist on the use of a condom as a condition to the granting of her consent to an act of intercourse. If the man agrees to that condition, then clearly the act of intercourse which follows is with her consent. If he surreptitiously removes or deliberately breaks the condom, that is an act of deception which is so closely connected to the act of intercourse itself, and with the nature of the act of intercourse, as to negate the consent which the woman has given – *Assange v Swedish Prosecution Authority*.[60]

2.79 A failure to disclose a sexually transmissible disease, or even an express deception as to infection, will not affect the issue of consent, even where the woman makes it a condition of agreeing to intercourse that the man is free of infection. The deception in such a case is as to the risk of infection rather than as to the nature or purpose of the sexual intercourse – *R v B*.[61]

2.80 Where a woman relies on a man's deception that he has had a vasectomy and would not otherwise have consented to unprotected sexual intercourse with him, the woman is deceived about the nature and quality of the ejaculate and therefore of the risks and possible consequences of unprotected intercourse. The deception involved relates not to the physical performance of the sexual act but to the risks or consequence associated with it. It is not sufficiently closely connected to the performance of sexual intercourse as to vitiate the consent given – *R v Lawrence*.[62]

60 A similar conclusion was reached by the Supreme Court of Canada in the case of *R v Hutchison* 2014 1 SCR 346 when it held that the complainer's consent to intercourse was vitiated by fraud because of the conduct of the accused in deliberately poking holes in the condom which he used, leading to the complainer becoming pregnant.

61 And the subsequent explanation at para 83 of the decision in *Assange v Swedish Prosecution Authority*. Failing to disclose an infection such as HIV to a sexual partner may constitute the offence of culpable and reckless conduct – see, eg, *HM Advocate v Mola* 2007 SCCR 124.

62 This decision has been the subject of substantial academic criticism – see, eg, Rook and Ward at paras 1.244 to 1.248.

2.81 Deception as to gender on the part of a sexual partner may *depending on the circumstances*[63] vitiate consent. Consent will be vitiated where a female agrees to have intercourse with a person who pretends to be a male but who is in fact a female – *R v McNally*.[64]

2.82 Deception as to identity will not affect the fact that consent was given to acts of intercourse, even if the deception went to the entire extent of the individual's background, beliefs and personality and where the woman concerned would not have entertained a relationship with the man had she known of his true identity – *R (Monica) v DPP*.[65]

2.83 If a man procures intercourse with a prostitute by the fraudulent promise of paying for her services free agreement is present on her part, even if the man never intended to, and did not, pay the sum agreed – *R v Linekar*.

Grooming

2.84 The practice of grooming, though not a legal term of art, is well recognised by the Scottish criminal courts, and is routinely referred to by the Appeal Court to characterise offending behaviour, to identify any similarities in behaviour for the purposes of mutual corroboration, and to evaluate the seriousness of it in sentencing appeals. There has not been any appellate consideration in Scotland of the extent to which grooming can vitiate consent, but cases have proceeded to trial – and resulted in convictions – where the Crown case has been that the complainer's consent has been vitiated by grooming. In putting its case on that basis, the Crown has relied on leading authorities in England and Wales, which recognise that grooming can, in certain circumstances, vitiate consent. It is instructive therefore to look at these authorities, their understanding of grooming, and the principles on vitiation of consent that emerge from them.

2.85 The term grooming has become so commonplace that it might be thought unwise to attempt a comprehensive definition now. Perhaps for that reason, the Court of Appeal of England and Wales has repeatedly declined to attempt such a definition, but has variously described grooming as 'cynical and manipulative behaviour designed to achieve a particular sexual objective';[66] 'trying to obtain the confidence of the intended victim and to break down that person's inhibitions';[67] and 'using

63 This was the cautious manner in which this proposition was stated by the LCJ in delivering the decision of the court in the case of *McNally*.

64 In the subsequent case of *R (Monica) v DPP* the ratio of *McNally* was explained as being that as a matter of common sense there is all of the difference in the world between sexual activity with a boy and similar activities with a girl.

65 Where an undercover police officer formed a relationship with an environmental activist who understood that he shared her core beliefs and would not have entered any form of relationship with him had she know the truth.

66 *R v Robinson* [2011] EWCA Crim 916 at para 22.

67 *R v H (J B J)* [2014] EWCA Crim 2873 at para 20.

an opportunity for contact in a way which opens the door to sexual offending'.[68] In *Robinson*, the appellant had initiated a relationship with his partner's teenage daughter, ZK, which progressed from touching to a full sexual relationship, against the background of spending a great deal of time with her, continually praising her, and then initiating sexual contact. ZK gave ambivalent evidence as to whether she wanted the sexual intercourse to happen; the trial judge concluded that there were passages in that evidence which would allow the jury to conclude that she submitted to intercourse rather than consented to it. In dismissing Robinson's appeal, the Court observed:

> 'Not all relationships with underage children can fairly be characterised as involving grooming, although many will. But even where they can, the fact of grooming plainly does not necessarily vitiate consent. Many a seducer achieves his objectives with the liberal and cynical employment of gifts, insincere compliments and false promises. But such manipulative and deceitful methods could not be relied upon to establish a lack of consent whenever the seduction was successful. The situation will often be no different where the complainant is under age. But where the exploitation is of a girl who is of an age where she does not, or may not, have the capacity to understand the full significance of what she is doing, and in particular, where, as here, there was evidence of acquiescence or acceptance rather than positive consent, we think that, as the judge found, it would be open to the jury to conclude that the complainant, perhaps out of embarrassment or some other reason, had in reality unwillingly gone along with the acts which she did not in fact wish to engage in.'

2.86 The Court went further in *R v Ali (Yasir)* where the appellants had been targeting young girls, often from troubled backgrounds, and driving them to out-of-the-way locations such as 'parties' at hotels, where they sexually assaulted and raped them, often after giving them alcohol.[69] There was no evidence of an express lack of consent by the girls, but the trial judge directed the jury to consider whether there was in fact genuine consent (and not merely submission) and, in so doing, to consider the position of young immature complainants, evidence of exploitation, and factors such as the age and maturity of each complainant, the history of the relationship between the parties and the nature of the sexual encounter, and the consumption of significant amounts of alcohol. The Court, in dismissing the appeals, observed (at paragraph 58):

> 'One of the consequences of grooming is that it has a tendency to limit or subvert the alleged victim's capacity to make free decisions, and it creates the

68 *R v I (M)* [2015] EWCA Crim 1375 at para 13. Rook and Ward at para 1.192 observe that the classic cases of grooming tend to involve the manipulation of an individual, often a teenage girl, so as to achieve and/or obtain opportunities for sexual exploitation of that individual. It can manifest itself in incremental steps such as providing: (i) time, attention and apparent friendship, sometimes over the internet; (ii) gifts; (iii) alcohol; and (iv) drugs. It may evolve into violence and threats of violence to ensure the sexual objective.

69 [2015] 2 Cr App R 33.

> risk that he or she simply submitted because of the environment of dependency created by those responsible for treating the alleged victim in this way. Indeed, the individual may have been manipulated to the extent that he or she is unaware of, or confused about, the distinction between acquiescence and genuine agreement at the time the incident occurred.'

2.87 It also emphasised that in cases in which a vulnerable or immature individual has allegedly been groomed by the defendant, the question of whether real or proper consent was given will usually be for the jury unless the evidence clearly indicates that proper consent was given.[70] The Court was also at pains to emphasise that the prosecution is not obliged to call overt evidence from the alleged victim to the effect that he or she did not consent, given that it is possible that the circumstances may have limited or distorted the individual's appreciation or understanding of his or her role in the sexual relations and the true nature of what occurred.[71]

2.88 The approach taken in *Robinson* and *Ali* was followed in *R v Usman and others*[72] (exploitation by various means of two care-experienced teenagers) and *R v Taylor* (sexual activity between a teacher and young pupil at a boarding school).[73]

2.89 We suggest that all four authorities are likely to be persuasive should any of the situations arise in a Scottish case. We would add that grooming is not limited to children. It can – and often does – involve the exploitation of other vulnerabilities. A common one is drug addition, where A provides drugs to B on the condition that B have sex with A. Much will depend on the circumstances. Setting aside cases of inability to consent because of intoxication, the voluntary supply and taking of drugs together will not, without more, amount to A's grooming of B and not vitiate B's consent. But if A's intention in supplying the drugs is to make B addicted or to feed B's existing addiction so that A can exploit that addiction to obtain sex from B, then A's behaviour may amount to vitiation of B's consent in the same way as any other manipulation of B for the purposes of sexual exploitation. There are likely to be other scenarios. In any case of grooming, as with consent generally, the questions are always: (i) whether A acted in the way alleged; (ii) whether the context is such that B did not freely agree to sexual activity.

Section 14 of the 2009 Act: asleep or unconscious

2.90 Section 14 of the 2009 Act provides that (in relation to sections 1 to 9 of the Act) a person is incapable while asleep or unconscious of consenting to any conduct.

2.91 This is an unambiguous statement that sexual activity with a sleeping person will constitute criminal conduct, since that person cannot consent whilst in

70 At para 61.
71 Para 56.
72 [2021] EWCA Crim 502.
73 [2022] EWCA Crim 1207.

that condition. Nor is it possible for consent to be given in advance to sexual activity whilst asleep. In the case of *GW v HM Advocate*[74] the court made it clear that consent must be given at the time of the sexual act and not at a point remote from it.[75] One of the important consequences which flows from the decision in *GW* is that since consent cannot lawfully be issued in advance, the question of whether a complainer consented to sexual activity on a particular occasion cannot be illuminated to any extent by prior expressions of interest in sexual activity with that person by the complainer. Any such evidence would be inadmissible as collateral and irrelevant.[76]

2.92 Furthermore, since a person is incapable while asleep or unconscious of consenting to any conduct, someone who appreciates that the person is asleep cannot reasonably believe that she is consenting.[77]

Section 15 of the 2009 Act: the scope of consent and withdrawal

2.93 Section 15 of the Act provides, in statutory form, the self-evident statement that consent to conduct does not of itself imply consent to any other conduct. It also provides that consent may be withdrawn at any time before or during the conduct, and if conduct takes place after consent has been withdrawn, it takes place, or continues to take place, without consent. Although uncontroversial in its language, section 15 provides the basis for many prosecutions for serious sexual offences, including rape. There are many examples of prosecutions which allege that sexual intercourse, which began as a consensual act, became non-consensual and constituted the crime of rape when person A is asked to withdraw his penis and refuses to do so, or when A engages in a different form of penetration without B consenting to that act. The section also underpins aspects of the jurisprudence relating to the application of section 275 of the 1995 Act by making it clear why evidence of prior sexual activity is irrelevant. Consent even shortly before a sexual encounter does not imply the presence of consent during a later event.[78]

Section 17: capacity of mentally disordered persons

2.94 Section 17 reads:

> **'Capacity to consent**
>
> (1) This section applies in relation to sections 1 to 9.

74 2019 JC 109.

75 In this regard the statutory provision departed from the recommendation made by the SLC.

76 *HM Advocate v JW* and *CH v HM Advocate* 2021 JC 45 at paras 61 and 65.

77 GW para 27. The circumstances in which reasonable belief in consent may be a live issue where the complainer maintains that she was asleep at the time of penetration will, at best, be vanishingly rare – *LW v HM Advocate* [2023] HCJAC 18 at para 19. See further at **2.114**.

78 SLC para 2.83.

(2) A mentally disordered person is incapable of consenting to conduct where, by reason of mental disorder, the person is unable to do one or more of the following—
(a) understand what the conduct is,
(b) form a decision as to whether to engage in the conduct (or as to whether the conduct should take place),
(c) communicate any such decision.

(3) In this Act, 'mental disorder' has the same meaning as in section 328 of the Mental Health (Care and Treatment) (Scotland) Act 2003 (asp 13) (and related expressions are to be construed accordingly).'

2.95 Section 17 has its origins in section 311 of the Mental Health (Care and Treatment) (Scotland) Act 2003. This Act codified the mental health law generally in Scotland and created two criminal offences in respect of sexual activity with a mentally disordered person: non-consensual sexual acts with a mentally disordered person (section 311), and an abuse of trust offence of engaging in sexual activity with a mentally disordered person while providing a care service to them (section 313).[79]

2.96 Section 311 had been enacted because of the problem, noted above, that the common law at the time provided little guidance on what consent meant. This made it particularly difficult to apply the common law in cases where a person had a mental disorder.

2.97 Section 311 was an offence in two parts. By section 311(1) and (2) it was an offence to engage in sexual intercourse or any other sexual act with or towards a mentally disordered person if the mentally disordered person either: (a) did not consent to the act; or (b) by reason of mental disorder, was incapable of consenting to the act.

2.98 By section 311(3), the mentally disordered person was to be regarded as not consenting if he or she purported to consent as a result of:
(a) being placed in such a state of fear; or
(b) being subjected to any such–
 (i) threat;
 (ii) intimidation;
 (iii) deceit; or
 (iv) persuasion,

as vitiated that person's consent.

2.99 This was the lack of consent part of the offence.

2.100 By section 311(4), a mentally disordered person was incapable of consent if he or she was unable to:

79 S 313 was re-enacted as s 46 of the 2009 Act, both of these ss are considered in Chapter 5. S 311 is considered in Chapter 12.

(a) understand what the act was;
(b) form a decision as to whether to engage in the act (or as to whether the act should take place); or
(c) communicate any such decision.

2.101 This was the lack of capacity part of the offence.

2.102 The SLC considered whether, in light of the consent model it proposed for the Act generally, there would be no need for section 311. It ultimately concluded that the better approach was to repeal section 311(3) because it would be confusing to have one definition of consent for general application and a different definition for a person with a mental disorder, but to retain and re-enact subsection (4) because of the value in having a provision on the capacity of someone with a mental disorder to consent. It emphasised, though, that the fact that someone has a mental disorder does not mean that he or she necessarily or always lacks capacity to consent.[80]

2.103 Section 17 thus re-enacts section 311(4). It is directed only to capacity to consent. Where, applying the definition of capacity in section 17, a mentally disordered person has no capacity, there is no consent, and the Crown needs to do nothing further to prove lack of consent.[81] Where a mentally disordered person has capacity to consent but the issue is whether he or she in fact consented, the general provisions in sections 12 to 15 apply.

2.104 The meaning of mental disorder in section 328 of the 2003 Act, adopted via section 17(5), is any mental illness, personality disorder or learning disability, however caused or manifested. By section 328(2), a person is not mentally disordered by reason only of any of the following:
(a) sexual orientation;
(b) sexual deviancy;
(c) transsexualism;
(d) transvestism;
(e) dependence on, or use of, alcohol or drugs;
(f) behaviour that causes, or is likely to cause, harassment, alarm or distress to any other person;
(g) acting as no prudent person would act.

Is there a limit to what can be consented to?

2.105 The core principle of respect for a person's sexual autonomy, which underpinned the SLC report led to the view that sexual practices involving consent should not, unless there are weighty overriding reasons, be subject to legal sanctions.[82]

80 Para 4.95 of the SLC's report.
81 Or, as it was put in *Winton v HM Advocate* 2016 SLT 393, the effect of the provision is that, where the requirements of s 17 are met, the Crown does not need to prove lack of consent. This was said in respect of s 1, the offence in that case, but it is suggested the same logic applies for ss 2 to 9.
82 Report para 5.19.

As the authors recognised, difficult issues arise when applying this principle to sexual activities which consist of sado-masochistic practices. In general terms, the infliction of violence is treated in Scots law as an assault, and the apparent consent of the 'victim' will be irrelevant, although the SLC's view seemed to be that the law of assault would not apply to activities to which all parties had given their consent for the purposes of sexual gratification.[83] Its view was that the matter should be expressly stated in law to remove any doubt. As a consequence, section 37 of the draft bill proposed that it would not be the crime of assault for a person aged 16 years or over to attack another person aged 16 years or over where the attack is carried out for the purpose of providing sexual gratification to either of them, that each agrees as to the purpose of the attack, consents to it and the attack is unlikely to result in serious injury. However, the Scottish Parliament declined to include the terms of this proposed provision within the 2009 Act.

2.106 The position in English law may not provide particularly helpful guidance given the difference between the law of assault as between England and Scotland. It may be noted though that the position in England and Wales appears to be that consent to participating in sado-masochistic practices which do not involve the infliction of serious bodily harm may mean that no offence is committed,[84] whereas if such practices involve the infliction of serious bodily harm, consent will not operate as a defence.[85] It may also be noted that the European Court of Human Rights has held that Member States are entitled to regulate, through the operation of the criminal law, activities which involve the infliction of physical harm, whether the activities occur in the course of sexual conduct or otherwise.[86]

REASONABLE BELIEF AS TO CONSENT

2.107 As noted above, the offences created in Part 1 of the 2009 Act are each defined by the absence of consent and the absence of a reasonable belief as to consent. It follows that in relation to belief in consent, the Act has in mind an objective assessment rather than a subjective one, an honest belief will not be sufficient. It would require to be based on reasonable grounds. The absence of a reasonable belief is a constituent element of the offence: the offence creating provisions do not provide for the defence of reasonable belief in consent.[87]

2.108 The decision in the case of *Graham v HM Advocate*[88] (in dealing with the offence of rape under section 1), acknowledged that an absence of a reasonable belief was an essential element of the offence but explained that it was not something which

83 Report para 5.23.
84 *R v Wilson* [1997] QB 47.
85 *R v Brown* [1994] 1 AC 212.
86 *Laskey, Jaggard and Brown v United Kingdom* (1997) 24 EHHR 39.
87 *Winton v HM Advocate* 2017 SCCR 320.
88 2017 SCCR 497.

required to be established by corroborated evidence.[89] The purpose of the statutory reference to a reasonable belief in consent was not to add a new requirement but simply to change that part of the mental element from an absence of an honest belief to an absence of a reasonable one. Whether a person had, or did not have, a reasonable belief was an inference to be drawn from proven facts[90] and a direction by a trial judge on reasonable belief was not required unless that issue was live.

2.109 This decision was intended to bring about a significant change in the practice adopted in charging juries in relation to Part 1 offences (most often in relation to charges of rape) which had, until then, generally been for judges to direct juries to the effect that both an absence of consent on the part of the complainer and an absence of reasonable belief as to consent on the part of the accused had to be established by the Crown by corroborated evidence, regardless of the nature of the defence put forward. Only a limited degree of success was obtained in securing this alteration until the issue was revisited in the subsequent case of *Maqsood v HM Advocate*.[91] In that case the court explained at paragraph 17 that:

> '... although a judge ought to continue to direct a jury that the definition of rape includes an absence of reasonable belief, no further direction on reasonable belief is required unless that is a live issue at trial. That issue will be live only in a limited number of situations in which, on the evidence, although the jury might find that the complainer did not consent, the circumstances were such that a reasonable person could nevertheless think that she was consenting. That does not normally arise, for example, where an accused describes a situation in which the complainer is clearly consenting and there is no room for a misunderstanding.'

2.110 The position is then that, in the vast majority of cases, if the relevant sexual activity is established, the only remaining question will be whether or not the complainer consented to that conduct. Circumstances which permit a conclusion that the complainer did not consent are likely to be sufficient to demonstrate the necessary *mens rea* on the part of the accused, namely that he had no reasonable belief that she was consenting.[92] It will only be in the unusual circumstance where it is accepted by the accused that the complainer was not consenting, but he contends that he thought she was, that the issue of whether a reasonable belief as to consent was held will fall to be determined. In this regard, it is important to note that for an issue about reasonable belief in consent to be live in any trial, such an issue would

89 We suggest that this is unaffected by *Lord Advocate's Reference No 1 of 2023*. *Graham* found that the Crown needs to establish penetration and lack of consent. *Lord Advocate's Reference No 1 of 2023* found that penetration and lack of consent do not need to be separately corroborated.

90 As had earlier been explained in *Spendiff v HM Advocate* 2005 1 JC 338.

91 2019 JC 45.

92 At para 26 in *GW v HM Advocate* the court explained the effect of the definition of rape introduced by s 1 of the 2009 Act was that 'The intention of the accused, other than in relation to penetration, ceases to be of direct relevance. The crime is committed if the act occurs without the complainer's consent. The mental element in the crime, if it arises at all, is restricted to reasonable belief.'

have to be raised in the evidence. It cannot simply be put before the jury by the accused's representative (or by the judge) as the 'defence position'.[93]

2.111 It may be that the question of whether a person had a reasonable belief in consent would be a live issue where the Crown case is based upon the premise that the complainer was so intoxicated as to be incapable of consenting, if this was put in issue by the defence.[94] Other circumstances might also allow this issue to be brought into focus. However it is clear that an accused person would not be able to assert that he had a reasonable belief in consent on the basis of having been told in advance by a complainer that she would agree to sexual activity at a later point,[95] or on the basis of an agreement in advance to engage in sexual activity when too intoxicated to then consent,[96] or on the basis of an agreement in advance to engage in sexual activity when asleep.[97] It would be most unlikely that an issue as to reasonable belief in consent could arise where there was evidence of intercourse having been achieved by the use of force.[98]

2.112 If a question of this sort is put in issue, then the terms of section 16 of the Act will be engaged. That section provides guidance as to how to determine whether or not a person has a reasonable belief as to consent. It states:

> 'In determining, for the purposes of Part 1, whether a person's belief as to consent or knowledge was reasonable, regard is to be had to whether the person took any steps to ascertain whether there was consent or, as the case may be, knowledge; and if so, to what those steps were.'

2.113 As the SLC observed, taking the approach to consent which they suggested would allow the law to adopt the position that if one person wants to have sex with another, and there is any doubt that the other person is consenting, then the obvious step to take is to ask.[99] Section 16 provides statutory underpinning for the obligation to take steps to enquire rather than to make assumptions about consent.

2.114 The opinion of the court delivered by the Lord Justice Clerk (Dorrian) in the case of *LW v HM Advocate*[100] gave important guidance on the proper context in which to consider the question of a reasonable belief in consent. The case concerned a complainer who was asleep at the time of sexual intercourse. The decision of the court emphasised that the question was not simply whether the accused thought that the complainer was awake, and thus capable of consenting, but whether there were objectively reasonable grounds for believing that she was in fact consenting. At paragraph 19 the Lord Justice Clerk explained:

93 The same applies to a defence of consent – *Bakhjam v HM Advocate* 2018 JC 127, *MacDonald v HM Advocate* 2020 JC 244, *W (A) v HM Advocate* 2022 JC 164.

94 As was acknowledged in *Nyiam v HM Advocate* 2022 JC 57.

95 *HM Advocate v JW* 2020 SCCR 174.

96 The SLC's recommendation that this should be possible was not accepted.

97 *GW v HM Advocate* 2019 JC 109.

98 *Flynn v HM Advocate* 2009 SCCR 651.

99 SLC report para 2.27.

100 [2023] HCJAC 18.

> 'The circumstances in which a reasonable belief in consent may be a live issue where the complainer maintains that she was asleep at the time of penetration will, at best, be vanishingly rare. It is obvious that this must be so, because the basis of any such assertion is that the complainer was, as a matter of fact, asleep, and incapable of consenting, but that the accused nevertheless maintains there were reasonable grounds to think that she was consenting to the conduct in question. This can only arise in very unusual and rare circumstances.'

2.115 At paragraph 23 of the decision the court had in mind the requirements of section 16 when it drew attention to the sort of steps that would be necessary as a minimum to begin to lay the basis for a claim of objectively reasonable belief in a case of this type.

2.116 As mentioned at **2.35** the approach taken in *LW v HM Advocate* would be equally applicable to a case where the complainer was said to be incapable of consenting through intoxication. The decision makes it clear that if the accused wished to argue that he had a reasonable belief in consent in such a case, the starting point would be that the complainer was, as a matter of fact, so intoxicated as to be incapable of consenting. The accused would then need to identify the steps he took which led him to the view that she was not so intoxicated as to be incapable of making a meaningful decision about her conduct and which led him to conclude that she did in fact consent to the behaviour engaged in. Once this position had been identified in evidence, and if it was accepted, the questions for the jury would be:

1. whether the account given by the accused constituted objectively reasonable grounds for believing that the complainer was capable of exercising meaningful consent, and
2. whether the account given by the accused constituted objectively reasonable grounds for believing that she did consent to the relevant conduct, despite in fact being incapable of doing so.

2.117 The same approach would apply to a case where the incapacity relied upon was mental disorder.

OTHER GENERAL PROVISIONS: THE ESTABLISHMENT OF A'S PURPOSE AND THE MEANING OF 'SEXUAL'

Section 49: establishment of purpose

2.118 Certain of the sections in Parts 1 and 4 of the 2009 Act specify activity which will constitute criminal conduct but attach the condition that the activity requires to have been engaged in for a particular purpose before the offence is committed.[101] That requirement is expressed in the same way throughout each of these sections and it is that the conduct must have been engaged in by person A for the purpose of:

[101] Ss 5, 6, 7, 8, 9, 22, 23, 24, 25, 26, 32, 33, 34, 35 and 36.

'(a) obtaining sexual gratification, or
(b) humiliating, distressing or alarming B.'

2.119 When it comes to determining what person A's purpose was, attention should be given to section 49 of the Act which provides that:

'(1) For the purposes of sections 5 to 9, 22 to 26 and 32 to 36, A's purpose was—
(a) obtaining sexual gratification, or
(b) humiliating, distressing or alarming B, if in all the circumstances of the case it may reasonably be inferred A was doing the thing for the purpose in question.
(2) In applying subsection (1) to determine A's purpose, it is irrelevant whether or not B was in fact humiliated, distressed or alarmed by the thing done by A.'

2.120 The effect of section 49 is that in determining purpose, the court is not directed towards assessing what the accused's actual purpose, or intention, was. The question of purpose falls to be determined as an objective test, and if it can reasonably be inferred that the perpetrator acted for one of the specified purposes that is sufficient, regardless of whether he did in fact obtain sexual gratification or whether person B was in fact humiliated, distressed or alarmed. Nor is it necessary for the conduct to be engaged in for the perpetrator's immediate sexual gratification. Future or deferred gratification is equally sufficient.[102]

2.121 When discussing the relevant offence creating sections in subsequent chapters mention is made of section 49.

Section 60: meaning of 'sexual'

2.122 In similar vein to the discussion in the previous paragraph, certain of the sections in Parts 1, 4 and 5 of the 2009 Act specify that for the conduct which is encompassed within the offence creating provision to be criminal it must be carried out 'sexually', or that 'sexual activity' requires to be participated in, or that the manner in which something is done is 'sexual'.[103] Certain of the sections which provide for defences to conduct which would otherwise be criminal refer to a 'sexual relationship'.[104] For the purposes of considering each of these qualifications attention should be given to section 60(2) which provides that:

'60. Interpretation

(2) For the purposes of this Act—
(a) penetration, touching, or any other activity,
(b) a communication,
(c) a manner of exposure, or
(d) a relationship,

102 *Buchan v Aziz* 2023 JC 51 at paras 24 and 25.
103 Ss 2, 3, 4, 5, 6, 7, 8, 11, 19, 20, 21, 22, 23, 24, 25, 29, 30, 31, 32, 33, 34, 35, 37, 42, and 46.
104 Ss 45 and 47.

is sexual if a reasonable person would, in all the circumstances of the case, consider it to be sexual.'

2.123 As with the approach to section 49, the test to be applied for the purposes of any of these qualifications is an objective one. The leading authorities are *Ferguson v HM Advocate* 2022 SCCR 26 and *Kennedy v PF, Aberdeen* [2024] HCJAC 47. In *Ferguson*, the court held that touching that is objectively sexual does not become non-sexual because the accused is intoxicated (paragraph 22 of the court's opinion; see also the discussion of *Ferguson* in the context of sections 2 and 3 of the 2009 Act in Chapter 3, footnote 13). In *Kennedy*, concerning a male stripper touching two women without their consent during his performance, the Appeal Court disapproved of the Sheriff Appeal Court case *PF, Edinburgh v Harper* [2024] SAC (Crim) 10 to the extent that it appeared to suggest that an accused's motivation is irrelevant to the objective analysis of whether something is sexual. The Appeal Court found that there was no reason to exclude an accused's motives from the equation, although what weight ought to be given to them will vary according to the particular facts. Equally, it reasoned, the context of the conduct will be a relevant factor to be weighed in the balance (paragraphs 19 and 20). The fact that the accused's motive might have been entertainment and not his own sexual gratification did not mean that the conduct was not sexual, and thus Kennedy's appeal against conviction was refused (paragraphs 20 to 23). In *Kennedy*, the Appeal Court did not disapprove of the result in *Harper*: that Harper's evidence that he had touched a woman's bottom in a bar as a joke did not mean that his conduct could not, on an objective view, be regarded as sexual. It is suggested therefore that *Harper* remains authority for the proposition that doing something for a joke does not of itself mean that it cannot be sexual and thus, if all the other factors in the case point to it being sexual and if it is done without consent, it can amount to an offence under the 2009 Act.

GENERAL TECHNICAL PROVISIONS

Alternative Offences

2.124 Section 50 of the 2009 Act provides for the power to convict after trial, either on indictment or on summary complaint, of an offence other than that charged. Subsection (1) provides for the general power by reference to Schedule 3, which specifies the alternative offences of which the accused may be convicted when charged under any of the offences created by sections of the 2009 Act, with the exception of sections 11 and 37.[105] The power to convict of an alternative offence is in addition to the general power to convict of an attempted crime, as provided for by section 294 and paragraph 10 of Schedule 3 to the 1995 Act. By way of example, where an offence of rape under section 1 is charged, if the jury is not satisfied that this crime was committed they may, if so satisfied, convict of any of the offences of:

105 S 11 creates the offence of administering a substance for sexual purposes. S 37 creates the offences of engaging while an older child in sexual conduct with or towards another older child and engaging while an older child in consensual sexual conduct with another older child.

- Sexual assault by penetration.
- Sexual assault.
- Having intercourse with an older child.
- Assault at common law.
- Assault with intent to commit rape at common law.
- Assault with intent to commit the offence of rape under section 1 of the Act.
- Assault with intent to commit the offence of rape of a young child.
- Abduction with intent to commit rape at common law.
- Abduction with intent to commit the offence of rape under section 1 of the Act.
- Abduction with intent to commit the offence of rape of a young child.
- An offence under section 1 (incest) of the Criminal Law (Consolidation) (Scotland) Act 1995.
- An offence under section 2 (intercourse with step-child) of that 1995 Act.

2.125 Subsections (2) to (4) of section 50 are new and did not feature in the SLC's recommendations. The purpose of these subsections is described in subsection (2). It is to allow the accused person to be convicted of an appropriate alternative 'older child offence' in circumstances where the necessary age is not established in evidence. This situation may arise in two different ways.

2.126 First, if the accused is charged with an offence against a young child, a necessary component of that charge will be that the child complainer was under the age of 13 years at the time of the offence. Section 50(3) allows the jury or court to return a verdict of guilty of an alternative offence in relation to an older child, ie one who has reached the age of 13 years but not 16 years, even if the Crown has failed to establish beyond reasonable doubt that the child had reached the age of 13 years. In other words, where there is confusion or uncertainty over whether the child was over or under 13 years at the time, the subsection permits the jury or court to proceed on the basis that she was at least 13 years old and to return a verdict of guilty of one of the older child offences specified in Schedule 3 as an alternative to the original charge brought.[106]

2.127 The second situation contemplated by these subsections is where the accused is charged with one of the older child offences specified in sections 28, 29 or 30. In relation to these offences an essential component is the age of the accused, he must have attained the age of 16 years. Section 50(4) recognises that in such cases an appropriate alternative verdict might be guilty of an offence under section 37, older children engaging in sexual conduct with each other. In order for an offence

106 Where an accused person is charged with an offence against an older child the necessary component is that the child was aged between 13 and 16 years at the time. If there is confusion or uncertainty about whether she was over or under 13 years at the time then, so long as the court or jury is satisfied that the child was under 16 years, the deeming provision found in ss 40 and 41 of the Act apply. The consequence is that the child is deemed to have attained the age of 13 and therefore to allow a conviction of the older child offence. This does not restrict the ability to return a conviction on a relevant alternative offence as permitted by s 50(1).

under this section to be committed, however, the person 'A' participant, the party who perpetrates the conduct, requires to be under 16 years of age. Section 50(4) permits a verdict of guilty to a relevant section 37 offence to be returned even where the Crown has not proved beyond reasonable doubt that the relevant participant was under 16 at the time. In other words, if returning an alternative verdict of a section 37 offence seems appropriate, the jury or court are not barred from doing so on account of confusion or uncertainty about the accused person's age.

2.128 The availability of an alternative verdict of a section 37 offence raises the possibility of what may be something of an anomaly. Section 37 is the concluding offence creating section in Part 4 of the Act, which deals with offences concerning children. By this stage of the Act, the legislation has dealt with sexual conduct directed towards a child under 13, where both the age of the Person 'A' participant and the issue of consent is irrelevant. It has dealt with sexual conduct directed towards a child aged between 13 and under 16 years where again the issue of consent is irrelevant, but the Person 'A' participant requires to be 16 years of age or older. Section 37 concludes this progression by addressing some specified acts of the most serious types of sexual conduct engaged in where both Person 'A' and Person 'B' are between 13 and under 16 years of age.

2.129 The section provides for two distinct offences. The first concerns the conduct perpetrated by the Person 'A' participant. If that person perpetrates any of the specified conduct, he (or she) commits the offence 'of engaging while an older child in sexual conduct with or towards another older child' – the section 37(1) offence. The second offence concerns the Person 'B' participant. If that person engages by consent in the conduct perpetrated by the Person 'A' participant that person commits the offence 'of engaging while an older child in consensual sexual conduct with another older child' – the section 37(4) offence.

2.130 Returning to Schedule 3, one finds that the section 37(1) offence is available as an alternative to charges brought under any of sections 18, 20, 28, 29 and 30. This is uncontroversial, as each of these sections identifies conduct on the part of Participant 'A' which constitutes a crime, just as section 37(1) does. However, the section 37(4) offence is also specified as an available alternative verdict in relation to charges brought under sections 20 and 30. This is difficult to understand, as each of sections 20 and 30 specify active conduct which requires to be perpetrated by the Person 'A' participant in order for criminal liability to arise. The section 37(4) offence can only be committed by the Person 'B' participant consenting to the acts being perpetrated against them. The alternative of the section 37(4) offence might perhaps be thought to be available where in a charge under either of sections 20 or 30 (and subject to the age requirements being met) the accused person's defence was that the complainer was in fact the party who behaved in the way specified in the charge towards him (or her) and that he (or she) consented to the acts specified.

2.131 It is rather difficult to envisage a prosecutor inviting such an alternative verdict in circumstances of the sort just canvassed. This highlights the fact that the availability of alternative offences does not imply that the judge in solemn proceedings ought to give directions on the possibility of returning one or more of the alternatives provided for. The general rule is set out in the case of *Duncan v HM Advocate*.[107] It is that the trial judge should only direct on verdicts in accordance with the manner in which the case has been presented to the jury by the parties and should not speculate upon areas of possible alternative verdicts which have not been canvassed in the evidence or formed part of the speeches to the jury. The judge may give directions on an alternative verdict if it is an obvious one based on the evidence and the public interest necessitates that the direction be given.

2.132 The need to direct on a matter not raised by parties ought to be a rare event. The decision of the Appeal Court in *Colley v HM Advocate*[108] provides a recent example of the importance of a trial judge directing the jury only on the issues as framed by the parties in the case and not giving directions on possible alternatives, even if raised by the jury.

Abolition of common law offences and continuity of law

2.133 The final two provisions to note in the 2009 Act are two important but related provisions: the abolition of common law offences in section 52 and the continuity of law provision in section 53.

Section 52: abolition of common law offences

2.134 Section 52 of the 2009 Act was brought into force on 16 December 2013.[109] It is in two parts. Section 52(a) provides that from that date onwards, the common law offences of rape, clandestine injury to women, lewd, indecent or libidinous practice or behaviour, and sodomy were abolished. Section 52(b) provides that insofar as the provisions of the 2009 Act regulated any conduct, they replaced any rule of law regulating that conduct. That does not abolish all of the common law offences concerning sexual behaviour altogether. The common law offences of indecent assault, assault with intent to rape, public indecency and other less frequently encountered criminal conduct remain in place, and we consider those offences in Chapter 10. Instead, the effect of section 52(b) is that if conduct amounts to an offence in the 2009 Act, then the Crown must bring a charge for that 2009 Act offence, not an offence at common law. For instance, if conduct amounts to sexual assault, contrary to section 3 of the 2009 Act, it is not competent for the Crown to bring a charge of indecent assault.

2.135 Section 52(b) does not, however, prevent conviction for a common law offence as an alternative to a 2009 Act offence when, at trial, the conduct is found not to amount

107 2018 SCCR 319.
108 HCA/2023/00010/XC.
109 SSI 2013/341.

to an offence under the 2009 Act but is found to amount to the common law offence. This is by application of paragraph 14(b) of Schedule 3 to the Criminal Procedure (Scotland) Act 1995, which provides that, where the facts proved under the indictment or complaint do not amount to a contravention of an enactment, but do amount to an offence at common law, it shall be lawful to convict of the common law offence. Thus, it remains possible for a person to be charged with, for instance, sexual assault, contrary to section 3 of the 2009 Act and instead to be convicted of indecent assault at common law. Finally, section 52(b) does not apply to conduct taking place before the entry into force of the 2009 Act, since the Act does not 'regulate' that conduct.

2.136 Section 52(b) also does not prevent the libelling of alternatives such as indecent assault and rape when the complainer is uncertain in her statement whether, for instance, an act of non-consensual anal penetration took place before or after 1 December 2010. In that case, paragraph 14(b) of Schedule 3 to the 1995 Act could again apply: if, after the evidence, the jury were satisfied that it took place after 1 December 2010, they would convict of the section 1 2009 Act alternative; if they were not so satisfied, then applying paragraph 14(b), they would convict of indecent assault.

Section 53: continuity of law

2.137 The continuity of law provision which is set out in section 53 of the 2009 Act is designed to address the situation which may arise if it is not clear whether particular conduct occurred before or after the coming into force of the new statutory offences. Subsection (1) anticipates that in this situation the accused will be charged with both the new offence as created by the Act and what is referred to as the 'existing offence'.[110]

2.138 The effect of the provision is that if it cannot be established beyond reasonable doubt that the conduct took place either after the coming into force of the new statutory provision, or before the abolition of the existing offence, but the offence[111] is otherwise established, then the accused should be convicted of the new offence unless the maximum penalty for the existing offence is less than the maximum penalty for the new offence, in which case he should be convicted of the existing offence. The provision is designed to ensure that the accused always benefits from the lower of the two penalties. Section 56 of the 2009 Act sets out a similar provision in relation to specified offences committed abroad where the question is whether the conduct occurred after the coming into force of section 55 of the 2009 Act or before the abolition of section 16B of the Criminal Law (Consolidation) (Scotland) Act 1995.

110 For the purpose of this transitional provision the existing offences are: rape at common law; clandestine injury; lewd, indecent or libidinous practice or behaviour; any other common law offence which was replaced by an offence under the Act; offences under the Criminal Law (Consolidation) (Scotland) Act 1995, ss 3, 5 and 6; and s 3 of the Sexual Offences (Amendment) Act 2000.

111 For these purposes any reference to an offence includes attempts, incitement, counselling or procurement and art and part participation, or an offence as modified by ss 16A or 16B of the Criminal Law (Consolidation) (Scotland) Act 1995 – s 53(5).

Chapter 3

The general offences under the 2009 Act

INTRODUCTION

3.01 In this chapter we consider Part 1 of the 2009 Act, which defines the general sexual offences which may be committed against a victim of any age. They are divided into contact offences (sections 1 to 3) and non-contact offences (sections 4 to 11).

3.02 The approach recommended by the SLC, and adopted in the legislation, was to remove sexual offences from the general category of the law on assault in order to give effect to the guiding principle that the law should promote and protect sexual autonomy. The Act uses the language of 'sexual assault' in various places, but the concept of violence does not feature in the definition of any of the Part 1 sexual offences. The inclusion of the word 'assault' does not incorporate the common law definition of this term.[1] The use of violence in committing any of the sexual offences identified constitutes an additional wrongdoing rather than being a necessary component.

3.03 An important distinction which arises between the two groups of offences is that the contact offences may be committed intentionally or recklessly,[2] whereas for each crime within the group of non-contact offences the perpetrator must act intentionally. The non-contact offences may be seen as falling into two further sub-groups, the coercive offences (sections 4, 5 and 6) and the remaining provisions (sections 7 to 11).

THE CONTACT OFFENCES – SECTIONS 1 TO 3

Section 1

3.04 Section 1 creates the statutory offence of rape. It provides that:

1 The classic definition of an assault at common law is an attack on another person carried out with evil intent.

2 Thus further distinguishing these offences from the crime of assault.

'(1) If a person ('A'), with A's penis—

(a) without another person ('B') consenting, and

(b) without any reasonable belief that B consents,

penetrates to any extent, either intending to do so or reckless as to whether there is penetration, the vagina, anus or mouth of B then A commits an offence, to be known as the offence of rape.

(2) For the purposes of this section, penetration is a continuing act from entry until withdrawal of the penis; but this subsection is subject to subsection (3).

(3) In a case where penetration is initially consented to but at some point of time the consent is withdrawn, subsection (2) is to be construed as if the reference in it to a continuing act from entry were a reference to a continuing act from that point of time.

(4) In this Act—

'penis' includes a surgically constructed penis if it forms part of A, having been created in the course of surgical treatment, and 'vagina' includes—

(a) the vulva,[3] and

(b) a surgically constructed vagina (together with any surgically constructed vulva), if it forms part of B, having been created in the course of such treatment.'

3.05 It follows that there are two components to the *actus reus* of the offence: penile penetration by the perpetrator of the vagina, anus or mouth of the victim and the lack of the victim's consent to this penetration.

3.06 The definition of the crime of rape does not direct attention to sex or gender but to the relevant body parts. Subsection (4) defines both penis and vagina as including such parts created in the course of surgical treatment. It follows that a person born with female sex who had an artificial penis but not a gender recognition certificate could commit the crime of rape.

3.07 The effect of subsections (2) and (3) is to make it clear that the term 'penetration' means more than solely the initial act of penetrating and is a continuing act. Accordingly, if sexual intercourse begins consensually but B then withdraws consent and A does not withdraw his penis, then the remaining conduct constitutes the offence of rape. Section 15 subsections (3) and (4) reinforce the fact that consent may be withdrawn at any time, including during the sexual act being engaged in,

3 The medical definition of the vagina is the lowest part of the female genital tract, the muscular tube which has the cervix (neck of the womb) at its upper end and the hymen or hymenal remnants) at its outer end. By virtue of s 1(4)(a) the 'vagina' is not restricted to its strict medical meaning and is to be interpreted for all purposes of the Act as including the vulva (the outer end of the vagina or the external female genitals which include the labia majora, labia minora and vestibule of the vagina). The same effect is achieved by s 79(9) of the Sexual Offences Act 2003.

and that if the conduct continues after consent has been withdrawn, such conduct continues without consent and therefore constitutes an offence (see further **2.93**).

3.08 The Act provides no guidance on how much, if any, time is allowed to permit the person concerned to realise that consent has been withdrawn and to act accordingly. In the case of *Mutebi v HM Advocate*[4] the Crown's submission appears to have been that there was no *de minimis* rule and that an offence was committed from the moment that withdrawal of consent was communicated, by whatever means. Whilst the court did not have to rule upon this submission, it did react with a degree of surprise to it. In delivering the opinion of the court Lord Brailsford stated:

> '... it is not necessary for us to express a concluded view on the prima facie stark submission that the mere indication – by a single, short word, of some unwillingness by one, previously willing, party further to continue in what is by its nature a passionate activity makes the other party guilty of a criminal offence if that party does not instantly desist, with no interval whatever for appreciation of the fact that consent has been revoked and react to it.'

3.09 Despite its rather unsympathetic reaction to the submission the court declined to offer any view of its own as to what sort of period of reaction time might be available. If such an issue were to arise the answer would no doubt depend upon the particular circumstance disclosed in the evidence relating to that case.

3.10 An offence under this section can be committed either directly, as the person engaged in the act of penetration, or in concert with such an individual.[5] Accordingly, a person without a penis could commit the offence by encouraging or assisting the perpetration of the crime by another.

3.11 The act of penetration has to be intentionally or recklessly achieved. Intending in this context means no more than that the person's act was done voluntarily or deliberately. That the offence of rape (and the other contact offences) can be committed in Scotland by a reckless act[6] which results in penetration distinguishes the Scottish legislation from the Sexual Offences Act 2003.

3.12 At paragraph 26 of its decision in the case of *GW v HM Advocate*[7] the court explained the effect of the definition of rape introduced by section 1 of the 2009 Act was that:

4 2014 SCCR 52.

5 S 293 of the 1995 Act provides that a person may be convicted and punished, for a contravention of any enactment, notwithstanding that he was guilty of such contravention as art and part only.

6 Prosecutions based on reckless conduct are likely to be rare but the type of circumstances which would be capable of underpinning an allegation of reckless penetration are not unknown. For example, where a man claimed that anal penetration had occurred accidentally whilst he was intending to engage in consensual vaginal penetration, the Crown would be capable of seeking a conviction based on reckless penetration where the woman had taken steps to prevent anal penetration and had made her objection to this type of conduct clear.

7 2019 JC 109.

> 'The intention of the accused, other than in relation to penetration, ceases to be of direct relevance. The crime is committed if the act occurs without the complainer's consent. The mental element in the crime, if it arises at all, is restricted to reasonable belief.'

3.13 As discussed at **2.20**, the issue of *mens rea* will likely be resolved in most cases by a determination of whether or not the complainer was consenting. If she was not, then the evidence relied upon to establish that aspect of the *actus reus* will likely be sufficient to demonstrate that the accused had no reasonable belief that she was consenting. If the issue becomes live, then attention has to be given to the terms of section 16 of the Act which requires that regard is to be had to whether the accused took any steps to ascertain whether there was consent and if so, what those steps were. Thus, again, the question of whether the accused person had a reasonable belief that the complainer was consenting will be determined on an objective assessment of whether he took sufficient steps to allow him reasonably to conclude that the complainer was consenting or by an objective assessment of what conclusion he ought reasonably to have arrived at in light of the steps he did take.

3.14 On conviction for a contravention of section 1 of the Act a person will be subject to the notification requirements specified in Part 2 of the Sexual Offences Act 2003.[8] The same result follows upon conviction for all of the other offences provided for in Part 1 of the Act.[9] The appliable periods during which a person will be subject to the notification requirements are set out in Chapter 18.

Attempt to rape

3.15 Section 294 of the 1995 Act provides that an attempt to commit any indictable crime is itself an indictable crime. Paragraph (10)(1) of Schedule 3 to the 1995 Act provides that where a completed offence is charged the accused may be convicted of an attempt to commit the offence. Accordingly, on a charge of rape under section 1, a person can be convicted of an attempted rape contrary to that section.[10]

8 2003 Act, s 80. This section also provides that a person who is found not guilty by reason of insanity is to be subject to the notification requirements. That term no longer features in Scottish criminal procedure and the relevant provisions are s 51A and 53E of the 1995 Act which provide for a special defence and acquittal of a person who is not criminally responsible for conduct constituting an offence if he was at the time unable by reason of mental disorder to appreciate the nature or wrongfulness of the conduct. Section 82 of the 2003 Act, which specifies the relevant notification periods, identifies periods applicable to individuals subject to a finding who have been admitted to hospital with or without a restriction order. This would appear to cover the situation of a person acquitted in terms of s 53E of the 1995 Act.

9 In relation to the offence of sexual exposure provided for by s 8 the notification requirements are only applicable if certain conditions are present. These are mentioned in the discussion on that section at **3.62**.

10 *RCB v HM Advocate* 2016 SCCR 374.

3.16 The various offences specified in Schedule 3 to the 2009 Act as alternative offences available to a charge of rape include assault with intent to commit the offence of rape under section 1. In this situation the conviction would be for an assault at common law with the intent to commit the statutory crime of rape. If such a verdict was to be left available to a jury the trial judge would require to give adequate directions on the common law offence of assault as well as the sexual offence of rape.

Section 2

3.17 Section 2 creates the offence of sexual assault by penetration. It provides that:

> '(1) If a person ('A'), with any part of A's body or anything else—
> (a) without another person ('B') consenting, and
> (b) without any reasonable belief that B consents,
>
> penetrates sexually to any extent, either intending to do so or reckless as to whether there is penetration, the vagina or anus of B then A commits an offence, to be known as the offence of sexual assault by penetration.
>
> (2) For the purposes of this section, penetration is a continuing act from entry to withdrawal of whatever is intruded; but this subsection is subject to subsection (3).
>
> (3) In a case where penetration is initially consented to but at some point of time the consent is withdrawn, subsection (2) is to be construed as if the reference in it to a continuing act from entry were a reference to a continuing act from that point of time.
>
> (4) Without prejudice to the generality of subsection (1), the reference in that subsection to penetration with any part of A's body is to be construed as including a reference to penetration with A's penis.'

3.18 As is stated in the Explanatory Notes accompanying the Act, there is a degree of overlap between the conduct which constitutes sexual assault by penetration under this section and that which constitutes rape under section 1. Although the SLC had initially considered that there should be a separate offence of non-penile penetration, its final view was that the law should mark out non-penile penetration as a specific sexual wrong but not as a separate offence, and it should instead be seen as one of the several forms of conduct which constitute sexual assault (paragraph 3.36). Thus, section 2 did not appear in the SLC's draft Bill or the Sexual Offences (Scotland) Bill as introduced. It was inserted at the recommendation of the Justice Committee. After taking evidence, the Justice Committee's view was that there should be such a separate offence in recognition of the comparable distress that the act is likely to cause the victim and that such an offence already existed in England and Wales.[11]

11 Justice Committee stage 1 report on the Sexual Offences (Scotland) Bill at para 97.

3.19 The scope of the offence of sexual assault by penetration is not as wide as the offence provided for by section 1. It is restricted to penetration of the vagina or anus and does not include penetration of the mouth. However, the use of the term 'anything else' in the first line of subsection (1) means that the offence can capture penetration by any other object or thing, including an animal or other living organism.[12]

3.20 The *actus reus* of this offence consists of penetrating sexually the vagina or anus of the victim and the absence of the victim's consent to this penetration. Subsections (2) and (3) mirror the effect of subsections (2) and (3) of section 1 in relation to the meaning of penetration and the effect of withdrawing consent.

3.21 The observations concerning the relevant *mens rea* as set out at **3.13** apply with equal force to an offence under section 2 of the Act, with one qualification. For an offence under section 2 to be committed, the relevant penetration has to fall within the concept of penetrating sexually. As discussed at **2.122**, content is given to the concept of 'sexually' for these purposes by section 60(2)(a) of the Act which provides that penetration, touching, or any other activity, is sexual if a reasonable person would, in all the circumstances of the case, consider it to be sexual. If this issue were to arise the jury would be directed to determine whether the penetration was or was not sexual on an objective basis.[13]

3.22 The purpose of the overlap between this offence and the offence of rape contained in section 1 (as explained in the Explanatory Notes) is to allow for the situation in which an individual may not know precisely what he or she was penetrated by. In addition, a child or a person with a learning disability may be able to explain being penetrated but may not be able to convey an understanding of whether it was by a penis or something else.

Section 3

3.23 Section 3 creates the offence of sexual assault. It provides that:

'(1) If a person ('A')—
(a) without another person ('B') consenting, and
(b) without any reasonable belief that B consents,

does any of the things mentioned in subsection (2), then A commits an offence, to be known as the offence of sexual assault.

12 The need for such a wide scope is demonstrated by the various examples of depravity which the courts have encountered – see, eg, *Williams* unreported 22 October 1999 (No.99/4704/R1) indecent assault committed by inserting live maggots into the victim's vagina.

13 See *Kennedy v PF, Aberdeen* [2024] HCJAC 47. For a similar approach in relation to section 7(1) (communicating indecently) see *Buchan v Aziz* 2023 JC 51 at para 24. See also the case of *Ferguson v HM Advocate* 2022 SCCR 26 for authority that an act of penetration or other relevant activity does not cease to be sexual on account of it being engaged in by the accused as an act of drunkenness. There is no dichotomy between drink-fuelled and overtly sexual assaults. The test is as set out in s 60. It is not a test of whether there was a significant sexual aspect to the person's conduct.

(2) Those things are, that A—

(a) penetrates sexually, by any means and to any extent, either intending to do so or reckless as to whether there is penetration, the vagina, anus or mouth of B,

(b) intentionally or recklessly touches B sexually,

(c) engages in any other form of sexual activity in which A, intentionally or recklessly, has physical contact (whether bodily contact or contact by means of an implement and whether or not through clothing) with B,

(d) intentionally or recklessly ejaculates semen onto B,

(e) intentionally or recklessly emits urine or saliva onto B sexually.

(3) For the purposes of paragraph (a) of subsection (2), penetration is a continuing act from entry until withdrawal of whatever is intruded; but this subsection is subject to subsection (4).

(4) In a case where penetration is initially consented to but at some point of time the consent is withdrawn, subsection (3) is to be construed as if the reference in it to a continuing act from entry were a reference to a continuing act from that point of time.

(5) Without prejudice to the generality of paragraph (a) of subsection (2), the reference in the paragraph to penetration by any means is to be construed as including a reference to penetration with A's penis.'

3.24 Section 3 continues to apply the underlying principle of autonomy by providing that the offence of sexual assault is committed if conduct occurs to which person B does not consent. However, the provision is prescriptive, in the sense that it then defines the various things which require to be done without consent so as to constitute the offence. Subsections (3), (4) and (5) mirror the import of subsections (2), (3) and (4) of section 2.

3.25 Once again there is an overlap between the provisions of section 3 and those of section 1. There is also a degree of overlap between the provisions of section 3 and those of section 2. The Explanatory Notes to section 3 state that this is deliberate and give the same rationale as is found in relation to the overlap between sections 1 and 2. There remains, however, something of a legislative curiosity which arises as a consequence of the choice of the Scottish Parliament to follow the English model of a separate offence of sexual assault by penetration. Section 1 extends the crime of rape to penetration of person B's mouth by person A's penis. The offence of sexual assault by penetration created by section 2 does not include penile, or any other form, of penetration of the victim's mouth. Section 3 defines sexual assault as including penetration, which is sexual, by any means, including a penis, of the victim's mouth. Accordingly, the crime of rape or the crime of sexual assault can be committed by penetration of the victim's mouth by the perpetrator's penis but the crime of sexual assault by penetration cannot be.[14]

14 The same drafting structure is repeated in the corresponding sections found within Part 4 of the Act in relation to the offences against young children and older children: see Chapter 4, **4.34–4.37** and **4.51–4.55**.

3.26 The issue of *mens rea* in relation to a section 3 offence is to be approached in the same way as it would be in respect of a section 2 offence. The question of whether any act of penetration, touching or any other activity is sexual also falls to be determined in the same fashion by reference to the provisions of section 60.

3.27 In the case of *Tait v HM Advocate*[15] the court was concerned with the offences specified in sections 19 and 20 of the Act, which provide for sexual assault by penetration on a young child and sexual assault on a young child. The decision is equally relevant to charges brought under sections 2 and 3. In that decision, the court emphasised that the statutory offence of sexual assault is a completely different entity from common law assault, with or without aggravations, pointing out that unlike common law assault, the statutory offence (as found in either section 3 or section 20) can be committed recklessly.[16]

THE NON-CONTACT OFFENCES

The coercive offences

3.28 In common with the structure of the rest of the Act, each of sections 4, 5 and 6 has a heading which introduces the nature of the conduct constituting the offence, and within the body of each section there is a provision which identifies the name by which each offence is to be known. The concept of coercion features in both the heading and body of each of these three sections. So section 4, for example, is headed 'Sexual coercion' and paragraph (b) provides that the conduct specified constitutes an offence 'to be known as the offence of sexual coercion'.

3.29 In ordinary language the concept of coercion implies the use of some form of compulsion, such as a threat or other form of pressure. Coercion can also operate as a distinct legal concept, providing a complete defence to what would otherwise be criminal conduct. By way of distinction, the legal concept of coercion only recognises a very limited form of compulsion. It normally or generally requires the person to have acted under threat of death or great bodily harm.[17]

3.30 This leads to the question of whether any form of compulsion is a necessary component in any of the sections 4, 5 or 6 offences. All three offences require intentional conduct on the part of the perpetrator but it may be helpful to consider each separately, as the section 4 offence includes active participation on the part of the victim whereas the remaining sections contemplate passive involvement.

15 2015 SCCR 308.

16 The subsequent aspects of the court's decision on what requires to be corroborated for the purposes of an offence of sexual assault or sexual assault on a young child must now be viewed as incorrect in light of the decision in *Lord Advocate's Reference No 1 of 2023* 2024 JC 140.

17 See *Thomson v HM Advocate* 1983 JC 69; Chalmers, J and Leverick, F, *Criminal Defences and Pleas in Bar of Trial* (W Green & Son 2006) Ch 5. See also *Van Phan v HM Advocate* 2018 SCCR 133 at paras 42 and 43.

Section 4

3.31 Section 4 creates the offence of sexual coercion. It provides that:

> 'If a person ('A')—
> (a) without another person ('B') consenting to participate in a sexual activity, and
> (b) without any reasonable belief that B consents to participating in that activity,
>
> intentionally causes B to participate in that activity, then A commits an offence, to be known as the offence of sexual coercion.'

3.32 In recommending the creation of this offence, the SLC saw the merit of its proposal as being that it would capture many types of sexual conduct to which the victim did not consent, and which did not necessarily involve contact between the offender and the victim, such as would be the case in conduct constituting the offence of sexual assault. The SLC gave various examples of circumstances which might constitute the offence of sexual coercion, including compelling a victim to have sex with a third party, or to have sexual contact with an animal, or an object, or with herself. It was also seen as capturing a situation of a woman compelling a man to have penetrative intercourse with her without his consent.[18]

3.33 Although the examples mentioned by the SLC did not involve sexual contact between the coercing party and the victim (other than the female rape example) the terms of the section as enacted are wide enough to cover circumstances in which B is coerced into participating in sexual activity with person A or with another person, or both. If the circumstances were that person A coerced person B into participating in sexual activity with him where person B did not consent to doing so there could be an overlap with the offences created in sections 1 to 3.[19] The clearest example would be where the nature of the coercion adopted was physical violence or a threat of violence by A. In this event, it seems likely that a charge under one or other of sections 1 to 3 would be more appropriately brought.

3.34 This analysis suggests that a charge of sexual coercion would mostly likely arise where B was coerced by A into engaging in some form of sexual activity either in the presence of A or as observed by him, for instance, over a webcam. It could also arise where A compelled B to take intimate images of B's own body and send them to him. Alternatively, the offence is commonly seen in High Court prosecutions where A coerced B into participating in sexual activity with another person, though in many such cases it would also be possible to prosecute A for rape on an art-and-part basis. Another common form now seen is coercion of B by A to do things to A, such as coercing B to insert objects into A's mouth or anus.

18 Report paragraphs 3.48 to 3.50.

19 S 3(2)(c) covers the situation where A engages in any other form of sexual activity in which A has physical contact with B.

3.35 It is obvious that the reference in section 4(b) to 'participate in a sexual activity' is wide enough to cover any form of conduct which is sexual in nature. The only limiting factor is found in the section 60(2) definition that penetrating, touching or any other activity is sexual if a reasonable person would, in all the circumstances of the case, consider it to be sexual. The more difficult aspect of the offence may be the question of what the section has in mind in requiring that person A should intentionally 'cause' person B to participate in sexual activity to which that person does not consent.

3.36 Despite the ways in which the SLC anticipated the operation of this offence, and the name given to it, there is no reference to compulsion (or force) in the statutory provision. The implication would seem to be that a person who does not consent to engage in sexual activity but is caused to do so must have been compelled or coerced in some fashion. That approach, which looks at the combined effect of the two components of the offence together, ie, cause and absence of consent, is logical and sensible. But the two components are separate and will require to be individually established, and the statute provides no guidance on what constitutes 'cause' in this context.

3.37 It would seem obvious that the legal requirements of the defence of coercion have no relevance, but that may not advance matters terribly far. Determining the question of causation can become intertwined with considerations concerning freedom of choice, consent and the ability of the victim to exercise an informed choice – see for example (in a different context) the competing approaches taken in the cases of *R v Kennedy (No 2)*[20] and *MacAngus v HM Advocate.*[21] Absent any suggestion of vulnerability or reckless conduct, if a person agrees to engage in sexual activity at the request of another, it would seem difficult to view it as having been 'caused' by the request. It will have occurred as an exercise of the free will of the consenting party.

3.38 In relation to 'causing' the suggested direction at page 118.30/133 of the Jury Manual is as follows:

> 'Causing simply means that there must be some direct connection between what the accused did and the complainer's resulting conduct. Causing does not need to involve compulsion. Physical contact between the accused and the complainer may be involved, but is not necessary.'

3.39 That suggested direction may well be correct but it will be essential in any prosecution under section 4 to keep in mind the twin requirements of causing and the absence of consent. If a person persuades an initially unwilling party to agree,

20 [2008] AC 269 Lord Bingham at para 14.

21 2009 SLT 137 Lord Justice General (Hamilton) at para 48. *Kennedy (No 2)* and *MacAngus* concerned the issue of manslaughter/culpable homicide charges for supplying a controlled drug to someone who dies after voluntarily taking it.

even reluctantly, to participate in sexual conduct then even if they are to be viewed as having caused that conduct to take place another essential element of the offence, the absence of consent, will no longer be present.

3.40 It is therefore difficult to contemplate conduct other than some form of compulsion or pressure which would cause a person to engage in sexual activity to which they did not consent. Violence or threat of violence would obviously suffice. Equally, if person B was financially dependent on her partner, person A, and he required her to participate unwillingly in a particular sexual activity as a condition of support, then the requirements of the section would be met. The matter may be different, however, if the 'cause' relied upon was inducement. Suppose person A offered to pay two women to engage together in sexual activity for him to observe but never had any intention of keeping his word, and declined to pay them at the conclusion. There may well have been a direct connection between what A did in making the offer and the resulting conduct which the women engaged in but a failure by A to keep to his side of the arrangement would not result in the conduct having been engaged in without the consent of the female participants.[22] So neither inducement nor an act of deception[23] on the part of person A which leads to person B participating in sexual activity which she would not otherwise have engaged in is likely to constitute the offence of sexual coercion.

3.41 Whatever its nature, what is clear is that some form of act is necessary to constitute 'causing' and mere looking on, or failure to prevent a third party engaging in sexual activity with the complainer, would be insufficient.

Sections 5 and 6

3.42 These sections provide, respectively, for the offence of coercing a person into being present during a sexual activity and the offence of coercing a person into looking at a sexual image. As with the section 4 offence, these provisions require the perpetrator to act intentionally in order for the offence to be committed. They each introduce a further qualification, which is that the relevant behaviour engaged in by the perpetrator has to be done for the purpose of obtaining sexual gratification, or of humiliating, distressing, or alarming the victim. The effect of this requirement is to ensure that the provisions have a proportionate effect. For example, to use the examples given by the SLC,[24] a couple who have intercourse in the same room as their infant child will not be guilty of the section 5 offence. For the same reason a teacher who shows pupils a sexual image for educational purposes will not be

22 *R v Linekar* [1995] QB 250. See **2.83**.

23 The approach taken in the case of *R v Devonald* [2008] EWCA Crim 527, a prosecution under the equivalent English provision to s 4, was doubted in the subsequent case of *R v B* [2013] EWCA Crim 823 and is out of kilter with the subsequent cases analysing the effect of deception. For a discussion of the impact of deception on free agreement see **2.73–2.83**.

24 At para 3.57.

guilty of a section 6 offence. Plainly, though, that will not allow any image at all, however graphic or far removed from an ordinary biology or sex education lesson, to be shown.

3.43 If sexual gratification is relied upon as the perpetrator's purpose, then that purpose must be to obtain sexual gratification from the knowledge or belief that the activity is being carried out in the victim's presence, rather than from the sexual activity itself.[25]

3.44 Section 5 provides that:

> '(1) If a person ('A')—
> (a) without another person ('B') consenting, and
> (b) without any reasonable belief that B consents,
> either intentionally engages in a sexual activity and for a purpose mentioned in subsection (2) does so in the presence of B or intentionally and for a purpose mentioned in that subsection causes B to be present while a third person engages in such an activity, then A commits an offence, to be known as the offence of coercing a person into being present during a sexual activity.
> (2) The purposes are—
> (a) obtaining sexual gratification,
> (b) humiliating, distressing or alarming B.
> (3) Without prejudice to the generality of subsection (1), the reference in that subsection—
> (a) to A engaging in a sexual activity in the presence of B, includes a reference to A engaging in it in a place in which A can be observed by B other than by B looking at an image, and
> (b) to B being present while a third person engages in such an activity, includes a reference to B being in a place from which the third person can be so observed by B.'

3.45 Subject to the other requirements, the offence is committed where the perpetrator engages in sexual activity in the presence of the victim, or where the perpetrator causes the victim to be present while a third person engages in sexual activity. Any activity is sexual if a reasonable person would, in all of the circumstances of the case, consider it to be sexual.[26] In either case, it is not necessary for the victim to have actually observed the behaviour. He or she might have closed their eyes or turned away. The intended victim might not even have been aware of the perpetrator's conduct. All that is necessary is that the constituent elements of the offence are present, namely intentional engagement in sexual activity in the presence of person B without that person's consent (or causing B to be present while a third person so behaves) and for one of the purposes mentioned.

25 See *R v B and L* [2018] EWCA Crim 1439 interpreting a similar provision in the Sexual Offences Act 2003.

26 S 60(2).

3.46 Despite the reference in subsection (1) to activity 'in the presence of B' and 'causing B to be present', subsection (3) makes it plain that there is no need for physical proximity. It is sufficient that the behaviour occurred in a place where it was capable of being observed by the victim. For example, it would be sufficient (assuming the other requirements were satisfied) for the conduct to occur in the garden of an adjoining house where the activity could be viewed by B.

3.47 Subsection 3 paragraph (a) excludes observation by looking at an image. The same result would appear to be implied by subsection (b) given the exclusion of image in paragraph (a) and the need for the third person to be observed by B. The effect of this is that the section 5 offence cannot be committed where person B is observing the sexual activity filmed by a webcam from a different location. This wording may be unnecessary given that section 6 creates the specific offence of coercing a person into looking at a sexual image.

3.48 Since this offence involves passive conduct on the part of the victim, simply being present when the relevant conduct occurs, 'coercing' might convey a rather misleading impression of this offence. All that is required is to deliberately create the circumstances necessary to allow for the victim's presence, or for the opportunity to observe what occurs, in the knowledge that she does not consent to being exposed to this activity and for the perpetrator's purpose to be as defined above.

3.49 When it comes to determining what the perpetrator's purpose was, attention should be given to section 49 of the Act which provides that the relevant purpose will be established if in all the circumstances of the case it may reasonably be inferred that the accused was doing the thing for the purpose in question.[27]

3.50 Section 6 provides that:

> '(1) If a person ('A') intentionally and for a purpose mentioned in subsection (2) causes another person ('B')—
> (a) without B consenting, and
> (b) without any reasonable belief that B consents,
> to look at a sexual image, then A commits an offence, to be known as the offence of coercing a person into looking at a sexual image.
> (2) The purposes are—
> (a) obtaining sexual gratification,
> (b) humiliating, distressing or alarming B.
> (3) For the purposes of subsection (1), a sexual image is an image (produced by whatever means and whether or not a moving image) of—
> (a) A engaging in a sexual activity or of a third person or imaginary person so engaging,
> (b) A's genitals or the genitals of a third person or imaginary person.'

27 See **2.120**.

3.51 The same requirements of intentionality, absence of consent[28] and purpose apply in relation to this offence as they do in relation to the section 5 offence. Section 49 applies the same objective test to purpose. As with a section 5 offence, causing is a straightforward consideration and requires no more than deliberately creating the circumstances in which the victim comes to look at the image. So surprising the victim with the image would suffice, subject to the remaining requirements of the offence being satisfied. Nor is it necessary for this offence to be committed in the presence of person A. Assuming the appropriate purpose in doing so and the absence of consent, the offence could be committed by sending an image, for example, of person A's penis, by text or email or other means to person B.

3.52 The definition of a 'sexual image' is provided for by subsection (3) and includes an image created in any manner which may be of a real person, or of an imaginary person, a cartoon, or the like. For the purpose of subsection 3(a) 'engaging in sexual activity' applies to any form of activity if a reasonable person would, in all of the circumstances of the case, consider it to be sexual.[29] Subsection (3)(b) makes it plain that an image of genitals, whether of a real person or an imaginary person, is to be considered a sexual image. The combined effect of paragraphs (a) and (b) is that images of any other body parts (for example of a woman's breasts) are only included when the image shows that body part and the person (real or imaginary) is engaging in sexual activity.

The remaining non-contact offences

3.53 Sections 7, 8, 9 and 11 create the remaining general non-contact offences.

Section 7

3.54 Section 7 creates the offence of communicating indecently. It provides that:

> '(1) If a person ('A'), intentionally and for a purpose mentioned in subsection (3), sends, by whatever means, a sexual written communication to or directs, by whatever means, a sexual verbal communication at, another person ('B')—
> (a) without B consenting to its being so sent or directed, and

28 It is not uncommon to encounter circumstances in which two people have been consensually exchanging images of an increasingly sexualised nature. If there comes a point at which one party complains that he or she did not consent to receiving a particular image then s 6, in common with the other offence creating provisions of Part 1 of the Act, caters for the situation in which A may have a reasonable belief that B was consenting to the conduct. If this situation arises then s 16 of the Act applies so as to require regard to be had to whether person A took any steps to ascertain whether there was consent and if so what those steps were. Similar circumstances may arise in connection with a s 7 offence. In his annotations to s 7 of the Act Sheriff Brown draws attention to the example of what he describes as the sending of a 'steamy text message'. We share his view that the Crown would be unlikely to prosecute in the circumstances which he describes and the same would likely apply to the example of the sharing of increasingly sexualised images which we have given.

29 S 60(2).

(b) without any reasonable belief that B consents to its being so sent or directed, then A commits an offence, to be known as the offence of communicating indecently.

(2) If, in circumstances other than are as mentioned in subsection (1), a person ('A'), intentionally and for a purpose mentioned in subsection (3), causes another person ('B') to see or hear, by whatever means, a sexual written communication or sexual verbal communication—

(a) without B consenting to seeing or as the case may be hearing it, and

(b) without any reasonable belief that B consents to seeing or as the case may be hearing it, then A commits an offence, to be known as the offence of causing a person to see or hear an indecent communication.

(3) The purposes are—

(a) obtaining sexual gratification,

(b) humiliating, distressing or alarming B.

(4) In this section—

'written communication' means a communication in whatever written form, and without prejudice to that generality includes a communication which comprises writings of a person other than A (as for example a passage in a book or magazine), and

'verbal communication' means a communication in whatever verbal form, and without prejudice to that generality includes—

(a) a communication which comprises sounds of sexual activity (whether actual or simulated), and

(b) a communication by means of sign language.'

3.55 The section 7 offence follows the familiar path of requiring intentional conduct on the part of the perpetrator, resulting in a consequence to which the victim did not consent, and that the conduct is engaged in for a particular defined purpose. Whether the communication falls to be described as sexual will be determined as before by reference to section 60(2) of the Act and purpose will be established by reference to section 49.[30]

3.56 For the purposes of subsection (1), sending or directing each have their ordinary meaning. Although person B must be the intended recipient of the communication, be it written or verbal, the commission of the offence is not dependant on the receipt of the communication by person B.

3.57 The requirement that the communication be written or verbal excludes the sending of images of any nature, although a comment or sound attached to such an image could constitute a sexual verbal communication and, in that fashion, amount to a commission of the offence. The sending of indecent images might be prosecuted under section 6 of the 2009 Act, section 127 of the Communications Act 2003,

30 In the same fashion as set out at **3.49** (in relation to s 5).

section 2 of the Abusive and Sexual Harm (Scotland) Act 2016 or as a contravention of section 38 of the Criminal Justice and Licensing (Scotland) Act 2003.[31]

3.58 For the purposes of subsection (2), intentionally causing another to see or hear a sexual communication means deliberately bringing about the circumstances in which person B sees or hears the relevant communication. The additional requirements of an absence of a reasonable belief that person B consents and person A's purpose of course also apply before the offence is committed.

Section 8

3.59 Section 8 creates the offence of sexual exposure. It provides that:

> '(1) If a person ('A')—
> (a) without another person ('B') consenting, and
> (b) without any reasonable belief that B consents,
> intentionally and for a purpose mentioned in subsection (2), exposes A's genitals in a sexual manner to B with the intention that B will see them, then A commits an offence, to be known as the offence of sexual exposure.
> (2) The purposes are—
> (a) obtaining sexual gratification,
> (b) humiliating, distressing or alarming B.'

3.60 The scope of this offence is narrow, in the sense that the perpetrator has to act deliberately with the intention of exposing his genitals in a sexual manner[32] to a particular person. The need for the same underlying purpose as specified in the preceding sections means that the offence will not be committed by a naturist in normal circumstances, or by someone who urinates in a public place (as does the requirement that the exposure must be in a sexual manner).

3.61 Whilst the term 'genitals' is not defined it ought to be given its normal meaning and would therefore exclude exposure of buttocks or breasts, even if done in circumstances which would otherwise satisfy the remaining tests in the section.

3.62 On conviction for an offence contrary to section 8 a person will be subject to the notification requirements specified in Part 2 of the Sexual Offences Act 2003 if:

- (a) the offender, in respect of the offence, is or has been—
  - (i) sentenced to a term of imprisonment, or
  - (ii) admitted to a hospital, or
- (b) the offender was 18 or over and the victim was under 18.

31 See, eg, *Sutherland v HM Advocate* 2017 SCCR 268, *McHugh v Harvie* 2015 SCCR 430.

32 That is, if a reasonable person would in all the circumstances consider it to be sexual.

Section 9

3.63 Section 9 creates the offence of voyeurism. It provides that:

> '(1) A person ('A') commits an offence, to be known as the offence of voyeurism, if A does any of the things mentioned in subsections (2) to (5).
> (2) The first thing is that A—
> (a) without another person ('B') consenting, and
> (b) without any reasonable belief that B consents,
> for a purpose mentioned in subsection (6) observes B doing a private act.
> (3) The second thing is that A—
> (a) without another person ('B') consenting, and
> (b) without any reasonable belief that B consents,
> operates equipment with the intention of enabling A or another person ('C'), for a purpose mentioned in subsection (7), to observe B doing a private act.
> (4) The third thing is that A—
> (a) without another person ('B') consenting, and
> (b) without any reasonable belief that B consents,
> records B doing a private act with the intention that A or another person ('C'), for a purpose mentioned in subsection (7), will look at an image of B doing the act.
> (4A) The fourth thing is that A—
> (a) without another person ('B') consenting, and
> (b) without any reasonable belief that B consents,
> operates equipment beneath B's clothing with the intention of enabling A or another person ('C'), for a purpose mentioned in subsection (7), to observe B's genitals or buttocks (whether exposed or covered with underwear) or the underwear covering B's genitals or buttocks, in circumstances where the genitals, buttocks or underwear would not otherwise be visible.
> (4B) The fifth thing is that A—
> (a) without another person ('B') consenting, and
> (b) without any reasonable belief that B consents,
> records an image beneath B's clothing of B's genitals or buttocks (whether exposed or covered with underwear) or the underwear covering B's genitals or buttocks, in circumstances where the genitals, buttocks or underwear would not otherwise be visible, with the intention that A or another person ('C'), for a purpose mentioned in subsection (7), will look at the image.
> (5) The sixth thing is that A—
> (a) installs equipment, or
> (b) constructs or adapts a structure or part of a structure, with the intention of enabling A or another person to do an act referred to in subsection (2), (3), (4), (4A) or (4B).
> (6) The purposes referred to in subsection (2) are—
> (a) obtaining sexual gratification,
> (b) humiliating, distressing or alarming B.

(7) The purposes referred to in subsections (3), (4), (4A) and (4B) are—
(a) obtaining sexual gratification (whether for A or C),
(b) humiliating, distressing or alarming B.'

3.64 As with the offence of sexual exposure created by section 8, the offence of voyeurism was not suggested by the SLC in its report. Both offences were introduced during the passage of the Bill through the Scottish Parliament. In the case of the section 9 offence, it was further amended before the Act was brought into force so as to include what is sometimes referred to as 'upskirting' by the introduction of subsections (4A) and (4B).[33] Whilst these two subsections address conduct which is indistinguishable from the relevant provision in the Sexual Offences Act 2003,[34] it is notable that the English provision extends the offending conduct to circumstances in which the perpetrator records an image of the victim breastfeeding a child, or of her re-arranging her clothing in the course of preparing to do so, or having just finished doing so.

3.65 The offence provided for by section 9 occurs when non-consensual conduct occurs for the purpose of obtaining sexual gratification, or humiliating, distressing or alarming the victim.[35] In summary, the conduct concerned involves:

- observing another person doing a private act;
- operating equipment with the intention of enabling the observation of the victim doing a private act;
- recording a person doing a private act with the intention that an image of that act will be looked at;
- operating equipment beneath the victim's clothing with the intention of enabling the victims genitals or buttocks or underwear to be observed;
- recording an image beneath the victim's clothing of the person's genitals and buttocks or underwear with the intention that the image will be looked at, and
- installing equipment or constructing or adapting a structure or part thereof with the intention of enabling someone to do one of the acts already described.

3.66 The provisions of section 9 appear to be modelled on section 67 of the Sexual Offences Act 2003. As with section 68(1) of that Act, section 10 of the 2009 Act provides for interpretation of some of the terms used in setting out the offence of voyeurism. It provides that:

'(1) For the purposes of section 9, a person is doing a private act if the person is in a place which in the circumstances would reasonably be expected to provide privacy, and—
(a) the person's genitals, buttocks or breasts are exposed or covered only with underwear,
(b) the person is using a lavatory, or
(c) the person is doing a sexual act that is not of a kind ordinarily done in public.

33 By s 43 of the Criminal Justice and Licensing (Scotland) Act 2010.
34 Sexual Offences Act 2003, s 67A.
35 To be determined by reference to s 49.

(2) For the purposes of section 9(3) operating equipment includes enabling or securing its activation by another person without that person's knowledge.
(3) In section 9(5), 'structure' includes a tent, vehicle or vessel or other temporary or movable structure.'

3.67 Each of sections 67 of the 2003 Act and section 9 of the 2009 Act has an accompanying interpretation section in identical terms. Accordingly, should any similar issues arise, cases decided in England and Wales are likely to provide guidance as to the meaning of the relevant terms.

3.68 The first point to consider in this context concerns the conduct involved in 'observing' a person doing a private act, as referred to in section 9(2). Despite the approach taken in the five preceding sections, which all specify the need for intentional conduct engaged in for the same underlying purpose (obtaining sexual gratification, or humiliating, distressing, or alarming B), the section 9(2) offence does not mention the need for the relevant observation to be engaged in intentionally. All of the offences specified in the remaining subsections of section 9 refer to the need for both a particular intention and purpose.

3.69 Nevertheless, the use of the verb 'observes' in section 9(2) connotes a deliberate decision on the part of the perpetrator to look at someone doing a private act as opposed to an accidental, careless or reckless perception of someone doing such an act.[36] The term is apt to cover observation by the naked eye or by the use of binoculars or the like and observing the victim in a mirror.

3.70 As can be seen from section 10, a person is 'doing a private act' if the person is in a place which, in the circumstances, would reasonably be expected to provide privacy and one or other of the conditions mentioned in subsection (1) paragraphs (a) to (c) is met. This imposes an objective test rather than directing consideration to the subjective view in fact held by the person observed. So the expectation of privacy must be a reasonable one in the circumstances. However 'a place' plainly allows the offence to be committed outside, such as in an enclosed garden or a remote rural location, provided that in the circumstances it could reasonably be expected to provide privacy.

3.71 The term 'breasts' which appears in section 10(1)(a) is unlikely to include the male chest.[37] The term 'underwear' has been held not to include bikini bottoms when worn as swimwear but that they may constitute underwear if the person chose to wear them as underpants.[38] The terms of section 9(4) are wide enough to extend the offence to secret filming by one of the participants to a consensual act of intercourse.[39]

36 *R v B* [2012] EWCA Crim 770.
37 *R v Bassett* [2008] EWCA Crim 1174.
38 *Police Service for Northern Ireland v MacRitchie* [2008] NICA 26. We would suggest that context is all important and that there may be many circumstances in which swimwear easily falls within the definition of underwear.
39 *R v Richards* [2020] EWCA Crim 95.

Section 11

3.72 Section 11 creates the offence of administering a substance for sexual purposes. It provides that:

> '(1) If a person ('A') intentionally administers a substance to, or causes a substance to be taken by, another person ('B')—
> (a) without B knowing, and
> (b) without any reasonable belief that B knows,
> and does so for the purpose of stupefying or overpowering B, so as to enable any person to engage in a sexual activity which involves B, then A commits an offence, to be known as the offence of administering a substance for sexual purposes.
> (2) For the purposes of subsection (1), if A, whether by act or omission, induces in B a reasonable belief that the substance administered or taken is (either or both)—
> (a) of a substantially lesser strength, or
> (b) in a substantially lesser quantity, than it is, any knowledge which B has (or belief as to knowledge which B has)
> that it is being administered or taken is to be disregarded.'

3.73 A person who has sexual activity with someone who is incapable of consenting through being stupefied or overpowered by the consumption of alcohol, or any other substance, commits a crime,[40] regardless of how that person came to be in that condition. However, the section 11 provision specifically criminalises the activity of administering or causing another to take a substance for the purpose of thereafter engaging in sexual activity with that person, or of permitting someone else to do so. The crime is one of purpose, and therefore it is immaterial whether sexual activity in fact occurs or not.

3.74 As the SLC explained in its report[41] the key element of this offence is that the victim is given the substance without her knowledge. The effect of subsection (2) is that a victim is to be deemed to be lacking knowledge of what she is consuming if a substance in greater strength or in greater quantity than she was expecting to consume is provided (for instance, a stronger drink or stronger dose of a drug than B was expecting).

3.75 The interplay between this section and sections 13(2)(a) and 14 is interesting. To commit the section 11 offence the perpetrator must administer the substance or cause the substance to be taken in circumstances where the victim is unaware that this has happened, and the perpetrator requires to lack reasonable belief that the victim knew about the administration or consumption of the substance. The purpose behind doing so has to be the intention to engage in sexual activity once the other party has become stupefied.

40 2009 Act, ss 13(1)(a) and 14.
41 Para 3.65.

3.76 Lack of knowledge by the victim and the perpetrator's purpose are no doubt linked together in the creation of this offence to give effect to the SLC's underlying view as to the importance of sexual autonomy. However, the context in which the SLC saw the principle of autonomy applying included the proposition that the law ought not to criminalise conduct which parties had agreed to enter into. In keeping with this approach, the SLC recommended that persons could agree in advance to have sex when they had reached such an intoxicated state as to be incapable at that point of giving consent and persons could agree in advance to allow intercourse whilst sleeping.[42] These recommendations were rejected by the Scottish Parliament.

3.77 The effect of the approach which is set out in section 11 is that if person B knows what is being administered, and is happy to consume the substance in the knowledge that person A will engage in sexual activity with her once she has been stupefied, the administrator of the substance will not commit the section 11 offence. However, if person A then goes on, as was planned, to have intercourse with person B after she has become stupefied, he still commits a sexual offence, since consent cannot be issued in advance and free agreement is absent where sexual conduct occurs at a time when the person is incapable because of the effect of alcohol or any other substance of consenting to it, or when the person is unconscious.

3.78 It is suggested that, in cases where a substance is administered without the knowledge of person B and then sexual intercourse takes place while B is incapacitated, a section 11 charge should be libelled with the section 1 rape charge (applying the rule on mixed charges in section 288BB of the 1995 Act). It is not necessary for the Crown to prove what substance has been administered, but in circumstances where it is not known what the substance is, the indictment should read 'with a substance to the prosecutor unknown'.

TABLE OF OFFENCES

3.79

Table 3.1

Offence	**Dates in force**	**Maximum sentence**
Section 1: rape	1 December 2010 to present	Life imprisonment and a fine
Section 2: sexual assault by penetration	1 December 2010 to present	Life imprisonment and a fine
Section 3: sexual assault	1 December 2010 to present	Summary: 12 months' imprisonment or a fine not exceeding the statutory maximum (or both) Indictment: life imprisonment or a fine (or both)

42 Report para 2.59.

Offence	Dates in force	Maximum sentence
Section 4: sexual coercion	1 December 2010 to present	Summary: 12 months' imprisonment or a fine not exceeding the statutory maximum (or both) Indictment: life imprisonment or a fine (or both)
Section 5: coercing a person into being present during a sexual activity	1 December 2010 to present	Summary: 12 months' imprisonment or a fine not exceeding the statutory maximum (or both) Indictment: 10 years' imprisonment or a fine (or both)
Section 6: coercing a person into looking at a sexual image	1 December 2010 to present	Summary: 12 months' imprisonment or a fine not exceeding the statutory maximum (or both) Indictment: 10 years' imprisonment or a fine (or both)
Section 7: communicating indecently	1 December 2010 to present	Summary: 12 months' imprisonment or a fine not exceeding the statutory maximum (or both) Indictment: 10 years' imprisonment or a fine (or both)
Section 8: sexual exposure	1 December 2010 to present	Summary: 12 months' imprisonment or a fine not exceeding the statutory maximum (or both) Indictment: five years' imprisonment or a fine (or both)
Section 9: voyeurism	1 December 2010 to present	Summary: 12 months' imprisonment or a fine not exceeding the statutory maximum (or both) Indictment: five years' imprisonment or a fine (or both)
Section 11: administering a substance for sexual purposes	1 December 2010 to present	Summary: 12 months' imprisonment or a fine not exceeding the statutory maximum (or both) Indictment: five years' imprisonment or a fine (or both)

Chapter 4

The offences against children under the 2009 Act

INTRODUCTION

4.01 Part 4 and Part 5 of the Sexual Offences (Scotland) Act 2009 are devoted to offences that are based on the protective principle, that is, the principle that the criminal law should give special protection to certain groups of people because their consent to sexual activity is, to use the word used by the Scottish Law Commission, problematic. Part 4 contains offences against children. Part 5 contains 'abuse of trust' offences: offences where the offender has either abused the trust of a child or abused the trust of a mentally disordered person. This chapter sets out the Part 4 offences. The following chapter sets out the Part 5 offences.

4.02 We discuss the structure of Part 4 and the rationale for that structure at **4.05–4.09** below, but in short, Part 4 contains two sets of offences: offences that can be committed against young children (those under 13) and offences that can be committed against older children (those between 13 and 16). These Part 4 offences deliberately mirror the wording of general offences in Part 1, and this chapter should be read along with the discussion of those offences in Chapter 3. We confine ourselves in this chapter to setting out the key differences for each Part 4 offence. Equally, the wording of the young and older children offences in Part 4 is often similar: for instance, the offences of causing a young child to participate in sexual activity (section 21) and causing an older child to participate in sexual activity (section 31) are identical, save for the necessary references to age. Again, to avoid repetition, when discussing the equivalent offence for older children, we have confined our analysis to noting the key components of that offence and how it differs from the equivalent offence against young children.

4.03 Before turning to each set of offences, we set out some general considerations on the Part 4 offences: the protective principle; the structure of Part 4 and the distinction in it between young and older children; the defences to Part 4 offences; the deeming provisions in sections 40 and 41; and the rules on alternative offences in section 50(2)–(4).

THE PROTECTIVE PRINCIPLE

4.04 The protective principle was one of the main guiding principles of the SLC's report. The SLC defined it as 'the idea that the criminal law should give special protection to those persons about whom consenting to sexual activity is problematic'.[1] It identified the categories of persons to whom the protective principle applied as: children; persons with a mental disorder; and persons over whom others hold a position of trust.[2] The SLC gave several rationales for the protective principle. One was that, for young children, the protective principle simply added to the consent principle: young children, because they could not consent to sexual activity, should be protected from it. But the SLC suggested that the protective principle went further and also applied in cases where the person to be protected could give consent (such as an older child or a person over whom others held a position of trust) but that consent was in some way underdeveloped.[3] In such cases, the protective principle acted to protect vulnerability and prevent exploitation; in such cases, the protective principle overrode the consent principle.[4] That is the philosophy that underpins both Parts 4 and 5 of the Act.

THE STRUCTURE OF PART 4 AND THE DISTINCTION BETWEEN YOUNG AND OLDER CHILDREN

4.05 The different rationales for the protective principle – that young children could never consent to sexual activity and thus ought to be protected from it, and that older children ought to be protected because their consent was underdeveloped – were carried forward into the structure of Part 4. The first part of Part 4, sections 18–27, creates offences against young children (those under 13). The second part of Part 4, sections 28–39, creates separate offences against older children (those aged between 13 and 16) and specifies the defences available to those offences. A final part, sections 40 and 41, creates deeming provisions to govern what should happen if, at trial, it becomes unclear whether the child is a young or older child, or when the accused's age becomes unclear. We consider these deeming provisions at **4.23–4.31** below.

4.06 The age of 13 was chosen as the dividing line between young and older children. As the SLC observed in its report, this distinction between young and older children already existed in Scots law. The offences against children which existed before the 2009 Act are discussed in Chapter 12: Historical offences, but as the SLC observed, the state of the law was unsatisfactory, using different cut-off ages for different offences and even different ages for each gender.[5] Principally, two ages

1 Para 1.28.
2 Ibid.
3 Para 4.8.
4 Para 1.28.
5 SLC report at para 4.15.

had been used. At common law, sexual intercourse with a girl under 12 was rape. By section 5(1) of the Criminal Law (Consolidation) (Scotland) Act 1995, it was an offence to have sexual intercourse with a girl under 13. The SLC recommended that the age should be 13, to avoid being seen to lower the level of protection set out in section 5(1) of the 1995 Act and to follow the Sexual Offences Act 2003, which also created young and older children offences for the rest of the UK and set the dividing line between those offences at 13.[6] In line with the gender-parity principle, the age of 13 in the 2009 Act applies equally to male and female children, significantly rationalising the law in this area.[7]

4.07 Having established the distinction between young and older children, Part 4 creates a series of offences for each group of children that mirror the equivalent general offences in Part 1, making the necessary changes to reflect the principles that: (i) young children cannot consent to sexual activity; (ii) the sexual activity with or towards older children should be criminalised to protect them, irrespective of whether they seem to consent to that sexual activity.[8] The Part 1 offences and their equivalents in Part 4 are set out in the table below. There is a final offence in Part 4: engaging while an older child in sexual conduct with or towards another older child (section 37(1) and (4)). This is a stand-alone offence and it is considered at **4.62–4.66** below.

Table 4.1

Part 1 offence	Equivalent offence against a young child	Equivalent offence against an older child
Section 1: rape	Section 18: rape of a young child	Section 28: Having intercourse with an older child
Section 2: sexual assault by penetration	Section 19: sexual assault on a young child by penetration	Section 29: engaging in penetrative sexual activity with or towards an older child
Section 3: sexual assault	Section 20: sexual assault on a young child	Section 30: engaging in sexual activity with or towards an older child

6 SLC report at para 4.24.

7 The pre-2009 Act offences and the different ages used to create offences involving boys and girls, are set out in Chapter 12.

8 With the exception of s 11, administering a substance for sexual purposes. It is not apparent from paragraphs of the SLC's report recommending such an offence why the SLC did not also recommend equivalent offences in Part 4. The thinking may simply have been that the offence is a general one (requiring A to administer a substance to, or to cause a substance to be taken by, B without B knowing and without any reasonable belief that B knows) and that, being based on a lack of knowledge by B rather than any concept of consent, can apply to young and older children without any need for changes.

Part 1 offence	Equivalent offence against a young child	Equivalent offence against an older child
Section 4: sexual coercion	Section 21: causing a young child to participate in a sexual activity	Section 31: causing an older child to participate in a sexual activity
Section 5: coercing a person into being present during a sexual activity	Section 22: causing a young child to be present during a sexual activity	Section 32: causing an older child to be present during a sexual activity
Section 6: coercing a person into looking at a sexual image	Section 23: Causing a young child to look at a sexual image	Section 33: causing an older child to look at a sexual image
Section 7(1): communicating indecently	Section 24(1): communicating indecently with a young child	Section 34(1): communicating indecently with an older child
Section 7(4): causing a person to see or hear an indecent communication	Section 24(4): causing a young child to see or hear an indecent communication	Section 34(2): causing an older child to see or hear an indecent communication
Section 8: sexual exposure	Section 25: sexual exposure to a young child	Section 35: sexual exposure to an older child
Section 9: voyeurism	Section 26: voyeurism towards a young child	Section 36: voyeurism towards an older child

4.08 A final aspect of the interplay between Part 1 and Part 4 calls for comment. For the reasons given above, when it comes to sexual activity with or towards a young child, consent is irrelevant. For that reason, sections 18–27, the offences against young children, omit all reference to consent, and those sections act as a code of bespoke offences against young children. This means that, when there is sexual activity with a young child, that activity can be charged under the appropriate offence in sections 18–27: normally, there will be no need to bring a charge involving a young child under Part 1. But it is slightly different for the offences against older children in sections 28–39. Although these older-child offences are drafted without any reference to consent, they are not to the exclusion of the offences in Part 1 of the Act.[9] It is perfectly consistent with the structure of the Act for sexual activity with or towards older children to be prosecuted under Part 1 of the Act, where there is an express lack of consent on the older child's part.

4.09 In that sense, it is not entirely accurate to say that consent is irrelevant or immaterial to the offences against older children in Part 4: it is relevant in determining

9 SLC report at para 4.43 and the Scottish Government's Policy Memorandum at para 108.

whether the appropriate charge is one under Part 1 or Part 4. For instance, if a person over 16 has sexual intercourse with an older child when the child clearly tells him that they do not want to have sex, though that would fall within the Part 4 offence of having intercourse with an older child (contrary to section 28), it is also the Part 1 offence of rape (contrary to section 1) and will always be indicted as such. The same is true for the other offences that may be committed against an older child in sections 29–32: any clear lack of consent on the older child's part (either stated by the older child or inferred from, say, the older child being asleep or too intoxicated) will bring the behaviour within the terms of the equivalent general offence in sections 2–5 in Part 1 of the Act and is likely to be charged as such. If there is no evidence of a clear lack of consent (express or inferred) then the appropriate offence is one under Part 4.

DEFENCES TO PART 4 OFFENCES

4.10 The Act spells out what is and what is not a defence to a Part 4 offence. It is convenient first to consider what is not a defence to a Part 4 offence, then to consider what is.

Defences not available to Part 4 offences

4.11 We turn first to what is not a defence to a Part 4 offence. First, section 27 of the Act makes clear that it is not a defence to an offence against a young child for the accused to believe that the child had attained the age of 13 years. When making this proposal, the SLC was confident that it would not breach the presumption of innocence in Article 6(2) ECHR because of the Court of Appeal Criminal Division's ruling to that effect in respect of section 5 of the Sexual Offences Act 2003 (rape of a child under 13) *R v G*.[10] After the SLC's report, that ruling was upheld by the House of Lords[11] and the European Court of Human Rights.[12] The argument had run that, by removing any reasonable-belief defence, a sexual offence against a young child became a strict-liability offence. Strict-liability offences can fall foul of the presumption of innocence if: (i) the definition of the strict-liability offence allows presumptions of fact or law to be drawn from facts proven by the Crown; and (ii) those presumptions are not confined within reasonable limits ('the *Salabiaku* principle'[13]). The argument was extensively considered and rejected by both the House of Lords and ECtHR. Both courts found that the term strict-liability offence was apt to mislead; even without the availability of the defence, the prosecution in any such case still has to prove that the sexual activity was done intentionally or

10 [2006] 1 WLR 2052.
11 [2009] 1 AC 92.
12 *G v the United Kingdom* [2012] Crim LR 46.
13 *Salabiaku v France* (1991) 13 EHRR 379.

recklessly. This, rather than doing the sexual activity in the knowledge that it is being done to a young child, is the *mens rea* of the offence. For that reason, both the House of Lords and the ECtHR found that section 5 of the 2003 Act was not a strict-liability offence and, in any event, it did not allow presumptions of facts and law to be drawn from the facts proven by the prosecution. The *Salabiaku* principle thus had no application. The point thus appears settled for section 27 of the 2009 Act too.

4.12 By section 39(7) of the 2009 Act, it is not a defence to any offence involving an older child to believe that the child has not attained 13 years, closing the potential loophole that A could be acquitted of an offence against an older child by claiming that he was trying to commit an offence against a young child.

4.13 Finally, it is no defence to the older-child offences to be married to or in a civil partnership with the older child. This was a defence to the offence of unlawful sexual intercourse with a girl aged between 13 and 16 years of age, contrary to section 5(3) of the Criminal Law (Consolidation) (Scotland) Act 1995: section 5(5). The SLC proposed retaining the defence, envisaging the situation where Scots law might recognise a foreign marriage or civil partnership where one of the parties was under 16.[14] The Scottish Government and Scottish Parliament disagreed. The Scottish Government Policy Memorandum noted that there was no such defence in England and Wales, that such a defence would be contrary to a founding principle of the then Bill that children under the age of 16 should be protected from premature sexual activity, and that a similar principle was found in Scotland's own laws on marriage and civil partnership.[15]

Defences to Part 4 offences

4.14 There are three defences to Part 4 offences. The first, contained in section 39(1), is that it is a defence to any of the offences involving an older child to have reasonably believed that the older child was over 16. The second defence, contained in section 39(3), also gives the accused (A) a defence to certain of the offences involving an older child when there is a difference in age between A and the older child (B) of less than two years (the proximity-of-age defence). The third defence is contained in section 51 of the Act. It gives a defence to inciting or being involved art and part in the commission of any Part 4 offence to those who may counsel or provide medical or other care and advice to a child.[16] Like all defences, all three defences place an evidential burden on the accused to lead evidence of them. Without such evidence, the defence will not be available, and the jury will be instructed that it does not arise for their consideration. With such evidence, it is for the Crown to prove that the defence is not made out. We consider the three defences in further detail below.

[14] Paras 4.65–4.70.

[15] Paras 136 and 137.

[16] It is also a defence to the two Part 5 offences: see Chapter 5.

The defence of reasonable belief as to the age of an older child

4.15 As stated above, by section 39(1), it is a defence to any of the older-child offences in Part 4 for an accused (A) to have reasonably believed that the older child (B) was over 16.[17] In proposing this defence, the SLC[18] and, in turn, the Scottish Government and Scottish Parliament recognised that offences against older children were different in this respect from offences against young children in that there may be greater scope for a defence of mistake as to an older child's age: the example given by the Scottish Government in its Policy Memorandum accompanying the Bill is of an accused meeting the child in a nightclub or other venue where only adults should be admitted.[19]

4.16 The defence applies whatever age A is. The previous rule – that only those under 24 could avail themselves of the defence to a charge of unlawful sexual intercourse with a girl aged over 13 and under 16 (contrary to section 5(3) of the Criminal Law (Consolidation) (Scotland) Act 1995) – was considered by the SLC to be lacking in any obvious principle. The Scottish Government agreed, observing in its Policy Memorandum that, in the nightclub example above, the accused might even have enquired as to the child's age and been shown some 'proof of age'. It added that it would be for the court (ie, factfinder) to decide on the credibility of the individual offering such a defence.[20]

4.17 As enacted, section 39(2) provided that the defence of reasonable belief was not available to A if:

(i) A had previously been charged with a relevant sexual offence (that is, an offence listed in Schedule 1 to the Act, which contains almost all sexual offences when they are committed against a person under 16 (section 39(2)(i));
(ii) A had a previous conviction for a relevant foreign offence committed against a person under 16 (section 39(2)(ii)); or
(iii) a risk of sexual harm order was in force in respect of A (section 39(2)(iii)).[21]

4.18 In *AB v HM Advocate*,[22] the Supreme Court found that section 39(2)(i) was incompatible with Article 8 ECHR and was thus not law. The Supreme Court observed that the reason which had been given for removing the defence for those who had been previously charged with a relevant sexual offence was that such persons had received an official warning about sexual offences with children. The Supreme Court found that the difficulty with that rationale was the width of the definition of relevant sexual offences in Schedule 1. Schedule 1 included not just offences against older children but also offences against other children and general offences like rape, where the question of age was irrelevant. There was then no rational connection

17 And in s 37(4), for B, an older child, to believe that A, also an older child, was over 16.
18 SLC report at para 4.33.
19 At para 134.
20 Ibid.
21 By s 39(2)(b), the same applies to B, when B is charged with an offence under s 37(4).
22 2017 SC (UKSC) 101.

between the warning and deterrence of the person who was charged with consensual sexual activity with older children. There would not always be an adequate basis in the earlier charge from which the charged person could infer an official warning about sexual behaviour with children under 16: there was no link between the earlier charge and the supposed warning about sexual activity with older children that the earlier charge gave.[23] As such, section 39(2)(i) was disproportionate and not law.

4.19 We make two points about the Supreme Court's judgment. First, it was concerned only with section 39(2)(i) and not section 39(2)(ia) or (ii) (the removal of the reasonable-belief defence in respect of those charges with a relevant foreign offence or those subject to a risk of sexual harm order). However, the breadth of the relevant foreign offences and the breadth of the grounds on which a risk of sexual harm order could be made mean that it is likely that those provisions would also be found to be incompatible with Article 8. Second, the problem in *AB* was the breadth of the list of relevant sexual offences in Schedule 1. The Supreme Court did not find that there could never be a rational link between certain sexual offences and the warning about sexual activity with older children that those offences could be said to give: both Lord Hodge and Lord Reed gave the example of a previous charge of sexual conduct with another older child, contrary to section 37.[24] Thus, if the list of relevant sexual offences were to be revised and restricted to purportedly consensual activity with older children (with similar restrictions placed on the references to foreign offences and risk of sexual harm orders), it may be that section 37(2) would then be found to be compatible with Article 8.

The proximity-of-age defence

4.20 By section 39(3), it is a defence to certain of the offences against older children that, when the conduct took place, the difference between A's age and B's age did not exceed two years. The aim of this defence is to protect those who have just turned 16. As the Scottish Government's Policy Memorandum observed, the Act prevents all sexual activity between those under 16 and those over 16 (even kissing and cuddling). Without the defence, a teenager's sixteenth birthday would cause them to commit an offence if, on that birthday, they had any sexual contact (even kissing and cuddling) with their 15-year-old boyfriend or girlfriend, even though that contact would have been lawful the day before. The SLC had proposed a formulation where A and B's ages were to be expressed in whole years and the defence was to apply if the difference between those two ages was not more than two (thus allowing the defence when A was 17 and a half and B 15).[25] This was rejected by the Scottish Government as allowing, at its extreme, a gap of nearly three years. It also created anomalies because it converted an effective age gap of two years

23 Lord Hodge at para 35; Lord Reed at para 66.
24 At paras 44 and 65 respectively.
25 S 27 of its draft Bill.

into three years if A's birthday is slightly before B's.[26] The solution proposed by the Scottish Government (and enacted by the Parliament) of a simple calendar difference of two years is, we suggest, clearer and provides a bright-line rule.

4.21 When the difference is less than two years, then by section 39(4)(d), A has a defence to any of the offences in sections 31–36. A also has a defence to the offence of engaging in sexual activity with or toward an older child (contrary to section 30), as long as the conduct alleged does not involve: penetration of B's vagina, anus, or mouth with A's penis; penetration of B's vagina or anus with A's mouth, tongue, or teeth; B's vagina, anus, or penis being touched sexually by A's mouth; A's vagina, anus or mouth being penetrated by B's penis; or A's vagina, anus or penis being touched sexually by B's mouth.[27] It is not a defence to a charge under section 28. In effect, these restrictions on the defence prohibit penetrative and oral sex between A and B. By doing so, they align the defence with the types of sexual activity that are permitted and prohibited between older children in section 37: see **4.63** below.

4.22 For sections 31–36, the wording of section 39 arguably goes further than it needs to and would appear to give an accused (A) a defence to charges under sections 31–36 irrespective of A's motives. For instance, it would theoretically, give A a defence to sexual exposure, contrary to section 35, even if A's purpose in sexually exposing himself was to humiliate, distress, or alarm B, as long as A could show he was, for instance, 16, and B was 15 at the time of the incident. The same is true if A carries out the acts criminalised in sections 32–34 with the same purpose. The statutory scheme is probably saved by the fact that, if B does not consent to any of these acts (and one would assume that any act carried out with the purpose of humiliating, distressing, or alarming B would not be with B's consent) then the appropriate charge would be the equivalent offence in sections 5–8 of Part 1 of the Act.

The section 51 defence for those counselling children

4.23 The third defence is contained in section 51. Section 51(1)(a) provides that a person (X) is not guilty of inciting, or being involved art and part in, an offence under Part 4 or 5 if, as regards another person (Y) (that is, a child or mentally disordered person), X acts with the purpose of: (i) protecting Y from sexually transmitted infection, (ii) protecting the physical safety of Y, (iii) preventing Y from becoming pregnant, or (iv) promoting Y's emotional well-being by the giving of advice. By section 51(1)(b), X must not be acting for the purpose of: (i) obtaining sexual gratification, (ii) humiliating, distressing, or alarming Y, or (iii) causing or encouraging the activity constituting the offence or Y's participation in it.

26 Scottish Government's Policy Memorandum at para 128.

27 By s 39(4)(a)-(c). As enacted, s 39(4)(c) gave A a defence to s 30 when the conduct involved ejaculation of semen onto B (s 30(2)(d)) but not when the conduct involved the sexual emission of urine or saliva onto B (s 30(2)(e)). This was because, as enacted, s 39(4)(c) only referred to s 30(2)(d) and not s 30(2)(e) too. That was put right by the Criminal Justice and Licensing (Scotland) Act 2010 which amended s 39(4)(c) to include s 30(2)(e).

4.24 Section 51 is a defence to all of the offences in Parts 4 and 5 of the Act. It seeks to protect those who counsel or give medical or other care to children (and, in Part 5, to mentally disordered persons). Its purpose is to allow, for instance, a doctor to provide contraception to a child without that being construed as inciting the child to have sexual intercourse. As the Scottish Government stated in its Policy Memorandum, without this provision, the provision of counselling services and other services intended to protect children from pregnancy or sexually transmitted infection might be put at risk.[28] The purpose of section 51(1)(b) is to limit the defence to situations where a person is acting in good faith and not with an interest in the sexual activity that the child (or mentally disordered person) might then engage in. Though the provision is primarily aimed at medical and other professionals, there is nothing in it to limit it to such persons; it would cover anyone who, in good faith, acts with one of the purposes specified in section 51(a).

AGE AND THE DEEMING PROVISIONS IN SECTIONS 40 AND 41

4.25 What if, in a trial for older-children offences, it becomes clear that sexual activity with a child has taken place but it is not clear whether the child was under 13 or between 13 and 16 at the time of that sexual activity? Equally, in a trial for section 37 offences (that is, A and B, older children, engaging in sexual activity with each other), what should happen if it is clear that sexual activity has taken place but it is unclear whether A and B were between 13 and 16 at the time of that sexual activity? Sections 40 and 41 provide for these eventualities by creating four 'deeming provisions'. The four deeming provisions work this way:

4.26 Deeming provision 1: This applies if A is charged with an offence under sections 28–36 or 37(1) (ie, an offence against an older child, B). If the Crown fails to establish that B was over 13 but the court/jury is satisfied that B was under 16, then B is deemed to have attained the age of 13.

4.27 Deeming provision 2: This applies if B is charged with an offence of sexual conduct with another older child under section 37(4). If the Crown fails to establish that A (B's sexual partner) was 13 or over but the court/jury is satisfied that A was under 16, then A is deemed to have attained the age of 13.

4.28 Deeming provision 3: This applies if A is charged with an offence of sexual conduct with another older child under section 37(1). If the Crown fails to establish that A was under 16 but the court/jury is satisfied that A was over 13, then A is deemed to have been under 16.

[28] At para 162.

4.29 Deeming provision 4: Like deeming provision 2, this applies if B is charged under section 37(4). If the Crown fails to establish that B was under 16 but the court/jury is satisfied that B was over 13, then B is deemed to have been under 16.

4.30 The deeming provisions have to be read in the statutory scheme as a whole. When an accused is charged with one of the older-child offences in sections 28–37, the young-child offences are not available as alternative offences (otherwise, an accused would be at risk of conviction for a more serious offence than he is charged with). This would mean that, without deeming provision 1, an accused would have to be acquitted even if it is established at his trial that he had been involved in sexual activity with a child under 16 simply because it was unclear whether the child was under 13 or between 13 and 16. In this way, although deeming provision 1 creates a presumption of fact (that B has attained the age of 13), it seeks to do so within reasonable limits: the alternatives would be either to allow acquittal, even though it is clear that sexual conduct with a child has taken place, or to add the young-child offences as alternatives to the older-child offences and to allow conviction for more serious offences than the accused is charged with.

4.31 Deeming provisions 2, 3 and 4 are slightly different. They operate to prevent acquittal in a section 37 case when it is clear that sexual activity with a child has taken place, but it has not been established that both A and B are between 13 and 16. There are no alternative offences to section 37(1) and (4) . Thus, without deeming provisions 2, 3 and 4, the alternatives would be to acquit the accused, even though it is clear that sexual conduct with a child has taken place, or somehow to add other Part 4 offences as alternatives to section 37(1) and (4), which would place the accused at risk of a more serious offence than he or she is charged with. Furthermore, adding other Part 4 offences as alternatives would not fit with the general statutory scheme because the other older-child offences in Part 4 can only be committed by those over 16. Adding other Part 4 offences as alternatives would therefore require changing the statutory scheme entirely, including removing the status of section 37(1) and (4) as discrete offences. By preventing outright acquittal but also preventing conviction for an offence any more serious than section 37(1)/(4), deeming provisions 2, 3 and 4 create presumptions of fact. But they seek to confine those presumptions of fact within reasonable limits that fit with the statutory scheme as a whole.

AGE AND ALTERNATIVE OFFENCES: SECTION 50(2)–(4)

4.32 We have dealt with the general concept of alternative offences under the 2009 Act at **2.124–2.132** in Chapter 2: The general provisions of the 2009 Act. The concept of alternative offences also applies to the Part 4 offences: Schedule 3 sets out the list of alternative offences that are available for each of the offences in Part 4. The two further rules, contained in section 50(2)–(4), that apply specifically in respect of Part 4 offences are also considered in Chapter 2: see **2.125–2.130**.

OFFENCES AGAINST YOUNG CHILDREN

4.33 With these general considerations, we turn first to the offences against young children contained in sections 18–26.

Section 18: rape of a young child

4.34 Section 18 enacts the SLC's recommendation that there should be a separate offence of rape of a young child. It provides that the offence of rape of a young child is committed when a person, with his penis, penetrates to any extent the vagina, anus, or mouth of a child under 13 years of age. As with section 1, the penetration may be intentional or reckless.

4.35 The wording of section 18 follows the wording of section 1 of the Act, but it will be apparent that there are key differences, consistent with the philosophy behind the offence. Most obviously, there are no references to lack of consent or reasonable belief in consent in section 18 because consent cannot be given, and thus there can be no reasonable belief in a consent that does not exist.[29] For the same reason, there is no reference, as there is in section 1(2) and (3), to penetration being a continuing act or to initial consent to penetration later being withdrawn. By contrast, the terms 'penis' and 'vagina' in section 18 have to be read in accordance with section 1(4) and the definitions given there because section 1(4) applies to the whole Act.

4.36 Section 18, like all provisions of the Act, is gender neutral and so can be committed against a male or female child. By Schedule 3, the alternative offences of sexual assault of a young child by penetration (section 19) and sexual assault of a young child (section 20) are available. Like section 1 rape, the various offences of assault with intent to commit certain sexual offences and abduction with the same intention are also available as alternative offences. As noted in Chapter 1, section 18 cases must be tried in the High Court of Justiciary.

Section 19: sexual assault on a young child by penetration

4.37 Section 2 of the Act creates the offence of sexual assault by penetration. As noted in Chapter 3 at **3.18**, this was inserted into the Sexual Offences Bill during its passage through the Scottish Parliament, and it followed that equivalent offences had to be inserted for young and older children. Section 19 is the equivalent offence to section 2 for young children. It is committed when a person (A), with a part of their body or anything else, penetrates the vagina or anus (but not mouth) of a young

[29] Confirmed in *Rae v HM Advocate* [2021] HCJAC 13, an appeal against sentence where the Court was prepared to treat a reasonable belief as a mitigating factor but one that could only be taken so far: the Lord Justice Clerk (Dorrian) at paras 22 and 23.

child. The Appeal Court found in *Tait v HM Advocate*,[30] that penetration requires to be corroborated because it is an element of the offence. That is to be doubted in light of *Lord Advocate's Reference No 1 of 2023*:[31] penetration remains an element of the offence, but, like all elements of a crime, it does not now need to be the subject of separate corroboration. As with section 18 (and indeed with all of the provisions in this part of Part 4), there are no references to consent in section 19. Like section 2(2), section 19(2) makes it clear that the penetration can be with A's penis and, as with section 2, the alternative offence of rape is not available but sexual assault and the various 'assault with intent' and 'abduction with intent' offences are available. Section 19 is triable on indictment only.

Section 20: sexual assault on a young child

4.38 Section 20 is the equivalent offence to section 3, sexual assault, when it is committed on a young child. The only difference is the omission of any reference to consent. As with section 3, it is committed when A does one or more of a list of five 'things' in subsection (2) of the provision. *Tait v HM Advocate* held that whichever 'thing' or 'things' the Crown libels becomes an essential fact which must be proved by corroborated evidence;[32] as we have noted in Chapter 3 at **3.17**, footnote 16 in respect of section 3 of the 2009 Act, that must now be viewed as incorrect in light of the decision in *Lord Advocate's Reference No 1 of 2023.*

Section 21: causing a young child to participate in a sexual activity

4.39 This offence is the equivalent of section 4 (sexual coercion). The key difference is that it does not refer to coercion or to absence of consent, for the same reasons that consent does not feature in any of the young child offences in Part 4. Section 21 will be made out when a person intentionally causes a young child to participate in a sexual activity: as with section 4, recklessness does not suffice.

Section 22: causing a young child to be present during a sexual activity

4.40 This offence is the equivalent of section 5 (coercing into being present during a sexual activity). Section 22 will be made out when a person (A) either intentionally engages in a sexual activity in the presence of a young child (B) or intentionally causes a young child to be present while a third person engages in such an activity. As

30 2016 SLT 495 at 499E-F. For an example of the offence being committed by spontaneous concert, see *Gay v HM Advocate* 2016 SCCR 87.

31 2024 JC 140.

32 *Tait v HM Advocate* 2015 SLT 495 at 500D.

with section 5, either means of committing the offence (that is, intentionally engaging in sexual activity or intentionally causing a young child to be present while a third person engages in sexual activity) must be with the purpose of obtaining sexual gratification or of humiliating, distressing or alarming the young child.

4.41 'Obtaining sexual gratification' does not mean obtaining sexual gratification from the sexual activity itself, but rather obtaining sexual gratification from the young child being present during the sexual activity. That is clear from the SLC report, which expressly recommended the inclusion of that phrase to ensure that section 5 has a proportionate effect (see Chapter 3 at **3.42**). That applies *a fortiori* to section 22 because one of the examples the SLC gave for limiting the scope of the section 5 offence is a married couple having sexual intercourse in a room which they share with their infant child.[33] Like section 5, in section 22 it is not necessary for the young child to actually see the sexual activity, merely that the young child was present and could have observed it.[34]

Section 23: causing a young child to look at a sexual image

4.42 Section 23 is the equivalent of section 6. Like section 6, section 23 requires an intention to show the sexual image with the purpose of either: (i) obtaining sexual gratification; or (ii) humiliating, distressing or alarming the viewer of the image, the young child. As we note in Chapter 3 (in respect of section 6), the inclusion of these purposes is designed to exclude, for instance, the situation where a teacher shows pupils a sexual image for educational purposes: see **3.42**.

Section 24: communicating indecently with a young child, etc

4.43 Section 24(1) and section 24(2) are the equivalents of section 7(1) and section 7(2) (the general offences of communicating indecently and causing someone to see or hear an indecent communication). There are three aspects of the offences in section 24 that call for separate comment.

4.44 First, section 24(1) and section 24(2) are subject to the same limiting principle as in section 7: that the purpose of sending or directing the communication (or causing such a communication to be seen) must either be: (i) sexual gratification; or (ii) humiliating, distressing, or alarming the young child. However, it is difficult to conceive of a sexual communication directed at a young child that would not have either of those purposes: while one can conceive of a legitimate purpose in showing a sexual image to a young child (the example of the biology or sex education lesson above), one cannot as readily conceive of a legitimate purpose in sending or directing sexual communications to a young child. For that reason, once the fact of

33 SLC report at para 3.57.
34 SLC report at para 3.60.

communication is established, not much is likely to be required to allow the inference that the purpose of the communication was either sexual gratification or humiliating, distressing or alarming the young child.

4.45 Second, the offence often arises when a person communicates with an undercover officer or a member of a private online child abuse activist group (OCAG), where the undercover officer/OCAG member is pretending to be a child.[35] In such cases, the appropriate charge is one of attempt to commit the offence, under the common law rule that one can attempt something that is factually impossible, provided that it is averred that the accused had the necessary *mens rea*.[36] Here, that will be met by averring that the accused intentionally attempted to send, direct, etc, the sexual communication to a young child.

4.46 Third, where the communications are with an OCAG member, the Appeal Court has found that no question of entrapment arises, though the Court preferred to consider the question as one of the fairness of the admission of the evidence obtained.[37] The Court also preferred to leave open the question of whether it would be different if the decoy had been a police officer, or the OCAG member acting as the decoy had been 'in cahoots' with the police or acting under the police's directions. Experience shows that the police do not act in concert with such groups, and wherever a police officer acts as a decoy, they ought to be careful to ensure that any discussion does not cross into entrapment.[38]

4.47 The Appeal Court also found that relying on the evidence of an OCAG member will not result in a breach of Article 6 or 8 ECHR. For Article 6, the domestic rules of evidence gave any accused the opportunity to object to the evidence and to question its provenance. For Article 8, any interference with private life was in accordance with the law for the purposes of Article 8(2) because the activities of such groups are subject to the common law and the interference was readily justified by being in the interests of public safety, the prevention of disorder or crime, and the protection of the rights and freedoms of others.[39] The Supreme Court upheld that conclusion and went further in finding that there was no interference with Article 8 when an accused communicates (or attempts to communicate) with a child in this manner.[40] The Appeal Court and Supreme Court considered these points in respect of a charge brought under section 34 (the equivalent offence when the communication

35 Sometimes referred to as 'paedophile hunter organisations' or 'paedophile hunter groups'.

36 *Docherty v Brown* 1996 JC 48 in particular the Lord Justice Clerk (Ross) at para 60.

37 *Quinn and Sutherland v HM Advocate* 2022 JC 131 per the Lord Justice General (Carloway) at paras 39 and 40.

38 For one case where police behaviour was found to have crossed the line into entrapment, particularly when the accused had not expressed any interest in sexual activity with children and had not reacted when that was first suggested by the police, see *HM Advocate v IP* 2017 SCCR 447. That was a case of attempting to engage in sexual activity with an older child, contrary to s 30, but the same principles on entrapment apply.

39 Ibid at paras 50 and 51.

40 *Sutherland v HM Advocate* 2020 SC (UKSC) 66.

is with an older child: **4.60** below)[41] but the same principles surely apply under section 24.

4.48 The alternative offences to section 24(1) and section 24(2) include the main other non-contact offences against children, but curiously also include the 'assault with intent' and 'abduction with intent' offences. These are not available as alternatives to section 23. It may be that they are included in respect of sections 24(1) and (2) to capture the situation where the intention behind the communications might be to prepare to commit those offences, but those alternatives will rarely arise in a typical case under section 24.

Section 25: sexual exposure to a young child and section 26: voyeurism towards a young child

4.49 Section 25 corresponds to section 8 and section 26 corresponds to section 9. Neither calls for substantial additional comment: the provisions follow the wording of their section 8 and section 9 counterparts, save for the necessary omission of any references to consent.

OFFENCES AGAINST OLDER CHILDREN

4.50 Two general points suffice to introduce the offences against older children in sections 28–37. First, only a person over 16 can commit an offence against an older child in sections 28–36. Second, it is, of course, a different matter for the discrete offences of older children engaging in sexual activity with each other, contrary to sections 37(1) and (4).

Section 28: having intercourse with an older child

4.51 As set out above, the policy behind the older children offences in Part 4 is that older children require to be protected from certain sexual behaviour, regardless of whether they might appear to wish to engage in that behaviour. The first and most important is protection from sexual intercourse with an older person. Section 28 thus makes it an offence for any person (A), who is 16 years of age or over to have sexual intercourse with an older child (B). Intercourse is the intentional or reckless penetration with A's penis, to any extent, of the older child's vagina, anus, or mouth. Section 28 is not a totally new offence: as detailed in Chapter 12: Historical offences,

41 And in respect of two further charges of attempting to cause an older child to look at a sexual image, contrary to s 33 of the 2009 Act, and attempting to meet a child for the purpose of engaging in unlawful sexual activity, contrary to s 1 of the Protection of Children and the Prevention of Sexual Offences (Scotland) Act 2005.

under section 5(3) of the Criminal Law (Consolidation) (Scotland) Act 1995 it was already an offence to have unlawful sexual intercourse with a girl over 13 and under 16. The principal change is the introduction of gender parity.

4.52 Section 28 is an alternative offence to rape, when that is alleged to have been committed against an older child. That has the effect that, if the defence to rape of an older child is one of consent, the accused is accepting that he is guilty of an offence under section 28. Though that can create difficulties in defending such cases, it is suggested that this is no different from many other crimes where, to advance a defence, one must accept guilt of a lesser offence (a plea of provocation in a murder trial, for instance, which is an acceptance of the offence of culpable homicide). It is common in such cases for the Crown to seek a conviction for rape and, in the alternative, conviction under section 28. Though the maximum penalties are 12 months' imprisonment (on summary conviction) and 10 years' imprisonment (on conviction on indictment), it is not unusual to see community sentences imposed, particularly on young offenders.

Section 29: penetrative sexual activity with an older child

4.53 Section 29 is the equivalent to sections 2 and 19. The wording of the offence is the same as in sections 2 and 19, but the name of the offence is not. Though the word assault is used in both section 2 (where the offence is called 'sexual assault by penetration') and section 19 (where it is called 'sexual assault on a young child by penetration'), it is avoided in section 29 (where the offence is simply called 'penetrative sexual activity with an older child'). The reason would seem to be to avoid the language of consent or lack of consent. Plainly, any penetrative sexual activity with someone over 16 is not an offence when the person consents to it, justifying the term 'assault' in section 2 when the person does not consent. In section 19, no young child could ever consent to such penetration, justifying the use of the word assault in that section.[42] In each case, assault connotes a lack of consent. But the purpose of section 29, like all of the offences against older children, is to criminalise particular types of sexual behaviour with older children, irrespective of whether the older child appears to consent to it. That is why the word assault is, properly, avoided in section 29: the offence is committed when the older child appears to consent to the penetrative sexual activity and when they do not, though of course any clear lack of consent will make the more appropriate charge one under section 2 of the Act.

[42] Though the name of the offence does not import the general assault into the offence: Sheriff Brown's commentary *Greens Annotated Acts: The Sexual Offences (Scotland) Act 2009* (2nd edn, W. Green 2015) p 23, with which the Appeal Court agreed in *Tait v HM Advocate* 2015 SLT 495 at 500C-D.

Section 30: engaging in sexual activity with or towards an older child

4.54 In its wording, section 30 is the equivalent to section 3 (sexual assault) and section 20 (sexual assault on a young child). The name of the offence omits any reference to sexual assault, for the same reasons as for section 29: the concept of assault is not relevant to an offence that can be committed irrespective of whether the older child appears to consent to the sexual activity or not. In all other aspects, the offence is identical to section 3.

4.55 'Sexual activity' in section 30, as with all references to 'sexual' in the Act, is defined with reference to section 60(2): that an activity is sexual if a reasonable person would, in all the circumstances of the case, consider it to be sexual. Sexual activity in section 30 is not necessarily the same as indecent activity. As the Appeal Court observed in *Wightman v HM Advocate*,[43] when considering a charge under section 30 against a tennis coach who asked an older child to remove his upper clothing in a tennis club changing room, filmed him undressing, and touched him on the body, there might be an overlap between 'sexual' and 'indecent' but this is not inevitable. Refusing the appeal, the Appeal Court observed that contact that involved merely touching another person, in a manner that could not reasonably be described as indecent, might nevertheless have a sexual motivation if an inference might properly be drawn that the person responsible for the touching obtained sexual gratification from it.[44]

Section 31: causing an older child to participate in a sexual activity

4.56 This offence is the equivalent of section 4 (sexual coercion) and section 21 (causing a young child to participate in a sexual activity). It will be made out when a person over 16 intentionally causes an older child to participate in a sexual activity.

Section 32: causing an older child to be present during a sexual activity

4.57 This offence is the equivalent of section 5 (coercing a person into being present during a sexual activity). It will be made out when a person (A), who is over 16 years of age, either intentionally engages in a sexual activity in the presence of an older child (B), or intentionally causes B to be present while a third person engages in such an activity. As with section 5, either means of committing the offence (that is, intentionally engaging in sexual activity or intentionally causing an older child to be present while a third person engages in sexual activity) must be with the purpose

43 2017 SCCR 437.

44 Lord Drummond Young at para 14, 443D-E.

of obtaining sexual gratification or of humiliating, distressing or alarming the older child.

4.58 As with section 22 (the equivalent offence for young children) 'obtaining sexual gratification' does not mean obtaining sexual gratification from the sexual activity itself, but rather obtaining sexual gratification from the older child being present during the sexual activity and, as with section 22, is not necessary for the older child to actually see the sexual activity, merely that he or she could have observed it.

Section 33: causing an older child to look at a sexual image

4.59 Section 33 is the equivalent of section 6 (coercing a person into looking at a sexual image) and section 23 (causing a young child to look at a sexual image). Like sections 6 and 23, it requires an intention to show the sexual image with the purpose of either obtaining sexual gratification or humiliating, distressing, or alarming the older child, and we repeat our comment made at **3.42** in respect of sections 5 and 23 that, while this is intended to allow the showing of images in the context of biology or sex education lessons, even with older children, this will not excuse the showing of any image, however graphic or far removed from an ordinary biology or sex education lesson.

Section 34: communicating indecently with an older child

4.60 The offences in section 34(1) and (2) are the equivalents of the offences in section 7(1) and (2) and section 24(2) and (2). The offences do not call for additional comment beyond those we have made in respect of section 24 above. The offences are frequently seen in conjunction with an offence of causing an older child to look at a sexual image, contrary to section 33 of the Act, and the offence of meeting a child following certain preliminary contact, contrary to section 1 of the Protection of Children and Prevention of Sexual Offences (Scotland) Act 2005. Where it is with the latter, if the accused is convicted, a custodial sentence is the norm.

Section 35: sexual exposure to an older child and section 36: voyeurism towards an older child

4.61 Section 35 corresponds to section 8 (the general offence of sexual exposure) and section 25 (the specific offence of sexual exposure to a young child). Section 36 corresponds to section 9 (the general offence of voyeurism) and section 26 (the specific offence of voyeurism towards a young child). In each case, the provisions follow the wording of their counterparts in sections 8 and 25, and sections 9 and 26.

Section 37: older children engaging in sexual conduct with each other

4.62 The SLC recommended that it should not be an offence for older children to engage in sexual conduct with each other. The Scottish Parliament disagreed and enacted section 37. It provides:

> **'37. Older children engaging in sexual conduct with each other**
>
> (1) If a child ("A"), being a child mentioned in subsection (2), does any of the things mentioned in subsection (3), "B" being in each case a child mentioned in subsection (2), then A commits an offence, to be known as the offence of engaging while an older child in sexual conduct with or towards another older child.
>
> (2) The child is a child who—
> (a) has attained the age of 13 years, but
> (b) has not attained the age of 16 years.
>
> (3) The things are that A—
> (a) penetrates sexually, with A's penis and to any extent, either intending to do so or reckless as to whether there is penetration, the vagina, anus or mouth of B,
> (b) intentionally or recklessly touches the vagina, anus or penis of B sexually with A's mouth.
>
> (4) In the circumstances specified in subsection (1), if B engages by consent in the conduct in question, then B commits an offence, to be known as the offence of engaging while an older child in consensual sexual conduct with another older child.
>
> (5) In paragraph (b) of subsection (3), the reference to A's mouth is to be construed as including a reference to A's tongue or teeth.'

4.63 The section could have been more simply drafted, but its effect is clear. It creates two offences: the section 37(1) offence of engaging while an older child in sexual conduct with or towards another older child, and the section 37(4) offence of engaging while an older child in consensual sexual conduct with another older child. By subsections (1) and (2), the two offences can only be committed by older children or by those deemed to be older children by virtue of the deeming provisions in sections 40 and 41. By subsection (3), the offences are limited to instances of: (a) penile intercourse (whether penile-oral, penile-vaginal or penile-anal); and (b) oral sex (whether performed on the vagina, anus, or penis). The second category was added to subsection (3) during the Act's passage through Parliament. Subsection (3) as enacted reflects the Parliament's desire not to criminalise all forms of sexual activity or experimentation between younger teenagers, but rather to prevent them from engaging in the most advanced forms of sexual activity.

4.64 Subsection (4) makes clear that if B consents to the sexual activity, he or she is also guilty of an offence (the second of the two offences). We make two points in respect of subsection (4). First, as Sheriff Brown notes in his commentary to the 2009 Act,[45] the wording of section 37(3) and (4) makes it possible for a person to be both A and B for the purposes of the section (for example, when B performs oral sex on A). We suggest that this is unavoidable in a provision that seeks to make clear that both A and B commit an offence if they engage in the sexual activity. In the highly unlikely event that both A and B were prosecuted, the charges would make it clear what each was accused of doing. Second, section 37(4) contains the only reference to B's consent in Part 4. This is unavoidable in a section which seeks to criminalise both A and B's behaviour: without the reference to B in subsection (4), B could, under the section, be guilty of an offence even if he or she did not consent to the sexual activity. If B does not consent, then it is still possible for A to commit the section 37(1) offence by doing any of the things mentioned in subsection (3). However, in those circumstances, A would not be charged under section 37: he or she would be charged with the appropriate offence under Part 1 of the Act (most likely rape or sexual assault).

4.65 Section 38 defines penetration and consent for the purposes of section 37. It uses the definitions contained in Part 1. Section 38(2) repeats the definition in section 1(2) that penetration is a continuing act from entry until withdrawal. Section 38(3)–(8) assists in defining when B will or will not be consenting for the purposes of section 37(4). It does so by incorporating the definitions of consent and related expressions that appear elsewhere in the Act: that consent means free agreement, that a person who is asleep or unconscious does not consent, that consent to one type of conduct does not imply consent to other conduct and that consent may be withdrawn at any time (and if it is withdrawn, any conduct taking place afterwards is without consent).

4.66 The question of criminalising sexual activity between teenagers (and if so, to what extent) was, and continues to be, the subject of some debate, as reflected in the disagreement between the SLC and the Scottish Parliament about whether such an offence should be included in the Act. We make three legal rather than policy observations. First, by dint of section 37(3) and its restriction of the offence to penile intercourse and oral sex, the offence is much more limited than the equivalent provision for England and Wales, section 13 of the Sexual Offences Act 2003. Section 13 extends all of the child-sex offences in sections 9–12 of the 2003 Act to those under 18. This includes, for instance, sexual touching, contrary to section 9 of the Act, making the type of sexual behaviour criminalised between teenagers in England and Wales much broader than in Scotland. Second, given the specific guidance to the police on when section 37 offences should be jointly reported to both the Crown and Scottish Children's Reporter Administration (see Chapter 13 at **13.19**), it is unlikely that the Crown in Scotland would ever prosecute a section 37 offence when that is the only offence on a complaint/indictment. Third, for this reason (and for the fact that one older child engaging in apparently sexual behaviour with another might be unlikely to wish to give evidence against their girlfriend/boyfriend) in practice

45 *Greens Annotated Acts: The Sexual Offences (Scotland) Act 2009* (2nd edn) p 66.

conviction under section 37 is likely only to arise when A is charged with non-consensual sexual behaviour towards B (for instance, rape, contrary to section 1) and section 37 is an alternative offence that the judge/jury can convict A of when it is not established that there was no consent from B.

TABLES OF OFFENCES

4.67

Table 4.2: The offences against young children in Part 4 of the 2009 Act

Offences against young children		
Offence	**Dates in force**	**Maximum sentence**
Section 18: rape of a young child	1 December 2010 to present	Life imprisonment and a fine
Section 19: sexual assault on a young child by penetration	1 December 2010 to present	Life imprisonment and a fine
Section 20: sexual assault on a young child	1 December 2010 to present	Summary: 12 months' imprisonment or a fine not exceeding the statutory maximum (or both) Indictment: Life imprisonment or a fine (or both)
Section 21: causing a young child to participate in a sexual activity	1 December 2010 to present	Summary: 12 months' imprisonment or a fine not exceeding the statutory maximum (or both) Indictment: life imprisonment or a fine (or both)
Section 22: causing a young child to be present during a sexual activity	1 December 2010 to present	Summary: 12 months' imprisonment or a fine not exceeding the statutory maximum (or both) Indictment: 10 years' imprisonment or a fine (or both)

Offences against young children		
Offence	**Dates in force**	**Maximum sentence**
Section 23: causing a young child to look at a sexual image	1 December 2010 to present	Summary: 12 months' imprisonment or a fine not exceeding the statutory maximum (or both) Indictment: 10 years' imprisonment or a fine (or both)
Section 24(1): communicating indecently with a young child Section 24 (2): causing a young child to see or hear an indecent communication	1 December 2010 to present	Summary: 12 months' imprisonment or a fine not exceeding the statutory maximum (or both) Indictment: 10 years' imprisonment or a fine (or both)
Section 25: sexual exposure to a young child	1 December 2010 to present	Summary: 12 months' imprisonment or a fine not exceeding the statutory maximum (or both) Indictment: 10 years' imprisonment or a fine (or both)
Section 26: voyeurism towards a young child	1 December 2010 to present	Summary: 12 months' imprisonment or a fine not exceeding the statutory maximum (or both) Indictment: 10 years' imprisonment or a fine (or both)

Table 4.3: The offences against older children in Part 4 of the 2009 Act

Offences against older children		
Offence	**Dates in force**	**Maximum sentence**
Section 28: having sexual intercourse with an older child	1 December 2010 to present	Summary: 12 months' imprisonment or a fine not exceeding the statutory maximum (or both) Indictment: 10 years' imprisonment or a fine (or both)

Offences against older children		
Offence	**Dates in force**	**Maximum sentence**
Section 29: engaging in penetrative sexual activity with or towards an older child	1 December 2010 to present	Summary: 12 months' imprisonment or a fine not exceeding the statutory maximum (or both) Indictment: 10 years' imprisonment or a fine (or both)
Section 30: Engaging in sexual activity with or towards an older child	1 December 2010 to present	Summary: 12 months' imprisonment or a fine not exceeding the statutory maximum (or both) Indictment: 10 years' imprisonment or a fine (or both)
Section 31: causing an older child to participate in a sexual activity	1 December 2010 to present	Summary: 12 months' imprisonment or a fine not exceeding the statutory maximum (or both) Indictment: 10 years' imprisonment or a fine (or both)
Section 32: causing an older child to be present during a sexual activity	1 December 2010 to present	Summary: 12 months' imprisonment or a fine not exceeding the statutory maximum (or both) Indictment: five years' imprisonment or a fine (or both)
Section 33: causing an older child to look at a sexual image	1 December 2010 to present	Summary: 12 months' imprisonment or a fine not exceeding the statutory maximum (or both) Indictment: five years' imprisonment or a fine (or both)
Section 34(1): communicating indecently with an older child Section 34(2): causing an older child to see or hear an indecent communication	1 December 2010 to present	Summary: 12 months' imprisonment or a fine not exceeding the statutory maximum (or both) Indictment: five years' imprisonment or a fine (or both)

Offences against older children		
Offence	**Dates in force**	**Maximum sentence**
Section 35: sexual exposure to an older child	1 December 2010 to present	Summary: 12 months' imprisonment or a fine not exceeding the statutory maximum (or both) Indictment: five years' imprisonment or a fine (or both)
Section 36: voyeurism towards an older child	1 December 2010 to present	Summary: 12 months' imprisonment or a fine not exceeding the statutory maximum (or both) Indictment: five years' imprisonment or a fine (or both)
Section 37(1): engaging while an older child in sexual conduct with or towards another older child Section 37(4): engaging while an older child in consensual sexual conduct with another older child	1 December 2010 to present	For both offences: Summary: 12 months' imprisonment or a fine not exceeding the statutory maximum (or both) Indictment: 10 years' imprisonment or a fine (or both)

Chapter 5

The abuse-of-trust offences under the 2009 Act

INTRODUCTION

5.01 Part 5 of the Sexual Offences (Scotland) Act 2009 created two offences in furtherance of the protective principle: sexual abuse of trust of a child (section 42) and sexual abuse of trust of a mentally disordered person (section 46). For each offence, we set out the elements of the offence and the defences to it. Before turning to the offences, it is helpful to place them in context by considering the previous abuse-of-trust offences which existed in Scots law, the reasons for reforming those offences in the 2009 Act, and the relationship between Part 1 of the 2009 Act and new offences created in Part 5.

PREVIOUS ABUSE-OF-TRUST OFFENCES IN SCOTS LAW

5.02 Sexual abuse-of-trust offences are not new in Scots law. The previous abuse-of-trust offences are considered in Chapter 12: Historical offences, but it suffices here to note that, immediately prior to the 2009 Act, there were two abuse-of-trust offences in respect of children in Scots law and one in respect of mentally disordered persons.

5.03 Section 3 of the Criminal Law (Consolidation) (Scotland) Act 1995 provided that a person over 16 who had sexual intercourse (that is, penile-vaginal intercourse) with a person under 16 was guilty of an offence if he was a member of the same household as the child and was in a position of trust or authority in relation to that child. Subsequently, section 3 of the Sexual Offences (Amendment) Act 2000 made it an offence for a person aged 18 or over to have sexual intercourse or to engage in any other sexual activity with a person under 18 where there was a position of trust between the parties. Section 4 of the 2000 Act defined various positions of trust with reference to the accused (A) looking after the person under 18 (B) in a place of detention, in local authority accommodation or foster care, in various types of hospitals and care institutions, or in full-time education at an educational establishment.

5.04 In the mental-health context, there have been offences in order to protect mentally-disordered persons since the middle of the eighteenth century.[1] Immediately before the 2009 Act, section 313 of the Mental Health (Care and Treatment) (Scotland) Act 2003 made it an offence for a person who was providing care services to a person who suffered from a mental disorder to engage in a sexual act with that person.[2]

THE REASONS FOR SEPARATE ABUSE-OF-TRUST OFFENCES IN THE 2009 ACT

5.05 The SLC queried whether these abuse-of-trust offences were necessary in light of the expanded approach to consent that it proposed for what was to become Part 1 of the 2009 Act. Ultimately, it considered that sexual abuse-of-trust offences had their own specific rationale: even if some instances of sexual contact with a person were wrong because of some characteristic of that person that might vitiate consent (such as age or mental condition), there was a separate and additional type of wrong where the perpetrator held a position of trust over the victim. It observed that, over and above the issue of consent, a person who held a position of trust over another was acting inconsistently with the duties imposed by that position if he engaged in sexual activity with that person.[3] For the SLC, it was also a consideration that the Sexual Offences Act 2003 had retained and widened the scope of abuse-of-trust offences for the rest of the UK, though as we shall see, the 2003 Act for the rest of the UK includes many more positions of trust than the 2009 Act does for Scotland.[4]

5.06 The SLC thus proposed retaining the substance of the three sexual abuse-of-trust offences set out above which existed in Scots law at the time of its report (section 3 of the Criminal Law (Consolidation) (Scotland) Act 1995, section 3 of the Sexual Offences (Amendment) Act 2000 and section 313 of the Mental Health (Care and Treatment) (Scotland) Act 2003), but made the following proposals to rationalise the law in this area.[5]

5.07 It proposed consolidating the two abuse-of-trust offences involving older children into one offence, the offence of sexual abuse of trust (now section 42 of the 2009 Act). It proposed that, for this offence, the relevant age should be the same for both family and other settings: 18 years of age.[6] For abuse of trust in family settings,

1 See Chapter 12 at **12.25**.

2 Extending to all those indirectly involved in providing care, such as those employed in, or contracted to provide services in or to, hospitals where the mentally disordered person was being given medical treatment and to the managers of such hospitals. There was also the general offence of non-consensual sexual acts with or towards a mentally disordered person in s 311 of the Act. See Chapter 12 at **12.26** for further details.

3 Para 4.107.

4 Ibid.

5 The SLC's proposals are at paras 4.110–4.134 of its report.

6 A position which accorded with, and effectively transposed, the EU Council Framework Decision of 22 December 2003 on combating the sexual exploitation of children and child pornography, which required the criminalisation of the sexual abuse of trust of children, and defined children as under 18.

the SLC proposed restricting the relationship to one where there were parental rights and responsibilities (or statutory equivalents), or where the person treated the child as a member of his or her family. It did so because it considered that, beyond these two situations, it was not clear that there could ever be a relationship of trust. It also proposed that the prohibited conduct should extend to all types of sexual conduct (both heterosexual and homosexual). Outside of the family setting, the SLC proposed extending the offence to those in part-time (and not just full-time education) and restricting the positions of trust to situations where the older person actually looked after the young person in question (rather than generally looking after persons under 18 in the place in question).

5.08 In respect of section 313 of the Mental Health (Care and Treatment) (Scotland) Act 2003, the SLC proposed repealing the provision and replacing it with a similar offence in a modified form. This modified offence became section 46 of the 2009 Act. The principal modification proposed by the SLC was changing the prohibited sexual conduct from engaging in 'sexual intercourse (whether vaginal or anal) … or any other sexual act' to just engaging in 'a sexual activity'.

5.09 All of these proposals, were accepted by the Scottish Government and enacted by the Scottish Parliament, save for the proposal to restrict the position of trust to situations where the older person actually looked after the young person in question, where a different legislative solution was found. We consider that solution at **5.15** below.

THE RELATIONSHIP BETWEEN PARTS 1 AND 5 OF THE 2009 ACT

5.10 Much of what was said on the relationship between Parts 1 and 4 of the Act at **4.07** to **4.09** of Chapter 4 applies to the relationship between Parts 1 and 5. Like the older-children offences in Part 4, any sexual activity where there is a clear lack of consent by the young or mentally disordered person, will be caught by, and charged under, Part 1 rather than Part 5. But when a person is charged with a Part 5 offence, any issue of consent does not arise. As it was put by the Lord Justice Clerk (Dorrian) in *CW v HM Advocate*,[7] a case where the sheriff had misdirected the jury that lack of consent was implied in section 42:

> 'The question of consent or lack of it is immaterial. It is not the case that lack of consent is implicit. Rather Parliament has decided that where a relationship of trust exists such conduct should constitute an offence regardless of whether the complainer consents or not.'

5.11 There is a further provision which, in the context of a mentally disordered person is relevant to the relationship between Part 1 and Part 5: section 17, a Part 1

[7] 2016 JC 148 at para 26.

provision, which defines when a mentally disordered person will be incapable of consenting to sexual conduct.

5.12 The origins and meaning of section 17 are set out in Chapter 2 at **2.94** to **2.104** One further comment on section 17 is necessary here to explain the relationship between Part 1 and Part 5. Section 17 applies only to sections 1–9 (that is, the Part 1 offences). That means sexual activity with a mentally disordered person falls to be considered slightly differently from the other offences based on the protective principle in Parts 4 and 5 of the Act. If there is sexual activity with a mentally disordered person, the evaluation of whether there is a lack of consent (express or inferred) has to be considered in the light of both the general provisions in Part 1 on consent *and* in light of section 17. If, applying both of those provisions, there is evidence of a lack of consent, then the appropriate charge is a Part 1 charge. Otherwise, provided there is a position of trust between the accused and the mentally disordered person as defined in section 46(2), then section 46 is the appropriate charge.

SECTION 42: SEXUAL ABUSE OF TRUST OF A CHILD

Elements of the offence

5.13 Section 42 provides that if a person (A) who has attained the age of 18 years: (i) intentionally engages in a sexual activity with or directed towards another person (B) who is under 18; and (ii) is in a position of trust in relation to B, then A commits the offence of sexual abuse of trust. The reason for not adding 'of a child' to the name of the offence is not apparent, but the import is clear. The offence cannot be committed recklessly. Confining the offence to intentional sexual activity is consistent with the philosophy behind the offence: preventing a person in a position of trust from sexually abusing that trust.

5.14 Section 43 defines five positions of trust:

(1) B is detained in an institution and A looks after persons under 18 in that institution.
This contemplates situations where, for instance, A is a prison officer in a young offenders' institution where B is detained.

(2) B is a resident in a home or other place in which accommodation is provided by a local authority under section 26(1) of the Children (Scotland) Act 1995 and A looks after persons under 18 in that place.
This covers all of the situations where a child is removed from his or her birth home and placed in foster, kinship or other care settings.

(3) B is accommodated and cared for in: a hospital; accommodation provided by an independent health care service or care home service; residential establishment; or accommodation provided by a school care accommodation

service or a secure accommodation service, and A looks after persons under 18 in that place.

In addition to hospitals, this covers the remainder of the places, of varying types and levels of security, where B might be cared for outside his or her birth home.

(4) B is receiving education at a school and A looks after persons under 18 in that school, or B is receiving education in a further or higher education institution and A looks after B in that institution.

This covers schools, colleges and universities.[8]

(5) B is a member of the same household as A and A either: (i) has or had parental responsibilities and rights for B (or fulfils them under an arrangement with someone who does) or (ii) treats B as a child of A's family.

This is the family setting provision which replaced section 3 of the Criminal Law (Consolidation) (Scotland) Act 1995 in line with the SLC's proposals.

5.15 Subsection (7) provides that A looks after a person if A regularly cares for, teaches, trains, supervises, or is in sole charge of the person. In situations (1) to (4), the reference to A 'looking after persons under 18' in the place in question is deliberate. Except for further or higher education institutions, it is not necessary that A is looking after B specifically in that place or institution; it suffices that A is looking after persons under 18 generally in that place or institution. A cannot thus pray in aid the fact that he or she works in the institution and, other than sexual activity with B, has not had contact with B. In this, the Act consciously departed from the SLC's proposal that, for a position of trust to arise, A should actually be looking after B in the place or institution.[9] The SLC's concern had been that, without such a qualification, the provision would be too wide in its scope. It gave the example of A being a lecturer in one subject on one campus, and B being a student in a totally different subject on a different campus.[10] The Bill as introduced followed the SLC's proposal. But at stage 2 the Bill was amended. This was done to preserve the position which existed under the Sexual Offences (Amendment) Act 2000, where it was not necessary that A looked after B specifically. To accommodate the SLC's concern, the stage 2 amendments also made an exception for higher or further education institutions, where A must actually be looking after B.[11]

5.16 Many of the terms used in section 43 to define these positions of trust are legislative terms of art. Section 44 is the interpretation provision which accompanies section 43. Section 44 does not define these terms itself but rather refers to other Acts of Parliament where these terms are set out. Care has to be taken. For instance, section 44 refers to the definition of school in the Education (Scotland) Act 1980.

8 This is because 'further or higher education institution' is now defined in s 44 as either a body listed in Sch 2 to the Further and Higher Education (Scotland) Act 2005 (which lists Scotland's colleges and universities), or as a college 'assigned to a regional strategic body' by a ministerial order made under s 7C(1) of that Act.

9 Para 4.131 of the SLC's report.

10 Para 4.131, footnote 140 to the SLC's report.

11 Official report of the Justice Committee, 31 March 2009.

There, in section 135, the term 'school' is broadly defined: there is no list of schools in the Act. But that is not true for all the places or institutions referred to in sections 43 and 44. Certain of these places or institutions are not so much defined as specified in the other legislative provisions. For instance, as stated above, an institution is not a 'further or higher institution' for the purposes of section 43 unless it is one of the colleges specifically named in the relevant legislation (or named in a ministerial order made under the legislation). Unlike the term 'school', there is no scope for interpretation: either the institution is on the list or it is not.

5.17 Section 42 is a focussed and narrowly drafted offence. It is limited to engaging in sexual activity. This is not the case for the Sexual Offences Act 2003, which, for the rest of the UK, criminalises not just engaging in sexual activity with or towards a child while in a position of trust but also, while in that position of trust, causing a child to engage in sexual activity, engaging in sexual activity in the presence of that child and causing that child to watch a sexual act (sections 17–19). There are also more positions of trust in the 2003 Act than in the 2009 Act. These cover virtually anyone who, in a public position, might have regular, unsupervised contact with a child, such as guardians ad litem or social workers: section 22 of the 2003 Act. Moreover, since the insertion of section 22A into the 2003 Act in 2022, the positions of trust now include sport coaches and anyone providing religious instruction to the child. The five positions of trust in section 42 of the 2009 Act are much more limited.[12]

Defences

5.18 By section 45, there are four defences to a charge under section 42. The first defence is if A reasonably believed B was over 18. This is self-explanatory and gives A the same defence he or she would have to an older-children offence under Part 4. The second defence is if A reasonably believed that B was not a person in relation to whom A was in a position of trust. Reasonable belief as to the position of trust is not as straightforward as reasonable belief as to age, not least because the 2009 Act departed from the previous formulation of this defence in the 2000 Act.[13] In the 2000 Act, it was a defence if A did not know, and could not reasonably have been expected to know, that B was a person in relation to whom he (A) was in

12 A curiosity of the Sexual Offences Act 2003 is that it creates jurisdiction for the courts in England and Wales over the Act's abuse-of-trust offences when they have been committed in Scotland: s 20 of the Act provides that 'anything which, if done in England and Wales, would constitute an offence under any of sections 16 to 19 [the abuse-of-trust offences], also constitutes that offence if done in Scotland'. This seeks to prevent persons in a position of trust in England and Wales evading prosecution by travelling, with the child, to Scotland. The curiosity is that the provision comes with none of the standard provisions that accompany (and limit) extra-territorial jurisdiction: a residence or nationality requirement, a dual-criminality requirement, or a need to seek the concurrence of the Law Officers in the other jurisdiction before prosecution.

13 Without, it appears, any intention to do that. The SLC agreed that the 2000 Act defences should continue to apply to the reformulated offence, but phrased its formal recommendation, recommendation 51 and its draft Bill, in terms of reasonable belief. The phrase was used in the Bill as introduced and has stayed in that form ever since.

a position of trust.[14] We suggest that, under section 42, the focus must be on what A reasonably believed about B, rather than what A reasonably believed about his position. If A reasonably believed that B was not someone within A's position of trust (for instance, A reasonably believed that B was not a pupil at his school) the defence would be available. The same must surely apply if A did not form any belief on the issue at all (that is, A simply did not know that B was within A's position of trust; for instance, A simply did not know that B was a pupil at his school), and A's lack of knowledge is a reasonable one.[15] However, it would not be available if A believed that his job or role was not one which created a position of trust; otherwise, A's ignorance of the law would be a defence. The third defence is that B was A's spouse or civil partner. The fourth is that, immediately before the position of trust came into being, a sexual relationship between A and B existed. The third and fourth defences cater for the situation (admittedly rare) where A and B legally marry or are in a relationship and, by happenstance, find themselves at the same institution. These defences do not apply to any position of trust which arises in the family setting (the fifth position of trust above: section 43(6) and 45(3)).[16]

SECTION 46: SEXUAL ABUSE OF TRUST OF A MENTALLY DISORDERED PERSON

Elements of the offence

5.19 Section 46(1) provides that if A:

> '(a) intentionally engages in a sexual activity with or directed towards a mentally disordered person ('B'), and
> (b) is a person mentioned in subsection (2),
>
> then A commits an offence, to be known as sexual abuse of trust of a mentally disordered person.'

5.20 The persons in subsection (2) are: (a) a person providing care services to B; or (b) a person who is employed in, is contracted to provide services in or to, or is a manager of, a hospital, independent health care service, or state hospital in

14 The formulation still used in the Sexual Offences Act 2003: s 16(1)(d), which makes it an element of the offence that A knows or could reasonably be expected to know of the circumstances by virtue of which he is in a position of trust in relation to B.

15 This is Professors Chalmers and Leverick's view in *Gordon, Criminal Law* (4th edn, Edinburgh University Press 2010) Vol 2 at para 39.53, though the authors also note, correctly, that this departs from the literal wording of the statute.

16 SLC said that the defence should not apply because it is highly unlikely that there could be a relationship of trust in this sense between married people and it viewed any such defence as unnecessary. In its annotation to this clause in its draft Bill (p 167), the SLC also observed that there was considerable doubt whether a position of trust could ever arise between spouses or those in any other lawful sexual relationship. The Scottish Government, at para 150 of its Policy Memorandum, considered it highly unlikely that a relationship of trust could ever arise between people who are married, in a civil partnership or had been in a sexual relationship with each other before the position of trust arose.

which B is being given medical treatment. All of the relevant terms are defined with reference to the definitions of 'care service', 'hospital' and 'state hospital' given elsewhere in primary legislation. Section 17(3) of the 2009 Act provides that 'mental disorder' has the same meaning as in section 328 of the Mental Health (Care and Treatment) (Scotland) Act 2003 and that related expressions – that is, 'mentally disordered person' – are to be construed accordingly.[17] By section 328(1), a mental disorder means any: (a) mental illness; (b) personality disorder; or (c) learning disability, however caused or manifested.[18] As with section 42, section 46 is confined to actually engaging in sexual activity with or toward B and requires that sexual activity to be intentional.[19]

Defences

5.21 By section 47, three defences exist. The first defence, in section 47(1), is that A reasonably believed that B did not have a mental disorder. Again, as with section 42/45 above, any lack of clarity in this defence is not helped by the 2009 Act's departure from the wording used in section 313 of the Mental Health (Care and Treatment) (Scotland) Act 2003.[20] This gave a defence when the person charged 'did not know, and could not reasonably have been expected to know' that the other person was mentally disordered (section 313(3)(a)(i)). As with section 42/45, we suggest it must also be a defence that A simply does not know of B's mental disorder and A's lack of knowledge is a reasonable one, rather than being confined to a situation where A has actively considered whether B has a mental disorder and concluded, on reasonable grounds, that B does not.[21] The second defence, also in section 47(1), is that A reasonably believed that he, A, was not a person in section 46(2), that is, a person who provides care services to B, or a person employed or otherwise working in a place where B is being given medical treatment.

5.22 The third defence is where there is a pre-existing intimate relationship between A and B. This third defence recognises that A may take on a carer role for

17 This is common: the provisions in the Criminal Procedure (Scotland) Act 1995 on mental disorder also refer to s 328.

18 It does not include: sexual orientation, sexual deviancy, transsexualism, transvestism, dependency on or use of alcohol or drugs, behaviour that causes or is likely to cause harassment, alarm or distress to another person, or acting as no prudent person would act: s 328(2).

19 Again, the equivalent provisions in the Sexual Offences Act 2003 are broader and include various non-contact sexual offences. The 2003 Act takes a slightly different approach to the concept of mental disorder and groups the offences into: offences against a person with a mental disorder impeding choice (ss 30–33), offences that are committed by inducement, threat or deception of a person with a mental disorder (ss 34–37), and offences committed by care workers caring for those with a mental disorder (ss 38–41).

20 Again, the fault appears to lie with the way the SLC expressed the defence in its draft Bill (s 35 of that draft Bill); Recommendation 41 in the body of the report was quite clear that the defence should be extended to a lack of knowledge on reasonable grounds.

21 The view of Professors Chalmers and Leverick in the fourth edition of *Gordon, Criminal Law,* Vol 2 at para 39.56, though they correctly note that this too is a departure from the literal wording of the statute.

his or her mentally disordered partner, B, and that continuing sexual activity in that relationship between A and B should not necessarily be seen as a breach of trust.[22] It has three forms. The first is if B is A's spouse or civil partner (section 47(2)(a)). The second is when A is providing care services to B and, immediately before he did, a sexual relationship existed between A and B (section 47(2)(b)(i)). The third is when A is a person in section 46(2)(b) and immediately before admission (or, for admission more than once, before B's last admission) there was a sexual relationship between A and B (section 47(2)(b)(ii)).

SPECIAL CAPACITY

5.23 The question arises whether the positions of trust defined in sections 42 and 46 are special capacities for the purpose of section 255 of the Criminal Procedure (Scotland) Act 1995. If they are, this would mean that the Crown would not have to prove that A occupied that position of trust, unless that fact were the subject of a preliminary challenge. For section 42, all the Crown would have to prove was that A engaged in sexual activity while B was under 18 and, where applicable, B was in a relevant place or institution. For section 46, all the Crown would have to prove is that B suffered from a mental disorder within the meaning of section 328 of the 2003 Act and, where applicable, was in a hospital, independent care service, or state hospital and was being given medical treatment there.

5.24 Sheriff Brown, in his commentary on these provisions, tends to the view that they are special capacity offences.[23] In the absence of any Appeal Court authorities on the matter, we are unable to express a concluded view. It is true that some of the positions of trust are sufficiently well-defined as to be special capacities (for instance, having parental responsibilities and rights). But others seem too open-textured for that to be the case. For instance, for the reasons given at **5.16** above, in certain cases, whether a place is a school for the purposes of sections 42–44 would be a question of whether, on the facts, it fell within the broad definition of school in section 135 of the Education (Scotland) Act 1980. So too whether A provided 'care services' to B for the purposes of section 46(2)(a). Moreover, the establishment of the position of trust in most of these cases requires more than A being in a particular place or position: in several of the positions of trust in section 42, A must be looking after persons under 18 in the place or institution where he or she works. In the family setting, he or she must be in the same household as B. And in section 46(2)(a), he or she requires to be *providing* care services to B. All of these are additional questions of fact on which it would appear the Crown would have to lead evidence to establish the position of trust. That would indicate that these are offences which do not fit easily with the concept of special capacity.

22 See the SLC report at para 4.123 endorsed in the Policy Memorandum at para 153.

23 *Green's Annotated Acts: The Sexual Offences (Scotland) Act 2009* (2nd edn) at pp 75 and 79.

TABLE OF OFFENCES

5.25

Table 5.1

The abuse-of-trust offences		
Offence	**Dates in force**	**Maximum sentence**
Section 42: sexual abuse of trust	1 December 2010 to present	Summary: 12 months' imprisonment or a fine not exceeding the statutory maximum (or both) Indictment: five years' imprisonment or a fine (or both)
Section 46: sexual abuse of trust of a mentally disordered person	1 December 2010 to present	Summary: 12 months' imprisonment or a fine not exceeding the statutory maximum (or both) Indictment: five years' imprisonment or a fine (or both)

5.26 There are few authorities to guide sentencing on the abuse of trust offences, but one is *Malcolmson v HM Advocate*.[24] There, the Appeal Court, having reviewed the equivalent English authorities and Sentencing Guidelines, imposed a *cumulo* sentence of 12 months' imprisonment for one offence contrary to section 3(1)(b) of the Sexual Offences (Amendment) Act 2000 and one offence contrary to section 42 of the 2009 Act. It emphasised that the five-year maximum sentence was an indication of the seriousness with which Parliament viewed this conduct and the need for young persons to be protected from sexual abuse and exploitation by persons entrusted with their care, welfare and education (at 1252A-B).

24 2021 SLT 1247.

Chapter 6

Further offences to protect children: the Protection of Children and Prevention of Sexual Offences (Scotland) Act 2005

INTRODUCTION

6.01 This chapter considers the offences created by the Protection of Children and Prevention of Sexual Offences (Scotland) Act 2005 ('the 2005 Act'). It considers first, the offence of meeting a child following certain preliminary contact (section 1 of the Act) and then the offences on child sexual services and child pornography (sections 9–12 of the Act).

SECTION 1: MEETING A CHILD FOLLOWING CERTAIN PRELIMINARY CONTACT

The elements of the offence

6.02 Section 1 of the 2005 Act criminalises the grooming of children. It was enacted because the Scottish Government considered that Scots law would be able to deal with most forms of grooming,[1] but was concerned that someone could carefully tailor their behaviour to ensure that they did not commit an offence during that grooming. To address that concern, section 1(1) to (3) provides that:

> '(1) A person ('A') commits an offence if–
> (a) having met or communicated with another person ('B') on at least one earlier occasion, A–
> (i) intentionally meets B;
> (ii) travels, in any part of the world, with the intention of meeting B in any part of the world; or

1 The examples given in the Scottish Government's Policy Memorandum accompanying the Bill were: the offence of fraud; offences under the Communications Act 2003; offences under the Civic Government (Scotland) Act 1982; the then common law offence of lewd, indecent or libidinous practice or behaviour; and breach of the peace (para 4 of the memorandum).

(iii) makes arrangements, in any part of the world, with the intention of meeting B in any part of the world, for B to travel in any part of the world;

(b) at the time, A intends to engage in unlawful sexual activity involving B or in the presence of B–

(i) during or after the meeting; and

(ii) in any part of the world;

(c) B is –

(i) aged under 16; or

(ii) a constable;

(d) A does not reasonably believe that B is 16 or over; and

(e) at least one of the following is the case–

(i) the meeting or communication on an earlier occasion referred to in paragraph (a) (or, if there is more than one, one of them) has a relevant Scottish connection;

(ii) the meeting referred to in sub-paragraph (i) of that paragraph or, as the case may be, the travelling referred to in sub-paragraph (ii) of that paragraph or the making of arrangements referred to in sub-paragraph (iii) of that paragraph, has a relevant Scottish connection;

(iii) A is a British citizen or resident in the United Kingdom.'

(2) In subsection (1) above–

(a) the reference to A's having met or communicated with B is a reference to A's having met B in any part of the world or having communicated with B by any means from or in any part of the world (and irrespective of where B is in the world); and

(b) a meeting or travelling or making of arrangements has a relevant Scottish connection if it, or any part of it, takes place in Scotland; and a communication has such a connection if it is made from or to or takes place in Scotland.

(3) For the purposes of subsection (1)(b) above, it is not necessary to allege or prove that A intended to engage in a specific activity.'

6.03 Section 1 is deliberately wide. The original version that was introduced in the Scottish Parliament limited the offence to those over 18. That was removed after the Parliament's Justice Committee heard evidence from the police and others that it was possible for those under 18 to groom others under 18, particularly more vulnerable children. For the same reason, there is no requirement that A must be older than the person he or she grooms.[2]

6.04 There is also no express proximity-of-age defence to section 1. It is suggested that this defence would, however, apply through reference in section 1(1)(b) to 'unlawful sexual activity'. If any sexual activity intended by A and B after they meet (or travel to meet) remains within the bounds of sexual activity permitted by

2 Justice Committee stage 1 report at paras 37–50.

Part 4 of the 2009 Act – that is, either the sexual activity permitted by section 37 or the sexual activity permitted by the proximity-of-age defence in section 39(4) – then their intended sexual activity would not be unlawful sexual activity for the purposes of section 1(1)(b) of the 2005 Act. That reading of the two Acts would remove several anomalies that might otherwise arise. For instance, without that reading of the two Acts, A and B, aged 16 and 15, could commit an offence under section 1 of the 2005 Act by agreeing, by text message, to meet to engage in sexual activity, even if, at their meeting, no sexual activity took place. By contrast, if A and B simply engaged in that sexual activity without any prior communication (for instance, by meeting at a house party and engaging in limited sexual activity in an upstairs bedroom) they would not commit an offence under the 2009 Act.

6.05 Each of the conditions in section 1(1)(a) to (e) must be met for an offence to be committed. In respect of each, we make the following comments:

(a) The grooming need only take place on one occasion before the meeting between A and B, before A travels to meet B, or before A makes arrangements for B to travel. The Bill as introduced initially referred to 'at least two earlier occasions'. This was reduced to one occasion on the recommendation of the Justice Committee, which was concerned that a particularly skilled paedophile could, in one communication, arrange a meeting with a vulnerable child.[3] Sub-paragraph (iii) of section 1(1)(a) was also added to the Bill to close the loophole that, to avoid prosecution, A would not meet or travel himself but would arrange for B to travel.[4] The communication does not need to be sexually explicit.

(b) As introduced, the Bill provided that, at the time of the meeting, travelling, or making of arrangements, A had to intend to do something that would, if done, constitute the commission of a 'relevant offence'. The Bill then went on to give a list of relevant sexual offences. This was changed to simply an intention on A's part to engage in 'unlawful sexual activity'. This was done at the request of COPFS. It was concerned that the court might require the Crown to prove precisely which of the relevant offences the accused intended to commit and that this would allow an acquittal if the Crown was not able to specify the exact offence that the accused had in mind.[5] The change to 'unlawful sexual activity' means that is not the case. This is put beyond doubt by section 1(3) and its provision that, for the purposes of section 1(1)(b), it is not necessary to allege or prove that A intended to engage in a specific activity. A does not need to intend for the unlawful sexual activity to take place at the meeting itself. It suffices that, at the time of doing any of the things in section 1(a)(i)–(iii), A intends to engage in unlawful sexual activity

3 Justice Committee stage 1 report at para 69, a recommendation with which then the Scottish Executive agreed: Justice Committee meeting 20 April 2005 at 1689–1690.

4 Ibid at 1690–1691.

5 Stage 3 Chamber debate, Deputy Minister for Justice (Hugh Henry) at 17548.

with or in the presence of B, irrespective of when A intends that unlawful sexual activity to happen. That is the reason for the phrase 'during or after the meeting' in section 1(1)(b)(i).

(c) The reference to 'a constable' was added during the Bill's passage through Parliament, in recognition of the possibility that A might think he is communicating with a child but in fact be communicating with an undercover police officer who is posing as a child.[6]

(d) A must have no reasonable belief that B is 16 or over.[7] The provision is a logical one: A can hardly be guilty of grooming a child if A does not believe it is a child he or she is talking to. But it is rarely seen in practice since, in most cases charged, the child (or undercover police officer) will say during the communications that he or she is under 16, often giving an exact age.

(e) This is, in effect, a jurisdiction provision. Section 1(1)(e)(i) and (ii), when read with section 1(2)(b), operate to mean the offence is committed (and the Scottish courts have jurisdiction) when: the initial meeting between A and B takes place in Scotland; the subsequent meeting, travelling, or making of arrangements take place in Scotland; or the initial communication between A and B is made from, to, or takes place in Scotland. On one view, section 1(1)(e)(i) and (ii) are unnecessary because if any of these things happened, then the ordinary, common-law rules on jurisdiction would give the Scottish courts jurisdiction,[8] but these express provisions ensure that there is no dubiety about that jurisdiction. Section 1(1)(e)(iii) is, in effect, an extra-territorial jurisdiction provision. Its effect is that, if A is a British citizen or UK resident,[9] then no part of the offence has to take place in Scotland for the Scottish courts to have jurisdiction and there is no need to consider whether anything done by A has a relevant Scottish connection. That is clear from the reference at the start of section 1(1)(e) to 'at least one of the following is the case' (ie, (i) or (ii) or (iii)).

6 This issue is discussed in Chapter 4 at **4.45** in respect of s 24 (communicating indecently with a young child).

7 The fact that absence of reasonable belief is an element of the offence would, on its face, seem to indicate that the Crown must prove this absence of reasonable belief, irrespective of whether A raises evidence of it at trial. The same is true for the other offences in the Act, where absence of reasonable belief as to age is also an element of the offences. But that view would not sit with *Graham v HM Advocate* 2017 SCCR 497 where, in the admittedly different context of rape, the Appeal Court found that, although an absence of reasonable belief was an essential element of the crime of rape, it did not require 'formal proof', in the sense of not requiring to be established by corroborated evidence, and that whether a person had, or did not have, a reasonable belief was an inference to be drawn from proven facts: see Chapter 2 at **2.108** and **2.109**. See also *Maqsood v HM Advocate* 2019 JC 45 at para 16 where this part of *Graham* was explained by the Lord Justice General (Carloway).

8 On these rules, see Chapter 1 at **1.13–1.24**.

9 On British citizenship and UK residency, see Chapter 1 at **1.44**.

SECTIONS 9–12: THE CHILD SEXUAL SERVICES AND CHILD PORNOGRAPHY OFFENCES

6.06 Sections 9–12 of the 2005 Act criminalise child pornography and the sexual exploitation of children. Their purpose was to transpose into Scots law Council Framework Decision 2004/68/JHA,[10] which obliged EU Member States to criminalise those offences. Under Article 1 of the Framework Decision, sexual exploitation was defined as: coercing a child into prostitution or pornographic performances; recruiting a child into prostitution or pornographic performances; and engaging in sexual activities with a child though coercion, money or other forms of payment, or abuse of a position of trust over the child.

6.07 There were already sexual abuse of positions of trust offences in Scots law and thus no transposition of this part of the Framework Decision was required.[11] For the other parts of the Framework Decision (the obligation to criminalise engaging in sexual activities with a child, child prostitution and child pornography), where transposition was necessary, the method of transposition chosen by the Scottish Government was to enact in Scots law the offences that already existed for the rest of the UK in sections 47–50 of the Sexual Offences Act 2003. The reason for this appears to have been that, when the Framework Decision was adopted, the UK Government's position was that there was no need to transpose it into English law because sections 47–50 already criminalised child pornography and sexual exploitation of children.[12] If that was correct, then the obvious method of transposition was to enact similar offences in Scots law. That produced sections 9–12 which replicate sections 47–50 in Scots law. Table 6.1 sets out the English offences in sections 47–50 and their equivalents in sections 9–12.

Table 6.1

Offence in England and Wales in the Sexual Offences Act 2003	Equivalent Scottish provision in the Protection of Children and Prevention of Sexual Offences (Scotland) Act 2005
Section 47: paying for sexual services of a child	Section 9: paying for sexual services of a child
Section 48: causing or inciting child prostitution or pornography (original offence)/causing or inciting sexual exploitation of a child (current offence)	Section 10: causing or inciting the provision by a child of sexual services or child pornography

10 On combating the sexual exploitation of children and child pornography. The Framework Decision has since been replaced by Directive 2011/93/EU.

11 See Chapter 5 at **5.13–5.18**.

12 That remained the position after the Framework Decision was replaced with the Directive. The UK Government continued to believe that the 2003 Act adequately complied with the Directive: see Rook and Ward paras 10.06–10.08.

Offence in England and Wales in the Sexual Offences Act 2003	Equivalent Scottish provision in the Protection of Children and Prevention of Sexual Offences (Scotland) Act 2005
Section 49: controlling a child prostitute or a child involved in pornography (original offence)/ controlling a child in relation to sexual exploitation	Section 11: controlling a child providing sexual services or involved in pornography
Section 50: arranging or facilitating child prostitution or pornography (original offence)/arranging or facilitating sexual exploitation of a child	Section 12: arranging or facilitating the provision by a child of sexual services or child pornography
Section 51 is the interpretation provision for this part of the 2003 Act.	Sections 13 and 19 are the interpretation provisions for this part of the 2005 Act
Section 78 is a general provision on the meaning of 'sexual'.	

6.08 There are differences between sections 47–50 and sections 9–12. The principal difference is that sections 47–50 of the 2003 Act were originally limited to child prostitution and child pornography; they have been amended since the entry into force of the Scottish 2005 Act so that they now refer to 'sexual exploitation of a child' rather than 'prostitution' or 'pornography'. We highlight the other, minor differences for each offence below but, despite these differences, the wording used in sections 9–12 remains similar (and in places identical) to the wording in sections 47–50. This means that judicial interpretation of sections 47–50 of the 2003 Act in England and Wales is likely to be particularly persuasive should any questions of interpretation of sections 9–12 arise in Scotland.[13]

6.09 We make five further introductory points about sections 9–12. The first is that, for the purpose of these offences, a child is someone under 18 (rather than someone under 16) because that is the definition of a child in Article 1 of the Framework Decision. For each of the offences, A (the accused) commits the offence: (i) if B (the complainer) is under 18 and A does not reasonably believe that B is aged 18 or over; or (ii) B is under 13. That is the same in the English offences in sections 47–50. Consent is not in issue for any of the offences: it does not matter if the child, even if aged 16 or 17, consents to the sexual activity.

6.10 The second point is that, although the offences in themselves are all triable either way, the seriousness of the offences means the Crown will almost always elect

[13] For the same reason, the full commentary on sections 45–51 in Chapter 10 of Rook and Ward may be of particular interest to Scottish readers.

to prosecute on indictment. The maximum sentences are set out in the table at the end of the chapter.

6.11 The third and related point is that, when the child is under 16, the offences are likely to overlap with other child-sex offences in Scots law. Section 14(1) of the Act addresses this by providing that sections 9–12 do not exempt any person from any proceedings for an offence which is punishable at common law or under any other enactment.[14] The provision has greater salience now than at its time of enactment given the child-sex offences now in Parts 4 and 5 of the 2009 Act. If the child is under 16, many of the situations that amount to an offence under sections 9–12 of the 2005 Act will also amount to an offence under Parts 4 and 5 of the 2009 Act. There are no guidelines for prosecutors on which charge to prefer when conduct would amount to both an offence under the 2005 Act and an offence under the 2009 Act. This is not the case in England and Wales where the CPS's guidance to prosecutors is that, where the child is under 13, prosecutors should charge an offence, if appropriate, under the young-child offences in sections 5–8 of the Sexual Offences Act 2003 (rape of a child under 13, etc) rather than sections 47–50.[15] It is thought, however, that should that situation arise in Scotland, the Crown would similarly prefer a charge under the young-child provisions in Part 4 of the 2009 Act to a charge under sections 9–12 of the 2005 Act.

6.12 The fourth point is the extra-territorial reach of sections 9–12. As enacted, the 2005 Act drew a distinction between section 9, which did not have extra-territorial reach, and sections 10–12, which did, in the sense that, as long as A did the act required for the offence, the sections 10–12 offences would be committed wherever in the world the child-complainer might be.[16] That distinction has been superseded by the Sexual Offences (Scotland) Act 2009. Sections 9–12 are all on the list of child-sex offences in Part 2 of Schedule 4 to the 2009 Act: that is, the list of child-sex offences over which the Scottish courts have extra-territorial jurisdiction. This significantly extends the reach of the offences in sections 9–12. The rules on precisely when the Scottish courts have extra-territorial jurisdiction over these offences and the other offences listed in Part 2 of Schedule 4 are set out in Chapter 1. In particular, Table 1.1 summarises the different rules that apply depending on whether the offences listed in Part 2 of Schedule 4 are committed elsewhere in the UK or in the rest of the world.

6.13 The fifth and final point is that the offences in sections 10–12 can be committed by corporate bodies and persons in positions of control within those bodies. Section 14A (a provision inserted into the 2005 Act by the Criminal Justice and Licensing (Scotland) Act 2010) provides that, where the offence is committed by a corporate body (that is, a company, partnership, or unincorporated association) and that is done with the consent or connivance of, or is attributable to any neglect on the

14 S 14(2) preserves the double-jeopardy rule by stating that nothing in ss 9–12 or 14 enables a person to be punished twice for the same offence.

15 Chapter 7 of the legal guidance to prosecutors on rape and sexual offences: Rape and Sexual Offences – Chapter 7: Key Legislation and Offences | The Crown Prosecution Service (cps.gov.uk).

16 By references to 'any part of the world' which appear in ss 10–12 but not s 9.

part of, a person within a defined role in the corporate body,[17] both the person and the corporate body commit the offence and can be prosecuted and punished accordingly. This would apply for instance, where a company that operates telephone sex lines employs people under 18 to take calls.

Section 9: paying for sexual services of a child

6.14 Section 9 makes it an offence to pay for the sexual services of a child. By section 9(1)(a) to (c), the offence has three elements:

(i) A intentionally obtains for himself or herself the sexual services of B;

(ii) Before obtaining those services, A either makes or promises payment for those services to B or a third person, or knows that a third person has made or promised such a payment; and

(iii) B is under 18 and A does not reasonably believe that B is aged 18 or over, or B is aged under 13.

6.15 The offence requires that A intends to obtain the sexual services and that A obtains them for himself or herself. The offence is completed when the sexual services are obtained. When they are not, the offence will be either an attempt or other inchoate offence, or, depending on the circumstances, one of the other offences in sections 10–12 of the Act. The same is true when A obtains the sexual services for another person.[18]

6.16 'Sexual services' are defined in section 9(3)(a) and (b) as:

'(a) the performance of sexual activity; or

(b) the performance of any other activity that a reasonable person would, in all the circumstances, consider to be for the purpose of providing sexual gratification'.[19]

6.17 For section (9)(3)(a), 'sexual activity' is further defined in section 19 of the 2005 Act as 'an activity that a reasonable person would, in all the circumstances, consider to be sexual'. It is designedly wider than prostitution and will include lap dancing, stripping, and telephone sex lines.[20] The purpose of section 9(3)(b) is to

17 For bodies corporate (that is, companies): a director, manager, secretary or similar officer. For a partnership: a partner. For an unincorporated association: a person concerned in the management or control of the association. See s 14A(1)(a)-(c).

18 The view taken by Rook and Ward for s 47 (paras 10.25 and 10.26).

19 This is slightly different from the equivalent offence in England in Wales, s 47 of the 2003 Act (paying for the sexual services of a child), which does not contain a definition of sexual services and which must be considered by reference to the general definition of 'sexual' in s 78 of that Act. S 78 provides that an activity is sexual if a reasonable person would consider that – (a) whatever its circumstances or any person's purpose in relation to it, it is because of its nature sexual; or (b) because of its nature it may be sexual and because of its circumstances or the purpose of any person in relation to it (or both) it is sexual. Given their similar terms, s 9(3) of the 2005 Act and s 78 of the 2003 Act are unlikely to return different answers to whether the services obtained are sexual. S 78 as applied to s 47 is discussed in Rook and Ward at paras 10.27–10.29.

20 The examples given at para 30 of the Explanatory Notes.

capture the situation where it is not immediately obvious that the activity is sexual but nevertheless it appears from the surrounding circumstances that A is deriving sexual gratification from what B is doing for or to A: for instance, the satisfaction of a sexual fetish.[21]

6.18 The references to 'a third person' contemplate the situation where B is exploited or controlled by a third person (for instance, a pimp) and A makes the payment or promise of payment to the third person rather than directly to B. 'Payment' is defined in section 9(2) as: 'any financial advantage, including the discharge of an obligation to pay or the provision of goods or services (including sexual services) gratuitously or at a discount'. It is identical to the definition in section 45 of the Sexual Offences Act 2003. The width of the definition is intended to capture all ways by which children may be exploited into providing sexual services.[22] The phrase 'including sexual services' within the definition of a payment catches the activities of paedophile rings whose members provide each other on a reciprocal basis with access to children whom they exploit sexually.[23]

Section 10: causing or inciting the provision by a child of sexual services or child pornography

6.19 This offence has two elements:

(i) A intentionally causes or incites B to become a provider of sexual services, or to be involved in pornography, in any part of the world; and

(ii) B is either aged under 18, and A does not reasonably believe that B is aged 18 or over, or B is under 13.

6.20 The offence is intended to cover situations where someone is, for example, recruiting children into the provision of sexual services or pornography,[24] though like all offences of causing or inciting a crime, the offence is arguably able to cover a wider range of situations than that.[25] Rook and Ward's commentary on the equivalent offence in England and Wales, section 48 of the 2003 Act, suggests that A commits the offence when A causes or incites B to be sexually exploited, but not when A causes or incites C to sexually exploit B. In those circumstances, the correct course would be to charge C with an appropriate substantive offence and to charge

21 A situation which, in England and Wales, would be considered by reference to the second limb of s 78, (b): 'because of its nature it may be sexual and because of its circumstances or the purpose of any person in relation to it (or both) it is sexual'.

22 The examples given in para 29 of the Explanatory Notes include the waiving of a debt, providing food or accommodation, and supply illegal drugs free or for less than street value.

23 See Rook and Ward at para 10.30.

24 Explanatory notes at para 33.

25 The possible form of direction on this offence in the Jury Manual suggests that juries should be directed that 'Causing simply means there must be some direct connection between the actions of the accused and what happened. No compulsion is needed. Inciting simply means actively encouraging.' Page 113.6/133.

A with aiding and abetting that offence.[26] If that reasoning is correct, it would hold for section 10 too, since the wording is materially the same. The second element of the section 10 offence, B's age, is the same as the age element in section 9.

6.21 Section 13 defines the terms used in section 10.[27] By section 13(1), a person is 'involved in pornography' if an indecent image of that person is recorded. Consistent with the use of the term 'indecent' elsewhere in Scots law, no further definition is provided, indecency being a question for the factfinder (judge or jury) to determine. The term 'become a provider of sexual services' is a new term in the 2005 Act: it does not appear in the equivalent section in the 2003 Act, section 48, where the original term was 'become a prostitute' and is now 'be sexually exploited'. Section 13(2) defines 'provider of sexual services' as a person (B) who, on at least one occasion and whether or not compelled to do so, offers or provides B's sexual services in return for payment or a promise of payment to B or a third person.[28] The reference to a third person in that definition is for the same reason as for section 9 above: to cover payment to a pimp or other person controlling or exploiting B. Section 13(3) gives the same definition of 'payment' as in section 9(2). It is not necessary that any payment or gain should find its way to A.[29] Finally, section 13(4) provides that 'sexual services' are: (a) the performance of sexual activity; or (b) the performance of any other activity that a reasonable person would, in all the circumstances, consider to be for the purpose of providing sexual gratification (that is, the same definition as used in section 9, the commentary for which see **6.17** above).[30]

6.22 The reference to '*become* a provider of sexual services' introduces an unfortunate uncertainty into the provision. On one reading, if B has provided sexual services in the past, A cannot commit the offence since B cannot be caused or incited to 'become' what he or she already is. This is a reading which the English authorities would appear to support.[31] On another reading, B becomes a provider of sexual services anew each time he or she provides sexual services. In the absence of any Appeal Court authority, we cannot express a concluded view, but the ambiguity

26 At para 10.53. The authors also suggest that A cannot cause or incite B to provide sexual services to A himself, though concede that the courts may be reluctant to construe the English provision that way: para 10.57.

27 The same definitions also apply to ss 11 and 12.

28 A definition almost identical to the original definition of 'prostitute' and to now the definition of 'sexually exploited' in s 51 of the 2003 Act.

29 This was an element of the offence in s 48 as introduced, but it was removed during its passage through Parliament: Rook and Ward at para 10.63.

30 And, by the same subsection, a person's sexual services are offered or provided to another person where such an activity (ie, a sexual activity) is offered to be performed or performed with or for the other person.

31 The English provision, before it was changed from 'become a prostitute' to 'be sexually exploited', turned on the meaning of 'become a prostitute'. Though that term as it appeared in s 48 was not considered by the Court of Appeal, the identical term in s 52 (the offence of causing or inciting prostitution for gain) was considered by the Court of Appeal in *R v Ubolcharoen* [2009] EWCA Crim 3263. The Court found that no s 52 offence would be committed where B had previously acted as a prostitute, even on a single occasion. For further discussion of the case and criticism of it, particularly when applied to s 48, see Rook and Ward at 10.58 and 10.130.

would be removed if the term were changed to 'causes or incites B to *provide* sexual services'. This would be consistent with the amended English provision which, as noted above, now refers to A intentionally causing or inciting B 'to be sexually exploited'.

6.23 Section 13(5) provides that this offence and the following offences in sections 11 and 12 are not committed by reason only of doing something within section 52(1) or 52A(1) of the Civic Government (Scotland) Act 1982. These sections relate to the taking, possession, and distribution of indecent images of a child. As a result, while taking an indecent photograph of a person under 18 would be an offence under these sections, it would not, without more, constitute the offence of causing a child to be involved in pornography.

Section 11: controlling a child providing sexual services or involved in pornography

6.24 This offence has two elements:

(i) A intentionally controls any of the activities of another person (B) relating to B's provision of sexual services or involvement in pornography in any part of the world; and

(ii) B is either aged under 18, and A does not reasonably believe that B is aged 18 or over, or B is under 13.

6.25 The offence is intended to cover situations where someone is, for example, acting as a pimp for a child involved in the provision of sexual services or controlling the movements of a child involved in pornography.[32] It is identical to section 49 of the 2003 Act, save for the reference to 'B's provision of sexual services or involvement in pornography', in place of which section 49 now simply refers to 'B's sexual exploitation'. The phrase 'controls any of the activities of another person (B)' is wide in two senses. First, the phrase covers any of the people who might be involved in the exploitation of B, for instance, the person who is not directly involved in offering B's sexual services, but who is responsible for ensuring B remains detained in a place where others then offer out B's sexual services. Equally, it would cover those higher in an organised-crime group, if there is sufficient knowledge as to demonstrate an intention to control B. Second, the phrase covers not just physical control of B, but also anything A might do to instruct or direct B's activities: what to wear, what to charge, etc.[33] It would thus also cover the employer-employee relationship, were A to employ B (a child) as stripper, lap dancer, or call handler for telephone sex lines. As with section 10, 'sexual services' and 'involved in pornography' carry the meanings

32 Explanatory notes at para 35.

33 That is the interpretation given by the Court of Appeal Criminal Division to the companion offence of controlling prostitution for gain, contrary to s 53 of the Sexual Offences Act 2003, where the same phrase appears: *R v Massey* [2007] EWCA Crim 2664. That interpretation accords with the view expressed by the Government when the Bill was debated in the House of Lords. See Rook and Ward at paras 10.77 and 10.147–10.152.

given in section 13: see **6.21** above. As with section 10, there is no requirement that A gain anything from his or her control of B.

Section 12: arranging or facilitating the provision by a child of sexual services or child pornography

6.26 The two elements of section 12 are:

(i) A intentionally arranges or facilitates the provision of sexual services in any part of the world by B, or B's involvement in pornography in any part of the world; and

(ii) B is either aged under 18, and A does not reasonably believe that B is aged 18 or over, or B is under 13.

6.27 The explanatory notes for this offence state that it is intended to cover situations where A is, for example, arranging clients for B or providing premises for the provision of sexual services or pornography to take place.[34] The explanatory notes for the equivalent English offence, section 50 of the 2003 Act, give further examples of delivering B to a place where he will be used to make pornography or making arrangements for B's prostitution (as the offence then was) to take place in a particular room.[35] All of these are consistent with the ordinary meanings of either 'arrange' or 'facilitate'[36] and it might be thought that little gloss on either term is required. It would be possible for A to be charged with attempting to commit the section 12 offence if, for instance, he or she attempts to arrange the provision of sexual services, but no arrangement comes to fruition.[37]

6.28 Section 12 would appear to cover many of the situations where A's activities would fall short of the control of B required for section 10.[38] The breadth of the terms 'arrange' and 'facilitate' suggest that there would, in some situations, be an overlap

34 Para 37.

35 Para 97. S 12 of the 2005 Act and s 50 of the 2003 Act are identical, save for the references in s 12 to B's 'provision of sexual services' or 'involvement in pornography' and simply B's 'sexual exploitation' in s 50.

36 The *Shorter Oxford English Dictionary* defines 'facilitate' as 'make easy or easier; promote; help forward (an action, result, etc.)' and 'arrange' in this context means either: (i) plan or settle beforehand the details of (something to be done); give instructions for, cause to take place; or (ii) come to an agreement or understanding (with a person, about something); settle or determine matters, take steps, make plans (about, for, to do).

37 The view of the Court of Appeal Criminal Division on the similar offence of arranging or facilitating the commission of a child sex offence (contrary to s 41 of the 2003 Act) in *R v R* [2008] EWCA Crim 619. R asked a prostitute to find a girl of 12 or 13 for sex; the prostitute refused and instead reported R to the police. The Court of Appeal reserved its view on whether the full offence had been committed since it found that, in any event, the case could proceed as an attempt to commit the offence. It found that the jury would be entitled to find that R's request was not simply preparatory. He need have done no more than make the request. Once that request had been accepted then something would have been arranged. The request was the final thing R needed to do before the full offence was committed: para 12.

38 The view of Rook and Ward on s 50 of the 2003 Act at para 10.94, though there do not appear to be any authorities on the point.

with causing or inciting B to become a provider of sexual services, contrary to section 11. It is therefore quite conceivable that, in any case where section 12 is libelled, the Crown would also libel alternative offences under section 10 or section 11.

TABLE OF OFFENCES

6.29

Table 6.2

The Protection of Children and Prevention of Sexual Offences (Scotland) Act 2005		
Offence	**Dates in force**	**Maximum sentence**
Section 1: meeting a child following certain preliminary contact	7 October 2005 to present	Summary: 12 months' imprisonment or a fine (or both) (NB: for this and all of the 2005 Act offences, initially, the maximum sentence on summary conviction was six months' imprisonment. This was increased from 10 December 2007 when section 45 of the Criminal Proceedings etc. (Reform) (Scotland) Act 2007 entered into force. Section 45 increased the maximum sentence in summary proceedings to 12 months' imprisonment.) Indictment: 10 years' imprisonment or a fine (or both)
Section 9: paying for sexual services of a child	7 October 2005 to present	Where the child is 16 or over: Summary: as above: initially six months' imprisonment; now 12 months' imprisonment or a fine (or both); Indictment: seven years' imprisonment or a fine (or both) Where the child is under 16: Summary: now 12 months' imprisonment or a fine (or both); Indictment: 14 years' imprisonment or a fine (or both)

The Protection of Children and Prevention of Sexual Offences (Scotland) Act 2005		
Offence	**Dates in force**	**Maximum sentence**
Section 10: causing or inciting the provision by a child of sexual services or child pornography	7 October 2005 to present	Summary: as above: initially six months' imprisonment; now 12 months' imprisonment or a fine (or both) Indictment: 14 years' imprisonment or a fine (or both)
Section 11: controlling a child providing sexual services or involved in pornography	7 October 2005 to present	Summary: as above: initially six months' imprisonment; now 12 months' imprisonment or a fine (or both) Indictment: 14 years' imprisonment or a fine (or both)
Section 12: arranging or facilitating the provision by a child of sexual services or child pornography	7 October 2005 to present	Summary: as above: initially six months' imprisonment; now 12 months' imprisonment or a fine (or both) Indictment: 14 years' imprisonment or a fine (or both)

6.30 The maximum sentences for the equivalent offences in sections 47–50 are the same, save that for section 47, where the maximum penalty is life imprisonment if the child is under 13 and there is penetrative sexual activity (a situation which, if it occurred in Scotland, would result in a charge under section 18 or 19 of the 2009 Act and thus carry the same maximum penalty). This would suggest that the detailed Sentencing Guidelines[39] for these offences would prove a useful cross check for Scottish sentencers.

6.31 Perhaps by oversight, sections 10–12 of the 2005 Act are not the criminal lifestyle offences for the purposes of the Proceeds of Crime Act 2002, whereas sections 48–50 are.

39 Available in the Crown Court sentencing guidelines section of the Sentencing Council's website www.sentencingcouncil.org.uk/crown-court/.

Chapter 7

Further offences to protect those in intimate relationships: stalking, intimate images and the Domestic Abuse (Scotland) Act 2018

INTRODUCTION

7.01 This chapter considers three offences:

- stalking (contrary to section 39 of the Criminal Justice and Licensing (Scotland) Act 2010);
- disclosing, or threatening to disclose, an intimate photograph or film (contrary to section 2 of the Abusive Behaviour and Sexual Harm (Scotland) Act 2016);[1] and
- abusive behaviour towards a partner or ex-partner (contrary to section 1 of the Domestic Abuse (Scotland) Act 2018).

7.02 The common feature of these offences is that they are directed at the protection of those in intimate relationships and they offer further protection to such persons than the general criminal law does. We include stalking among these offences because although it can be directed at persons not personally known to the offender, it is most commonly seen in the context of intimate relationships, often shortly after those relationships have ended.[2]

STALKING: SECTION 39 OF THE CRIMINAL JUSTICE AND LICENSING (SCOTLAND) ACT 2010

Background

7.03 Section 39 of the Criminal Justice and Licensing (Scotland) Act 2010 creates the offence of stalking. It was introduced to the Criminal Justice and

1 The aggravation of any offence when it causes physical or psychological harm to a partner or ex-partner, introduced by s 1 of the 2016 Act, is considered in Chapter 20.

2 The most recent figures are for 2022 to 2023. In that year, of the 921 stalking charges that were reported to COPFS, 485 (53%) were identified as domestic abuse.

Licensing (Scotland) Bill, an omnibus Bill, at stage 2 by opposition amendment.[3] The opposition amendment was initially opposed by the Scottish Government, which considered that the offence did not go as far as the new offence it proposed in the Bill, the offence of threatening or abusive behaviour in what was to become section 38(1) of the Act. The Scottish Government came to support the opposition amendment and proposed, at stage 3, a number of amendments to clarify and strengthen the offence, including that threatening or abusive behaviour, contrary to section 38(1), be an alternative offence when a person is charged with a stalking, contrary to section 39.

7.04 Scotland, like the rest of the United Kingdom, was relatively late in creating the specific offence of stalking: similar laws were introduced in Australia and Canada in the mid-1990s.[4]

7.05 There were two main reasons for creating the specific offence in the Criminal Justice and Licensing (Scotland) Act in 2010. The first was that previously, some of the conduct now called stalking was prosecuted as breach of the peace. That approach was foreclosed by the High Court of Justiciary's ruling in *Harris v HM Advocate*[5] that breach of the peace required a public element, in the sense of causing or threatening to have caused disturbance to the public peace. The second reason was that it was considered that prosecution for breach of the peace had hidden the specific practice of stalking and that it was necessary to recognise, through a specific criminal offence, the practice, its prevalence and its consequences for those affected.

7.06 The essence of the offence is a course of conduct involving specific acts that might not themselves be criminal but cause fear and distress either as a result of

3 Rhoda Grant MSP, after work with Action Scotland Against Stalking, which had campaigned for the introduction of a specific offence to cover stalking. See the official report of the Justice Committee of 13 April 2010 at https://archive2021.parliament.scot/parliamentarybusiness/Bills/16193.aspx.

4 See the Victorian Law Reform Commission Stalking consultation paper, July 2021, Chapter 5: Criminal Law Responses to Stalking at para 5.2, fn 144, and the offence of criminal harassment in s 264 of the Canadian Criminal Code, added in 1993.

5 2010 JC 245. The follow-up case, *Harris v HM Advocate (no 2)* 2011 JC 125 is illustrative of the differences between breach of the peace at common law and stalking in s 39, but also of the extent to which the offences may still overlap. In *Harris (no 2)* the same accused was charged on an indictment containing, *inter alia* charges of breach of the peace. These were: sending an ex-partner numerous letters and text messages (charge 4 on the indictment); repeatedly sending emails to the ex-partner's daughter at her workplace (charge 5); sending envelopes with distressing and embarrassing communications to various persons at the daughter's workplace (charge 8); fitting a tracking device to the ex-partner's car and using it to follow her (charge 9); and fitting a tracking device to a car used by the ex-partner and her daughter (charge 10). He took preliminary pleas to the relevancy of these charges. Charges 4, 5 were found to be irrelevant as they lacked the necessary public element. Charge 8 was not. Charge 10, involving only the fitting of the device, was irrelevant, but at the preliminary stage, the Appeal Court was not prepared to find that charge 9, which additionally involved following the ex-partner in public places, was irrelevant. Though not referring explicitly to s 39 (the 2010 Act had only just received Royal Assent and had not yet entered into force), the Appeal Court did observe that both charge 9 and charge 10 constituted unusual forms of stalking.

a combination of those acts or in the context of a relationship between accused and complainer.[6]

The elements of the offence

7.07 By section 39(1)-(4) of the 2010 Act, A stalks B if:

(a) A engages in a course of conduct,
(b) either: (i) A engages in the course of conduct with the intention of causing B to suffer fear or alarm; or (ii) A knows, or ought in all the circumstances to have known, that engaging in the course of conduct would be likely to cause B to suffer fear or alarm; and
(c) A's course of conduct causes B to suffer fear or alarm.

7.08 By section 39(6), 'course of conduct' involves conduct on at least two occasions and 'conduct' is:

(a) following B or any other person,
(b) contacting, or attempting to contact, B or any other person by any means,
(c) publishing any statement or other material: (i) relating or purporting to relate to B or to any other person, or (ii) purporting to originate from B or from any other person,
(d) monitoring the use by B or by any other person of the internet, email or any other form of electronic communication,
(e) entering any premises,
(f) loitering in any place (whether public or private),
(g) interfering with any property in the possession of B or of any other person,
(h) giving anything to B or to any other person or leaving anything where it may be found by, given to or brought to the attention of B or any other person,
(i) watching or spying on B or any other person,
(j) acting in any other way that a reasonable person would expect would cause B to suffer fear or alarm.

7.09 There are, then, three elements to the offence:

(i) A's course of conduct;
(ii) the *mens rea* of either intending B to suffer fear or alarm or being reckless as to B suffering fear or alarm; and
(iii) A's course of conduct actually causing B to suffer that fear or alarm.

7.10 For the first element, course of conduct is a familiar term in Scots law; its definition in this context of conduct on at least two occasions is no different from the term's meaning elsewhere in the criminal law. The list of activities constituting 'conduct' for the purpose of the offence is extensive. It was said by the Government

6 Intervention of Rhoda Grant MSP, introducing the amendment to create s 39 at the Justice Committee meeting on 13 April 2010. See the official report of the meeting at https://archive2021.parliament.scot/parliamentarybusiness/Bills/16193.aspx.

in the stage 3 debate to be exhaustive rather than illustrative,[7] but it is subject to the catch-all in (j) of 'acting in any other way that a reasonable person would expect would cause B to suffer fear or alarm'.[8] Of the specific instances on the list, (b) deliberately refers to 'attempting to contact' so that it can include voicemail messages or emails that may or may not be read, and the generality of the reference in (b) to 'any means' is to ensure that the provision does not become outdated by technological developments.[9]

7.11 The second element concerns intention or knowledge. It is a standard *mens rea* requirement, requiring the prosecution to prove, either expressly or by inference, that A intended to cause fear or alarm or was reckless as to his or her course of conduct having that effect. The third element requires proof that A's behaviour in fact causes the person being stalked, B, to suffer fear or alarm: B must be aware of the behaviour (or become aware of it), and as result, suffer that fear or alarm.[10] The references to fear or alarm in both the second and third elements were the result of Government amendments moved at stage 3 of the Bill's passage through Parliament. Originally, after stage 2 the Bill had referred to causing B '(i) to suffer physical or psychological harm, or (ii) apprehension or fear for B's own safety or for the safety of any other person' (and the *mens rea* requirement referred to causing such harm or arousing such apprehension or fear in B). At stage 3 that was changed to simply 'fear or alarm' after concerns expressed by Crown Office about the difficulty of proving psychological harm: fear or alarm, by contrast, was a test the courts were used to applying in breach of the peace cases.[11]

7.12 The second and third elements were described by the Appeal Court in *Miller v HM Advocate*[12] as critical requirements of the offence. The Court emphasised that, in any trial, the focus should not just be on showing that the course of conduct took place, but on also showing that the course of conduct satisfies the second and third elements of the offences. The convictions in that case were quashed because neither the procurator fiscal nor the sheriff provided the jury with a clear route to finding that behaviour by a father and daughter, ostensibly to persuade their partner/mother to return to the family home, was done in concert and with the necessary intention to cause her fear and alarm. This may appear obvious, because it is true for any offence that the prosecution must establish that all of its elements took place, but it is particularly necessary for it to be kept in mind in relation to this offence,

7 A Government amendment changed the original draft to make this clear, the original referring to 'conduct includes (but is not limited to)' and the section as enacted reading 'conduct means'. Official report of the stage 3 debate, 30 June 2010, Kenny MacAskill MSP.

8 It is noteworthy that s 2A of the Protection from Harassment Act 1997, which created the offence of stalking in England and Wales, adopted the Scottish list but declined to include (e) entering any premises and (h) giving anything to B, etc.

9 Official report of the stage 3 debate, 30 June 2010, Kenny MacAskill MSP.

10 It will be a misdirection, though not necessarily a material one resulting in a miscarriage of justice, to fail to direct the jury that they require to find it proved that actual fear and alarm was caused: *McBride v HM Advocate* [2016] HCJAC 66 at paras 10 and 11.

11 Official report of the stage 3 debate, 30 June 2010, Kenny MacAskill MSP.

12 2022 JC 33.

where, given the breadth of examples of conduct in section 39, otherwise lawful and innocent behaviour only becomes criminal by demonstrating that the second and third elements of the offence are present.

7.13 The issue has arisen twice in decided cases as to whether the Crown is entitled to rely on previous criminal behaviour by the accused to explain why the course of conduct he or she is charged with meets the second and third elements of the offence. The Appeal Court had no difficulty with that in *Behan v PF, Hamilton*.[13] In the reported case *PF Dunfermline v Ogilvie*[14] the sheriff sustained a defence preliminary plea, against a common law docket appending to a complaint because he considered it to be collateral, unnecessary to prove the charge and prejudicial. The latter appears to have been wrongly decided. The sheriff does not appear to have been taken to *Behan* and, in any event, to have erred in considering that, because it is the course of conduct that requires to cause fear or alarm, not any extraneous incident, that extraneous incident is not relevant and is collateral and inadmissible. Leading evidence of, and asking a court to consider, previous criminal behaviour might be collateral in the strict sense to the charge on an indictment, but that is always so for dockets, and it does not of itself make the evidence irrelevant and thus inadmissible: previous behaviour is undoubtedly relevant to why a complainer might have a subjective fear or alarm at unsolicited conduct from a previous partner in a way they would not from any other person. Nor is leading such evidence automatically prejudicial or unfair as long as care is taken in the drafting of the docket, and in the leading of evidence related to it so as, for instance, not to reveal any previous criminal convictions.

Defences

7.14 Section 39(5) gives A three defences to the offence, requiring A to show that his or her course of conduct:

(a) was authorised by virtue of any enactment or rule of law,
(b) was engaged in for the purpose of preventing or detecting crime, or
(c) was, in the particular circumstances, reasonable.

7.15 The first is self-explanatory, and the third is a form of the reasonable excuse defence seen daily in the courts, which is assessed objectively by the judge or jury. The second has not been the subject of any direct judicial consideration in Scotland, but the equivalent wording in the Protection from Harassment Act 1997 has proven problematic. The difficulty is that, under both section 39 of the 2010 and the 1997 Act, the wording suggests that A only has to believe (whether reasonably or not) that his course of conduct was necessary to prevent or detect crime. However, such a wholly subjective test is obviously problematic. In the

13 [2013] HCJAC 118.
14 2020 SLT (Sh Ct) 144.

civil case *Hayes v Willoughby*,[15] concerning an action for damages for harassment under the 1997 Act, the Supreme Court recognised this difficulty. It found that while 'purpose' was a subjective state of mind and could not be subject to a wholly objective test, the necessary control mechanism lay in the concept of rationality. This applied a minimum objective standard to the defendant's mental process by importing: a requirement of good faith; a requirement of some logical connection between the evidence and the reasons for the course of conduct; and an absence of arbitrariness, of capriciousness, or of reasoning so outrageous as to be perverse. It is not certain that the Scottish criminal courts would adopt the same approach. *Hayes* is significant for Lord Reed's dissent that Parliament did not provide for such a rationality test, that a statute should not be construed as extending criminal liability beyond the limits which Parliament enacted, and criminal liability would turn on a subtle distinction between irrationality and unreasonableness, which would create particular difficulties in giving clear directions to juries.

Sentencing

7.16 The maximum sentences for stalking are: (a) on conviction on indictment, to imprisonment for a term not exceeding five years, or to a fine, or to both; (b) on summary conviction, to imprisonment for a term not exceeding 12 months, or to a fine not exceeding the statutory maximum, or to both.

Alternative offences

7.17 By section 39(8) and (9), abusive or threatening behaviour, contrary to section 38 of the 2010 Act, is an alternative offence to stalking.

Extra-territorial jurisdiction

7.18 The Scottish courts have jurisdiction to try the offence of stalking when the course of conduct consists of or includes conduct outside the United Kingdom by a United Kingdom national or someone habitually resident in Scotland: section 39A of the 2010 Act, in force from 29 June 2021.[16] The practical effect of the change is likely to be seen in cases where the course of conduct takes place partly in Scotland and partly outside the United Kingdom, though it is not limited to such cases and is capable of being committed wholly outside the United Kingdom. Like all offences, when it takes place partly in Scotland and partly in the rest of the United Kingdom, the common law rules on jurisdiction over cross-border offences apply (see Chapter 1, **1.22**).

15 [2013] 1 WLR 935, [2013] UKSC 17.

16 As noted in Chapter 1, this removes the anomaly that a person might stalk and then commit a sexual offence against another outside the UK, but, before s 39A, the latter and not the former could be tried in the Scottish courts.

The prohibition on an accused conducting his own defence

7.19 An accused will generally be prohibited from personally conducting his or her own defence in a section 39 trial. Although stalking is not one of the offences to which the automatic prohibition in section 288C of the 1995 Act applies, the court can make an order prohibiting personal conduct of the defence if there is a substantial sexual element to the alleged stalking: section 288C(3) and (4). Equally, if the offence is alleged to have been committed against a partner or ex-partner, the complaint or indictment will likely carry the statutory aggravation in section 1 of the Abusive Behaviour and Sexual Harm (Scotland) Act 2016, in which case, by section 288DC, the prohibition will also apply. Finally, in stalking cases, complainers are deemed vulnerable witnesses (section 271(1)(c)(v)), giving the court the power to prohibit the personal conduct of the defence if satisfied that it is in the interests of the vulnerable witnesses to do so (section 288F).

INTIMATE IMAGES: SECTION 2 OF THE ABUSIVE BEHAVIOUR AND SEXUAL HARM (SCOTLAND) ACT 2016

The background to section 2

7.20 Section 2 of the 2016 Act is part of a worldwide trend towards the criminalisation of the sharing of intimate images without consent. The practice of sharing such images without consent is sometimes called 'revenge pornography' in reference to the practice of sharing sexual images in revenge for ending a relationship. The term is misleading. There may be nothing pornographic or even sexual about the images (and even if there were, the term 'pornography' would be to judge the victim rather than perpetrator). Also, the motivation may be something other than revenge; often, it is the exercise of control during or after a relationship, though, of course, the offence is not limited to those in relationships. The practice of sharing such images accelerated in around 2012 as smartphones became everyday items, and films and photographs could be more easily taken, retained indefinitely and quickly shared. The first laws specifically criminalising the practice were enacted in 2013: the first appears to have been the South Australian Summary Offences (Filming Offences) Amendment Act 2013, passed in March 2013. Since then, many, if not all, common-law and European countries have passed similar laws, either by enacting specific criminal provisions or tightening existing criminal privacy laws to make clear that they cover the practice.[17]

17 Up-to-date and authoritative comparative studies are hard to come by simply because of the pace at which countries are now legislating to criminalise the practice, but see the Law Commission's consultation on reforming the offence in England and Wales *Intimate Image Abuse*, 26 February 2021, which, in addition to commentary on the Scottish legislation, analyses intimate-images offences in Australia, Canada, Ireland and New Zealand.

7.21 The immediate impetus for criminalising the practice in Scotland through section 2 of the 2016 Act was the enactment of sections 33 to 35 of the Criminal Justice and Courts Act 2015, which created a similar offence for England and Wales.[18] The Scottish Government's Policy Memorandum on the 2016 Act sets out its reasons for creating the offence. It is instructive in explaining both the rationale for the offence and the way in which it has been framed. It records that, while existing offences such as blackmail might cover the practice, a new offence made it clear to victims and potential perpetrators that the practice was criminal.[19]

7.22 The Policy Memorandum also records that the Scottish Government considered and rejected a number of alternative approaches to the offence. It rejected replicating sections 33 to 35 of the Criminal Justice and Courts Act 2015, which limited the offence to disclosure with an intention to cause distress. The Scottish Government considered that this was not broad enough and that the offence should also be committed when the accused was reckless as to whether the complainer would be caused fear, alarm or distress.[20] The Scottish Government also considered (against the views of a majority of its consultees) that the offence should be limited to films and photographs and not include other intimate communications such as letters, emails or voice-mails: it believed that it would be very difficult to provide a clear definition of an intimate written or recorded communication that was compatible with freedom of speech.[21]

7.23 The Scottish Government also rejected suggestions for a broad breach-of-privacy offence, which it considered would be considerably wider than necessary to deal with the core harm of sharing intimate images and might inadvertently criminalise the ordinary use of social media and photo-sharing sites.[22] It also rejected (again against the views of a majority of the consultees) a subjective definition of an intimate image, where an image might be intimate if both the person featured and the person sharing it considered it to be so (for instance, showing a person who normally wore a headscarf without one). It considered that this risked perpetuating the very ambiguity in the law which a specific offence sought to address.[23] In focussing on intimate images and in providing an objective definition of intimate images, the Scottish legislation has remained within the mainstream of both European and common-law responses.

18 Now replaced, by the Online Safety Act 2023 which inserted ss 66B-D into the Sexual Offences Act 2003.

19 Paras 25, 26 and 33.

20 Para 34. This was a key point of difference between the Scottish offence and the English offence as it originally appeared in s 33 of the Criminal Courts and Justice Act 2015. The offence, as it now appears in s 66B of the Sexual Offences Act 2003, does now contain a version of the offence, in subsection (1), where A will commit the offence by sharing an image if B does not consent and A has no reasonable belief in consent and thus the offence can be committed without any need to show alarm, distress or humiliation. The version of the offence in subsection (2), where A commits the offence with the intention of causing B alarm, distress or humiliation, does not include a provision where A is reckless as to the causing of alarm, distress or humiliation.

21 Para 35.

22 Para 36.

23 Para 37.

Save for one change by the Parliament, which we record below, section 2 (and its interpretative provisions in section 3) were passed without amendment.

The elements of the offence

7.24 Section 2(1) provides that A commits an offence if:

'(a) A discloses, or threatens to disclose, a photograph or film which shows, or appears to show, another person ("B") in an intimate situation,

(b) by doing so, A intends to cause B fear, alarm or distress or A is reckless as to whether B will be caused fear, alarm or distress, and

(c) the photograph or film has not previously been disclosed to the public at large, or any section of the public, by B or with B's consent.'

(i) Discloses or threatens to disclose

7.25 The offence can be committed in two ways: disclosing a photograph or film, or threatening to disclose a photograph or film. 'Disclose' will normally carry its ordinary meaning, and the offence is often committed by sending the images by email or text message to other people, posting on social media or, less frequently, on websites specifically created for this purpose.[24] Subsection 2 does, however, provide an additional clarification of what disclosure means, providing that: 'a photograph or film is disclosed if it, or any data or other thing which is capable of being converted into it, is given, shown or made available to a person other than B'. That has three effects. First, it makes clear that A cannot plead that he or she has not disclosed the photograph or film simply because he or she has sent it to another in an encoded or encrypted file. Second, it makes clear that A does not commit the offence by sending the photograph or film to B. Third, it makes clear that there is no requirement to send the image: it can be committed simply by showing it to another.

7.26 There is no requirement that A and B be in a relationship (or have been in a relationship), nor even have met each other, as long as the requisite *mens rea* is met, though plainly that will be so in the majority of cases. By the same token, the offence is not limited to the first person to disclose the image: anyone who forwards the image, or who receives it and shows it to another person, is equally guilty of disclosing the image, provided they too have the requisite *mens rea* (on which see **7.29** below). In such situations, though, where there have been repeated disclosures through a chain of people, the Crown might take a pragmatic approach and focus any prosecution on the first or principal person to disclose, that person being the source of the harm to B.

24 S 4 and Sch 1 make special provision for 'providers of information society services' such as mobile telephone companies so that they do not commit the offence merely by acting as conduit, or caching or hosting the photographs or films. It makes no difference if the disclosure is restricted to friends or another restricted audience: *F (D) v PF, Dundee* [2023] SAC Crim 1; 2023 SLT (SAC) 17 at para 28.

7.27 The inclusion of threatening to disclose within the offence drew near unanimous support from consultees, with the Policy Memorandum recording that responses focussed on the powerful and harmful effect such threats could have.[25] The section is not clear on whether, when a threat of disclosure is made, the photograph or film must actually exist for the offence to be committed and, if it does exist, that it is in fact an intimate image. While section 2(1)(a) refers to a threat to disclose *a* photograph or film, section 2(1)(c), the third element of the offence, refers to *the* photograph or film not having previously been disclosed to the public at large, which suggests that one must exist (and if it does, that it is of the type contemplated by the legislation). On the other hand, one can easily envisage a scenario where A tells B that he has surreptitiously taken an intimate photograph of her and threatens to disclose it, and in those circumstances, it is arguable that it may be sufficient that A implies with sufficient credibility that a photograph or film of that type exists.[26]

7.28 The reference to 'shows, or appears to show' means the offence covers the disclosure of any film or photograph which has been altered to show B in an intimate situation (sometimes called 'photoshopping' or, in this context, 'deepfake porn').[27] It obviously covers the situation when A deliberately sets out to create a realistic image of B in an intimate situation and to deceive others that it is really B in the photograph or film, but it is less obvious that it would cover an image that is obviously fake and would not lead anyone to believe that it is truly B in the photograph or film (superimposing B's face on a cartoon drawing, for instance). While even obviously fake photographs might have a harmful effect on the person depicted in them, it may be that in that situation, the court would decline to find that the image truly appears to show B in an intimate situation.

(ii) The *mens rea* requirement: intention to cause, or recklessness as to causing, fear, alarm or distress

7.29 As noted above, the offence can be committed either by an intention to cause fear, alarm, or distress to B, or by recklessness as to whether B will be caused fear, alarm or distress. In *F (D) v PF, Dundee*,[28] the appellant had uploaded images of himself and his then partner in intimate situations to a website, and sought to conceal his ex-partner's identity by obscuring her eyes. At trial, the sheriff found that

25 Para 42. The English offence has since been amended to include threatened disclosure: s 69(2) of the Domestic Abuse Act 2021.

26 To remove similar dubieties in the English offence, s 33(2A) provided that it is not necessary for the prosecution to prove that the photograph or film referred to in the threat exists or, if it does exist, that it was in fact a private sexual photograph or film (the term used at that time in the English legislation). The same provision now appears in s 66B(7) of the Sexual Offences Act 2003, which now uses the term 'a photograph or film which shows or appears to show a person in an intimate state'.

27 The original English offence required B to appear in the private sexual photograph or film. S 66B adopted the Scottish terminology of 'shows, or appears to show'.

28 [2023] SAC (Crim) 1; 2023 SLT (SAC) 17.

the appellant had been reckless as to whether his partner would be caused fear, alarm or distress. On appeal, the appellant submitted that, although the offence could be committed recklessly, the mischief the offence sought to address was the same as the equivalent English offence, the mischief of revenge pornography. The Sheriff Appeal Court rejected that submission. It found that the offence was not restricted to revenge pornography (para 24) and that the offence would be committed if an individual failed to give thought to or was indifferent as to the foreseeable effect upon the complainer of such a disclosure (para 25). Applying that test, the appellant had acted not just carelessly but recklessly. Though he had obscured the complainer's face, he had failed to give any thought to, or was indifferent to, the possibility of jigsaw identification by those who knew the parties (para 27). By uploading the images, the appellant had no control over what other users might do with them, and he ought to have been aware of the possibility that other users might share them more widely (para 28).

(iii) No previous disclosure of the photograph or film

7.30 The third element of the offence – that the photograph or film has not previously been disclosed to the public at large, or any section of the public, by B or with B's consent – appears to cover the situation where A does nothing more than share a photograph or film that others have already, though it carries the critical qualification that B must have consented to other people having that photograph or film already. Since this is an element of the offence, it will be necessary for the prosecutor to lead evidence (usually from B) that the item has not previously been disclosed to the public at large, or any section of it, with B's consent. If A does not know that B did not consent to that previous sharing, then A might have a defence under section 2(3) (see **7.35–7.37** below).

The definitions of 'intimate situation', 'film' and 'photograph'

7.31 Section 3 gives definitions of the key terms in section 2: 'intimate situation', 'film' and 'photograph'. By section 3(1), a person is in an intimate situation if—

'(a) the person is engaging or participating in, or present during, an act which—
 (i) a reasonable person would consider to be a sexual act, and
 (ii) is not of a kind ordinarily done in public, or
(b) the person's genitals, buttocks or breasts are exposed or covered only with underwear.'

7.32 As noted above, this is an objective definition. The first limb, in section 3(1)(a), provides, in effect, a definition of private sexual acts. The reference to 'not of a kind ordinarily done in public' will exclude photographs or films of B engaging, whether in private or in public, in less intimate sexual behaviour such as kissing or holding hands. The second limb, section 3(1)(b), is the reason the offence covers intimate images and not merely sexual images. It means the offence can be committed not only when B was photographed or filmed engaging in a sexual act, but also when B was just naked or only partially clothed: showering, changing clothes, etc. It also means the offence is committed when A discloses photographs that might have been surreptitiously taken of B in public: so-called 'upskirting' or 'downblousing' photographs.

7.33 'Film' means a moving image in any form, whether or not the image has been altered in any way, that was originally captured by making a recording, on any medium, from which a moving image may be produced, and includes a copy of the image (section 3(2)). 'Photograph' means a still image in any form, whether or not the image has been altered in any way, that was originally captured by photography, and includes a copy of the image (also section 3(2)). Though it might have been thought that definitions of common words like 'film' and 'photograph' were unnecessary, there does appear to have been some utility in including definitions because it provided an opportunity to make clear that the offence is still committed even if the film or photograph has been altered (that is, the deepfake or photoshopped scenario discussed above) and that they include copies.

Defences

7.34 There are five defences to the offence. Four are set out in section 2(3). The fifth is set out in section 2(5). For each, section 2(6) places the usual evidential burden on the defence to adduce sufficient evidence to put the defence in issue and a legal burden on the prosecution to negative the defence.

The section 2(3) defences

7.35 Section 2(3) provides:

> 'In proceedings for an offence under subsection (1), A has a defence if any of the following facts is established—
> (a) B consented to the photograph or film being disclosed,
> (b) A reasonably believed that B consented to the photograph or film being disclosed,
> (c) A reasonably believed that disclosure of the photograph or film was necessary for the purposes of the prevention, detection, investigation or prosecution of crime, or
> (d) A reasonably believed that disclosure of the photograph or film was in the public interest.'

7.36 Subsection (4) further provides that:

> 'For the purposes of subsection (3), consent to the photograph or film being disclosed may be –

(a) consent which is specific to the particular disclosure or (as the case may be) the particular threatened disclosure, or
(b) consent to disclosure generally where that consent covers the particular disclosure or (as the case may be) the particular threatened disclosure.'

7.37 We suggest that the first two defences, (a) and (b), are self-explanatory and, though consent and reasonable are not defined in the statute, they carry the same meaning as they do in other sexual offences. Subsection (4) is also self-explanatory: if B consents to A disclosing or threatening to disclose the intimate photograph or film, or B consents to A disclosing or threatening to disclose intimate photographs or films generally (in terms that may be taken to cover the disclosure of the particular photograph or film), then A has a defence. Consent for the purposes of the defence is not consent to any sexual act that might be the subject of the photograph or film but rather to disclosure of the photograph or film: plainly, though, lack of consent to the sexual act will almost certainly imply lack of consent to disclosure of the photograph of film.

7.38 The third defence, (c), will apply if, for instance, A comes into possession of a film or photograph that shows (or A reasonably believes it shows) B engaging in a criminal act, whether a sexual offence or another offence, whilst B is in a state of undress and A discloses that film to the police.

7.39 The fourth defence, (d), is wider than the original version of the English defence, which only covered journalistic activity.[29] 'Public interest' is not defined in the 2016 Act but would, we suggest, carry the same meaning as the term carries in other areas of law such as defamation or human rights law, including that the public interest is not the same as what the public is interested in. Though broader than the journalistic-activity defence originally in the English legislation, it contemplates similar scenarios, for instance newspapers publishing pictures of public figures engaging in improper sexual activity.

The section 2(5) defence: public places

7.40 Section 2(5) provides:

'In proceedings for an offence under subsection (1), A has a defence if the following matter is established—
(a) B was in the intimate situation shown in the photograph or film,
(b) B was not in the intimate situation as a result of a deliberate act of another person to which B did not agree, and

[29] Now replaced, for the subsection (1) version of the offence in s 66B, with a general reasonable excuse defence: s 66B(8). That reasonable-excuse defence does not apply to the other forms of the offence, in subsections (2) and (3), where A discloses the image to alarm, distress or humiliate B, or for the purpose of A or another person obtaining sexual gratification.

(c) when B was in the intimate situation—
   (i) B was in a place to which members of the public had access (whether or not on payment of a fee), and
   (ii) members of the public were present.'

7.41 Section 2(5) has two effects. The first, and, from the legislative materials, the express purpose of section 2(5), is to exclude from the offence photographs or films taken when people are deliberately naked in public: naked protestors or streakers at sporting events are the examples given in the legislative materials.[30] The second effect is to exclude the disclosure of photographs or films of B in public places, such as public swimming pools or public beaches, where it is in the nature of the place for people to be partially dressed. Section 2(5)(c)(i) is a novel definition of a public place (appearing for the first time in legislation) but, it is suggested, a workable one. By section 2(5)(c)(ii), the defence does not apply if B is alone in a public place (either completely or only accompanied by people known to B) and thus would have had a reasonable expectation of privacy when the photograph or film was taken. Section 2(5)(b) was the only substantive amendment to section 2 during its passage through the Scottish Parliament. It is an important one. It means the defence is not available when B is in the intimate situation against his or her will.

7.42 Section 2(5)(a) to (c) are objective matters, drafted without reference to A's state of knowledge. They do not therefore give A a defence if, for instance, A reasonably believed B was willingly in the intimate situation but was in fact not, or A reasonably believed the place in which the photograph or film was taken was a public place when it in fact was not. It may be though that, in that situation, the Crown would have difficulty showing that A acted with the necessary *mens rea* for the offence in section 2(1)(b) (intending to cause B fear, alarm or distress or being reckless to that effect). It may also be that that A would have a defence that he or she reasonably believed B consented to disclosure.

Sentencing

7.43 Section 2(7) sets the maximum penalties for the offence: on summary conviction, 12 months' imprisonment or a fine (or both); and, on conviction on indictment, five years' imprisonment or a fine (or both). The offence has attracted both custodial and community disposals.[31] In *Shanks v PF, Glasgow*,[32] the Sheriff Appeal Court took the statutory maximum sentences to be an indication of how seriously Parliament viewed the offence and left undisturbed a sentence of 135 hours' unpaid work for threatening to disclose images of an ex-partner to her children,

30 The Explanatory Notes at para 17 and the Policy Memorandum at para 30.

31 One custodial disposal was *Kennaway v HM Advocate* [2019] HCJAC 11, where a sentence of two years' imprisonment for sending images to the complainer's new boyfriend was reduced to one on appeal, albeit in the context of a 12-charge indictment involving assaults, threatening and abusive behaviour, and bail offences.

32 [2018] SAC (Crim) 18; 2018 SLT (Sh Ct) 417.

which it characterised as abusive. It found that the sentence was within the upper end of the range open to the sheriff. In *F (D) v PF Dundee* (see **7.29** above), the Sheriff Appeal Court found a community disposal (rather than an absolute discharge) was appropriate for when the offence, though committed recklessly, involved a breach of trust over a period of time for personal gain.

7.44 Section 2 is not an offence to which the notification requirements in Part 2 of the Sexual Offences Act 2003 automatically apply. They will only apply if, in the usual way, the sentencer considers that there is a significant sexual aspect to the offence: paragraph 60 of Schedule 3 to the Act. For discussion of paragraph 60 and section 2, see Chapter 20 at **20.60–20.70**.

SECTION 1 OF THE DOMESTIC ABUSE (SCOTLAND) ACT 2018

Background

7.45 The Domestic Abuse (Scotland) Act 2018 (DASA) is the most significant change to the prosecution and trial of sexual offences since the Sexual Offences (Scotland) Act 2009. This is because the course of abusive behaviour towards a partner or ex-partner which section 1 of the Act criminalises can include anything that amounts to sexual violence, or any sexual offending which would amount to abusive behaviour. This means that sexual offences, which would previously have appeared on separate charges, can be included in a single charge under section 1 as part of a single alleged course of conduct by an accused towards his or her partner or ex-partner. The consequence has been that sexual offences, and often the most serious sexual offences, which would otherwise have required separate charges and thus separate corroboration, have instead come to be included in section 1 charges, where the requirement is instead for corroboration of the course of abusive behaviour.

7.46 The Act was passed with the near unanimous support of the Scottish Parliament and with very little amendment to the Bill as introduced. The primary policy objective of section 1 of the Act was to ensure that the criminal law reflects the view that: (i) domestic abuse can often be a course of conduct which takes place over a sustained period of time; and (ii) the course of conduct can consist of both physical violence and threats, and psychological and emotional abuse.[33] These are now the key components of the offence. The reason for defining the offence as a course of conduct was to reflect how victims actually experienced domestic abuse.[34] The reason for the width of the definition was a desire to create a general offence to cover the wide range of conduct that can make up a pattern of abusive behaviour within a relationship.[35]

33 Para 4 of the Scottish Government's Policy Memorandum on the Bill.

34 Para 5.

35 Para 22.

7.47 That can be seen in the express rejection of two approaches by the Scottish Government. In introducing the new offence, the Scottish Government rejected first, the possibility of relying on the existing criminal law to prosecute perpetrators of domestic abuse since this would require prosecutions to focus on individual incidents of domestic abuse, which did not recognise that domestic abuse was often a pattern of behaviour sustained over a considerable period of time.[36] The existing law also made it difficult to prosecute on-going psychological and emotional abuse where there was no physical violence or overt threats.[37] Secondly, the Scottish Government rejected importing the offence of controlling or coercive behaviour in an intimate or family relationship from England and Wales.[38] It considered that this would not avoid an overlap with existing offences such as threatening or abusive behaviour, contrary to section 38 of the Criminal Justice and Licensing (Scotland) Act 2010. Furthermore, there would be cases where behaviour that might appear innocuous would be clearly seen as psychologically abusive when viewed in the context of past threats or violence. Equally, threats that might seem low-level if viewed in isolation would not be when seen against a background of on-going psychological abuse. It was thus considered extremely useful for prosecutors to be able to libel the accused's entire course of conduct under a single charge of domestic abuse. Finally, it was considered that the English approach did not allow the wide range of conduct constituting domestic abuse to be contained in one offence.[39]

7.48 The express inclusion of sexual violence within the offence received very little attention either in the Policy Memorandum or in the Parliament's consideration of the Bill, and there seems to have been little appreciation of the effect it would have on the prosecution of sexual offences, particularly in the High Court. The Policy Memorandum refers, for instance, to the need to have a maximum penalty of 14 years' imprisonment for the offence to ensure that the High Court had appropriate sentencing powers to deal with 'the small number of most serious cases'. This has not

36 Para 53.

37 Para 54.

38 In s 76 of the Serious Crime Act 2015. Ireland has enacted a similar offence: s 39 of the Domestic Violence Act 2018. Northern Ireland has followed the Scottish model and enacted a specific domestic abuse offence: s 2 of the Domestic Abuse and Civil Proceedings Act (Northern Ireland) 2021.

39 Paras 55–59. The Policy Memorandum does not give examples of offending that would not be caught by the English offence but would be caught by the Scottish offence. The language of the Scottish offences is certainly wider, referring to abusive behaviour rather than controlling or coercive behaviour and referring to physical or psychological harm rather than fear of violence or serious alarm or distress. But any differences are lessened by the Statutory Guidance issued in respect of s 76 which gives examples of controlling or coercive behaviour that include all of the behaviour referred to in s 2 of DASA (the section which defines abusive behaviour for the purposes of the Scottish offence): *Controlling or Coercive Behaviour in an Intimate or Family Relationship: Statutory Guidance Framework*, December 2015 at page 4. An even longer list of examples is given in the CPS Guidance: https://www.cps.gov.uk/legal-guidance/controlling-or-coercive-behaviour-intimate-or-family-relationship.

been the experience. Section 1 DASA charges now feature regularly in High Court indictments.[40]

The elements of the offence

7.49 There are three elements to the offence (or, as the Act puts it 'conditions' to be met):

- (i) A engages in a course of behaviour which is abusive of a partner or ex-partner (B) (section 1(1));
- (ii) a reasonable person would consider the course of behaviour to be likely to cause B to suffer physical or psychological harm (section 1(2)(a)); and
- (iii) either the accused intended by the course of abusive behaviour to cause B to suffer physical or psychological harm, or was reckless as to the causing of such harm (section 1(2)(b)).

(i) The first element: engaging in a course of behaviour which is abusive of a partner or ex-partner

7.50 This is the key element of the offence and the Act defines its terms in some detail. Someone is a person's partner if they are: (a) spouses or civil partners of each other, (b) living together as if spouses of each other, or (c) in an intimate personal relationship with each other (section 11(2)). Ex-partner is to be determined accordingly (section 11(3)). By section 7, the matter of B being A's partner or ex-partner is taken to be established unless the matter is challenged by preliminary objection.

7.51 A 'course of behaviour' involves behaviour on at least two occasions (section 10(4)). Thus, a single incident of abuse, however severe, will not be an offence under section 1 of DASA. There is no specified maximum period of time between the two occasions beyond which a course of behaviour cannot be said to exist, but plainly the closer in time, and the more occasions of behaviour, the greater the likelihood of there being a course of behaviour.

7.52 'Behaviour' is behaviour of any kind including, for example: (i) saying or otherwise communicating something as well as doing something; and (ii) intentionally failing to do something, saying or otherwise communicating something (section 10(2)). The intention of these provisions is to make clear that behaviour can include things said, silence, and omissions, all of which, in the right context, can be abusive and can cause psychological harm.

40 DASA charges are not separately recorded in SCTS's *Quarterly Criminal Court Statistics* series. COPFS's *Domestic Abuse and Stalking Charges in Scotland* series does not distinguish between solemn Sheriff Court proceedings and High Court proceedings but does record that, for 2022–23, 38% of DASA charges were prosecuted at solemn level and 62% at summary level.

7.53 With that broad definition of behaviour in mind, the next question is what is abusive behaviour? The Act does not attempt an exhaustive definition, but section 2 'elaborates' on what behaviour is abusive. Section 2(2) provides that it includes:

'(a) behaviour directed at B that is violent, threatening or intimidating;

(b) behaviour directed at B, at a child of B or at another person that either –

  (i) has as its purpose (or among its purposes) one or more of the relevant effects set out in subsection (3), or

  (ii) would be considered by a reasonable person to be likely to have one or more of the relevant effects set out in subsection (3).'

7.54 That is a two-part definition. The first, in section 2(2)(a), is directly abusive behaviour: the kind that could be prosecuted under existing laws, but that also might form part of a pattern of abuse. The second is behaviour that is abusive because of its effects. It is intended to capture behaviour that is abusive because it is coercive, or controlling, or otherwise amounts to psychological or emotional abuse.[41] That is the reason for the reference in section 2(2) to 'relevant effects'. Section 2(3) then gives a list of those relevant effects. Slightly unusually, the Explanatory Notes for the Act, when commenting on each relevant effect, gives numerous examples of behaviour that would have that effect (paras 18–23). Though they are not endorsed by the Parliament, they do provide some guide to the breadth of the offence, and we therefore reproduce them below. The relevant effects in section 2(3) are:

(a) making B dependent on, or subordinate to, A

7.55 The Explanatory Notes examples: preventing the victim from having access to money, forcing the victim to leave their job, taking charge of household decision-making to the exclusion of the victim or treating the victim as a domestic slave.

(b) isolating B from friends, relatives or other sources of support

7.56 Controlling the victim's movements or access to their phone or other forms of communication, not allowing visits from or to the victim's friends or family, or deliberately failing to pass on messages from friends or family.

(c) controlling, regulating or monitoring B's day-to-day activities

7.57 Checking the victim's phone, e-mail or social media use, controlling what clothes the victim can or cannot wear, or placing unreasonable requirements on the victim to, for example, prepare meals in a particular way at a particular time every day.

41 Policy Memorandum at para 32.

(d) depriving B of, or restricting B's, freedom of action

7.58 The Explanatory Notes (at para 21) state that this addresses behaviour which 'robs victims of their autonomy'. The examples are: preventing the victim from attending work or college, preventing the victim from leaving the house alone, insisting on accompanying the victim to medical appointments, or taking decisions for the victim in relation to private, individual matters that a person would normally decide for themselves.

(e) frightening, humiliating, degrading or punishing B.

7.59 Abusive name-calling, threats of self-harm, playing mind games with the victim that cause them to doubt their sanity, controlling the victim's access to the toilet or forcing the victim to eat food off the floor.

7.60 Though section 2 is deliberately wide in scope, it is important to remember that the behaviour must be 'directed at B' (if it is violent, threatening, or intimidating) or 'directed at B, at a child of B[42] or at another person' (if it has as its purpose, or would be considered by a reasonable person likely to have, one or more of the 'relevant effects'). 'Behaviour directed at a person' is behaviour, however carried out; it includes conduct towards property and conduct through making use of a third party, as well as behaviour in a personal or direct manner (section 10(3)). The reference to 'conduct towards property' is designed to include matters such as threats to abuse a family pet (and no doubt abuse of the pet itself), and vandalism of personal property.[43] The property need not belong to the complainer.[44] The reference to 'making use of a third party' is said, in the Explanatory Notes, to include getting another person to spy on or report on the activities of the complainer.[45] Despite the breadth of these definitions, the behaviour must still be 'directed' at a person. Behaviour that might cause the complainer to be humiliated but is not directed at the complainer is not caught. For instance, taking the example given in the Policy Memorandum, if A has an affair, then that might cause A's partner, B, to be humiliated, but it is not, without more, directed at B: it is simply carried out or undertaken with another person.[46]

42 The child must be a person under 18 years of age: s 2(4)(b).

43 The examples in para 36 of the Policy Memorandum.

44 Ibid and para 53 of the Explanatory Notes.

45 At para 54.

46 Para 37 of the Policy Memorandum. In *Walker v PF, Dunoon* [2022] SAC (Crim) 9, which quashed the appellant's conviction for loitering outside his daughter's school, where he was seen by his ex-partner, the Sheriff Appeal Court found that the sheriff's findings-in-fact did not support the inference that this was directed against his ex-partner, the complainer, and that the sheriff had failed to address that question when repelling a submission of no case to answer. Although that appears correct, neither the sheriff nor the Sheriff Appeal Court appear to have considered that the offence could still be established if the behaviour was directed at the daughter.

(ii) The second element: that a reasonable person would consider the course of behaviour to be likely to cause B to suffer physical or psychological harm

7.61 The second, objective element of the offence has two effects. The first, and stated purpose of this element of the offence,[47] is to ensure that innocuous behaviour that might have one of the relevant effects (such as a work/childcare arrangement that has the effect of making one partner financially dependent on the other simply because the two partners decide together that one will work, and one will care for their children) is not inadvertently brought within the offence. The second effect is that it ensures that a course of behaviour that is clearly intended to cause B to suffer physical or psychological harm is still caught by the legislation even if B, for whatever reason does not in fact suffer any harm. Thus section 4(1) of the Act makes clear that there is no requirement to prove that B actually suffered physical or psychological harm from the course of behaviour. Equally, in respect of behaviour directed at B, a child of B or another person, there is no requirement to show that the behaviour actually had any of the relevant effects in section 2(3): section 4(2). This was considered appropriate to ensure that the court could take into account any particular vulnerability of the victim, without requiring proof of harm because this would require the victim to give evidence of it, and risk re-traumatisation.[48] The reality though is that the offence is unlikely to be established without the evidence of the victim in some form, the court will want to hear evidence of what harm is caused (if only for sentencing purposes), and the Act itself does not preclude the Crown from leading evidence of the harm: section 4(3).

(iii) The third element: either the accused intended by the course of abusive behaviour to cause B to suffer physical or psychological harm, or was reckless as to the causing of such harm

7.62 The third element is a standard *mens rea* requirement of either intention to cause harm or being reckless as to the causing of that harm. The Policy Memorandum states that its purpose is to avoid the offences either being triggered or not triggered by the simple fact that behaviour may not have the effect that it would be expected to have on the victim. The approach is said to ensure that the focus remains on the offender's behaviour and not on the victim's reaction.[49] This is unclear. Such considerations would appear to relate to the absence of any requirement to prove that B actually suffered harm (see the second element of the offence at **7.61** above), but at any rate, it is a standard *mens rea* requirement which avoids A engaging in a course of abusive behaviour then claiming that he or she did not intend that behaviour to cause any harm.

47 Para 42.
48 Para 44.
49 Para 48.

7.63 In *Walker v PF, Dunoon*,[50] the Sheriff Appeal Court found that neither requirement was met by the appellant loitering outside his daughter's school, where his ex-partner saw him. The background appears to have been a contact dispute over the daughter. The Court found it difficult to see how the sheriff could have concluded the appellant's behaviour was reckless, when the appellant had taken legal advice before attending the school. The Court's finding that there could be no intention to cause harm is less clear as it does not appear to have been expressly addressed by the Court. The Court appears to have founded on the fact there was no finding-in-fact that the complainer was frightened by the appellant's behaviour, though that would have no direct bearing on the presence or absence of the *mens rea* when the actual harm to the complainer is of course not a requirement of the offence.

Aggravation in relation to a child

7.64 Section 5 provides for the offence to be aggravated by reason of involving a child, when that is specified in the complaint or libelled in the indictment. The offence can be so aggravated in three ways:

- (i) if A directs behaviour at a child or makes use of a child in directing behaviour at B, the partner or ex-partner (section 5(2));
- (ii) a child sees or hears, or is present during, an incident of behaviour that A directs at B as part of the course of behaviour (section 5(3)); or
- (iii) a reasonable person would consider the course of behaviour, or an incident of A's behaviour that forms part of the course of behaviour, to be likely to adversely affect a child usually residing with A or B (or both) (section 5(4)).

7.65 The three forms of the aggravation are designed to cover situations where A directs behaviour at a child so as to make B fearful for the safety or well-being of the child (and thus frighten or control B); A uses the child to spy on B; or the child sees or hears A's abuse of B (this latter form seeking to reflect the harm caused to children by domestic abuse).[51] The child does not need to have been aware of A's behaviour, to have understood the nature of it or to have been adversely affected by it: section 5(5). Evidence from a single source is sufficient to prove the aggravation: section 5(6). The three forms of the aggravation can apply separately or in combination: section 5(8). There is no requirement that the child be A's child or B's child.

The reasonableness defence

7.66 The Act provides only one defence for A: that the course of behaviour was reasonable in the particular circumstances (section 6(1)). The Explanatory Notes give the examples of the accused acting in order to protect the household finances where their partner is suffering from a gambling addiction; preventing their partner from

50 [2022] SAC (Crim) 9.
51 Paras 88–90 of the Policy Memorandum.

associating with certain persons or frequenting certain places if they are recovering from alcohol or drug addiction; and restricting the freedom of movement of a partner who is suffering from dementia.[52] Section 6(2) places an evidential burden on the defence to adduce sufficient evidence to put the defence in issue and a legal burden on the prosecution to negative the defence.

The place of sexual offences in section 1 DASA charges

7.67 As the explanatory notes to the Act state (at paragraph 23), sexual offences can appear within a section 1 DASA libel for three reasons. First, as noted above, section 2(2)(a) states that behaviour which is abusive of B includes 'behaviour directed at B that is violent, threatening or intimidating' and section 2(4) expressly provides that this reference to violent behaviour includes sexual violence as well as physical violence. Second, applying the second part of the definition of abusive behaviour in sections 2(2)(b) and (3), non-violent sexually abusive behaviour may also be abusive because of its effect. The 'relevant effect' most likely to be engaged by a sexual offence committed by A against B is section 2(3)(e): that it has the effect of frightening, humiliating, degrading, or punishing B. There will be few, if any, sexual offences that do not meet this definition. Third, non-violent sexually abusive behaviour may also be considered threatening or intimidating in terms of section 2(2)(a).

7.68 The inclusion of sexual behaviour within section 1 of DASA has led to the charge that the Crown can circumvent the ordinary rules on corroboration by including sexual offences within DASA libels; that sexual offending which would previously have required corroboration need not do so if the sexual offence is included in a DASA charge and other incidents in that charge are corroborated. In *M v HM Advocate*, unreported, 11 May 2023, the Appeal Court had no difficulty in finding that it was competent to include sexual behaviour within DASA charges. The Appeal Court endorsed the opinion of Lord Matthews at first instance in *DF v HM Advocate*, unreported, 10 August 2021 that section 1 of DASA extended to sexual behaviour and that there was nothing incompetent in libelling what could also be charged as rape within a charge under that section (para 8). Equally, there was no requirement that such a case be tried in the High Court (ibid), though the Crown's general approach is to indict such cases in the High Court.

7.69 *DF* is notable for its extended analysis of whether sexual offending can be found to be part of the same course of behaviour as other offending in the libel. Having reviewed the Scottish and English authorities on analogous offences which are constituted by a course of conduct, Lord Matthews concluded that: (i) the acceptance by the jury on corroborated evidence that two episodes of abusive behaviour had been proved would suffice for conviction of the offence; (ii) whether the jury could also convict of the uncorroborated elements would depend on whether or not they

[52] Para 42.

were satisfied that those uncorroborated elements formed part of the same course of behaviour; (iii) there required to be some sort of nexus or link between the various elements, otherwise they would be simply separate incidents and not part of a course of conduct; (iv) whether or not that link exists will depend on the evidence in each case; (v) it might be found if the jury were satisfied, for example, that there was a continuity of purpose in the accused's behaviour; (v) it was not necessary that the individual incidents require to be of the same kind or of a similar kind to the full extent required by *Moorov*; (vi) it will always be open to an accused to submit that there is no case to answer where the evidence does not support a course of conduct (para 39).

7.70 In considering what is necessary for corroboration of the offence, the Appeal Court in *CA v HM Advocate*[53] endorsed the first two of these points (see the section on corroboration at **7.72** below). The Appeal Court did not expressly disapprove points (iii)–(vi), and, in particular, the requirement for some sort of nexus or link between the various elements in a section 1 DASA libel. However, it did not expressly endorse them either, and instead approved a direction which made no reference to a need for a nexus or link. *CA* was in turn approved in *McKenzie v HM Advocate* 2024 JC 121, where again these points in *DF* were neither expressly approved nor expressly disapproved. The same approach was also taken in *Bain v HM Advocate*,[54] where the appellant expressly contended that there should be a jury direction on the need for a nexus or link between an averment of sexual misconduct and the other averments in the libel, but the appeal was refused. The court in *Bain* had no difficulty with the trial judge's direction to the jury that they could only return a verdict of guilt on an element which was only spoken to by one witness (ie the complainer) if it was 'part of the same course of abusive behaviour'. It observed that the jury must have believed the complainer in relation to the sexual element under consideration and must have accepted that the sexual element formed part of the course of conduct (para 9).

7.71 Given that the Appeal Court has now, on three occasions, declined to endorse what was said in *DF* about the need for a nexus or link, it might be thought that whether there is a course of abusive behaviour (and whether any averments of sexual misconduct form part of that course of behaviour) is now simply a jury question. If that is so then, although the Appeal Court has not yet said so, it may be that a DASA course of abusive behaviour now falls to be considered in the same way as any other course of conduct: as with other courses of conduct, it will only be when, on no possible view, could it be said that the individual incidents were component parts of a course of conduct that submission of no case to answer (either on the libel or an averment in it) should be upheld and the matter withdrawn from the jury.[55]

53 2023 JC 8.

54 [2024] HCJAC 16.

55 See further Chapter 19 at **19.67** and **19.90**.

Corroboration

7.72 *CA v HM Advocate* determined what is required for corroboration of a section 1 DASA charge. It found that section 1 created a new offence of a course of behaviour which enables abuse of various types taking place over a period of time to be prosecuted as a single offence. It is the course of behaviour which is the core of the offence. Thus, it is the course of behaviour – in other words, proof of behaviour on at least two occasions – which must be established by corroborated evidence. Once there is corroborative evidence of this kind, it is open to the jury to determine that other incidents equally form part of the course of conduct, even though spoken to by only one witness (para 10 and para 13 quoting with approval Lord Matthews in *DF*). The approach to corroboration set out in *CA* was endorsed in *McKenzie v HM Advocate*, cited above, where the Court reiterated that the offence was committed by engaging in a course of behaviour, that it would be sufficient to prove two incidents of the course of behaviour and that this would entitle the jury to convict of the remaining, albeit uncorroborated, aspects if they were part of the same course of conduct (at para 9). The point is thus now clear. Two of the incidents in the libel must be proven by corroborated evidence. Thereafter, the jury/judge can find the remainder of the incidents proven on the evidence of one witness (usually the complainer) if those incidents are part of the same course of abusive behaviour as the two corroborated incidents.

Extra-territorial jurisdiction

7.73 As discussed in Chapter 1, the offence is one over which the Scottish courts have extra-territorial jurisdiction. By section 3 of the 2018 Act, they will have that jurisdiction when the course of behaviour occurs wholly or partly outside the UK and the accused is either a UK national or is habitually resident in Scotland. This is most commonly seen when the majority of the course of behaviour takes place in Scotland, but certain particularly abusive acts have taken place when the partners are on holiday. When part of the course of behaviour takes place in the rest of the UK and part in Scotland, the ordinary common law rules on jurisdiction in cross-border offences will apply, this being the stated intention of the Scottish Government during the Bill's passage through the Scottish Parliament (see Chapter 1 at **1.41**).

Alternative offences

7.74 Section 38 (threatening and abusive behaviour) and section 39 (stalking) are alternative offences to a section 1 DASA charge: section 8 of DASA.

Prohibition of personal conduct of defence

7.75 The prohibition on an accused personally conducting his or her defence applies to the offence: section 288DC of the 1995 Act. The prohibition on sexual-history or character evidence in section 274 does not automatically apply and will require a separate order of the court: see Chapter 13 at **13.63–13.65**.

Sentencing

7.76 By section 9, the maximum sentences are: (a) on summary conviction, to imprisonment for a term not exceeding 12 months or a fine not exceeding the statutory maximum (or both); and (b) on conviction on indictment, to imprisonment for a term not exceeding 14 years or a fine (or both). The maximum sentences were chosen to reflect the fact that the offence could consist of a course of behaviour that took place over many years. The Scottish Government's Policy Memorandum also records that it initially preferred a maximum sentence of ten years' imprisonment. This was changed after consultation to 14 years' imprisonment: as noted above, the reason was to ensure that the High Court had appropriate sentencing powers to deal with 'the small number of most serious cases'.[56] As also noted above, that has not been the experience, and section 1 DASA charges are now frequently seen in the High Court. The Scottish Government was, however, correct that the maximum sentence of 14 years' imprisonment gives the High Court an appropriate sentencing power for the cases it sees. It is common for High Court cases to involve a course of abusive behaviour over years and to include multiple incidents of both serious sexual and physical violence, often against several ex-partners. Such cases have attracted High Court sentences, with the Court willing to sentence such cases as it would cases where multiple incidents of sexual or physical violence are libelled on separate charges.

TABLE OF OFFENCES

7.77

Table 7.1

Offence	Dates in force	Maximum sentence
Stalking: section 39 of the Criminal Justice and Licensing (Scotland) Act 2010	13 December 2010 to present	Summary: 12 months' imprisonment or a fine not exceeding the statutory maximum (or both) Indictment: five years' imprisonment or a fine (or both)

[56] Para 50 of the Policy Memorandum.

Table 7.1 *Further offences to protect those in intimate relationships*

Offence	Dates in force	Maximum sentence
Disclosing, or threatening to disclose, an intimate photograph or film: section 2 of the Abusive Behaviour and Sexual Harm (Scotland) Act 2016	3 July 2017 to present	Summary: 12 months' imprisonment or a fine not exceeding the statutory maximum (or both) Indictment: five years' imprisonment or a fine (or both)
Abusive behaviour towards partner or ex-partner: section 1 of the Domestic Abuse (Scotland) Act 2018	1 April 2019 to present	Summary: 12 months' imprisonment or a fine not exceeding the statutory maximum (or both) Indictment: 14 years' imprisonment or a fine (or both)

Chapter 8

Further offences to protect vulnerable groups from sexual exploitation

INTRODUCTION

8.01 This chapter considers the offences in Scots law which protect vulnerable groups from sexual exploitation. It is in four parts.

8.02 Part 1 considers the offences of human trafficking and holding another in slavery or servitude/requiring another person to perform forced or compulsory labour in, respectively, sections 1 and 4 of the Human Trafficking and Exploitation (Scotland) Act 2015. These offences are included because one of the main purposes of human trafficking is the sexual exploitation of the victim and one of the main forms of servitude/forced or compulsory labour is the forced provision of sexual services. These offences are often prosecuted on indictments that also contain charges of rape or sexual coercion under sections 1 and 4 of the Sexual Offences (Scotland) Act 2009, the child-specific offences contained in Part 4 of the 2009 Act, or the other offences protecting children from sexual exploitation in sections 9 to 12 of the Protection of Children and Prevention of Sexual Offences (Scotland) Act 2005.

8.03 Part 2 considers the offences directed at the sexual exploitation of others by organised prostitution, and the allied offences that seek to protect particularly vulnerable people from organised prostitution. These offences are contained in sections 7 to 13 of the Criminal Law (Consolidation) (Scotland) Act 1995.

8.04 Part 3 considers the offences of solicitation in section 11(1)(b) of the 1995 Act, section 46 of the Civic Government (Scotland) Act 1982 and section 1 of the Prostitution (Public Places) (Scotland) Act 2007.

8.05 Part 4 briefly considers the offences of female genital mutilation, virginity testing and hymenoplasty contained in the Prohibition of Female Genital Mutilation (Scotland) Act 2005 and the Health and Care Act 2022.

THE HUMAN TRAFFICKING AND EXPLOITATION (SCOTLAND) ACT 2015 OFFENCES

Section 1: human trafficking

8.06 The purpose of section 1 of the Human Trafficking and Exploitation (Scotland) Act 2015 was to create a single offence of human trafficking dealing with all of the forms of exploitation that trafficking can involve. It replaced the existing offences in section 22 of the Criminal Justice (Scotland) Act 2003 and sections 4 and 5 of the Asylum and Immigration (Treatment of Claimants, etc) Act 2004.[1] The Act passed through the Scottish Parliament virtually in tandem with the Modern Slavery Act 2015, and the Human Trafficking and Exploitation (Criminal Justice and Support for Victims) Act (Northern Ireland) 2015, which also consolidated and strengthened the criminal law on human trafficking for the rest of the UK.

8.07 Section 1 was heavily amended at stage 2 of its passage through the Scottish Parliament: the initial version was felt by the Justice Committee and consultees to have too great an emphasis on the need for travel and not to align with definitions contained in the international instruments on human trafficking.[2] Therefore, section 1(1) as enacted simply states that a person commits an offence if he: (a) takes a relevant action; and (b) does so with a view to another being exploited. By section 1(2), a 'relevant action' is: (a) the recruitment of another person; (b) the transportation or transfer of another person; (c) the harbouring or receiving of another person; (d) the exchange or transfer of control over another person; or (e) the arrangement or facilitation of any of the actions mentioned in (a) to (d). It is irrelevant whether the other person (that is, the person being trafficked) consents to any part of the relevant action: section 1(3).[3] A person takes a relevant action 'with a view to another person

1 S 22 of the 2003 Act criminalised trafficking for the purpose of prostitution or the making or production of indecent or obscene material. Section 4 of the 2004 Act criminalised trafficking for other forms of exploitation such as slavery or forced labour. Both were repealed by the 2015 Act with effect from 17 December 2016.

2 See official report of stage 2 proceedings, 16 June 2015, Cabinet Secretary for Justice at p 15. The principal international texts are the 2000 UN Protocol to Prevent, Suppress and Punish Trafficking in Persons, Especially Women and Children ('Palermo Protocol'), the 2005 Council of Europe Convention on Action against Trafficking in Human Beings, and the EU Anti-trafficking Directive, Directive 2011/36/EU. The initial wording of s 1 as introduced was very similar in wording to the equivalent provision in the Modern Slavery Act 2015 and Human Trafficking and Exploitation (Criminal Justice and Support for Victims) Act (Northern Ireland) 2015. Section 1 as enacted is closer to the wording of the international instruments.

3 The same provision exists in s 2(2) of the Modern Slavery Act 2015 and in their commentary on it Rook and Ward suggest that while the complainant's consent is irrelevant to whether or not they have been trafficked, it is nonetheless something that may go to the question of the defendant's intent. They ask: 'if the defendant believes that the complainant is consenting to the travel and subsequent work that they are made to undertake, can it be said that they are acting with a view to exploiting them?' (para 11.132). We respectfully disagree. All the Crown requires to prove is that A acts with the view to B being exploited. B might consent to travel (and even to, say, prostitution on arrival) but that does not mean that A does not act with a view to B engaging in prostitution. Whatever B does or wishes, A still acts with a view to B being engaging in the activity which, the Act says, is exploitation. Further, the aim of the legislation is to suppress travel for certain purposes (prostitution, slavery, etc), even if, without that element of travel there might be no offence. B's consent, on that view, is irrelevant to A's intentions.

being exploited' if: (a) the person intends to exploit the other person (in any part of the world) during or after the relevant action; or (b) the person knows or ought to know the other person is likely to be exploited (in any part of the world) during or after the relevant action: section 1(4).

8.08 Section 3 defines exploitation. There are four situations in which a person is exploited:

(i) slavery, servitude and forced or compulsory labour;
(ii) prostitution and sexual exploitation;
(iii) removal of organs or other parts of the body; and
(iv) inducement by force, threats or deception to provide services or benefits (or enabling another to acquire those benefits).[4]

8.09 We restrict our commentary to prostitution and sexual exploitation, but slavery and other forced labour is considered below in respect of section 4 of the Act. By section 3(3)–(5), prostitution and sexual exploitation covers three scenarios:

- the accused exercises control, direction or influence over prostitution by the trafficked person in a way which shows that the accused is aiding, abetting or compelling the prostitution (section 3(3));
- the accused involves the trafficked person in the making or production of obscene or indecent material (section 3(4));[5]
- the trafficked person is the victim of conduct which involves the commission of one of the main statutory sexual offences in Scots law or would constitute such an offence were it done in Scotland (section 3(5)).[6]

8.10 The first two categories replicate the earlier version of the offence in section 22 of the Criminal Justice (Scotland) Act 2003. The third category is new in Scots law, but equivalent wording is used in section 3(3) of the Modern Slavery Act 2015 and section 3(3) of the Human Trafficking and Exploitation (Criminal Justice and Support for Victims) Act (Northern Ireland) 2015. The combined effect of the three categories is to make section 1 a wide offence.

4 The first three follow the definition of exploitation in the international texts and similar definitions appear in the equivalent Acts for England and Wales and Northern Ireland.

5 Construed in accordance with s 52(1)(a) of the Civic Government (Scotland) Act 1982 and including images within s 51A of that Act: see Chapter 9.

6 The offences are: ss 1, 2, 7 and 10 of the Criminal Law (Consolidation) (Scotland) Act 1995 (incest, intercourse with a step-child, procuring of prostitution, and seduction, prostitution, etc of a girl under 16 by someone having parental responsibilities); ss 9 to 12 of the Protection of Children and Prevention of Sexual Offences (Scotland) Act 2005 (sexual services of children and child pornography); and all of the offences in Parts 1, 4 and 5 of the 2009 Act. The reference to conduct that 'would constitute such an offence were it done in Scotland' captures the situation where the sexual exploitation takes place outside Scotland and so includes, for instance, the situation where the victim is trafficked out of Scotland for the purposes of sexual exploitation elsewhere.

8.11 Sections 6 and 7 provide that the offence is aggravated when committed against a child (section 6) or when it is committed by a public official (section 7).[7] Section 5 provides for a general aggravation of any offence when it is connected with human trafficking. As with all statutory aggravations, the aggravations in sections 5 to 7 must be libelled in the indictment or complaint. In each case, evidence from a single source is sufficient to prove the aggravation.

8.12 As stated in Chapter 1, section 1 has extra-territorial effect. A UK national, habitual resident or body incorporated in the UK can commit the offence regardless of where the relevant action for the offence takes place (section 2(1) and (2)); any other person commits the offence if any part of the relevant action takes place in the United Kingdom or the relevant action is taken with a view to a person arriving in or entering into, departing from, or travelling within the United Kingdom (section 2(3)).

Section 4: slavery, servitude and forced labour

8.13 Article 4 of the European Convention on Human Rights prohibits slavery, servitude and forced or compulsory labour. ECHR Contracting States have a positive obligation to prevent it and to criminalise it. Section 4 seeks to fulfil that obligation. Similar provisions are found in section 1 of the Modern Slavery Act 2015 and section 1 of the Human Trafficking and Exploitation (Criminal Justice and Support for Victims) Act (Northern Ireland) 2015.

8.14 Section 4 is short and straightforward. Section 4(1) provides that a person commits an offence if he or she: (a) holds another person in slavery or servitude (and the circumstances are such that the person knows or ought to know that the other person is so held); or (b) requires another person to perform forced or compulsory labour (and similarly, the circumstances are such that the person knows or ought to know that the other person is being required to perform such labour). 'Knows or ought to know' is a standard, objective *mens rea* of knowledge or constructive knowledge.

8.15 Section 4(2) provides that these references to holding a person in slavery or servitude or requiring a person to perform forced or compulsory labour are to be construed in accordance with Article 4.[8] That requires consideration of how these terms have been interpreted by the European Court of Human Rights and, in

7 S 7 was in the original Bill as introduced. S 6 was added at stage 2 by opposition amendment (Alison McInnes MSP). Though not expressly stated in either case, both appear to implement in part Art 24 of the Council of Europe Convention, which obliges signatories to ensure that the offence of trafficking is aggravated by: (a) endangering the life of the victim; (b) being committed against a child; (c) being committed by a public official; (d) being committed within the framework of a criminal organisation. Though again there was no express consideration of whether it was unnecessary to legislate to implement (a) and (d), it is suggested that the latter would be covered by the aggravation of connection with serious organised crime in s 29 of the Criminal Justice and Licensing (Scotland) Act 2010 and the former, in appropriate cases, by the common law aggravation of 'to the danger of life'.

8 Similar provisions are contained in s 1(2) of the Modern Slavery Act 2015 and s 1(2) of the Human Trafficking and Exploitation (Criminal Justice and Support for Victims) Act (Northern Ireland) 2015.

turn, requires the Appeal Court to adopt a dynamic construction of section 4 and, if necessary, revise any interpretations it has given to the terms in section 4 if the definition of these terms evolves in the Strasbourg jurisprudence.[9]

8.16 In *Miller v HM Advocate*,[10] the sheriff had read that jurisprudence and had crafted her directions based upon it. The Appeal Court, having reviewed the same jurisprudence, approved the sheriff's directions. The Appeal Court observed 'slavery' carries connotations of ownership: it is 'the status or condition of a person over whom any or all of the powers attaching to the right of ownership are exercised'.[11] 'Servitude' is the obligation to provide one's services that is imposed by the use of coercion. It involves aggravated forced or compulsory labour in which the person feels his condition is permanent and unlikely to change. It is sufficient if the person's understanding is brought about or kept alive by those responsible for the situation. It is a particularly serious form of denial of freedom, including, in addition to the obligation to provide certain services to another, the obligation to live on the other person's property.[12] We detect no change in the Strasbourg jurisprudence on these definitions since *Miller* was decided.

8.17 *Miller* did not consider the term 'forced or compulsory labour'. In the text of Article 4 itself,[13] and in the Strasbourg jurisprudence, this is a single term or concept rather than two separate ones of 'forced labour' and 'compulsory labour'. The term means 'all work or service which is exacted from any person under the menace of any penalty and for which the said person has not offered himself voluntarily'.[14] The word 'penalty' is used in a broad sense: it may go as far as physical violence or restraint, but it can also take subtler forms, of a psychological nature, such as threats to denounce victims to the police or immigration authorities when their employment status is illegal.[15] In the context of forced prostitution, the Strasbourg Court has stressed that 'force' may encompass subtle forms of coercive conduct.[16]

8.18 As with section 1, the purpose of section 4 is to criminalise A's exploitation of B, including A's exploitation of B's consent to the work performed in circumstances where other, less vulnerable people might not have given that consent. To that end, section 4(3) and (4) provide two further aids to assessing whether a person has been

9 But with the lower courts, in the usual way, remaining bound by any binding Appeal court authority, notwithstanding any subsequent Strasbourg jurisprudence to the contrary.

10 2019 JC 61.

11 See *Miller* at paras 8 and 21. This, as the Court noted, is the classic definition of slavery in the 1926 Slavery Convention, adopted by the ECtHR in *Siliadin v France* (2006) 43 EHRR 16 at para 122.

12 *Miller* at para 21, based on *Siliadin* above, *Van Droogenbroeck v Belgium* (1982) EHRR 443 at para 124 and *CN and V v France*, no. 67724/09, 11 January 2013 at para 91.

13 Particularly Art 4(3), which states: 'For the purpose of this Article the term "forced or compulsory labour" shall not include…' and goes on to list four categories of work that will not constitute 'forced or compulsory labour'.

14 *Van der Mussele v Belgium*, 23 November 1983, Series A no. 70 at para 32, applying the definition used in the International Labour Organisation Convention No. 29, concerning Forced or Compulsory Labour.

15 *CN and V v France* at para 77: see n 12 above.

16 *SM v Croatia* [GC], no. 60561/14, 25 June 2020, at para 301.

held in slavery or servitude, or required to perform forced or compulsory labour. Section 4(3) provides that, in determining that, regard is to be had to any particular personal circumstances of the person (for example, the person being a child, their age, family relationships or health) that may make the person more vulnerable. Section 4(4) provides that the consent of the person does not preclude a determination that they are being held in slavery or servitude, or required to perform forced or compulsory labour.

SEXUAL EXPLOITATION, ORGANISED PROSTITUTION AND ASSOCIATED OFFENCES

8.19 This section sets out the offences in sections 7 to 13 of the Criminal Law (Consolidation) (Scotland) Act 1995. Their common theme is the suppression of sexual exploitation of others through prostitution. In each case the offence is committed by the person procuring, controlling or profiting from the prostitution, rather than the person physically providing the sexual services. The sections have been heavily amended to repeal certain of the offences contained in them. In this chapter, we refer only to the offences currently in force. Certain of the repealed offences in the 1995 Act are considered in Chapter 12. The 1995 Act is, as its name suggests, a consolidation Act. Many of the offences in it were derived, with little or no amendment, from the Sexual Offences (Scotland) Act 1976 and ultimately from the Criminal Law (Amendment) Act 1885 and Immoral Traffic (Scotland) Act 1902. We have referred where appropriate to cases decided under the previous Acts.

Section 7: 'procuring'

8.20 Section 7, in its current form,[17] criminalises four forms of procurement or attempted procurement, each set out in section 7(1). It criminalises procuring or attempting to procure:

(a) any woman under 21 years of age or girl to have unlawful sexual intercourse with any other person or persons in any part of the world;
(b) any woman or girl to become a common prostitute in any part of the world;
(c) any woman or girl to leave the United Kingdom, with intent that she may become an inmate of or frequent a brothel elsewhere; or

17 S 7(2) also criminalised: (a) procuring or attempting to procure, by threats or intimidation, unlawful intercourse in any part of the world; (b) procuring the same by false pretences or false representations; and (c) applying or administering to, or causing to be taken by, any woman or girl any drug, matter or thing, with intent to stupefy or overpower so as to enable any person to have unlawful sexual intercourse with the woman or girl. S 7(3) provided that inducing a married woman to have sexual intercourse by impersonating her husband was deemed to be rape. Both were replaced and repealed by the Sexual Offences (Scotland) Act 2009 with effect from 1 December 2010.

(d) any woman or girl to leave her usual place of abode in the United Kingdom, with intent that she may, for the purposes of prostitution, become an inmate of or frequent a brothel in any part of the world.

8.21 Of the four, (c) and (d) will now have some overlap with human trafficking in section 1 of the 2015 Act (see above). All four editions of *Gordon, Criminal Law* have noted the absence of reported Scottish cases on the meaning of 'procure', but have gone on to note the English case of *R v Christian*[18] as likely to be persuasive should the point ever arise.[19] *Christian* found that, for the purposes of procuring a woman to be a prostitute, it was not aimed at brothel-keepers but rather at those who get girls by fraud or persuasion, or by inviting them to prostitution if they cannot get money in any other way. Rook and Ward (at para 10.129) also cite *Christian* with approval, adding (on the basis of *R v Broadfoot*)[20] that it requires the accused to bring about a course of conduct that the prostitute would not have embarked on spontaneously or of her own volition. For the uncertainty created by the use of the word 'become' in (b), see our comments in Chapter 6, **6.22** and further discussion there of the English authority *R v Ubolcharoen*.[21]

8.22 It has been quite some time since the meaning of 'brothel' (either in section 7(1)(c) or sections 8, 11 and 12 of the 1995 Act or under previous statutes) has been considered by the Appeal Court. The last reported decision of note appears to have been *Milne v Nicol*,[22] where the Appeal Court was content that, on its facts, a boarding house to which prostitutes began bringing their clients was a brothel. Extended reviews of the English case law are set out in the fourth edition of *Gordon, Criminal Law* at 41.03 and Rook and Ward at 13.23 to 13.31. Rook and Ward distil the requirements in the English case law to: (i) that the premises be a house or building (or part thereof); (ii) that it be used by more than one person (that is, not just a place from which a single prostitute plies their trade); (iii) that it be used for the purposes of sex (though not necessarily in return for financial or other reward). That captures the essence of what is an ordinary term, but in the absence of any recent Scottish authority, we offer no view on the correctness of those requirements or on whether the Scottish courts would follow the English authorities, many of which date from the sixties and earlier.

Section 8(3): abduction and unlawful detention

8.23 Section 8(3)[23] makes it an offence for a person to detain any woman or girl against her will either: (a) in any premises with the intent that she have unlawful

18 (1913) 23 Cox CC 541.

19 See, most recently, the fourth edition at para 41.06.

20 [1976] 3 All ER 753).

21 [2009] EWCA Crim 3263.

22 1965 SCCR (Supp) 8.

23 Until its repeal by Criminal Justice (Scotland) Act 2003 on 27 June 2003, s 8(1) made it an offence for any person who, with intent that any unmarried girl under the age of 18 years should have unlawful sexual intercourse with men or with a particular man, took or caused to be taken such girl out of the possession and against the will of her father or mother, or any other person having the lawful care or charge of her.

sexual intercourse with men or with a particular man; or (b) in any brothel. By section 8(4) detention is deemed to occur when the person, with the intent to compel or induce the women or girl to remain, withholds her clothing ('wearing apparel') or property, or threatens legal proceedings if she takes away any clothing lent or supplied. Section 8(4) does not of course exclude detention by other means. For this offence, there is likely to be significant overlap with section 4 of the Human Trafficking and Exploitation (Scotland) Act 2015 to the stage where any prosecution is likely to be under that section rather than section 8(3).

Section 9: permitting a girl to use premises for intercourse

8.24 A person commits an offence under section 9 if, being the owner or occupier of any premises (or having, acting or assisting in the management or control of any premises), he or she induces or knowingly suffers any girl under 16 to use those premises for the purpose of having unlawful sexual intercourse with men or with a particular man. 'Suffers' simply means 'permits'. Section 9(2) gives the defence that the person had reasonable cause to believe the girl was over 16. That is at odds with most other statutes because it applies irrespective of the age of the girl: most other statutes do not allow a defence of reasonable belief when the girl is under 13. Clearly, though, the younger the girl, the less likelihood of showing a reasonable belief that she is over 16. Section 9(2A) provides that this defence is not available to someone who has previously been charged with a relevant sexual offence, convicted of a relevant foreign offence or in respect of whom a sexual harm order in force but the lawfulness of this provision must be doubted in light of *AB v HM Advocate*[24] (see Chapter 4 at **4.18** and **4.19**).

8.25 There is a substantial overlap between this offence and section 12 of the Protection of Children and Prevention of Sexual Offences (Scotland) Act 2005: arranging or facilitating the provision by a child of sexual services or child pornography. Anyone permitting a girl to use premises for intercourse, contrary to section 9 of the 1995 Act, is likely to be facilitating the provision of sexual services by the girl, contrary to section 12 of the 2005 Act, and it may be that, in such a case, the Crown would prefer a charge under the more modern 2005 Act.

Section 10: seduction, prostitution, etc, of a girl under 16

8.26 Section 10 is directed at those with parental responsibilities for, or those having charge or care of, a girl under 16. Under section 10(1), any person with those responsibilities, or with that charge or care, commits an offence if he or she causes or encourages: (a) the seduction or prostitution of the girl; (b) unlawful sexual intercourse with the girl; or (c) the commission of an indecent assault upon her.

24 2017 SC (UKSC) 101.

'Parental responsibilities' means parental responsibilities as that term is defined in section 1(3) of the Children (Scotland) Act 1995.[25] No definition of charge or care is given.

8.27 By section 10(2), a person is deemed to have caused or encouraged these matters in (a) to (c) if he knowingly allows the girl to concert with, or to enter or continue in the employment of, any prostitute or person of 'known immoral character'. The offence is not limited only to that situation, simply that the person is *deemed* to have caused or encouraged the matters in (a) to (c) in that situation.

8.28 By section 10(3), the offence is also committed if the person causes or encourages the commission of one of the sexual offences in sections 19 to 26 and 29 to 36 of the 2009 Act.[26] The reason for not including section 18 (rape of a young child) and section 28 (intercourse with an older child) in section 10(3) would appear to be that causing or encouraging the intercourse required for those sections is already caught by section 10(1)(b) above: causing or encouraging 'unlawful sexual intercourse' with the girl.

Section 11: trading in prostitution and brothel-keeping

8.29 Section 11 creates three offences. Section 11(1)(a) makes it an offence for a male person to knowingly live wholly, or in part, on the earnings of prostitution (most commonly, though not limited to, 'pimping'[27]). By section 11(3), unless the accused can satisfy the court to the contrary, the offence is deemed to have been committed if the accused is proven either: (i) to live with or to be habitually in the company of a prostitute; or (ii) to have exercised control, direction or influence over the movements of a prostitute in such a manner as to show that he was aiding, abetting or compelling her prostitution with any other person or generally. A woman who is proven, for gain, to have exercised similar control, direction or influence, is, by section 11(4), liable to the same penalties for the offence and may be convicted on an art-and-part basis of the offence under section 11(1)(a).[28] The offence is rarely employed and it is suggested that any particularly egregious pimping (through force or other means) would be charged as requiring another person to perform forced or

25 The list of those who have parental responsibilities is given in s 3 of the Children (Scotland) Act 1995. These are: the child's mother; his or her father when married or in a civil partnership with the mother at conception or subsequently, or when registered on the birth certificate; parents by virtue of the Human Fertilisation and Embryology Act; and anyone given parental responsibilities by a court order (such as adoptive parents or guardians).

26 Before the entry into force of the 2009 Act, s 10(3) provided that the offence applied to a contravention of s 6 of the 1995 Act (indecent behaviour towards a girl between 12 and 16): that is, a s 10 offence would be committed if a person with parental responsibilities or charge or care of a girl under 16 caused or encouraged a s 6 offence.

27 The equivalent English offence was held to apply to taxi drivers knowingly conveying clients to prostitutes in *Calvert v Mayes* [1954] 1 QB 342 and *R v Farrugia* (1979) 69 Cr App R 108. It can also be satisfied by knowingly letting accommodation: *Soni v HM Advocate* 1970 SLT 275 (decided under the previous version of the offence in the Immoral Traffic (Scotland) Act 1902).

28 *Reid v HM Advocate* 1999 JC 54.

compulsory labour, contrary to section 4 of the Human Trafficking and Exploitation (Scotland) Act 2015 above.

8.30 The second offence is in section 11(1)(b), which makes it an offence for a male person in any public place to persistently solicit or importune for immoral purposes. This section 11(1)(b) offence is considered in the section on solicitation below at **8.39** and **8.40**.

8.31 The third offence is in section 11(5). This criminalises brothel keeping. The offence is committed by: (a) any person who keeps or manages or acts or assists in the management of a brothel; (b) any tenant, lessee, occupier or person in charge of any premises who knowingly permits such premises (or any part it) to be used as a brothel or for the purposes of habitual prostitution; and (c) any lessor or landlord (or his/her agent) who lets premises (or any part of it) knowing that the premises (or any part of it) are or are to be used as a brothel, or is wilfully a party to the continued use of the premises (or any part of it) as a brothel. For the meaning of brothel, see **8.22** above. This offence and the following offence in section 12 apply equally to heterosexual and homosexual activity: section 12A.

Section 12: allowing a child to be in a brothel

8.32 Section 12 makes it an offence for any person having parental responsibilities for, or having charge or care of, a child over 4 and under 16 years of age to allow that child to reside in or frequent a brothel. Like section 10 of the Act, 'parental responsibilities' means parental responsibilities as that term is defined in section 1(3) of the Children (Scotland) Act 1995.

Section 13: living on the earnings of another from male prostitution

8.33 Section 13 originally criminalised a range of homosexual offences, including, in section 13(9), knowingly living wholly, or in part, on the earnings of another from male prostitution. The other offences initially contained in section 13 – to the extent that they are ever likely to be prosecuted now – are discussed in Chapter 12. The only remaining part of section 13 is section 13(9), which now simply provides that a person who knowingly lives wholly or in part on the earnings of another from male prostitution shall be liable: (a) on conviction on indictment, to imprisonment for a term not exceeding seven years, to a fine, or to both; (b) on summary conviction, to imprisonment for a term not exceeding 12 months, to a fine not exceeding the statutory maximum, or to both.[29]

[29] Until 12 December 2010, the maximum sentences were, on summary conviction, six months' imprisonment and, on indictment, two years' imprisonment. Until 30 November 2010, s 13(9) also covered soliciting or importuning any male person for the purpose of procuring the commission of a homosexual act. This part of s 13(9) was repealed by the Sexual Offences (Scotland) Act 2009.

SOLICITATION

8.34 Although prostitution is not a crime in Scotland, there are three offences covering solicitation of prostitution. Section 46 of the Civic Government (Scotland) Act 1982 criminalises solicitation by prostitutes themselves. Section 11(1)(b) of the Criminal Law (Consolidation) (Scotland) Act 1995 criminalises solicitation on behalf of a prostitute. Section 1 of the Prostitution (Public Places) (Scotland) Act 2007 criminalises solicitation of a prostitute by a client/purchaser.

Section 46 of the Civic Government (Scotland) Act 1982

8.35 Section 46(1) of the Civic Government (Scotland) Act 1982 creates a single offence of soliciting and importuning by prostitutes that can be committed in three ways. It provides that a prostitute (whether male or female) who for the purposes of prostitution: (i) loiters in a public place; (ii) solicits in a public place or in any other place so as to be seen from a public place; or (iii) importunes any person who is in a public place is guilty of an offence.

8.36 'Loiters', 'solicits' and 'importunes' are not defined but little difficulty arises in this context. Loiter, in its ordinary meaning, is clear, meaning to linger in a place. Solicit and importune overlap in meaning (importune, in its modern definition, just means to solicit for the purposes of prostitution) but the meaning of the statute is clear: offering oneself as a prostitute.

8.37 The offence can only be committed by a prostitute. This is a special capacity: that is, it will be averred in the complaint and held as admitted unless challenged. When challenged it will be necessary for the Crown to prove that the person was a prostitute prior to soliciting on the occasion alleged.[30]

8.38 'Public place' is defined by section 133 of the 1982 Act as any place (whether a thoroughfare or not) to which the public have unrestricted access including the doorways or entrances of premises abutting on any such place; and any common passage, close, court, stair, garden or yard pertinent to any tenement or group of separately owned houses. Section 46(2) extends that definition to include: (a) any place to which at the material time the public are permitted to have access, whether on payment or otherwise; and (b) any public conveyance other than a taxi or hire car.

Section 11(1)(b) of the Criminal Law (Consolidation) (Scotland) Act 1995

8.39 Section 11(1)(b) makes it an offence for a male person in any public place to persistently solicit or importune for immoral purposes. The original intention of Parliament in passing it has been lost in the mists of time because the provision has been successively re-enacted without discussion or amendment since it was first

[30] *White v Allan* 1985 SLT 396 and *Allan v McGraw* 1986 SCCR 257.

enacted in section 1 of the Vagrancy Act 1898 and section 1 of the Immoral Traffic (Scotland) Act 1902. Both Professors Chalmers and Leverick in the fourth edition of *Gordon, Criminal Law*[31] and Professor Gane in *Sexual Offences*[32] are clear that it applies to a person who solicits on behalf of a prostitute but are not able to say with certainty that it also applies to someone seeking sex from a prostitute. The point has become moot with the passage of the Prostitution (Public Places) (Scotland) Act 2007.

8.40 'Solicit' and 'importune' carry the same meaning as they would in section 46 above. From the English authorities on similar enactments, 'persistently' is understood to be on at least two occasions.[33]

Section 1: Prostitution (Public Places) (Scotland) Act 2007

8.41 The original purpose of the Prostitution (Public Places) (Scotland) Bill 2006 was to repeal section 46 and have a single regime applying equally to purchasers and sellers of sex. The purpose was to shift the focus from prosecution of sellers of sex to prosecution of buyers because until that point there was no statutory offence of a solicitation that covered purchasers.[34] Under this regime, it would have been an offence for either a purchaser and seller to solicit sex in a public place, or to loiter in a public place for that purpose. In each case, however, the soliciting or loitering would have to take place in circumstances in which a reasonable person would consider it likely to cause alarm, offence, or nuisance. After criticism from the Local Government and Transport Committee,[35] the Bill was heavily amended before enactment. The Bill was re-drafted to refer only to purchasers and, at the same time, to retain section 46. This was done because of the Committee's concerns that a new offence covering both purchasers and sellers would lead to more prosecutions of sellers. It was also thought that repealing section 46 and creating a single offence covering both purchasers and sellers would not achieve the Bill's aim of shifting the focus to prosecution of buyers.[36] It is not entirely clear why it was thought that limiting the new offence to purchasers *and* retaining section 46 would achieve that purpose, but that was the approach taken. The need to show a likelihood of alarm, offence or nuisance was also removed because of the Committee's concern that it

31 At para 41.12.

32 Gane, C, *Sexual Offences* (Butterworths, 1992) at p 157.

33 *Darroch v DPP* (1990) 91 Cr App R 378.

34 See paras 2, 5 and 6 of the Policy Memorandum for the Bill: https://archive2021.parliament.scot/S2_Bills/Prostitution%20(Public%20Places)%20(Scotland)%20Bill/b69-introd-pm.pdf. It would be possible for a purchaser's behaviour to amount to a breach of the peace at common law, but only if the manner in which the soliciting took place was such as to cause alarm to ordinary people and threaten serious disturbance to the community such that the normal elements of breach of the peace, set out in *Smith v Donnelly* 2002 JC 65 at para 17, are met. The application of breach of the peace to sexual misconduct generally is discussed in Chapter 10 and in the fourth edition of *Gordon, Criminal Law* at para 47.15.

35 Local Government and Transport Committee, 1st report, 2007 (Session 2) Stage 1: Report on the Prostitution (Public Places) (Scotland) Bill: https://archive2021.parliament.scot/S2_LocalGovernmentandTransportCommittee/Reports/lgr07-01.pdf.

36 Committee report at paras 14, 26 and 114.

would lead to zones where, so long as trade was conducted discreetly away from the public, no offence would be committed.[37]

8.42 Section 1 of the Prostitution (Public Places) (Scotland) Act 2007 therefore creates two offences: soliciting and loitering, in each case applying only to purchasers. Section 1(1) provides that a person who, for the purpose of obtaining the services of a person engaged in prostitution, solicits in a relevant place commits an offence. It is immaterial whether or not the accused is on public transport or (to include kerb crawlers) in a motor vehicle: section 1(2)(a) and (b). It is also immaterial whether or not the person solicited is in fact engaged in prostitution (section 1(2)(c)): the purchaser who approaches someone thinking that he or she is a prostitute but who is in fact not is just as guilty of the offence.

8.43 Section 1(3) covers loitering. It provides that a person who loiters in a relevant place so that in all the circumstances it may reasonably be inferred that the person was doing so for the purpose of obtaining the services of a person engaged in prostitution commits an offence. Again, it is immaterial whether or not the accused is on public transport or in a motor vehicle: section 1(4). The addition of a reference to a motor vehicle in section 1(4) was an amendment insisted on by the Committee to ensure that kerb crawlers would also be covered by the loitering offence and not just the soliciting offence.[38]

8.44 For the purposes of both offences, 'a relevant place' is simply a public place either as that term is defined in section 133 of the Civic Government (Scotland) Act 1982 or a place to which, at the material time, the public are permitted to have access (whether on payment or otherwise): section 1(6). For the purposes of section 1(1), it includes a place visible from a public place (ibid).

8.45 The offences in the 2007 Act are the subject of Lord Advocate's guidelines to the police.[39] The guidelines state that the offences should not be regarded as minor and there is a strong presumption in favour of formal action, even in respect of first offenders (paragraph 11). The use of direct measures (such as warnings or fixed penalty notices) is not appropriate (paragraph 12), but the guidelines do allow for local enforcement strategies appropriate to the needs of communities (paragraphs 13 and 14) and for the exercise of discretion in individual cases (paragraph 15).

FEMALE GENITAL MUTILATION, VIRGINITY TESTING AND HYMENOPLASTY

8.46 These offences reflect the Scottish and Westminster Parliaments' desire to eliminate cultural practices which infringe on female sexual autonomy.

37 Ibid at para 87.
38 Para 3 of its report.
39 https://www.copfs.gov.uk/publications/lord-advocate-s-guidelines-soliciting-and-loitering-offences/.

8.47 The current law on female genital mutilation is contained in the Prohibition of Female Genital Mutilation (Scotland) Act 2005.[40] Section 1 makes it an offence to excise, infibulate or otherwise mutilate the whole or any part of the labia majora, labia minora, prepuce of the clitoris, clitoris or vagina of another person. There is a defence in section 1(3) and (4) for any medical professional who performs a surgical operation necessary for the person's physical or mental health or surgery connected with labour or birth. By section 3 it is an offence to aid, abet, counsel, procure or incite someone to commit the offence, including someone outside the UK. The two offences have extra-territorial effect for UK nationals or residents (section 4).[41]

8.48 Conducting virginity testing and hymenoplasty (reconstructing the hymen) were criminalised by the Health and Care Act 2022 on the basis that there is no known examination that can prove whether a woman has had vaginal intercourse and no clinical reason for hymenoplasty, and thus that each practice is a form of honour-based abuse.[42] For Scotland, the virginity-testing offences are contained in sections 140–142 of the 2022 Act and cover virginity testing itself (section 140), offering to carry it out (section 141), and aiding, abetting, counselling, procuring, or inciting it (section 142). The hymenoplasty offences are: section 152, carrying out hymenoplasty; section 153, offering to carry it out; and section 154, aiding, abetting, counselling, procuring, or inciting it. The six offences have extra-territorial effect.

TABLES OF OFFENCES

8.49

Table 8.1

The Human Trafficking and Exploitation (Scotland) Act 2015 offences		
Offence	**Dates in force**	**Maximum sentence**
Section 1: human trafficking	31 May 2016 to present	Summary: 12 months' imprisonment or a fine (or both) Indictment: life imprisonment or a fine (or both)

40 This replaced the Prohibition of Female Circumcision Act 1985. The corresponding legislation for the rest of the United Kingdom is the Female Genital Mutilation Act 2003.

41 When it enters into force, s 5Q of the Act, a provision inserted by the Female Genital Mutilation (Protection and Guidance) (Scotland) Act 2020, will also create a series of offences relating to breach of female genital mutilation protection orders (orders created by the 2020 Act, but also yet not in force). No date for the entry into force of the 2020 Act has been fixed.

42 See for instance UK Government's multi-agency guidance on virginity testing and hymenoplasty at https://www.gov.uk/government/publications/virginity-testing-and-hymenoplasty-multi-agency-guidance/virginity-testing-and-hymenoplasty-multi-agency-guidance#:~:text=multi%2Dagency%2Dguidance-,Purpose%20of%20the%20guidance,these%20things%20outside%20the%20UK.

The Human Trafficking and Exploitation (Scotland) Act 2015 offences		
Offence	**Dates in force**	**Maximum sentence**
Section 4: slavery, servitude and forced or compulsory labour	31 May 2016 to present	Summary: 12 months' imprisonment or a fine (or both) Indictment: life imprisonment or a fine (or both)

Sexual exploitation, organised prostitution and associated offences: the Criminal Law (Consolidation) (Scotland) Act 1995		
Offence	**Dates in force**	**Maximum sentence**
Section 7: procuring	1 April 1996 to present	Summary: 12 months' imprisonment (initially three months until 10 December 2007 when section 45 of the Criminal Proceedings etc. (Reform) (Scotland) Act 2007 entered into force) Indictment: two years' imprisonment
Section 8: abduction and unlawful detention	1 April 1996 to present	Summary: initially three months' imprisonment, now 12 months (section 45 of the 2007 Act) Indictment: two years' imprisonment
Section 9: permitting a girl to use premises for intercourse	1 April 1996 to present	When the girl is under 13: indictment-only offence and a maximum sentence of life imprisonment When the girl is between 13 and 16: summary 12 months' imprisonment; indictment two years' imprisonment
Section 10: seduction, prostitution, etc of a girl under 16	1 April 1996 to present	Summary: initially three months' imprisonment, now 12 months' imprisonment (section 45 of the 2007 Act) Indictment: two years' imprisonment

Table 8.1 *Further offences to protect vulnerable groups from sexual exploitation*

Sexual exploitation, organised prostitution and associated offences: the Criminal Law (Consolidation) (Scotland) Act 1995		
Offence	**Dates in force**	**Maximum sentence**
Section 11: trading in prostitution and brothel-keeping Section 11(1)(a): imprisonment or a fine knowingly living on the earnings of prostitution (For section 11(1)(b), see the section on the solicitation offences below) Section 11(5): brothel keeping	1 April 1996 to present	For both section 11(1)(a) and section 11(5): Summary conviction: 12 months' imprisonment or a fine (or both) Indictment: seven years' imprisonment or a fine (or both)
Section 12: allowing a child to be in a brothel	1 April 1996 to present	Summary: initially six months' imprisonment (now 12 months' imprisonment by virtue of section 45 of the 2007 Act) or a fine (or both) Indictment: six months' imprisonment or a fine (or both)
Section 13(9): living on the earnings of another from male prostitution	1 April 1996 to present	Summary: initially six months' imprisonment (now 12 months' imprisonment by virtue of section 45 of the 2007 Act) or a fine (or both) Indictment: seven years' imprisonment or fine (or both)

Solicitation		
Offence	**Dates in force**	**Maximum sentence**
Section 46 of the Civic Government (Scotland) Act 1982	1 April 1983 to present	Summary only: fine at level two on the standard scale (currently £500)

Solicitation		
Offence	**Dates in force**	**Maximum sentence**
Section 11(1)(b) of the Criminal Law (Consolidation) (Scotland) 1995	1 April 1996 to present	Summary: 12 months' imprisonment Indictment: two years' imprisonment
Section 1 of the Prostitution (Public Places) (Scotland) Act 2007 (soliciting and loitering by purchasers)	15 October 2007 to present	Fine not exceeding level three on the standard scale (currently £1,000)

Prohibition of Female Genital Mutilation (Scotland) Act 2005		
Offence	**Dates in force**	**Maximum sentence**
Section 1: female genital mutilation	1 September 2005 to present	Summary: initially six months' imprisonment (now 12 months' imprisonment by virtue of section 45 of the 2007 Act) or a fine (or both) Indictment: 14 years' imprisonment or a fine (or both)
Section 3: aiding and abetting female genital mutilation	1 September 2005 to present	Summary: initially six months' imprisonment (now 12 months' imprisonment by virtue of section 45 of the 2007 Act) or a fine (or both) Indictment: 14 years' imprisonment or a fine (or both)

Health and Care Act 2002		
Offence	**Dates in force**	**Maximum sentence**
Section 140: virginity testing	1 July 2022 to present	Summary: 12 months' imprisonment or a fine (or both) Indictment: five years' imprisonment or a fine (or both)

Table 8.1 *Further offences to protect vulnerable groups from sexual exploitation*

Health and Care Act 2002		
Offence	**Dates in force**	**Maximum sentence**
Section 141: offering to carry out virginity testing	1 July 2022 to present	As above
Section 142: aiding or abetting, etc, a person to carry out virginity testing	1 July 2022 to present	As above
Section 152: carrying out hymenoplasty	1 July 2022 to present	As above
Section 153: offering to carry out hymenoplasty	1 July 2022 to present	As above
Section 154: aiding or abetting, etc, a person to carry out hymenoplasty	1 July 2022 to present	As above

Chapter 9

Obscene material, extreme pornography and indecent images offences

INTRODUCTION

9.01 We set out in this chapter the main offences relating to obscene material, extreme pornography and indecent images of children. The first two are relatively rare, though the latter has figured in High Court indictments alongside other charges of serious contact offending. The internet has led to a sharp increase in cases involving indecent images of children and such charges are commonly seen in Sheriff Court indictments and, occasionally, in the High Court of Justiciary if the accused has a record of analogous offending. The provisions concerning these various offences are contained in sections 51 to 52C of the Civic Government (Scotland) Act 1982 ('the 1982 Act'). The structure of this part of the Act is to provide for an offence creating provision and to set out the basis upon which a defence will be available to a person accused of a relevant offence, with the onus being on the accused to establish that defence on the balance of probabilities.

OBSCENE MATERIAL

9.02 For practical purposes the publishing, selling or distributing of obscene materials is governed by section 51 of the Civic Government (Scotland) Act 1982.[1]

9.03 Section 51 subsection (1) of the 1982 Act provides that it shall be an offence to display any obscene material in a public place or in any other place where it can be seen by the public. Subsection (2) provides that it shall be an offence to publish, sell[2] or distribute or, with a view to its eventual sale or distribution, make, print or keep any obscene materials. A separate offence is created by subsection (2A) which provides that any person who: (a) is responsible for the inclusion of any obscene

1 It may still be an offence at common law to publish an obscene work which is intended to corrupt public morals – see *Gordon, Criminal Law* (4th edn, Sweet & Maxwell 2016) para 50.01.

2 Which includes offers for sale – *Rees v Lees* 1996 SCCR 601.

material in a programme included in a programme service;[3] or (b) with a view to its eventual inclusion in a programme so included, makes, prints, has or keeps any obscene material, commits an offence.

9.04 'Material' includes any book, magazine, bill, paper, print, film, tape, disk or other kind of recording (whether of sound or visual images or both), photograph, drawing, painting representation, model or figure.[4]

9.05 The 1982 Act does not provide any guidance on what constitutes 'obscene' for the purposes of these provisions. The common law position is that material is obscene if it is likely to deprave or corrupt the morals of those subjected to it.[5] This would be the test to be applied by the decision maker in determining whether the statutory meaning of obscene had been made out.

9.06 For the purposes of section 51 a 'public place' means any place (whether a thoroughfare or not) to which the public have unrestricted access and includes the doorways or entrances of premises abutting on any such place and any common passage, close, court, stair, garden or yard pertinent to any tenement or group of separately owned houses. The meaning also extends to any place to which at the material time the public are permitted to have access, whether on payment or otherwise.[6]

9.07 The offences created by section 51 do not apply in relation to any matter included in the performance of a play, which includes dramatic pieces and ballet.[7]

9.08 In a prosecution for an offence under section 51 it will be a defence for the person accused to prove that he used all due diligence to avoid committing the offence.[8]

9.09 The offences provided for by section 51 are not specified within Schedule 3 to the Sexual Offences Act 2003 as being included within those which attract the notification requirements of Part 2 of that Act. However paragraph 60 of Schedule 3 provides that the court may, in imposing sentence, determine that there was a significant sexual aspect to the offender's behaviour in committing the offence and order that the requirements should apply.

EXTREME PORNOGRAPHY

9.10 Section 51A of the 1982 Act provides that it shall be an offence for a person to be in possession of an extreme pornographic image, namely an image which is

3 S 51(8) provides that 'programme' and 'programme service' have the same meaning as in the Broadcasting Act 1990.
4 S 51(8).
5 *Ingram v Macari* 1983 JC 1.
6 S 51(8) and s 133.
7 S 51(6). The definition of a 'play' is given in the Theatres Act 1968, s 18(1).
8 S 51(4).

obscene, pornographic and extreme. The provision was inserted into the 1982 Act by the Criminal Justice and Licensing (Scotland) Act 2010 and is modelled on the equivalent provision applicable in the rest of the UK, section 63 of the Criminal Justice and Immigration Act 2008; although there are some differences between section 51A and section 63,[9] should any questions of interpretation arise, any judicial decisions on section 63 are likely to be persuasive in the Scottish courts.

9.11 For the purposes of section 51A, an image is to be viewed as a moving or still image made by any means, or data stored by any means which is capable of conversion into such an image[10]. An image is to be defined as being obscene by applying the common law test mentioned at **9.05**. An image will be pornographic if it is of such a nature that it must reasonably be assumed to have been made solely or principally for the purpose of sexual arousal.[11]

9.12 Subsections (4) and (5) provide guidance on how to determine whether an image which forms part of a series of images is to be viewed as pornographic. The question is to be determined by reference to the image itself and any context for the image which is provided by the series of images and its context within that series. Where an image may be viewed as pornographic if considered on its own, it may be found not to be pornographic if it forms an integral part of a narrative constituted by a series of images which are not of such a nature that they must reasonably be assumed to have been made solely or principally for the purpose of sexual arousal.

9.13 Subsection (6) provides that an image is to be considered 'extreme' if it depicts in an explicit and realistic way any one of five specified things, namely:

- an act which takes or threatens a person's life.
- an act which results, or is likely to result, in a person's severe injury.
- rape or other non-consensual penetrative sexual activity.
- sexual activity involving (directly or indirectly) a human corpse.
- an act which involves sexual activity between a person and an animal (or the carcase of an animal).

9.14 In determining whether an image depicts any of the acts mentioned regard may be had to how the image is or was described, any signs accompanying it and,

9 In s 51A the image must be obscene, pornographic and extreme; in s 63, the image must be extreme and pornographic, but there is no direct requirement that the image be obscene, rather that it be 'grossly offensive, disgusting or otherwise of an obscene character'. In s 51A, one of the ways an image will be extreme is if it depicts any severe injury; the equivalent provision in s 63 requires severe injury to the anus, breasts or genitals. Likewise, an image will be extreme for the purpose of s 51A if it depicts the taking or threatening of a person's life; s 63 refers only to threatening a person's life. S 51A but not s 63 gives further guidance on assessing whether an image depicts an act (by looking at how the image is described, any sounds and context): subsection (7). The defence that the accused directly participated in the act depicted extends in s 51C(4)(e), but not s 63, to the situation where the animal or its carcase was not real.

10 S 51A(9).

11 S 51A(3).

where the image forms an integral part of a narrative constituted by a series of images, any sounds accompanying the series and the context provided by that narrative.[12]

Excluded images

9.15 Certain kinds of images, known as 'excluded images', do not fall within the scope of the extreme pornography provisions and no offence is committed by their possession. An excluded image is one which is all or part of a 'classified work', meaning a video work in respect of which a classification certificate has been issued by a designated authority. The consequence of this is that films classified under the Video Recordings Act 1984 fall to be viewed as classified work for these purposes.[13] An image will no longer be classified as an excluded image if it is extracted from a classified work and it must reasonably be assumed to have been extracted from the work solely or principally for the purpose of sexual arousal. In determining whether this was the purpose of any such extraction, regard may be had to how the image was stored, how the image is or was described, any sounds accompanying the image and, where the image forms an integral part of a narrative constituted by a series of images, any sounds accompanying that series and the context provided by that narrative.[14]

Defences

9.16 Certain defences are provided for within the ambit of the extreme pornography provisions. Section 51C subsections (1) and (2) provide that it will be a defence for the person charged to establish that he had a legitimate reason for being in possession of the image concerned, or that he had not seen the image concerned and did not know nor had any cause to suspect it to be an extreme pornographic image, or that he was sent the image concerned without any prior request having been made by or on behalf of him and did not keep it for an unreasonable time. Where a 'legitimate reason' defence is advanced, it will be a pure question of fact, for the court (or jury) to determine, in each individual case whether or not the defence has been established. In conducting such an assessment the court (or jury) will be entitled to bring a measure of scepticism to bear upon the inquiry and should not conclude too readily that the defence is made out.[15]

9.17 Section 51C subsections (3) and (4) provide that it will be a defence for the person charged to establish that he directly participated in the act depicted in the image and that it did not actually have the characteristics specified in section 51A(6).

12 S 51A (7).
13 S 51B(1), (2) and (5).
14 S 51B(3) and (4).
15 *Atkins v DPP* [2000] 1 WLR 1427 dealing with the defence available to a charge of possessing an indecent photograph where the same wording appears.

So, for example, it would be open to the accused to establish that the act depicted in the image did not actually take or threaten a person's life, or that none of the other examples specified in that subsection were in fact present. This defence is not available if the accused shows, gives or offers for sale the image to any person who is not also a direct participant in the act depicted.[16] As with the defence provided for by section 51, it will be for the person charged to establish any of the section 51C defences on the balance of probabilities.

Notification requirements

9.18 On conviction for an offence under section 51A of the 1982 Act the offender will be subject to the notification requirements specified in Part 2 of the Sexual Offences Act 2003 if certain conditions are met. These are that the offender was aged 18 or over and is sentenced in respect of the offence to a term of imprisonment of more than 12 months and the court determines that it is appropriate that Part 2 of the Act should apply in relation to him.[17]

INDECENT PHOTOGRAPHS OF CHILDREN

9.19 The acts of taking, making, showing and distributing indecent photographs of children each constitute a criminal offence, as does the possession of such images. Sections 52 to 52C of the 1982 Act set out the relevant statutory provisions. As with the preceding provisions relating to obscene material and extreme pornography, the structure of this part of the 1982 Act is to provide for an offence creating provision and to set out the basis upon which a defence will be available to a person accused of a relevant offence, with the onus being on the accused to establish that defence on the balance of probabilities. Separately, these provisions identify certain other circumstances in which criminal liability will not attach to an individual who commits what would otherwise be an offence under the relevant provision.

9.20 The conduct criminalised by these sections of the 1982 Act constitutes a serious form of offending:

> 'Viewing, downloading and distributing indecent images of children is part of the process of child sexual abuse. Each photograph represents the serious abuse of the child depicted. Those who access this material through the internet bear responsibility for the abuse by creating a demand for the material …. Such offences can properly be said to contribute to the pain, discomfort and fear suffered by children who are physically abused, and to the psychological harm

16 S 51C(5).

17 Sexual Offences Act 2003, Sch 3 para 44A.

that the children concerned would suffer from knowing that others would get perverted pleasure from looking at the material.'[18]

9.21 The literature review on offences involving indecent images of children, published by the Scottish Sentencing Council in August 2022, notes at page 7 that:

> 'Research on IIOC [Indecent images of children] victims has found that the production of IIOC can cause severe, long-term psychological, and emotional harm, including damage to a child's sense of privacy, dignity, and autonomy, all exacerbated by knowing that the images continue to be out in the world for others to view indefinitely. Victimisation as a child can lead to a number of serious challenges in adult life, including shame, anxiety, suicidal ideation and relationship problems.'[19]

The taking, making, distributing and showing offences

9.22 Section 52(1) of the 1982 Act provides that:

> '(1) Any person who –
> (a) takes, or permits to be taken, or makes, any indecent photograph or pseudo-photograph of a child;
> (b) distributes or shows such an indecent photograph or pseudo-photograph;
> (c) has in his possession such an indecent photograph or pseudo-photograph with a view to its being distributed or shown by himself or others; or
> (d) publishes or causes to be published any advertisement likely to be understood as conveying that the advertiser distributes or shows such an indecent photograph or pseudo-photograph, or intends to do so,
> shall be guilty of an offence under this section.'

9.23 For the purposes of the offences created by this section, a 'child' is any person under the age of 18.[20] A wide range of types of evidence may be available to establish this essential fact (including expert evidence). The person depicted in a photograph is to be taken as having been under 18 at the material time if it appears from the evidence as a whole that he or she was under that age.[21] It is not necessary for the Crown to prove that the child was any particular age, and it is not necessary to prove that the accused knew the age of the person depicted.[22]

9.24 A photograph includes a film, or copy of either, and any form of video recording, as well as a negative and data stored on a computer disc or otherwise

18 *HM Advocate v Graham* 2011 JC 1, the Lord Justice Clerk (Gill) at para 28.

19 It also notes at the same page that there is little support in the literature for the proposition that viewing indecent images of children is a gateway to committing contact offences against children.

20 1982 Act, s 52(2). As originally passed the Act defined a child as a person under the age of 16. The change in age applied from 7 October 2005 by virtue of s 16 of the Protection of Children and Prevention of Sexual Offences (Scotland) Act 2005.

21 S 52(2), *Griffiths v Hart* 2005 SCCR 392.

22 *R v Land* [1999] QB 65.

which is capable of conversion into a photograph. The term also includes a tracing or other image, whether made by electronic or other means which is not itself a photograph or pseudo-photograph but which is derived from the whole or part of such.[23] A pseudo-photograph is an image, however produced, which appears to be a photograph or a copy of a pseudo-photograph, or data stored which is capable of being converted into a pseudo-photograph. Any such pseudo-photograph shall be treated as showing a child if the impression conveyed by it is that the person shown is a child. The same consequence follows where the predominant impression conveyed is that the person shown is a child, even if some of the physical characteristics shown are those of an adult.[24]

9.25 The 1982 Act does not provide a definition of what is meant by 'indecent', nor is the term defined in case law. An image will be viewed as indecent if it affronts the sensibilities of the average citizen in contemporary society, or if it lies outwith the recognised contemporary standards of common propriety. The same picture of an adult might not be indecent whereas one of a child might be.[25]

9.26 In order to take, to permit to be taken, or to make an indecent photograph of a child, the person concerned has to act deliberately, intending so to do in the knowledge that the image is likely to be an indecent photograph or pseudo-photograph. The term 'makes' includes the act of downloading indecent images from the Internet or bringing into existence the data stored on a disc.[26] In assessing the issue of *mens rea* the context in which a photograph was taken may be relevant, as it might raise the question of whether the accused acted in a sufficiently deliberate way or whether the photograph was taken more or less accidentally. Context is irrelevant to the assessment of whether the photograph is indecent. That cannot be assessed by reference to any extraneous circumstances.[27]

9.27 A person distributes or shows an indecent photograph if he parts with possession of it, or exposes it, or offers it for acquisition by another person.[28] It will be sufficient to establish the necessary *mens rea* of the offence under section 52(1)(c) (that a person has in his possession an indecent photograph with a view to it being distributed or shown by himself or others) that the accused held indecent images within a shared folder with a file sharing function which has been enabled, regardless of whether any other user accessed the relevant files. A further offence of distributing or showing such an indecent photograph under section 52(1)(b) is committed when

23 S 52(8) and (9).

24 Section 52(2A), (2B) and (2C).

25 The Jury Manual at pp 83.3/133 and 79.6/133. The references to 'average citizen' and 'recognised contemporary standards of common propriety' appears to be based on the definition of indecency in the public indecency case *Webster v Dominick* 2005 1 JC 65 at para 58. The test is little, if at all different, from the test in the rest of the UK: applying the recognised standards of propriety (*R v Stamford* [1972] 2 QB 391 at 398, approved again in *R v Miles* [2015] 2 Cr App R 22 at para 19).

26 *Smart v HM Advocate* 2006 SCCR 120, *Longmuir v HM Advocate* 2000 SCCR 447, *HM Advocate v Graham* 2011 JC 1.

27 *Bruce v McLeod* 1998 SCCR 733.

28 S 52(4).

another person accesses the images within that shared folder.[29] A person can possess images with a view to distribution to others or showing to others if this is one of his reasons for possessing, even if it is not the primary reason.[30]

9.28 Section 52B of the 1982 Act[31] provides for exceptions to liability to any of the offences set out in section 52(1)(a), (b) or (c). The exception arises in relation to what would be a section 51(1)(a) offence where the child who is depicted in an image was over 16 (or the accused reasonably believed that to be so), the accused and the child were married, in a civil relationship or in an established relationship at the relevant time and the child consented to the act which would otherwise constitute the offence (or the accused reasonably believe that to be so). In relation to what would otherwise be a section 51(1)(b) offence, the same circumstances require to exist for the exception to apply but in addition the showing or distributing of the photograph must only have been to the child. In relation to what would otherwise be a section 51(1)(c) offence, the same circumstances as apply to the section 51(1)(a) exception must apply, but in addition, the accused must have had the photograph in his possession with a view to its being shown or distributed only to the child. There is an evidential burden placed on the accused to raise any of these issues.[32] Each exception applies where the photograph is of the child alone or with the accused. They do not apply if the photograph shows any other person.[33]

9.29 A defence is available to a person charged with an offence of distributing or showing an indecent photograph or pseudo-photograph (section 52(1)(b)), or an offence of having in his possession such an indecent photograph or pseudo-photograph with a view to its being distributed or shown by himself or others (section 52(1)(c)). In such circumstances it will be open to the accused to establish, on the balance of probabilities, that he had a legitimate reason for distributing or showing the photograph, or having it in his possession, or that he had not himself seen the photograph and did not know, nor had any cause to suspect, it to be indecent.[34]

9.30 Where a 'legitimate reason' defence is advanced it will be a pure question of fact, for the court (or jury) to determine, in each individual case, whether or not the defence has been established. In conducting such an assessment the court (or jury) will be entitled to bring a measure of scepticism to bear upon the inquiry and should not conclude too readily that the defence is made out.[35]

9.31 A person convicted of an offence under section 52 of the 1982 Act will be liable to the notification requirements specified in Part 2 of the Sexual Offences Act

29 *Peebles v HM Advocate* 2007 JC 93 (paras 30 and 31).

30 *R v Dooley* [2006] 1 WLR 775.

31 As introduced by s 16 of the Protection of Children and Prevention of Sexual Offences (Scotland) Act 2005.

32 S 52C.

33 S 52B(9).

34 S 52(5). The provision imposes a reverse onus on the accused rather than merely an evidential burden – *McMurdo v HM Advocate* 2015 SCCR 271.

35 *Atkins v DPP* [2000] 1 WLR 1427.

2003 if certain conditions are met. These are that: (a) the child in the image was under 16 years old and the offender: (i) was 18 years old or over; or (ii) is sentenced in respect of the offence for a term of at least 12 months' imprisonment, or (b) the court determines that it is appropriate to order that the requirements should apply.[36]

The possession offence

9.32 Section 52A(1) of the 1982 Act provides that:

> '(1) It is an offence for a person to have any indecent photograph or pseudo-photograph of a child in his possession.'

9.33 The same definitions of child, photograph and pseudo-photograph as apply in section 52 apply to the offence created by this section.

9.34 For a person to be in possession of an indecent image requires both knowledge and control. In modern times, the vast majority of cases involving possession of indecent images involve downloading and storage on a computer or other electronic storage systems. Accordingly, the concepts of knowledge and control require to be understood in the context of the functioning and operation of computer systems.

9.35 The requisite knowledge is established where the accused is shown to have known of the 'things' which were in his control, even although it is not proved that he had knowledge of the quality or content of the things. Photographs include data stored on a computer disc or other electronic means which is capable of conversion into a photograph. So where indecent images of children are stored on computer discs, it will be sufficient for the Crown to establish that the accused was aware that he had discs which contained data. Once that is established the onus passes to the accused to establish the statutory defence if he wishes to do so.[37] Evidence of deleting files may go to demonstrate knowledge of the presence of relevant data.[38]

9.36 The element of control which is necessary for the concept of possession of an image requires a person to be able to do something with it. The image does not have to be readily within reach, however, and can be stored elsewhere. Files containing indecent images which have been deleted by the computer user may still be within the person's control if they are retrievable by the use of specialist software and deleting an image may demonstrate control in the sense of being able to do something with it.[39] More than one person may be in possession of indecent images stored on a computer system if each have access to the computer and are aware of the storage of the indecent images.[40]

36 Sexual Offences Act 2003, Sch 3, para 45.
37 *Redpath v HM Advocate* 2019 SCCR 266.
38 *Georgiou v HM Advocate* [2020] HCJAC 38.
39 *Harris v HM Advocate* 2012 SCCR 234.
40 *Harris v HM Advocate*.

9.37 An exception to liability to what would otherwise constitute an offence under section 52A is provided for by section 52B(7) in similar circumstances to the exceptions which apply to the section 52(1) offences. This exception will apply where the child who is depicted in an image was over 16 (or the accused reasonably believed that to be so), the accused and the child were married, in a civil relationship or in an established relationship at the relevant time and the child consented to the photograph being in the accused's possession (or the accused reasonably believe that to be so). As with the exceptions mentioned above, an evidential burden will be imposed on an accused who wishes to raise the applicability of this exception.[41]

9.38 It will be a defence for a person charged with possession of indecent images to prove that he had a legitimate reason for possessing the image, or that he had not himself seen the image and did not know, nor had cause to suspect, it to be indecent, or that the image was sent to him without any prior request by him or on his behalf and that he did not keep it for an unreasonable time.[42] The observations concerning a 'legitimate reasons' defence as made at **9.16** apply with equal force to a prosecution brought under this section.

9.39 A person convicted of an offence under section 52A of the 1982 Act will be liable to the notification requirements specified in Part 2 of the Sexual Offences Act 2003 if certain conditions are met. These are that: (a) the child in the image was under 16 years old and the offender, (i) was 18 years old or over, or (ii) is sentenced in respect of the offence for a term of at least 12 months imprisonment; or (b) the court determines that it is appropriate to order that the requirements should apply.[43]

Classification of images

9.40 On 30 April 2007, the Sentencing Council for England and Wales issued a definitive guideline on the Sexual Offences Act 2003. In that definitive guideline, the Council set out a table of indecent images categorised 1 to 5 depending upon a description of the content of the image. Since the case of *HM Advocate v Graham* in 2010 (2011 JC 1), the Scottish courts have adopted the use of this system of categorisation. The 2007 guideline was superseded in 2014 and is now to be found in a stand-alone document dealing just with indecent images of children.[44] A three-level category system (A, B and C) is now in use. Category A covers images involving penetrative sexual activity, or sexual activity with an animal or sadism. Category B covers non-penetrative sexual activity. Category C covers other indecent images not falling within categories A or B.

41 S 53C.

42 S 52A(2). The onus will be on the accused to establish this on a balance of probabilities – *McMurdo v HM Advocate* 2015 SCCR 271.

43 Sexual Offences Act 2003, Sch 3, para 46.

44 Sentencing Council for England and Wales, Possession of indecent photographs of child/photographs of children (2022) (IIOC Guideline).

9.41 Classification according to the three-level category system is done by the police, using the national Child Abuse Image Database (CAID). CAID is now used by all UK police forces; Police Scotland joined in July 2015. Images are stored in CAID with any unique hashes, keywords or metadata that can be used to identify the image. Any completely new image obtained by the police is graded according to the three-level category system by police officers from three different forces, producing an approved or 'trusted' grade for that image. When an image is seized, it is uploaded to see whether it is completely new or it matches any image already on the database. This can be done by comparing the image's metadata or other electronic identifying features, or by techniques such as facial recognition. If the image matches one already on the database, the seized image will automatically be assigned the same grade as already on the system, obviating the need for officers to look at and grade every image they seize. A report is then prepared on the image or images seized, detailing how many images were seized at each grade. In most cases, such as when the images are clearly indecent, this removes the need for anyone in the case – whether prosecution, defence or court – to have to look at the images, and allows for the category and description of the images to be agreed.[45]

9.42 The Sentencing Council's definitive guideline also identifies various factors which may be treated as aggravating an offence of possessing, distributing or producing indecent images:

- Age and/or vulnerability of the child depicted.
- Discernible pain or distress suffered by child depicted.
- Period over which images were possessed, distributed or produced.
- High volume of images possessed, distributed or produced.
- Placing images where there is the potential for a high volume of viewers.
- Collection includes moving images.
- Attempts to dispose of or conceal evidence.
- Abuse of trust; child depicted known to the offender.
- Active involvement in a network that produces indecent images.
- Commercial exploitation and/or motivation.
- Deliberate or systematic searching for images.
- Large number of different victims.
- Child depicted intoxicated or drugged.

45 See *R v Pinkerton* [2017] 4 WLR 65 per Treacy LJ at para 28. In *HM Advocate v Graham* 2011 JC 1 at paras 48–50, the Court found that a judge sentencing for such images has a discretion on whether to look at a representative sample. This has never been overruled, but in light of the way the CAID works, the reference at para 50 of *Graham* to the practice of the Crown making an agreed sample available to the Court is now no longer the practice. In the event of a trial, the images recovered and that they depict children ought normally to be the subject of a joint minute, if this can be agreed. If it cannot, then absent any defence objection, police officers can speak to what the images contain, thus obviating the need for the jury to see the images: *Leadbetter v HM Advocate* 2021 JC 130 at paras 22 and 30. In the unlikely event that it becomes necessary to prove that children are depicted, this does not require to be the subject of technical or scientific evidence (ibid, para 25).

TABLE OF OFFENCES

9.43

Table 9.1

Offence	Dates in force	Maximum sentence
Section 51(1): displaying any obscene material in a public place	1 July 1984	Summary: Initially six months' imprisonment or a fine (or both); increased to 12 months' imprisonment from 10 December 2007 by section 45 of the Criminal Proceedings etc. (Reform) (Scotland) Act 2007 Indictment: two years' imprisonment or a fine (or both) For offences committed on or after 28 March 2011: Summary: 12 months' imprisonment or a fine (or both) Indictment: where the obscene material includes an extreme pornographic image 5 years' imprisonment or a fine (or both) in any other case three years' imprisonment or a fine (or both)
Section 51(2A): responsible for the inclusion of any obscene material in a programme included in a programme service	1 January 1991	As above
Section 51A: possession of an extreme pornographic image	28 March 2011	Summary: 12 months' imprisonment or a fine (or both) Indictment: three years' imprisonment or a fine (or both)
Section 52: taking, making, distributing and showing indecent images of children	1 July 1984	Summary: Initially six months' imprisonment or a fine (or both); increased to 12 months' imprisonment from 10 December 2007 by section 45 of the 2007 Act Indictment: (since 27 June 2003) 10 years' imprisonment or a fine (or both)
Section 52A: possession of an indecent image of a child	29 September 1998	Summary: Initially six months' imprisonment or a fine (or both); increased to 12 months' imprisonment from 10 December 2007 by section 45 of the 2007 Act Indictment: (since 27 June 2003) five years' imprisonment or a fine (or both)

Chapter 10

The remaining common law sexual offences

INTRODUCTION

10.01 Although most sexual offences in Scots law are now found in statutes, there is a clutch of common law offences which are still seen regularly in sexual offences cases in the Scottish criminal courts, and which were not abolished by section 52(a) of the Sexual Offences (Scotland) Act 2009.[1] We set them out here. The important feature is that they are not sexual offences in themselves. Instead, they are either ordinary common law offences that can be aggravated by an element of indecency or sexual intention, or they are public order offences that might (and often do) include a sexual element.

10.02 Before turning to these remaining common law offences, it is appropriate to reiterate the terms of section 52(b) of the 2009 Act (discussed in Chapter 2 at **2.134–2.136**): that in so far as the provisions of the Act regulate any conduct, they replace any rule of law regulating that conduct. That does not abolish these common law offences altogether. Instead, the effect of section 52(b) is that if conduct amounts to an offence in the 2009 Act, then the Crown must bring a charge for that 2009 Act offence, not an offence at common law, though the common law offence will remain available as an alternative verdict in application of paragraph 14(b) of Schedule 3 to the 1995 Act. Section 52(b) does not apply to conduct taking place before the entry into force of the 2009 Act, since the Act does not 'regulate' that conduct.

INDECENT ASSAULT

10.03 The classic statement of the modern law of indecent assault was set out in *Grainger v HM Advocate*:[2]

1 S 52(a) only abolished rape at common law, clandestine injury to women, lewd, indecent or libidinous practice or behaviour, and sodomy: see Chapter 2 at **2.134**.

2 2006 JC 141 per Lord Justice Clerk Gill at para 17.

> 'Indecent assault is not, in our view, an independent sexual offence. It need not be, and generally is not, libelled as a nomen juris. It is essentially an assault aggravated by indecency in the manner of its commission. That aggravation does not take the assault into a separate category of crime (cf *Gordon, Criminal Law*, paras 29.04, 29.24). Whether or not an assault is aggravated in this way is to be judged, in our view, by an objective standard (*Gordon; Macdonald, Criminal Law*, pp 117–119). An assault may have the quality of indecency irrespective of the accused's intention or motive.'

10.04 On the basis of this statement of the law, the SLC recommended retaining the common law on indecent assault, foreseeing that there might be still some assaults that did not fall within the definition of the new offence of sexual assault which it proposed but that were nevertheless indecent (paragraphs 3.46 and 3.47 of its report).

10.05 That was the course taken in the 2009 Act. However, as the SLC also intended, the retention of the common law on indecent assault is subject to the rule in section 52(b) of the Act: that, in so far as the Act regulates any conduct, it replaces any rule of law regulating that conduct. Put simply, if conduct that would amount to indecent assault also amounts to an offence under the Act, the Act replaces the common law on indecent assault. This means that, for any conduct taking place after the entry into force of the 2009 Act, the Crown cannot bring a charge of indecent assault if the conduct would also amount to an offence under the 2009 Act, most obviously sexual assault contrary to section 3.

10.06 The definition of sexual assault in section 3 is wider than the definition proposed by the SLC. Indeed, it was widened by the Parliament to include the SLC's example of an assault that might be indecent but not sexual: A urinating on B. Section 3(2)(e) provides that this, if this is done 'sexually', will be one of the five 'things' in section 3(2) that will constitute sexual assault. It is possible – just – to conceive of a situation where A might do this to B without doing it 'sexually' such that A's conduct is not sexual assault but is indecent assault. However, even that example shows how difficult it is to think of examples of conduct that will not amount to sexual assault, contrary to section 3 but will amount to indecent assault at common law. Both Professor Chalmers and Sheriff Brown in their commentaries on the 2009 Act suggest that this limits the ambit of indecent assaults to assaults in which indecency is only one of the components.[3] This may be so, but in any such case, it would be open to the Crown to libel a composite charge of sexual assault contrary to section

[3] Chalmers, J, *The New Law of Sexual Offences in Scotland* (W. Green 2010), paragraph 2.13, cited with approval by Sheriff Brown, *The Sexual Offences (Scotland) Act 2009* (2nd edn) in his commentary on section 52 at page 87.

3 and an ordinary assault at common law.[4] Finally, assault at common law (so called in Schedule 3 to the 2009 Act) is available as an alternative verdict to a charge under section 3.[5] Bearing in mind that indecent assault is only assault aggravated by indecency, this suggests that it is open to a court/jury to convict of indecent assault when not satisfied that a sexual assault has taken place, though again this is unlikely to arise in practice.

10.07 These comments on the unlikelihood of indecent assault charges now being brought apply to conduct taking place after the entry into force of the 2009 Act. For conduct that took place before the 2009 Act, prosecutions for indecent assault are still common. A frequent example is penile penetration of the anus where there was no consent or where there was no capacity to consent. That is, of course, now rape, contrary to either section 1 or section 18 of the Sexual Offences (Scotland) Act 2009, and will be charged as such if the conduct takes place after the entry into force of the 2009 Act. However, when the conduct is alleged to have occurred before the 2009 Act, then it will, as a matter of Crown policy, be charged as indecent assault, not sodomy. In such a case, the charge will be expressly libelled as indecent assault, that 'you, A, did indecently assault B and did penetrate his/her anus with your penis'.

10.08 Although indecent assault is, in the words of *Grainger*, an assault aggravated by indecency and not an independent sexual offence, the term does have a legal meaning that is independent from the general law of assault – and is, in effect, treated as a separate offence – in two contexts. Indecent assault is included in the list of sexual offences in section 288C of the 1995 Act, the offences in respect of which the accused is prohibited from conducting his or her own defence. It is also included in the list of offences to which the automatic notification requirements under Part 2 of the Sexual Offences Act 2003 apply: see paragraph 40 of Schedule 3 to the Act. However, by paragraph 60 the notification requirements can also apply if the court determines that there was a significant sexual aspect to the offender's behaviour in committing the offence. The notification requirements and the concept of a 'significant sexual aspect' are discussed in Chapter 20 , but their application has led the Appeal Court to revisit the observation in *Grainger* that indecent assault need not be, and generally is not, libelled as a *nomen juris*. In *Hay v HM Advocate*[6] and *Thompson v Dunn*[7] the Appeal Court found that, where the Crown insists that an

4 One such example is *JGW v HM Advocate* 2013 SCCR 152, where, after discussions with the Crown and after significant discussion within Crown Office, involving a Law Officer, the accused pled guilty to a charge that 'On 16 March 2011 at [address] you J G W did assault R M, born 24 April 2008, … punch her on the head, bite and scratch her on the body, seize her by the body, force her legs apart, penetrate her vagina with your fingers, penetrate her anus with your fingers and strike her on the vagina, all to her severe injury.' The Appeal Court did not find it surprising that the sentencing judge in that case rejected both the Crown and defence submissions that this was not an indecent assault and concluded for himself that it was. While this is undoubtedly correct, it does not detract from the point that, in such a case, the better course is surely for the Crown to libel a composite 2009 Act/common law charge.

5 Assault at common law is also an alternative to offences under ss 1–3, 5, 6, and 18–21.

6 2012 SCCR 281.

7 2012 SCCR 298.

alleged assault is indecent and should therefore, on conviction, result automatically in notification under paragraph 40, it should give express notice of that in the libel itself: that is, the libel should specifically allege indecent assault.[8] Where the Crown has not, it remains open to the sentencing judge, having heard representations from the accused, to conclude that what occurred was an indecent assault such that the notification requirements apply.[9]

ASSAULT WITH INTENT TO RAPE

10.09 Assault with intent to rape,[10] like indecent assault, is not an independent sexual offence. Instead, it is an aggravated assault; it is part of the category of assaults that are aggravated by an intention to commit another crime. Since the core of the offence is assault and the intent to commit the crime of rape an aggravation, it follows that there are three versions of the offence: assault with intent to commit rape at common law; assault with intent to commit rape under section 1 of the Act; and assault with intent to commit the offence of rape of a young child (the section 18 offence).[11] None of these permutations exclude the assault also being aggravated by other circumstances, such as the causing of severe injury, permanent disfigurement or danger to life.

10.10 Like all assaults that fall into this category, the offence is generally reserved for situations where the accused's actions fall short of attempting the other offence. Thus, it will generally only be charged when A has assaulted B and it can be inferred that the reason for A's assault was an intention to rape B, but A's actions fall short of attempted rape. The distinction between assault with intent to rape and attempted rape is necessarily fact-specific and can often be a fine one, but it will arise in circumstances such as A forcing B into a private place such as a bedroom, A pinning B down or otherwise restraining B, A assaulting B so that B does not move or resist for fear of further violence, or A forcibly removing B's clothing. It might also arise when B is asleep, intoxicated, or unconscious and A removes B's clothing with the intention of having sexual intercourse with B while she remains in that state and is unable to give consent. These are all examples only.[12] The search in such a case is for any circumstances from which it may be inferred that the purpose of A's assault is

8 *Thompson* at para 9; *Hay* at para 45.

9 *JGW v HM Advocate* 2013 SCCR 152 at para 10.

10 Or, in the older writings, 'assault with intent to ravish' (the two meaning the same thing).

11 And s 288BC of the Criminal Procedure (Scotland) Act 1995 provides that the specification in the charge that the offence is with intent to rape may be given by referring to sections 1 or 18 of the 2009 Act (that is, in addition to referring to rape at common law). The current edition of Jury Manual comments (at p. 118.20/133) that 'presumably there could be an offence of sexual assault under s 3 of the 2009 Act with intent to commit the statutory crime of rape'. It is not clear why this should be so. Assault with intent to rape is the common law offence of assault aggravated, at common law, by the intention to commit another crime. It is not clear why a new statutory offence should automatically carry common law aggravations and the SLC was clear s 3 adopts the *nomen juris* of assault but does not import the general law of assault. Also, in contrast to assault with intent to rape, sexual assault with intent to rape is not listed as an alternative verdict in Sch 3.

12 Recent examples of libels of assault with intent to rape appear in *Paterson v HM Advocate* 2019 SCCR 338 and *Liddell v HM Advocate* 2013 SCCR 541.

to rape B but where A's actions have fallen short of attempted rape. Since the *actus reus* is assault and the intent to rape is an aggravation only, the intent to rape does not need to be established by corroborated evidence.

ABDUCTION WITH INTENT TO RAPE

10.11 Just as assault can be aggravated by an intention to commit another crime, so too can abduction. Abduction, a common law offence, is deliberately carrying off someone against their will or detaining them against their will, in each case without lawful authority. It does not require the use of physical force. In cases of young children who cannot consent, it does not require showing that the carrying off or detention was against the child's wishes. Abduction with intent to rape is, therefore, an abduction where the circumstances are such that it can be inferred the accused's intention was to commit rape. As with assault with intent to rape, there are three versions of the offence to reflect the three versions of rape: abduction with intent to commit rape at common law; abduction with intent to commit the offence of rape under section 1 of the 2009 Act; and abduction with intent to commit the offence of rape of a young child under section 18 of the 2009 Act.[13]

PUBLIC INDECENCY

10.12 Plainly, not all sexual conduct in public will be criminal, but it will be criminal if it is indecent and thus constitutes the offence of public indecency. The modern law of public indecency begins with the Appeal Court's decision in *Webster v Dominick*[14] that shameless indecency was not an offence, but that indecent conduct would amount to an offence in two scenarios: (i) when it was directed at an individual; and (ii) when it is carried out in public. The Court in *Webster* stated that the first was lewd, indecent or libidinous practice or behaviour (when directed against a specific victim whom the law protected, ie, when directed at a child), and the second should carry the *nomen juris* of public indecency. The Court in *Webster* (per Lord Justice Clerk Gill at paragraphs 50–58) defined the offence of public indecency at some length. The definition can be summarised as follows:

(i) The offence has two elements: the act itself and the effect of it on the minds of the public. It is sufficient for liability that, on an objective assessment, the conduct complained of should cause public offence.

(ii) Whether a particular act is indecent will depend on the circumstances of the case judged by social standards that will change from age to age. These will be the standards that would be applied by the average citizen in contemporary society. How such standards are applied in an individual case will depend on the time, place and circumstances of the conduct complained of.

13 See s 288BC, discussed at n 11 above.

14 2005 1 JC 65.

(iii) The paradigm case is that of indecent exposure, but the crime may extend to any other form of indecency, for example sexual intercourse in public view or the making of indecent actions or gestures in a stage show. Whether or not such indecency is committed for sexual gratification is irrelevant to liability, being a matter of motive.
(iv) The crime does not extend to consensual sexual conduct committed in private; nor to the private showing of indecent films and videos; nor to the selling of indecent publications. Nor does it extend to conduct witnessed only by persons who wish to see it – for example, performances by strippers or plays with scenes of nudity and the like – except perhaps where the conduct is such as to offend even members of a consenting audience.
(v) Whether the crime extends to conduct that is not of a sexual nature is a question that can be decided if and when it arises.[15]
(vi) As to the public element of the crime, the test is not whether the conduct occurs in a public place in any technical sense. Conduct falling within the definition could take place on a private occasion if it occurred in the presence of unwilling witnesses or if it occurred on private premises but was nonetheless visible to the public.

10.13 In *DF v Griffiths*,[16] where police officers followed a prostitute and her client to a cemetery and surreptitiously observed her performing oral sex on him, the Appeal Court reserved its opinion on whether the conduct must actually be seen by the public rather than by police officers.[17] It did, however, address the *mens rea* of the offence, finding that, before an accused could be guilty of public indecency, the circumstances had to show either that he intended to be seen or was recklessly indifferent as to whether or not he was observed.[18] The reading in of that *mens rea* requirement avoids criminal liability where, for instance, a two people retreat to a secluded but public spot where there is little likelihood of being seen, engage in sexual activity and, wholly by chance, are discovered by a member of the public.

10.14 We make three further comments on the nature of the offence in the sexual context. First, as a public order offence, public indecency is a different offence from sexual exposure, contrary to section 8 of the 2009 Act. That is only committed when A intentionally exposes his or her genitals in a sexual manner to an individual, B, with the purpose either of obtaining sexual gratification or of humiliating, distressing or alarming B. Public indecency, which does not require the indecency to be directed

15 In *Clark v HM Advocate* 2008 JC 390 at para 19 Lord Eassie gave the examples of a streaker at a sporting event, a political protestor 'mooning', naked swimmers at a pool or river, naked bathers at beach, and a dramatist using nudity to shock or confront what he considers to be prudery in society. See *Robertson and Gough v HM Advocate* 2008 JC 146 per Lord Justice Clerk Gill at para 77 (observing that offence was committed by appearing in court naked).

16 2011 JC 158.

17 Para 11; cf. *Barrie v Nisbet* 2013 SCCR 16 (public masturbation in the street observed by a police officer who was driving past).

18 Para 12.

towards anyone, which has a different *mens rea* and which is not limited to exposure of the genitalia, is a broader offence than section 8.

10.15 Second, while broader than sexual exposure, the offence is circumscribed by the need, when judging whether the conduct is indecent, to apply the standards of the average citizen in contemporary society. The offence, in so far as it relates to sexual activity in public, does not apply to all sexual activity in public, only those sexual acts that society considers are not appropriate for public places. Although this will ultimately be a question for the factfinder in any given case, we do not think any judge or jury would have difficulty in drawing the line between what is and what is not appropriate sexual behaviour in public.

10.16 Third, there might well be a case where the offence is made out by conduct taking place in private, for instance, conduct that goes beyond what a private group or paying audience wishes or expects to see, in which there might be interesting questions as to how far beyond the expectations of the audience the conduct has to go before it becomes indecent. However, the most common version of the offence is simply sexual activity taking place in public which has been witnessed by unwilling members of the public: the couple in *McNair v Murphy*[19] who engaged in oral sex on the back seat on the top floor of a double-decker bus and were captured on CCTV remain a typical example.[20]

10.17 The notification requirements only apply to the offence if: (a) a person (other than the offender) involved in the offence was under 18; and (b) the court determines that there was a significant sexual aspect to the offender's behaviour in committing the offence: paragraph 41A of Schedule 3. In *McNair*, one of the other passengers on the bus was a primary-school child accompanied by an adult. The Court found that this was sufficient for the first limb to apply: it was sufficient that a child was present and therefore exposed, or potentially exposed, to McNair and his companion's act of indecency. Involvement for the purpose of paragraph 41A did not require anything further where the essence of the offence was exhibitionist behaviour with a sexual aspect (paragraph 6 per Lord Brodie).

BREACH OF THE PEACE

10.18 Breach of the peace involves conduct severe enough: (i) to cause alarm to ordinary people; and (ii) to threaten serious disturbance to the community.[21] The latter is the necessary public element of the offence,[22] which is met either by the conduct taking place in public or, if taking place in private, either causing a disturbance or potential disturbance among those present or carrying a realistic risk of discovery by

19 2015 SCCR 306.
20 See too *Barrie* at n 17 above.
21 *Smith v Donnelly* 2002 JC 65 at para 17.
22 *Harris v HM Advocate* 2010 SCCR 15.

third parties.[23] Sexual misconduct is, of course, capable of amounting to a breach of the peace; indeed, throughout the history of the offence, sexual misconduct has been a relatively common form of the offence. However, care must now be taken for three reasons.

10.19 First, in many of the older cases, the conduct involved sexual activity in public but that sexual activity was not directed at any particular person. A common example was masturbation in public.[24] It is suggested that, although there is no bar to such cases being prosecuted as breaches of the peace, after *Webster v Dominick*, they are now better seen as examples of public indecency.

10.20 Second, for sexual conduct in public that is directed at a particular person, there are several statutory offences other than those in the Sexual Offences (Scotland) Act 2009 that may now cover the conduct. Thus, to take a common example from the older authorities, following someone for sexual purposes will now likely amount to either threatening and abusive behaviour, contrary to section 38 of the Criminal Justice and Licensing (Scotland) Act 2010[25] or stalking, contrary to section 39 of the same Act. There is no general rule that, where a statutory alternative to a common law offence exists, the Crown must charge the statutory offence,[26] but in many cases it will be appropriate, and good practice, to do so.

10.21 Third, where the conduct said to amount to breach of the peace would also amount to an offence under the Sexual Offences (Scotland) Act 2009 it is not just a matter of good practice to bring a charge under the Act, it is a requirement: section 52(b) of the Act, discussed above. That means many of the older cases would now require to proceed as 2009 Act charges.[27] For instance, the touching in *Paterson v HM Advocate*[28] if it took place today, would require to proceed as sexual assault, contrary to section 3 (or the equivalent offences in sections 20 or 30 for young and older children). Unwanted sexual activity directed towards a person, such as

23 *Harris* at para 25.

24 See, for instance, *Halcrow v Shanks* 2012 SLT 579 and *McGuire v Dunn* [2012] HCJAC 86.

25 See *Burnett v Hamilton* [2017] SAC (Crim) 4 (a stranger approaching a 14-year-old, asking her where she lived and inviting her to go home with him). On s 38, see too *M (K) v PF, Edinburgh* [2022] SAC (Crim) 2 (a man entering an address uninvited, in a state of undress and cupping his naked genitals).

26 Compare the position in England and Wales since *R v Rimmington and Goldstein* [2006] 1 AC 459 per Lord Bingham at para 30, that while it cannot be said that conduct might never be lawfully prosecuted as a common law crime where it fell within the terms of a specific statutory provision, good practice and respect for the primacy of statute required that conduct falling within the terms of a specific statutory provision should be prosecuted under that provision unless there was good reason for doing otherwise.

27 For an early but full and section-by-section analysis of the overlap between breach of the peace and the 2009 Act, see Ferguson, P, *Breach of the Peace* (Dundee University Press 2013) at pages 67–70. See also the classification of reported breach of the peace cases by type of conduct in Appendix B.

28 2008 JC 327. This involved two incidents of sexual activity towards a 17-year-old girl by a family friend 20 years her senior: one when he asked her to sit on his knee during a driving lesson and she could feel his erection; the other when he cuddled her tightly in the family kitchen.

masturbating out of a window towards a neighbour,[29] would require to proceed under section 5 (coercing a person into being present during a sexual activity). Many of the other cases of inappropriate or unwanted sexual comments, such as those in *Biggins v Stott*[30] and *Bowes v Frame*,[31] would require to proceed as communicating indecently, contrary to section 7, particularly since the breath of that offence was confirmed in *Buchan v Aziz*.[32] Intentionally exposing one's genitals to a stranger (such as in *Heatherall v McGowan*[33]) would be sexual exposure, providing it was done in a sexual manner and with the necessary purpose of obtaining sexual gratification or humiliating, distressing or alarming the complainer. The peeping-Tom activities in *MacDougall v Dochree*[34] and *Bryce v Normand*[35] would require to proceed as voyeurism, contrary to section 9, provided that the person observed is doing a private act as that term is defined in section 10.

10.22 There is, though, a small residue of sexual misconduct for which breach of the peace will be an appropriate and relevant charge. This will arise principally in three situations.

10.23 First, there might still be some sexual misconduct in public that will not amount to a 2009 Act offence but will amount to a breach of the peace. This can happen in cases that fall just short of 2009 Act offences. For instance, it may have been doubt as to whether a section 5 offence was made out which led the Crown to libel breach of the peace in *PF, Falkirk v BY*.[36] In that case, the complainer was a patient waiting in a single-occupancy room in a hospital ward when the accused, a doctor,

29 Compare the pre-2009 Act case of *Hutchison v HM Advocate* 1998 SLT 679, charged as a breach of the peace, and the post-2009 Act case of *HM Advocate v Taylor* 2019 JC 71, charged as a s 5 offence. *Taylor*, which gave rise to the doctrine of single-complainer mutual corroboration, is discussed at greater length in Chapter 19 at **19.79–19.83**.

30 1999 JC 298. The appellant, a 36-year-old man, repeatedly invited a 13-year-old child who had been playing hide-and-seek in the street with her friends to come up to his flat, offering her money and telling her, 'you ken what it's for', which the complainer suspected was a reference to sex.

31 2010 JC 297, concerning a taxi driver's sexualised questions and remarks towards a 14-year-old passenger. Cf. *Angus v Nisbet* 2011 JC 69 where the Appeal Court, while approving of the result in *Bowes*, found that the offence was not established by the appellant passing a note to a 15-year-old newspaper girl with his mobile telephone number on it, asking her to keep in touch. See also *McConachie v Shanks* 2019 SC (SAC) 1, where the appellant, a 65-year-old man, intermittently smiled and winked at a 12-year-old boy while they were on a bus; the man had then written his name, address and phone number on his bus ticket and, as he was getting off the bus, left it on the boy's gym bag, which was resting on the boy's lap, and gestured for the boy to telephone him. The Sheriff Appeal Court found the facts to be closer to *Angus* than *Bowes*. There had been no conversation or physical contact, beyond placing the ticket on the gym bag. This was inappropriate and imprudent conduct, but not breach of the peace. There is a reasonable contrary view that this case was closer to *Bowes*: unlike *Angus*, a young child was involved, the appellant's behaviour went beyond the passing of a telephone number, and his remarks to the young child, if not explicitly sexual, were implicitly so.

32 2023 JC 51.

33 2014 JC 8.

34 1992 JC 154. The accused was discovered in a toilet cubicle using a hole in the wall to look at naked women sunbathing in an adjoining solarium.

35 1997 SLT 1351. The appellant, from either a front garden or the street, videoed his 15-year-old neighbour undressing. He was unobserved taking the video but later showed it to another neighbour.

36 16 January 2015, unreported.

walked in and began excitedly rubbing his private parts over his clothing, causing the complainer to pull the room's alarm cord. It was not in dispute that the accused's conduct was such as to cause severe alarm. The issue was whether the necessary public element had been met, and the Court had no difficulty in finding that it had: the room was one to which all staff and visitors had access, and nothing turned on the hospital practice of knocking on room doors before entering. The accused's conduct was such that anyone encountering or discovering it would be likely to react in a serious way, such that it threatened serious disturbance to the community.

10.24 Equally, there might well be instances of unwanted sexual attention where the accused does not communicate indecently but none the less causes alarm by the unwanted sexual attention he directs at another, in which case breach of the peace, not section 7 of the 2009 Act, will be the appropriate charge. An example is *Montgomery v Harvie*.[37] The accused had, on three occasions, stared continuously at children from his van and, on one of the occasions, tried to entice a child into his van with sweets; the van contained a mattress and bedding. The Appeal Court found that the offence of breach of the peace was made out because it was not simply that the accused had stared at children, but that he had done so repeatedly and over prolonged periods (paragraph 15). The attempt to entice an eleven-year-old boy into a van containing a mattress and bedding also meant the offending contained a significant sexual aspect (paragraph 18).[38]

10.25 Similarly, the peeping-Tom who repeatedly looks into bedroom windows with the hope of seeking someone doing a private act, but does not in fact see anything, will not commit voyeurism, contrary to section 9, but might commit a breach of the peace.[39] So too cases of photography where the images taken are for sexual gratification but are not of someone doing a private act.

10.26 That issue arose in *AB v PF, Hamilton*.[40] The appellant, a schoolteacher, had, in furtherance of a fetish for seeing children performing fireman's lifts, taken photographs and videos of his pupils at gym lessons and photographs of pupils at a local football field, and had told the police that the school was aware that the gym lessons were recorded. His conviction for breach of the peace was quashed on other grounds relating to the police's recovery of the photographs and videos, but the Sheriff Appeal Court, in *obiter dicta*, found that, although the conduct would have caused legitimate alarm and distress, the conduct did not amount to breach of the

37 2015 JC 223.

38 From the pre-2009 Act cases, see *Faroux v Brown* 1996 SCCR 891. Although the conviction in that case was quashed on other grounds, the charge of breach of the peace for driving past three young girls, lowering the driver's window, and slowly perusing them from head to feet, would be a relevant and appropriate charge today. So too the charges in *Hay v HM Advocate* 2014 JC 19 (driving past, and staring, nodding and gesturing at young girls to come over to the accused's car). On a post-2009 Act case that arguably fell short of indecent communication but did amount to a breach of the peace, see *McConachie v Shanks* 2019 SC (SAC) 1 discussed at n 31 above.

39 The facts in *Raffaelli v Heatly* 1949 JC 101, which laid down the principle that peeping-Tom activities amount to a breach of the peace.

40 2024 SC (SAC) 35.

peace because there was no evidence of a realistic risk of discovery, nor any grounds on which the sheriff could infer such a risk.[41]

10.27 Second, there might be cases where the accused pursues a course of conduct and where part of that conduct amounts to a 2009 Act offence and part of it does not, in which case it may be appropriate for the Crown to libel both the 2009 Act offence and breach of the peace together. The conduct in *Carpenter v Hamilton*[42] (jumping out of bushes at a woman, making suggestive noises, and running after her) and *Anoliefo v HM Advocate*[43] (where some of the charges variously involved approaching women, following them, asking them into his car or back to his home, and, in some cases, making sexual remarks to them) are both examples of conduct where, today, a mixed breach of the peace/2009 Act charge under section 288BB of the Criminal Procedure (Scotland) Act 1995 would be appropriate (on such mixed charges see Chapter 13 at **13.51–13.53**).[44]

10.28 Third, there might be cases where there is simply no relevant 2009 Act offence or, indeed, any other statutory offence. In *Stewart v Lockhart*[45] the accused was seen by police officers at 10.20 pm walking in the red-light district of Aberdeen. He was dressed in female clothing and was carrying a lady's umbrella and handbag. He was wearing rouge, eye shadow and lipstick. When he saw the police, he moved quickly into another street. The appellant was arrested, charged, and convicted of breach of the peace on the basis of the factual finding that there was a very real possibility he would be approached by a man, or even by several men, looking for the services of a female prostitute who would be annoyed to discover a male in

41 It is not apparent why, assuming they were admissible, the appellant's own admissions to what he had been doing (apparently taking the photographs openly) and where he had been doing it (in a school gym class and at a local football field) were not sufficient evidence of a realistic risk of discovery or, at the least, evidence from which a sheriff could infer a realistic risk of discovery. It is not speculation or conjecture to consider ways in which that risk might realistically come to pass: that is inherent in any exercise of determining whether there is a realistic risk of something happening. This was the approach taken in *MacDougall v Dochree* 1992 JC 154, discussed at n 34 above (the Lord Justice Clerk (Ross) at 159 and Lord McCluskey at 161). Indeed, contrary to the basis upon which the appeal was argued, it is not apparent that the conduct was even private, such as to require recourse to the rules on realistic risk of discovery. The local football field and, arguably, the school gym were public places and there does not appear to have been anything surreptitious in the taking of the photographs/videos at either place.

42 1994 SCCR 108.

43 2012 SCCR 657.

44 As further such examples, see also *Kearney v Ramage* 2007 SCCR 35 (approaching the complainers, making explicit comments and inviting them home, and in one case, seizing her by the hand); *M v HM Advocate* 2012 SLT 147 (engaging ten- and eleven-year-olds in conversation, asking if he could tickle their legs, attempting to entice them into his care, offering a lift home on the promise not to tell their parents, and returning twice to the locus); and *Dudley v HM Advocate*, 3 November 2004, unreported (telephoning women, claiming to be a police officer, telling them they were in danger of men breaking into their houses, asking about their underwear and making other sexual remarks to them). See though *Bartkus v Harvie* [2015] HCJAC 25, a post-2009 Act case which proceeded solely as a breach of the peace case. The appellant had, on four occasions, visited a lingerie shop, followed the sales assistants at length, stood too close to them, and made sexualised remarks to them. The Appeal Court had little difficulty in finding the offence established (albeit at the lower end of offending): the appellant's conduct had gone well beyond the merely irritating or uncomfortable.

45 1990 SCCR 390.

such circumstances and might cause a disturbance. The Appeal Court upheld his conviction on that basis. *Stewart* is an example of a case where unconventional sexual conduct can amount to a breach of the peace, not because unconventional sexual conduct per se is a breach of peace but rather because the unconventional sexual conduct in a particular context can cause the necessary alarm and threat to serious disturbance. Not all such unconventional sexual conduct will meet that test and such cases are likely to receive closer scrutiny from the appeal courts than might have previously been the case. For instance, in *Wotherspoon v Orr*,[46] the appellant, a man, had been convicted of breach of the peace for wearing a bra at his front door and windows and once rubbing his nipple. In quashing the conviction, the Appeal Court was clear that the appellant's conduct might have been exhibitionist, provocative and even perverse, but none of those descriptions rendered it criminal.

10.29 For obvious reasons, the notification requirements in Part 2 of the Sexual Offences Act 2003 do not automatically apply upon any conviction for breach of the peace. However, as noted above, under paragraph 60 of Schedule 3, the notification requirements can apply if the court determines that there was a significant sexual aspect to the offender's behaviour in committing the offence. Breach of the peace convictions have generated much of the case law on paragraph 60 and the meaning and application of the term 'significant sexual aspect'. That case law is discussed at **20.58** and following in Chapter 20.

BESTIALITY AND NECROPHILIA

10.30 These practices rarely trouble Scots criminal law, save that they are sometimes seen in possession of extreme pornography cases, and we comment on them for the sake of completeness only. The view of the successive authors of *Gordon, Criminal Law* is that bestiality is certainly a crime when committed by a man and might be a crime when committed by a woman.[47] The view of Professors Chalmers and Leverick in the fourth edition is that it is unclear whether necrophilia is a crime.[48] Those views were shared by the Scottish Law Commission in its discussion paper and final report on *Rape and Other Sexual Offences*.[49] In the absence of any recent decided cases on the matter, we cannot add to that analysis. In *HM Advocate v Gibson and Corrigan*, the second accused was charged with breach of the peace for sexually touching the body of the deceased (after her murder by the first accused), and for this and for attempting to defeat the ends of justice received a *cumulo* sentence of nine years' imprisonment.[50]

46 2018 JC 79.

47 First edition at pages 836–837; second at para 34.03; third at para 34.04; fourth at para 41.26.

48 At para 41.27.

49 On bestiality, see the discussion paper at para 6.38. On necrophilia, see the discussion paper at 6.41 and the final report at para 5.28.

50 The sentencing statement incorrectly refers to sexual assault. The charge was one of breach of the peace. https://judiciary.scot/home/sentences-judgments/sentences-and-opinions/2023/09/04/hma-v-connor-gibson-and-stephen-corrigan

TABLE OF OFFENCES

10.31

Table 10.1

The remaining common law offences		
Offence	**Dates in force**	**Maximum sentence**
Indecent assault	N/A – common law offence	Life imprisonment
Assault with intent to rape	N/A – common law offence	Life imprisonment
Abduction with intent to rape or ravish	N/A – common law offence	Life imprisonment
Public indecency	N/A – common law offence	Life imprisonment
Bestiality	N/A – common law offence	Life imprisonment
Necrophilia	*Quaere* whether this is an offence	If an offence, life imprisonment like all common law offences

Chapter 11

Incest

INTRODUCTION

11.01 This short chapter sets out the historical and current offences on incest. There is value in considering the historical and current offences together because the current law as contained in the Criminal Law (Consolidation) (Scotland) Act 1995 ('the 1995 Act') is a re-enactment of the previous law, with some changes, and it is instructive to trace the law's development from the Incest Act 1567 to the 1995 Act.

INCEST BEFORE THE CRIMINAL LAW (CONSOLIDATION) (SCOTLAND) ACT 1995

11.02 The crime of incest was originally, and for centuries thereafter, prosecuted as a contravention of the Incest Act 1567. The crime was constituted by an act of sexual intercourse between two people related to each other within the forbidden degrees specified in Leviticus Chapter 18. Relationships by affinity were in the same position as blood relationships. The crime was committed by both parties.

11.03 There were some questions as to the extent of the prohibitions envisaged in Leviticus (for example, whether it was incest for an uncle to have intercourse with his niece or for a man to have intercourse with his deceased wife's sister) and some other unsatisfactory consequences. For example, incest could not be committed with illegitimate blood relations. Clarification of the scope of the offence was provided by section 13 of the Criminal Procedure (Scotland) Act 1938, which confirmed that it was not incest for sexual relations to occur between parties such as a man and his deceased wife's sister, or a woman and her deceased husband's brother, and by the Marriage (Scotland) Act 1977, which specified the relevant relationships by consanguinity and by affinity.

11.04 The Incest Act 1567 was repealed by the Incest and Related Offences (Scotland) Act 1986, which restricted the scope of the offence to specified relationships of consanguinity or adoption. The 1986 Act also introduced an offence involving intercourse with a stepchild and an offence of having intercourse with a child under 16 years of age whilst in a position of trust. The 1986 Act achieved these changes by inserting a series of provisions into the Sexual Offences (Scotland) Act 1976: section 2A (incest), section 2B (intercourse with a stepchild) and section 2C (intercourse in a position of trust with a child under 16).[1] These provisions were in turn replaced by sections 1 to 3 of the Criminal Law (Consolidation) (Scotland) Act 1995. A more detailed discussion on this area of the law can be found in *Gordon, Criminal Law*, second edition, Chapter 35.

INCEST AND INTERCOURSE WITH A STEPCHILD IN THE CRIMINAL LAW (CONSOLIDATION) (SCOTLAND) ACT 1995

11.05 The current law of incest and intercourse with a stepchild remains as in the Criminal Law (Consolidation) (Scotland) Act 1995 and is unaffected by the Sexual Offences (Scotland) Act 2009 because, in its report on Rape and Other Sexual Offences, the SLC saw no case for expanding the law as it is in the 1995 Act.[2] This contrasts with the approach in England and Wales, where the current law of incest and related crimes was modernised by the Sexual Offences Act 2003.[3] Many of the instances in which incest or sexual intercourse with a stepchild take place will now also be covered by the child and abuse-of-trust offences in Parts 4 and 5 of the 2009 Act, but the offences are still occasionally seen in historical sexual offences cases, and incest remains a separate crime from the Part 4 and 5 offences because it can also occur between consenting adults.

Section 1: incest

11.06 Section 1 of the 1995 Act criminalises sexual intercourse by men and women when that sexual intercourse is with a person related to them within certain specific degrees of relationship. These specific degrees are set out in the following table, which is contained in section 1 itself. A man will commit incest if he has sexual intercourse with any of the people in column 1. A women will commit incest if she has sexual intercourse with any of the people in column 2. In each case, sexual intercourse means penile-vaginal intercourse, the meaning of sexual intercourse at the time of the 1995 Act.

1 Section 2C is considered in Chapter 12 at **12.22**.
2 Para 5.3 of its report.
3 The 2003 Act separated the law of incest into two sets of offences: sexual activity with a child family member in s 25 (which does not criminalise the child with whom sexual activity occurs, only the person engaging in sexual activity with the child) and sex with an adult relative in ss 64 and 65 (which criminalises both consenting parties). It also expanded the offence from penile-vaginal intercourse to penile-oral penetration and any form of anal or vaginal penetration with a part of the body or anything else (in ss 64 and 65) and all forms of sexual touching (in s 25). The previous provisions were contained in ss 10 and 11 of the Sexual Offences Act 1956.

Table 11.1: Degrees of Relationship

Column 1	**Column 2**
1. Relationships by consanguinity	
Mother	Father
Daughter	Son
Grandmother	Grandfather
Grand-daughter	Grandson
Sister	Brother
Aunt	Uncle
Niece	Nephew
Great grandmother	Great grandfather
Great grand-daughter	Great grandson
2. Relationships by adoption	
Adoptive mother or former adoptive mother	Adoptive father or former adoptive father
Adopted daughter or former adopted daughter	Adopted son or former adopted son
3. Relationships by virtue of Part 2 of the Human Fertilisation and Embryology Act 2008	
Mother	Father
Daughter	Son
Second female parent by virtue of section 42 or 43 of that Act	

11.07 Section 1 is thus gender neutral, applying in the same way and to the same degrees of relationship for men and women. That in turn means that it is possible for both partners in the sexual intercourse to commit the offence. It is, however, limited to heterosexual intercourse.

11.08 Section 1(2) specifies that the degree of relationship exists:

'(a) whether it is of the full blood or the half blood; and

(b) even where traced through or to any person whose parents are not or have not been married to one another.'

11.09 Subsection (a) means that, for instance, a man who has sex with his half-sister is as guilty as a man who has sex with his sister. Subsection (b) simply means that, for instance, a man who has sex with his sister is guilty of the offence irrespective of whether his and his sister's parents were married to each other.[4] The

[4] This was the position under the previous provision in s 2A of the Sexual Offences Act 1976. Before that, relationships by affinity had to be constituted on the basis of a consummated marriage: Scottish Law Commission, *The Law of Incest in Scotland*, 1980 at paras 2.7 and 2.8.

need for there to be a blood relationship excludes sexual intercourse with the spouses or partners of family members: if a man has a blood uncle (that is, the brother of his mother or father), it is not an offence for the man to have sexual intercourse with his uncle's wife.

11.10 The table is an exclusive list: section 1(3) provides that, for the avoidance of doubt, sexual intercourse between persons who are not related to each other in the degrees referred to in the table is not incest.

11.11 There are three defences to a charge of incest, each for the accused to prove:

(1) The accused person did not know and had no reason to suspect that the person with whom he or she had sexual intercourse was related in a degree so specified (section 1(1)(a)).

(2) The accused person did not consent to have sexual intercourse, or to have sexual intercourse with that person (section 1(1)(b)).

(3) The accused person was married to that person, at the time when the sexual intercourse took place, by a marriage entered into outside Scotland and recognised as valid by Scots law (section 1(1)(c)).

11.12 The first is the standard *mens rea* requirement: the lack of *mens rea* is a defence to the act. The second protects the party who did not consent, though, of course, if the case papers show a clear lack of consent to the intercourse by a female relative (or an inability by young age to consent), a charge of rape is likely to be preferred to one of incest. The third protects consensual sexual intercourse in foreign marriages as long as those marriages are recognised in Scots law.

Section 2: intercourse with a stepchild

11.13 Section 2 of the 1995 Act criminalises intercourse with a stepchild in certain, limited situations. It provides that any stepparent or former stepparent who has sexual intercourse with his or her stepchild or former stepchild shall be guilty of an offence if that stepchild is either: (i) under the age of 21 years; or (ii) has at any time before attaining the age of 18 years lived in the same household and been treated as a child of his or her family.

11.14 Section 2, like section 2B of the Sexual Offences (Scotland) Act 1976 before it, thus circumscribes the offence so that it only applies to those relationships where either: (i) the stepchild is considered in need of protection (because he or she is under 21); or (ii) by having lived in the same household and having been treated as a child of the accused's family, is in the same position as any natural child, and thus any sexual intercourse should be treated in the same way as sexual intercourse between a parent and his or her natural child.

11.15 There are four defences, each for the accused to prove:

(1) that he or she did not know and had no reason to suspect that the person with whom he or she had sexual intercourse was a stepchild or former stepchild (section 2(a));
(2) that he or she believed on reasonable grounds that that person was of or over the age of 21 years (section 2(b));
(3) that he or she did not consent to have sexual intercourse, or to have sexual intercourse with that person (section 2(c)); and
(4) that he or she was married to that person, at the time when the sexual intercourse took place, by a marriage entered into outside Scotland and recognised as valid by Scots law (section 2(d)).

11.16 The first is a standard lack of *mens rea* defence. The second is a standard reasonable belief defence. The third and fourth are the same defences as for incest and the same comments we have made for them above apply.

Proceedings for offences under sections 1 and 2

11.17 Section 4 of the 1995 Act governs the forum for proceedings under sections 1 and 2 and the maximum sentences for each offence. Proceedings may be brought on indictment or, if the Lord Advocate directs, on summary complaint: section 4(1). Summary proceedings may be brought within six months of the date on which evidence sufficient in the opinion of the Lord Advocate to justify the proceedings comes to her knowledge: section 4(2).[5]

Table 11.2: The historical incest offences

The historical incest offences		
Offence	**Dates in force**	**Maximum sentence**
Incest Act 1567	1567 to 31 October 1986	Life imprisonment
Section 2A of the Sexual Offences (Scotland) Act 1976: incest (as inserted by the Incest and Related Offences (Scotland) Act 1986)	1 November 1986–31 July 1997	Summary: three months' imprisonment Indictment: life imprisonment
Section 2B of the Sexual Offences (Scotland) Act 1976: intercourse with a stepchild (as inserted by the Incest and Related Offences (Scotland) Act 1986)	1 November 1986–31 July 1997	As above

5 And a certificate from the Lord Advocate to that effect is conclusive: s 4(4).

Table 11.3: The current offences

The current law in the Criminal Law (Consolidation) (Scotland) Act 1995		
Offence	**Dates in force**	**Maximum sentence**
Section 1: incest	1 April 1996 to present (relationships in part 3 of the degree-of-relationships table – that is, those created by virtue of the Human Fertilisation and Embryology Act 2008 – from 6 April 2009 onwards)	Summary: 12 months' imprisonment (initially three months until 10 December 2007 when section 45 of the Criminal Proceedings etc. (Reform) (Scotland) Act 2007 entered into force) Indictment: life imprisonment
Section 2: intercourse with a stepchild	1 April 1996 to present	Summary: as above; initially three months, now 12 months' imprisonment Indictment: life imprisonment

Chapter 12

Historical offences

INTRODUCTION

12.01 This chapter covers historical sexual offences. Though of diminishing importance, such offences continue to be prosecuted as adults make allegations later in life against family members and others who might have been in a position of trust during their childhood. There is then some value in setting out, if briefly, the main offences that applied and that are still regularly seen in sexual offences cases. The offences are, for the most part, self-explanatory. Often though, the greatest difficulty for practitioners when dealing with historical sexual offences is knowing which offence applies at any given date, a difficulty not helped by the fact that different common law and statutory offences applied to male and female complainers, with different sentences, at different times. To help, Tables 12.1 to 12.5 at the end of the chapter set out the relevant dates for each offence, which age and gender it applies to, and the maximum sentences for it. We have divided the offences into five categories: (i) general offences; (ii) offences of unlawful sexual intercourse against children; (iii) other sexual offences against children short of intercourse; (iv) abuse-of-trust offences; and (v) offences against those with a mental disorder. The tables also follow this categorisation.

GENERAL OFFENCES

Rape at common law

12.02 The common law crime of rape was committed where a man penetrated the vagina of a woman with his penis without her consent and where he knew that the woman was not consenting, or was reckless as to whether she was consenting. There was no need for the woman's will to be overcome by force.[1] In the case of females who were under the age of 12 the absence of consent was presumed as a matter of law. The act of penetration was the only necessary element of the completed crime. Consent for common law purposes was given its normal meaning[2] but, as was

1 *Lord Advocate's Reference No 1 of 2001* 2002 SCCR 435.
2 *Marr v HMA* 1996 SCCR 696.

discussed in *HM Advocate v SM (No 1)*,[3] there is little, if anything, to distinguish the common law concept of consent from free agreement. A man was reckless as to whether the woman was consenting if he failed to think about, or was indifferent to, whether the woman was consenting.[4] The relevant *mens rea* as constituted by being reckless has often been described as an absence of honest belief.

12.03 Despite some confusion in the authorities which existed for a period of time following the decision in *McKearney v HM Advocate*,[5] it is clear that the requisite mental element in the common law crime of rape (as with the statutory offence) is an inferential fact to be drawn from the primary facts and is not something which requires to be proved by corroborated evidence.[6] Although the absence of an honest belief that the woman was consenting was an essential element of the common law crime,[7] this issue would require to be raised in the evidence before it could become a live matter requiring direction from the trial judge.[8]

Clandestine injury

12.04 Clandestine injury was the offence which occurred when a man had intercourse with a woman who was asleep or unconscious[9] and, therefore, not in a position either to consent or to withhold her consent. Such conduct did not constitute rape because of the perceived need for the woman's will to have been overcome by force.[10] The decision in *Lord Advocate's Reference No 1 of 2001* had the effect that all instances of clandestine injury were instances of rape. The offence was probably redundant as from the date of the decision in that case.

Sodomy

12.05 The crime of sodomy at common law consisted of the penetration of the anus of one male by the penis of another.[11] Both parties were guilty of the offence. Homosexual behaviour short of sodomy was not a crime at common law. This was

3 2019 JC 176 and see **2.56**.

4 *Lord Advocate's Reference No 1 of 2001* per Lord Justice General Cullen at paras 29 and 44.

5 2004 JC 87.

6 *Spendiff v HM Advocate* 2005 1 JC 338, *Maqsood v HM Advocate* 2019 JC 45, *Graham v HM Advocate* 2017 SCCR 497, *Briggs v HM Advocate* 2019 SCCR 323, *Duthie v HM Advocate* 2021 JC 207.

7 *Meek v HM Advocate* 1982 SCCR 613.

8 *Doris v HM Advocate* 1996 SCCR 854.

9 Through a fit, drink or the like – Macdonald, *A Practical Treatise on the Criminal Law of Scotland* (5th edn, W Green 1948) page 120.

10 *Charles Sweenie* (1858) 3 Irvine 109; *Rodgers v Hamilton* 1994 SLT 822.

11 Macdonald page 149, *Gordon, Criminal Law* para 34.01. When sodomy was an offence, both the second and third editions of *Gordon* (both at para 34.01, fn 5) considered whether it included non-consensual penetration of a woman's anus but observed that the point was academic given that the behaviour was covered by indecent assault. The point will now never be resolved, particularly given the Crown's policy of charging all acts of non-consensual anal penetration as indecent assault.

changed by section 11 of the Criminal Law Amendment Act 1885, which provided that acts of gross indecency between two or more men, whether committed in public or in private, constituted criminal conduct. The statute did not define gross indecency and no judicial definition has been attempted,[12] but it must have been intended to refer to conduct short of sodomy.

12.06 The impact of the common law of sodomy was restricted by section 80 of the Criminal Justice (Scotland) Act 1980, which came into force on 1 February 1981. It provided that a homosexual act[13] in private would not be an offence provided that the parties consented thereto and were aged at least 21 years. An act was not to be treated as being done in private if more than two persons participated or if it occurred in a place to which the public had access. Section 13 of the Criminal Law (Consolidation) (Scotland) Act 1995 and subsequent amendments to that provision had the effect of reducing the relevant age requirement, in stages, to 16 years and removing the stipulation that the act was only to be viewed as taking place in private when it involved no more than two participants.

12.07 The Crown now considers it inappropriate to libel charges of sodomy: all non-consensual penile-anal penetration alleged to have taken place before the entry into force of the Sexual Offences (Scotland) Act 2009 is now libelled as indecent assault (on which offence, see Chapter 10, **10.03–10.08**).

UNLAWFUL SEXUAL INTERCOURSE WITH CHILDREN

Rape of a girl at common law

12.08 From at least the time of the institutional writers until its abolition by section 52 the Sexual Offences (Scotland) Act 2009,[14] it was rape at common law for a man to have penile-vaginal sexual intercourse[15] with a girl less than twelve years old (that being the age of puberty), irrespective of any purported consent by the girl. The offence was occasionally referred to as 'constructive rape', reflecting the fact that lack of consent was inferred or presumed from the age of the girl. The maximum sentence was life imprisonment.

12 For a helpful review of the term see *R v Holmes* [2023] EWCA Crim 58.

13 A homosexual act was defined as sodomy or an act of gross indecency by one male person with another male person.

14 As set out in Chapter 2 at **2.134**, s 52 abolished the common law offences of rape, clandestine injury to women, lewd, indecent or libidinous practice or behaviour, and sodomy. Unlike most of the 2009 Act, which entered into force on 1 December 2010, s 52 did not enter into force until 16 December 2013, meaning these common law offences still existed until 15 December 2013.

15 Penile-anal and penile-oral intercourse between a man and a girl would not have amounted to common law rape. They would have been charged as indecent assault or lewd, indecent and libidinous practice and behaviour. The Crown's policy now is to charge indecent assault.

The statutory offences of unlawful sexual intercourse with girls

12.09 Successive statutes extended the protection against unlawful sexual intercourse to older girls up to the age of 16 (sexual intercourse being understood to be penile-vaginal intercourse). The first was the Criminal Law Amendment Act 1885. Section 4 made it an offence to have, or to attempt to have, intercourse with any girl under 13. The maximum sentence for having intercourse was life imprisonment. The maximum sentence for attempting to have intercourse was two years' imprisonment. Section 5 made it an offence to have, or attempt to have, intercourse with any girl over 13 but under 16. The maximum sentence under section 5 was two years' imprisonment.

12.10 Sections 4 and 5 of the 1885 Act were replaced by the Sexual Offences (Scotland) Act 1976. Section 3(1) of the 1976 Act criminalised sexual intercourse with a girl under 13. Section 3(2) criminalised attempting to have sexual intercourse with a girl under 13. Section 4(1) criminalised having, or attempting to have, sexual intercourse with a girl over 13 but under 16. Section 4(1) is now an obsolete offence because proceedings had to be brought within one year of the commission of the offence. That time bar would not, however, prevent the sexual intercourse being the subject of a charge under section 5 of the Sexual Offences (Scotland) Act 1976 (statutory lewd and libidinous conduct towards a girl between 12 and 16), for which there is no such time bar: see **12.19** below. For all these offences in the 1976 Act, the maximum penalties were the same as in the 1885 Act.

12.11 The 1976 Act offences were replaced by section 5 of the Criminal Law (Consolidation) (Scotland) Act 1995.[16] Section 5(1) criminalised sexual intercourse with a girl under 13, again with a maximum sentence of life imprisonment.[17] Section 5(2) criminalised attempting to have sexual intercourse with a girl under 13, with a maximum sentence of three months' imprisonment on summary conviction and, initially, two years' imprisonment on conviction on indictment. This was increased to ten years' imprisonment by the Crime and Punishment (Scotland) Act 1997. Section 5(3) criminalised having, or attempting to have, sexual intercourse with any girl over 13 but under 16. Initially the maximum sentence under section 5(3) was two years' imprisonment: this too was increased to ten years' imprisonment by the 1997 Act. Initially, no prosecution could commence under section 5(3) more than one year after the commission of the offence: section 5(4). This was removed on 7 October 2005 by the Protection of Children and Prevention of Sexual Offences (Scotland) Act 2005. As with the 1885 and 1976 Acts, it was a defence to a charge under section 5(3) for an accused to have a reasonable cause to believe: (a) that the girl was his wife; and (b) for a man under 24 years of age who had not previously

16 The 1976 Act was not repealed until the Crime and Punishment (Scotland) Act 1997, which did so with retroactive effect from 1 April 1996, date of entry into force of the Criminal Law (Consolidation) (Scotland) Act 1995: para 6 of Sch 1 to the 1997 Act.

17 The practice was, and remains, to charge common law rape when the girl was under 12 and to charge under s 5(1) when the girl was between 12 and 13.

been charged with a 'like offence', that the girl was 16 years of age or over: section 5(5)(a) and (b).[18]

12.12 Section 14 of the Criminal Law (Consolidation) (Scotland) Act 1995 contains an important provision on alternative verdicts. It provides that, when a person is tried for rape at common law or an offence under section 5(1) of the Act, the jury can convict of the alternative offences in section 5(2) and section 5(3), and of indecent assault.[19] This can still sometimes arise in trials for rape of a child under 12. It can arise either: (i) when the complainer is unsure in her evidence whether penetration took place (in which case the jury can convict of offence of attempted sexual intercourse under section 5(2) or the common law offence of indecent assault); or (ii) when she is unsure of her age at the time of the offence (in which case the jury can convict of the section 5(3) offence of sexual intercourse with a girl between 13 and 16).

Unlawful sexual intercourse with boys

12.13 Before the 2009 Act, penile penetration of the male anus without consent (whatever the age of the complainer) would have amounted to the common law crime of sodomy but, as stated above, the Crown now considers it inappropriate to libel charges of sodomy. Now, as with all cases of non-consensual penile-anal penetration, the appropriate charge where there is clear lack of consent by a male child to penile-anal intercourse will be indecent assault.

12.14 If the complainer was under 14 at the time, a charge of lewd, indecent or libidinous practice or behaviour at common law (see **12.16** below) could also be brought. For a complainer over 14 but still a child at the time of the incident, if the complainer purported to consent to the penile-anal penetration, the matter is not likely to be prosecuted because all of the relevant statutory offences are time barred. For instance, the most recent statute, section 13(5) of the Criminal Law (Consolidation) (Scotland) Act 1995, which made it an offence for a man to have penile-anal intercourse with a male child under 16, also included a time-bar preventing prosecution more than one year after the offence (section 13(11)). The

18 S 5(6) defined a 'like offence' as: s 5(3) itself; the previous version of the offence in s 4(1) of the 1976 Act; s 10(1) of the 1976 Act (permitting a girl to use a premises for intercourse); ss 5 and 6 of the Criminal Law Amendment Act 1885 (respectively, unlawful sexual intercourse with a girl between 13 and 16 years of age and an owner/occupier permitting unlawful intercourse on his premises); s 6 of the Sexual Offences Act 1956 (the equivalent offence to s 5(3) in England and Wales); from 1 May 2004 onwards, the child-sex offences in ss 9 to 14 of the Sexual Offences Act 2003; and s 9(1) of the 1995 Act (permitting a girl to use premises for intercourse).

19 There are two further alternative offences: s 7(2) of the 1995 Act (certain forms of procuring sexual intercourse) and s 7(3) (sexual intercourse by impersonation of a woman's husband). Neither is likely now to arise, but they none the less remain available.

same is true for the previous provision, section 80 of the Criminal Justice (Scotland) Act 1980.[20]

SEXUAL OFFENCES AGAINST CHILDREN NOT INVOLVING INTERCOURSE

12.15 Where the sexual behaviour with or towards a child did not involve sexual intercourse, the principal offence that applied was lewd, indecent or libidinous practice or behaviour.[21] This was initially a common law offence. It was extended by a series of statutes beginning with the Criminal Law Amendment Act 1922. We consider first the common law offence then the statutory versions.

Lewd, indecent or libidinous practice or behaviour at common law

12.16 The essence of lewd, indecent or libidinous practice or behaviour at common law was engaging in indecent conduct with or towards a child below the age of puberty with or without their consent.[22] The age of puberty was taken to be 12 for a girl and 14 for a boy. The offence thus applied to girls under 12 and boys under 14.

12.17 The nature of the offence was re-stated, with examples, in *Webster v Dominick*.[23] The offence is a form of indecent conduct. The indecent conduct becomes lewd, indecent, and libidinous when it is directed against 'a specific victim who is within the class of persons whom the law protects' (that is, children under the relevant age). It may be committed by indecent physical conduct, but need not

20 For penile-anal intercourse between an adult male and a male teenager aged 14 or 15 occurring before 1980, prosecution for gross indecency under either s 7 of the Sexual Offences (Scotland) Act 1976 or s 11 of the Criminal Law Amendment Act 1885 would theoretically be possible, but unlikely to arise. The passage of time and the factual scenario required for such a prosecution mean any case is extremely unlikely to arise. If it did, the Crown, for good policy reasons, is unlikely to rely on statutes that did not seek specifically to protect children from adults but rather sought to criminalise sexual intercourse between consenting adult men.

21 The name of the offence as it appears in statute, though often called, and referred to in indictments as, 'lewd, indecent *and* libidinous practice *and* behaviour'. It is often referred by the shorthand names 'lewd and libidinous practices', 'lewd and libidinous conduct', 'indecent practices' or, in the headings in the relevant statutes, 'indecent behaviour'. 'The common law and statutory versions are sometimes distinguished by referring to 'common law lewd and libidinous conduct' and 'statutory lewd and libidinous conduct'.

22 There is some authority that the common law offence could be committed on children above the age of puberty: see *Batty v HM Advocate* 1995 JC 160, where the Appeal Court observed that the age of the complainer will not be a critical factor, so long as the conduct complained of falls within the scope of the crime of shameless indecency (164F-G). But shameless indecency was found not to be a criminal offence in *Webster v Dominick* 2005 1 JC 65, which casts significant doubt on whether the decision in *Batty* was correct. The issue is unlikely ever to be resolved: the Crown is unlikely ever to test the point by charging the common law offence for an older child when the statutory alternatives exist.

23 2005 1 JC 65 per Lord Justice Clerk Gill at para 49.

be. It may be committed by taking indecent photographs of the child, indecent exposure to the child, showing the child indecent photographs or videos, or other indecent conduct carried out in the child's presence. It may also be carried out by lewd conversations (whether face to face, by telephone or online). The essence of the offence is 'the tendency of the conduct to corrupt the innocence of the complainer'.[24] The Appeal Court later confirmed in *Sommerville v HM Advocate*[25] that there is no need to prove an intention to corrupt the innocence of the complainer or an intention to obtain sexual gratification – all that is required is that the accused intended to do the acts alleged.

Statutory lewd and libidinous conduct offences

12.18 The protection of girls (and only girls) from lewd and libidinous conduct was extended from those under the age of puberty to those over it by a series of statutes.

12.19 The first was section 4(1) of the Criminal Law Amendment Act 1922, which made it an offence to engage in lewd and libidinous conduct with a girl over 12 and under 16. There was no defence as to a belief that a girl was over 16. The maximum penalties were three months' imprisonment on summary conviction and two years' imprisonment on conviction on indictment. Section 4(1) of the 1922 was then replaced, in identical terms, by section 5 of the Sexual Offences (Scotland) Act 1976, again with the same penalties. The final form of the offence, again covering girls over 12 but under 16, appeared in section 6 of the Criminal Law (Consolidation) (Scotland) Act 1995. Initially, the maximum penalties were as they had been in the 1922 and 1976 Acts: thus, between, 1 April 1996 and 31 July 1997, the penalties were three months' imprisonment on summary conviction and two years' imprisonment on indictment. The maximum penalty for conviction on indictment was increased on 1 August 1997 to ten years' imprisonment. [26] While section 6 did not include a defence on the basis of a reasonable belief as to the girl's age, in *H v Griffiths*, the Appeal Court found that, absent any provision to the contrary, the offences included a *mens rea* requirement, that is, that the prosecution required to prove the accused knew that the girl was under 16 years of age.[27]

Non-intercourse offences involving older boys

12.20 The position in respect of older boys (that is, those between 14 and 16) is more complicated. For any sexual act falling short of intercourse with a boy under 14,

[24] A tendency found in the French kiss of an adult of a child: *Moynagh v Speirs* 2003 SCCR 765.

[25] 2010 SCCR 299. See too *Casey v HM Advocate* 2010 JC 197.

[26] By the Crime and Punishment (Scotland) Act 1997. By Art 4 of Statutory Instrument 1997/1712, the change was not retroactive: the penalty for an offence committed before 1 August 1997 is unaffected.

[27] 2009 SCCR 312.

the offence of lewd, indecent or libidinous practice or behaviour at common law is available, just as it is for a girl under 12. But the statutes that extended that offence (the 1922, 1976 and 1995 Acts) only applied to girls. Thus, if an adult engaged in any sexual conduct with or towards a boy aged 14 or 15, the question of which, if any, charge to bring depends on: (i) whether the boy purported to consent to the sexual conduct; and (ii) the gender of the adult. If an adult of either gender engaged in sexual conduct with a boy aged 14 or 15, and the boy clearly did not consent, the offence of indecent assault would be appropriate. If the boy purported to consent to the sexual conduct, and the adult was female, no offence would be committed.[28] If the boy purported to consent to the sexual conduct, and the adult was male, at the time of the offence it would have been possible to bring a charge under section 80 of the Criminal Justice (Scotland) Act 1980 or, subsequently, section 13(5) of the Criminal Law (Consolidation) (Scotland) Act 1995. However, both provisions contained time bars preventing prosecution from 12 months after the offence. The result is that any historical sexual conduct between an adult male and a boy aged 14 or 15 who purported to consent would not now be prosecuted.[29]

HISTORICAL ABUSE-OF-TRUST OFFENCES

12.21 There were three offences which criminalised the abuse of trust of a child by having sexual intercourse with that child.

12.22 Section 2C of the Sexual Offences (Scotland) Act 1976[30] made it an offence for a person over 16 to have sexual intercourse with a child under 16 when: (i) he or she was a member of the same household as that child; and (ii) was in a position of trust or authority in relation to that child. The defences were: a belief on reasonable grounds that the child was over 16; that the accused did not consent to have sexual intercourse; or was married to the child at the time by a marriage entered into outside Scotland and recognised as valid by Scots law.

12.23 Section 2C was re-enacted in identical terms in section 3 of the Criminal Law (Consolidation) (Scotland) Act 1995 and remained in force until its repeal by the Sexual Offences (Scotland) Act 2009.

12.24 Section 3 of the Sexual Offences (Amendment) Act 2000 was the precursor to section 42 of the 2009 Act (for which, see Chapter 5 at **5.13–5.18**). It made it an offence for a person over 18 (A) to have sexual intercourse (whether vaginal or anal), or to engage in any other sexual activity with or directed towards a person under 18 (B), when in a position of trust in relation to that person. The positions of trust, defined in section 4, covered: places of detention; accommodation for children in local authority or similar care; hospitals and similar places of care; and full-time

28 Subject to any possible abuse-of-trust offence, set out at **12.24** below.

29 Again subject to any possible abuse-of-trust offence.

30 Inserted by s 1 of the Incest and Related Offences (Scotland) Act 1986.

educational institutions.[31] In each case, A had to be looking after persons under 18 at that place. 'Looking after' was defined in section 4(7) as being regularly involved in caring for, training, supervising or being in sole charge of such persons. By section 3(2), the defences to a charge under section 3 were that: (i) A did not know, and could not reasonably have been expected to know, that B was under 18; (ii) A did not know, and could not reasonably have been expected to know, that B was a person in relation to whom he was in a position of trust; and (iii) A was lawfully married to, or (from 5 December 2005) in a civil partnership with, B. Section 3(3) also excluded relationships where, before the commencement of the Act, A was in a position of trust in relation to B and a sexual relationship existed between them.

OFFENCES AGAINST A PERSON WITH A MENTAL DISORDER

12.25 The common law would appear to have held that a woman who suffered from a sufficient degree of mental disorder would not be capable of consenting to an act of intercourse. Whilst this question was not what fell to be decided in the case of *Charles Sweenie*[32] the judges did express this view in various ways. What form of disorder would be necessary to place a woman into this category was not explored in anything other than the most general fashion. Subsequently, commencing in 1885, various statutory provisions regulated sexual intercourse with women who were mentally impaired by creating offences which were available as alternatives to a charge of rape.[33] Section 13 of the Criminal Law (Consolidation) (Scotland) Act 1995 gave protection to men who suffered from what was called mental deficiency of such a degree as to render them incapable of living an independent life, or of guarding against serious sexual exploitation.

12.26 The Mental Health (Care and Treatment) (Scotland) Act 2003 sought to reform this area of legislation by introducing an underlying approach which took much more account of autonomy. The aim was to focus on criminalising sexual behaviour, which was abusive or exploitative, whilst recognising the right of adults with learning disabilities to choose to enter into sexual relationships.[34] The scope of the legislation was also widened to cover people with mental disorders generally, rather than being restricted to people with learning disabilities, to apply equally to men and women and to cover other sexual acts in addition to intercourse. There were two offences: sections 311 and 313. Section 311 provided that any sexual act engaged in with a mentally disordered person was criminal if that person did not consent to

31 The terms varied slightly over time as the wording of s 4 was changed to reflect statutory definitions contained, and from time to time changed, in other Acts.

32 (1858) 3 Irvine 109.

33 Criminal Law Amendment Act 1885, s 5(2), the Mental Deficiency and Lunacy (Scotland) Act 1913, s 46, the Mental Health (Scotland) Act 1960, s 96, and the Mental Health (Scotland) Act 1984, s 106.

34 See The Millan Committee report on the Review of the Mental Health (Scotland) Act 1984, Chapter 21, paras 32 and 33. The recommendations of this report led to the passing of the Mental Health (Care and Treatment) (Scotland) Act 2003.

the act or was incapable of doing so. The section identified certain circumstances in which the mentally disordered person would be regarded as not consenting or being incapable of consenting. It also provided for a defence for a person charged under the section to prove that he did not know and could not reasonably have been expected to know that the other person had a mental disorder and was incapable of consenting to the sexual act. Section 313 made it an offence for a person who was providing care services to a person who suffered from a mental disorder to engage in a sexual act with that person.[35] There were also defences based on reasonable lack of knowledge that the person was mentally disordered, for spouses and civil partners, and for those in prior sexual relationships. Sections 311 and 313 were repealed by the 2009 Act and replaced by section 17 of that Act (the general provision on consent and mental disorder) and by section 45 (the offence of sexual abuse of trust of a mentally disordered person): see, respectively, Chapter 2 at **2.94–2.104** and Chapter 5 at **5.19–5.22**.

TABLES OF OFFENCES WITH RELEVANT DATES

12.27

Table 12.1: General historical offences

Offence	Dates in force (inclusive)	Gender of complainer	Gender of accused	Maximum Sentence
Rape at common law	Until 15 December 2013	Female	Male	Life imprisonment
Clandestine injury	Until 15 December 2013	Female	Male	Life imprisonment
Sodomy NB not now prosecuted	Until 15 December 2013	Male *Quaere* whether it extended to female complainers	Male	Life imprisonment

[35] It extended to all those indirectly involved in providing care, such as those employed in, or contracted to provide services in or to, hospitals where the mentally disordered person was being given medical treatment, and to the managers of such hospitals.

Table 12.2: Unlawful sexual intercourse with children

Offence	Dates in force (inclusive)	Gender and age of complainer	Gender of accused	Maximum Sentence
Rape of a girl under 12 at common law	Until 15 December 2013	Female child under 12	Male	Life imprisonment
Defilement of (ie, sexual intercourse with) a girl under 13: section 4 of the Criminal Law Amendment Act 1885	1885 to 14 December 1976	Female child under 13	Male	Life imprisonment (two years for attempt)
Defilement of (ie, sexual intercourse with) a girl between 13 and 16 years of age: section 5(1) of the Criminal Law Amendment Act 1885	1885 to 14 December 1976	Female child between 13 and 16	Male	Two years' imprisonment (the same for attempt)
Intercourse with a girl under 13: section 3(1) of the Sexual Offences (Scotland) Act 1976	15 December 1976 to 31 March 1996	Female child under 13	Male	Life imprisonment
Attempting to have intercourse with a girl under 13: section 3(2) of the Sexual Offences (Scotland) Act 1976	15 December 1976 to 31 March 1996	Female child under 13	Male	Summary: three months' imprisonment Indictment: two years' imprisonment
Intercourse with (or attempting to have intercourse with) a girl between 13 and 16: section 4(1) of the Sexual Offences (Scotland) Act 1976	15 December 1976 to 31 March 1996	Female child between 13 and 16	Male	Summary: three months' imprisonment Indictment: two years' imprisonment

Offence	**Dates in force (inclusive)**	**Gender and age of complainer**	**Gender of accused**	**Maximum Sentence**
Intercourse with a girl under 13: section 5(1) of the Criminal Law (Consolidation) (Scotland) Act 1995	1 April 1996 to 30 November 2010	Female child under 13	Male	Life imprisonment
Attempting to have unlawful sexual intercourse with a girl under 13: section 5(2) of the Criminal Law (Consolidation) (Scotland) Act 1995	1 April 1996 to 30 November 2010	Female child under 13	Male	Summary: 12 months' imprisonment (initially three months until 10 December 2007 when section 45 of the Criminal Proceedings etc. (Reform) (Scotland) Act 2007 entered into force) Indictment: from 1 April 1996 to 31 July 1997: two years' imprisonment from 1 August 1997 to 30 November 2010: ten years' imprisonment

Offence	Dates in force (inclusive)	Gender and age of complainer	Gender of accused	Maximum Sentence
Intercourse with (or attempting to have intercourse with) a girl between 13 and 16: section 5(3) of the Criminal Law (Consolidation) (Scotland) Act 1995	1 April 1996 to 30 November 2010	Female child between 13 and 16	Male	Summary: initially three months' imprisonment; then, from 10 December 2007, 12 months' imprisonment (section 45 of the 2007 Act) Indictment: from 1 April 1996 to 31 July 1997: two years' imprisonment from 1 August 1997 to 30 November 2010: ten years' imprisonment

Table 12.3: Non-intercourse offences against children

Offence	Dates in force (inclusive)	Gender and age of complainer	Gender of accused	Maximum Sentence
Lewd, indecent or libidinous practice or behaviour at common law	Until 12 December 2013	Female child under 12 Male child under 14	Male or female	Life imprisonment
'Statutory lewd and libidinous conduct': section 4(1) of the Criminal Law Amendment Act 1922	1922 to 14 December 1976	Female child between 12 and 16	Male or female	Summary: three months' imprisonment Indictment: two years' imprisonment

Offence	**Dates in force (inclusive)**	**Gender and age of complainer**	**Gender of accused**	**Maximum Sentence**
Indecent behaviour (ie, statutory lewd and libidinous conduct) towards a girl between 12 and 16: section 5 of the Sexual Offences (Scotland) Act 1976	15 December 1976 to 31 March 1996	Female child between 12 and 16	Male or female	Summary: three months' imprisonment Indictment: two years' imprisonment
Indecent behaviour (ie, statutory lewd and libidinous conduct) towards a girl between 12 and 16: section 6 of the Criminal Law (Consolidation) (Scotland) Act 1995	1 April 1996 to 30 November 2010	Female child between 12 and 16	Male or female	Summary: initially three months' imprisonment; then, from 10 December 2007, 12 months' imprisonment (section 45 of the 2007 Act) Indictment: from 1 April 1996 to 31 July 1997: two years' imprisonment from 1 August 1997 to 30 November 2010: ten years' imprisonment

Table 12.4: Abuse-of-trust offences against children

Offence	Dates in force (inclusive)	Gender and age of complainer	Gender and age of accused	Maximum Sentence
Intercourse in position of trust with a child under 16: section 2C of the Sexual Offences (Scotland) Act 1976	1 November 1986 to 31 March 1996	Female child under 16 Male child under 16	Male or female over 16	Summary: three months' imprisonment Indictment: life imprisonment
Intercourse in a position of trust with a child under 16: section 3 of the Criminal Law (Consolidation) (Scotland) Act 1995	1 April 1996 to 30 November 2010	Female child under 16 Male child under 16	Male or female over 16	Summary: initially three months' imprisonment; then, from 10 December 2007, 12 months' imprisonment (section 45 of the 2007 Act) Indictment: life imprisonment
Abuse of a position of trust: section 3 of the Sexual Offences (Amendment) Act 2000	8 January 2001 to 30 November 2010	Female child under 18 Male child under 18	Male or female over 18	Summary: initially six months' imprisonment or a fine (or both); then, from 10 December 2007, 12 months' imprisonment (section 45 of the 2007 Act) Indictment: five years' imprisonment or a fine (or both)

Table 12.5: Offences against persons with a mental disorder

Offence	**Dates in force (inclusive)**	**Gender of complainer**	**Gender of accused**	**Maximum Sentence**
Unlawful and carnal knowledge (or attempting to have unlawful carnal knowledge) of any female 'idiot or imbecile woman or girl': section 5(2) of the Criminal Law Amendment Act 1885	1885 to 14 December 1976	Female	Male	Two years' imprisonment
Protection of 'defectives' from acts of sexual immorality, procuration, etc: section 46 of the Mental Deficiency and Lunacy (Scotland) Act 1913	1913 to 1960	Female	Male for offence of unlawful carnal knowledge; male and female for ancillary offences	Two years' imprisonment
Protection of female 'defectives': section 96 of the Mental Health (Scotland) Act 1960	1960 to 29 September 1984	Female	Male for offence of unlawful sexual intercourse; male and female for ancillary offences	Two years' imprisonment

Offence	**Dates in force (inclusive)**	**Gender of complainer**	**Gender of accused**	**Maximum Sentence**
Protection of mentally handicapped females: section 106 of the Mental Health (Scotland) Act 1984	30 September 1984 to 4 October 2005	Female	Male for offence of unlawful sexual intercourse; male and female for ancillary offences	Two years' imprisonment or a fine
Homosexual act with a male person suffering from a mental deficiency: section 13(3) and (5) of the Criminal Law (Consolidation) (Scotland) Act 1995	1 April 1996 to 4 October 2005	Male	Male	Summary: three months' imprisonment or a fine Indictment: two years' imprisonment or a fine (or both)
Non-consensual sexual acts with or towards a mentally disordered person: section 311 of the Mental Health (Care and Treatment) (Scotland) Act 2003	5 October 2005 to 30 November 2010	Male or female	Male or female	Substantive offence Summary: initially three months' imprisonment or a fine (or both); then, from 10 December 2007, 12 months' imprisonment (section 45 of the 2007 Act)

Offence	Dates in force (inclusive)	Gender of complainer	Gender of accused	Maximum Sentence
Non-consensual sexual acts with or towards a mentally disordered person: section 311 of the Mental Health (Care and Treatment) (Scotland) Act 2003 – *contd*	5 October 2005 to 30 November 2010	Male or female	Male or female	Indictment: life imprisonment Aiding, abetting, etc Summary: initially three months' imprisonment or a fine (or both); then, from 10 December 2007, 12 months' imprisonment (section 45 of the 2007 Act) Indictment: two years' imprisonment or a fine (or both)
Sexual activity with or towards a mentally disordered while providing care services to that person: section 313 of Mental Health (Care and Treatment) (Scotland) Act 2003	21 March 2005 (for the purpose of making regulations 5 October 2005 (date it took effect) To 30 November 2010	Male or female	Male or female	Summary: initially three months' imprisonment or a fine (or both); then, from 10 December 2007, 12 months' imprisonment (section 45 of the 2007 Act) Indictment: two years' imprisonment or a fine (or both)

Part II

The Investigation, Prosecution and Trial of Sexual Offences

Chapter 13

The investigation and prosecution of sexual offences

INTRODUCTION

13.01 With few exceptions (such as private prosecutions and certain Armed Forces cases), sexual offences in Scotland are investigated by the police, reported by them to COPFS, and prosecuted by COPFS in the public interest. In that, they do not differ from the investigation and prosecution of other offences in Scotland. There are, though, certain special features of the investigation and prosecution of sexual offences and we set out these special features in this chapter. The recovery and analysis of medical evidence and forensic scientific evidence in sexual offences cases are set out separately in Chapters 15 and 16.

13.02 The Victims and Witnesses (Scotland) Act 2014 and the Victim Code for Scotland promulgated under it impose a series of statutory duties on the Chief Constable and Lord Advocate towards victims and witnesses during the investigation and prosecution of crime (and, by extension, those in Police Scotland and COPFS acting under their authority). The Act also gives victims and witnesses a series of rights during the investigation and prosecution of offences (victim is used in the Act to mean someone who is or appears to be a victim: section 1(1)). Many of these rights and duties, such as the right of a victim to receive information about the case, apply in all cases. Others either specifically apply to sexual offences cases or have a particular resonance in such cases. An example of the former is the right under section 8 of the Act to specify the gender of an interviewer, which we discuss at **13.03** below. An example of the latter is the right to review of a decision not to prosecute, which we discuss at **13.34–13.36** below.

THE POLICE INVESTIGATION

Initial briefing reports

13.03 Police investigations into allegations of sexual offending will almost always begin with a member of the public reporting the allegation to the police. When that happens, the police will speak to the complainer and ascertain, in brief terms, the nature of the allegation. Nothing more than the nature of the allegation is taken from the complainer. This is deliberate: the details of the allegation are to be taken later by a specially-trained officer – a sexual offences liaison officer (SOLO: see below). The officer to whom the allegation is first made will note the details of the allegation on a standard form called a 'rape and serious sexual offences initial briefing report' (IBR). The IBR also requires the officer to note any visible injuries to the complainer and his or her demeanour, both of which may be relevant as corroboration for the allegation. To ensure compliance with section 8 of the Victims and Witnesses (Scotland) Act 2014 (the right, noted above, to specify the gender of an interviewing officer), the officer completing the IBR is also required to ask the complainer if he or she prefers to be interviewed by a male or female SOLO and to note any preference expressed. The IBR will be lodged as Crown production should the case be prosecuted and, depending on how close in time the noting of the IBR is to the allegation, the officer completing it may be called as a witness, often to speak to the complainer's distress or to the making of a *de recenti* statement or both.

Sexual offences liaison officers

13.04 Sexual offences liaison officers are specialist police officers who trained to a Police Scotland national standard in the investigation and gathering of evidence in sexual offences cases. A SOLO is appointed to a complainer throughout the duration of the investigation and will be responsible for noting the complainer's statement, arranging any forensic medical examination, and providing regular updates and support during the investigation. As of 12 June 2023, there were 636 trained SOLO officers serving with Police Scotland.[1]

The police taking of evidence: statements, VRIs, JIIs and Bairns' Hooses

13.05 Once a SOLO has been allocated to a case, he or she will conduct an interview with the complainer to take the complainer's evidence of what is alleged to have happened. There are three ways in which that evidence may be taken.

Statement taking

13.06 The first, and still the most common, is by noting the complainer's statement. The practice is not for statements to be taken at a police station: the statement will normally be taken either at the complainer's home or, if the complainer is to be medically examined, at a hospital, or at a Sexual Assault Response Coordination Service (SARCS). Other than this, the statement will be taken in the usual way: the

1 Police Scotland Freedom of Information Response, FOI 23-1194, available on the Police Scotland website.

police officer will ask questions to obtain the complainer's version of events and then write up the statement in prose form, read it back and invite the complainer to sign each page. It is not uncommon, particularly in cases of several allegations or a prolonged course of conduct, for several statements to be taken over a number of interviews.

Visually recorded interviews

13.07 The second, and still at the pilot stage,[2] is the use for adult complainers of visually recorded interviews (VRIs), where the complainer is interviewed by a qualified SOLO in a police station (or other appropriate location) and the interview is recorded. Like JIIs for children (see below), the object is to allow the VRI to be played at trial as part of, or wholly instead of, evidence-in-chief. At the time of writing, the use of VRIs rather than traditional statement taking from adult complainers remains the exception to the rule.[3]

Joint investigative interviews

13.08 The third method the police use to take evidence is a joint investigative interview (JII). This is used to take the evidence of children and, in contrast to VRIs for adult complainers, is the norm. The SOLO conducts the interview with a social worker. The aim of the interview is twofold: to take the child complainer's evidence for the purposes of the criminal investigation (the SOLO's role in the interview) and to identify any child-protection concerns that might need social work to intervene, for instance to remove the child from the family home to a place of safety (the social worker's role in the interview). Generally, the SOLO will lead the interview, asking questions to elicit the child complainer's account. Once that is done, there will then be a short break to review matters, and then the social worker will ask any further questions he or she considers necessary to fulfil his or her role. The interview is recorded and thus may be used as all or part of the child's evidence-in-chief at trial, if an application is made to use it as a prior statement under section 271M of the 1995 Act.[4]

2 There was always a discretion for the police to take adult complainers' evidence in this way, but it has been rarely used, until Police Scotland began piloting VRIs for adult complainers in 2019. That pilot has continued in various forms since then.

3 The Victims, Witnesses and Justice Reform (Scotland) Bill will place an obligation on the Sexual Offences Court to enable all vulnerable complainers' evidence to be given in advance of a hearing, but this need not see a shift towards the systematic use of VRIs since there will remain the option of taking that evidence on commission.

4 On which see Chapter 17. There is, since the abolition of the competency test for witnesses by s 24 of the Vulnerable Witnesses (Scotland) Act 2004, no requirement for the JII to be preceded by any form of oath (or any other check on the child's ability to understand and tell the truth), but paras 100 and 101 of the guidance on the context of such interviews (see n 6 below) is that the interviewer should make clear to the child at the start of the interview the importance of telling the truth and giving the child's own account.

13.09 There are two main policy documents which govern the conduct of such interviews. The first is the Scottish Child Interview Model, which emphasises the need for proper planning of interviews, properly structured interviews, and proper consideration of the child's needs before, during and after the interview.[5]

13.10 The second stems from section 7 of the Victims and Witnesses (Scotland) Act 2014 which directs those carrying out a JII of a child to have due regard to any guidance issued by the Scottish Ministers about the carrying out of such interviews. The current guidance was published in 2011.[6] The guidance is general, applying equally to JIIs in sexual offences and other offences, but two parts of the guidance apply in particular to sexual offences. The first part is the section on 'seeking clarifications' (paras 138–148), which underlines the importance of ensuring that it is clear what sexual acts or conduct the child is describing, and the acceptable and unacceptable means of obtaining clarifications. The second part is that, when the interview is disclosable, appropriate arrangements for the defence to attend and view it in private should be made, and that any request to view the recording should be refused if it would put the child at risk of harm or be incompatible with their Article 8 ECHR rights: paras 216–221.

13.11 JIIs are not always used as evidence-in-chief. The quality of the sound and video can vary, depending on where they are recorded. Most are recorded in police stations or at the child's school and are recorded by the police themselves rather than audio-visual experts. Moreover, the dual-purpose of a JII – the open-ended taking of evidence for the police investigation and the identification for social work of any child protection concerns – can often mean that not all of the interview will be admissible as evidence. JIIs thus often require heavy editing before they can be used as evidence-in-chief and often further questioning will be necessary, meaning that the child will often have to give evidence at a commission.

Bairns' Hooses

13.12 In 1998, Iceland introduced *Barnahus* (children's houses), where children's evidence in criminal cases can be taken without their needing to come to court to give evidence. The model has been widely copied, first in the other Nordic countries and then more widely across Europe as a means of complying with the various EU instruments and Council of Europe Conventions on child victims, such as the duty to adapt procedures to the needs of children, to prevent delay in taking their evidence,

5 See https://www.cosla.gov.uk/about-cosla/our-teams/children-and-young-people/joint-investigative-interviews-of-child-victims- and-witnesses.

6 https://www.gov.scot/binaries/content/documents/govscot/publications/advice-and-guidance/2011/12/guidance-joint- investigative-interviewing-child-witnesses-scotland/documents/0124263-pdf/0124263-pdf/govscot%3Adocument/0124263.pdf.

to limit the number of interviews and medical examinations during an investigation, and to avoid, where possible, the need for children to give evidence in court.[7]

13.13 In its original, Icelandic form, the Barnahus is quite literally a house consisting, at a minimum, of a series of specialist rooms: a waiting room; an interview room where the child's oral evidence is taken and recorded (by one professional with others watching from an observation room); a room for medical examination and the taking of forensic samples; and a room in which therapy, support and mental health assessment and treatment can be provided after the child's evidence is taken. The house itself will usually have more than one of each of these rooms: for instance, there will be different waiting and interview rooms for younger and older children, and these rooms will be differently decorated and furnished for each age group. Though there have been some adaptations as the Barnahus model has been rolled out across Europe, there has been little change to the core four rooms of the original Icelandic Barnahus. The key features remain: (i) simultaneously assessing any child protection needs and taking the child's evidence for criminal proceedings; (ii) that all forms of investigation, evidence-taking and support for the child is done in the same house, obviating the need for the child to be interviewed at a police station, medically examined in a clinic, and so on; (iii) that the house is exclusively used as a Barnahus; (iv) that the house is a private place and, in appearance, unlike a police station or clinic, and the rooms in it are designed, furnished and decorated in an age-appropriate manner.

13.14 The introduction of the Barnahus model to Scotland has been in gestation since 2019. At the time of writing, the Scottish Government has identified six test sites for a pilot scheme of Barnahus – to be known as 'Bairns' Hooses' – with a national roll out to follow thereafter.[8] One such Bairns' Hoose is now operational for the North Strathclyde sheriffdom and at the time of writing, it has taken the evidence of over 90 children. One of the authors has visited it. It is carefully modelled on, and in some ways goes beyond, both the original Icelandic model and current international standards. The only substantive departure from the original model is that forensic medical examinations are not conducted at it, and it remains to be seen how such examinations could be done at the site whilst complying with the national standards on ensuring the integrity of forensic samples (see Chapters 15 and 16).

7 The PROMISE Barnahus network maintains a website www.barnahus.eu which contains information on the original model and how it is being applied and developed in different European countries. It also maintains and develops the Barnahus Quality Standards, which guide the model's adaptation and implementation in different countries, and a compendium of law and guidance on how the model can implement the various EU instruments and Council of Europe Conventions on child victims and the criminal justice system. These include: Directive 2012/29/EU (the Victims' Rights Directive); Directive 2011/93/EU (the Child Sexual Abuse Directive), Directive 2011/36/EU (the Anti-Trafficking Directive), the Council of Europe Convention on Action against Trafficking in Human Beings, and the Council of Europe Convention on Protection of Children against Sexual Exploitation and Sexual Abuse ('the Lanzarote Convention').

8 Information on the proposed Bairns' Hooses and their roll out can be found at www.bairnshoosescotland.com.

13.15 Despite how impressive the first Bairns' Hoose is, there are a number of challenges to setting up a Bairns' Hoose such as finding, buying and re-purposing a suitable residential property and, once this is done, securing funding for the house's ongoing operational costs. Given Scotland's geography, any truly national roll out will also require a high number of houses so that no child has to travel an excessive distance to attend one. It may therefore be some years before the Barnahus model becomes standard practice in Scotland and the current practice – where children are interviewed at police stations, then taken to hospitals or clinics for medical examination, and provided with separate support through social services or the NHS – is likely to continue for some years.

Pro-active investigations

13.16 The nature of the allegation made by a complainer may lead the police to begin a 'pro-active' investigation into others who may have been the subject of similar offending. This type of investigation often arises when the allegation is made by an ex-partner or family member, and often when the allegation is non-recent or 'historical' (that is, the offending is alleged to have taken place more than one year ago). In such cases, the police will identify other family members or ex-partners of the suspect and will contact them to ascertain whether they wish to make any allegations. The same approach is taken to domestic-abuse allegations. It is common to see cases at the solemn level that involve either multiple family members or multiple ex-partners (or both) that have started from a pro-active investigation triggered by the allegations of a single family member or ex-partner, and for the final indictment in such cases to include a number of allegations of domestic, physical and sexual abuse against a series of ex-partners and family members.

Reporting to COPFS and joint reporting to COPFS and SCRA

13.17 As with all police investigations, if a police investigation into alleged sexual offending concludes with the arrest and charge of a suspect, or if the police have evidence that would justify charging a person they cannot find, then they must report the case to the Procurator Fiscal (ie, to COPFS). This allows COPFS to decide whether to prosecute, a decision exclusively for the Crown in Scotland. The duty to report is now contained in section 20(1)(d) of the Police and Fire Reform (Scotland) Act 2012. The report is prepared by a police officer on a national standard form, the Standard Prosecution Report (SPR): the police officer who prepares the report becomes the 'reporting officer' in the case. The content of the SPR and the material which must accompany it are set out in the publicly available 'Case Reporting Standard Operating Procedure document'.[9]

9 https://www.scotland.police.uk/spa-media/s5mj2mwo/case-reporting-sop.pdf.

13.18 Primary legislation has slightly modified the procedure for children. Previously, for any child under 16 or for any 16 or 17-year-old subject to supervision under the Children's Hearing system, if a report was made to COPFS, then under section 61 of the Children's Hearings (Scotland) Act 2011, police also had to make a report to the Principal Reporter (ie, to the Scottish Children's Reporter Administration (SCRA)). A report to the Principal Reporter is the first step in the case being dealt with by the Children's Hearing System. With the entry into force of the Children (Care and Justice) (Scotland) Act 2024, this obligation on the police now applies to all those under 18: that is, it now includes all 16 and 17-year-olds, not just those who are subject to supervision.[10]

13.19 The process of making a report to COPFS and the Principal Reporter is called 'joint reporting'. Since the obligation to jointly report only applies when a report is made to COPFS and not when the police choose only to make a report to the SCRA, Lord Advocate's guidelines to the police govern which cases should be jointly reported. The Lord Advocate issued the current version of the guidelines in December 2021.[11] Under those guidelines, the principal category of cases that should be jointly reported are offences which require to be prosecuted on indictment or which are so serious as normally to give rise to solemn proceedings. Further guidance is given on what offences fall into this category, and this covers a number of sexual offences:

(i) those offences which require by law to be prosecuted on indictment (which includes rape at common law, section 5(1) of the Criminal Law (Consolidation) (Scotland) Act 1995, and sections 1, 2, 18 and 19 of the Sexual Offences (Scotland) Act 2009);

(ii) those normally indicted in the High Court of Justiciary (which includes attempted rape, incest and related offences);

(iii) offences normally prosecuted on indictment (which includes assault with intent to rape);

(iv) The Sexual Offences (Scotland) Act 2009 offences that can be prosecuted on indictment (that is, all of the offences in the 2009 Act).

13.20 For (iv), if the police have any doubt about whether to jointly report, they are directed to seek the advice of sexual offences prosecutors in COPFS. Further, in assessing whether an offence under section 37 of the 2009 Act (older children engaging in sexual conduct with one another) should be jointly reported, the police are directed to have regard to a non-exhaustive list of nine indicators designed to enable them to determine whether the offence is merely sexual experimentation or something more serious and concerning.

10 S 1 of the 2024 Act changed the definition of 'a child' in the Children's Hearing (Scotland) Act 2011 from those under 16 to those under 18: see s 199 of the 2011 Act as amended by the 2024 Act.

11 https://www.copfs.gov.uk/publications/lord-advocate-s-guidelines-offences-committed-by-children/html/.

13.21 The purpose and advantage of joint reporting is that it allows for communication between COPFS and SCRA before COPFS takes any decision that the child should be prosecuted rather than considered by the Children's Hearing System. A binding agreement between COPFS and SCRA governs this process.[12] Under the agreement, the rebuttable presumption[13] is that the child will be referred to the Children's Hearing system rather than prosecuted. This is no different for sexual offences.

THE PROSECUTION OF SEXUAL OFFENCES

13.22 For adults, and for children where the decision is to prosecute rather than refer to the Children's Hearing system, there are a number of preparatory steps COPFS will take before a complaint or indictment is served in a sexual offences case. Before outlining those steps, it is worth setting out some of the situations in which the Crown will decide *not* to prosecute sexual offences in Scotland, and the applicable legal and policy frameworks for such decisions. These are in addition to cases where, applying the Prosecution Code, the Crown considers that a prosecution should not take place.[14]

13.23 Other than referral of children to the Children's Hearing system, the two main instances where there might not be a prosecution in a sexual offences case are where there is a decision to 'divert' the accused from prosecution and into social-work programmes, or where the complainer has difficulty engaging with COPFS, simply fails to engage with COPFS or positively does not wish the prosecution to proceed (so-called 'reluctant complainers').

Diversion from prosecution

13.24 Diversion from prosecution is the decision by the Crown to refer an accused to social work (or other agencies) to address the underlying causes of the alleged

12 Entitled '*Decision making in cases of child accused.*' The agreement was last updated in September 2023 and is available at: https://www.copfs.gov.uk/publications/decision-making-in-cases-of-child-accused/html/.

13 Consideration of whether the presumption is rebutted in any given case is governed by factors enumerated in the agreement such as the gravity of the offence and a pattern of serious offending by the child, weighed against other factors such as the best interests of the child and whether the Children's Hearing system is most likely to suitably address the child's needs and behaviour. The views of both the child and any victim (who may also be a child) must also be considered.

14 Evidential and public-interest considerations govern the decision as to whether there should be a prosecution. Evidential considerations include whether there is sufficient admissible, credible and reliable evidence. Credibility and reliability are treated slightly differently in the Code. Where there are grave and substantial concerns as to the reliability of essential evidence, criminal proceedings will not be appropriate. Where there are concerns regarding the credibility of the evidence, the prosecutor may take account of this in assessing whether there is sufficient evidence.

offending.[15] Diversion ought to be considered when there is an identifiable need which has contributed to the offending. The assessment is always whether diversion or prosecution is in the public interest. No offence is automatically excluded from consideration for diversion,[16] but the more serious the case, the less likely it is that diversion will be considered to be in the public interest. Consideration will also be given as to whether it would be in the public interest for prosecution to take place so that the court can make ancillary orders such as making the offender subject to the notification requirements under the Sexual Offences Act 2003 or making non-harassment orders so as to protect complainers.

13.25 Diversion involves asking the accused whether they would accept diversion. If they are willing to do so, they will be referred to and assessed by social work. If that assessment is favourable, then the accused will undergo whatever social-work programme has been identified as suitable. Once the accused has completed the programme, social work will prepare a completion report. Upon receipt of that report, COPFS will take the final decision as to whether to discontinue the proceedings: a positive report will usually result in a decision that no proceedings will be taken. The views of any complainer are also taken during this process.[17]

13.26 One of the challenges in diversion is that the availability of programmes for sexual offending varies between local authorities and it is not unusual to find that one local authority has programmes in place whereas another, often in an adjoining area, does not have those programmes. That should not lead to a postcode lottery: there is no requirement that a specific social-work programme be available before diversion is possible, and if no programme is said to be available, the local authority may be requested to produce a bespoke one.

13.27 For obvious reasons, the nature of social-work programmes, the needs they seek to address and thus the offences and offenders to which they might apply are not publicly discussed. That is particularly so in sexual offences cases. It suffices perhaps to say that, in assessing whether any given offender should be considered for diversion, the challenge is to ensure that diversion is used appropriately and that appropriate weight is given to factors such as the seriousness of the offence, the presumptions against prosecution that apply to those under 18, the views and rights of complainers, and the likelihood of social-work programmes being able to address any identified needs.

13.28 In July 2023, the Lord Advocate announced a review of diversion from prosecution for sexual offences. At the time of writing, the review is ongoing.

15 See Community Scotland's *National Guidelines on Diversion from Prosecution in Scotland*: https://communityjustice.scot/wp-content/uploads/2023/11/national-guidelines-on-diversion-from-prosecution.pdf at page 3 (introduction).

16 Ibid at page 4.

17 The process is set out in detail in the *National Guidelines on Diversion from Prosecution*, cited above, at pages 4 to 10.

Reluctant complainers

13.29 It is well recognised in Scotland and elsewhere that, in sexual offences cases and particularly those where the complainer and accused have been in an intimate relationship, there may be many reasons why a complainer might struggle to engage with the prosecution or not wish to give evidence. These can include ongoing trauma because of the offence, fear of the accused or others, fear of what the criminal justice process and giving evidence might involve, and frustration at any delays in the case coming to trial.

13.30 COPFS has a policy for such cases,[18] the stated focus of which is on not compelling complainers to testify, but at the same time making clear that the decision on whether a case will be prosecuted is one to be taken by the Crown in the public interest. As such, the policy requires prosecutors to attach very significant weight to the attitudes and views of the complainer whilst also weighing factors such as the dynamics of coercive control that may be present in the case, the nature of the offending behaviour, the risk posed by the accused, and the Crown's own responsibilities (including those under the ECHR to prosecute rape and other serious sexual offences and domestic abuse).

13.31 In any case where the complainer is reluctant, the duty on prosecutors is to explore the reasons for the complainer's reluctance, and to work, where possible, with other agencies to address these reasons and to provide support to the complainer. The purpose of exploring those reasons is twofold: (i) to discover whether there is anything that can be done to address that reluctance (for instance, addressing a fear of giving evidence in court by exploring the possibility of special measures such as evidence by commission or by live link); and (ii) to ensure that, if there is nothing that can be done to address that reluctance, the complainer is making a fully-informed decision not to engage and is aware of all of the consequences that might flow from a decision to discontinue proceedings.

13.32 Where the Crown decides to proceed with a case despite the complainer's reluctance or difficulty in engaging, the policy does not exclude that there may be cases where it might be necessary to seek a warrant from the court when a complainer refuses to attend to give evidence. The policy states the expectation that such cases will be exceptionally rare. They do, however, arise. An example is in a two-complainer case that depends entirely on mutual corroboration where, after the first complainer has given evidence, the second complainer refuses to give evidence. In any rape case, the Advocate Depute is required to seek Law Officer approval before moving for a warrant for a complainer.

18 Reluctant complainers in cases of rape and serious sexual offending policy, March 2018. https://www.copfs.gov.uk/publications/reluctant-complainers-in-cases-of-rape-and-serious-sexual-offending-policy/html/.

Discontinuing rape prosecutions

13.33 On 21 January 1982, as a result of public concern over the Crown's decision to discontinue proceedings in the 'Carol X' rape case, the Law Officers of the day made identical statements to each House of Parliament. The statements informed the Parliament that, on the instruction of the Lord Advocate, no decision to discontinue proceedings in any case of murder or rape would be taken before the hearing of evidence had begun without being referred to the Lord Advocate for decision.[19] In other words, from that date on, no prosecutor (in practice, no advocate depute) could discontinue proceedings for murder or rape in advance of trial without the approval of a Law Officer; at trial, the decision remained one for the advocate depute. The core principle remains as the Law Officers stated in 1982, but it has evolved slightly. It will apply to any decision to discontinue proceedings after an accused has been placed on petition: any decision to discontinue before that stage does not require approval. It also now applies in cases where the evidence has begun: if, during a trial, it appears to an advocate depute that a charge of rape should be withdrawn, he or she will be required to seek Law Officer approval. It will also apply: (i) to charges of indecent assault where that charge is used to prosecute historical conduct that would, if committed today, amount to rape (for instance, penile-anal penetration without consent); and (ii) any averment in a section 1 Domestic Abuse (Scotland) Act 2018 charge that alleges non-consensual sexual intercourse (whether penile-anal, penile-oral, or penile-vaginal).

The decision not to prosecute: the victim's right to review scheme

13.34 Section 4 of the Victims and Witnesses (Scotland) Act 2014 requires the Lord Advocate to make and publish rules about the process for reviewing, on the request of a person who is or appears to be a victim in relation to an offence or alleged offence, a decision of the prosecutor not to prosecute a person for that offence or alleged offence. The purpose of section 4, and the rules the Lord Advocate has made under it, were to give effect to the right to review of a decision not to prosecute that was created by Article 11 of Directive 2012/29/EU ('the Victims' Rights Directive').

13.35 The Lord Advocate's Rules took effect in July 2015 and are publicly available.[20] The right to review applies to decisions to take no action in a case reported by Police Scotland (or other reporting agency), or to stop or discontinue a case once court proceedings have started (but not where the decision is taken mid-trial by withdrawing a charge). The Rules exclude certain decisions and situations from the right to review: decisions taken by the court; decisions where one charge is stopped

19 The case was later the subject of a private prosecution *X v Sweeney* 1982 JC 70; see the unsuccessful appeal against conviction, *Sweeney v X* 1982 SCCR 509.

20 https://www.copfs.gov.uk/publications/lord-advocate-s-rules-review-of-a-decision-not-to-prosecute/html/.

or discontinued (or changed) but the court proceedings for other substantial and significant charges with the same victim continue; where a plea has been accepted; where the case has been dealt with by use of a direct measure (like a warning letter or fiscal fine); where the case has been referred to the Children's Reporter; or where the accused has been told that the proceedings have been stopped or discontinued.

13.36 Any victim can apply for a review. The application for review should normally be made within one month of the date the victim learns of the decision. The review will be taken by a lawyer ('a reviewer') who was not involved in the original decision, and he or she will consider the case papers and obtain any further information which may be required to take the decision. The reviewer will consider if the decision not to prosecute was reasonable, having regard to all the circumstances and in line with the Prosecution Code and COPFS prosecution policies. The review will ordinarily be completed within 20 working days. The Rules also allow for a person to request and receive more information about a decision not to prosecute, instead of or before deciding whether to exercise their right to review.

The decision to prosecute: preparation of the case by COPFS

13.37 The decision to prosecute in the High Court is taken by Crown Counsel (the collective term for the Law Officers and Advocates Depute) and in all other cases by Procurators Fiscal, all applying the test for prosecution as set out in the Prosecution Code: that there is sufficient admissible, reliable and credible evidence of a crime committed by the accused and that prosecution is in the public interest. Summary sexual offences cases are prepared by local offices around the country. Sheriff and jury sexual offences cases are prepared by regional specialist sexual offences teams. High Court sexual offences cases are prepared by national specialist sexual offences teams. These are accredited prosecutors and staff who have undergone training in the preparation and prosecution of such cases. The core task in all cases is the amassing and analysis of witness statements, productions and labels upon which a complaint or indictment can be prepared and served, but there are also a number of aspects of pre-trial preparation of a case which apply in sexual offences cases. We set these out before outlining some of the special rules and considerations that apply to the drafting of indictments or complaints in sexual offences cases.

Engaging complainers

13.38 Once a case is reported by the police to COPFS, the responsibility for providing information and support to a complainer passes from the police to COPFS. Contact between COPFS and the complainer will be made by a combination of the case preparer (a Procurator Fiscal Depute or other COPFS official responsible for preparing cases for trial); solemn legal managers (SLMs senior lawyers in COPFS responsible for supervising the preparation of cases); officials from COPFS's Victim

Information and Advice (VIA) service; and, in the latter stages of preparation, the Procurator Fiscal Depute or Advocate Depute who will conduct the trial or take the complainer's evidence at a commission.

13.39 Case preparers and SLMs will be responsible for conducting any precognition of the complainer (and what to precognosce on will very much be a judgement for them); for ascertaining the complainer's level of engagement; for discussing with the complainer whether it may be necessary to obtain personal or sensitive records such as medical records; and for providing basic information on the nature of the case (such as whether it is a single or multiple complainer case) and likely timescales.

13.40 VIA's role involves maintaining regular contact with the complainer and regularly providing information on the process and likely timescales; referring the complainer to other support organisations, if needed; identifying any vulnerabilities that might make special measures while giving evidence appropriate; and taking the complainer's views on those special measures.

13.41 The Procurator Fiscal Depute or Advocate Depute who conducts the trial/commission is required to meet the complainer in advance of the trial/commission – if necessary more than once – to explain the process and to discuss and alleviate any concerns the complainer might have about it.

Recovery of sensitive personal records

13.42 By their nature, sexual offences cases may require the Crown to obtain and, if necessary disclose, private information about a complainer. This is done in accordance with COPFS's Sensitive Records Policy.[21] Two scenarios fall to be distinguished.

13.43 First, when the Crown seeks to obtain medical records to evidence injuries to a complainer, it will write to the record holder to obtain them under the authority of the petition warrant in the case.

13.44 Second, different considerations apply to 'sensitive records' (defined in the policy as including, but not restricted to, medical, psychiatric or psychological, counselling, social work, education and employment records). Under the policy, recovery of such sensitive records is only to take place when necessary, and with due regard to the right to respect for private and family life in Article 8 ECHR and, where applicable, the United Nations Convention on the Rights of the Child. Normally, the complainer's or other witness's informed consent will be sought. If consent is not given, the records can be obtained by seeking a warrant from the court, but before seeking such a warrant, the policy requires that the matter be referred to Crown

[21] https://www.copfs.gov.uk/publications/sensitive-personal-records-policy/html/#:~:text=In%20the%20case%20of%20%27Sensitive,part%20of%20the%20actual%20record.

Counsel for a decision on whether to seek the warrant or discontinue the prosecution on some or all of the charges. The procedure on petitions for recovery of sensitive records (either by the Crown or defence) and the principles governing whether the court should give its authority to the recovery of such records is set out in Chapter 14 at **14.17–14.27**.

13.45 After the Crown has obtained either the consent of the complainer/witness or the authority of the court for the recovery of the records, the policy sets detailed rules on recovering the records, assessing them for relevancy and materiality, and for further consultation with the complainer/witness before disclosure, either to the defence or, occasionally, to expert witnesses.

Disclosure of evidence

13.46 The Crown's disclosure obligations are no different in sexual offences cases: the Crown must disclose all the evidence it proposes to rely on at trial and any other information which meets the test for disclosure in Part 6 of the Criminal Justice and Licensing (Scotland) Act 2010. There are, though, some specific practices which apply in sexual offences cases. Under paragraph 26.8 of the statutory code of practice issued by the Lord Advocate under section 164 of the 2010 Act,[22] the ordinary practice of providing the defence with electronic or physical copies of information, will not apply to information of a personal and highly sensitive nature when disclosing copies may either be extremely distressing to any individual or where the information consists of indecent images or other images of extreme pornography.[23] The code also states that the exception applies to police recordings of vulnerable witnesses being interviewed (that is, JIIs or VRIs); instead, arrangements should be made for the defence to view the recording at a Procurator Fiscal's office or police station.

Indicting sexual offences

13.47 There are a number of rules both in statute and at common law which regulate how indictments are framed in sexual offences cases. Most flow from the requirement – and one of the cornerstones of Scottish criminal procedure – that the Crown must give fair notice to the accused of the evidence it intends to lead at trial.[24] Four rules are of particular importance and relevance in sexual offences cases: implied latitude and exceptional latitude in stating the date of an offence, mixed charges, evidential charges, and dockets.

22 https://www.copfs.gov.uk/media/03znmxlq/code-of-practice-disclosure-of-evidence-in-criminal-proceedings.pdf.

23 Such images are rarely, if ever, shown to the Crown itself. Most images are graded by the Child Abuse Image Database: see Chapter 9 at **9.41**. When devices with such images are seized, the Crown's policy is not to return the device to the owner.

24 See *Nelson v HM Advocate* 1994 JC 94.

Implied latitude and exceptional latitude in specifying the date of the offence alleged

13.48 In historical cases or cases of repeated offending over the course of a relationship, the complainer may not be able to state with certainty when the alleged offending took place. Three rules apply. First, when a crime is libelled to have occurred on a specific date, there is an implied latitude in the indictment or complaint of three calendar months;[25] thus, if a crime is libelled as having occurred on 10 July 2024, the implied latitude runs from 1 June to 31 August 2024.[26] Second, the Crown is permitted to libel a crime as having been committed between two dates, if what is alleged is a continuous crime taking place over a considerable period of time.[27] Third, the Crown is permitted an exceptional latitude (sometimes called an unusual latitude) to libel a crime or crimes as having occurred not on a specific date but rather between two dates. The Crown will be permitted to do so when it can show sufficient reason for that latitude: that is, when it can show why more accurate and sufficient detail could not be given[28] and when it can show that due diligence has been taken to limit the latitude of time, for instance by thoroughly investigating the complaints.[29] The Crown often seeks to meet this requirement by obtaining housing or other records to show when the complainer or accused lived at the address, attended the school, etc, where the offending is alleged to have taken place.

13.49 This exceptional latitude is now commonplace in sexual offences cases. It has been allowed in sexual offences involving young children since the 1930s, if what is alleged is a course of criminal conduct.[30] Indeed, it has been allowed for all sexual offences since the time of the Institutional Writers, either when the nature of the offence alleged is that it has occurred on various occasions or over a long course of time,[31] or if a long period has elapsed between the date of the crime and the date of trial such that witnesses cannot be expected to remember specific dates.[32] These are usually the two reasons why the Crown will seek to libel a sexual offence or offences as having occurred between two dates. In such cases, the libel will read 'between [first date] and [second date], both dates inclusive, at [place] you, John Smith, did…'.

25 Hume, ii, 221; Alison, ii, 251, preserved in para 4(1) of Sch 3 to the 1995 Act.

26 Hume, ii, 221 (using the example of 10 July 1796).

27 See the reset cases *HM Advocate v McDonald* (1888) 1 White 593 and *Maguire v HM Advocate* (1908) 5 Adam 539.

28 *Ogg v HM Advocate* 1938 JC 152 based on Alison, ii, 256–257.

29 *Stewart v HM Advocate* 2005 SCCR 635 at para 21. *Stewart* recognised (at para 22) that when historical complaints are eventually made there may be a lack of precision about dates, and that there were difficulties for the appellant in that case where such a wide latitude was to be taken. It went on to observe that these were difficulties for both defence and Crown, and that allowance could be made both in the conduct of the defence and the trial judge's directions to the jury for such difficulties as the appellant might face. It is suggested that these observations apply generally to such cases.

30 *HM Advocate v AE* 1937 JC 96.

31 See Hume, ii, 222–223; and Alison, ii, 256.

32 Macdonald, 218; Hume, ii, 223; Alison, ii, 257; and *HM Advocate v James Stewart* (1875) 3 Couper 147.

13.50 If the complainer speaks to the offending occurring in a narrower timeframe than libelled, the Crown will be expected to move to amend the indictment/complaint to reflect that narrower timeframe. If the complainer speaks to a wider or totally different timeframe, the rules on amendment of the indictment/complaint in sections 96/159 will apply: amendment will be permissible to cure any discrepancy or variance between the indictment/complaint and the evidence given, unless the court sees just cause to the contrary; no amendment may be authorised which changes the character of the offence charged; and if the accused is prejudiced by any amendment made, the court must grant such remedy, by adjournment or otherwise, as appears to the court to be just.[33]

Mixed charges

13.51 Normally, unless libelling a course of conduct or a series of similar offences, one charge in an indictment or complaint should cover one crime. Section 288BB of the Criminal Procedure (Scotland) Act 1995 – inserted by the Criminal Justice and Licensing (Scotland) Act 2010 – allows for two particular exceptions in sexual offences cases.

13.52 First, it allows for an indictment or complaint to include a charge which covers more than one offence under the Sexual Offences (Scotland) Act 2009. There are all sorts of permutations. One of the most common is a charge which alleges sexual assault, contrary to section 3 of the 2009 Act, and rape, contrary to section 1, where the sexual assault takes place shortly before, during or shortly after the rape (though there is no requirement in section 288BB that the two offences be proximate in time). In such situations, it is common for the Crown to move to delete the reference to the more minor charge at the close of the Crown case or at the end of all the evidence in a case, so that the jury can focus on the more serious charge, and the judge does not need to direct them on the elements of the offence of the minor charge.[34]

13.53 Second, section 288BB also allows for a charge to cover both a 2009 Act offence and any other act or omission, 'except by way of reference to a statutory offence'. The provision could have been more simply drafted but the Explanatory Notes (at para 296) make clear that the intention is to allow a charge which covers a

33 On amendment to bring dates into line with a complainer's evidence, see *McCafferty v HM Advocate* 2020 SCCR 105 at para 17. When the Crown libels a timeframe rather than a specific date, it is unclear whether the implied latitude applies. *Creighton v HM Advocate* (1904) 4 Adam 356 is authority for the proposition that the implied latitude cannot apply when the period specified spans more than one month because that would create ambiguity as to when the implied latitude begins and ends. *Andrew v HM Advocate* 1982 SCCR 539 is authority for the proposition that the implied latitude does not apply even when the period specified falls entirely within a single calendar month, but the correctness of *Andrew* was doubted in *Kearney v Ramage* 2007 SCCR 35.

34 The minor charge might be left in where it is of a similar order of offending to the more serious charge. An example would be a charge that includes a s 1 rape and a particularly serious s 2 sexual assault by penetration, particularly if injury is caused by the latter.

2009 Act offence and a common law offence (and only a common law offence). For instance, it allows a charge covering assault at common law and rape under section 1. This frequently occurs when an assault takes place shortly before, during or shortly after the rape. Judges will usually direct juries that references to common law crimes such as assault are included in the charge as narrative only.

Evidential charges

13.54 Evidential charges are those included on an indictment or complaint to allow the Crown to lead evidence of criminal behaviour that is relevant to proof of the main charge or charges on the indictment or complaint. They are called evidential charges because their purpose is to allow the Crown to lead that evidence; the Crown normally does not seek a conviction on such charges and will withdraw them at the close of the Crown case or the end of all the evidence in the case. Evidential charges that are commonly seen in sexual offences indictments are: charges of threatening or abusive behaviour, contrary to section 38 of the Criminal Justice and Licensing (Scotland) Act 2010 (to lead evidence of such behaviour by the accused, either before, during or after the alleged sexual offence, where that might be relevant to explaining how sexual activity came to take place and why the complainer did not consent to it); and charges under the Misuse of Drugs Act 1971 (to lead evidence either that the accused took drugs or supplied drugs to the complainer before the alleged sexual offence, where that might be relevant either to the accused's *mens rea* or the complainer's capacity to consent).[35] The Crown seldom, if ever, seeks a conviction for such charges in High Court cases. The evidence led remains available for the jury to consider if relevant to the remaining charges,[36] including for mutual corroboration.[37]

Dockets

13.55 A docket is a note appearing after the charges on an indictment or complaint. It gives notice that the Crown might lead evidence that the accused has committed a crime not covered by the charges on the indictment. There are two forms: 'common law docket' and a docket under section 288BA of the 1995 Act. The difference is that if the subject of the docket is sexual, the docket will be under the authority of section 288BA; if not, it will be a common law docket.

13.56 The authority for including a common law docket on an indictment or complaint is the Appeal Court's *obiter dictum* suggesting the practice in *Fraser v HM Advocate*,[38] quoted with approval in *HM Advocate v Moynihan*.[39] That *obiter*

35 Despite the prevalence of certain drugs such as cannabis, for the time being the taking of any illegal drugs by a complainer will require a Crown section 275 application because it implies bad character. Such applications are usually granted.

36 *McDonald v HM Advocate* 1995 SLT 1101; and *HM Advocate v Mair* 2014 JC 137.

37 *Cannell v HM Advocate* 2009 SCCR 207 at para 34; *Lauchlan and O'Neill v HM Advocate (no 2)* 2015 JC 75 at para 27.

38 2014 JC 115 at para 50.

39 2019 SCCR 61 at para 12.

dictum has never been disapproved and the practice of common law dockets is now well established.

13.57 Section 288BA provides that an indictment or complaint may include a docket which specifies any act or omission that is 'connected with a sexual offence'. By subsection (2), an act or omission is connected with a sexual offence if it:

'(a) is specifiable by way of reference to a sexual offence, and
(b) relates to—
    (i) the same event as the offence charged, or
    (ii) a series of events of which that offence is also part.'

13.58 Paragraph (a) means that the act or omission must be capable of being described as a sexual offence, and paragraph (b) means that the evidence must be relevant to the offence or offences charged.[40] Paragraph (b)(ii) makes clear that this can include a course of conduct, so the docket can be included for the purposes of mutual corroboration. By subsection (4), it does not matter whether the act or omission, if it were instead charged as an offence, could not be competently tried by the court. This allows the docket to cover: acts or omissions committed outside Scotland;[41] ones for which the accused has already been convicted or acquitted (in Scotland or elsewhere, provided no mention is made of the fact of conviction);[42] ones for which the relevant offence would be time-barred;[43] ones for which the Crown has renounced the right to prosecute;[44] and ones for which the accused would, if the conduct occurred now, be under the age of criminal responsibility.[45] The reason this is possible is that including such acts or omissions in a docket does not amount to trying the accused for that conduct: the docket is 'background material which may, or may not, assist in establishing facts relevant to the proof of one or more of the formal charges in the indictment'.[46]

13.59 Section 288BA(5) states that, where, under subsection (1), a docket is included on an indictment or complaint, it is to be presumed that the accused has been give fair notice of the prosecutor's intention to lead that evidence and that the evidence is admissible as relevant.

40 *Moynihan* n 39 above at para 19.

41 See, *mutatis mutandis*, *Lauchlan and O'Neill (no 2)*, cited above, approved on this point in *Moynihan* at para 9.

42 Previous convictions: *Moynihan*, cited above. Previous acquittals: *Kerr v HM Advocate* 2016 JC 32 and *Fisher v HM Advocate* 2023 JC 21 (this including, per *Kerr*, a plea of not guilty accepted by the Crown). For convictions, this includes cases where the accused pled guilty. No issue will arise from the difficulties to the defence, as a result of that guilty plea, in cross-examining the docket witness on his or her account: the Appeal Court found in *HM Advocate v Adams* 2021 JC 87 (a case concerning a guilty plea in England and Wales) that this was no different from the situation where the accused might accept his guilt of part of the libel in an indictment. For previous acquittals, *Fisher* also found that docketing a previous acquittal did not infringe the presumption of innocence in Art 6(2) ECHR or violate the right to private life in Art 8. The Supreme Court refused permission to appeal on 12 May 2022.

43 *HM Advocate v AD* 2018 JC 109.

44 See *Moynihan* at para 9.

45 *Deeney v HM Advocate* 2021 SCCR 222.

46 *HM Advocate v AD*, cited above, at para 32.

13.60 The docket, whether at common law or under section 288BA, will be drafted without including the name of any crime.[47]

Pre-trial applications

Applications for special measures

13.61 When drafting an indictment or complaint, the Crown will also consider what special measures to seek on behalf of complainers or other witnesses. The views of the complainer/witness will be taken by COPFS's Victim Information and Advice service (VIA), who will also seek to identify particular vulnerabilities that might make a special measure necessary or more suitable. It remains for the Crown to decide which is the most appropriate special measure to seek. For instance, though there might be a recorded VRI or JII that could be used as a prior statement and stand as the witness's evidence-in-chief at trial, the Crown may take the view that, because of concerns as to the quality of the VRI/JII (and those concerns could be as simple as concerns over the sound or video quality in the recording), it is better not to use the VRI/JII and to take the evidence anew, either at a commission or at the trial itself.

13.62 Once a view has been reached, a vulnerable witness notice or application will be drafted, intimated to the defence and lodged with the Court. Where it is proposed to use a VRI/JII as a prior statement, the Crown will identify any parts of it that can be edited out as irrelevant (for instance, any general questions at the start that were designed to build a rapport with the witness) or inadmissible (for instance, any inadmissible hearsay), and will seek to agree such edits with the defence ahead of any first diet or preliminary hearing. Any application to take the evidence of a witness from abroad or elsewhere in the United Kingdom will usually be drafted at this stage.

Applications to prevent the personal conduct of a defence and for section 274 to apply to the case

13.63 These two situations are related but not always the same. With the exception of JP court proceedings, the prohibition on the personal conduct of a defence applies

47 A typical example is: 'TAKE NOTICE that in terms of section 288BA of the Criminal Procedure (Scotland) Act 1995 the Crown intends to lead at your trial that: on [date] at [locus] you [accused] did restrain [witness], c/o Police Service of Scotland, Edinburgh, struggle with her, pull down her lower clothing and penetrate her vagina with your penis.' In accordance with Practice Note No 2 of 2016, when the indictment is read to the jury as required by s 88(5) of the 1995 Act, any docket under s 288BA should also be read to the jury and a copy of the docket should be provided to the jury. Though not covered in the Practice Note, the same will apply to any common law docket. The Practice Note also states that judges may wish to include an explanation of the purpose of the docket in their introductory remarks to the jury (though of course the reason the act or omission is in the docket and not a charge will not usually be explained to them).

to all sexual offences listed in section 288C of the 1995 Act. By section 288DC it also applies all domestic abuse cases.[48]

13.64 There is, though, something of an anomaly between section 288C and section 288DC. The prohibition on the personal conduct of a defence only applies to the offences listed in 288C and only to any other offence if the court is persuaded that there appears to be a substantial sexual element in the alleged commission of that other offence: section 288C(4). The restriction in section 274 on sexual history and bad character evidence only applies to those sexual offences specified in section 288C or when the court has made an order under section 288C(4). The anomaly arises because domestic abuse cases are not on the list in section 288C and nothing in section 288DC itself automatically extends the restriction in section 274 to them.

13.65 At the time of writing, the Scottish Government's intention is to introduce an amendment to the Victims, Witnesses, and Justice Reform (Scotland) Bill to remove this anomaly, at least where the domestic abuse contains a sexual element. As matters stand, the anomaly has two consequences. First, in any case which does not involve an offence listed in 288C or is not a domestic abuse case, if the Crown considers that the accused should be prohibited from conducting his or her own defence, then it must make an application to the court and satisfy the court that section 288C(4) applies: that is, that there appears to be a substantial sexual element in the alleged commission of the offence. Second, in any domestic abuse case where the Crown considers that the restriction in section 274 should apply, then similarly the Crown must make an application to the court under section 288C(4). Such applications ought normally to be prepared at the same time as any other pre-trial Crown application. For the courts' duties under section 288C and 288DC, see Chapter 14 at **14.28–4.38**.

Orders for lifelong restriction: notices under section 210B(2)

13.66 Section 210B of the 1995 Act allows the Crown, upon conviction, to move the court to make a risk assessment order, the means by which the court can consider whether the criteria for imposing an order for lifelong restriction are met. The Crown can only make such a motion if it has given the accused notice of its intention to do so: section 210B(2). The Crown serves such a notice in a minority of High Court cases (most risk assessment orders are made by the High Court on its own motion) but, if served, any such notice will normally be served with the indictment.

Crown section 275 applications and precognition on all section 275 applications

13.67 Crown section 275 applications – for instance, to lead evidence of sexual activity shortly before the incident libelled or to lead evidence of drug use by a

48 That is, where the charge is a contravention of s 1(1) of the Domestic Abuse (Scotland) Act 2018 or when the offence is alleged to be aggravated by abuse of a partner or ex-partner under s 1(1)(a) of the Abusive Behaviour and Sexual Harm (Scotland) Act 2016. The same exception is made for JP court proceedings.

complainer which has led to intoxication and an inability to consent – are usually drafted at the same time as any indictment or complaint, though often they are not finalised until the case is being prepared for a first diet/preliminary hearing.

13.68 One of the other pre-trial responsibilities of the Crown is the precognition of complainers on section 275 applications and the communication of the complainer's comments of the accuracy of any allegations in the application and any objections she might have to it, a responsibility arising from the full-Bench decision in *RR v HM Advocate*.[49] The responsibility applies to both Crown and defence applications. In respect of Crown applications, the complainer's views will be taken when the application is first drafted. In respect of defence applications, the views will be taken when the application is received (in practice in the week before the preliminary hearing). When it has not been possible to obtain those views before the preliminary hearing (the tight timescale of seven-days before a preliminary hearing for lodging a section 275 application can often make it difficult to contact the complainer and arrange precognition before the preliminary hearing), the court's consideration of the application may be deferred to a continued preliminary hearing to allow time for that to be done. The case preparer usually carries out the precognition.

Service of the indictment or complaint

13.69 Once an indictment or complaint has been drafted, it will be signed. In solemn cases the indictment is served; in summary cases, the accused will be cited to appear. In sexual offences and domestic abuse cases, the indictment or citation must be accompanied by a notice advising the accused that he or she is prohibited from conducting his or her own defence, that it is in his or her interest to get the professional assistance of a solicitor and that if he or she does not, the court will appoint one.[50] When doing so, the Crown will also serve a signed copy of the accused's previous convictions and a statement of uncontroversial evidence (SOUE) under section 258 of the 1995 Act. In sexual offences cases, the SOUE will normally invite agreement on matters such as: identification (that when a complainer or other witness refers in his or her evidence to 'John Smith' or 'John', he or she is referring to the accused, John Smith; a matter of importance if the witness is giving evidence with special measures which means he or she cannot identify the accused in court); uncontroversial medical or scientific evidence; and, often in historical cases or cases involving offences committed in the course of intimate relationships where the offences are alleged to have been committed in the family home, that the accused and/or complainer lived at certain addresses during certain periods.

49 2021 JC 167.

50 For solemn cases, ss 66(6) and (6A), and for summary cases, s 140(2A) of the Criminal Procedure (Scotland) Act 1995. In solemn cases, when the accused already has a solicitor, that notice and a second notice of service, required s 66(6C) of the 1995 Act, will be served on the solicitor.

Chapter 14

The trial of sexual offences

INTRODUCTION

14.01 In this chapter we discuss aspects of the scheme for preliminary hearings and first diets and draw attention to matters which arise in the context of the trial of sexual offences, or which may have a particular importance in such prosecutions. The general provisions of the scheme of course apply to prosecutions charging sexual offences as they apply to any other form of prosecution on indictment. However, important discrete considerations arise in relation to the prosecution of sexual offences. These matters are discussed more fully below. One consideration which arises with particular importance in the prosecution of sexual offences concerns the detailed provisions which apply in relation to taking the evidence of vulnerable witnesses. Given the importance and complexity of these provisions we have dealt with them separately in Chapter 17.

PRELIMINARY HEARINGS AND FIRST DIETS

14.02 The scheme for preliminary hearings was introduced in 2005 as a case management procedure for all cases prosecuted in the High Court. It was subsequently extended to include cases prosecuted on indictment in the sheriff court where the case management procedure takes place at first diets.[1]

The procedure leading up to the hearing

14.03 The outline of the scheme is that the accused person is indicted by the Crown to attend at a preliminary hearing or first diet. When the procedures were

1 The scheme was introduced into the High Court as a consequence of the recommendations made in the 2002 Review of the Practices and Procedure of the High Court conducted by Lord Bonomy. The scheme for the management of solemn cases in the sheriff court, which largely mirrors the High Court scheme, was introduced by the Criminal Justice (Scotland) Act 2016 following on from the recommendations set out in the Bowen report (The Independent Review of Sheriff and Jury Procedure, Sheriff Principal Bowen (2010)).

first introduced, and as extended to the sheriff court, a timetable for the holding of a preliminary hearing (or first diet) and a trial diet, was fixed which distinguished between accused persons who were on bail (or otherwise at liberty) and those who were remanded in custody. Unless the accused person was remanded in custody, a preliminary hearing (or first diet) required to be held within a period of 11 months of the first appearance on petition and the trial diet required to be commenced within a period of 12 months from that same date. For those remanded in custody the relevant periods were 110 days and 140 days from the date of full committal.[2]

14.04 The current position is governed by the amendments brought about by the Coronavirus (Recovery and Reform) (Scotland) Act 2022 for accused persons who appeared on petition after 1 October 2022. For those who are not remanded in custody, the preliminary hearing (or first diet) requires to be held within 17 months of first appearance on petition and the trial diet within 18 months of that date. For those remanded in custody the relevant periods are 290 days and 320 days from full committal.[3] Any of the periods mentioned may be extended on application made to it by the court.[4]

14.05 The Crown and the defence are each required to prepare a written record of their state of preparation, which must be lodged with the court in advance of a preliminary hearing (or first diet).[5] Amongst other steps to be taken, any vulnerable or child witnesses which the party intends to call must be identified in the written record. In addition to preparing this document the accused is required to lodge a defence statement at least 14 days before a preliminary hearing (or first diet)[6] which must set out the matters specified in section 70A(9) of the 1995 Act. Further statements should be lodged prior to the commencement of the trial intimating any change in circumstances or confirming that there has been no change.[7]

The conduct of the hearing

14.06 The statutory provisions governing the procedure to be carried out at preliminary hearings (and first diets) are to be found between sections 71 and 75 of the 1995 Act. A number of Practice Notes issued by the Lord Justice General also

2 S 65 of the Criminal Procedure (Scotland) Act 1995.

3 These periods will apply to 30 November 2024 unless a later date is specified by regulation – s 52 of the 2022 Act and SSI 2023/360. S 52(3)(b) provides that a date later than 30 November 2025 may not be specified. It remains to be seen what will happen when the temporary provisions expire.

4 S 65(3).

5 Ss 71C and 72E. The written records for first diets and preliminary hearings require to be in accordance with Form 9.3A and Form 9A.4 respectively of the Act of Adjournal (Criminal Procedure Rules) 1996. The Criminal Courts Practice Note No 3 of 2015 and The High Court of Justiciary Practice Note No 1 of 2005 provide general guidance in relation to the conduct of first diets and preliminary hearings.

6 S 70A(2) and (3).

7 S 70A(4). The obligation to lodge a 'no change' statement appears to be largely ignored in practice.

provide guidance as to the conduct of preliminary hearings, some of which will be looked at in more detail below.

14.07 In general terms, the case management procedures are similar as between first diets and preliminary hearings. The court is to dispose of any preliminary pleas,[8] objections to the admissibility of evidence or other preliminary issues,[9] to ascertain which witnesses are required and to identify the extent to which parties have complied with the duty to seek agreement of evidence.[10]

14.08 Decisions in respect of how the evidence of vulnerable or child witnesses is to be taken may be dealt with administratively in advance, but any that remain undetermined must be addressed at the hearing.[11] Professional and police witnesses who are able to give evidence remotely are also to be identified (this is the practice in High Court cases but does not yet seem to be prevalent in cases prosecuted on indictment in the sheriff court). A 'ground rules hearing'[12] may need to be convened alongside the preliminary hearing or first diet. Any application made under section 275 of the 1995 Act must be adjudicated upon. This will include the Crown providing the court with the views of the complainer on any such applications (whether made by the Crown or defence).

14.09 The court will also consider whether any special defence of consent is in the proper form (such as there being no reference in it to reasonable belief if that is not an issue in the case and conversely, it being included if it is). Practices vary, but in cases where there is a special defence of consent to more than one charge, many judges will wish there to be separate special defences to each charge (that is, in separate documents), rather than a single special defence.

14.10 There will also be discussion of a joint minute. The expectation from the court is that a joint minute is agreed by the time of the preliminary hearing and is not submitted as a 'draft joint minute'. In cases where the defence is one of consent, the expectation (and usual practice between Crown and defence) will be that penetration will be agreed in the joint minute, thus obviating, in many such cases, the need for scientific evidence to be led.[13] It is common in cases where a child or vulnerable witness gives evidence with special measures (and thus cannot carry out a dock identification of the accused) for a joint minute to agree identification.[14] Medical and scientific evidence will also, in so far as possible, be agreed.

8 As defined in s 79(2)(a).

9 As defined in s 79(2)(b).

10 The duties of the court in first diets and preliminary hearings are set out in ss 71 and 72 of the 1995 Act.

11 For a discussion as to the procedures surrounding such decisions see Chapter 17.

12 See **17.31–17.39**.

13 In the form 'on [date] at [locus] the accused, John Smith, penetrated the mouth/anus/vagina of Jane Smith with his penis/finger.'

14 Usually in the form: 'when Jane Smith refers in her evidence to 'John' or 'John Smith', she is referring to the accused, John Smith.' This will apply in cases where identification is not an issue in the case, for instance because penetration is accepted or the complainer has identified the accused at a VIPER parade.

14.11 At the conclusion of the preliminary hearing (or first diet) the court will consider any application for the extension of the relevant time limits which might be necessary in view of the anticipated trial diet, fix a trial diet and, where the accused person is on bail, review the conditions of bail and if appropriate to do so fix bail on different conditions.[15]

14.12 In order that the defence may properly be in a position to prepare its case in advance of the preliminary hearing (or first diet) a statutory duty is imposed upon the Crown to disclose the information which it is likely to lead by way of evidence at the trial, along with any information held by the Crown which would materially weaken that evidence or strengthen the accused's case.[16] The statute requires the disclosure of this material to be made as soon as practicable after the accused appears for the first time on petition (or on indictment if he did not previously appear on petition). The Crown's Disclosure Manual and the Code of Practice[17] issued in terms of section 164 of the Criminal Justice and Licensing (Scotland) Act 2010 Act set out the mechanics and timescales for compliance with the statutory duties which COPFS staff are expected to comply with.

14.13 In light of these procedures the court will expect that each party will have undertaken whatever case preparation is necessary in advance of the preliminary hearing (or first diet). As Lord Bracadale stated in providing general guidance as to the conduct of preliminary hearings in the case of *HM Advocate v Forrester*:[18]

> 'Parliament had in contemplation that the preliminary hearing would be the end-point of preparation rather than the starting point.'

14.14 It follows that at the hearing the presiding judge or sheriff will expect to examine closely the respective state of preparation for trial of each party along with the extent to which the other duties specified have been complied with. In terms of section 72(6)(b)(iv) the court is given the power to dispose of:

> 'any other matter which, in the opinion of the court, could be disposed of with advantage before the trial;'

14.15 When taken along with the power in section 72D(4) to:

> '... ask the prosecutor and the accused any question in connection with any matter which it is required to dispose of or ascertain under section 72 of this Act.'

it is clear that the court is capable of exercising a wide-ranging case management power at either a preliminary hearing or first diet. Parties may expect this power to be used with particular focus in determining which witnesses are necessary and what areas of evidence are capable of being agreed.

15 Ss 71B and 72A.
16 S 121 of the Criminal Justice and Licensing (Scotland) Act 2010.
17 COPFS Code of Practice: Disclosure of evidence in criminal proceedings.
18 2007 SCCR 216.

14.16 A continuation of the preliminary hearing (or first diet) ought to be a most unusual occurrence. One exception that does arise in practice is when the views of a complainer on a section 275 application have not been obtained in time for the preliminary hearing (which can arise if the application is late or has been lodged just within the seven-day time-limit). There, the obligation on the court to have the complainer's views before ruling on the application will justify continuing that issue to a continued preliminary hearing; all other matters in the case will still be decided at the preliminary hearing. If any ongoing preparation is necessary in advance of the trial diet the court will likely nevertheless fix a trial diet at the preliminary hearing and identify a timeframe within which the relevant preparations are to be carried out.

RECOVERY OF SENSITIVE RECORDS

14.17 In some circumstances, the defence may wish to obtain records held by other parties relating to the complainer or other witnesses. Examples include medical records, social work records, school records, telephone records and social media records. An accused person has, of course, no automatic right of access to records of any sort concerning other individuals, far less any right to access sensitive documents such as medical records. Nevertheless, the High Court of Justiciary has always had power at common law[19] to grant access to any form of record held by another on application made to it by way of petition for an order granting commission and diligence for recovery of the documents (or other items) in question.

14.18 For proceedings in the High Court, this remains the appropriate procedure where the items sought are held by third parties. If they are in the possession of the Crown an order for production may be sought.[20] In sheriff court proceedings (or in proceedings before a JP court) section 301A of the 1995 Act now allows a sheriff to make an order granting commission and diligence for the recovery of documents or an order for the production of documents.

14.19 The Crown's approach to the recovery of sensitive records which it may require for the presentation of its own case is set out in its policy document 'Sensitive personal records policy'.[21] Where a complainer (or other witness) does not consent to the recovery of any such sensitive records as the Crown may consider necessary an application will be made to the court in the same manner as applies to an application made on behalf of the accused.[22]

14.20 A petition for commission and diligence should be accompanied by a specification of documents which must identify the records, or documents, which

19 *HM Advocate v Hasson* 1971 JC 35, *McLeod v HM Advocate (No. 2)* 1998 JC 67.

20 *McLeod v HM Advocate* at page 69E.

21 See Chapter 13 at **13.42** and n 21 in that chapter.

22 The Crown's policy document at para 38 requires the witness to be informed of their right to object to recovery and of the right to Legal Aid to represent the witness before the court for this purpose – see **14.21**.

the applicant seeks to recover. The documents must be sufficiently identified by description and by date range. On a petition being presented, the court will consider whether to grant an order for service on the Crown (in the case of a defence application), any havers and any interested parties. If it decides to do so it should fix a date for a hearing which may coincide with the date for a preliminary hearing or first diet. In both the High Court and the sheriff court the Scottish Courts and Tribunal Service will facilitate service of the application on the complainer or witness if this is not known to the accused.

14.21 The most commonly encountered petitions seek recovery of documents or records concerning personal data relating to a witness, usually the complainer. In such circumstances, it is likely that the Article 8 ECHR rights of the person concerned will be engaged.[23] If this is the case, the person whose records it is sought to recover has the right to be heard on the application. Legal aid provision exists to assist with representation in relation to proceedings concerning an application for an order of recovery of documents in connection with criminal proceedings in which that person's medical records or other sensitive documents are sought.[24] This can include challenging a first instance decision by appeal, either in terms of section 301A(5) if the application is initiated in the sheriff court or by way of petition to the nobile officium if the application relates to High Court proceedings.[25] The haver of any document sought will also have the right to be heard in opposition to any application, regardless of whether the person to whom the records relate chooses to do so.

14.22 The test which requires to be met in presenting a petition for commission and diligence was set out in the opinion of the Lord Justice General in the case of *McLeod v HM Advocate (No. 2)* at page 80. He explained that the accused person[26] must satisfy the court by averments in the petition (as supplemented by oral submissions) that the recovery of the documents sought will serve a proper purpose and that it is in the interests of justice to grant the order sought. This in turn means that the court must be satisfied that an order for the production of the particular documents would be likely to be of material assistance to the proper preparation or presentation of the accused's defence (or the party's case). Thus, in an application on behalf of an accused person he will need to show how the documents relate to the charge or charges which he faces and the proposed defence to them. If the court is minded to grant the order sought, or a restricted version of it, a commissioner may, if necessary, be appointed to take relevant extracts from the body of documents recovered.

23 Medical records and telephone records have been held to fall within this category – *Z v Finland* (1997) 25 EHRR 371, *F v Scottish Ministers* 2016 SLT 359, *Halford v United Kingdom* (1997) 24 EHHR 523, *Saber v Norway* [2020] ECHR 912, *AR v HM Advocate* [2019] HCJ 81. Social work records and records kept by educational establishments or employers concerning the person would also seem to engage the right to respect for private life and correspondence.

24 The Advice and Assistance (Proceedings for Recovery of Documents) (Scotland) Regulations 2017 (SSI 2017/291).

25 *JC Petitioner* 2020 JC 155.

26 The same test would require to be met in an application made by the Crown.

14.23 Petitions on behalf of the accused seeking the recovery of documents such as medical records, social work or educational records have often proceeded upon the proposition that the information contained therein will be relevant to an assessment of the credibility and reliability of the complainer (or other witness). In any application for commission and diligence, but perhaps more particularly when such a contention is advanced, the court requires to consider the purpose to which the accused wishes to put the material sought. It will require to be satisfied that the material sought is capable of being used evidentially in the manner contemplated in the petition.

14.24 In general, matters of credibility and reliability fall to be determined by the jury (or sheriff) upon their assessment of the witness and the testimony given without the contribution of opinion evidence from others, be they lay or expert witnesses. As discussed at **18.13** and **18.55** if a witness has an objective medical condition bearing upon his or her credibility then (and only then) expert medical evidence of that condition and its general effects may be admissible either at common law or in terms of section 275(1)(a)(ii) of the 1995 Act.

14.25 The consequence of this limited extent to which evidence can be led impacting on the credibility or reliability of a witness is that any application which seeks recovery of documents with this aim in mind will require to contain sufficient by way of vouched averments to satisfy the court that the underlying purpose can properly be achieved.[27]

14.26 In the case of *Procurator Fiscal Falkirk v BM*[28] the Sheriff Appeal Court issued a judgment concerning an application for recovery of telephone records acknowledging that such an application engaged the complainer's rights in terms of Article 8 and emphasising that the procedure for recovery of sensitive personal records applied with equal vigour to such an application. When discussing that procedure the SAC emphasised the importance of vouched intimation of an application for commission and diligence providing the complainer with an explanation of where and when the application was to be heard along with information setting out the complainer's right to be heard on the application, her right to apply for legal advice

27 In *JC Petitioner* the application presented by the accused facing trial on charges of rape and assault of his former partner contained averments that the complainer suffered from poor mental health, had anger management issues and might have a personality disorder. The complainer had mentioned in her statement to the police that she had suffered from mental health problems since her teenage years. In recalling the order of the first instance court granting the commission and diligence the Appeal Court noted that the accused's petition contained no examples of how any condition which the complainer was said to be suffering from manifested itself, gave no examples of situations in which the complainer had given false accounts of events as a consequence of her illness and gave no information about any treatment or medication supplied to the complainer. It also noted that those who acted for the accused were not in possession of any medical advice vouching the contention that the description of the complainer's mental health was consistent with any known medical condition which would manifest itself in a lack of reliability or truthfulness. In these circumstances the Appeal Court concluded that there was no basis set out upon which an order for recovery of medical records could be granted.

28 2024 SLT (SAC) 7.

and assistance for that purpose and the possible availability of legal aid. In relation to determining any such application the SAC emphasised that regardless of the position taken by the Crown, it was incumbent on the sheriff hearing it to properly consider the application by reference to the test set out in *McLeod v HM Advocate (No.2)*. It was accordingly necessary for the accused in that case to specify why the production of the complainer's telephone records would be of material assistance to the presentation of his case.

14.27 It is equally competent to present a petition for the recovery of property rather than documents. Such an application requires to meet the same tests as set out above and the haver (or person whose Article 8 rights may be affected by recovery) will have a right to be heard.[29] It should be noted however that the power which a sheriff may exercise in terms of section 301A of the 1995 Act is restricted to recovery or production of documents. Accordingly, any petition seeking recovery or production of property in relation to proceedings in the sheriff court would have to be presented to the High Court (as was the case in relation to documents prior to the introduction of section 301A).

THE PROHIBITION OF PERSONAL CONDUCT

14.28 With the exception of JP court proceedings, an accused person (regardless of gender or sex) is prohibited from personally conducting any evidential hearing in a sexual offences case or a domestic abuse case.[30] The types of case in which the prohibitions apply are specified in sections 288C(2) and 288DC(1) of the 1995 Act. Section 288C applies the prohibition to the whole spectrum of cases which involve criminal sexual conduct, or an attempt to commit such an offence. It also includes a provision allowing the court to apply the prohibition in the case of an offence other than one specified if satisfied that there appears to be such a substantial sexual element to the commission of the offence charged that it ought to be treated in the same way.[31] Section 288DC applies the prohibition to cases where a charge under section 1(1) of the Domestic Abuse Act (Scotland) 2018 is brought or to a case in which a charge is aggravated in terms of section 1(1) of the Abusive Behaviour and Sexual Harm (Scotland) Act 2016.[32]

29 *AR v HM Advocate* [2019] HCJ 81. In that case the accused sought an order for recovery of the complainer's mobile telephone in order to extract text messages passing between him and the complainer.

30 1995 Act ss 288C and 288DC. This includes a hearing at which evidence is taken before a commissioner. Ss 288E and 288F contain provisions which allow the court to prohibit personal conduct of the case by the accused in other non-sexual cases where a child under 12 or a vulnerable witness is to give evidence.

31 S 288C(4). The test is not whether the sexual element was a substantial part of the charge but whether the charge contained a sexual element which was itself substantial. The court may make an order prohibiting the accused from conducting his own defence even if he is represented at that time – *HM Advocate v S(R)* 2023 JC 1.

32 Where the offence charged is libelled as being aggravated by involving abuse of a partner or ex-partner.

14.29 If either sections 288C or 288DC apply, the court must ascertain at the preliminary hearing (or first diet) whether the accused has instructed legal representation for the purpose of the conduct of his case. Section 288D gives the court power to appoint a solicitor to act in the proceedings where the accused has not engaged one, or has dismissed the solicitor, or the solicitor has withdrawn from acting. If a solicitor is appointed to act by the court that solicitor cannot be dismissed by the accused, nor is he obliged to comply with any instruction from the accused to dismiss counsel. A solicitor so appointed remains under a duty to ascertain and act upon the instructions of the accused, insofar as it is appropriate to do so, but if the accused refuses to give instructions, or gives inadequate or perverse instructions, the solicitor's duty is restricted to acting in the best interests of the accused.

14.30 In by far the vast majority of cases, accused persons charged with serious offences, whether of a sexual nature or otherwise, instruct solicitors to represent them. It is not, however, unknown for the court to find itself required to exercise its powers of appointment under section 288D. In such circumstances questions might arise as to the extent of the function of the appointed lawyer. For example, once a lawyer is appointed is the accused prohibited from cross-examining any witnesses, including police officers and forensic scientists and from examining defence witnesses? In a case where an accused person faces a number of charges of both a sexual and non-sexual nature in relation to the same complainer (assuming that section 288DC does not apply) is the prohibition restricted to the sexual offences? What is the position where an accused person appears on an indictment with a number of complainers where some will give evidence in support of charges of a sexual nature and others will give evidence in support of charges of a nonsexual nature?

14.31 There is no Scottish authority which provides guidance in relation to any of these questions, although in practice, in the few cases where defence representatives have been appointed by the court in terms of section 288D they have conducted the entire defence on the accused's behalf and no such issues have arisen for resolution.

14.32 On this occasion no real assistance can be gained from considering the operation of the equivalent legislation applicable in England and Wales, which is quite different in its terms. The relevant provisions are contained within Chapter II of the Youth Justice and Criminal Evidence Act 1999 between sections 34 and 38 under the heading of:

> 'Protection of witnesses from cross-examination by accused in person.'

14.33 These provisions make it plain that the prohibition is against cross-examination of a witness who is either a child witness or a complainant in connection with a sexual offence.[33] They have no broader impact and in the case of *Abbas v CPS*[34]

[33] The court may also direct that the accused may not cross-examine other particular witness if the quality of the evidence to be given by that witness is likely to be diminished if the cross-examination is conducted by the accused in person – s 36.

[34] [2015] 2 Cr App R 11.

(where the relevant witness was the complainant) it was confirmed that the role of an advocate appointed by the court to act under these provisions was restricted to cross-examination of the complainant. The court noted that the lawyer no longer has a role in the proceedings thereafter but, if he is prepared to stay and assist the defendant on a pro bono basis, there was nothing in the Act to prevent him from doing so.

14.34 By way of immediate contrast the heading to section 288C in the 1995 Act reads:

> 'Prohibition of personal conduct of defence in cases of certain sexual offences.'

14.35 The current version of the section as read in light of the relevant definitions provides that:

> 'an accused person charged with *a sexual offence* is prohibited from conducting his case in person at a hearing at which a witness is to give evidence *in the course of proceedings in respect of the offence*' (emphasis added).

14.36 It is of interest to note that from the introduction of the section in 2002 up until the most recent amendment introduced by section 69 of the Criminal Justice and Licensing (Scotland) Act 2010, the effect of the prohibition was that the accused person charged with a sexual offence was 'prohibited from conducting his defence in person at the trial'. That statement carried a plain meaning that the accused could have no role in the examination of witnesses at his trial, at least where he faced only charges of a sexual nature. Subsequent amendments extended the prohibition to preliminary hearings and victim statement proofs until the current wording was introduced by the 2010 Act. The focus is now on any form of hearing at which any witness is to give evidence in the course of proceedings in respect of the sexual offence.

14.37 The Explanatory Notes to the 2010 Act state that section 69 extends the existing provisions that 'prevent an accused person conducting their own defence in certain cases'. There is no hint anywhere in the legislative progression of an intention to limit the extent of participation by the court appointed lawyer to cross-examination of the complainer in a sexual offences case, as is the case with the legislation applying to England and Wales. So in the straightforward case of a single complainer speaking to one or more charges of a sexual nature it is clear that the accused is prohibited from conducting any part of the proceedings at which a witness is to give evidence. This conclusion is reinforced by the terms of section 288D(5)[35] which provide that when a solicitor is appointed he has the same obligations and the same authority as if engaged by the accused. An accused person who engages a solicitor in the ordinary fashion cannot conduct any part of the proceedings whilst his solicitor remains instructed.

14.38 We suggest that the matter is just as straightforward where the accused appears on an indictment or summary complaint relating to a mixture of sexual and

35 Which is not replicated in the provisions within the Youth Justice and Criminal Evidence Act 1999.

non-sexual charges against the same, or more than one complainer, even if some of such complainers speak only to non-sexual offences. This is because the trigger which acts to prohibit the accused from conducting his case in person is the presence on the indictment (or summary complaint) of a sexual offence charge and a hearing in the course of the proceedings for that offence. The trial will constitute the proceedings for that offence, regardless of whether there are other charges on the same indictment. Once the appointment provision is triggered in this fashion, the court appointed lawyer has the same obligations and authority as if engaged by an accused. That means he or she conducts the whole case. This would include any witness examined at a sentencing diet, for instance, an assessor who had prepared a risk assessment report in connection with the possible imposition of an order for lifelong restriction.

JURY DIRECTIONS IN SEXUAL OFFENCES CASES

14.39 Juries in sexual offences cases will receive a series of directions designed to counter what are often referred to as rape myths. The current directions have their origin in the mandatory directions which judges are required to give pursuant to sections 288DA and 288DB of the 1995 Act. Further changes were introduced by the Jury Manual when it was updated in August 2023. It is instructive to consider first section 288DA and section 288DB, then the judicial decisions, research and other findings which led to the 2023 changes to the Jury Manual, and finally the seven specimen directions which the Jury Manual now contains (at pp. 12.9/133 and following).

The statutory framework: the mandatory directions in sections 288DA and 288DB

14.40 Section 6 of the Abusive Behaviour and Sexual Harm (Scotland) Act 2016 introduced sections 288DA and 288DB into the 1995 Act. This reflected the first occasion on which the Scottish Parliament had imposed a statutory duty requiring particular statements to be made as part of the legal directions given by the presiding judge in a Scottish criminal trial.

14.41 Sections 288DA and 288DB apply in a trial on indictment for a sexual offence.[36] These sections apply where evidence is led, or a question is asked, suggesting that the complainer had delayed in telling anyone about, or reporting, the commission of the offence (section 288DA), or where evidence is given, or a question

36 Sexual offence is defined, for the purposes of s 288DA, with reference to the relatively comprehensive list of sexual offences in s 210A of the 1995 Act: see s 288D(4). For s 288DB, 'sexual offence' is confined by subsection (7) to the main contact sexual offences at common law and in ss 1–4 of the 2009 Act and thus does not include, for instance, inchoate offences. It is suggested that the effect of s 288DB is to make the direction mandatory for these offences, but does not prevent a trial judge from giving a direction in a trial for any other offence if he or she considers it appropriate.

is asked, suggesting that the sexual offences activity took place without physical resistance on the part of the complainer or without the accused using physical force to overcome the will of the complainer (section 288DB).

In these situations, the trial judge is required when charging the jury to advise that there can be good reasons why a person might not tell others about the commission of a sexual offence, report it, or delay in doing such things (section 288DA(2)), or that there can be good reasons why a person against whom a sexual offence is committed might not physically resist or that there can be good reasons why a person may, in committing a sexual offence, not need to use physical force to overcome the will of the person against whom the offence is committed (section 288DB(2) and (5)). The judge is required to advise that delay, lack of physical resistance and a lack of force do not necessarily indicate that an allegation is false.[37]

The 2023 Jury Manual changes

14.42 From the introduction of these two sections until August 2023, the guidance given to judges within the Jury Manual as to how to comply with these statutory duties consisted of little more than a suggested reading of the terms of the relevant provision during the course of the judge's charge delivered at the end of the case.

14.43 In the amendments introduced to the Jury Manual in the August 2023 update, a new approach to the practical method of complying with the duties imposed by sections 288DA and 288DB was set out, along with a revised emphasis on the content of the directions which it is suggested that judges should give. A brief examination of the circumstances within which the provisions were introduced and a look at some subsequent developments may provide a context within which to understand the perceived importance of the information which the statute requires to be conveyed and the emphasis which is now laid upon these directions in the Jury Manual.

The background to the mandatory directions

14.44 When the Abusive Behaviour and Sexual Harm (Scotland) Bill was considered by the Justice Committee of the Scottish Parliament the Committee noted that the proposition set out in the Bill was that there were misconceptions in the minds of juries that required to be tackled. At paragraph 135 of the Justice Committee's stage 1 report it turned to the evidence supporting that proposition stating:

37 The judge need not give the relevant direction if in the circumstances of the case no reasonable jury could consider the evidence of delay, lack of resistance or lack of force, to be material to the question of whether the offence charged is proved (section 288DA(3) and section 288DB(3) and (6).

> 'The Policy Memorandum does not quote any hard evidence backing its view that juries have biases in relation to the two matters covered in the Bill, and that these cause the wrong verdict to be reached. It notes 'concerns being expressed' about ill-founded misconceptions. It states that 'it is thought' some members of the public think that a sexual assault is always violent and that a victim is likely to try to physically resist their attacker. And it says that 'it has been suggested' that jurors may consider that an allegation is false if the victim took time to report it.'

14.45 Despite drawing attention to the basis upon which the proposition in the Bill was supported by the Policy Memorandum[38] a majority of the members of the Committee supported the introduction of the proposed mandatory directions on the ground that:

> '… they would appear to do no more than ensure that judges provide relevant factual information to juries to inform their deliberations and, in so doing, help ensure that these directions are delivered more consistently than is currently the case.'[39]

Further developments

14.46 In the time which has passed since this proposal was put before the Scottish Parliament what have come to be called 'rape myths' have been commented upon in reported decisions in both Scotland and in England and Wales. They have also been the subject of a number of research projects and academic articles.

14.47 In delivering the judgment of the Court of Appeal in the case of *CM v R*[40] Lord Justice Leveson stated at paragraph 23 that:

> 'In recent years, the courts have increasingly been prepared to acknowledge the need for a direction that deals with what might be described as stereotypical assumptions about issues such as delay in reporting allegations of sexual crime and distress (see, for example, *R v MM* [2007] EWCA Crim 1558 , *R v D* [2008] EWCA Crim 2557 and *R v Breeze* [2009] EWCA Crim 255).'

14.48 In delivering the opinion of the court in the case of *Donegan v HM Advocate*[41] the Lord Justice Clerk (Lady Dorrian) stated at paragraphs 51 and 56:

> 'It is not uncommon for victims of sexual assaults to delay making reports, to stagger reporting or make inconsistent statements in doing so. This is recognised to such a degree that measures are in place, namely section 288DA

38 The committee did call for evidence from Prof. Vanessa Munro to speak to research which she had conducted into jury attitudes at rape trials under English law using mock trials.

39 Stage 1 report para 179.

40 [2010] EWCA Crim 1578.

41 2019 JC 81.

of the Criminal Procedure (Scotland) Act 1995, to demystify myths and misunderstandings that a jury may otherwise have as to these matters.

...

In recent years, in line with the approach in other jurisdictions, notable steps have been taken in Scotland seeking to address and demystify for court users various supposed 'myths' associated with the reporting of and the reliability of rape allegations; and to improve the experiences of those involved and those giving evidence.'

14.49 In delivering the judgment of the Court of Appeal in the case of *R v Jemma Beale*[42] Lady Justice Hallett stated at paragraph 35:

> 'We need no persuading that myths and stereotypes about rape complainants still persist, and if the evidence of a complainant is to be assessed fairly the trial judge should give the guidance suggested by the Judicial College. It is part of the trial judge's overall duty to ensure the trial is fair. The courts have a far greater understanding now of the need to ensure that complainants in sexual cases are treated properly and that no one who has been raped should be deterred from coming forward for fear of how they will be treated in court.'

14.50 In her review of research studies published in 2020 'What do we know about rape myths and juror decision making?'[43] Professor Leverick concluded that those studies provided:

> '... overwhelming evidence that jurors take into the deliberation room false and prejudicial beliefs about what rape looks like and what genuine rape victims would do and that these beliefs affect attitudes and verdict choices in concrete cases. This evidence is both quantitative and qualitative.'[44]

14.51 The findings of the Scottish Government funded research into a large-scale mock jury study were published in 2019.[45] In their 2021 article[46] on the findings of their research study Professors Chalmers, Leverick and Munro stated that:

> 'We found considerable evidence of the expression of problematic attitudes towards rape complainers during deliberations. These included the belief that a 'real' victim would have extensive external and internal injuries and would resist by inflicting injuries on her attacker and shouting for help, that even a short delay in reporting is suspicious, and that false allegations are commonly made by women and difficult to refute.'

42 [2019] EWCA Crim 665.

43 (2020) 24(3) *International Journal of Evidence and Proof* 255–279.

44 Page 273.

45 Ormston, R, Chalmers, J, Leverick, F, Munro, V, and Murray, L, 'Scottish jury research: findings from a large scale mock jury study', Scottish Government (2019).

46 Chalmers, J, Leverick, F, Munro, V, 'The provenance of what is proven: exploring (mock) jury deliberation in Scottish rape trials' (2021) 48 *J. Law Soc.* 226–249 at 248.

14.52 Two subsequent research projects conducted in New Zealand have added to the body of information available. In the first, the researchers looked at aspects of the deliberations of jurors in actual rape trials. In the second they compared the conduct of rape trials when conducted before a jury as against those conducted before a single judge, again using the materials from actual cases. The first of these studies concluded that jurors:

> '... accepted stereotypical ideas about the behaviour of victims during and after sexual offending and viewed complainants as less credible when they did not act as jurors expected them to.'

and that

> '... it is clear that some juries or jurors use cultural misconceptions about sexual violence.'[47]

14.53 The second study noted that:

> '... credibility in reliance on rape myths and misconceptions formed a significant part of the cross-examination of complainants ....'[48]

The new 2023 directions

14.54 The Judicial Institute for Scotland has drawn upon some of these research findings and decisions in drafting the current advice on delivering mandatory directions provided to Scottish judges in the Jury Manual.[49] The guidance is provided in a section of the general guidance on charging the jury headed 'Addressing Rape myths and stereotypes'.

14.55 This section takes account of the practice which has been in place since July 2020 by which jurors are given a written note of the general legal directions which apply in every case at the commencement of the trial and before evidence is led. They are then taken through those directions by the presiding judge who delivers them orally in the traditional fashion whilst the jurors have the document before them.

47 Tinsley, Y, Baylis, C, and Young, W, ''I Think She's Learnt Her Lesson': Juror Use of Cultural Misconceptions in Sexual Violence Trials' (2022) 52(2) *Victoria University of Wellington Law Review* 463–486 at 474 and 485.

48 McDonald, E, *In The Absence of a Jury* (Canterbury University Press 2022) page 275.

49 The Jury Manual also references the article by Professor Thomas – 'The 21st Century Jury: Contempt, Bias and the Impact of Jury Service' (2020) 11 *Crim. Law Review* 987–1011. In that article Professor Thomas concludes at page 1004 that 'previous claims of widespread 'juror bias' in sexual offence cases are not valid'. A critique of Professor Thomas's findings is set out at pages 468/469 of Tynsley et al. Professor McDonald observes at page 26 of her book that 'The Thomas research finding is in conflict with a range of empirical projects across multiple jurisdictions over many years that examined the content and process of deliberations. This suggests it might be problematic to assume that, just because real jurors on an attitudinal survey claimed not to believe rape myths, these culturally embedded beliefs will not impact deliberations in actual trials.'

14.56 The section then sets out seven specimen directions which are considered to be appropriate in sexual offences cases and which may be made use of according to the circumstances of the case.

14.57 The first suggested direction is for inclusion in the introductory written directions. It is as follows:

> 'It may be that you come to this trial with assumptions about the crime of rape/sexual assault/sexual abuse and the circumstances in which it happens. You must now set them aside.
>
> You have taken a legal oath or affirmation to well and truly try the accused and give a true verdict according to the evidence. So you must not let any false assumptions or misleading stereotypes about [rape or other sexual offence(s)] affect your decision in this case.
>
> I will give you the legal definition of [specify relevant sexual offence(s)] as it applies in this case at the end of the trial and you must apply that definition.
>
> Let me explain what the courts have learned through experience about [rape and] sexual offences generally.
>
> 1. There is no typical crime of [rape or typical sexual offence].
> 2. There is no typical [rapist or sex offender].
> 3. There is no typical person that is [raped or sexually assaulted/abused].
> 4. [Rape or other sexual offences] can take place in almost any circumstances. It/They can happen between all different kinds of people, quite often when the people involved are known to each other or related.
> 5. There is no typical response to [rape/sexual offences]. People can react in many different ways to being [raped/sexually assaulted/abused]. These reactions may not be what you would expect or what you think you would do in the same situation. Some people may tell someone about it straight away, others may not feel able to do so until later whether out of fear or shame or for other reasons.
> 6. There is no typical response from a complainer who is asked about [rape/sexual offences]. People who have been [raped/sexually assaulted/abused] may present in many different ways when they are asked about it. They may be visibly emotional or show no obvious emotion.
>
> So I repeat, each of you must make sure that you do not let any false assumptions or stereotypes about [rape/sexual offences] affect your verdict.'

14.58 It can be seen that these introductory directions are sharply focussed on the need to be aware of, and to avoid being influenced by, misconceptions about how the crime of rape, or other sexual offences, may occur and how the victims of such conduct might react. These directions may be seen as a precursor to the mandatory directions required to be included in the judge's charge to the jury by section 288DA and 288DB. The second to seventh specimen directions are designed either to be given in the judge's charge or at the end of a particular witness's evidence.

14.59 The second specimen direction is on consent and reminds juries that consent is situation specific, that there is no need for violence, protest, resistance or injury, and that rape or sexual assault can happen within relationships. The third and fourth specimen directions are designed to replace the previous guidance on how to comply with the duties imposed by sections 288DA and 288DB. Assuming that the circumstances of the case require it, the suggested section 288DA direction (the third specimen direction in the set of seven) includes the following:

> '… When you come to consider your verdict, you will have to consider why a report was not made earlier but you must not assume that because it was delayed it is untrue. The fact that a complaint is made late does not necessarily make it untrue. Experience shows that it is *very common* (emphasis added) for a person who has been sexually assaulted/abused not to tell anyone about it for a long time and some sexual crimes are never reported.
>
> You will need to bear in mind that there can be good reasons why a person against whom a sexual offence is committed may not tell anyone about it, may not report it or may delay in doing so.
>
> You should look at all the circumstances. *Experience shows* (emphasis added) that different people react to situations in different ways. Some people may tell someone about it straight away. But others do not feel able to do so. This can be out of shame, shock, confusion or fear of getting into trouble, not being believed, or causing problems for other people.'

14.60 There is a supplementary direction which can be used in child-abuse cases, which gives the additional reasons why a child might not speak out at the time of the abuse.

14.61 The suggested section 288DB direction (the fourth in the series) includes the following:

> '… When you come to consider your verdict, you will have to consider if these matters are of any significance. You will need to bear in mind that there can be good reasons why unwanted sexual activity can take place without someone using physical force to overcome the will of the complainer or without physical resistance from the complainer.
>
> The fact that a person has not used physical force or that the complainer has not physically resisted does not necessarily mean that the allegation is false.
>
> *Experience has shown* (emphasis added) that different people can respond to unwanted sexual activity in different ways. Some may protest and physically resist throughout the event. Others may not. This may be out of fear, or because they are not a very forceful person, or for other reasons.'

14.62 The fifth specimen direction concerns prior inconsistent statements by complainers and directs juries to bear in mind that trauma can account for such inconsistencies. The sixth covers the case of the complainer who gives evidence of a background of domestic abuse and cautions the jury that they should not fall into the trap of assessing the complainer's behaviour by how they, the jury, may or may not have acted.[50] The seventh concerns the presence or absence of emotion during questioning and directs the jury that the presence or absence of emotion or distress when giving evidence is not a good indication of whether the person is telling the truth or not.

14.63 From the above discussion it can be seen that the suggested directions crafted by the Judicial Institute now go much further than merely to repeat the terms of the statutory provisions. They now proceed upon a clear acceptance of the proposition originally set out in the Policy Memorandum attached to the Abusive Behaviour and Sexual Harm (Scotland) Bill, namely that there were misconceptions in the minds of juries that required to be tackled. The suggested directions go significantly further than the rationale for supporting the proposed directions in the Bill as explained by the Justice Committee, namely that they do no more than ensure that judges provide relevant factual information to juries to inform their deliberations. The combination of the introductory written directions, and the suggested other directions, provide the selected jurors with information about the experience of the court drawn from other cases and demonstrate a focussed effort on the part of the court to recognise and dispel an underlying body of misconceptions which researchers and others have drawn attention to over many years.

50 In DASA cases, from March 2024, this may be given as part of the introductory directions at the start of the case.

PART III

Evidence in Sexual Offences Cases

Chapter 15

Medical evidence in sexual offences cases

Dr Deborah Wardle

Consultant in Genitourinary Medicine and Sexual Health; Lead Consultant, West of Scotland Sexual Assault Services; Associate Post Graduate Dean (Forensics) NHS Education for Scotland

INTRODUCTION

15.01 This chapter sets out the role of medical evidence in sexual offences cases in Scotland. Much medical evidence is obtained by examination of adult or adolescent complainers within seven days of the incident at one of Scotland's sexual assault referral centres: a Sexual Assault Response Co-ordination Service (SARCS).[1] The first part of the chapter explains how these centres came to be and sets out their key features. The second part outlines what happens when someone attends a centre and the means by which evidence is collected. The third part sets out means by which a forensic medical examination in a sexual offences case is documented, including how information is recorded in the standardised national forms created for this purpose. The fourth part summarises the interpretation of the main clinical findings from a medical examination in sexual offences cases and their possible legal significance.

SEXUAL ASSAULT EXAMINATION SERVICES IN SCOTLAND

The history of sexual assault referral centres in Scotland

15.02 In April 2007, Scotland's first sexual assault referral centre became operational. Archway, Glasgow, began as a Scottish Government funded pilot, externally evaluated by London Metropolitan University, to ensure a co-ordinated response to sexual violence. It was recognised that victims of sexual violence needed a safe place, located within the NHS, where they could access immediate medical and psychological support, in parallel with forensic evidence collection, whether or not they chose to engage with the criminal justice system.

1 Children and adolescents are examined within the National Health Service (NHS) child protection paediatric services, with the exception of the West of Scotland service, which manages adolescent disclosures. Forensic medical examinations of children are often undertaken in a children's healthcare facility with two examiners present: a paediatrician and a forensic physician. Where a single clinician possesses all the skills required for appropriate examination and management of older children, they would perform the examination, as is the case in the West of Scotland SARCS service where children over the age of 13 years reporting a recent event are examined in a SARCS. A child would never be examined without their informed consent.

15.03 Thereafter, a review by Her Majesty's Inspectorate of Constabulary in Scotland (HMICS) in 2017 and the establishment of a Chief Medical Officer's Forensic Taskforce, led to the establishment of similar regional services in the north, east, and west of Scotland. Rather than a single physical location for each service, and to cater for remote and rural areas of Scotland, the concept of a SARCS was developed. The aim is for various professionals and experts to collaborate to deliver consistent, person-centred, trauma-informed healthcare and forensic medical services; to provide access to recovery for victims; and to transfer forensic medical examinations of complainers out of police settings and into the NHS.[2]

Features of SARCS

Site set-up

15.04 The SARCS centres tend to be in places accessible by public transport. They may be in a standalone building and are not necessarily close to any other healthcare facilities. Signage is discrete and generic and avoids reference to the type of services delivered.

15.05 There are several rooms within the centre: a waiting area, a consultation room and a forensic examination room. Attendance is by arrangement to guard against contamination of any samples obtained and to maintain the forensic integrity of the centre. There is only ever one complainer present in a centre at any time to minimise the risk of DNA transfer between cases.[3] The average time at the centre – to allow for consultation, assessment, management of clinical risks, forensic examination, the taking of samples, and planning to ensure the complainer's future safety – is around three hours.

Forensic integrity and contamination control

15.06 Forensic medical examinations at SARCS follow the national decontamination guidance issued by the Scottish Police Authority (SPA). This ensures the forensic integrity of any evidential samples and mitigates the risk of DNA transfer and contamination.[4] The guidance requires quarterly environmental monitoring of examination suites and the use of protective clothing by anyone

2 One aspect of the plan included a focus on ensuring the adequate staffing with female clinicians, to recognise that many complainers preferred female examiners. This is in line with the obligation in s 9 of the Victims and Witnesses (Scotland) Act 2014 to give any complainer the opportunity to request that any such medical examination be carried out by a registered medical practitioner of a sex specified by them.

3 The equipment and furniture coverings in all rooms are wipe-down materials. Any items used by the complainer are single use, eg tissue packs rather than boxes and individual shower packs. There are no magazines, plants or extraneous materials in forensically secure areas.

4 See the section in Chapter 16 on avoiding DNA contamination in sexual offences casework at **16.41** and **16.42**.

handling any samples seized. Samples are taken in a particular order as described in the Faculty of Forensic & Legal Medicine (FFLM) recommendations (see further **15.18** and **15.19** below.[5] While extreme care and caution is taken when taking samples at a crime scene or analysing samples in forensic laboratories, in sexual offences cases there is the added complexity that the complainer is part of the crime scene. The process of taking samples is thus performed with awareness of the potential risk of emotional or situational triggers for re-traumatisation, particularly during a genital examination.

THE CARE AND MEDICAL EXAMINATION PROCESS

Considerations before the medical examination

15.07 Many complainers will be brought to a SARCS by the police after a report of an allegation of sexual offending. Others may attend a SARCS after seeking advice and information from other health services (such as GPs, sexual health clinics, or pharmacies), having been offered a referral to a SARCS to discuss the option of a forensic medical examination, with or without the involvement of the police. The Forensic Medical Services (Victims of Sexual Offences) (Scotland) Act 2021 gives victims of sexual offending the right to refer themselves for forensic medical examinations without the need to first disclose to the police.[6] Since the entry into force of the 2021 Act, people have increasingly contacted SARCS for information and advice.[7] An individual may thus choose to access SARCS for support only and decline the offer of a forensic medical examination if they have no intention of ever reporting to the police. Unless there are safeguarding concerns, the decision of a competent adult must be respected.

15.08 When a complainer has made a report to the police, it is the responsibility of the police Sexual Offences Liaison Officer (SOLO) to explain to the complainer the services available at a SARCS and obtain oral consent to arrange the complainer's attendance. A SOLO will call ahead to the SARCS, providing the sexual offences

5 *Recommendations for the collection of forensic specimens from complainants and suspects*, January 2024 available at: https://fflm.ac.uk/wp-content/uploads/2024/01/Recommendations-for-the-Collection-of-Forensic-Specimens-FSSC-Jan-2024.pdf. FFLM guidance is reviewed twice a year by a scientific subcommittee that includes representation from SPA, providing an opportunity for queries on current practice and suggestions to receive consideration and inform positive changes in future guidance.

6 This gives them time to decide if they wanted to report an incident, whilst ensuring potential evidence is not lost. If a person decides not to report, they can ask for the stored evidence to be destroyed. If they decide to report, Police Scotland will collect and keep the evidence. If unreported within 26 months, the evidence will be destroyed, although the option to report a crime will remain.

7 For instance, in the financial year 2023–24, 556 people in total were supported by the West of Scotland SARCS: 361 cases were seen for a forensic medical examination (of whom 83 adolescents), and a further 195 people did not attend for a forensic examination but were supported by the service in other ways.

examiner with briefing details that allow clinicians to consider both the health and forensic priorities, and to prepare the centre for the complainer's arrival.

15.09 Those who self-refer (often via the NHS inform website) have an opportunity to discuss their concerns, priorities, and options with SARCS staff before making a decision on whether to undergo a forensic medical examination. If any immediate health concerns are noted, complainers are directed to accident and emergency departments for initial assessment first as there are no acute medical services within SARCS. Once medical priorities are addressed, the complainer is preferably transferred to the SARCS for forensic capture in a forensically clean environment.

15.10 On arrival at the centre, complainers are introduced to the staff who will be involved with them during their visit. Names and roles, rather than ranks and titles, are used to avoid the introduction of any power imbalance and avoid re-traumatisation. In cases where the complainer attends with the police, the examiner will clarify with the police officer the details which were provided prior to attending and will add any additional details that have been obtained since the initial discussion. Simultaneously, in a separate consultation room, the nurse will discuss with the complainer the process in the centre and answer any questions they may have. The examiner will then leave the police in the briefing room and both a forensic and a health consultation will take place with the complainer, whilst the nurse prepares the forensic examination room.

The initial consultation

15.11 The consultation will begin with a medical assessment which includes clinical risk assessments for pregnancy and transmission of sexually transmitted infections (STIs) including HIV. Existing support mechanisms will be explored, including the risk of any harmful coping strategies, whether escalating or recurring, such as self-harm, alcohol, or substance use, and enquiring about suicidal ideation. Any pre-existing physical or mental health problems that may have contributed to the appearance of injuries or could potentially impact on the complainer's ability to give evidence will be recorded.

15.12 To minimise the risk of re-traumatisation, the examiner will sensitively and succinctly describe their understanding of events from the discussions that have already taken place. The examining clinician will ask the complainer if there is any other information that would help to ensure that appropriate samples are taken.

15.13 Written consent is obtained to clarify that the complainer understands the process of forensic capture and the information sharing that will take place between professionals to support their health and any ongoing investigation. In addition to confirming what has been agreed, the consultation also allows for the complainer to highlight anything that they do not want to happen and what they might choose to decline. Consent is a dynamic process that can be withdrawn at any time: complainers are reminded that the examination will stop if they want it to.

15.14 Health needs that require admission or assessment in acute hospital sites are a priority over forensic capture. If someone is required to have hospital assessment before attendance at a SARCS and deemed too unwell to then be transferred to a SARCS, or in situations where a complainer with dementia would be distressed by moving from the familiarity of residential care to allow examination in a forensic facility, the sexual offences examiner will assess whether an 'off-site' examination can be arranged to gather evidence. This involves the sexual offences examiner and forensically trained nurse attending the hospital site or care home, taking their equipment with them.

The medical examination

15.15 Following the initial forensic/clinical consultation, the complainer will be taken through to the examination room. In addition to theatre scrubs, staff will don additional protective clothing prior to the examination to avoid transfer of their DNA to any samples taken.[8] The examination room has an examination couch covered with a disposable couch cover. A colposcope and viewing screen is also present.[9] There are work surfaces of sufficient length to allow the swabs to be used for examination to be laid out ready for use.

15.16 Complainers will be asked to change into a hospital gown in a bathroom available for the complainer's use only.[10] A blanket is used to keep them suitably covered and they are asked to take a seat on the examination couch. In police-referred cases, the SOLO is then invited into the room to corroborate that the examination took place. A curtain is positioned to separate the SOLO from view of the examination. One of the roles of the forensically trained nurse during the examination is to corroborate the samples taken as described by the examiner and they also sign the swabs and samples. The swabs taken by the examiner are passed by the nurse to the SOLO. The SOLO is responsible for packaging samples.[11] An equivalent worktop space is provided on the police side of the curtain to allow the SOLO sufficient space to sign, label with the site and time taken, package and seal productions in tamper-proof evidence production bags. All swabs and bags are countersigned by the examining clinician to maintain the chain of custody. In self-referred cases, samples are stored with an appropriate chain of custody.

8 This includes a theatre cap, facemask, over-sleeves, if arms are bare, or a theatre gown and two pairs of vinyl gloves. The first pair remain on the hands and only the outer pair are changed when examining different parts of the body. This reduces the risk of the examiner's skin cells being shed into the room during glove changes.

9 This is a magnifying light source that can be used to record digital images of ano-genital examinations. It is not a requirement to use it in all cases; however, it tends to be used where genital injuries are present. This allows the examination to proceed at the usual pace, allowing the examiner the ability to review images and documentation of injuries once the complainer leaves.

10 This is often within the forensic suite.

11 They wear gloves whilst handling samples.

15.17 One part of the examination is referred to as the 'top to toe' survey. This involves a visual inspection of the complainer starting at the head and working down to the feet. The patient remains covered throughout and is never naked: only the section being assessed is exposed and it is re-covered before moving to another area. This visual inspection allows identification of injuries, which are noted on body diagrams along with written descriptions, noting the presence or absence of features that support a particular mechanism of injury. Relevant negative findings are also noted. If appropriate, skin swabs are taken from injuries or, alternatively, from areas where injuries are absent but where contact with a suspect has been described.

15.18 Any ano-genital examination begins only when the complainer is ready and when it is clear how they will indicate if they want the examination to stop. First, a visual inspection for any external injury takes place. Samples are then taken. A moistened cotton-tipped swab is rolled over the skin with moderate pressure, followed by a second dry swab, allowing any previously dried biological material to be lifted onto the swab. Sampling before any touching or movement of the skin with gloved hands allows for safe investigation into the presence of suspect DNA, whilst avoiding the loss of evidentially valuable material onto the examiner's gloves. The sampling order, as described in the FFLM guidance,[12] aims to allow analysis of suspect DNA present as a result of the sexual offending reported and to avoid the risk of transferring any suspect DNA as a consequence of the forensic examination.

15.19 Female genital samples are taken from 'the outside in': external skin swabs from the labia majora and labia minora are taken ahead of 'internal' swabs from the lower vagina,[13] upper vagina and cervical os (the opening into the uterus at the upper end of the vagina). Low vaginal swabs are then taken whilst carefully examining the folds of hymenal tissue for injury using a cotton-tipped swab.

Table 15.1: Anatomical terms

Anatomy	Definition
Posterior fourchette	Junction of labia minora posteriorly
Vestibule	Area between labia minora containing openings of urethra and vagina and Bartholin's glands
Fossa navicularis	Lowest part of the vestibule bounded anteriorly by hymen and posteriorly by posterior fourchette (boat-shaped space)
Hymenal tissue/ remnants	Tissue which partially or completely surrounds the vaginal opening
Perineum	The bridge of skin between genitalia and the perianal area

12 See n 5 above.

13 The medical definition of vagina differs from the legal definition. Medically, the vagina begins at the introitus (the opening of the vagina), extending inwards and ending at the cervix (neck of the uterus). The 'legal vagina' includes both the vulva and the medical vagina: see Chapter 3 at n 3.

15.20 For male genital samples, the FFLM order of sampling advises a moistened then a dry swab used to sample the skin of the penile shaft. This is followed by swabbing of the internal aspect of the retracted foreskin (if present), and the coronal sulcus or area at base of the head (glans) of the penis in the same manner. The glans penis is then swabbed.

15.21 Where anal penetration is reported, or where there is amnesia of events and a complainer consents to examination of likely sites of penetration, swabs are taken from the external perianal skin surrounding the anus (the opening of the anal canal). Swabs are then taken from the anal canal (approximately 3-5cm in length and sensitive to pain). This is followed by insertion of a lubricated, clear rounded plastic device, known as a proctoscope, into the anal canal. The internal section of the device can be removed once in place to allow visualisation of the rectum, the lining of which is darker in appearance than the anal canal. The rectum experiences dull sensation rather than pain. Use of the proctoscope allows for rectal swabs to be taken under direct vision. If the complainer is unable to tolerate this procedure, a swab is inserted directly into the rectum (8-15cm in length). It is referred to as a 'blind' rectal swab as it is not taken under direct vision.

The timeframe for obtaining forensic samples

15.22 The usual timeframe for obtaining forensic samples during a medical examination is within seven days of an incident. There may be circumstances – for example, complainers detained against their will with no showering facilities, or elderly and people living alone with dementia and minimal self-hygiene – where samples are retrievable beyond this timeframe. The police may also have taken 'early evidence samples': non-intimate samples that may include mouth swabs and mouth rinse in cases involving oral penetration (ahead of the buccal DNA elimination sample), urine, tissue paper, tampons, toothbrushes, vomit, clothing articles such as underwear, or items reported to have been grabbed at or removed by a suspect. When a pregnancy results from sexual violence, there is the possibility that products of conception may be seized as evidential samples. Police Scotland have developed management pathways in collaboration with the NHS to ensure a considered and sensitive approach to the discussion and retrieval of such material. This includes careful pre-arrangement of procedures to ensure appropriate packaging and collection with an intact chain of evidence to maximise the evidential value of such samples.

After the medical examination

15.23 Once any samples have been taken, the SOLO (if present) will be asked to leave the room and wait in the briefing room. This allows any clinical work to be undertaken in medical confidence. This may include, for example, coil insertion as emergency contraception or Hepatitis B vaccination to reduce the risk of infection transmission. There are facilities for complainers to shower after the examination, if they choose to.

15.24 Once all forensic and clinical assessments are completed, the examiner will verbally brief the officer regarding their findings (or absence of findings) and their interpretation to assist with any ongoing investigation.

15.25 The forensic suite is 'decontaminated' after the patient leaves. This involves disposal of any extraneous items used by the complainer (for instance, paper cups or tissues) and cleaning of all rooms used by the complainer during an attendance, including the patient shower room, with a solution approved by the Scottish Police Authority (SPA) that denatures DNA as per the national forensic cleaning protocol. This ensures the unit is forensically cleaned and minimises the risk of DNA transfer between cases.

DOCUMENTING THE MEDICAL EXAMINATION

The national form

15.26 Any medical examination at a SARCS is documented on a standard national form, the *Sexual Offences against Adults National Form*.[14] It is derived from the Form used in the initial Archway pilot and it has been in use across Scotland since 1 December 2010. The form (and an equivalent form for adolescents) comprises two main sections: the medical assessment section, and the forensic examination section.

The medical assessment section

15.27 The medical section is kept in medical confidence by the SARCS and not submitted to the police. It supports assessment and management of immediate clinical risks and information sharing with other professionals to support aftercare and recovery, reducing the need for patients to have to retell their account and the associated risk of re-traumatisation. As with all medical notes, these are accessible by court order if deemed necessary and appropriate to do so.

The forensic assessment section

15.28 The separate 'Forensic Examination' section of the form was developed in collaboration with health professionals, Police Scotland, COPFS and SPA Forensic Services to ensure the efficient and effective documentation of the forensic medical

14 The form is the product of 2017 standards produced by Healthcare Improvement Scotland, entitled *Healthcare and Forensic Medical Services for People who have experienced Rape, Sexual Assault or Child Sexual Exploitation: Children, Young People and Adults*.

examination and to assist investigation and prosecution of sexual offences. The forensic documentation is completed contemporaneously and should be available for collection by the police within 24 hours of an examination with brief witness statements from the examining clinician and forensically trained nurse present at the examination. It is submitted as a production and often available for clinicians to refer to if called to give evidence in court. Elements of the form, such as completed body maps, may be used to explain any positive findings to the jury.

15.29 This part of the form contains:

- Documentation of consent to the forensic medical examination.
- The briefing details provided by the investigating police officer(s) summarising the time, location, and nature of the incident, early evidence samples taken and any preference regarding the gender of the examining clinician.
- A section recording any additional information provided directly to the clinician by the complainer, visibly distinct from that provided in the officer's briefing.
- Any sexual contact in the week prior to the incident, along with any knowledge of vasectomy in any male partners. This assists SPA Forensic Services in any forensic analysis.
- Other activities since the incident including showering, bathing, or changing clothes or sanitary wear that may potentially lessen the opportunity for isolation of suspect DNA.
- The suspect's details, if known, to assist in searching the DNA database.
- The start time of the examination, allowing confirmation of the time between the incident and examination.
- The complainer's height and weight. These are details required in toxicological assessments for 'back calculations' in order to assess alcohol levels at the time of the incident if the allegation is that consent was absent due to intoxication.
- The complainer's size and stature. When compared with the suspect, these may be significant in understanding the dynamics of any restraint used in non-consensual acts.
- Details of the head-to-toe survey, including a description of the complainer's demeanour such as observed distress.
- Details of any ano-genital examination, with descriptions of any injuries annotated on body maps.
- Confirmation of the sites sampled or articles seized, together with the lot number and expiry date of sterile water ampules used to moisten swabs and single-use lubricant sachets used on medical devices during the examination.
- Details of any clinical information that may impact on the presence or appearance of injuries.

15.30 A copy of the forensic examination section of the national form must be submitted with the productions lodged by the police when transferred to the SPA Forensic Services laboratory. This assists in prioritising sample testing.

Distress and other emotional states

15.31 If there is evidence that the complainer was distressed when attending a SARCS, the clinician may be called to give evidence of that distress, in addition to their evidence on any of the interpretations of the forensic medical examination. It is therefore prudent to document that distress and any adaptions which were made during a complainer's attendance to avoid potential triggers and reduce the risk of re-traumatisation, since this will show that the clinician was aware of and managed that distress.

Summary of findings

15.32 The final section of the forensic documentation is the summary of findings, providing the opportunity to reflect and summarise the salient points in the forensic process, including the outcome of the examination with professional medical interpretation. When read in isolation, a sound 'summary of findings' should focus on pertinent points and provide a clear snapshot of the clinician's encounter with the case, signposting other professionals to additional salient parts of the forensic documentation. This summary section provides an opportunity to review both positive findings and the absence of findings on examination, alongside the details of the incident available to the examiner at the time of the examination (for example, an absence of injury where grabbed, or the likely absence of genital injuries). Any less routine samples taken for forensic analysis in response to incident details that might be of particular significance may be highlighted here. The conclusion should include a professional opinion with documentation of reasoning.

Photography

15.33 In police-referred cases, where a digital image might assist with the description of an injury, arrangements are made to organise photography by a police photographer if it is acceptable to the patient/complainer to do so. Photographs of non-genital injuries may be taken whilst in the forensic suite if a crime-scene photographer is available to attend. In self-referred cases, where there is access to a hospital medical illustration department, photography will be arranged and stored as a medical record for a period of up to 26 months or until the complainer decides to report to Police Scotland. In some rural and remote areas with less access, staff are trained to take photographs.

15.34 Non-genital injuries associated with the incident may result from reports of restraint and be indicative of an absence of consent. A photograph of the patterned nature of such injuries, for instance fingertip bruising, may be a useful adjunct to the documentation in the forensic notes and on body maps. To photograph body parts, the complainer's body needs to be in anatomical position, that is, with arms slightly away from the sides of the body and palms facing forward, allowing the use of fixed anatomical landmarks to note the position of injuries. One photograph is taken with, and one without, a forensic scale to provide a perspective on the size of the injuries.

15.35 Injuries are documented by numbers or letters and the descriptions tend to be listed separately from the image. Using letters or numbers to differentiate between different injuries on body maps allows for a medical witness to refer to annotated body maps whilst referring to descriptions documented in a separate section to assist them, exposing jurors only to the descriptions of injuries that are deemed relevant to the case. Photography is an adjunct to, and not a replacement for, written description and annotation on body maps. The documented description and body maps completed by the examining clinician take precedence over photographic images that may or may not reflect the description of the appearance at the time of the examination.[15]

15.36 Body maps may contain images that may or may not be relevant to the case. Such findings could include healed self-harm scars. These may be unrelated to the case; however, they are clinically relevant. An exacerbation of harmful coping strategies, such as self-harm by cutting, may exacerbate or recur in response to managing distress. Findings from any subsequent examination in response to such behaviours can be compared with documentation made at the time of the examination. Alternatively, the onset of self-harm may pre-date the examination, perhaps coinciding with the onset of grooming and chronic abuse.

CLINICAL FINDINGS AND THEIR POTENTIAL LEGAL SIGNIFICANCE

15.37 As noted above, the forensic medical examiner's summary of findings outlines their professional interpretation of the outcomes of the examination in relation to the details of the incident available to them. This section highlights aspects that might bear importance in the investigation and prosecution of these incidents.[16]

Neutrality of absence of genital findings

15.38 It is more common than not to find an absence of visible genital injuries following a disclosure of non-consensual sexual intercourse, with more than half of the complainers having no detectable injuries. Even in those who report no previous

15 The same is valid for colposcopic images. It is worth noting that colposcopic images are stored in medical confidence and are not seized as a production. The intimate nature of colposcopic images makes their use in a court setting extremely unlikely.

16 When medical evidence may be corroborative and the principles to be applied, particularly in light of the case of *Meighan v HM Advocate* 2022 JC 10, is considered in Chapter 19 at **19.42–19.49**.

sexual experiences, an absence of genital injury does not exclude penetration. Contrary to myths and misperceptions, the hymen is not always injured on first sexual contact. The absence of genital injuries is a neutral finding and neither confirms nor refutes a lack of consent. However, when genital injuries are observed it is consistent with, though in isolation not conclusive of, an absence of consent.

Anal injuries

15.39 Lacerations are the most frequently described anal injury. Some studies have demonstrated that anal injuries, although more likely to be absent, are found more commonly in male complainers than female. A fresh laceration may be identified through bleeding and a lack of signs of healing. Bruising, abrasions, erythema (redness) or oedema (swelling) may be noted on examination of the perianal skin, anal canal or rectum during a forensic medical examination.

Injury mechanisms

15.40 Some mechanisms of injury have associated features. An abrasion is caused by superficial disruption of the outer layer of the skin (epidermis) caused by the movement of a rough surface against the skin (or vice versa). A wide abrasion is known as a graze and a linear abrasion as a scratch. The surface may appear raised at one end of the injury and this may indicate the direction of the force. Crescenteric-shaped abrasions can result from abrasions by fingernails. Debris such as fibres from a carpet may be present. Fresh bleeding may assist in ageing an injury or scab formation might be indicative of a healing, less acute injury.

15.41 Lacerations or 'splits' in the skin are caused by blunt force trauma and, unlike incisions, a laceration has irregular edges. Debris may be present, and tissue may bridge the injury. Genital lacerations are superficial splits in the skin caused by overstretching of the tissue whilst attempting penetration and may not contain the features sometimes present in non-genital sites. The midline area at the posterior fourchette is a commonly reported site when acute lacerations are noted to be present. Incisions are caused by sharp objects such as knives, cause well-defined injuries, and may be deep and bleed profusely. An incision that is wider than it is deep may be referred to as a 'slash' injury.

15.42 Bruising is caused by leakage of blood from vessels into the surrounding tissue. Bruises may not appear immediately and may be distant from the injury due to gravity. Colour changes with time are due to the degradation of the pigment haemoglobin in the blood. Colour changes occur at different rates and may appear different on paler and darker skin tones. A yellow bruise is at least 18 hours old; however, colour assessment is subjective and not all bruises progress to a yellow colour. Applied pressure or a ligature impedes blood return to the heart resulting in raised pressure in small blood vessels and leakage of blood and the development of bruises less than 2mm in size. These appear above the level of the constraint and are referred to as petechial haemorrhages (or 'petechiae'). In addition, petechiae can appear on the skin where there has been pinching or twisting (direct damage) with other petechiae in the whites of the eyes, caused 'indirectly' as a consequence of a rise in intravascular pressure.

15.43 Patterned bruising is a term used when an injury reflects the object which caused it such as the sole of a shoe. Fingertip bruising is a cluster of small, oval or discoid bruises. They may be present on the arms or inner thighs and supportive of an account of sexual assault if restraint or force was used. They may be present in the axillae (armpits) if a victim has been dragged. Bite marks, sometimes noted by the presence of two crescenteric bruises, are best examined by a forensic odontologist. In addition to swabs taken to analyse the possibility of saliva from a suspect, photographic techniques can assist in obtaining identification features.

Non-fatal strangulation

15.44 Non-fatal strangulation (NFS) is a high-risk indicator of escalating violence. There is no safe way to strangle, with potential short- and long-term sequelae including memory loss, vascular tears, and strokes. Non-fatal strangulation may leave bruises at the point of pressure by hands or ligature, with petechial (pin-prick) haemorrhages above the level of restriction, including in the eyes. Observation for potential signs and assessment of symptoms is imperative to support further assessment of potential internal injuries. Absence of symptoms does not negate an account of strangulation.

Children

15.45 Younger children may not recognise abuse for what it is, making it crucial for professionals to recognise indicators of risk. Most childhood disclosures are therefore delayed due to lack of awareness and relate to less recent events where the opportunity for capture of biological material has passed. Forensic examinations performed after the DNA persistence window will not therefore provide an opportunity for the forensic capture of a suspect's DNA. However, forensic medical examination of an otherwise sexually naive child may still be advised by clinicians (a 'non-acute forensic examination'). This is because there may be physical findings, such as healed injuries, that are consistent with child sexual abuse. In the event of a finding of sexually transmitted infections in a previously sexually inexperienced child, expert interpretation would be required to determine whether this might be indicative of abuse, or may be explained by vertical transmission during pregnancy or birth.

Older persons

15.46 Women who have passed the age of menopause are more likely to experience genital injuries. This is consistent with physiological changes such as decreased elasticity and thinning of genital tissue resulting from a lowering of the hormone oestrogen. Incidents are more likely to occur in their own homes or in care facilities. Underreporting can arise because of pre-existing vulnerabilities such as dementia and because of the possibility that those in positions of care or responsibility are responsible for the abuse. As with sexually inexperienced younger patients, the presence of some STIs may be of forensic significance and might be associated with the incident if a complainer reports having been sexually inactive for a number of years prior to the assault. It is worth noting that some sexually transmitted infections are asymptomatic and may pre-date the incident. The potential forensic significance of the presence or absence of STIs requires expert interpretation.

Chapter 16

Forensic scientific evidence in sexual offences cases: from crime scene to court

Dr Nighean Stevenson

Forensic Lead (DNA Interpretation), Forensic Services, Scottish Police Authority

INTRODUCTION

16.01 This chapter provides a general overview of forensic science as it applies in sexual offences cases. First, it sets out the role of SPA Forensic Services in providing forensic scientific analysis in Scotland and the main types of sexual offences cases currently submitted to SPA Forensic Services for analysis. Then, it sets out the general principles on which cases are evaluated and results reported, including the structure of, and standards used in, Joint Forensic Science Reports (JFSRs). It then outlines the main techniques for the detection of body fluids and DNA profiling, and the interpretation of those results in sexual offences cases, including some of the considerations important to the forensic scientist when formulating opinions in relation to DNA and other scientific evidence. It concludes with a brief section on textile damage interpretation in the context of sexual offences cases. The chapter is not a comprehensive review of forensic techniques or scientific literature, rather it is intended as guidance for legal practitioners on DNA and other scientific evidence in sexual offences cases in Scotland.

SPA FORENSIC SERVICES

16.02 SPA Forensic Services, part of the Scottish Police Authority (SPA), is *the* provider of forensic services to the criminal justice system in Scotland, delivering a high quality and vital service to meet the expectations of the Scottish public and to deliver SPA's Forensic Strategy 'Scientific Excellence for Safer Communities'. Its unique crime-scene-to-court model enables Forensic Services to provide a coordinated response from the crime scene, through search, recovery, and analysis, to the reporting of evidence and provision of expert-witness testimony in court.

16.03 Forensic Services currently employs approximately 600 staff, 70% of whom are scientists. Within the biology discipline, there are approximately 70 Senior Forensic Scientists. They undergo rigorous training and competency testing prior to being authorised by the Scottish Government for the purposes of section 280(4) of the Criminal Procedure (Scotland) Act 1995. These Senior Forensic Scientists are supported in their examinations by 50 Forensic Examiners and Analysts whom they instruct to undertake specific duties.

Quality Standards

16.04 Forensic reporting, as well as the scientific procedures contained therein, are audited and accredited by the UK Accreditation Service (UKAS) to ISO17025 to ensure quality standards are met. In England and Wales, legislation exists, the Forensic Science Regulator (FSR) Act 2021, which sets a statutory code of practice for some forensic activities. This does not apply in Scotland, however SPA Forensic Services is consulted and contributes to the FSR guidance and codes, and aims to align its own practice with them in the majority of situations where our legal system permits. SPA Forensic Services also has obligations under the Scottish Biometrics Commissioner (SBC) Code of Practice to safeguard biometric data (such as DNA profiles or fingerprints) under the Scottish Biometrics Commissioner Act 2020.

Profile of sexual offences cases submitted to SPA Forensic Services

16.05 The role of forensic scientific evidence in sexual offences casework can be extremely significant. The last few years has seen a significant increase in the number of sexual offences cases submitted to the SPA Forensic Sciences Laboratory (See Figure 16.1). Sexual offences casework accounts for approximately 50% of all violent crime casework submitted to the biology discipline and around 35% across all scientific disciplines within Forensic Services.

16.06 There are several reasons why there are increasing numbers of sexual offences cases being submitted. One is improved scientific technologies and the ability to obtain reportable DNA results from more challenging samples. For example, in the past, large amounts of semen were often required in order to achieve reportable results, whereas results can now be obtained from trace levels of semen or from other cellular material. For example:

- The enhanced discriminating power and sensitivity of new DNA technologies such as GlobalFiler™ ('DNA24') can yield DNA results from low level and degraded samples.
- The ability to interpret and provide statistical evaluations of ever more complex mixtures of DNA using probabilistic genotyping software (STRmix™).
- The ability to specifically target tiny amounts of male DNA in a background of vast amounts of female DNA on a vaginal swab using Y-STR DNA analysis can provide results in digital or penile penetration without ejaculation.

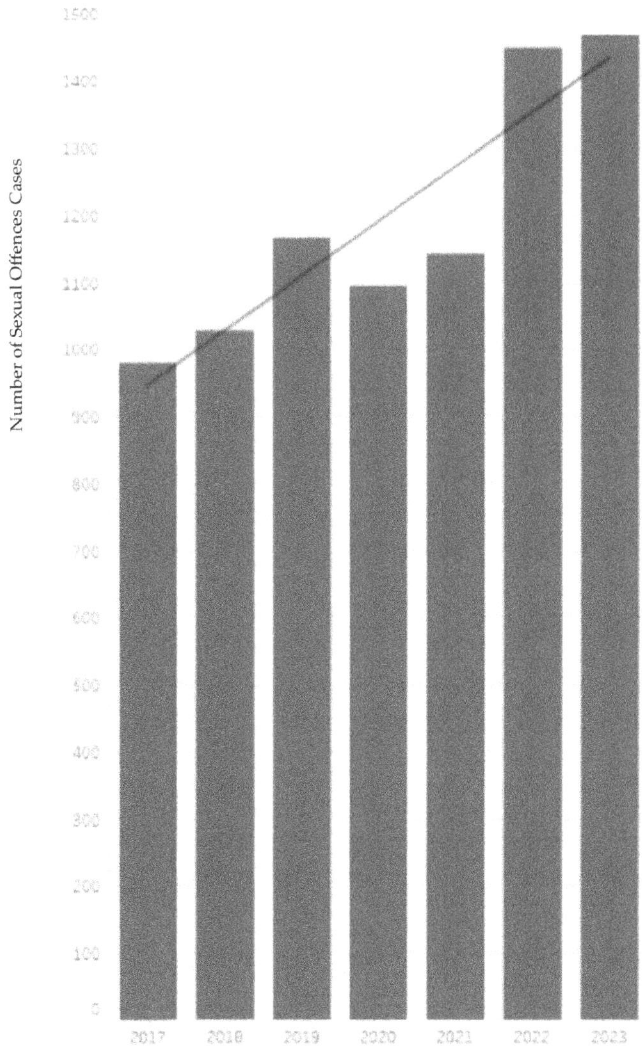

Figure 16.1: Trends in sexual-offences cases submitted to Forensic Services (2017/23), showing a general upward trend; 2020/21 saw a slight dip in submissions due to Covid-19.

16.07 Another contributing factor is cases where the issue is one of consent being submitted for examination when in the past they may not have been. In such cases, where the complainer and suspect both state that sexual intercourse took place, the forensic scientist cannot address consent; this is for the jury to consider. However, the forensic scientist may be able to provide evidence which corroborates sexual intercourse.

WHEN CAN FORENSICS ASSIST IN SEXUAL OFFENCES CASES?

16.08 The most common type of evidence sought during a forensic examination of a sexual offences case is DNA evidence originating from body fluids, the presence of which may provide evidence to address sexual activity. Table 16.1 summarises the main sections of the Sexual Offences (Scotland) Act 2009 where forensic analysis can assist.

Table 16.1: Summary of forensic requests for Sexual Offences (Scotland) Act 2009 cases. This is outlined only for adults (≥ 16 years), but the equivalent sections relating to children and young people also apply.

2009 Act	Offence	Sexual Activity	Forensic Biology Request
Section 1	Rape	Penetration of the vagina, anus or mouth with a penis	Identify any evidence to assist in addressing if sexual intercourse took place
Section 2	Sexual assault by penetration	Penetration of the vagina or anus with any body part (including a penis) or object	Identify any evidence to assist in addressing if penetration of the body orifice took place
Section 3	Sexual Assault	Sexual touching, external ejaculation, sexual transfer of urine or saliva	Identify any evidence to assist in addressing if (sexual) contact took place

16.09 Many sexual offences cases involve the identification of semen. However, the presence of other body fluids such as vaginal material, saliva, blood or faecal material may also assist, as can the presence of DNA from other sources (such as skin cells), comparison of hairs or fibres, and textile damage.

16.10 Before considering the technical processes involved in body fluid examinations and DNA analysis and interpretation, and textile damage, it is worth considering the examination, evaluation and reporting approach taken by forensic scientists, specifically in relation to sexual offences casework.

CASE EVALUATION AND REPORTING OF FORENSIC EVIDENCE

16.11 Forensic scientists follow a logical framework extending from designing an examination strategy through to evaluation of results in the context of the case circumstances. Where possible, forensic results are considered against an opposing set of propositions to allow a meaningful evaluation of their observations by a jury in relation to the offence (see Figure 16.2). This evaluative framework is advocated by the European Network of Forensic Science Institutes and the DNA commission of the International Society of Forensic Genetics.

Principles for evaluation of forensic evidence

16.12 Three principles underpin the evaluation of forensic evidence:

1. Observations should be evaluated within a framework of circumstances; this relies on information provided to the scientist by the police, COPFS, defence, healthcare professionals, etc.
2. Observations should be evaluated with respect to at least two competing propositions, for example:
   a. The prosecution hypothesis (Hp) – eg, the complainer reported that the suspect had sexual intercourse with them.
   b. The defence hypothesis (Hd) – eg, the suspect stated that sexual intercourse did not take place. In the absence of an Hd, the scientist may propose a reasonable proposition based on the case circumstances.
3. The expert should only consider the probability of the evidence *given* the propositions, and not the probability of the propositions themselves; the latter is for the jury to consider given all of the evidence provided to them.

16.13 Within the evaluative framework, there is a hierarchy of issues that the forensic scientist can address, which ultimately ends at trial where the jury, not the scientist, makes an assessment of innocence or guilt at the offence level (see Figure 16.2). In general, it is preferable to address the more helpful activity level (eg, 'did the accused have sexual intercourse with the complainer?', or indeed 'did not'). However, sometimes the necessary background information or data is not available to allow an activity-level evaluation, or the remit of the examination may simply be source level (eg, 'did the semen on the swab come from the accused?').

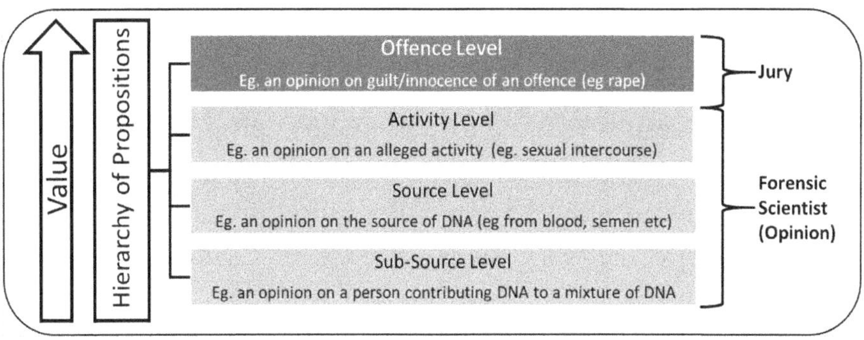

Figure 16.2: Forensic interpretation is the evaluation of the probative value of scientific findings and their significance within the evaluative framework and case circumstances. The jury will consider this in combination with other evidence presented to them.

Case assessment and interpretation

16.14 The evaluative framework starts at an early stage (see Figure 16.3). When a case is received at the laboratory, the first step is to fully assess the case and combine the information provided with the expectations in relation to the competing propositions. It is during this initial phase that published data, relevant casework data, and experience are considered to establish expectations in relation to the specific circumstances and opposing propositions. This is carried out without bias, based on the information available and prior to any laboratory examinations.

16.15 Thereafter, an examination strategy is devised, and results are compiled and interpreted. The requirement in Scots law for corroboration extends to the examination strategy, the examinations themselves and the interpretation of results. In practice, at least two scientists formulate their own interpretation and opinions independently.

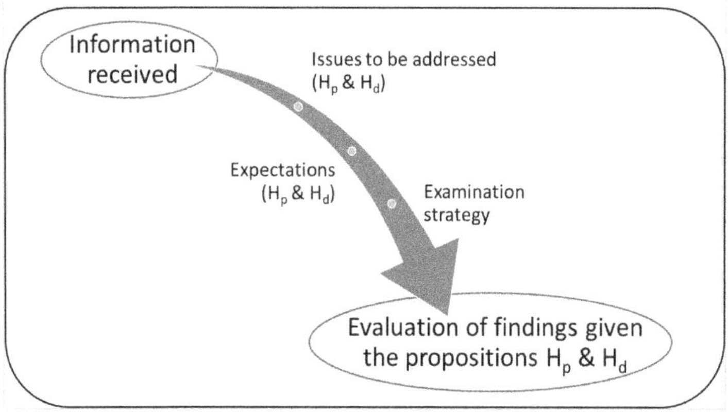

Figure 16.3: The Case Assessment and Interpretation (CAI) process within the evaluative framework.

Evaluation of results relating to activity-level propositions

16.16 The final stage of the framework is evaluation. There are two main approaches to evaluating forensic results: the evaluative approach and the investigative approach.

The evaluative approach

16.17 The evaluative approach follows Bayes' theorem, which describes the probability of an event based on prior knowledge of conditions that might be related to the event. In forensic science, findings are evaluated against the allegation and any known defence position, considering them in the context of the case circumstances, propositions, and expectations, all of which were outlined during the case assessment phase. The forensic scientist may then give an opinion on the likelihood of the results given the propositions (see Box 16.1 for a case example). It is crucial that the scientist is not drawn into giving an opinion on the propositions themselves: this is the 'prosecutor's fallacy' and is discussed at **16.33** and **16.34** below.

Box 16.1: Case example – Evaluative Approach

Case circumstances (information provided by the police):

- The complainer, Ms C, reported to the police that she met the suspect, Mr S, for the first time at a party and that he had penile-vaginal intercourse with her without consent. She reported the incident to the police and underwent a forensic-medical examination approximately 48 hours later.
- Mr S stated to the police that he had never met Ms C. Swabs from his penis were recovered approximately 60 hours later.
- Vaginal and penile swabs were submitted to the laboratory for analysis along with relevant reference DNA samples.
- We were requested to examine items to assist in addressing whether or not Mr S had sexual intercourse with Ms C.

Case assessment and propositions:

Hp: Mr S had penile-vaginal intercourse with Ms C (we cannot address consent).

- Expectations given Hp – If Mr S had penile-vaginal intercourse with Ms C and there was internal ejaculation, there is an expectation of recovering semen from Mr S on vaginal swabs taken 48 hours later. If there was no ejaculation, there is a low expectation of recovering DNA from skin cells transferred from the penis to the vagina, and a low expectation of recovering DNA from Ms C's vagina on Mr S's penile swabs given they were taken 60 hours later.

Hd: Mr S had never met Ms C. Therefore, the Hd proposition can be extended to: Mr S did not have penile-vaginal intercourse with Ms C.

- Expectations given Hd – we would not expect to detect semen or DNA from Mr S on Ms C's vaginal swabs or DNA from Ms C on Mr S's penile swabs.

Examination strategy and interpretation:

- The internal vaginal swabs from Ms C were examined and semen was detected. A DNA profile was obtained that matched that of Mr S (*sub-source level*).
- A statistical evaluation of the match was carried out (see later section).
- The source of the DNA was attributed to semen (*source-level opinion*).
- The penile swabs were examined and only DNA matching that of Mr S was detected (this was not unexpected given the expectations outlined in relation to both the Hp and Hd – neutral evaluation).

Evaluation:

- The results from Ms C's vaginal swabs would be explained if semen from Mr S had been deposited thereon.
- Overall, the findings could be explained if Mr S had sexual intercourse with Ms C, as stated by Ms C, but are not readily explained if Mr S had never met Ms C, as stated by Mr S.*
- We are not able to comment on the issue of consent (this is 'offence level' and for the jury to consider).

**In some situations, forensic providers can offer a level of support to the results in relation to the opposing propositions.*

The investigative approach

16.18 Investigative reporting provides explanations for technical/factual findings and is used when it is not possible to consider competing propositions. There are many case situations, particularly in sexual offences casework, where there is little or no clear information available, either from the complainer or suspect. For example, if the complainer has amnesia, or if the suspect is not identified or gave a no-comment police interview. In such situations, the scientist generates (often numerous) explanations for observations and may give an opinion as to how likely the results are if a certain activity occurred rather than another (see Box 16.2 for a case example). When this type of opinion is given, alternative explanations would be considered.

Box 16.2: Case example – Investigative Approach

Case circumstances (information provided by the police):

- The investigative approach, using the same example outlined in Box 16.1, but here Ms C was intoxicated and had no memory of events at the party. She awoke to find her clothes dishevelled, had vaginal pain and believed that there may have been sexual intercourse. She was medically examined 48 hours later.
- There is no suspect and, at this point, there is no crime.
- Vaginal swabs were submitted to the laboratory for analysis along with relevant reference DNA samples to assist in addressing whether or not there had been sexual intercourse/contact.

Case assessment and propositions:

Hp: Unknown, but consider that an unknown person had sexual contact with Ms C and/or penetrated Ms C's vagina (given the vaginal pain).

- Expectations given Hp – the expectations in this situation are wide ranging, and each of our expectations would be assessed separately considering the propositions.

Hd: None at this time, but alternative propositions would be considered under Hp, including no sexual intercourse/contact or considering social contact only.

Case examination and interpretation:

- The internal vaginal swabs from Ms C were examined and semen was detected. A DNA profile was obtained that was loaded to the DNA Database and a match with a named individual was obtained. The name was disclosed to the police.

Evaluation:

- In our opinion, the presence of semen on the vaginal swabs could be explained if the person identified from the DNA Database had sexual intercourse with Ms C.
- Evaluation per se is not appropriate given there are no competing propositions to consider. However, an opinion may be provided to the police in order to advance the investigation.

Evaluation in sexual offences cases

16.19 As discussed at **16.16–16.18** above (on evaluation of results relating to activity-level propositions), results can often be explained by alternative scenarios or propositions. Ideally and where possible, it is preferable to provide a level of support for the results given these alternative propositions, if known. This may not be entirely possible prior to court. However, by engaging in discussion during examination-in-chief/cross-examination/re-examination of the forensic scientist using meaningful specific scenarios, it may be possible to discuss levels of support for opposing activity-level propositions in sexual offences cases. For example:

- Semen on internal vaginal swabs might be explained by penile-vaginal intercourse with ejaculation or by penetration of the vagina with an object bearing semen. It may be that this is as far as the interpretation can go. However, the distribution of semen and the sperm score are crucial in assessing the likelihood of the results given the alternative propositions (see Figures 16.3 and 16.6 and **16.46** and **16.47** below); thus a level of support for the propositions may be possible. For instance, if it is proposed that the results from the vaginal swabs are from penetration with an object bearing semen (rather than intercourse with ejaculation) but a large amount of semen was detected on the internal swabs, and is within the range expected for the timescale between the incident and the medical examination, then it may be possible to give an opinion on the results being unlikely to be from penetration with an object. This is not an exclusion: scientists are often unable to exclude due to the large amount of (often unknown) variables, such as the sperm count of the suspect, the amount of semen that was present on the inserted object, the extent of washing, physical activity, etc.

- DNA on internal vaginal swabs might be explained by digital or penile penetration without ejaculation or penetration of the vagina/anus with an object bearing DNA. The distribution of the DNA and the anatomical location are crucial. For instance, if DNA is detected on internal vaginal swabs but not externally, then it may be possible to give an opinion on the results being more likely if penetration took place than if it did not. Again, many variables affect such interpretations.
- A mixture of semen and cellular DNA on bedding might be explained by penile-vaginal penetration with ejaculation where the semen drained from the vagina onto the bedding, as reported by a complainer. However, an alternative explanation might be that the semen and cellular DNA were deposited at different times. The appearance of the staining, whether it is mixed with another body fluid, DNA amounts, and/or results from background samples to address general levels of DNA on the bedsheet (see background DNA section) are crucial.

The Joint Forensic Science Report (JFSR)

16.20 The reporting of the scientific findings is the conclusion of the framework of evaluation used by forensic scientists. The goal is to make the report informative and understandable. This requires striking a balance between brevity and comprehension while maintaining the truth to produce a consistent, unbiased product which follows a logical framework.

16.21 Forensic scientists have a duty to assist the court by explaining the significance of their findings within the context of the case in a logical, balanced, and transparent fashion. Generally, the scientific aspects of the Joint Forensic Science Report (JFSR) are arranged as follows:

1. **Information provided section** The report outlines the information which is relevant to the purpose of the forensic examination and provides details of the propositions on which the scientist has based their evaluations, and which were outlined in the case assessment phase. This information can come from sources including the police, COPFS, defence and medical professionals.
2. **Outline of evaluative framework** Given the nature of investigations and criminal proceedings, further relevant information may come to light at a later date. Therefore, the report contains a proviso that, if further information becomes available, the interpretation of the findings may need to be re-evaluated. It should be noted that the propositions themselves are not adapted in light of the forensic results obtained, rather the results are considered in relation to any alternative propositions.
3. **Results** The examinations and forensic findings are reported in this section, generally at sub-source and source level (see Figure 16.2).
4. **Interpretation and conclusion section** This is where an evaluation of the results at activity level are reported, if appropriate, relating them back to the opposing propositions and expectations that were outlined in the case assessment stage.

5. **Technical information** To assist with comprehension, technical information relating to the relevant scientific techniques used in the case are included as an addendum rather than within the main body of the report for brevity. These are intended as a reference; however, if technical information is required in court, asking the scientist to paraphrase relevant sections is advisable rather than asking for sections to be read out.

KEY TECHNICAL PROCESSES

16.22 Locard's exchange principle that every contact leaves a trace was first proposed by Edmond Locard in the early 1900s. The principle states that the perpetrator of a crime will bring something into the crime scene and leave with something from it, and that both can be used as forensic evidence. This principle still holds true today and underpins virtually every forensic-examination strategy.

16.23 However, in practice, the challenge is often finding that trace and, if found, identifying who left it, how and when, and what it means in the context of the case circumstances. Due to the discriminating power and acceptance of DNA evidence, it is more often the latter issues that are disputed in court, rather than, for example, *whose* DNA was deposited on the item.

16.24 The following sections outline some of these issues and key technical processes, with a focus on their application in sexual offences casework.

DNA PROFILING

16.25 DNA (or deoxyribonucleic acid) is the genetic material found in most cells in the body and is inherited from a person's parents with half coming from the person's mother and half from their father. DNA is the blueprint for life and determines characteristics such as a person's hair and eye colour, and their physical appearance. It is generally accepted that no two individuals will have the same DNA, with the exception of identical twins.

16.26 Importantly for forensic evidence, an individual's DNA is the same no matter the source within the body. The most commonly encountered sources of DNA in forensic science are components of blood, sperm, vaginal cells, saliva, hair, and skin cells. Due to the enormous size and complexity of DNA in its entirety, forensic scientists can only look at a small portion of it which is known to differ between unrelated individuals: a DNA 'profile'. DNA profiling in Scotland uses DNA24 which looks at 24 different regions (loci or alleles) of the DNA. Other forensic providers in the UK use different DNA profiling kits which look at 17 regions of DNA, all of which overlap with those in DNA24. These regions help discriminate between individuals, which can be very useful to the criminal justice system for identification purposes if a match between a crime sample profile and a DNA reference profile is found.

Statistical evaluation of forensic DNA evidence

16.27 Despite DNA in its entirety being unique to an individual (identical twins excepted), we cannot assume a DNA *profile* is unique. Therefore we need to consider there being another known person with the same matching DNA profile. To address this, a match between the DNA profile from a crime sample and that of a named individual is statistically evaluated in order to provide information regarding the relevance of the match and convey the probative value of the DNA findings.

16.28 The likelihood ratio (LR) is seen as the most appropriate way to convey the relative support for the weight of DNA evidence under competing hypotheses. The LR approach is based on Bayes' theorem where the probability of the DNA profiling findings is expressed as a ratio of two probabilities of the same evidence under different hypotheses.

16.29 The likelihood ratio is represented by the formula:

$$LR = \frac{\mathbf{Pr}[E|Hp]}{\mathbf{Pr}[E|Hd]}$$

16.30 The likelihood ratio (***LR***) is the ratio of the probability (**Pr**) of finding the evidence (***E***) (ie, the DNA profile) given (|) the prosecution hypothesis (***Hp***) over the probability of finding the evidence given the defence hypothesis (***Hd***).

16.31 In terms of DNA evidence, if a match with the DNA profile of the person of interest (***Mr X***) is obtained, the likelihood ratio could be expressed as follows:

$$\text{LR} = \frac{\textbf{Pr}[\textit{DNA match}|\textit{(if) Mr X is the source of the DNA}]}{\textbf{Pr}\ [\textit{DNA match}|\textit{(if) someone else is the source of the DNA}]}$$

16.32 In words, this could be expressed as 'the DNA match is (y) times more likely if the DNA was from Mr X rather than from another individual unrelated to them' (where (y) is the calculated statistic, eg, one billion).

The prosecutor's fallacy

16.33 The appropriate interpretation of likelihood ratios is not intuitively obvious, and it is during the forensic scientist's testimony of the likelihood ratio that difficulties can be encountered in court. The DNA statistic relates to the likelihood of obtaining the DNA profile if Mr X left the DNA. It does *not* relate to the likelihood of Mr X leaving the DNA. This is a confusion with the posterior probabilities and is known as 'transposing the conditional' or 'the prosecutor's fallacy'.

16.34 In the context of DNA evidence, the statement 'it is a billion times more likely that the DNA originated from Mr X rather than another individual' is transposed and is incorrect. On the other hand, the statement 'the results (the DNA profile) are one billion times more likely if the DNA originated from Mr X rather than another individual' is correct because it is referring to the likelihood of the match. The difference is subtle, but it is incorrect for a scientist to agree to the first statement, and for this reason they will often correct paraphrased statements from a lawyer when giving evidence.

Mixed DNA profiles

16.35 When a sample is tested and more than two DNA types are detected at a single region then, in general, DNA from more than one person must be present. This is termed a mixed DNA profile. The different donors to the profile may be contributing different relative amounts and these can be described using terms such as major, minor, and trace level contributors.

16.36 Statistical calculations relating to contributors in mixed DNA profiles can be more complex than for single-source profiles. This is often because many different combinations of the DNA types present could explain any given mixed profile. Statistical evaluations are often still possible due to the use of probabilistic genotyping software, such as STRmix™, which considers all the information within the DNA profile to produce a likelihood-ratio evaluation of the result. However, sometimes a mixed DNA profile may be unsuitable if it is of a very low level, of poor quality, or too complex such that it is not possible to confidently determine the number of contributing individuals.

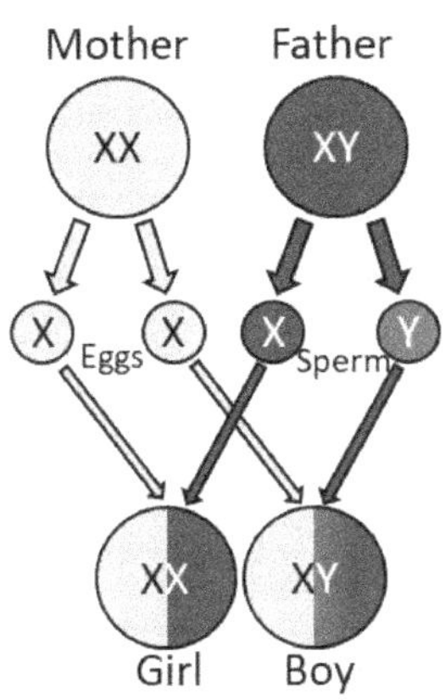

Figure 16.4: The inheritance of the sex chromosomes: the Y chromosome is inherited as a haploid (only one set of the Y chromosome is inherited from the father); therefore, the Y chromosomes are identical between father/brother/son.

Y-STR DNA profiling

16.37 Y-STR DNA profiling is a relatively recent addition to the forensic scientist's toolkit, and one which has a particular benefit in sexual offences casework. The Y chromosome is only present in biological males and is passed from father to son virtually unchanged (see Figure 16.4). Because most sexual offences cases involve a male accused and a female complainer, the exclusivity of the Y chromosome to males can be used to great effect as evidence in these cases.

16.38 Y-STR DNA profiling is used as a supplementary procedure to regular DNA profiling. With regular DNA profiling, any male DNA present at a very low level in, for example, a vaginal swab, would be masked by the large amount of female DNA present in such samples. However, by specifically targeting only the Y chromosome, the female DNA is not profiled and effectively ignored. There are a wide variety of situations where Y-STR profiling is useful, some of which are outlined in Table 16.2.

Table 16.2: Examples of when Y-STR DNA profiling might be used in casework primarily to detect cellular DNA transfers; this is not an exhaustive list.

Reported activity	Sample type
Digital penetration of a female by a male	Intimate vaginal/anal swabs
Penile penetration of a female without ejaculation	Intimate vaginal/anal/oral swabs for cellular DNA transfer
Section 3 of the Sexual Offences (Scotland) Act 2009 ('touching' case)	Relevant body swabs and/or clothing
Deposition of azoospermic semen (eg, from a vasectomised male)	Intimate swabs, body swabs or clothing
Extended time interval between the incident and the collection of intimate/ body swabs	Intimate swabs, body swabs or clothing (trace level semen)

Limitations of Y-STR DNA profiling

16.39 While Y-STR profiling can be extremely useful, it has practical limitations:

- It is unable to distinguish between male relatives: due to the way the Y chromosome is inherited, males with the same paternal lineage (fathers, sons, brothers) share the same Y-STR profile.
- It is less discriminating with the maximum reported statistic generally being around 20,000 compared with the one billion which is often the reported statistic with regular DNA24 profiling. This is partly due to the way statistics are calculated where non-linked frequency information for DNA regions from separate chromosomes in DNA24 can be multiplied together (the product rule), thus producing vast numbers. The different DNA areas in Y-STR profiling are all on the same chromosome, therefore the product rule cannot be used.

- Currently, there is no UK or Scottish criminal DNA database of Y-STR profiles and therefore no ability to load to or search unknown Y-STR profiles for intelligence purposes.
- Very low level and complex mixed Y-STR DNA profiles are often unsuitable for interpretation, given insufficient information or complexity of the profile.

16.40 Despite these limitations, Y-STR profiling has proved extremely useful in numerous sexual offences cases (see Box 16.3 for an example).

Box 16.3: Case Example – Y-STR (Digital-Vaginal Penetration)

- The complainer, Ms C, reported to the police that an unknown male digitally penetrated her vagina. Intimate swabs were taken from Ms C approximately 12 hours following this incident and were submitted to the laboratory for analysis along with relevant reference DNA samples. No other items were available. No suspect was initially identified.
- The internal vaginal swabs from Ms C were analysed using standard DNA profiling and only DNA from Ms C herself was detected.
- The swabs were further analysed using Y-STR DNA profiling and a Y-STR profile was obtained from the low vaginal and vulval swabs. Ms C's regular sexual partner's DNA profile was compared to this Y-STR DNA profile and was found not to match.
- As this was a Y-STR profile, no search of the DNA Database was possible. Therefore there were no further forensic opportunities at this time.
- A month after the incident, a suspect, Mr S, was identified. Mr S gave a 'no comment' police interview.
- A reference DNA sample from Mr S was submitted to the laboratory at this time and the Y-STR DNA profile from the vaginal swabs was found to match that of Mr S (statistically evaluated).
- An explanation for the scientific findings from Ms C's vaginal swabs could be that Mr S digitally penetrated Ms C's vagina.
- Of course, as with most forensic DNA evidence, other explanations can be explored by the prosecution, defence, or other scientific specialists.

Avoiding DNA contamination in sexual offences casework

16.41 Given the sensitivity of DNA profiling, DNA contamination becomes an increasing risk. Accidental contamination can occur during any stage of the investigation, including during sampling in a forensic medical examination (FME), recovery of items of clothing and packaging of evidential items and swabs. Forensic Services have extremely rigorous controls in place to limit contamination within the laboratory and procedures to identify contamination if it occurs. Rigorous counter-contamination procedures are particularly important in sexual offences cases due to expectations of recovering high amounts of DNA from body fluids such as semen and vaginal material, both of which have greater potential to contaminate other items because they are rich sources of DNA.

16.42 It is extremely important to have confidence in any results from an intimate swab: for example that it originates from the anatomical area from which it was sampled, rather than being introduced by some other mechanism. In order to address contamination the following procedures are in place:

- The avoidance of contamination between anatomical areas during sampling of intimate swabs by use of a speculum or proctoscope by a Sexual Offences Examiner (SOE). Forensic scientists require a basic knowledge of how and from where samples are taken by SOEs. This is crucial in order for scientists to evaluate the probative value of results. For example, knowledge of where the endocervix is in relation to the vulva is important as the presence of semen on the former can support penile penetration of the vagina whereas the latter may not. Also of importance is confidence that any semen introduced to the endocervix was not as a result of the sampling process itself due to knowledge of how a speculum is used. However, it should be noted that any detail of how a particular set of swabs was taken and the detail of how a speculum would reduce or avoid contamination is not for the scientist to consider and any such opinions must be given by the SOE.
- The DNA Elimination Database: a database containing DNA profiles of Forensic Services laboratory staff and visitors as well as SOEs and associated NHS staff. This allows scientists to identify accidental contamination of samples by laboratory and NHS staff.
- DNA Decontamination Protocol and Environmental Monitoring Regime. These were developed under the remit of the Chief Medical Officer's Taskforce, in consultation with SPA Forensic Services. They were introduced as a consequence of the Forensic Medical Services (Victims of Sexual Offences) (Scotland) Act 2021, which places a duty on health boards to provide forensic medical examinations to possible victims of sexual offences and to retain any evidence obtained during such examinations (sections 1, 2 and 6 of the Act). Together, these procedures align forensic medical examination facilities with Forensic Services' laboratory anti-contamination procedures.

THE DETECTION OF BODY FLUIDS IN SEXUAL OFFENCES CASES

16.43 The presence of semen on items, such as intimate swabs or clothing, is arguably the most common body fluid of interest in sexual offences cases as it can support some form of sexual activity. However, other body fluids, such as blood, vaginal fluids, saliva, urine and faeces, can also be of evidential value. In order to assist in locating body fluid staining on items for further testing or DNA analysis, 'presumptive' chemical tests are often used. The following sections describe the basic composition of some of the most relevant body fluids, the tests used to help identify them, and the interpretations that can be made at activity level. This is not an exhaustive list, and other scientific evidence, such as textile damage interpretation, hair and fibre comparisons, can also be relevant.

The detection and identification of semen

16.44 Semen is a fluid made up of secretions from the male reproductive organs and contains a number of constituents, including acids, spermatozoa (sperm) and enzymes including acid phosphatase (AP). The methods used to detect and analyse semen are generally more complex than those used for other body fluids, primarily due to a specialised extraction procedure known as the differential extraction process (discussed at **16.48–16.58** below).

The Acid Phosphatase (AP) test

16.45 The AP test is a presumptive chemical test which can indicate the presence of semen. The AP test is extremely versatile and can be used on swabs, clothing, carpets, furniture, car seats, etc (Figure 16.5).

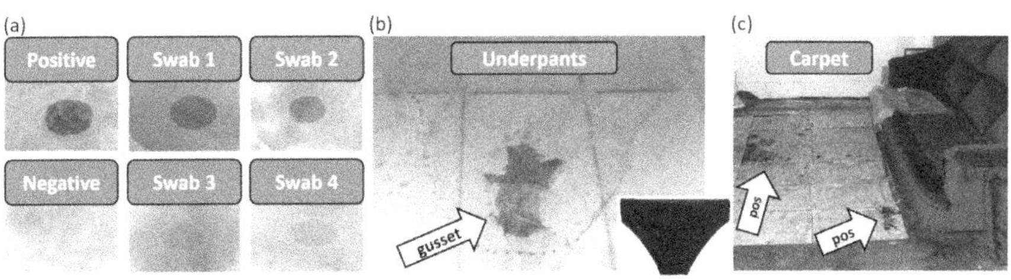

Figure 16.5: (a) AP testing of swabs: positive and negative control results are shown and portions of swabs 1-4, showing the range of positive reactions (purple colour change); (b) AP testing on a pair of underpants worn after sexual intercourse where semen has drained from the vagina onto the gusset; (c) AP testing of a carpet where sexual intercourse is reported to have taken place. (Nighean Stevenson)

The confirmatory test for semen: the detection of sperm

16.46 The AP test is a useful screening technique, but it only indicates the possible presence of semen. In order to confirm the presence of semen, a microscopic examination of a portion of the sample would thereafter be carried out. If sperm cells are observed microscopically, this confirms the presence of semen in the sample.

A standard sperm scoring system is used to give an approximation of the amount of sperm in the sample (Figure 16.6). This can help direct how samples would be analysed for DNA and can be informative when considering 'Time Since Intercourse' (TSI) interpretations (see **16.59–16.62**).

16.47 On occasion, semen may not contain any sperm (azoospermic semen) or contain very few sperm (oligospermic semen). This can occur if a male has been vasectomised or has a medical condition. In such situations, it may not be possible to confirm the presence of seminal fluid due to the lack of sperm cells. Furthermore, given that the majority of DNA in seminal fluid is from sperm, difficulties may be encountered in determining from whom any seminal fluid could originate. However, with the advent of additional presumptive testing (such as Choline or RSID-Semen™) and Y-STR profiling, it may still be possible to give an opinion on the presence of seminal fluid and from whom it may have originated.

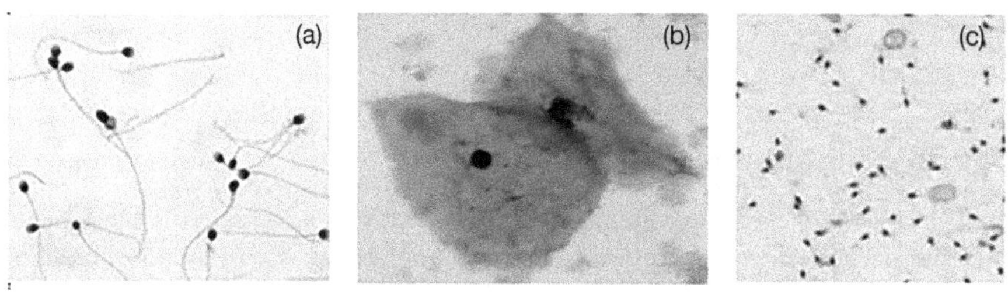

Standard Sperm Microscopy Scoring System	(d)
NEG	No sperm
Trace	Fewer than 10 sperm
1+	Sperm hard to find
2+	Some sperm in some fields
3+	Many or some sperm in most fields
4+	Many sperm in every field
(T)	Indicates sperm with the presence of tails

Figure 16.6: Microscopy of (a) sperm cells (x40 magnification); (b) nucleated epithelial cells (x40 magnification); (c) mix of sperm and nucleated epithelial cells (x20 magnification); and (d) standard sperm scoring system used in Time Since Intercourse studies.[1]

1 Allard, JE, 'The collection of data from findings in cases of sexual assault and the significance of spermatozoa on vaginal, anal and oral swabs' (1997) 37(2) *Science & Justice* 99–108.

The extraction of semen samples: the differential extraction process

16.48 The differential extraction technique is a well-established process whereby any sperm cells present within a sample are separated from any other cellular material (see Figure 16.7 below). The differential extraction process can be complex for the jury (and lawyers) to grasp. Generally, the fine detail of the process is best avoided in court, unless of course this aspect of the evidence is not agreed. The process can nevertheless be summarised as follows.

16.49 The extraction and analysis of sperm cells and other cellular material follows a two-step extraction process, resulting in two fractions which can be analysed separately to obtain DNA profiles from each fraction:

- **'Sperm' fraction** This contains sperm cells if they were present in the sample; if no/very few sperm were present in the sample, the 'sperm' fraction will not yield a DNA profile, or it may yield only a DNA profile from the donor of the swab. This is the reason why, on occasion, only female DNA is detected in a so-called sperm fraction. This is often described by scientists as 'carry-over'.
- **'Cellular' fraction** This contains any other cells in the sample, for example epithelial cells from the lining of the vagina.

16.50 It should be noted that this process attempts to concentrate the sperm and cellular material in each fraction. However, material can carry over from one fraction to the other due to incomplete separation.

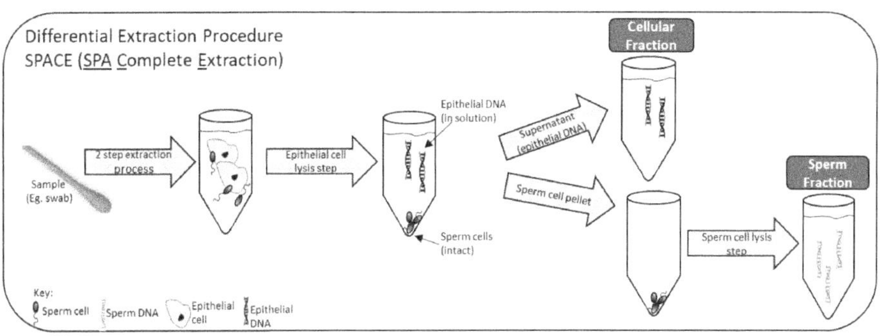

Figure 16.7: The differential extraction procedure: SPA Complete Extraction (SPACE). At the conclusion a cellular fraction and a sperm fraction is obtained which is thereafter analysed to produce a DNA profile from each fraction.

16.51 It is well established that the differential extraction process generally results in the recovery of lower levels of DNA when compared to regular DNA extraction procedures. Nevertheless, in some situations, it has an important place in the forensic scientist's toolkit. It has two key uses: (i) to avoid masking of one cell type with another; and (ii) to attribute DNA to semen. These are discussed in the following two sections.

Use of the differential extraction process to avoid masking

16.52 A specific complexity with the analysis of intimate swabs is masking of sperm DNA by the complainer's own DNA. By separating the sperm cells (of interest) from the donor's own vaginal/anal/mouth cells (not of interest), the successful DNA analysis of small amounts of sperm can be achieved without overwhelming the sample with the donor's own DNA. Therefore, intimate swabs, where the presence of semen is expected (or suspected) and the identification of semen is the primary purpose of the examination, are generally processed using the differential extraction process and the sperm fraction analysed to help identify DNA from semen.

Attribution of DNA to semen

16.53 The ability to attribute the source of DNA in a sample to a particular body fluid, such as semen, can be very informative and can elevate support for a DNA result from sub-source level to source level and ultimately activity level (Figure 16.2 and **16.13** above). This permits the forensic scientist to provide an opinion on sexual intercourse which is far more helpful to the court than simply addressing source or sub-source level propositions.

16.54 For example, for a sample such as a semen stain on a bedsheet which had drained from the vagina ('drainage stain'), if the sample was processed without the differential extraction technique, a mixed DNA profile of a male and female might be obtained (sub-source level). However, it would not be known if the male DNA could be from semen or from another source. By contrast, if the differential extraction procedure is used and the presence of semen is confirmed (using microscopy), if a male DNA profile is obtained from the sperm fraction, an opinion can be drawn on the source of this male DNA being semen (source level). Ultimately an opinion may thereafter be drawn that an explanation for the findings could be sexual intercourse (activity level).

16.55 Scientists are comprehensively trained and have been competency tested in order to give impartial opinions on body-fluid attribution. These opinions are based on the results from the tests being used, validation studies, experience and peer-reviewed published data. For example, when providing an opinion on DNA being attributed to semen, a combination of some or all of the following may be considered (see later for details on these tests):[2]

2 Similar considerations are relevant for attribution to other body fluids. However, for some body fluids there are no chemical tests available (eg, vaginal fluid), or there is variability and/or cross reactivity with other substances (eg, saliva). Furthermore, an opinion on the attribution of DNA to vaginal material or cellular material is often equivocal and is largely based on experience of relative DNA amounts, together with experience and expectations given the propositions. The value of casework experience and access to extensive empirical datasets collected over many years should not be underestimated.

- Presence of 'visible' staining (either by eye, with alternative light sources or mixed with another visible body fluid, eg, blood).
- Chemical tests: eg, the Acid Phosphatase (AP) test.
- Visualisation of spermatozoa (sperm) microscopically.
- Relative amounts of DNA across the two fractions of a differential extraction.
- Expectations based on published data, casework data and experience.

16.56 Usually the scientist's opinion that a DNA profile is likely to be from semen should be sufficient. For brevity and comprehension of the report, the presence of the donor's DNA on a sample where it is expected (such as an intimate swab), may not always be specifically described. Furthermore, the description of the differential extraction process may not always be specifically referred to in the report.

Situations where the differential extraction process might not be used

16.57 Given the compromise between the benefits of the differential extraction process (see above) and the lower recovery of DNA from samples compared with a direct extraction of a sample, there may be situations where intimate swabs would not be extracted using a differential extraction, for example, intimate swabs when digital penetration or penile penetration without ejaculation/with a condom has been reported. In those situations, semen is not expected. Therefore the focus is on maximising the recovery of DNA from the sample rather than being able to attribute DNA to semen.

16.58 However, the greatest compromise comes when a complainer has no recollection of events. In such circumstances, the benefits of using a direct extraction to increase the chances of finding any DNA on intimate swabs might outweigh the risk of not being able to attribute DNA to semen. Such processing decisions are taken on a case-by-case basis.

'Time Since Intercourse' (TSI) interpretations

16.59 In some cases, an opinion may be possible on when sexual intercourse took place relative to when intimate samples were collected. This can be particularly useful in, for example, a domestic situation where sexual intercourse itself is not disputed, rather when the intercourse took place is not agreed. In order to give opinions on so-called 'Time Since Intercourse' (TSI) interpretations, competing propositions are evaluated where the scientist assesses the likelihood of the findings if the sexual intercourse took place × versus *y* days prior to the recovery of the intimate samples.

16.60 Key to TSI interpretations is a knowledge of the retention of semen in body orifices and expectations of sperm scores for given timeframes (see Figures 16.6 and 16.8, and Table 16.3). When semen is deposited in the vagina or anus following sexual intercourse, that semen will drain out by gravity over time. The rate of drainage and loss of semen from body orifices is variable and dependent on a number of factors. The following are examples which would be expected to increase the rate of semen loss from the vagina, anus and/or mouth:

- Physical activity.
- Bleeding (from an injury or menstruation).
- Washing and bathing.
- Wiping.
- Position after deposition (upright rather than supine or prone).
- Eating, drinking or brushing teeth (oral penetration).
- Defaecation (anal penetration).

16.61 The specific, post-incident activities of the complainer are not always known in forensic science casework, thus making it difficult to fully determine expectations for loss of semen from the body orifice. However, certain inferences and generalities can be drawn from published data, casework data and experience in relation to specific case propositions and expectations given the amount of sperm identified microscopically within the body orifice. Table 16.3 summarises timescales when the recovery of forensic medical samples are advised. This is based on the maximum times observed in published data, but in reality, the timescales for semen loss can be much lower. Furthermore, the loss of semen from body orifices is generally exponential (See Figure 16.8).

16.62 By using a combination of such published data, casework data and relevant casework experience, as well as expectations given the case circumstances, on occasion scientists can give an opinion relating to Time Since Intercourse (TSI). Generally, such opinions are only possible where the results (sperm scores) are evaluated against competing propositions, namely sexual intercourse taking place x or *y* days prior to medical examination. See Box 16.4 for a case example.

Table 16.3: Maximum timeframes for recovery of forensic medical samples and their relevance to the forensic examination.
Source: Faculty of Forensic and Legal Medicine (FFLM), *Recommendations for the collection of forensic specimens from complainants and suspects.*

Sample type	Reason for analysis	Timeframe for sample recovery
Vaginal swabs	For sperm	Up to seven days
Vaginal swabs	For seminal fluid (AP testing)	Up to three days
Anal/rectal swabs	For semen	Up to three days
Vaginal/rectal swabs	For cellular DNA (eg, digital penetration or penile penetration without ejaculation)	Up to two days
Mouth swabs/ rinse	For semen	Up to two days

Sample type	Reason for analysis	Timeframe for sample recovery
Skin/fingernails	For cellular DNA or semen	Subject to abrasion/washing
Penile swabs	For cellular DNA or semen	Up to three days
Clothing – unwashed	For semen (AP) or cellular DNA	Until washed
Clothing – washed	For sperm (with specific target area identified)	N/A

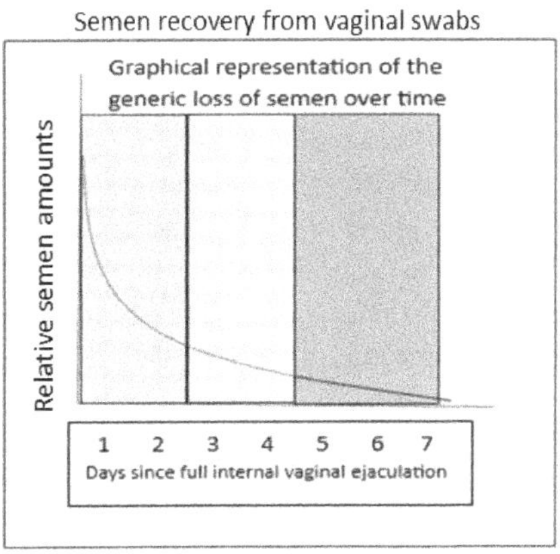

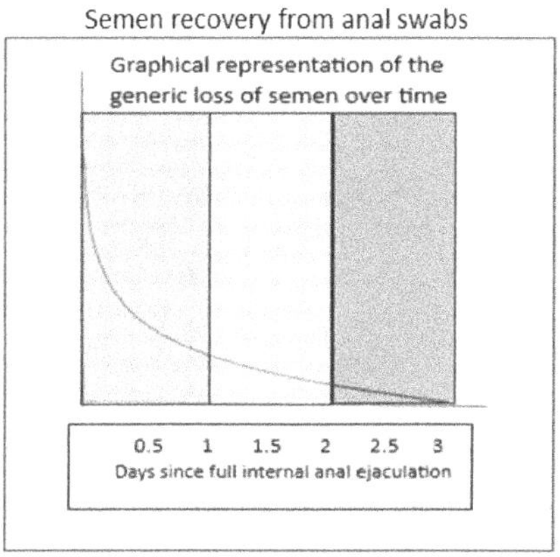

Figure 16.8: Graphical representation of the approximate expectations for recovery of semen from vaginal and anal swabs (in days – note the different scales for vaginal and anal swabs). The shaded areas indicate red, amber and green zones which relate to guidance around medical examination timeframes. (Used with kind permission of the Faculty of Forensic and Legal Medicine (FFLM)).

Box 16.4: Case Example – Time Since Intercourse (TSI)

- The complainer, Ms C, reported to the police that her partner, Mr S, had non-consensual vaginal intercourse with ejaculation on 10 February.
- Ms C underwent a forensic medical examination on 11 February.
- Mr S was interviewed by the police and stated that he had consensual intercourse with Ms C on 9 February and there was no further intercourse thereafter.
- The propositions for evaluation:

$$\frac{\textit{Hp = sexual intercourse on 10 February}}{\textit{Hd = sexual intercourse on 9 February}}$$

- Results: semen which matched the DNA profile of Mr S was detected on Ms C's vaginal swabs (*3+ sperm score using the standard sperm microscopy scoring system*).
- Evaluation – the amount of semen is more readily explained if sexual intercourse took place on 10 February as stated by Ms C rather than on 9 February as stated by Mr S.

The detection of vaginal material

16.63 Vaginal fluid consists of several components including water, acids and alcohols. It also contains cells from the vaginal wall known as nucleated epithelial cells or NECs. NECs from the vagina are a rich source of DNA, as are NECs from the lining of other body orifices (for example, the mouth and anus). There are currently no definitive tests for vaginal material. However, on occasion, an opinion of findings can be given based on the amount of DNA recovered and/or the presence of visible staining. As described previously, this involves an evaluation of the findings under opposing propositions, such as the DNA is from vaginal material versus the DNA is from another source (for example, skin cells). Within the report, this might lead to an interpretation of the findings in relation to the information received, for example, see Box 16.5.

Box 16.5: Case Example – Opinion on vaginal DNA

- The complainer, Ms C, reported to the police that Mr S, whom she had met for the first time that evening, had non-consensual penile-vaginal intercourse with her.
- Ms C did not consent to a forensic medical examination.
- Mr S was interviewed by the police and denied sexual intercourse but stated they had cuddled while wearing clothes. Penile swabs were recovered 24 hours later.
- The propositions for evaluation:

$$\frac{\textit{Hp = penile – vaginal intercourse}}{\textit{Hd = no sexual intercourse but contact via cuddling}}$$

- Results – a relatively* large amount of DNA was detected on the penile swabs; the major contributor in the DNA profile was attributable to Ms C (statistically evaluated).
- Evaluation – The findings are more readily explained if Mr S had penile-vaginal intercourse with Ms C, as stated by Ms C, than if Mr S only cuddled Ms C, as stated by Mr S.

**Relative to the amount of DNA from the donor on his own penis, also based on data and casework.*

16.64 It should be noted that this evaluation is opinion-based; casework experience and data contribute to the ability of the scientist to give such opinions. Other items which might be examined for vaginal material include the inside front of male underwear worn after sexual intercourse, condoms, inserted objects, and fingernails.

The detection of saliva

16.65 Saliva consists of 99.5% water, with the remainder containing salts, proteins, and enzymes (eg, amylase). Saliva initiates the digestion of starches using α-amylase and it is the activity of this enzyme that forensic testing detects using Phadebas™ testing. This test is a 'presumptive' test and can indicate the presence of saliva.

16.66 However, it is not specific for saliva and positive test results can be obtained from other substances, including sweat, vaginal fluid, urine and some detergents. Furthermore, the presence of amylase activity varies greatly between individuals: some do not produce any detectable amylase activity and an individual's amylase activity varies throughout the day. Nevertheless, it can be a useful test when used in conjunction with other results (such as relative DNA amounts) and when used to assess opposing propositions based on case circumstances. For example:

- If it is present on a complainer's underwear, it can provide support for cunnilingus.
- On the inside front of a suspect's underwear, it can provide support for penile-oral penetration.
- If mixed with semen, for instance, on a sleeve or bedding, it can provide support for penile-oral penetration.
- On a breast swab or bra it can provide support for licking of the breast.

The detection of blood

16.67 Blood consists of plasma, red blood cells (which contain haemoglobin), white blood cells (which contain DNA) and platelets. The test for blood is a 'presumptive' test which, together with visual appearance and DNA results, can indicate the presence of blood. The Kastle-Meyer (KM) test gives a positive reaction (pink colour change) in the presence of the peroxidase-like activity of haemoglobin of the red blood cells.

16.68 The identification of blood can provide support for sexual assault, for example:

- On the inside front of a suspect's underwear or penile swab, it can provide support for penile-vaginal/anal penetration.
- On a suspect's fingernail swab, it can provide support for digital-vaginal/anal penetration.
- If mixed with semen as a drainage stain on bedding, it can provide support for penile-vaginal/anal penetration.

- If present on intimate swabs, it can provide support for blood being present in the vagina/anus at the time of the medical examination.[3]

The detection of faecal material

16.69 Faeces contain urobilinogen, a breakdown product of red blood cells in the intestine, and is the basis of the forensic test for faeces. A secondary test relies on microscopy to detect breakdown products of undigested food such as plant cells, starch grains, etc. There is no chemical screening test for faeces; instead, sight or odour can be used to identify samples for further testing.

16.70 The identification of human faecal material may be required in cases involving anal penetration by an object. The presence of faecal material on penile or fingernail swabs, or on the inside front of underpants, may be of evidential value, albeit this can be limited due to the low expectation of DNA recovery from faecal material.

Non-specific body fluid detection: Alternative Light Sources (ALS)

16.71 One of the challenges encountered by scientists can be the identification of body fluids or other trace evidence to select for further analysis, particularly on large items or where the body fluid is not coloured. A tool which can be useful is light sources that produce light in narrow wavelength bandwidths of the visible spectrum (for example, in the violet or blue regions of the visible spectrum). When illuminated by such light sources, some body fluids (such as semen or saliva) and trace evidence (such as textile fibres or cellular deposits) may fluoresce.

16.72 The visualisation of fluorescence using alternative light sources is entirely 'non-specific' to any given body fluid, and many other substances, such as food stuffs or other liquids, can also fluoresce. Therefore, to confirm the presence of a specific body fluid, any staining identified by fluorescence must be further presumptively tested and/or DNA tested.

Section 3 of the Sexual Offences (Scotland) Act 2009: sexual touching cases

16.73 There is currently no test available to detect skin cells, therefore, the examination of items to assist in addressing contact between individuals generally

3 It should be noted that this does not necessarily indicate an injury; there is currently no test available to Forensic Services to determine if blood is menstrual or peripheral (from an injury). Further, there may be no correlation between the presence of blood at the time of the medical examination and what was present at the time of the incident.

relies on DNA evidence alone (so-called 'touch DNA'). When someone touches a surface, it is possible that their DNA will be deposited thereon. DNA transferred in this way will generally not be visible, therefore, a specific target area is required. The amount of DNA transferred is dependent on several factors including how much DNA was originally present, the duration of the contact, whether or not there was movement (friction) and the nature of the target surface (for instance, if it is porous or non-porous).

16.74 The persistence of any DNA transferred onto the target surface is variable and dependent on several factors including whether or not it was washed, wiped or subject to the elements, the use of that item thereafter or whether or not it was subject to friction to remove DNA.

16.75 Generally in casework, the amount of DNA transferred and the detail surrounding what may have affected its persistence on an item would not be known. Neither would it be known when any DNA was transferred. Therefore, consideration must be given to the DNA being transferred before, or after, the incident. Nevertheless, scientists may be able to evaluate findings in relation to the information provided by the complainer, suspect and witnesses.

Primary versus secondary transfer of DNA

16.76 A person's DNA might be present on a surface they have never touched via a secondary transfer. For example, if person A's DNA is left on an item through handling or wearing, and then this item comes into contact with another item, some of person A's DNA may be transferred. Consequently, under certain circumstances, person A's DNA can be detected without A having directly handled the second item.

16.77 In general, more DNA will be transferred in the primary transfer than it will in a subsequent secondary transfer, because some of the DNA will always remain on the first surface. Therefore, it is expected to see a loss of available DNA with each subsequent transfer (tertiary and beyond). However, without knowing how much DNA was transferred originally, or the factors affecting its persistence on a surface, this can be difficult to assess.

Background DNA

16.78 Another complexity in assessing the relevance of any DNA transfers detected is a knowledge of how much DNA might be expected on an item or surface from non-crime related, legitimate contact. In such situations, a knowledge of the legitimate or social contact would be assessed alongside the information relating to the reported sexual contact and how the items were seized, packaged and stored. Using this information, a target area would be sampled, and an appropriate equivalent sized area (or areas) would be sampled to assess the level of background DNA on the item(s). Using this information, as well as published data, casework experience, and DNA amounts, in some situations the results might be evaluated under alternative propositions. See Box 16.6 for an example.

Box 16.6: Case Example – Background DNA Evaluation

- The complainer, Ms C, reported to the police that Mr S put his hand inside her underwear and digitally penetrated her vagina. They were known to each other and had spent the evening together where they had been in direct contact while fully clothed.
- Mr S was interviewed by the police and denied sexual contact but stated they had cuddled while fully clothed.
- Ms C's underwear was recovered and submitted for examination. No other items were available.
- The propositions for evaluation:

$$\frac{\textit{Hp} = \textit{digital – vaginal penetration}}{\textit{Hd} = \textit{non-sexual contact while fully clothed}}$$

- Results – a relatively large amount of DNA attributable to Mr S was detected on the inside of the underwear compared to the outside (statistically evaluated).
- Evaluation – The findings are more readily explained if Mr S digitally penetrated Ms C's vagina, as stated by Ms C, than if Mr S only cuddled Ms C, as stated by Mr S.*

**Note that the scientist is not ruling out one or other proposition; this is merely an opinion on the likelihood of the results given the alternative propositions, based on the information provided and the expectations for non-intimate transfer on underwear (from peer reviewed controlled experiments and extensive casework data/experience).*

TEXTILE DAMAGE INTERPRETATION

16.79 Textile damage interpretation plays an important role in forensic examinations, particularly in sexual assaults where the presence of, for example, tears, burst fastenings or distortion of fabric can provide support of a struggle. By examining the overall damage features and microscopic examinations of the edges of the damage, opinions can be given on how the damage had been created (for example by pulling) or how recent the damage is, and hence more likely to be associated with the incident rather than old or wear damage that was already present. Care must be taken when describing damage as 'recent' as it could have been created some months or years before but stored unworn. Therefore, it is generally more correctly described as being unaffected by washing or wear rather than simply recent.

GLOSSARY

16.80

AP	Acid Phosphatase
ALS	Alternative Light Source
DNA	Deoxyribonucleic Acid
DNA24	GlobalFiler™ DNA profiling
FFLM	Faculty of Forensic & Legal Medicine
FME	Forensic Medical Examination
FSR	Forensic Science Regulator
Hd	Defence Hypothesis
Hp	Prosecution Hypothesis
JFSR	Forensic Science Report
LR	Likelihood Ratio
NEC	Nucleated Epithelial Cells
SOE	Sexual Offences Examiner
SPA	Scottish Police Authority
STR	Short Tandem Repeat
Sperm	Spermatazoa
TSI	Time Since Intercourse
Y-STR	Y chromosome Short Tandem Repeat

FURTHER READING

16.81 Faculty of Forensic & Legal Medicine guidelines: https://fflm.ac.uk.

Making Sense of Forensic Genetics: https://senseaboutscience.org.

Forensic DNA Analysis: a primer for courts: https://royalsociety.org/-/media/about-us/programmes/science-and-law/royal-society-forensic-dna-analysis-primer-for-courts.pdf.

ENFSI Guideline for Evaluative Reporting in Forensic Science: https://enfsi.eu/wp-content/uploads/2016/09/m1_guideline.pdf.

Chapter 17

Special measures in sexual offences prosecutions

INTRODUCTION

17.01 In this chapter we discuss the various special measures available to assist witnesses who are classed as vulnerable when giving their evidence. We consider the different approaches and procedures which apply when dealing with child witnesses, deemed vulnerable witnesses and other vulnerable witnesses. We have sought to take account of recent developments in this area brought about by both reviews and legislation. We have set out to explain the effect of the provisions which currently apply and to identify the future effect of other provisions which are yet to be brought into force.

THE UNDERLYING RATIONALE FOR PROVIDING SPECIAL MEASURES

17.02 The court has long had available to it the power to order that special measures should be available to assist witnesses in giving their evidence in sexual offences prosecutions. Section 92(3) of the Criminal Procedure (Scotland) Act 1995[1] provides that from the commencement of the leading of evidence in a trial for 'rape or the like' the judge may cause all persons other than the accused and counsel and solicitors to be removed from the courtroom. This power has been exercised consistently over very many years to exclude the public when the complainer in a sexual offences case gives evidence from within the courtroom, or by live television link to the courtroom. It is also exercised when a complainer's prior statement is read out in court and when recordings of any Joint Investigative Interviews or commission hearings are played. The press are permitted to stay in all circumstances.

1 Which repeats the provision set out in s 145(3) of the Criminal Procedure (Scotland) Act 1975. S 50(3) also provides that in certain circumstances the evidence of a child may be given with members of the public excluded.

17.03 In the case of *Hampson v HM Advocate*[2] the court held that it had the common law power and duty to regulate proceedings as to the manner in which witnesses might give evidence when it was necessary to meet the requirements of justice in a particular case.[3] Section 271G of the 1995 Act expressly preserves the common law powers to authorise any special measure for taking the evidence of any person.

17.04 The current statutory provisions regulating the giving of evidence by special measures require that the parties bring to the court's attention the fact that a witness they intend to cite may be a vulnerable witness. Applying the appropriate level of assessment, the court will then determine whether a witness is vulnerable and, if so, which special measure or measures ought to be authorised.

17.05 The relevant provisions are set out in the 22 sections which comprise sections 271 to 271M of the 1995 Act. The original provisions have been subject to various amendments, most recently by the Vulnerable Witnesses (Criminal Evidence) (Scotland) Act 2019. The statutory arrangements are somewhat detailed and complex, with frequent cross-referencing between sections, but the underlying aim is straightforward. It is that vulnerable witnesses ought to be assisted in giving their evidence to its best effect by allowing for departures from the historic common law rule that evidence should be given from within the courtroom in the presence of and in the sight of the accused.

Who are vulnerable witnesses?

17.06 Vulnerable witnesses are those who are to give evidence in any hearing in criminal proceedings in either the High Court or the sheriff court (solemn or summary) and who fall within the definition set out in section 271.[4] The importance of this provision in sexual offences cases is that complainers in a prosecution for virtually any criminal sexual conduct are classed as 'deemed vulnerable witnesses', as are complainers in trafficking, stalking and domestic abuse cases.[5]

17.07 Any witness under 18 years of age is defined as a child witness for the purpose of the regime of special measures and also falls to be classed as a vulnerable witness.[6]

17.08 Any other witness may be classed as vulnerable if there is a significant risk that the quality of the evidence to be given by the witness will be diminished by mental disorder, or fear or distress in connection with giving evidence at the hearing,

2 2003 SLT 94.

3 Such as authorising the witness to give evidence whilst screened from the view of the accused even where that measure was not available in terms of a statutory power.

4 S 288G of the 1995 Act gives Scottish Ministers power to provide by statutory instrument that any of the statutory vulnerable witness provisions should apply to proceedings in the district court. To date no such order has been made but the common law powers mentioned would be capable of being exercised in that court.

5 S 271(1)(c) and (5).

6 S 271(1)(a) and (5). The witness requires to be under 18 at the commencement of proceedings which is defined in subsection (3) as the date when the accused appeared on petition, or in any other case on the date when the indictment or complaint is served on the accused.

or there is considered to be a significant risk of harm to the person by reason only of the fact that he or she is to give evidence in the proceedings.[7]

Taking the evidence of vulnerable witnesses

17.09 Both child witnesses and deemed vulnerable witnesses have the right to give evidence with the benefit of one or more of the available special measures.[8] The special measures available are identified in section 271H as:

(a) taking of evidence by a commissioner;
(b) use of a live television link;
(c) use of a screen;
(d) use of a supporter;
(e) giving evidence in chief in the form of a prior statement;
(ea) excluding the public during the taking of the evidence.

17.10 The detailed provisions governing the use of each special measure are separately set out in sections 271I, 271J, 271K, 271L, 271M and 271HB respectively.

The original standard special measures

17.11 It has been common for many years for complainers in sexual offence prosecutions to give evidence by way of a live television link from another part of the court building, or with the use of a screen in court and/or with the use of a supporter. The evidence of children has also been taken in similar fashion for many years. These three special measures (live links, screens and supporters) were the original 'standard special measures', as provided for by section 271A(14). The benefit of this classification has been that the court would authorise the giving of evidence by a child or deemed vulnerable witness with the use of standard special measures without any further assessment of the appropriateness of the measures sought: in practice, the measures sought have invariably been a supporter and then either a live link or screen. The developments concerning the classification of standard special measures are discussed below.

The Vulnerable Witnesses (Criminal Evidence) (Scotland) Act 2019 changes

17.12 More recently the approach to taking the evidence of vulnerable witnesses has been given detailed attention. The Scottish Courts and Tribunal Service conducted a judicially led evidence and procedure review ('the SCTS review') which recommended that:[9]

7 S 271(1)(b) and (d).
8 S 271A(1).
9 SCTS Evidence and Procedure Review – Next Steps (February 2016) para 74.

> '... there should be a systematic approach to the evidence of children or vulnerable witnesses in which it should be presumed that the evidence in chief of such a witness will be captured and presented at trial in pre-recorded form; and that the subsequent cross-examination of that witness will also, on application, be recorded in advance of trial.'

17.13 Subsequently, the report on improving the management of sexual offence cases chaired by Lady Dorrian[10] included as its first recommendation three propositions:

(a) police interviews with complainers in serious sexual offences should be video recorded to capture the evidence of the witness at the earliest possible opportunity and that the recording should be used as the evidence in chief of the witness (visually-recorded interviews or VRIs: see Chapter 13 at **13.07**);
(b) until this could be achieved, in any case where the police statements have not been recorded in a manner which would allow their use as evidence in chief, the whole evidence of the witness should be pre-recorded on commission, at the earliest opportunity in the proceedings with that recording then constituting the evidence of the witness at trial; and
(c) ground rules hearings should be introduced for any occasion when a complainer is to give evidence on commission or at trial.

17.14 The Vulnerable Witnesses (Criminal Evidence) (Scotland) Act 2019 seeks to give statutory effect to the recommendations of the SCTS review by introducing various new sections into that part of the 1995 Act which governs how vulnerable witnesses are to be treated and provides for some important modifications concerning special measures. Not all of the provisions have as yet been brought into force and so the current position continues to develop. The statutory intent is clear though. It is that in all relevant solemn proceedings[11] where a child witness or a deemed vulnerable witness is to give evidence, the evidence of that witness should be pre-recorded. This should mean:

10 SCTS final report from the Lord Justice Clerk's Review Group – Improving the Management of Sexual Offence Cases March 2021.

11 As defined in s 271BZA(2) this means proceedings in respect of an offence of murder, culpable homicide, assault to the danger of life, abduction, plagium, a sexual offence to which s 288C applies, an offence under any of ss 140 to 142 and 152 to 154 of the Health and Care Act 2022 (offences relating to virginity testing and hymenoplasty), an offence under s 1(1) of the Domestic Abuse (Scotland) Act 2018, an offence that is aggravated as described in s 1(1)(a) of the Abusive Behaviour and Sexual Harm (Scotland) Act 2016, or an offence that would have fallen to be viewed as so aggravated if s 1 of the Abusive Behaviour and Sexual Harm (Scotland) Act 2016 had been in force when the offence was allegedly committed, an offence of human trafficking (see s 1 of the Human Trafficking and Exploitation (Scotland) Act 2015), an offence under s 4 of the Human Trafficking and Exploitation (Scotland) Act 2015 (slavery, servitude and forced or compulsory labour), an offence under s 1 of the Prohibition of Female Genital Mutilation (Scotland) Act 2005 (offence of female genital mutilation), an offence under s 3 of the Prohibition of Female Genital Mutilation (Scotland) Act 2005 (aiding and abetting female genital mutilation), or an attempt to commit any of these offences. This section only applies this definition to child witnesses but, when brought into force, s 271BZD will give Scottish Ministers the power to extend its application to deemed vulnerable witnesses.

- that the witness gives evidence before a commissioner in advance of the trial, or a prior statement given by the witness is used as the evidence in chief of the witness;
- where a prior statement is so used the cross-examination and any re-examination should be conducted before a commissioner;
- where the witness gives evidence before a commissioner for any purpose he or she will in addition be entitled to have the benefit of a supporter;
- the taking of evidence before a commissioner, the use of a prior statement as evidence in chief and the availability of a supporter will become known as the standard special measures for child and deemed vulnerable witnesses.

17.15 The rule requiring pre-recording has to date only been brought into force for child witnesses, and only in relation to proceedings in the High Court. It does not currently apply in relation to proceedings in the sheriff court. The rule has not yet been brought into force at all in relation to deemed vulnerable witnesses. The Scottish Ministers will have power to do so by regulation once section 3 of the 2019 Act (which will insert section 271BZD to the 1995 Act) is brought into force.

17.16 An overview of the effect of the statutory provisions which takes account of the amendments contained in the 2019 Act can be set out at this stage, with a more detailed analysis of the relevant provisions being undertaken below:

Child witnesses

- Child witnesses in relevant High Court proceedings are currently entitled, as of right, to the special measures of giving evidence before a commissioner, having a prior statement being introduced as their evidence in chief and having a supporter. These are the standard special measures for this class of witnesses in light of the application of section 271BZB.
- When the provisions of section 1 of the 2019 Act are fully brought into force child witnesses in relevant proceedings prosecuted on indictment in the sheriff court will also be entitled, as of right, to the special measures of giving evidence before a commissioner, having a prior statement being introduced as their evidence in chief and having a supporter. At that point these will be the standard special measures for this class of witnesses.
- Meantime, child witnesses in any proceedings prosecuted at either solemn or summary level in the sheriff court will be entitled, as of right, to the special measures of giving evidence by way of a live television link, the use of a screen in court and the use of a supporter. These are the current standard special measures for this class of witnesses as specified in section 271A(14).

Deemed vulnerable witnesses

- When section 3 of the 2019 Act is brought into force, and implemented by regulation, deemed vulnerable witnesses in relevant High Court proceedings and (depending upon the extent of the application by regulation) in relevant solemn proceedings in the sheriff court, will be entitled, as of right, to the special measures of giving evidence before a commissioner, having a prior statement being introduced as their evidence in chief and having a supporter. At this point these will be the standard special measures for this class of witnesses.

- Meantime, deemed vulnerable witnesses in any proceedings on indictment or at summary level, will be entitled, as of right, to the special measures of giving evidence by way of a live television link, the use of a screen in court and the use of a supporter. These are the current standard special measures for this class of witnesses as specified in section 271A(14).
- Regardless of the class to which any particular witness belongs, the other special measures remain available, subject to certain limitations as to their use in the case of child witnesses.

A further look at the relevant provisions

The rule requiring pre-recording of evidence

17.17 Since at present the rule only applies to child witnesses, consideration of its scope and application begins with section 271BZA of the 1995 Act. That section applies where a child witness is to give evidence in relevant solemn proceedings. Relevant proceedings are proceedings in respect of a sexual offence (or one of the other offences specified in subsection (2)). When this section applies its effect is to create a rule that the court will order the pre-recording of all of the child witness's evidence. This will be achieved by ordering that the evidence is to be taken by a commissioner, in accordance with section 271I, or given in evidence in chief in the form of a prior statement in accordance with section 271M (most commonly a video of a Joint Investigative Interview),[12] or by a combination of the two. The application of the rule is triggered by the presence of one of the specified offences listed in subsection (2) as a charge on the indictment. It does not matter whether the child witness is giving evidence in support of such a charge or not and it does not matter whether the child witness is a complainer or not.

17.18 Although the section applies the rule where the child witness is to give evidence in proceedings involving a relevant offence in all solemn proceedings, it has to date been brought into effect only in relation to proceedings in the High Court.[13]

17.19 Only limited exceptions to the rule requiring pre-recording are available. The first is if the giving of all of the child's evidence in advance would give rise to a significant risk of prejudice to the fairness of the hearing or to the interests of justice and that risk significantly outweighs any risk of prejudice to the interests of the child.

12 On Joint Investigative Interviews, see Chapter 13 at **13.08–13.11**.

13 Vulnerable Witnesses (Criminal Evidence) (Scotland) Act 2019 (Commencement No 1 and Transitional Provisions) Regulations 2019/392 reg 2 and Sch 1.

The second is where the child witness is aged 12 or over, expresses a wish to give evidence at the hearing and it would be in the child's best interests to do so.[14]

17.20 Where the rule requiring pre-recording applies, the special measures of taking evidence by a commissioner, giving evidence in chief in the form of a prior statement and the use of a supporter are to be considered the standard special measures.[15]

17.21 Where the rule does not apply there is no barrier to the court nevertheless granting an order under sections 271I or 271M, if satisfied that it is appropriate to do so. For example, authority could be (and often is) sought to take the evidence of a child by a commissioner when the child is to give evidence in sexual offence proceedings taking place in the sheriff court either on indictment or at summary level.

17.22 Section 271B provides for arrangements that may be made in connection with the evidence of a child who is under 12 years and is to give evidence in specified proceedings.[16] This section was in force prior to the amendments brought about by the 2019 Act and is not restricted to solemn proceedings. It provides that where a child who is under the age of 12 expresses a wish to be present in the courtroom to give evidence the court must make an order which has that effect, unless the court considers that it would not be appropriate for the child to be present.[17] It provides for other special measures to be granted where the child does not express such a preference and emphasises the priority to be given to measures which avoid the need for the child to be in the courtroom.[18] However section 271B is amended by section 2 of the 2019 Act so as to make it plain that it does not apply in any case where the rule requiring pre-recording is triggered[19] (ie, at present in solemn proceedings for a relevant offence conducted in the High Court).

Extending the scope of the rule requiring pre-recording of evidence

17.23 The broader scope of the SCTS review recommendation is encapsulated in what will become section 271BZD of the 1995 Act. That section will give to the Scottish Ministers the power to make regulations extending the rule on pre-recording evidence in section 271BZA so that it also applies to deemed vulnerable witnesses in relevant solemn proceedings, or to make a range of different provisions for different descriptions of vulnerable witnesses or different courts.

14 S 271BZA subsections (7) and (8). Where an exception to the rule is established other special measures such as enabling the witness to give evidence at the trial using a live television link may be ordered.

15 S 271BZB (2).

16 These are listed in s 271B(2). They comprise some but not all of the offences listed in s 271BZA(2).

17 By, for example, making an order that the child gives evidence with the use of a screen and a supporter.

18 Subsections (5) and (6).

19 S 271B(7) provides that the section does not apply in a case to which s 271BZA applies.

17.24 Although introduced by the 2019 Act, this section has not at the date of writing been brought into force. Nevertheless, it is now commonplace, at least in the High Court, for the Crown to make an application to permit the evidence of a deemed vulnerable complainer to be taken by a commissioner, as recommended in Lady Dorrian's review, and for such applications to be granted. Once section 271BZD is in force, and if the Scottish Ministers make the appropriate regulations, then the application of section 271BZD subsections (1) and (2) will have the effect of meaning that taking evidence by a commissioner, giving evidence in the form of a prior statement and the use of a supporter will become the standard special measures for complainers in sexual offences cases prosecuted in the High Court and at solemn level in the sheriff court.

The taking of evidence by a commissioner

17.25 The first of the two methods by which the rule requiring pre-recording can be complied with is the making of an order that the evidence of the witness is to be taken by a commissioner. Section 271I of the 1995 Act governs the procedure which applies when this special measure is to be used. The special measure of taking evidence by a commissioner may of course be used in relation to a vulnerable witness even if the rule requiring pre-recording is not triggered.

17.26 Where the trial is to take place in the High Court the commissioner is to be a judge and in other cases a sheriff. The witness may attend to give evidence in the room where the proceedings are to take place, or they may give evidence to the commissioner from a different location by live television link.[20] In either case the accused is not to be present in the same room as the witness[21] but adequate arrangements to permit him to watch and hear the proceedings have to be identified.

17.27 The commission proceedings will be video recorded and the recording will be available at the trial as the witness's evidence. An order that the relevant witness's evidence should be taken by commissioner may be applied for and made in advance of an indictment having been served.[22]

17.28 The Crown and defence legal representatives will be expected to engage in a pre-commission familiarisation process with the witness, as facilitated by a representative of the Victims and Information Advice service.[23] The wearing of wigs and gowns will be dispensed with and the commissioner, witness and lawyers

20 Commission hearings are intended to take place at SCTS facilities called 'evidence suites' located in Glasgow, Edinburgh, Aberdeen and Inverness. Different locations may be specified if necessary.

21 S 271I(3)(a) provides that the accused shall not be present in either location except by leave of the court on special cause shown.

22 S 271I(4A).

23 The High Court of Justiciary Practice Note No 1 of 2024 (see **17.33**) provides at para 15 that where practitioners are to meet a witness before the commission, it will be presumed that defence counsel will make themselves available to do so unless they have given notice to the contrary at a ground rules hearing or preliminary hearing and satisfied the court at that hearing of the reason.

will remain seated throughout the commission. The questions to be asked of the witness must be crafted and determined according to the process and principles discussed at **17.34 –17.38** below. Section 274/275 apply to commission hearings and commissioners have the power to rule on these matters at commissions.[24] Where the commissioner is a judge or a sheriff (as they invariably are), they have the power to rule on other objections to evidence that might arise.[25]

17.29 After a commission hearing has taken place, a copy of the commission recording disc will be made available to each of the parties who will be under a duty to view and listen to it in order to check that it is fit for use at trial[26] and to agree any edits to it. When fixing a commission hearing, the court will make an order requiring each party to advise in writing within a specified time period that they have complied with this duty and directing them to address any issues identified, or to bring these to the attention of the court in advance of the trial diet.

17.30 If the rule requiring pre-recording has been dispensed with in the case of a child witness, or a different special measure has been authorised in relation to another type of vulnerable witness, the scheme is flexible enough to allow the court to authorise a commission to take place, either on the motion of a party or of its own volition. It may do so at any time, including during the course of the trial and even after the particular witness has commenced giving evidence.[27]

Ground rules hearing

17.31 In any case where the court makes an order that the evidence of a witness is to be taken by commissioner it must fix what is known as a 'ground rules hearing'.[28] The ground rules hearing is to be presided over by a judge of the court which appointed the commissioner, or the commissioner appointed to take the evidence. It will normally be fixed to take place at the same time as a first diet or preliminary hearing. The purpose of the ground rules hearing is to ensure that the proceedings at the commission can proceed effectively, having taken account of all relevant considerations which apply to the particular witness, or witnesses, to give evidence at that commission.

17.32 The steps which must be undertaken at the ground rules hearing are set out in section 271I(1ZD).[29] In addition to disposing of any application to allow the

24 S 271I(5) and (6).

25 Criminal Procedure Rule 22.12(3). This is different from the rule that applies to the now little used procedure for commissions under s 272(1)(b) of the 1995 Act, where the power to rule on objections does not exist: see Rule 24.4(3).

26 This duty is specified in para 13 of Practice Note No 1of 2024.

27 S 271D allows the court to review an earlier order, including one allowing the witness to give evidence without the benefit of any special measure, and to replace it with an order authorising the use of such special measure as the court considers most appropriate.

28 S 271I(1ZA).

29 The references to the commissioner are to include the judge presiding at a ground rules hearing which is conjoined with any other form of hearing.

admission of evidence made under section 275 of the 1995 Act and considering whether the commission proceedings may proceed on the date fixed or require to be postponed, the court is required to:

a. ascertain the length of time the parties expect to take for examination in-chief and cross-examination, including any breaks that may be required;
b. to the extent that the commissioner considers it appropriate to do so, decide on the form and wording of the questions that are to be asked of the vulnerable witness;
c. if the commissioner considers it appropriate to do so, authorise the use of a supporter at the proceedings, in accordance with section 271L;
d. if the commissioner considers that there are steps that could reasonably be taken to enable the vulnerable witness to participate more effectively in the proceedings, direct that those steps be taken;

(…)

g. consider and, if appropriate, make a decision on, any other matter that the commissioner considers could be usefully dealt with before the proceedings take place.

17.33 In order properly to perform its function at the ground rules hearing, the court will require to be informed of all relevant issues concerning the vulnerable witness. This will include any significant communication or comprehension difficulties and any requirement for breaks. Where a psychologist has been instructed to examine the witness the relevant report should be available to the court. The High Court of Justiciary Practice Note No 1 of 2024 now provides comprehensive guidance on the preparation of an application or notice seeking the special measure of taking evidence by a commissioner, and on the matters which the court will wish to consider at a hearing on any such application or notice at a preliminary hearing or ground rules hearing. The Practice Note reflects and gives detailed content to the statutory provisions. It replaces the Practice Note No 1 of 2017. Accordingly, it ought to be viewed as the starting point for any practitioner who is engaged in proceedings involving a witness who may give evidence before a commissioner.

17.34 The extent to which the court will feel it necessary to decide on the form and wording of questions to be asked will depend upon the information provided to it concerning the individual witness but the 2024 Practice Note requires the appropriate form, wording and scope of questions to be identified in the vulnerable witness notice or application. The guidance on written questions set out in the High Court of Justiciary Practice Note No 1 of 2019 remains in place. That Practice Note explains that, as a general rule, in the case of child witnesses under the age of 12 written questions will be called for, as they will be in the case of any witnesses with significant communication or comprehension difficulties. This requirement can be dispensed with if the court is satisfied that the evidence of the witness can properly be adduced without prior approval of the questions.

17.35 In the case of children over the age of 12 written questions may still be required having regard to the child's best interests and the information available as to the child's abilities. If the court determines that the submission of written questions is appropriate then each party will be entitled to see the questions proposed by the other in order that a comprehensive understanding of what the witness is to be asked may be reached. The defence will not be entitled to assert that they have a right to keep their line, or content, of questioning from the Crown until the witness gives evidence.

17.36 In preparing written questions, and in the conduct of hearings without prior determination of the questions to be asked, the court will expect that the legal representatives acting will be familiar with and apply the guidance given in the 2019 Practice Note. The evidence of child and vulnerable witnesses should entail the least number of questions consistent with the duties of the respective representatives and the evidence should be taken as speedily as is possible. Questions should be simple and straightforward. Tagged or hypothetical questions should be avoided, as should complex syntax. Those eliciting the evidence of vulnerable and child witnesses must bear in mind the limitations of the witness and the questions posed should be crafted according to the principles set out in the Practice Note and the guidance provided by the Advocates Gateway website.[30]

17.37 It is now generally accepted that it is not appropriate for defence practitioners to 'put the defence case' by way of proposition in cross-examination to a child witness giving evidence at a commission (or when giving evidence in any other manner) but the 2024 Practice Note specifies that this is a matter to be canvassed with the parties at the ground rules or preliminary hearing with reference to the observations in *R v Lubemba*[31] and *R v Barker.*[32]

17.38 A further practical consideration which may arise at a ground rules hearing concerns whether the witness will require to be shown or to discuss any documentary or physical production during the course of his or her evidence before the commissioner. This may include referring the witness to a prior statement. Suitable arrangements will need to be identified to permit these steps to be achieved and the arrangements may vary according to whether the evidence is to be given directly to the commissioner or through a live television link.

17.39 In order to assist parties in their preparation for ground rules hearings and to assist the court in focussing on the issues to be discussed, a pro-forma commission checklist must be completed by both Crown and defence and lodged in advance of the ground rules hearing (in practice before the first diet or preliminary hearing). This requires the parties to provide answers to some 25 questions designed to ensure that

30 www.theadvocatesgateway.org.

31 [2015] 1 WLR 1579.

32 [2011] Crim LR 233.

full attention has been given to the issues required to be addressed by the statutory provision and the relevant parts of the 2017 and 2019 Practice Notes.[33]

Evidence by way of prior statement

17.40 The remaining method of complying with the rule requiring pre-recording of evidence is the making of an order allowing the witness's evidence in chief to be given in the form of a prior statement in accordance with section 271M of the 1995 Act. As with the special measure of taking evidence by a commissioner, this special measure may be used in relation to a vulnerable witness even if the rule requiring pre-recording is not triggered.

17.41 This special measure may be utilised where a qualifying statement made by the witness is lodged in evidence. That statement may then be admissible as the witness's evidence in chief, or as part of the witness's evidence in chief, without the witness being required to adopt or otherwise speak to the statement in giving evidence. As with any other form of testimony, rules regarding admissibility require to be met. Accordingly, section 271M(2) provides that the admissibility of a prior statement is governed by subsection (3). That subsection provides that section 260 of the 1995 Act applies to a statement for these purposes as it does to a prior statement referred to in that section but with some minor adjustments. The consequences are:

1. before a prior statement can be admitted as a witness's evidence in chief the content, or passages to be led, must constitute matters of which direct oral evidence by the witness would be admissible if given in the course of the proceedings;
2. the statement must be contained in a document;[34] and
3. at the time the statement was made the person who made it would have been a competent witness in the proceedings.

17.42 Subject to these considerations, a statement includes any representation, however made or expressed, of fact or opinion but does not include a statement in a precognition other than a precognition on oath.[35] A statement is contained in a document where the person who makes it makes the statement in the document personally, makes a statement which is, with or without his knowledge, embodied in a document by a person who has direct personal knowledge of the making of the statement, or approves the document as embodying the statement.[36]

17.43 Statements to be introduced for this purpose are generally video recorded as part of a Joint Investigative Interview or take the form of a Visually Recorded

33 A copy of the Checklist is Appendix 1. Presumably in completing the checklist, practitioners will also have to have regard to the 2024 Practice Note.

34 For these purposes 'document' includes, in addition to a document in writing, any map, plan, graph or drawing; any photograph; any disc, tape, soundtrack or other device in which sound may be recorded and reproduced therefrom and any film, negative, tape, disc or other device in which visual images are recorded so as to be capable of being reproduced – s 262(3).

35 S 271M(5) applying s 262(1) of the 1995 Act.

36 S 262(2).

Interview. It is clear, however, that in appropriate circumstances documents such as written statements, or transcripts of interviews, may be capable of being introduced as the witness's evidence in chief. In whatever form it exists, the statement will be played or read out at trial without the witness having to adopt or speak to it in court. The usual practice is for a police officer to read out the prior statement (where it is in a document) or for the JII/VRI simply to be played as the witness's evidence, often with a transcript being distributed so that the jury can follow along if the sound quality of the JII/VRI is imperfect.

17.44 Where this special measure is authorised the rule requiring the pre-recording of all of the witness's testimony, if triggered, will mean that the court will in addition order that cross-examination and any re-examination should take place in front of a commissioner in advance of the trial. A ground rules hearing will also require to be fixed in this event.

17.45 Where this special measure is authorised but the rule requiring pre-recording does not apply, it may still be appropriate for the court to order that cross-examination and re-examination should take place in front of a commissioner (with a ground rules hearing) but it may, alternatively, be that these stages in the evidence of the witness can take place in court with the benefit of a different form of special measure.

17.46 Certain particular considerations arise when the special measure of giving evidence in chief by way of prior statement is utilised. The statement may not have been elicited with the rules of evidence in mind and it may contain inadmissible hearsay, discussion of criminal conduct which does not feature in the case against the accused, reference to previous convictions, or information which would constitute a breach of section 274 of the 1995 Act if admitted. Various practical methods of addressing these issues are available, such as editing or redacting the offending passages or avoiding playing or reading out those passages. The expectation is that these passages will be identified by the first diet/preliminary hearing so that the court knows which parts of the prior statement it is authorising to form part of the witness's evidence and which parts it is not.

Evidence of identification

17.47 If either of the two special measures being discussed are utilised it is likely that thought will have to be given to how evidence of identification is to be elicited. The ordinary method of dock identification will be unavailable. In the case of a commission, the accused and the witness will not be in the same room and in the case of a prior statement the whole point is to allow the evidence in chief to be given without having to ask the witness questions. This issue will require to be addressed at a preliminary hearing (or first diet) or at a ground rules hearing (the same point will arise if the witness is to give evidence by live television link to the court or with the benefit of a screen in court). If the witness has identified the accused at an identification parade section 281A of the 1995 Act provides for a presumption that the person identified is the person of the same name who appears as the accused.[37] The common law rules of evidence also allow for identification to be established in other ways. A third party may give evidence that the witness identified the accused to him as the person involved[38] or may give evidence of the way in which the witness generally referred to the accused person, for example as dad or uncle.[39] As a consequence of these methods of identification being available the Crown will frequently serve a statement of uncontroversial evidence specifying the fact of identification by the witness of the accused[40] or a joint minute of agreement agreeing the fact of identification will be entered into.

Review of special measures

17.48 Section 271D of the 1995 Act sets out the circumstances in which the court may review the arrangements for taking the evidence of a vulnerable witness. In broad terms, the court may, at any stage, vary an earlier order providing for a special measure or, where no special measure has been ordered, it may authorise the use of a special measure. Different considerations apply depending upon whether an earlier order did or did not have the effect of enabling all of the witness's evidence to be taken in advance and according to whether the rule requiring pre-recording applied.[41]

Vulnerable witness notices and applications

Child or deemed vulnerable witnesses

17.49 The process for authorising special measures for witnesses under the age of 18, or for complainers in sexual offences cases,[42] envisages that the parties will bring relevant information to the court's notice. When a party cites, or intends to cite, a child witness or a deemed vulnerable witness the provisions contained within

37 The presumption arises where the witness and the person identified are named in the report of the identification parade, the report is lodged as a production and the Crown has served on the accused a copy of the report along with a notice that it is intended to rely on the presumption. The presumption will not apply if the accused challenges the facts stated in the report. The section specifies time limits for both the service of a notice and any challenge.

38 *Muldoon v Herron* 1970 JC 30.

39 Evidence of identification by implication can be sufficient in circumstances extending beyond family members – see, eg, *Robson v HM Advocate* 1996 SCCR 340 and *Murphy v HM Advocate* 2007 SCCR 532 as discussed in Chapter 19 at **19.09–19.10**.

40 S 258 of the 1995 Act provides that if such a statement is served within the relevant time period and is not challenged then any fact specified shall be deemed to be conclusively proved. The court also has the power to disregard any challenge which it considers to be unjustified.

41 S 271BZC restricts the court's ability to review orders where s 271BZA applies. Subsections (3A) to (3C) of s 271D restrict the court's ability to review orders enabling a witness's evidence to be given in advance in other circumstances.

42 Deemed vulnerable witnesses are those who fall within the specification given in s 271(1)(c).

section 271A must be complied with. The overarching requirement is that the citing party is required to lodge with the court what is called a 'vulnerable witness notice' and at the same time to intimate that notice to the other parties to the proceedings.

17.50 In summary, the vulnerable witness notice must provide sufficient information about the witness to make it clear that he or she falls within the relevant definition. It must specify the special measure considered to be the most appropriate for the purpose of taking that witness's evidence, or state the party's view that the witness should give evidence without the benefit of any special measure. If a measure other than a standard special measure is specified in the notice there requires to be provided a summary of any views expressed by the witness and, where the witness is a child witness, the views of that witness's parent (except where the parent is the accused).[43]

17.51 The party concerned must lodge the vulnerable witness notice with the court by what is referred to as 'the required time', which means at any time before a date has been fixed for a preliminary hearing, a first diet or a hearing at which evidence is to be given. If a date for such a hearing has been fixed then the notice requires to be lodged no later than 14 days before the preliminary hearing, 7 days before the first diet or 14 days before any other hearing at which evidence is to be given. On cause shown the court may allow a vulnerable witness notice to be lodged after the required time.[44]

17.52 Once a vulnerable witness notice has been lodged the court will consider the notice in the absence of the parties. Assuming the court is satisfied that the witness is either a child or a deemed vulnerable witness, the procedure which then follows depends upon the type of special measure specified in that notice. If a standard special measure is specified, the court shall immediately, or no later than 14 days after receipt, make an order authorising the use of that measure.[45] No objection can be taken if a standard special measure is specified in the vulnerable witness notice.[46]

17.53 If something other than a standard special measure is specified then the court may not consider authorising that measure until at least seven days and no more than 14 days have passed. This is to allow for any other party to lodge with the court a notice objecting to the special measure sought. The court may then authorise the use of the non-standard special measure specified, or authorise the giving of evidence without the benefit of any special measure. Before taking either step the court will require to be satisfied that it is appropriate to make the order sought. In assessing this the court will have regard to the best interests of the witness and take account of the views expressed by that witness.[47] Where the witness is a child witness aged 12 and over, it shall be presumed that he or she is of sufficient age and maturity to form a view. In such circumstances if the views expressed by the child witness

43 This is the effect of s 271A subsections (2), (3), (3A) and s 271E subsection (2).
44 S 271A(13A) and (4).
45 S 271A(3A) and (5)(a)(i).
46 S 271A(4A).
47 S 271E(1) and (2).

are inconsistent with any views expressed by the witness's parent the views of the witness shall be given greater weight.[48]

17.54 If a non-standard special measure is specified in the vulnerable witness notice, or if it is suggested that the witness should give evidence without the benefit of any special measure, and the court is not satisfied that it is appropriate to authorise the measure on the basis of the information provided, then it shall fix a hearing to dispose of the application.[49] If the preliminary hearing or first diet is yet to be held, the vulnerable witness notice will be considered at that hearing. At the hearing, the notice will be determined after oral submissions from the parties and taking account of any further relevant information or materials.

17.55 A duty is also imposed on the court to order a party to lodge a vulnerable witness notice if it appears that the party intends to call a child witness or a deemed vulnerable witness to give evidence but has not lodged an appropriate notice.[50]

Other vulnerable witnesses

17.56 The provisions which apply when a party cites or intends to cite a vulnerable witness who is not a child witness or a deemed vulnerable witness are set out in sections 271BA and 271C.

17.57 Section 271BA imposes a duty on a party to the proceedings who intends to cite a witness, who is other than a child witness or a deemed vulnerable witness, to take reasonable steps to carry out an assessment to determine whether the witness is likely to be a vulnerable witness and, if so, what special measure ought to be used for the purpose of taking that person's evidence. Such an assessment requires to take account of the best interests of the person concerned, any views expressed by that person and the general considerations informing vulnerability set out in section 271(2). These direct attention to matters such as the nature and circumstances of the offence to which the proceedings relate, the nature of the evidence likely to be given, the relationship between the person and the accused, the person's age and maturity, any relevant behaviour towards that person by others, the social and cultural background and ethnic origins of the person, the person's sexual orientation, domestic and employment circumstances, religious beliefs or political opinions and any physical disability or impairment which the person has.

17.58 If, having taken account of this duty of assessment, the party considers that the relevant witness is likely to be a vulnerable witness then the party requires to make an application to the court known as a 'vulnerable witness application'.[51] The application must provide sufficient information concerning the witness to

48 S 271E(1), (2) and (3).
49 S 271A(5)(c).
50 S 271A(6) and (7).
51 S 271C(2).

demonstrate that he or she falls within the relevant definition. It must also specify the special measure thought to be the most appropriate and contain a summary of any views expressed by the witness and any other information as may be appropriate.[52] Such an application requires to be made no later than 14 days before a preliminary hearing, seven days before a first diet and 14 days before any other hearing at which evidence is to be given. The application requires to be intimated to the other parties to the proceedings who will be entitled not later than seven days after the application has been lodged to intimate an objection to the special measure specified. On cause shown, the court may allow a vulnerable witness application, or an objection notice to be lodged after the required time.

17.59 As with vulnerable witness notices, the court will in the first place consider the application in the absence of the parties. The initial step to be taken is distinct however, as the court first requires to be satisfied that the witness is a vulnerable witness. For this purpose the court requires to return to the provisions of section 271 of the 1995 Act and ask itself whether either of the two definitions apply,[53] namely:

- i is there a significant risk that the quality[54] of the evidence to be given by the person will be diminished by reason of mental disorder or fear or distress in connection with the giving of evidence; or
- ii is there considered to be a significant risk of harm to the person by reason only of the fact that the person is giving or is to give evidence.

17.60 In assessing these questions the court must take into account:

- (a) the nature and circumstances of the alleged offence to which the proceedings relate,
- (b) the nature of the evidence which the person is likely to give,
- (c) the relationship (if any) between the person and the accused,
- (d) the person's age and maturity,
- (e) any behaviour towards the person on the part of–
  - (i) the accused,
  - (ii) members of the family or associates of the accused,
  - (iii) any other person who is likely to be an accused or a witness in the proceedings, and
- (f) such other matters, including–
  - (i) the social and cultural background and ethnic origins of the person,
  - (ii) the person's sexual orientation,
  - (iii) the domestic and employment circumstances of the person,
  - (iv) any religious beliefs or political opinions of the person, and
  - (v) any physical disability or other physical impairment which the person has,

as appear to the court to be relevant.[55]

52 S 271C(3).
53 S 271(1)(b) and (d).
54 Which means its quality in terms of completeness, coherence and accuracy – s 271(4).
55 S 271(2).

17.61 In addition to taking account of these factors the court must also take account of the best interests of the witness and any views which the witness may themselves have expressed in determining whether it is satisfied that the witness falls to be classed as vulnerable.[56]

17.62 If the court is satisfied on this first consideration it will then go on to consider whether the special measure specified is the most appropriate for the purpose of taking that witness's evidence and whether it is appropriate to make an order such as is sought. In deciding on these questions the court will have regard to the possible effect on the witness if required to give evidence without the benefit of any special measure, whether it is likely the witness would be better able to give evidence with that benefit and the general considerations informing vulnerability as set out in section 271(2) and referred to above.[57] It must also at this stage again take into account the best interests of the witness and any views expressed by that person.[58] Having taken these steps, if the court is satisfied that it should make the order sought it shall do so. If it is not, it shall fix a hearing.[59] At that hearing the same tests will be considered with the benefit of oral submissions from the parties and any further information or materials which may assist. Such a hearing may be held in chambers on the application of the party intending to cite the witness or on the court's own motion.[60]

The accused as a vulnerable witness

17.63 An accused person may fall within the class of vulnerable witnesses defined in section 271(1) either by virtue of age or by virtue of the matters set out in subparagraphs (b) and (d) of that subsection.[61] Section 271F provides for the ways in which sections 271, 271A, 271B, 271C, 271D, 271E, 271M, 271H and 271I are each to be read for the purposes of an accused person who may be, or is, to be treated as a vulnerable witness.

17.64 Where an accused person is under 18, a vulnerable witness notice may be lodged on his behalf in terms of section 271A on a contingent basis. If no such notice is lodged and it appears to the court that if he were to give evidence he would be a child witness, then the court shall order the party to lodge a vulnerable witness notice in the same manner as applies in respect of other apparent child witnesses. As with other child witnesses, an accused person who is classed as a child is entitled to the benefit of one or more of the special measures in giving evidence. However, section 271F(8)(a) provides that the accused person is not entitled to the benefit of the special

56 S 271(4A).
57 S 271C(8).
58 S 271E(1) and (2).
59 S 271C(5).
60 S 271C(9).
61 Mental disorder, fear or distress or a significant risk of harm by reason only of requiring to give evidence in the proceedings.

measures of a screen or of exclusion of the public. That apart, the accused who is a child witness is of right entitled to the benefit of the standard special measures of a live television link and the use of a supporter.[62]

17.65 Whilst the rule requiring the pre-recording of a child's evidence found in section 271BZA does not apply to the accused, an accused person who is a child, or would otherwise be classed as a vulnerable witness, may still apply to the court for authority to have their evidence taken by a commissioner or to give evidence in chief in the form of a prior statement. Section 271F(7) provides for section 271M (the section governing the use of a prior statement as a special measure) to be read so as to include the accused and subsection (8)(b) provides that the prohibition against an accused being present in the room where commission proceedings are taking place does not apply where it is the accused who is receiving the benefit of this special measure. The circumstances in which an accused person might seek authority to give evidence with the benefit of one or other of these special measures are likely to be rare.

17.66 Where it appears that an accused person would be a child witness if he were to give evidence then the duties under section 271A are triggered in respect of his representatives and the court. A vulnerable witness notice must be lodged or ordered to be lodged: section 271F(2) read with section 271A.

17.67 Where an accused person who is not a child wishes the benefit of a special measure, should he decide to give evidence, then a vulnerable witness application will require to be lodged on his behalf in the same manner as set out above: section 271F(3) and (4) read with section 271C.

17.68 The assessment of whether the accused falls to be classed as a vulnerable witness will be undertaken by the court in a similar manner as in the case of other witnesses who are the subject of vulnerable witness applications. The court will require to determine this question in light of the definitions in section 271(1)(b) and (d). In so doing it will require to take account of the general vulnerability characteristics set out in section 271(2) (as quoted at **17.60** above) but with certain modifications. Instead of taking account of what is set out at paragraph (c) (the relationship (if any) between the person and the accused) the court must have regard to whether the accused is to be legally represented at the hearing and, if not, his entitlement to be so represented. Furthermore, instead of considering the factors specified at paragraph (e), the court shall take account of any behaviour towards the accused on the part of any co-accused or any person who is likely to be a co-accused in the proceedings, any witness or any person who is likely to be a witness in the proceedings, or members of the family or associates of any such persons.[63]

62 Ss 271F(2) and 271A(5)(a)(i). The accused child witness does not benefit from the modification to the standard special measures provided to other child witnesses by s 271BZB(2) since the accused falls outwith the scope of s 271BZA.

63 S 271F(1).

17.69 Thereafter, if the court is satisfied that the accused should be classed as a vulnerable witness it will consider whether to authorise the use of the special measure specified, or any other special measure, in the same way as when determining these matters in relation to other vulnerable witness applications. The only exception is that in taking account of the general vulnerability characteristics for this purpose it shall do so in their modified form.[64]

The proposed Sexual Offences Court

17.70 As discussed in Chapter 1, the Victims, Witnesses, and Justice Reform (Scotland) Bill currently before the Scottish Parliament proposes to introduce a Sexual Offences Court. Sections 57–61 of the Bill contain provisions designed to ensure that, with some modifications, the scheme for the taking of evidence from vulnerable witnesses is extended to the new court.

The effects of the modifications

Ground rules hearing

17.71 Where any vulnerable witness[65] is to give evidence at a hearing in the course of proceedings in the Sexual Offences Court a 'vulnerable witness ground rules hearing' must be fixed. The purpose of that hearing is to ascertain how the witness's evidence is to be taken and to make any order in relation to the necessary special measure as may be appropriate. The judge of the Sexual Offences Court will also undertake the same case management functions as are prescribed for a ground rules hearing fixed when evidence is to be taken by a commissioner.[66]

Pre-recording of evidence

17.72 Section 59 of the Bill proposes to introduce a rule that the evidence of a 'vulnerable complainer' must be given in advance.[67] This is to be achieved by the court making an order that the vulnerable complainer's evidence is to be taken by a commissioner or given in evidence in chief in the form of a statement. Similar exceptions to the proposed rule apply as are set out at **17.19** above in relation to the current rule requiring pre-recording.

64 S 271F(2), (3) and (4).

65 Applying the s 271 definitions.

66 S 58 proposes to introduce s 271AZA to the 1995 Act. Subsection (2)(c) to (d) of that new section lists the same case management duties as are found in s 271I(1ZD).

67 In terms of the Bill a vulnerable complainer is a person against whom a sexual offence is alleged to have been committed or a complainer who otherwise falls to be treated as a vulnerable witness in terms of the s 271 definition, for example a complainer speaking to a non-sexual violent assault – s 59(7) of the Bill.

17.73 Where the Sexual Offences Court orders that the vulnerable complainer's evidence is to be taken by a commissioner, a judge of the Sexual Offences Court will be appointed so to do. The arrangements for this proposed procedure as set out in the Bill are generally the same as apply currently in terms of section 271I.[68]

17.74 Where the Sexual Offences Court orders that the vulnerable complainer's evidence is to be given in the form of a prior statement the same provisions and restrictions apply as in relation to the procedure which currently applies in terms of section 271M, with the exception that it is expressly stated that the prior statement is not required to be included in any list of productions lodged by the prosecutor.[69]

68 S 60 of the Bill.
69 S 61 of the Bill.

Chapter 18

Restrictions on sexual history and character evidence

INTRODUCTION

18.01 In this chapter we set out the restrictions on sexual history and character evidence in Scots law, both at common law and in section 274 of the Criminal Procedure (Scotland) Act 1995. We set out first the relationship between the common law and section 274, then the restrictions which apply at common law because of the common law rules against collateral and otherwise irrelevant evidence. We then turn to the content of sections 274 and 275 and the circumstances in which evidence will be prohibited by section 274, but may be elicited if an application under section 275 is made and granted by the court. In doing so, for the assistance of practitioners in this field, we have sought to distil the judicial guidance on how applications under section 275 to admit sexual history or character evidence should be drafted. We then set out how such applications are considered by the courts. The chapter concludes by addressing some of the procedural matters that govern sections 274 and 275, and the consequences of a successful application under section 275.

18.02 We have not, in this chapter, engaged in any comparative analysis between the Scottish provisions and the equivalent provisions elsewhere. There are two reasons for this. The first is that since the seminal decision of the Supreme Court of Canada in *R v Seaboyer*,[1] restrictions on sexual history and bad character evidence in sexual offences cases have been enacted in virtually every common law jurisdiction and it would be impossible, within the constraints of this chapter, to provide a succinct comparative analysis of all of them. The second is these statutory schemes vary considerably in their wording such that the courts, here or elsewhere, have rarely found it helpful, in interpreting their own statutory schemes, to look at the interpretation of different wording in the statutory schemes of other jurisdictions. One brief point may, however, be made. In its comparative study of these different schemes, the Law Commission for England and Wales considered the Scottish scheme, like the Canadian scheme on which it is drawn, to be one of 'structured discretion', that is, one that neither wholly excludes such evidence, nor requires the automatic admission of sexual history or bad character evidence when certain

1 [1991] 2 SCR 577.

common law or statutory criteria are met, nor leaves the matter entirely to judicial discretion.[2] We would agree with that categorisation.

THE RELATIONSHIP BETWEEN THE COMMON LAW AND SECTIONS 274 AND 275

18.03 The general common law of evidence operates to govern the extent to which evidence of a witness's character can be admitted as competent and relevant testimony in a criminal trial of any nature. Section 274 of the 1995 Act contains a provision which sits within the scheme of the general law of evidence and creates a statutory prohibition on the introduction of evidence bearing on the sexual history, character or credibility and reliability of complainers in sexual offences cases. Section 275 provides for circumstances in which evidence otherwise prohibited by section 274 may nevertheless be admitted.

18.04 When these two statutory provisions are seen in their proper context it becomes clear that their application cannot be understood by looking at them in isolation. They do not provide for a stand-alone assessment of admissibility. They operate so as further to restrict the leading of evidence which would otherwise be held to be admissible by the operation of the general law of evidence.

18.05 What this means for the admission of evidence concerning a complainer in a sexual offences case is that a three-stage process of assessment requires to be undertaken. The first matter to be determined is whether the proposed evidence is admissible in terms of the general law of evidence. If it is not, that is an end of the matter and the evidence cannot be admitted. If the proposed evidence should pass this threshold the second matter to be determined is whether it falls within the scope of the section 274 prohibition. If it does, the third matter to be assessed is whether it may nevertheless be admitted through the operation of section 275.

18.06 The interplay between the common law and sections 274 and 275 was discussed in the Full Bench decision in the case of *CJM v HM Advocate*,[3] the import of which was succinctly summarised by the Lord Justice Clerk at paragraph 36 of her opinion in the Full Bench case of *CH v HM Advocate*:[4]

> 'The decision in *CJM* may be summarised thus: (i) evidence is only admissible if it is relevant; (ii) evidence is relevant if it makes a fact in issue more or less probable: the testimony must have a reasonably direct bearing on the subject-matter of the prosecution; this would exclude collateral evidence; (iii) if evidence is inadmissible at common law it is inadmissible under the statute; (iv) the very nature of the statutory provisions is to restrict the admissibility of

2 *Evidence in Sexual Offences Prosecutions: A consultation paper*, 23 May 2023. Chapter 4 covers sexual history evidence. The Scottish scheme is considered at paras 4.138 and following.

3 2013 SCCR 215.

4 2021 JC 45.

evidence permissible at common law, not to expand it; (v) the former common law exceptions regarding the moral character of complainers was 'swept away' by the legislation; and (vi) the conditions for an exception within sec 275 are cumulative.'

THE APPLICATION OF THE GENERAL LAW OF EVIDENCE

18.07 It follows from the passage noted above that evidence which is irrelevant is never admissible. Thus, even evidence which is not in dispute but which fails to meet the test of making a fact in issue more or less probable and have a reasonably direct bearing on the subject matter of the prosecution, will still be inadmissible.[5] For the reasons discussed below, evidence will be irrelevant if it is collateral. This is of particular importance when considering evidence which seeks to undermine or attack the character of a witness.

18.08 Generally speaking, evidence of this sort is inadmissible at common law because it is collateral to the facts in issue. A jury requires to determine the credibility and reliability of witnesses having regard to their demeanour in court, the inherent likelihood of their account and the manner in which these accounts dovetail with other evidence in the case.[6]

18.09 In delivering her opinion in the case of *CH v HM Advocate*,[7] the Lord Justice Clerk observed that the reason for excluding evidence of collateral issues was set out clearly in Walker and Walker, *Law of Evidence in Scotland* (paragraph 7.1) where the authors explained that:

> 'A 'collateral issue' is one which runs parallel to a fact in issue but evidence of it is generally inadmissible on grounds of relevance, because the existence of the collateral fact does not have a reasonably direct bearing upon a fact in issue and thus does not render more or less probable the existence of that fact, and it is inexpedient to allow an inquiry to be confused and protracted by enquiries into other matters.'

18.10 In the case of *Brady v HM Advocate*,[8] Lord Justice Clerk Ross explained the justification for the rule as being:

> 'The existence of a collateral fact does not render more probable the existence of the fact in issue; at best a collateral matter can have only an indirect bearing on the matter in issue; a jury may become confused by having to consider collateral matters and may have their attention diverted from the true matter in issue.'

5 See, eg, *CH v HM Advocate* at para 70.
6 *G v HM Advocate* 2010 SCCR 589 at para 90.
7 2021 JC 45 at para 38.
8 1986 JC 68.

18.11 There can be exceptions to the rule in criminal cases in situations where the collateral fact is 'instantly verifiable and cannot be challenged'. So the dishonesty of a witness can be proved but only by reference to an established fact in the form of a previous conviction.[9] In a case of assault an accused person is entitled to prove the quarrelsome disposition of the alleged victim by the use of previous convictions for violence, if it is relevant to do so, such as where self-defence or provocation are pled. Evidence of specific acts of violence may not however be led.[10]

18.12 The application of the common law rule on the need for evidence to pass the test of relevance is discussed in the following paragraphs in relation to three circumstances: evidence of medical conditions affecting credibility, evidence of sexual activity either prior to or subsequent to an alleged sexual offence and evidence of non-sexual conduct.

The common law rule on medical conditions affecting credibility

18.13 The common law of evidence recognises that in limited circumstances, evidence may be admitted to show that a witness suffers from an objectively diagnosed medical condition affecting his credibility. So whilst it would not be competent to lead evidence from a person that a witness was not likely to be telling the truth, or had a propensity to lie, if a witness has an objective medical condition bearing upon his credibility or reliability then medical evidence of that condition and its general effects may be admissible.[11]

The common law rules on prior or subsequent sexual conduct

18.14 As discussed previously in Chapter 3, the principle of autonomy underpins the entire approach of the Sexual Offences (Scotland) Act 2009. That principle is expressed in what was said by Lady Hale in the case of *R v Cooper*[12] when she explained that:

> 'It is difficult to think of an activity which is more person – and situation – specific than sexual relations. One does not consent to sex in general. One consents to this act of sex with this person at this time and in this place.

9 There is not an unfettered right to lead evidence of a witness's previous convictions for dishonesty. The common law permits that a witness may be examined on a prior conviction for dishonesty so long as the conviction may reasonably be viewed as bearing on the credibility of the evidence which the witness may give. This will depend on the facts in issue in the case as well as factors such as the nature, frequency, and age of the convictions. In a case to which s 274 applies, the evidence would additionally require to meet the test for admissibility provided for by s 275 – *DM v HM Advocate*, unreported 21 March 2024 (HCA/2023/00645).

10 *G v HM Advocate* 2010 SCCR 589 at para 91, *CJM v HM Advocate* 2013 SCCR 215 at para 32. See also the decision of Lord Macfadyen in *Maan (Habib) Petitioner* 2001 SCCR 172 at para 30.

11 *McBrearty v HM Advocate* 2004 SCCR 337 at para 49; *CJM v HM Advocate* at para 38.

12 [2009] UKHL 42 at para 27 as quoted with approval by the Lord Justice General in *GW v HM Advocate* 2019 JC 109 at para 31.

Autonomy entails the freedom and the capacity to make a choice of whether or not to do so. This is entirely consistent with the respect for autonomy in matters of private life which is guaranteed by art.8 of the European Convention …'.

18.15 In the case of *GW v HM Advocate*,[13] the court made plain that, as a matter of law, consent to a sexual act requires to be given at the time of that act and not at a point remote from it. As a consequence, the question of consent in relation to a particular act is, generally speaking, not illuminated to any extent by prior expressions of interest in sexual conduct made by one party to another, or by expressions of interest in any particular type of sexual activity.[14] Evidence of this sort will in many cases fall to be viewed as collateral and thus will fail to pass the common law test of relevancy and will be inadmissible.

18.16 For the same reason, evidence of prior consensual sexual conduct between the parties is not normally relevant to the question of whether consent was present on a subsequent occasion.[15] Such evidence does not become relevant based upon a proposition that it shows the 'full picture' of the parties' relationship, nor upon a proposition that it demonstrates the 'real' level of prior association between the parties.[16]

18.17 In most circumstances, evidence of consensual sexual conduct said to have occurred after an alleged non-consensual act would be viewed as irrelevant, having no bearing on the question of whether the previous act was consented to and having no bearing on the complainer's credibility in describing that allegedly non-consensual act.[17] However the circumstances in which such issues arise will inevitably be fact specific to at least some degree and the decision in the case of *Oliver v HM Advocate*[18] may be thought to provide support for the proposition that it would be wrong to assume that such evidence could never pass the test of relevancy. The decision of the court was to the effect that evidence of continued co-habitation and consensual sexual intercourse was capable of having a bearing on the credibility of the complainer in relation to her account of the prior sexual assault libelled against the accused. The court's view was that evidence of this sort, so long as confined to the immediate aftermath of an alleged event, would not be collateral (and in that case of sufficient probative value to be admissible). Lord Menzies, who was a member of the Bench in *Oliver*, subsequently explained that the 'immediate aftermath' should be reckoned in hours and not days.[19]

13 2019 JC 109.

14 *HM Advocate v JW* 2020 SCCR 174.

15 *J (S) v HM Advocate* 2020 SLT 642 Lord Turnbull at paras 56 and 57, Lord Pentland at para 79, as approved by the Court in *CH v HM Advocate*.

16 *L v HM Advocate* 2018 JC 182, *SJ v HM Advocate* at para 57.

17 *Thomson v HM Advocate* HCJAC 13 December 2019, unreported, *HM Advocate v JW*, *CH v HM Advocate* per the Lord Justice Clerk at para 64.

18 2020 JC 119.

19 *CH v HM Advocate* at paras 83–86.

18.18 Subsequent analysis has tended to distinguish the case of *Oliver* on the basis of its unusual factual circumstances. These included the Crown's acceptance that the complainer continued to stay with the appellant and had consensual intercourse with him in the immediate aftermath of the alleged incident, meaning that there was little or no risk that the jury would be distracted by an exploration of evidence of a collateral matter which was itself disputed. A further circumstance of some importance was that the proposed evidence was said to have a bearing on the question of consent at the time of the events charged and the Crown did not challenge the relevancy at common law of the evidence for that purpose.

18.19 However, even with these circumstances kept firmly in mind, the approach taken in *Oliver* does not sit well alongside the views expressed by the Lord Justice Clerk in giving the leading opinion in *CH v HM Advocate* at paragraph 64, nor with the decision in *HM Advocate v JW*[20] as approved by the Appeal Court. It may therefore be that its influence in determining future applications will turn out to be very limited.

18.20 The circumstances in which questions of the relevance of other sexual conduct generally arise are where the representatives of the accused wish to lead evidence of other sexual activity, or evidence of amorous interest, between the accused and the complainer. It may transpire that the account which it is proposed to lead is not accepted by the complainer. This will often lead to the proposed evidence being viewed as collateral and therefore irrelevant. The observation made by Lord Menzies concerning the evidence which it was proposed to lead in *CH v HM Advocate*[21] is capable of providing general guidance as to why such evidence is not admitted:

> 'In the present case the appellant seeks to give evidence that the complainer had consensual sexual intercourse with him some hours after the event libelled. The complainer denies this. This is about as far from 'instantly verifiable material which cannot be challenged' as it is possible to imagine. If allowed, it would give rise to a real risk that the jury would be distracted from the central issue, namely, whether the appellant committed the crime libelled, and would focus on the collateral matter, namely whether the appellant and the complainer had consensual sexual intercourse the following morning.'

18.21 In assessing the relevance of evidence concerning other sexual conduct, the courts have made it plain that there may be circumstances in which evidence of, for example, a previous act of intercourse could be relevant to the issue of whether the complainer consented on a subsequent occasion. The point which has been clearly articulated is, that in such a case, particular circumstances would have to be identified to demonstrate what was said to be the connection between what would otherwise be

20 2020 SCCR 174, upheld on appeal in *JW v HM Advocate*, 27 February 2020, unreported: see *CH v HM Advocate* at para 63.

21 At para 88.

seen as unrelated events.[22] Similarly, evidence of other sexual conduct might pass the test of relevancy if it is designed to provide an alternative explanation for injuries, or for the presence of scientific evidence, such as DNA.[23] Any such proposed evidence which passes the common law test of relevancy will then fall to be assessed against the tests set out in sections 274 and 275.

Non-sexual conduct at common law

18.22 Alleged non-sexual conduct by a complainer may of course also fail to meet the common law test of relevance. Examples of such evidence held to be irrelevant and inadmissible at common law include evidence of prior allegedly false allegations, or attempting to induce another to make false allegations[24] and evidence that a complainer had falsely claimed to be pregnant with the accused's child at a point after the crime was said to have been committed.[25]

SECTIONS 274 AND 275

18.23 The operation of sections 274 and 275 can be considered in overview before turning to look more closely at the detail of the respective provisions.

18.24 Section 274 does four things:

1. It prohibits the court from allowing evidence or questioning concerning the complainer's character.
2. It prohibits the court from allowing evidence or questioning about the complainer's sexual history.
3. It prohibits the court from allowing evidence or questioning about any non-sexual 'behaviour' on the part of the complainer which is not broadly contemporaneous with the events charged and which would be designed to show that she/he in fact consented to those acts, or to show that she/he is not a credible or reliable witness.
4. It prohibits the court from allowing evidence or questioning designed to show that the complainer has ever been subject to a condition or pre-disposition such as would suggest that she/he consented to the acts concerned or was not a credible or reliable witness.

18.25 The prohibitions apply to the Crown as well as to the defence. Indeed, it is now as common to find Crown section 275 applications to admit evidence struck at by

22 *L v HM Advocate* at para 14.

23 *J (S) v HM Advocate* at para 77.

24 *M (M) v HM Advocate (No 2)* 2007 SCCR 159, Lord Johnston at para 26; *CJM v HM Advocate* 2013 SCCR 215.

25 *Kerseboom v HM Advocate* 2017 JC 47; *RN v HM Advocate* 2020 JC 132.

section 274 as defence applications.[26] If both parties wish to lead the same evidence, it is not sufficient that one party make an application; the Crown and defence require to make separate applications to lead the same evidence.[27]

18.26 Section 275 provides that the court can, on an application made to it, mitigate the effects of the section 274 prohibitions and allow the proposed evidence to be admitted if satisfied of a three-stage cumulative evaluation:

1. the proposed evidence passes a test of specificity;
2. the proposed evidence passes a test of relevance; and
3. the proposed evidence passes a test of assessment.

Section 274

18.27 Section 274 provides:

'Restrictions on evidence relating to sexual offences

(1) In the trial of a person charged with an offence to which section 288C of this Act applies, the court shall not admit, or allow questioning designed to elicit, evidence which shows or tends to show that the complainer–
   (a) is not of good character (whether in relation to sexual matters or otherwise);
   (b) has, at any time, engaged in sexual behaviour not forming part of the subject matter of the charge;
   (c) has, at any time (other than shortly before, at the same time as or shortly after the acts which form part of the subject matter of the charge), engaged in such behaviour, not being sexual behaviour, as might found the inference that the complainer–
      (i) is likely to have consented to those acts; or
      (ii) is not a credible or reliable witness; or
   (d) has, at any time, been subject to any such condition or predisposition as might found the inference referred to in sub-paragraph (c) above.

(2) In subsection (1) above—

'complainer' means the person against whom the offence referred to in that subsection is alleged to have been committed; and

the reference to engaging in sexual behaviour includes a reference to undergoing or being made subject to any experience of a sexual nature.'

18.28 As noted above, section 274 operates as a restricting force on the common law rules so as to prohibit the introduction of certain types of testimony which the

[26] Usually to lead an accused's account in police interview, or evidence of the taking of drugs by the complainer (insofar as relevant to a lack of capacity to consent), or sexual activity shortly before the subject matter of the charge.

[27] The view expressed in the Preliminary Hearings e-Bench Book at para 9.8, relying on s 275(3) and (7), *RN v HM Advocate* and an unreported interlocutor in *Jordan Garry v HM Advocate*, 17 March 2021.

law of evidence would otherwise class as admissible. For practical purposes it applies in every case where the accused is charged with an offence of a sexual nature.[28] It introduces a rule which the court is required to comply with (the court *shall* not admit), rather than a power which the court may or may not use according to the exercise of its discretion. The policy which lies behind the legislation is to protect complainers from unfair and intrusive attacks on their character and on their past sexual and other behaviour. It aims to prevent the leading of evidence in the belief that a complainer's previous sexual experience or sexual reputation makes it more likely that she would have consented to sexual relations with the accused and makes it less likely that she is a credible witness.[29] While the obvious focus of the section 274 prohibition is on questioning of the complainer, the section applies to evidence elicited from any source which is designed to show, or tends to show, any of the matters specified in subsection (1)(a) to (d).

18.29 The scope of the prohibition is very wide. Subsection 1(a) prohibits the eliciting of evidence designed to attack the complainer's character in relation to any matter. So, for example, evidence of dishonesty, even as vouched by previous convictions, would be prohibited.

18.30 Subsection 1(b) prohibits the eliciting of evidence about the complainer's sexual behaviour at any time other than that which forms part of the subject matter of the charge. For these purposes sexual behaviour includes being made subject to any experience of a sexual nature.[30] For sexual behaviour to be viewed as forming part of the subject matter of the charge it would require to be libelled within the charge.[31] It follows that if either the Crown or defence wish to lead evidence that sexual activity occurred of a type which is different from, or additional to, that which is specified in the charge they must make an application under section 275.

18.31 The scope of subsection (1)(b) also excludes anything done to the complainer by someone other than the accused, as such conduct would not be the subject matter of the charge. Accordingly, if the accused's position should be one of incrimination he will require to make an application under section 275 for authority to elicit any evidence concerning the incriminee's conduct towards the complainer.[32] The reference to 'sexual behaviour' in this subsection is wide enough to include things said by way of flirtatious or seductive conduct[33] but it does not include a period of

28 It applies in the trial of a person charged with any of the offences listed in s 288C of the 1995 Act and any charge in respect of which the court has made an order under s 288C(4): see Chapter 14 at **14.28**.

29 *DS v HM Advocate* 2007 SC (PC) 1 per Lord Rodger of Earlsferry at para 57.

30 Section 274(2).

31 *CH v HM Advocate* at para 74.

32 *L (J) v HM Advocate* 2021 JC 83. It should be noted that the court emphasised the need for the proposed evidence to demonstrate that the incriminee was the only person responsible for offending against the complainer, in other words it needed to demonstrate that the accused had not done so in addition.

33 *DS v HM Advocate* at para 77.

cohabitation. So the statutory prohibition does not prevent an accused person from establishing in evidence that he and the complainer had at one time lived together.[34]

18.32 Subsection 1(c) prohibits the eliciting of evidence designed to show that the complainer has at any time engaged in any other type of behaviour, ie, non-sexual behaviour, which might found the inference that she was likely to have consented to the sexual acts libelled or is not a credible or reliable witness. This prohibition does not apply if the behaviour took place shortly before, at the same time as, or shortly after the events libelled. Thus any form of evidence about behaviour outwith this period which is designed to undermine the credibility or reliability of the complainer is prohibited.

18.33 The qualification to the prohibition within this subsection means that evidence designed to show that the complainer had consumed, or was under the influence of alcohol at around the time of the events libelled is unlikely to fall within its scope. However, evidence that the complainer was behaving in a sexually disinhibited way as a consequence of being intoxicated at or around the time of the events libelled would fall within the scope of the prohibition specified in subsection 1(b).[35]

18.34 For the purposes of subsection (1)(c) 'behaviour' does not, in general, include non-sexual things said by a complainer to a third party which bear upon his or her credibility or reliability. So a comment by a complainer to another that she had consented to sex with the accused would not fall within the prohibition. However a statement made in the course of shouting or screaming, or in the course of verbal abuse may well constitute 'behaviour' for the purposes of this subsection and require an application under section 275 to authorise its admission in evidence.[36] A helpful analysis of what can constitute 'behaviour' for the purposes of subsection 1(c) can be found in the Preliminary Hearings e-Bench Book at paragraph 9.11.2 to the following effect:

> 'Behaviour can, in some circumstances, be constituted by the complainer saying things, but it does not encompass prior inconsistent statements about the incident itself. What a complainer may have said about something else which is not the subject matter of the charge may not be permissible even as a prior inconsistent statement if it seeks to elicit material prohibited by section 274 and will not be admissible if it seeks to introduce irrelevant or collateral material. It should be recalled that section 263(4) requires that examination on any different statement must be 'pertinent to the issue at the trial' which will

34 *DS v HM Advocate* paras 46 and 75. Any such evidence would of course still have to pass the common law test of relevancy.

35 As the Lord Justice Clerk stated at para 74 of her opinion in the case of *CH v HM* Advocate: 'On its own, the fact that a complainer was intoxicated is not something which would obviously require an application under section 275.'

36 *DS v HM Advocate* at paras 46 and 77.

have a bearing on judicial decision-making at both preliminary hearing and trial.'

18.35 Subsection 1(d) acts so as to prohibit the leading of evidence designed to show that the complainer has suffered from a medical condition, or some form of predisposition, which may found the inference that she consented to the acts libelled or is not a credible or reliable witness. This subsection therefore prohibits the type of evidence which would otherwise meet the common law test identified in *McBrearty v HM Advocate*.[37]

Section 275

18.36 Section 275 provides:

'Exception to restrictions under section 274

(1) The court may, on application made to it, admit such evidence or allow such questioning as is referred to in subsection (1) of section 274 of this Act if satisfied that–

(a) the evidence or questioning will relate only to a specific occurrence or occurrences of sexual or other behaviour[,][38] or to specific facts demonstrating–

(i) the complainer's character; or

(ii) any condition or predisposition to which the complainer is or has been subject;

(b) that occurrence or those occurrences of behaviour or facts are relevant to establishing whether the accused is guilty of the offence with which he is charged; and

(c) the probative value of the evidence sought to be admitted or elicited is significant and is likely to outweigh any risk of prejudice to the proper administration of justice arising from its being admitted or elicited.

(2) In subsection (1) above–

(a) the reference to an occurrence or occurrences of sexual behaviour includes a reference to undergoing or being made subject to any experience of a sexual nature;

(b) 'the proper administration of justice' includes–

(i) appropriate protection of a complainer's dignity and privacy; and

(ii) ensuring that the facts and circumstances of which a jury is made aware are, in cases of offences to which section 288C of this Act applies, relevant to an issue which is to be put before the jury and commensurate to the importance of that issue to the jury's verdict …'.

37 2004 SCCR 337.

38 Subsection (a) requires to be read as if there were, after the word 'behaviour', a comma so that the words after 'demonstrating' apply only to specific facts – *DS v HM Advocate* at paras 47 and 71.

18.37 Any party to a case who wishes to lead evidence otherwise prohibited by section 274 requires to make an application in terms of section 275(1) to the court for authority to admit that evidence. An application requires to be made in writing in compliance with form 21.5 of the Act of Adjournal (Criminal Procedure) Rules 1996[39] and intimated to the other parties in the case. The application requires to be lodged no later than 7 clear days before the preliminary hearing if the proceedings are in the High Court and otherwise not less than 14 clear days before the trial dict. An application made outwith these timescales can only be considered by the court on special cause shown.[40] Special cause does not imply an enhanced level of cause, it means that the cause must be special to the case and not one that applies in all or most cases.[41]

The nature and content of an application made under section 275(1)

18.38 Before turning to look at the ways in which the court will assess an application of this sort it may be helpful to take account of what is required of the application itself in terms of its content. Any such application requires to pay close attention to the requirements of section 275(3). That subsection provides that the application must set out:

(a) the evidence sought to be admitted or elicited;
(b) the nature of any questioning proposed;
(c) the issues at the trial to which that evidence is considered to be relevant;
(d) the reasons why that evidence is considered relevant to those issues;
(e) the inferences which the applicant proposes to submit to the court that it should draw from that evidence;
(f) any other information as is of a kind specified for the purposes of this paragraph in Act of Adjournal.

18.39 Form 21.5 in effect mirrors this subsection by requiring that the application should address, in five numbered paragraphs, the matters set out in paragraphs (a) to (e).

18.40 Despite common practice in the years following upon the introduction of the section in its present form, it has now become clear that these requirements impose exacting standards as to the content of an application of this sort. The requisite detail contemplated by each paragraph of section 275(3) must be set out in an informative and comprehensive manner. Bald assertions will not be sufficient to

39 A copy of the form is Appendix 2.
40 S 275B(1).
41 *Doran v HM Advocate* 2023 JC 149. The court noted that it was the responsibility of counsel rather than the instructing solicitor to draft and lodge such an application (para 4).

meet the demands of the subsection, and the court will be entitled to refuse to hear an application which is deficient in content.[42]

18.41 Each aspect of section 275(3) should be addressed separately in respect of each piece of evidence or proposed questioning. Three cases in particular have provided guidance for the drafting of an application of this sort: *HM Advocate v A*,[43] *RN v HM Advocate*,[44] and *CH v HM Advocate*.[45]

18.42 The import of these decisions may be summarised as follows.

A preamble

18.43 In comments subsequently approved in *RN* and *CH,* Lord Brodie in *A* observed that the parties will be familiar with their respective cases. The court, on the other hand, cannot know precisely how it is proposed to prosecute and to defend the charge. If it is to make a decision on a section 275(1) application the court is likely to require some information, specific to the instant case, and in sufficient detail to allow it to understand why it is being invited to admit otherwise inadmissible evidence. On this basis the Preliminary Hearings e-Bench Book states at paragraph 9.4 that:

> 'It would assist the court if applications contain a concise synopsis of this kind but it should be made plain in the application that it is a preamble as opposed to the narrative in which the applicant seeks to meet the requirements imposed by section 275(3).'

18.44 This preamble should usually be one paragraph at the start of the application.

Paragraph 1 of the application

18.45 This should address paragraph (a) of section 275(3). It must set out a statement of the evidence which it is proposed to lead or elicit. This paragraph does not direct the drafter to the questions proposed but to a narrative providing an explanation of what factual circumstances the proposed evidence will establish, be they related to behaviour, character or condition. For example, the application may set out an account of conduct which it is said the complainer engaged in and which witnesses can speak to this or these events. Equally, the application may set out conduct which it is contended provides an explanation for the allegation made against the accused. The drafter will require to specify the particular behaviour which the applicant seeks to establish in evidence, whether sexual or otherwise, by reference to what occurred,

42 *HM Advocate v G (J)* [2019] HCJ 71 at paras 35 and 36, as quoted with approval in *RN v HM Advocate* 2020 JC 132 at para 26.

43 2008 SCCR 84.

44 2020 JC 132.

45 2021 JC 45.

when, where and as observed or heard by whom. If the proposed evidence should be directed towards character the application must specify how the complainer is to be characterised and on what basis. If the application concerns a condition or predisposition specific facts about what this is and how it is to be demonstrated will require to be set out.

Paragraph 2

18.46 This must address paragraph (b) of section 275(3). The drafter of the application will need to turn his or her attention to the questions which it is proposed to ask, and of which witnesses, with the aim of establishing the account set out in the first paragraph of the application. In other words the application will need to show how, in terms of questioning, the evidence specified in the first part of the application is to be elicited. At this stage the application will require to do more than simply set out what questions are proposed or what propositions are to be put. Importantly, it will require to explain the evidential basis for the questions or propositions. This is to enable the court to be satisfied that the proposed evidence is competent and that there is, or can be, a proper foundation for any propositions or assertions which it is suggested ought to be permitted. So, for example, the court will require to be satisfied that the accused or another competent and available witness will be in a position to give admissible evidence in support of any proposition specified as part of a proposed question in this paragraph. In relation to a condition, the court will need to be satisfied as to the medical basis of the suggested condition and that any expert to whom the proposed questioning is to be directed is qualified to give evidence of the sort which is sought to be elicited.

Paragraph 3

18.47 Here, the drafter must identify and specify the issues at trial to which the proposed evidence is said to be relevant. It will not be sufficient to simply state that the issues are credibility and reliability. The drafter should have in mind that the information required to satisfy paragraphs (c), (d) and (e) of section 275(3) must flow in a cohesive, understandable and persuasive manner. Accordingly this part of the application ought to inform the content of the next two parts (addressing paragraphs (d) and (e)).

Paragraph 4

18.48 Here the drafter must explain why it is contended that the evidence proposed is relevant to the issues identified (that is, address the test of relevancy in section 275(1)(b)).

Paragraph 5

18.49 Here, the drafter of the application must set out the inferences which it is contended should be drawn from the proposed evidence. In coming to this paragraph the information set out in relation to numbered paragraphs 3 and 4 ought to lead logically to a proper inference which the applicant wishes the court to draw, ie, one which may legitimately be drawn from admissible evidence and which arises reasonably from the proposed evidence founded upon. The drafting of the application will require to make it clear that the suggested inference is not based simply on supposition or speculation. By this stage the combined effects of numbered paragraphs 3, 4 and 5 should have made it plain to the court why any questions designed to elicit evidence of the complainer's character or sexual history have an important part to play in the proper determination of the Crown's case. Equally, they should have made it plain why any questions concerning other behaviour by the complainer, or a condition or predisposition, have an important part to play in determining the complainer's credibility or reliability, or showing that she was likely to have consented to the acts charged.

The test in section 275(1)(c)

18.50 Finally, though it is not specified in form 21.5, the application will require to explain why the probative value of the evidence which it is sought to lead outweighs the risk to the proper administration of justice (the test in section 275(1)(c)).[46]

The application as an advocacy document

18.51 Amongst the best advice which could be kept in mind in seeking to follow these requirements is that given by Lord Brodie in the case of *HM Advocate v A* when he mentioned the benefit of having regard to the role of the application as an advocacy document. As he explained, it should be seen and drafted as a means of informing the court as to why the application is being made and as an aid in persuading the court that the cumulative tests set out in section 275(1)(a) to (c) are met.

The disposal of applications made under section 275(1)

18.52 The statutory provisions which govern an application to lead evidence otherwise prohibited are, of course, only engaged if the court is satisfied that the proposed evidence is admissible at common law. If this hurdle is crossed the court has to consider, in sequence, each of the three tests set out in section 275(1) paragraphs

46 *Watt v HM Advocate* [2023] HCJAC 2 at para 25.

(a), (b) and (c). All three tests require to be met.[47] This is the process through which, for example, an accused may obtain authority to elicit evidence of the complainer's record of previous convictions for dishonesty.[48]

18.53 In presenting an application to admit evidence under section 275(1), it should be kept in mind that an absence of objection from the other parties to the case will not be determinative and indeed may be of little importance. There requires to be a judicial determination in respect of each aspect of any application and the court is not entitled to abrogate responsibility for addressing the issues which arise in detail simply because, for example, the Crown does not oppose an application.[49]

Section 275(1) paragraph (a)

18.54 The test in paragraph (a) is one of specificity. The questions to be determined will be different according to the basis of the application. Where it is sought to lead evidence of behaviour the question will be whether the occurrences of sexual or other behaviour involved are sufficiently described and set out. Where the application seeks to lead evidence of the complainer's character the questions will be whether the characterisation which is to be advanced and the basis for that are both adequately explained by setting out specific facts. Where the application is based on a condition or predisposition to which the complainer has been subject there will again be two questions. First, whether the facts relied upon describe that condition or predisposition with sufficient clarity and detail and, second, whether the effect which it is contended flows from that condition or predisposition is made sufficiently clear.

18.55 Whilst subsection (1)(a) contemplates the admission of evidence of 'a condition or predisposition' which might impact on credibility or reliability or found an inference that the complainer is likely to have consented to the conduct charged, the provision does not introduce any lower test than that provided for by the common law. The statutory exception requires the 'condition or predisposition' to be one which is objectively diagnosable in medical, notably psychiatric, terms.[50]

18.56 In determining whether this test of specificity has been met the court will be looking to the terms of the application to assess whether the statement of the evidence which it is proposed to lead sets out a sufficiently specific narrative of events. A further aspect of this assessment is whether a proper foundation for the propositions or questions to be put is demonstrated. At this stage of its assessment the court is likely to be focussing on the first two paragraphs of the application.

47 'The important point to note is that such questioning or the admission of such evidence will only be permitted if the court has been persuaded that it passes the three tests' – *DS v HM Advocate* 2007 SC (PC) 1 per Lord Hope at para 28.

48 The case of *DM v HM Advocate,* unreported 21 March 2024 (HCA/2023/00645), provides an example of the need for evidence of such previous convictions to pass the s 275 tests. It also demonstrates that these tests fall to be applied to proposed evidence of this type with the same rigour as applies to any other proposed evidence.

49 *RN v HM Advocate* at para 20.

50 *JC v HM Advocate* 2020 SCCR 151 at para 30.

Section 275(1) paragraph (b)

18.57 If the first test in section 275(1) is met the test of relevancy set out in 275(1)(b) then requires to be addressed. Since the general common law test of relevancy will, by definition, already have been met, the purpose of the statutory direction to determine whether 'that occurrence or those occurrences of behaviour or facts are relevant to establishing whether the accused is guilty of the offence with which he is charged' requires to be understood. It may help to start by recognising that the context in which the present provisions were introduced by the Sexual Offences (Procedure and Evidence) (Scotland) Act 2002 is that the preceding provisions had failed to provide complainers with an appropriate level of protection from attacks on their character which could not reasonably be countered within the confines of a criminal trial. In discussing the evolution of the statutory provisions in the case of *CJM v HM Advocate*[51] the then Lord Justice Clerk (Lord Carloway) noted that in restricting the admissibility of evidence in relation to sexual offences section 274 repeats much of what already exists in the common law. He explained this as follows:

> 'This is understandable in the context of a situation in which neither the common law rules nor the original terms of section 274 were being adequately enforced by the courts for the protection of complainers from irrelevant or inexpedient attacks on their character. Rather, the inclusion of an 'interests of justice' exception to these terms had seen evidence being admitted, upon the basis of that exception, even when it ought to have been excluded at common law on the basis of expediency in the context of the administration of justice generally and the need to protect witnesses from attacks on their character which cannot reasonably be countered within the context of a criminal trial (see eg 'Redressing the Balance', paragraph 97). Furthermore, the lack of any mention of relevancy in the provisions exacerbated the matter (Sexual Offences (Procedure and Evidence) (Scotland) Bill, policy memorandum, paragraph 18) and diverted attention from that core issue.'

18.58 The underlying aim of the legislation as explained in the policy memorandum as set out at paragraph 20 is informative. It states:

> 'The reforms contained in this Bill are designed to prevent the use of irrelevant evidence, and discourage the use of evidence of limited relevance where the primary purpose of such use is to undermine the credibility of the complainer, or divert attention from the issues a jury requires to determine. The intention is to provide a greater degree of focus, requiring the courts to take time to consider in detail whether and how evidence is truly relevant and the extent to which it may divert attention onto issues which are not relevant.'

18.59 With this understanding of the background to the introduction of a statutory requirement to assess relevancy in mind it is clear that the test in section 275(1)(b) requires the court to assess the explanation set out in paragraph 4 of the application

[51] 2013 SCCR 215 at para 42.

through a very focused lens. The court will require to look closely at the question of the effect which establishing the facts specified will have in determining the guilt of the accused. The court will be looking to understand the precise issue to which the evidence relates, why the evidence relates to that issue and what consequence logically flows from establishing the evidence proposed. Beyond considering the explanation set out in paragraph 4 of the application the court will also require to focus on the content of paragraphs 3 and 5.

Section 275(1) paragraph (c)

18.60 If both of the first two tests set out in section 275(1) are met then the court must turn its attention to the third test as set out in paragraph (c). At this stage of the process the court requires to engage in an assessment of the proposed evidence in the circumstances of the particular case. In this exercise the court is not considering whether the evidence has probative value, that test must already have been passed in addressing paragraph (b). Nor is the court's decision based purely on whether the evidence has significant probative value, although that test will need to be met. The evidence cannot be admitted unless the court is satisfied that its probative value will be significant to the extent that it may be said to outweigh any risk of prejudice to the proper administration of justice. This exercise involves an assessment of the appropriate protection of a complainer's privacy and dignity and, separately, an assessment of the proportionality of admitting the evidence. This assessment of proportionality is what is encompassed in the requirement set out in section 275(2)(b)(ii) which directs the court to ensure that:

> '… the facts and circumstances of which a jury is made aware are … relevant to an issue which is to be put before the jury and commensurate to the importance of that issue to the jury's verdict'.

The view of complainers

18.61 What is involved at this final stage is a balancing exercise between the probative value of the evidence proposed and prejudice to the complainer in the form of a potential interference with her Article 8 ECHR rights.[52] In order to undertake this exercise, the court must have information on the complainer's position in relation to what is proposed in the application. It will be important to know whether any propositions as to fact are accepted by the complainer or are contentious. In order to assess to what extent a particular line of questioning may impinge upon a complainer's dignity and privacy the court will require to know what the complainer's attitude to the line of questioning is. The Crown is therefore under a duty, both under section 1

52 The right to respect for private and family life, which would include the right to privacy in respect of her previous sexual conduct and experiences – *R v T* (CA) [2002] 1 WLR 632 at para 38; *Y v Slovenia* (2016) 62 EHRR 3.

of the Victims and Witnesses (Scotland) Act 2014 and Article 8 ECHR, to ascertain the complainer's position in relation to a section 275 application and to present that position to the court, irrespective of its own attitude to it or the application.[53] The Victims, Witnesses, and Justice Reform (Scotland) Bill which is currently before the Scottish Parliament, if enacted, will give complainers statutory rights in relation to information concerning an application made under section 275. It will also provide complainers with the right to make submissions to the court on the accuracy of the content of any application and whether the evidence should be admitted through independent legal representation. A right to appeal is also contemplated within the Bill's provisions. At present, it is competent for a complainer to challenge a decision to grant a section 275 application by way of a petition to the nobile officium.[54]

The power to hear evidence

18.62 Before deciding on an application the court is entitled in terms of section 275(5) to hear evidence for the purpose of reaching its decision. Practice suggests that the circumstances in which it will be necessary to use this power will arise very rarely.

Conditions

18.63 If having heard an application a court is satisfied that it should be granted, either in whole or in part, it may authorise the leading of the evidence identified subject to any condition which appears necessary or appropriate and may order that the evidence shall only be admitted subject to compliance with directions which it may choose to issue.[55] A condition to be imposed may consist of a limitation on the extent to which the evidence admitted may be argued to support a particular inference specified in the condition.[56]

The requirement on the court to give reasons for its decision

18.64 If the court authorises the eliciting or admission of evidence then section 275(7) requires it to state what evidence or questioning it is permitting and to state the reasons for concluding that the evidence may be admitted, along with a statement of the issues at the trial to which the court considers that the evidence so authorised is relevant. This is an important provision as it ensures that at a subsequent trial (or when taking evidence on commission) the presiding judge is informed as to the extent of the evidence or questioning to be permitted and the purpose behind doing

53 *RR v HM Advocate* 2021 JC 167.
54 *RR* at paras 38 and 39.
55 S 275(6).
56 S 275(8).

so, thus enabling him or her to monitor compliance with the earlier decision. As was stated in *HM Advocate v Selfridge,*[57] the fulfilling by the preliminary hearing judge of the obligation placed on him by section 275(7) is critical for the benefit of the trial judge, who must have a clear understanding of the extent to which questioning has been authorised.

Review and variation of a decision under section 275

18.65 Section 275(9) gives power to the court to review and vary a decision authorising the admission of evidence made on the determination of an application under section 275(1). This is a very wide power which may be exercised at any time, including during the trial of the accused person.[58] The court may limit the extent of evidence earlier authorised on a partial basis or it may disallow the entirety of the questioning which had previously been authorised. The only restriction on the extent of this power is that the court may not extend the grant of the earlier authority.[59] Nor is the exercise of the power dependent upon a change in circumstance. The court may exercise the power 'as it thinks fit'. The power may be exercised by the trial judge *ex proprio motu* in light of developments at the trial or the way in which evidence has emerged. Equally, the power may be exercised on the motion of one of the parties to the case. This does not confer an opportunity for the party concerned to obtain a general reconsideration of an application or to revisit submissions which were previously rejected. To justify making the motion the party concerned must be able to identify a sound basis for the proposed limitation, such as the prospect of the admission of clearly irrelevant and inadmissible evidence or some other material factor which is likely adversely to affect the fairness of the trial.[60]

Unnecessary applications

18.66 Finally, it should be noted that in the case of *P (M) v HM Advocate*[61] the court disapproved of a practice in which applications included proposed questions or evidence for which it was maintained an application was in fact unnecessary. As the court explained, the procedure contained within section 275 was not designed to provide for a general ruling on admissibility. Accordingly, any application which asserts on its face that it is unnecessary, or where counsel so submits, will be viewed as incompetent and refused on that ground.

57 [2021] HCJAC 2 at para 43.

58 *W (J) v HM Advocate* 2021 SCCR 281.

59 In the case of *Moir v HM Advocate* 2005 1 JC 102 at para 43 the court referred to the trial judge having the power to limit *or extend* a grant of authority already made. As noted in *JW v HM Advocate* the reference to extending the grant is clearly incorrect.

60 *JW v HM Advocate* at paras 24 and 25.

61 2022 SCCR 1.

18.67 The Preliminary Hearings e-Bench Book does however, add that, if in response to submissions on a properly made application the court concludes that the evidence is admissible at common law, and is not prohibited by section 274, the wording of the decision should not say that the application is unnecessary; it should state that the evidence does not fall foul of any of the prohibitions in section 274.[62]

The consequence of a successful application

18.68 There is a particular consequence which may need to be kept in mind in deciding whether to make an application under section 275(1) which arises out of the provisions contained within section 275A. If the accused person has what is described as a 'relevant conviction', namely a previous conviction for a sexual offence,[63] and if the court allows any part of an application, then the prosecutor is required to place before the presiding judge any such previous convictions. The prosecutor has no discretion in this matter. This step having been taken, the conviction is to be brought to the attention of the jury or taken into consideration by the judge in summary proceedings, whether or not the accused gives evidence or has made any form of pre-trial statement.

18.69 The import of section 275A was considered by the Privy Council in the case of *DS v HM Advocate*[64] where it was found to be compliant with the accused's right to a fair trial. The Board's decision made it plain that the purpose in leading evidence of previous convictions in this fashion went beyond merely contributing to an assessment of the accused person's credibility.[65]

18.70 As Lord Hope explained at paragraph 43:

> '... section 275A must be approached on the basis that the main reason why previous relevant convictions are to be disclosed or taken into consideration is because they may be regarded as relevant to the accused's propensity to commit other sexual crimes. A further reason is that they may have a bearing on the accused's credibility, if this is put in issue, as compared with that of the complainer.'

18.71 Lord Rodger gave a similar explanation of the purpose of the provision at paragraph 84 where he stated:

> '... the jury are entitled to have regard to the accused's previous convictions when deciding whether the Crown has proved its case. In other words, when assessing the credibility and reliability of the evidence on which the Crown

62 At para 9.7.

63 S 275(10) defines what constitutes a previous relevant conviction.

64 2007 SC (PC) 1.

65 This may be contrasted with the current position where evidence of an accused person's previous convictions are elicited in non-sexual cases. In the Full Bench decision of *Leggate v HM Advocate* 1988 JC 127, the court held that such evidence is only permitted for the bearing which it may have on the accused person's credibility and is not relevant to his guilt.

relies, the jury are entitled to take account of the fact that, on one or more occasions, the accused was prepared to go further than the law permits in pursuit of sexual pleasure. Of course, where the accused has made a mixed statement or gives evidence, the fact that he has previously offended in this way may also have a bearing on the credibility of his version of events.'

18.72 The fact that a jury will be entitled to take account of such previous convictions for these purposes does not mean that the introduction of a previous relevant conviction constitutes evidence that the crime charged has been committed by the accused, nor is it capable of providing corroboration of the evidence of the complainer or any other witness on whom the Crown relies to prove the case.[66]

18.73 The fact that Scottish courts and Scots lawyers do not have experience of the application of the English law doctrine of similar fact evidence may mean that there is a lack of clarity around the meaning of and value to be attributed to the concept of 'propensity'. To date no guidance has been given in any reported decisions from the Scottish courts, which may in itself be a reflection of how rarely the statutory provision is engaged.[67]

18.74 Whilst the prosecutor has no discretion in placing any previous relevant convictions before the judge, section 275A(2) allows the accused to object to the convictions being laid before the jury, or being taken into consideration in summary proceedings. The grounds upon which objection may be stated are set out in subsection (4), the most relevant of which is that the disclosure of the conviction would be contrary to the interests of justice. Subsection (7) provides that when entertaining an objection based on this ground the court shall, unless the contrary is shown, presume that the disclosure of, or taking into consideration of, a conviction is in the interests of justice. However, this subsection has been interpreted as setting out no more than the default position that will apply if no objection is made. If an objection is made, then it should be considered on its merits and the presumption is to be disregarded by the court in deciding the question of what weight it should attach to that objection.[68]

Multiple charge indictments

18.75 The prohibition on leading evidence contained within section 274 bears to apply:

'(1) In the trial of a person charged with an offence to which section 288C applies, …'

and the effect of the prohibition is that:

66 *DS v HM Advocate* at paras 53 and 86.

67 At para 53 of the decision in *DS v HM Advocate* Lord Hope suggested that directions modelled on the decision in *R v Hanson* (which he quoted from) may be appropriate.

68 Lord Hope at para 48 of *DS v HM Advocate*.

'the court shall not allow questioning … which shows or tends to show that the complainer …' (is not of good character, etc).

18.76 In recent years there has been a substantial increase in the number of cases alleging multiple partner abuse and abuse perpetrated over many years. Some of these cases involve a mixture of charges alleging sexual and non-sexual violent conduct. This raises the question of whether an accused is required to submit an application under section 275(1) to authorise questioning in relation to any charges of non-sexual violence. Where the accused person faces both charges of a sexual and a non-sexual nature in relation to the same complainer the assumption in practice appears to be that it is necessary to do so. This view is supported by the Preliminary Hearings e-Bench Book at paragraph 9.11.5. However the issue was not brought into direct focus in either of the two cases cited in support of that interpretation and a different view was expressed by Lord Justice Clerk Gill in *MM v HM Advocate*[69] where, in an obiter comment, he rejected this interpretation and stated that it was plain that the introductory words of the section meant the trial of the accused on the relevant charge.

18.77 It is suggested that the interpretation contained within the Preliminary Hearings e-Bench Book is correct. If this was not the case then, for example, evidence could be admitted without the prior scrutiny of the court which was relied upon to attack the credibility or reliability of the complainer if it was argued that this evidence related to a non-sexual charge of violence. However, evidence once admitted is generally treated as being evidence at large. Thus any such evidence would be capable of affecting the credibility or reliability of the complainer in general unless the court was prepared to give directions to the effect that this evidence could be taken into account in respect of some charges but not others. This would seem to require the trial judge to introduce a layer of unrealistic complexity and expectation. Furthermore, unless the prohibition is seen to apply to all charges on an indictment alleging both sexual and non-sexual violence against the same complainer the accused would be able to avoid engaging the otherwise mandatory provisions of section 275A by arguing, for example, that evidence impacting on the character of the complainer was elicited in response to one of the charges of non-sexual violence. Again, this would seem to conflict with the assumption that evidence once admitted was at large and this result would be inconsistent with the policy of balance which lay behind the introduction of section 275A.

18.78 In setting out this analysis we recognise that the issue has not been the subject of an authoritative ruling to date. We also recognise that the question may become further complicated in a case where a single accused person faces charges concerning different complainers, some of whom allege sexual offending and some non-sexual violent offending. Similar complications may arise in a case with multiple accused persons in relation to the same complainer where some face charges of a sexual nature and some do not.

[69] 2005 1 JC 102 at para 28.

18.79 In our view, questioning of a complainer who spoke to only non-sexual offences, or questioning by an accused who was only charged with non-sexual offences would seem to be beyond the scope of the section 274 prohibition. This appears to follow from the terms of the first sentence of section 274(1) (as quoted above) and from the definition of 'complainer' set out in subsection (2) which is:

> '… the person against whom the offence referred to in (subsection (1)) is alleged to have been committed …'.

18.80 The prohibition therefore appears to affect a person who is charged with a sexual offence (specified in section 288C) and restricts that person's right to question or elicit evidence about the complainer identified in that charge.

Section 288BA dockets

18.81 The use of dockets specifying conduct connected with a sexual offence charged in the indictment or complaint is dealt with in Chapter 13 at **13.55–13.60**. It will be apparent that witnesses who give evidence of conduct specified in such dockets may be recounting events of serious sexual misconduct directed against them by the accused. In terms of policy there is no reason why such witnesses ought not to be given the protection afforded by the terms of sections 274 and 275 to complainers in the same case. However, there is at present an apparent anomaly in that docket witnesses do not fall within the definition of 'complainer' for the purposes of section 274.

18.82 The clearest example of the effect of this anomaly may be seen in the case of a witness who gave evidence against the accused in an earlier trial in which she was a complainer on a charge of rape. Her questioning would have been controlled and supervised by the court through the provisions of sections 274 and 275. If the witness is later called to give that same evidence again when speaking to a docket in the trial of the accused in respect of a different complainer she will not be entitled to the protection of these statutory provisions. She will, however, have the protection of the common law rules of evidence on collateral issues and relevancy generally, set out above. Although there is no direct authority on the point, we would suggest that it is different when the docket relates to behaviour directed at someone who is also a complainer on the indictment. In such a case, a section 275 application will be necessary to lead the docket evidence. The complainer enjoys the protection of section 274 precisely because she is a complainer in the case. The behaviour in the docket is struck at by section 274 because it is not the subject matter of any charge on the indictment, and section 274 extends to sexual behaviour which a complainer undergoes or is made subject to: section 274(2). The Crown's policy is thus to make a section 275 application in this situation. If this is correct, then it serves to underline the anomaly between the protections afforded to complainers and docket witnesses. At the time of writing, the Scottish Government's intention is to introduce an amendment to the Victims, Witnesses, and Justice Reform (Scotland) Bill to remove this anomaly.

Appeals against section 275 decisions

18.83 There is, with the leave of the preliminary-hearing judge or first-diet sheriff, a right of appeal against the decision to grant or refuse a section 275 application: section 74 of the 1995 Act. As with all appeals from preliminary hearings or first diets, leave to appeal must be sought at the first diet/preliminary hearing itself and immediately following the decision on the section 275 application: Criminal Procedure Rules 9.5 and 9A.6. As stated at **18.61** above, a complainer may challenge a decision to grant a section 275 application by petition to the nobile officium.

Further unresolved matters

18.84 Before leaving our consideration of the issues which arise in this chapter, it is worth mentioning some further as yet unresolved questions which may require the attention of the court in due course. In the absence of any authoritative ruling our views are set out on a most tentative basis.

Relationship evidence

18.85 In many cases in which charges of sexual offending are prosecuted the parties will have been in a relationship, either cohabiting or non-cohabiting, either at the time of the alleged offending or prior to it. Since the decision in the case of *Moir v HM Advocate*[70] in 2005, as reinforced by observations in the Privy Council case of *DS v HM Advocate*[71] in 2007, it has been understood that leading evidence of the fact of cohabitation does not fall within the scope of the section 274 prohibition. However, the interplay between section 274 and evidence of cohabitation was not the issue for determination in these cases and the context in which the submission concerning cohabitation was focussed is not brought out in either decision. Nevertheless, in *Moir* the Lord Justice Clerk (Lord Gill) rejected the submission that section 274 was engaged by evidence of cohabitation. His view was straightforward – a prior course of cohabitation would not constitute engaging in sexual behaviour not forming part of the subject matter of the charge.[72] That view was endorsed by Lord Rodger of Earlsferry in delivering his opinion in *DS* where he stated:

> 'I have no doubt that the Lord Justice Clerk was correct … to reject the submission that a period of cohabitation could constitute 'sexual behaviour' for the purposes of section 274(1)(b).'[73]

18.86 In our view, the import of these statements should be weighed carefully. The concern in the mind of the counsel who advanced the submission in *Moir*

70 2005 1 JC 102.
71 2007 SC (PC) 1.
72 At para 27.
73 At para 75.

may have been that to elicit evidence that a couple were married, or had lived in a cohabiting relationship, would be to introduce, at least by implication, evidence that they had engaged in sexual behaviour together during the course of at least some of that relationship, and at a time prior to the events of the charge. On this view, evidence of cohabitation would be struck at by that part of section 274(1) which prohibits evidence which '*tends to show*' that the complainer has at any time engaged in sexual behaviour not forming part of the subject matter of the charge. However, it appears to be clear from what both Lord Rodger and Lord Gill said that evidence of cohabitation simply does not constitute what is prohibited, ie, evidence of sexual behaviour. The passage of his opinion in which Lord Rodger explains his reasoning lends support to this analysis:

> 'Whatever the ultimate significance of such evidence turned out to be, it could never have been the intention of the legislature to prevent an accused from leading evidence and asking questions to show that he and the complainer had at one time lived together. After all, to say that two people have lived together for five years is to make a statement, not about their sexual behaviour, but about their way of life, which encompasses much more than any sexual relationship. Equally, to ask whether the complainer formerly lived with the accused for a year is to ask whether they shared a way of life, not to ask about the complainer's sexual behaviour. This can be tested by attempting to apply sec 275(1)(a) which is designed to allow the defence to lead evidence or to ask questions relating 'to a specific occurrence or occurrences' of the sexual behaviour envisaged in section 274(1)(b). It is really impossible to apply that provision to evidence relating to a period of cohabitation of the complainer and the accused.'

18.87 Accordingly, evidence of cohabitation neither shows nor tends to show that the complainer has engaged in sexual behaviour not forming part of the subject matter of the charge. If this analysis is correct, and we respectfully suggest that it is, then it ought to extend to all long-term intimate relationships, whether cohabiting or non-cohabiting.[74] We consider that this conclusion also withstands Lord Rodger's test of attempting to apply section 275(1)(a) to it. On this view an application under section 275 would not be necessary in order to lead evidence of the fact that the parties were in a long-term relationship, whether cohabiting or not.

18.88 What is missing in this whole discussion of course is the need, as a preliminary, for any evidence of relationship, either marriage, cohabitation or something else, to pass the common law test of relevancy. Nothing which was said in either *Moir* or *DS* diminishes this need or gives support to a proposition that such evidence is necessarily relevant.

18.89 There will often be some circumstances in which evidence of cohabitation could pass the test of relevancy. It might, for example, explain how the parties came

74 *CH v HM Advocate* 2020 SCCR 410 at para 132.

to be at the locus together. Equally, evidence of cohabitation might relevantly be led by the Crown to explain a series of rapes which were said to have occurred when the accused came home from spells of working away or after nights out drinking. The same might be said where similar evidence was to be led where the parties were in a non-cohabiting relationship. In the absence of such a relevant link however the presiding judge would require to be astute to ensure that the ordinary and now well-known rules governing the admissibility of evidence in this area were adhered to.

18.90 What of short-term relationships? In our view the circumstances are different here. Any such relationship would likely lack the characteristics of status, commitment, or way of life such as would allow it to encompass 'much more than any sexual relationship'. Even if the court was persuaded that evidence to the effect that the parties had been going out for a short period was relevant at common law, that evidence would, in our view, likely carry with it the implication that they had been engaging in sexual behaviour not forming part of the subject matter of the charge. If it does carry that implication, it would necessitate an application in terms of section 275.

18.91 Whilst it is impossible to draw a clear dividing line, what can perhaps be said with confidence is that the shorter the period of the relationship the more likely it is that section 274 would be engaged by an attempt to lead evidence of its existence.

Aggravations under section 1 of the Abusive Behaviour and Sexual Harm (Scotland) Act 2016

18.92 Where sexual offences are said to have occurred whilst the parties were in a relationship the relevant charges will now commonly include an aggravation under section 1 of the Abusive Behaviour and Sexual Harm (Scotland) Act 2016 (ABSHA). The aggravation applies where it is libelled within a charge that the offence is aggravated by involving abuse of the partner or ex-partner of the person committing the offence and it is proved that the person intends to cause the partner or ex-partner physical or psychological harm, or, in certain circumstances, is reckless as to whether such harm is caused. Where it arises this is an important aggravation, as the court must take it into account in determining the appropriate sentence and must also explain the effect given to the aggravation, or explain why it has had no effect on sentence.[75]

18.93 The status of partner for the purpose of the aggravation has a broad definition. It applies where the parties are spouses or civil partners, are living together as spouses, or are in an intimate personal relationship with each other.[76] The term ex-partner is construed accordingly. Therefore a couple who were boyfriend

75 ABSHA, s 1(5).
76 S 1(6).

and girlfriend (or in a same-sex relationship) can be classed as partners,[77] whether or not they lived together at any stage and without their relationship having to have subsisted for any particular period of time. The relevant status is established through a presumption which arises when a statement that the person was the other person's partner or ex-partner is included in the charge.[78] It can be challenged by the accused giving notice by way of a preliminary objection.

18.94 Given the method of establishing the necessary relationship, it is obvious that a statement to the effect that the parties were partners will constitute a relevant averment in a charge. It may also be thought to carry with it the implication that the parties have engaged in sexual behaviour on occasions other than those specified in the charge.

18.95 Despite this the Crown do not submit applications under section 275 of the Act in support of these averments. That might be thought to reflect the understanding of the cases of *Moir* and *DS* as discussed above. That would not, however, explain the lack of a section 275 application in a case concerning a boyfriend and girlfriend where the aggravation of being partners was based on them being in an intimate personal relationship. The better view may therefore be that in light of the statutory presumption the status of partner, regardless of its underlying basis, is established without the need for evidence and it is only the admission of evidence, or questioning designed to elicit evidence, which is prohibited by section 274.

18.96 This leads into the question of what effect a challenge by the accused to the statutory presumption has. Such challenges are rare, but in such an event the Crown will require to establish in evidence, to the satisfaction of the jury, that the parties were partners, according to one or other of the limbs of the statutory definition. Where the parties were married, or were civil partners, this will be achieved very straightforwardly through the complainer's evidence as supported by production of the relevant certificates. Where they were living together as if spouses this may be established through the evidence of the complainer about this fact as supported by various other types of evidence, such as friends and family members who were aware of their circumstances, or evidence of documentation such as property deeds, council tax records or the like. Eliciting evidence to establish that the parties were partners in these ways would not seem to engage the section 274 prohibition: on the analysis in *Moir* and *DS*, the effect of the evidence would be only to establish a status or way of life.

18.97 However, where the Crown seeks to support the aggravation by way of evidence to establish that the parties were in an intimate personal relationship the

77 Para 12 of the Explanatory Notes to ABSHA states that the phrase 'intimate personal relationship' is intended to cover relationships between boyfriends and girlfriends (including same sex relationships), although the relationship need not be sexual. Other family relationships and other types of relationship (eg, between friends or business partners or work colleagues) are not covered by the aggravation.

78 S 1A(1).

position may be different. Such a relationship need not be sexual but often will be. Often the relationship can be established by asking the complainer to describe the nature of her relationship with the accused. Should the Crown need to establish the relationship/aggravation by asking about any sexual aspect to the relationship, for instance in anticipation of cross-examination suggesting that there was no relationship, or only friendship, a Crown section 275 application would be necessary.

18.98 We would also suggest that the same approach would apply to any charge under section 1 of the Domestic Abuse (Scotland) Act 2018 if an order is made under section 288C to the effect that section 274/275 should apply in the case. This is because the 2018 Act works in a similar way to the 2016 Act: by section 7 of the 2018 Act, the fact that the accused and complainer were partners is to be presumed unless challenged. As such, the status of partner, regardless of its underlying basis, will be established without the need for evidence and there will be no infringement of section 274 because it is only the admission of evidence, or questioning designed to elicit evidence, which is prohibited by section 274. Again, the matter might be different if there is a challenge and the Crown requires to lead evidence.

18.99 For the sake of completeness, we record that an alternative approach would be to argue that any aggravation under the 2016 Act is part of the subject matter of the charge, thus any evidence in support of it would not fall foul of section 274. However, we suggest that there are perhaps two principal difficulties with such an argument. First, for the purposes of section 274(1)(b) the term 'the subject matter of the charge' has been construed narrowly. At paragraph 74 in the case of *CH v HM Advocate* the Lord Justice Clerk (with whom the majority of the other judges agree) explained it in this way:

> 'unless a particular type of sexual conduct is libelled within the charge it cannot be the subject-matter of the charge.'

18.100 The second difficulty is that while an aggravation is part of the charge, in the sense that it is contained within the wording of it, it has a standing which is distinct from the charge. An aggravation of the sort under discussion depends on the relationship between the parties, something which is additional to and separate from the acts which constitute the offence. It is ancillary to the charge and can only be engaged once the charge is established. The charge may be established whether or not the aggravation is. These facts would tend to suggest that it is something other than the subject matter of the charge.

Chapter 19

Corroboration

INTRODUCTION

19.01 Before 18 October 2023, any discussion of corroboration (in sexual offences or otherwise) would have required to start by stating the proposition that corroboration is required for each of the elements of a crime and then gone on to set out which forms of evidence could corroborate each of those elements. For instance, for rape, where the elements of the crime are of course penetration and a lack of consent, it would have been necessary to outline which forms of evidence could corroborate penetration and which a lack of consent. That discussion would have required the caveat that, as result of the ruling in *Smith v Lees*,[1] the observed distress of a complainer after the incident could only corroborate her lack of consent to what had happened but not what had happened, and thus could not, for instance, corroborate penetration.

19.02 On 18 October 2023 that approach to the individual elements of a crime was swept away by a bench of seven judges in *Lord Advocate's Reference No 1 of 2023*.[2] The Court overruled *Smith v Lees*, holding that distress could corroborate a complainer's account of what had happened, and went further, finding that it was not necessary to corroborate each of the elements of a crime; the Crown only needs to lead evidence that corroborates a complainer's (or other eyewitness's) account of the crime.

19.03 What has not changed in light of *Lord Advocate's Reference No 1 of 2023* is that there are broadly two types of corroboration: conventional corroboration (that is, where one source of evidence about a crime, usually a complainer's account, is corroborated by other evidence of that same crime), and mutual corroboration (where two or more witnesses' accounts of different crimes can corroborate each other, when those witnesses speak to a course of criminal conduct by an accused).

19.04 We first set out the main principles of corroboration as they now apply as a result of *Lord Advocate's Reference No 1 of 2023*. We then consider conventional

1 1997 JC 73.
2 2024 JC 140.

corroboration and the main forms of evidence that are used in sexual offences cases. Finally, we consider mutual corroboration and its contemporary application, including the recent doctrine of 'Ricky Taylor' or 'single-complainer *Moorov*' corroboration.

THE GENERAL PRINCIPLES OF CORROBORATION

19.05 The basic rule of corroboration was re-stated in *Lord Advocate's Reference No 1 of 2023* at paragraphs 1 and 235: no-one can be convicted on the testimony of one witness alone; corroboration (that is, evidence from another source) is required. From this basic rule, three other principles follow:

1. What requires to be proved by corroborated evidence is the case against the accused. This means there has to be evidence from two sources: first, that the crime libelled was committed and secondly, that it was the accused who committed it.
2. The evidence against the accused can come from any of the following: the direct/eyewitness testimony of two or more witnesses; from one eyewitness and circumstantial evidence; or from two or more sources of circumstantial evidence.
3. To be corroborative, evidence does not need to be incriminating in itself and does not need to be more consistent with the direct evidence than with the accused's account: evidence can corroborate a principal/direct source of evidence if it confirms or supports that direct evidence.

19.06 Each of these principles is considered further below.

That the crime libelled was committed

19.07 From 1910, the date of the decision in *Lockwood v Walker*,[3] to *Lord Advocate's Reference No 1 of 2023*, corroboration that the crime was committed was understood to mean that there had to be corroboration of each of the elements of the crime. As noted above, *Lord Advocate's Reference No 1 of 2023* held that this was incorrect: there is no requirement to prove the separate elements in a crime by corroborated evidence. The consequences are far-reaching, particularly so in sexual offences cases. Before *Lord Advocate's Reference No 1 of 2023* it was often necessary in sexual offences cases for the Crown to lead medical or scientific evidence to corroborate the sexual act (eg, penetration) and then to lead separate evidence of distress or other circumstantial evidence to corroborate the complainer's lack of consent to that act. Now, either the medical/scientific evidence or the evidence of distress will suffice to corroborate the complainer's account.

3 1910 SC (J) 3, (1909) 6 Adam 124.

That it was the accused who committed it

19.08 Corroborating that it was the accused who committed the crime is rarely problematic in sexual offences cases. Evidence that corroborates that the sexual act took place (for instance the finding of the accused's DNA on the complainer or her clothing) will, *a fortiori*, corroborate the fact that it was the accused who carried out the sexual act. In cases where the defence is one of consent, the issue of identity will obviously not arise.[4]

19.09 The point does occasionally arise in historic cases where, because of the passage of time the complainer cannot identify the accused or cannot remember the exact name of the person who carried out the acts alleged. In such cases, there is no rule that the complainer must identify the accused directly (either by dock identification or at a VIPER parade); it remains open to the Crown to establish by circumstantial evidence that the accused was the person responsible. In *Robson v HM Advocate*[5] the accused, Michael Robson, was charged with lewd, indecent or libidinous practice or behaviour towards two children. Both children spoke of the offences being by a nightwatchman called Mike. The children's parents identified the accused in court as a nightwatchman who had been friendly with the children and their family and was known to them as Mike. The Appeal Court held that, having regard to the circumstantial detail to which the parents were able to speak, their evidence was sufficient to enable the jury to draw the inference that the appellant was the man described by the complainers as the offender.

19.10 Similarly, in *Murphy v HM Advocate*,[6] the accused was charged with assaulting children at school where he was employed. Four complainers made a dock identification, another two wrongly identified a co-accused who was not involved in the charges against the accused, and the remaining complainers were not asked to make a dock identification. However, all of the complainers referred to their assailant as 'Brother Benedict'. The appeal was refused. For those complainers who had not been asked to identify the accused or who had wrongly identified the co-accused, the Crown was entitled to rely on the evidence of each complainer that the perpetrator was Brother Benedict and the evidence of the identifying complainer that the accused was Brother Benedict. The circumstantial evidence identifying the perpetrator and the accused as the same Brother Benedict was sufficient to allow the jury to draw the inference that all of the charges had been committed by the accused.

19.11 A different result was reached – it is suggested correctly – in *P v Williams*.[7] P was charged with assaulting his former partner, K, and his son, aged 10. K identified P in court as the person responsible. The son and P's stepdaughter gave evidence

4 The sexual act between the accused and complainer will be agreed in a joint minute. A standard form of wording is: 'on [date] at [locus] the accused, John Smith, penetrated the mouth/anus/vagina of Jane Smith with his penis/finger.'

5 1996 SCCR 340.

6 2007 SCCR 532.

7 2005 SCCR 234.

from behind screens and their evidence was that 'Dad' or 'Big B' was the person responsible. However, neither made a visual identification of P in court. P appealed against his conviction. He argued that the only source of identification came from his former partner K and that there was no corroboration of her identification of him. The appeal was allowed. K was the only witness who spoke to the link between the accused and the man described by the son and stepdaughter as 'Dad' or 'Big B': there was no other source of evidence of that link.

Corroboration by direct or circumstantial evidence

19.12 The need for two sources of evidence does not mean two eyewitnesses.[8] Setting aside for a moment the doctrine of mutual corroboration, the case against an accused can be proven by two eyewitnesses, by an eyewitness and circumstantial evidence, or entirely by circumstantial evidence.

19.13 Sexual offences cases where the Crown case is based on the evidence of two eyewitnesses are relatively rare, though it most often happens in cases of public indecency or sexual exposure. Instead, the most common is evidence from the complainer (that is direct, eyewitness evidence of what has happened to her) and circumstantial evidence supporting her account.[9] Although less common, it is by no means unusual to find sexual offences cases that are based entirely on circumstantial evidence. This is usually seen in cases where the complainer cannot remember what has happened, often as a result of intoxication. A charge of rape or sexual assault might, in such a case, be proven by a finding of the accused's DNA or semen in the complainer's vagina and evidence from eyewitnesses that the complainer would have been too intoxicated to consent to sexual activity. We consider such cases further at **19.52–19.58**.

To be corroborative, evidence only needs to confirm or support the direct evidence

19.14 The modern authority is *Fox v HM Advocate*.[10] There, a Full Bench overruled *Mackie v HM Advocate*[11] which had found that circumstantial evidence which was equally consistent with an accused's account could not amount to corroboration. Drawing on the Institutional Writers' understanding of corroboration, the Full Bench in *Fox* held that this was incorrect. It was sufficient that there was independent evidence that confirmed or supported the direct evidence. To be corroborative, the evidence did not need to be incriminating in itself.

8 Hume, ii, 384. Burnett at 516 and 518. Alison, i, 89.

9 The other common form is of course mutual corroboration, regarded, at least by the court in *Moorov*, as a form of circumstantial evidence.

10 1998 JC 94.

11 1994 JC 132.

19.15 *Fox* was approved in *Lord Advocate's Reference No 1 of 2023* and has become embedded in the courts' approach to corroboration. This aspect of corroboration is most commonly seen in cases where the Crown relies on medical or scientific evidence to corroborate a complainer's account. The presence of the accused's semen, other bodily fluids or hair on the complainer's body or clothing might be explained by other forms of contact, or might be explained by a different episode of consensual sexual intercourse but, applying *Fox*, that is of no moment: as long as the medical or scientific evidence confirms or supports the complainer's account (that is, one explanation for that evidence is the account given by the complainer), then it will be capable of providing corroboration. That is not to say that it will necessarily be regarded by the factfinder (judge or jury) as corroborative. The factfinder is always entitled to find that the better explanation is the account given by the accused. It is simply to say that, as long as the evidence supports or confirms the direct evidence in the case, it is capable in law of providing corroboration and that there is thus a sufficiency of evidence.

CONVENTIONAL CORROBORATION

19.16 The types of evidence that are capable of corroborating a sexual offences case are never closed but four categories commonly arise: admissions by the accused; *res gestae* statements, *de recenti* statements and distress on the part of the complainer; medical and scientific evidence; and other forms of circumstantial evidence.

Admissions

19.17 Statements by the accused after an incident often feature as Crown evidence in sexual offences trials. In historical cases, they can arise when complainers or other family members confront accused persons about behaviour which took place long ago. In contemporary cases, they can arise when the accused and complainer exchange text or social-media messages after the incident.[12] It is well established that an accused's admissions – express or implied, equivocal or unequivocal – can be corroborative. Two recent appeals, *CR* and *Lingard*, confirm that admissions in sexual offences cases are to be analysed in the same way as admissions made in any other case. Those appeals were taken on the basis of two earlier sexual offences cases, *Gracie v HM Advocate*[13] and *G v HM Advocate*,[14] where the convictions were quashed because comments made by the accused could not properly be regarded as admissions of criminal conduct. In *Gracie*, there was no specific context in which the accused's comment to a family member that he would be pleading guilty was

12 See, for instance, *LW v HM Advocate* 2023 JC 184 at para 5.
13 2003 SCCR 105.
14 2012 SLT 999.

made. In *G*, the accused was confronted about matters a complainer had written about in her diary, a diary which had not been produced in evidence. In response, the accused was reported to have said that, 'he did not mean to' and 'did not know why he had done it'. The Appeal Court found that there was insufficient means of identifying the nature of the conduct to which the accused's comments related.[15]

19.18 *Gracie* and *G* were first reviewed in *CR v HM Advocate*,[16] a case which also concerned statements made by an accused when confronted with allegations of historic sexual abuse of family members. The Appeal Court held that whether, and to what extent, a comment or reply made by an accused person may properly be regarded as an admission is a fact-specific question, the answer to which depends on the nature and content of the comment and the circumstances in which it is made (at paragraph 15). The Court found *Gracie* and *G* to be readily distinguishable, on the basis that CR's admissions were clearly in response to allegations of having abused one of the complainers in the case, but was at pains to point out that, if the impression had been gained from *Gracie* and *G* that only unequivocal admissions in the clearest terms could provide corroboration, that was not consistent with long-established authority on admissions, or with *Fox* discussed above (that, to be corroborative, evidence does not require to be more consistent with guilt than with innocence; it is sufficient if it is capable of providing support for or confirmation of, or fits with, the principal source of evidence).[17]

19.19 *CR* was approved in *Lingard v HM Advocate*,[18] where a similar submission was made that text messages from the accused to a complainer were, at most, an admission to some form of wrongdoing but had not been made in response to any specific allegation about the charges libelled and were thus irrelevant and inadmissible. The Appeal Court rejected that submission, observing that the only thing the appellant was alleged to have done to the complainer was the conduct libelled in the charges relating to her. That being so, the jury would be entitled, though not bound, to hold that what the accused said in the text messages amounted to an admission that he had conducted himself as libelled in those charges.

15 See too *Branney v HM Advocate* 2014 SCCR 620, another historical case, where the answer, made in response to an accusation of molestation, 'It didn't start until she was 21', was found to be a mixed statement and thus capable of being construed as an admission, but was insufficiently specific to be construed as an admission of penetration. There being no other evidence corroborating penetration, the conviction for rape was quashed. There was a further comment, made by the appellant when told the matter would be reported to the police, 'My life is crap anyway. Do as you like.' *Branney* was not considered in *CR* or *Lingard*. If it were decided now, it is arguable that the admissions were no less specific than the admissions in *CR* and *Lingard* (particularly *Lingard*). Nor, in light of *Lord Advocate's Reference No 1 of 2023* and *Taylor* would the result necessarily be the same. Penetration would not have required separate corroboration and there were separate charges involving the same complainer which were corroborated by other witnesses and thus single-complainer mutual corroboration/*Ricky Taylor* corroboration would now apply. *Branney* was also disapproved in *Lord Advocate's Reference No 1 of 2023* for having apparently proceeded on the basis that *mens rea* required corroboration: para 123.

16 2022 JC 235.

17 Para 19.

18 2024 JC 46.

19.20 In *M (W) v HM Advocate*,[19] there were admissions in general terms to assaulting children and a failure in the same conversation to respond to the statement 'well, stop hitting them'. The Appeal Court found that the same principles on admissions apply where the significance of the evidence is that an accused has failed to respond or react to an allegation in circumstances where that failure could be regarded as criminative.[20] In M's case, the failure to respond to the statement also had to be read in the context of the general admissions made.[21] However, the Court also stressed that it was important to distinguish a case where an admission is relied upon as the primary evidence in a circumstantial case, from one where it is relied upon as corroboration of other evidence which constitutes the primary evidence. In the former, the nature of the surrounding circumstances may be such that only a clear and unequivocal admission, made in the context of a specific allegation, or lack of reaction to a clear allegation, may be sufficient for the purpose. It stressed that everything depends on the context.[22]

19.21 An accused's reaction in the absence of any express words can also be corroborative: see *Adamson v HM Advocate*,[23] where the fact that the accused, upon being told that an allegation of rape was not to be reported to the police, sat down and began crying could be corroborative. It was for the jury to choose whether the reaction was relief that a well-founded accusation of rape was not to be investigated by the authorities or relief that an ill-founded, malicious accusation of that kind was not to be taken further.[24]

19.22 There are still, though, limits on what can legitimately be regarded as an admission, and whether a statement is reasonably capable of bearing the inference that it is an admission to a crime remains a question of law for the judge, not a question of fact for the jury.[25] In *C (L) v HM Advocate*,[26] the issue was whether the accused had continued to have sexual intercourse with the complainer after she told him to stop because it was sore. The accused gave statements in his police interview that he 'maybe went in a bit too hard' and the complainer was sore, and it was his fault 'because I'd gone in'. The Appeal Court found that these statements were not reasonably capable of bearing the inference that the appellant was admitting that he persisted with penetration after consent had been withdrawn. Indeed, the only reasonable inference was that he was accepting responsibility for the complainer feeling sore. The conviction was therefore quashed.

19 2022 JC 248.
20 At para 11. On the failure to respond to allegations generally, see *Campbell v HM Advocate* 2022 JC 243.
21 At paras 13–14.
22 Para 12.
23 2012 JC 27 at paras 14 and 15.
24 Para 14.
25 *C (L)*, cited at n 26 below, at para 17; *Kelly*, cited at n 27 below, at para 16.
26 [2022] HCJAC 47.

19.23 In *Kelly v HM Advocate*,[27] the accused was convicted of rape while the complainer was asleep. The Crown relied on an exchange where the complainer confronted the accused about waking her up (but made no mention of sexual misconduct) and the accused promised never to do so again. The Appeal Court quashed the conviction. The most that could be said was that the accused accepted waking up the complainer. For the jury to read any more into it was to indulge in speculation and to stretch the plain meaning of the words beyond breaking point. It is simply not tenable to interpret an admission of waking up the complainer as amounting to an admission of sexually assaulting and raping her.

Res gestae statements, *de recenti* statements and distress

19.24 One of the most common forms of corroboration in sexual offences cases is distress, that is to say evidence from an eyewitness or other independent source (such as CCTV) that the complainer was distressed and that this distress was because the complainer was subjected to a sexual act that took place without her consent.

19.25 Before 30 November 2024, it would have been impossible to set out the law on distress without considering the law on *res gestae* statements and *de recenti* statements. This is because, while *Lord Advocate's Reference No 1 of 2023* sought to simplify the law in this area by recognising the practical reality that statements made at the time of an incident or shortly afterwards are often (but not always) accompanied by distress, it nevertheless maintained a distinction between three categories of statements: *res gestae* statements, *de recenti* statements accompanied by distress, and *de recenti* statements unaccompanied by distress. *Lord Advocate's Reference No 1 of 2023* found that the first two of these were corroborative; the third was not and, in accordance with the decision of seven judges in *Morton v HM Advocate*,[28] was admissible only for showing that the complainer had been consistent and that her account was not an afterthought.

19.26 The nine-judge decision on 30 November 2024 in *Lord Advocate's References Nos 2 and 3 of 2023* [2024] HCJAC 43 removed that distinction. It found that *res gestae* and *de recenti* statements should be treated in the same way for evidential purposes: both are corroborative of a complainer's account and both are corroborative without the need for them to be accompanied by distress: paragraphs 87 and 110 of the Lord Justice General's opinion. There is still a distinction between a *res gestae* statement and a *de recenti* statement, and the fact that the latter is now corroborative even when it is not accompanied by distress invites careful consideration of what a *de recenti* statement is. We therefore consider these questions before setting out the law on distress as it applies after *Lord Advocate's Reference No 1 of 2023* and *Lord Advocate's References Nos 2 and 3 of 2023*. We emphasise, however, that since *Lord Advocate's References Nos 2 and 3 of 2023*, the important

27 2024 SCCR 247.

28 1938 JC 50 at 53 per Lord Justice Clerk Aitchison.

point is that both *res gestae* and *de recenti* statements are now corroborative even when they are not accompanied by distress.

What is meant by a *res gestae* statement and what is meant by a *de recenti* statement

19.27 *Lord Advocate's References Nos 2 and 3 of 2023* clarified the difference between a *res gestae* statement and a *de recenti* statement. In short, *res gestae* statements are just one type of *de recenti* statement (the kind made during or shortly after a crime), and *de recenti* statements are a much broader, and longer-lasting, category of statement. The following additional points might be made about each type of statement.

19.28 As stated above, a *res gestae* statement is one made during the crime or when there is a 'close association' with the crime (that is, shortly after it): see Lord President (Normand) in *O'Hara v Central SMT* 1941 SC 363 at 381, quoted in *Lord Advocate's Reference No 1 of 2023* at paragraph 73, and referred to in *Lord Advocate's References Nos 2 and 3 of 2023* at paragraph 102.[29] The statement must be made during or shortly after the crime and not after an interval, which would allow time for reflection and concocting a story.[30] As it is real evidence, a *res gestae* statement is – and has always been – capable of providing corroboration without more (that is, without the need for it to be accompanied by distress); this was not changed by either *Lord Advocate's Reference No 1 of 2023* or *Lord Advocate's References Nos 2 and 3 of 2023.*

19.29 A *de recenti* statement is an account given by a complainer after, but as a reaction to, the event (ie the crime): *Lord Advocate's References Nos 2 and 3 of 2023* at paragraph 54. It is a consequence and continuation of the *res gestae* but it is not (or need not be) the same as, or part of, the *res gestae*, (paragraph 87). In *Lord Advocate's References Nos 2 and 3 of 2023*, one of the questions the Lord Advocate asked of the Court was, 'At what point does a statement cease to be *de recenti*,

[29] Although the point has been somewhat superseded by *Lord Advocate's References Nos 2 and 3 of 2023*, it bears observing that *Lord Advocate's Reference No 1 of 2023* overruled *Cinci v HM Advocate* 2004 JC 103, which had taken a much more restrictive approach and had found that a complainer's statements that the accused had raped her, made in a state of distress when she and the accused had been discovered in a shower cubicle, could not be regarded as part of the *res gestae* because the statement was not made at the time of the crime, but rather shortly afterwards. That was found to be wrong in *Lord Advocate's Reference No 1 of 2023*: *res gestae* statements are not limited to those made during the crime, but include those made shortly afterwards too.

[30] See Lord President (Normand) in *O'Hara* at 381, quoted in *Lord Advocate's Reference No 1 of 2023* at para 73. It is for the factfinder to determine when an incident has come to an end: *O'Shea v HM Advocate* 2015 JC 201 at paras 37 and 40. See also *HM Advocate v Hutchison* 2013 SCCR 479 where, even before *Lord Advocate's Reference No 1 of 2023*, the statement 'he has battered me really badly and I can't get away', sent during the accused's detention of the complainer, was part of the *res gestae* and thus corroborative.

and hence corroborative, and become instead inadmissible hearsay?'[31] The Court answered this question by stating (at paragraph 110) that:

> 'A statement ceases to be de recenti when it ceases to be 'recent' following upon the commission of the crime, or is not provided to the [complainer's] first natural confidante … .'

19.30 We suggest that, in respect of this answer, it is important to bear in mind three further points.

First, some further guidance is given at paragraph 105 of the Lord Justice General's opinion. There, the Lord Justice General observed that a *de recenti* statement will generally be one that is the natural outpouring of feelings aroused by the recent injury (ie the crime) and still unsubsided. A statement made in those circumstances will be admissible. However, where there has been a lapse of time, which has raised a substantial risk of concoction, the statement may be regarded as inadmissible (ie no longer admissible because it is no longer a *de recenti* statement). This of course echoes the circumstances in which a statement will no longer be regarded as a *res gestae* statement.

Second, properly read, the answer given by the Appeal Court means a statement can be corroborative in two scenarios: (i) it is recent; or (ii) it is not recent but it has been made to a first natural confidante. In other words, a statement can still qualify as a corroborative, *de recenti* statement even if it is not recent but has nevertheless been made to the first natural confidante. This will arise, for instance, in the situation where the complainer had good reason not to speak to the first people she met but rather waited to speak to her natural confidante when she first saw him/her. The Lord Justice General's opinion refers to the case of *Robert Henderson*[32] as a useful illustration of the correct approach (the facts of the case are discussed at paragraph 65 of the Lord Justice General's opinion, and it is approved at paragraph 105). There, the rape was alleged to have taken place on a Thursday night. On returning home, the complainer did not disclose to the people who were in her house that Thursday night (and explained why), but disclosed to two natural confidantes, one on the Friday and the other on the following Wednesday. Both statements to the natural confidantes were admitted.

Third, in determining whether a statement is *de recenti*, in sexual offences cases and in cases involving children a greater and considerable latitude should apply: *Lord Advocate's References Nos 2 and 3 of 2023* at paragraphs 54 and 104. This confirms both the traditional position in the eighteenth- and nineteenth-century cases and the 2017 ruling in *Wilson v HM Advocate*.[33]

31 The form in which the question was re-formulated at para 2 of the Lord Justice General's opinion. The original question was: 'If a *de recenti* statement on its own is corroborative, at what point in time or in what circumstances does that statement stop being corroborative and become inadmissible hearsay?'

32 (1836) 1 Swin 316.

33 2017 JC 135 at para 34.

19.31 Three further points arise as to the admission of *res gestae* and *de recenti* statements to corroborate a complainer's account.

19.32 First, in the case of both a *res gestae* statement and a *de recenti* statement, there is no requirement that the complainer gives evidence that she made the statement; it is sufficient that the hearer of the statement gives evidence of it.[34] It is good practice, however, in any trial where such a statement is to be led from the hearer that the complainer is also examined on it.[35]

19.33 Second, as well as being corroborative in themselves, the words spoken by the complainer can also be used to link any accompanying distress to the offence: *Wilson v HM Advocate*;[36] and *Hogg v HM Advocate*.[37] It is thus legitimate to ask a witness who is speaking to a complainer's distress what she said while she was distressed and, equally, to ask a complainer what she said to others and how she felt while saying it.

19.34 Finally, *Lord Advocate's References Nos 2 and 3 of 2023* confirmed that *res gestae* and *de recenti* statements can corroborate both the complainer's account of the crime and the identity of the perpetrator.[38] This means that a complainer's *res gestae* or *de recenti* statement 'John Smith raped me' is corroborative both of the rape and that John Smith was the person responsible. We suggest that this, when taken with the greater or considerable latitude that should apply in sexual offences case in determining whether something is a *de recenti* statement, may be the most consequential part of *Lord Advocate's References Nos 2 and 3 of 2023*.

Distress

19.35 Evidence of a complainer's physical condition after an incident – that is to say injuries to his or her person – has always been used as corroboration in sexual offences cases. Evidence of a complainer's emotional condition after an incident has had a patchier history in Scots law. Although there are references in Alison[39] to a complainer's 'condition' being corroborative, and discussion in Hume[40] of the case of *James Wilson* (1813) where a complainer's 'great trepidation' and 'subdued

34 *Ahmed v HM Advocate* 2010 JC 41.

35 *Ahmed* at para 17.

36 2017 JC 135 at para 35.

37 2024 JC 54 at para 35.

38 Paras 106 to 109 of the Lord Justice General's opinion and the answer to the second question posed by the Lord Advocate, recorded at para 110.

39 Vol i at 244 and 247 (for complainers in robbery cases). See also most particularly Vol i at 222: 'In cases of rape, perhaps more than any other crime, it is indispensable to look minutely into the accounts told by the woman, and the support which they receive from the other circumstances of the case…The principal point to attend to is, whether her statement, in regard to the violence used, is duly corroborated; and this is done in the most unexceptional way by such physical appearances as afford real evidence of the truth of her story, and after that by the evidence in regard to her subsequent disclosure of the crime to her relations… .'

40 Vol i at 308, fn 1.

state' after a rape were part of the evidence supporting her account, the modern law on distress in Scotland only dates from the 1975 case of *Yates v HM Advocate*, which appears to be the first modern case where the Crown relied on distress – there described as the complainer's 'dramatically shocked condition' – as a means of corroborating a complainer's account of a sexual offence.[41]

19.36 From *Yates* the law then evolved to the point – decided by the Full Bench of five judges in *Smith v Lees* – that a complainer's distress could only be corroborative of a lack of consent to a sexual act, but not corroborative of the sexual act itself. That, as noted above, was overruled by the Full Bench of seven judges in *Lord Advocate's Reference No 1 of 2023*, which held that there was no requirement to prove the separate elements of a crime by corroborated evidence and that distress which is observed by a third party *de recenti* is capable of corroborating a complainer's account that she had been raped (or by extension, subjected to any other sexual act).[42]

What is meant by distress?

19.37 Distress is the term used in the authorities but it is important to emphasise that this is something of a shorthand term. The term used in *Moore v HM Advocate*[43] and quoted with approval in *Ferguson v HM Advocate*[44] is 'the shocked condition or distress of the complainer', and there are earlier passages in *Moore* referring simply to the 'condition'.[45] In *Wilson v HM Advocate*,[46] the Appeal Court, in *obiter dictum*, was also prepared to contemplate evidence from a complainer's mother of her daughter being uncharacteristically inward and sleeping excessively as indicative of a distressed state and thus corroborative.

19.38 The Commonwealth authorities also use a number of terms in addition to distress, such as 'emotional condition',[47] 'emotional state'[48] and 'post-event demeanour'.[49] We suggest that there is some force in looking beyond the term distress alone and instead to what each of these terms seeks to articulate. If distress is corroborative, it is because it is generally accepted that being subjected to a crime is a negative experience likely to provoke a negative emotional reaction, and distress is one form in which that negative emotional reaction might be manifested and observed by others. If that is so, there is no reason to limit the principle to distress and to exclude other forms of negative emotional reaction to a crime: this branch of

41 1990 JC 378 (27 May 1976, addendum to *Moore v HM Advocate* 1990 JC 371); and 1977 SLT (Notes) 42.
42 At paras 235 and 236.
43 1990 JC 371 at 377.
44 2019 JC 53 at para 14.
45 At 375.
46 2017 JC 135 at paras 8 and 31.
47 *Murphy and others v R* [1977] 2 RCS 603.
48 *S v Hammond* [2004] ZASCA 71; [2004] 4 All SA 5 (SCA).
49 *R v JAA* 2011 SCC 17. 'Demeanour' was also used by the Court of Appeal of England and Wales in *R v Khan (Waqaar)* [2021] EWCA Crim 142.

corroboration is, we suggest, directed at any observed change in the complainer that might be attributed to the trauma of having experienced a sexual or other crime. We therefore suggest that both the *obiter dictum* in *Wilson* and the wider approach taken in the Commonwealth authorities are correct, and thus, that this category of evidence is not limited to distress in the popular sense of that word alone.

19.39 The distress must be observed *de recenti*.[50] There is, though, no fixed time period in which the distress must be seen: *Moore*, cited above; *Hogg v HM Advocate*.[51] The Sheriff Appeal Court has also found that there is no obligation on the Crown to explain longer intervals between the incident and the distress: *Singh v PF, Kilmarnock*.[52] The court observed (at paragraph 40) that to find otherwise would be to endorse rather than dispel what have come to be known as 'rape myths' and would fly in the face of the legal directions which tell juries that there is no typical response to sexual offending[53] and that there may well be delays in disclosure or indeed displays of emotion. This is not to say, however, that the length of time between the incident and the showing of distress is irrelevant. The shorter the interval, the more likely it is that the condition is spontaneous and independent, and thus evidence in itself of what occurred. The longer the interval, the more important it becomes to examine what happened during that period (*Hogg* at paragraph 28).

19.40 *De recenti* distress on its own is corroborative: all that *Lord Advocate's Reference No 1 of 2023* changed is the extent of its corroborative nature; it now corroborates the whole of the complainer's account, not just a lack of consent.[54]

19.41 It follows from this that where there is either: (i) no *res gestae* statement; or (ii) no *de recenti* statement, but there is distress on its own, it is permissible to lead evidence of that distress and to rely on it as corroborating the complainer's account. This is always as long as it can be shown: first, that the distress is in part caused by the crime and not wholly by some other cause (*Hogg* at paragraph 27);[55] and, second, where there is a longer interval between the incident and the showing of distress, that there is an explanation for that longer interval. Examples of distress that are not accompanied by a *de recenti* statement are: distress captured on CCTV and distress

50 *Lord Advocate's Reference No 1 of 2023* at paras 236–240.

51 2024 JC 54 at paras 27–29.

52 2023 SLT (SAC) 202.

53 On which see Chapter 14 at **14.39–14.63**.

54 *Lord Advocate's Reference No 1 of 2023* at paras 238–240.

55 It bears stressing that the distress need not be wholly attributable to the crime. As it was expressed in *Hogg* at para 27, 'distress may have corroborative value where the jury can be satisfied that the distress was a genuine and spontaneous reaction to, and was caused by, the conduct complained of rather than wholly a reaction to something extraneous.' This is consistent with the earlier authorities of *Drummond v HM Advocate* 2015 SCCR 180 at para 15 and *Dalton v HM Advocate* 2015 SCCR 125 at para 41, which observed that the fact that the distress might have been caused in whole or in part by some other incident, such as a physical assault, is irrelevant to this pure issue of sufficiency. It is for the jury to determine whether the distress was properly attributable, at least in part, to the complainer's account of a sexual offence. Indeed, as the court observed in *Dalton*, it would be highly artificial to attempt to separate those elements of distress which might be attributable to a lack of consent to a sexual act and what might be attributable to a physical assault before or after the sexual act.

in a child too young to articulate what has happened to them. In such situations, provided that there is some other means of relating the distress to the crime, the distress is still corroborative.

Medical and scientific evidence

Medical evidence

19.42 Medical evidence in sexual offences cases usually means evidence of injury to the anus or vagina, or evidence of injury to other parts of the body: see Chapter 15 at **15.37–15.43**.

19.43 Evidence of injury to the anus or vagina is not limited to observed injuries but can also include evidence from a forensic medical examiner seeing the complainer in pain, particularly extreme pain, in those private parts.[56] A renal/urinary tract infection has also been found to be corroborative of intercourse.[57]

19.44 Evidence of injury to other parts of the body can include evidence of bruising to the upper body (led in support of an account of being hit or held down) or bruising to the legs (led in support of an account of 'separation injuries' – the legs being forced part). Other injuries commonly seen in sexual assaults are 'love bites' (and in serious cases, simple bite marks), but other marks such as scratches and other abrasions are often seen. In domestic abuse cases, where manual strangulation is a common form of physical abuse, provided the allegations are made promptly, it is possible to see evidence of compression of the neck's skin, or fingernail or other marks to the neck.

19.45 *Meighan v HM Advocate* is now the leading authority on medical evidence and corroboration in sexual offences cases, particularly because the Appeal Court reviewed the recent research and leading works on the genital and other injuries in sexual offences cases and their evidential significance. We suggest that four principal points should be taken from the Court's decision.

19.46 First, it is legitimate for a forensic medical examiner (FME) to give evidence not just of any injuries she has observed, but any pain the complainer is observed to be in: medical professionals are usually skilled in detecting whether complaints of pain are genuine, fabricated or exaggerated.[58]

19.47 Second, while it is not permissible for a FME to give the opinion that there has been a forceful sexual assault (that being an opinion on the ultimate issue),[59] it is legitimate for an FME to be asked about whether injuries are consistent with an assault, for the FME to say how those injuries compare with others the FME has

56 See *Meighan v HM Advocate* 2022 JC 10 at paras 8, 10, 72 and 77.

57 *Adamson v HM Advocate* 2012 JC 27 at paras 13 and 15.

58 Para 72.

59 Para 68.

seen, and for the FME to evaluate genital injuries in the context of other injuries observed on the complainer (or any pain she is observed to be in).[60]

19.48 Third, on bodily injuries generally, it is axiomatic that injuries may be caused by trauma arising from consensual or non-consensual activities. However, where there are multiple sights of injury, they are nevertheless indicators of violent activity, whether consensual or not. They are supportive of an account (ie, a complainer's account) which describes the use of force, even if there might be a contrary explanation.[61] (In this, it is suggested that the Court's conclusion is simply the application of the principle of *Fox* to medical evidence.)

19.49 Fourth, the same considerations apply to genital injuries. Such injuries are corroborative of the use of force. The use of force is indicative of a lack of consent, even if the injuries might also be consistent with consensual sexual activity.[62] Genital injuries, even when taken in isolation from other injuries or other evidence in a case, are more consistent with non-consensual activities because, as the Appeal Court found to be clear from the materials it had reviewed, multiple injuries are more commonly seen in cases of non-consensual intercourse.[63] Although a single genital injury may not in some cases yield an inference of consent, the greater the incidence of injuries, the more likely it is that the complainer did not consent.[64]

Scientific evidence

19.50 Scientific evidence in sexual offences cases is commonly seen in two forms. The first is forensic toxicology evidence, which is led to support an account that the complainer was too intoxicated by drink or drugs to consent to sex. Toxicological evidence, though relevant and admissible, comes with two caveats: (i) unless specimens are obtained very soon after the incident, it is difficult to conduct the necessary 'back calculations' to determine the level of intoxication at a particular moment in time; and (ii) forensic toxicologists will usually be unable to say exactly what effect alcohol or other intoxicants might have had on the complainer's capacity to consent.[65]

19.51 The second common form of scientific evidence in sexual offences cases is that discussed in Chapter 16, trace evidence: the finding of the accused's DNA, semen or other bodily fluids on the complainer's body or clothing, or vice versa

60 Paras 75–77.
61 Para 73.
62 Para 74
63 Para 80.
64 Ibid.
65 See, though, *HM Advocate v I (M)* 2022 SCCR 188, an intoxication case where the police attended shortly after the incident and the complainer was found to have a blood-alcohol concentration of between 265 and 340 mg per 100 ml at the time of the incident. The forensic scientist, in the usual way, was unable to say what effect the alcohol would have had, but the Appeal Court found that one of the adminicles corroborating the complainer's inability to consent was that the level of alcohol would have been sufficient in many people to induce a comatose state or even to cause death.

(ie, the finding of the complainer's DNA, etc, on the accused's body or clothing). The extent to which such evidence will be corroborative of a complainer's account of non-consensual penetration or other sexual contact will of course depend on the facts of the case and where the trace evidence is found, but a relatively wide approach is now taken. Examples include: the finding of the accused's pubic hair in the complainer's underpants;[66] the accused's semen mixed with the complainer's DNA on a duvet cover;[67] and the accused's DNA on the inside of the complainer's pants (this in addition to a bruise on her breast and evidence of her and the appellant being left alone in a bedroom).[68] In all of these cases, the trace evidence was found to be corroborative.

Other forms of circumstantial evidence

19.52 It is common to see a Crown case consisting mainly – and in some cases entirely – of circumstantial evidence when the allegation is that the complainer was either asleep, unconscious or too intoxicated to consent to sexual activity. In the latter case, it may well be that the complainer will be unable to remember what has happened. This, though a point the defence may make to the jury, is not fatal to a prosecution,[69] and the fact that the complainer does not remember may well be indicative of a degree of intoxication that made capacity to consent impossible, particularly if the complainer says that she would never have consented in the circumstances in which the sex took place.

19.53 Four cases illustrate the point and the types of circumstantial evidence that may be corroborative in such cases and indeed any other sexual offences case where the issue is one of consent.

19.54 In *Spendiff v HM Advocate*[70] the complainer, aged 18, had been staying with the appellant, aged 43, and his family after a dispute with her parents. After an evening drinking at the pub with the appellant and others, the complainer woke to find the appellant penetrating her with his penis. The Court found 'ample' corroboration in the following points: the complainer had returned home earlier than the appellant and was in bed at the material time; she was in a state of undress; the appellant returned at a time when the complainer would be expected to be asleep; there was no prior sexual relationship between them; there was a significant discrepancy in their ages; they had returned separately to the house; the complainer moaned when the appellant tickled her foot, which he took as an invitation when it was at best neutral; afterwards, the appellant followed the complainer into the street, but lost her and went to his mother's house, then

66 *Munro v HM Advocate* 2015 JC 1 at para 7.

67 *Palmer v HM Advocate* 2016 SCCR 71 at paras 10 and 11.

68 *Guthrie v HM Advocate* 2022 JC 201 at para 49.

69 See *R v H* [2007] EWCA Crim 2056.

70 2005 1 JC 338.

returned home; he came close to admitting in police interview that the complainer told him to stop; and he could give no explanation for the complainer's running from the house in a state of distress.[71]

19.55 In *Wright v HM Advocate*[72] the complainer and appellant were neighbours. On the day of the incident, she had the flu and took medication. That evening, she, her brother and her husband had some drinks. Her brother left and she went to bed, wearing a nightdress, with the blinds in the room closed and the light off. She woke to the appellant having sex with her. Her evidence was that she did not expect him to be in the house. He ran out. Still wearing her nightdress, the complainer banged on his front door to find her husband there. Her husband had apparently gone there. The husband's evidence was that, upon going next door, the appellant had poured him a large drink and, when the husband mentioned that he had left his cigarettes in his own house, the appellant offered to fetch them but had been gone for five to ten minutes. On finding her husband, the complainer told him what happened and was in a state of distress. The defence was one of consent. The Appeal Court found that there was sufficient evidence that the complainer had been asleep. Her account of the earlier part of the evening (of being unwell, drinking and taking medication, and then retiring to bed) was confirmed by her husband. The time of the incident – some 30 to 90 minutes after she had gone to bed – was supportive of her account of being asleep. Her husband had gone out without her and there was, of course, his account of her shouting for him, while in her nightdress and in considerable distress.

19.56 *HM Advocate v L*[73] is also illustrative of the sort of circumstantial evidence that will be corroborative in cases where there is no prior sexual relationship between the complainer and the accused. The complainer and her boyfriend visited his uncle, where she drank a bottle of Buckfast wine. The boyfriend and another relative went to another family home to sleep, leaving her with the accused. She drank more alcohol and gave evidence that she had fallen asleep on the sofa. She woke to find the accused having sex with her and left the house in distress. She also gave evidence that, whenever she had sex with her boyfriend, they used a condom. The accused admitted sexual intercourse but said the complainer had been a willing participant and he had stopped when she changed her mind. He had not worn a condom. The trial judge accepted that, in addition to the complainer's distress, corroboration could come from: the quantity of alcohol the complainer had taken; the time of the incident (3.20 am); that the amount of alcohol caused all of the parties to fall asleep (including the accused who had said that he fell asleep before the incident); that the

71 Paras 19 and 34.

72 2005 SCCR 780.

73 2008 SCCR 51. This is a first-instance decision on a defence submission of no case to answer. It too was disapproved in *Lord Advocate's Reference No 1 of 2023* at para 123 for suggesting, contrary to *Spendiff*, that *mens rea* required corroboration and for erring its consideration of *Fox*. For present purposes, nothing turns on this: the errors on *mens rea* and *Fox* meant the trial judge applied too high a test in assessing corroboration, and thus, the evidence identified by him as corroborative would, *a fortiori*, be corroborative in light of *Lord Advocate's Reference No 1 of 2023*.

complainer had left her mobile phone at the house (suggesting she left in a hurry); that the complainer and her boyfriend always used a condom, but the accused had not worn one; the age gap between the complainer and the accused; that the accused was the uncle of the complainer's boyfriend; and the absence of any prior sexual intercourse between the accused and complainer.

19.57 Finally, the Appeal Court quashed a trial judge's decision to sustain a submission of no case to answer in *HM Advocate v I (M)*,[74] where the complainer had given evidence of drinking during the day, being in a bar with the accused, whom she had never met before, and then of her next memory being in a room at a hotel and the police coming in. There was evidence of her intoxication from the barmen, from a taxi driver who refused the accused's request to take them to the hotel and instead phoned the police, from the hotel receptionist, and from the police officers who arrived in the hotel room and found the complainer with her top on inside out and not wearing any underwear, and unable to remember what had happened moments previously. There was scientific evidence of penetration and toxicology showing the complainer's blood-alcohol levels and there was CCTV from the bar and hotel showing the complainer's intoxication.[75] The Court held that the evidence of the complainer's heavy intoxication, the taxi driver's concerns at what might happen to her at the hotel and the state in which the police found her was sufficient for the jury to infer a lack of capacity to consent to sexual intercourse. The case is also notable for the Court's quotation with approval of Hallett LJ's observation in *R v H*[76] that it will rarely be open to a judge to sustain a no-case-to-answer submission where the evidence is of a young woman, 'alone at night and vulnerable through drink, [who] is picked up by a stranger who has sex with her within minutes of meeting her'.

19.58 It is suggested this dictum is correct. The fact that there has been no prior sexual relationship between the accused and the complainer can be corroborative in certain cases, notwithstanding the case law on sexual-history evidence at common law and under sections 274 and 275 of the 1995 Act. This is because, while under that case law, prior sexual relations between the accused and complainer are normally not relevant to the question of consent, the converse is not true: if there has been no prior sexual relationship (or even no relationship at all), then, in the circumstances described in *Spendiff, Wright, L* and *I (M)* above, that is relevant to the question of whether the complainer would have consented in the circumstances described. A jury is entitled to weigh the inherent unlikelihood of consent to sexual intercourse with someone whom the complainer has either had no sexual relationship with or no relationship at all, particularly if there are other circumstances in the case which suggest that the complainer would not have wanted sexual intercourse with anyone

74 2022 SCCR 188.

75 This point is discussed at n 65 above.

76 [2007] EWCA Crim 2056.

(such as being ill in *Wright*) and thus, *a fortiori*, not with someone she did not know or with whom she had no prior sexual relationship.

MUTUAL CORROBORATION

19.59 The doctrine of mutual corroboration has become so engrained in the law of sexual offences in Scotland, and the leading case on it, *Moorov v HM Advocate*,[77] has become so celebrated, analysed and discussed like few other cases in Scots criminal law, that it is easy to overlook two basic facts. First, as the Appeal Court observed in *Adam and Daisley v HM Advocate*,[78] the doctrine of mutual corroboration was not created in *Moorov*; *Moorov* merely set out its parameters. The doctrine itself can be found in the Institutional Writers and the practice of the Scottish courts as early as 1738.[79] Second, the doctrine is not unique to Scots law. The significance of *Moorov* is that it was the first case in the common law world to develop significantly the doctrine and the first to use the term mutual corroboration to describe it. For that reason, it has been almost as influential outside Scotland as within it. Although the doctrine of mutual corroboration has been largely, though by no means entirely, supplanted by the doctrine of similar-fact evidence in the rest of the common-law world, *Moorov* was influential in the development of both mutual corroboration and similar-fact evidence by the English courts in the 1970s and, from there, to Ireland and the Commonwealth. This explains why, whenever mutual corroboration or similar-fact evidence is considered in those jurisdictions, *Moorov* is still regularly cited with approval.[80]

19.60 Like all common law rules of evidence, the doctrine of mutual corroboration has evolved over the years. We summarise the basic parameters of mutual corroboration as set out in *Moorov*, before turning to how *Moorov* is now applied. Finally, we consider one form of the doctrine which has come to the fore in recent years: 'Ricky Taylor' or single-complainer mutual corroboration.

77 1930 JC 68.

78 2020 JC 141 at para 27.

79 The July 1738 trial of Thomas Souter and James Hog, discussed in Hume, ii, at 385. See too Alison, ii, at 552. The fullest discussion, with reference to the early, pre-*Moorov* authorities, is in Dickson, ii, at para 1808. See also, as an example of a pre-*Moorov* case applying the doctrine in a substantially similar form to that later set out in *Moorov*, *HM Advocate v M'Donald* 1928 JC 42.

80 See, in the Supreme Court of the United Kingdom, the Northern Irish case *R v Mitchell* [2017] AC 571. In the Supreme Court of Ireland, *DPP v Limen* [2021] IESC 8. In Australia, see, for instance, *Pfennig v R* (1995) 182 CLR 461; *R v Copeland* [2010] SASCFC 11; and *R v Liddy* [2002] SASC 19. In England and Wales, see *R v Kilbourne* [1973] AC 729; and *R v Boardman* [1975] AC 421, both of which relied heavily on *Moorov* and provide much of the foundation for how mutual corroboration and similar-fact evidence has been applied in Ireland and the Commonwealth: see, for instance, the citation of *Kilbourne* and *Broadman*, with the passages in which they relied on *Moorov*, in the Canadian cases *R v Grimaldi* [1978] 1 WWR 264 and *R v Vetrovec* (1980) 58 CCC (2d) 537.

186 Argyle Street, Glasgow in 1930. The Moorov sign can be seen in the right-hand side of the photograph with further signs in the first-floor windows. Source: Glasgow City Archives.

Moorov

19.61 The facts, though well known, are worth stating again. Samuel Moorov ran a drapery wholesaler at 186 Argyle Street. On 7 May 1930, he was convicted after trial in the High Court of Justiciary at Glasgow of seven charges of assault and nine charges of indecent assault of various women in his employment.[81] For three of the charges, there was conventional corroboration of the complainer's evidence. For the remainder, there was only the evidence of the relevant complainer. The assault charges spanned seven years (1923 to 1930) and the indecent assault charges three years (1927 to 1930). The trial judge in his charge separated the charges into two groups, the assault charges and the indecent assault charges, and directed the jury that for those charges in which there was only a single witness they could find corroboration in the evidence of the other women who spoke to an offence in the same group. Moorov appealed his conviction on those charges.

[81] The separation was somewhat artificial. The physical assault charges were in reality less serious indecent assaults involving kissing, tickling and the like. All of the charges would now constitute sexual assault.

19.62 A Full Bench of seven judges refused the appeal in respect of indecent assault charges but, influenced in large part by the fact that one of the assault charges took place in 1923, four years before the next charge in that group, allowed the appeal in respect of the assault charges.[82] In doing so, the Full Bench had no difficulty that corroboration could work in the way set out by the trial judge. Their greater concern was setting out the parameters of what, for the first time, they called mutual corroboration. There were different expressions used by the six judges who gave opinions, but the key features were:

(i) For mutual corroboration to apply, it was not enough for the charges to involve the repeated crimes; a disposition or susceptibility towards a type of offence was not enough.[83]

(ii) Instead, what was required was a connection or nexus of time, character and circumstances between the charges which showed an underlying unity between them, in the sense of showing that they formed part of a systematic course of criminal conduct.[84]

19.63 Beyond those two parameters, the Court was reluctant to set down any general rule on the application of the doctrine, emphasising the need to look at the circumstances of the offences and declining to lay down any rule on what would or would not demonstrate the necessary underlying unity or course of conduct. For instance, in passages with which none of the other judges appear to have taken issue, and which have ever since been regarded as correctly stating the law, Lord Justice Clerk (Alness) and Lord Sands were clear in rejecting the suggestion that the doctrine was limited in time, though Lord Sands accepted this would be an important factor in determining whether there was a course of conduct.[85]

19.64 There have been various attempts by the Appeal Court down the years to state succinctly the principle. In 2021, a Full Bench in *Duthie v HM Advocate*,[86] drawing on *Ogg v HM Advocate*,[87] the previous Full Bench decision in *MR v HM Advocate*[88] and *Adam v HM Advocate*,[89] endorsed this formulation:

> 'The testimony of one witness about one crime may be corroborated by a second witness's testimony about another crime where there are similarities in time, place and circumstances in the crimes such as demonstrate that the individual incidents are component parts of one course of conduct persistently pursued by the accused.'[90]

82 Lord Justice Clerk (Alness) and Lord Ormidale dissented in respect of the physical assault charges.
83 Lord Justice General (Clyde) at 75–76; Lord Justice Clerk (Alness), setting out the Institutional Writers, at 79–80; Lord Anderson (also quoting Alison) at 85; Lord Sands at 88–89.
84 Lord Justice General (Clyde) at 73–74.; Lord Justice Clerk (Alness) at 80; Lord Anderson at 85; Lord Sands at 88–89; Lord Blackburn at 92; Lord Morison at 94.
85 Lord Justice Clerk (Alness) at 82; Lord Sands at 88–89.
86 2021 JC 207.
87 1938 JC 152 at 57 and 158.
88 2013 JC 212 at para 20.
89 2020 JC 141 at para 28.
90 At para 19.

19.65 The Jury Manual at 24.3/133 observes that the reference to 'time, *place* and circumstances' is out of kilter with the conventional expression of 'time, *character* and circumstances'. That is so, but little turns on it: both formulations will include the same type of offending and the Full Bench in *Duthie* went on to use the conventional expression in the next paragraph of its opinion, saying:

> 'Before looking to see whether there is proof of a course of conduct, there first has to be a search for similarities in the time, character and circumstances.'

The contemporary approach to mutual corroboration

19.66 For much of its history, the jurisprudence on mutual corroboration involved the courts weighing any similarities and differences between the charges (both in the types of charges libelled and in conduct alleged) and considering any time gaps between those charges so as to determine whether the doctrine can apply. Where the courts found that the doctrine could not apply, either because the differences between the charges outweighed the similarities or because of time gaps between the charges, they upheld submissions of no case to answer or quashed convictions.

19.67 There has been a shift away from that approach in recent years and towards leaving the decision as to whether the doctrine can apply to the jury. The Full Bench in *Duthie* made clear that a submission of no case to answer should only be sustained when, on no possible view, could it be said that the individual incidents were component parts of a course of conduct persistently pursued by the accused.[91] Underpinning that shift – and thus the contemporary approach to the doctrine – is the Appeal Court's stated attempt to keep pace with the modern societal understanding of sexual and other conduct and, in particular, what are perceived to be characteristic links between the perpetration of different types of sexual and physical abuse especially, but not exclusively, of children and young persons.[92] For this reason, the Appeal Court has also said that, in applying the doctrine, it will proceed on its own developing knowledge of sexual and other behaviour and how one type of illegal activity can often be intimately connected with other types of different, but still illegal, acts.[93]

19.68 Although 'on no possible view' is a high test, it still invites consideration of when the doctrine can apply: that is, what similarities in time, character and circumstance have been found by the Appeal Court to be sufficient to allow a jury to decide whether to apply the doctrine in the case before it (sometimes called the 'requisite similarities'). It is convenient to consider 'time' separately, then 'character' and 'circumstance' together because they substantially overlap.

91 Para 25, confirming the earlier authorities on this point which date from *Reynolds v HM Advocate* 1995 JC 142.

92 See the Full Bench decision in *MR v HM Advocate* 2013 JC 212 at para 17, reiterated by the Full Bench in *Duthie* at para 20.

93 *MR* at para 17.

19.69 Before doing so, it bears emphasising that the Appeal Court has never said that all three need to be present for the doctrine to apply and, indeed, in one of the first cases after *Moorov* to apply it, *Ogg v HM Advocate*,[94] the Court was clear that the presence of all three features was not essential for the doctrine to apply.[95] Thus while it is always useful, for analytical purposes, to look at how each of the elements has been considered, the question always returns to whether there is an underlying unity to the accused's conduct such as to show a course of criminal conduct systematically pursued by him.

Time

19.70 Although *Moorov* and all subsequent authorities have declined to apply a hard-and-fast rule to time gaps between offences and have always said that there is no maximum period beyond which the doctrine cannot apply, until *Adam* and *Duthie* much of the case law on mutual corroboration turned on: (i) whether the time gap between offences was too long for the doctrine to apply; and (ii) in any case of a lengthy time gap, whether (and if so, what) special, compelling or extraordinary circumstances might be required to overcome that gap.[96] *Adam* and *Duthie* appear to have settled both questions.

19.71 In *Adam*, the Court rejected any suggestion that special circumstances were required in cases involving offending against children, observing that, in such cases, the peculiar nature of the crime means such special, compelling or extraordinary circumstances already exist.[97] Nor is there any need for evidence which might explain the time gap,[98] though in some cases, such as offending in families, this gap might be explained by the complainers being of different generations.[99]

19.72 The Full Bench in *Duthie* extended that ruling to all cases, not simply those involving offending against children.[100] It stated that it is not the case that, as a matter of law, in a lengthy time-gap case, there require to be special, compelling or extraordinary features. It found that the judge may elect to explain that there is a long time-gap and that, because of that, the similarities would require to be strong ones

94 1938 JC 152.

95 At 157 (per Lord Justice Clerk (Aitchison)).

96 See the authorities reviewed in *Russell v HM Advocate* 1990 JC 177, where the Appeal Court had cause to remark (at 184) that, although no hard-and-fast rule could be laid down, it was significant that there had been no case in which the doctrine was applied where there was an interval of three years or more. On the origin of the dicta that, in cases of a longer time-gap, a particularly unusual similarity could overcome the time gap, see *Dodds v HM Advocate* 2003 JC 8 at 12, quoting *Tudhope v Hazleton* 1984 SCCR 455 at 460.

97 At para 35. See thus *DW v HM Advocate* 2023 SCCR 248, which found it was a question for the jury whether the doctrine could apply across a time gap of 17 years.

98 See *DW* at para 19.

99 *B (R) v HM Advocate* 2017 JC 278 at para 30.

100 At para 28.

compared with those needed for incidents closely linked in time, but a direction in those terms is not essential.[101]

Character and circumstance

19.73 Consideration of similarities in character and circumstance has generally revolved around whether such similarities can exist between different crimes, different types of complainers and, less frequently, different places where the offences are alleged to have taken place.

19.74 **Different crimes**: A lesser charge can provide corroboration for a more serious charge (and vice versa) and the fact that the crimes libelled have different names does not prevent the doctrine applying; it is the underlying similarity of the conduct described, not the label attached to it, which must be examined.[102] It is a question of fact and degree and, as the Full Bench observed in *MR* (at paragraph 20), often one requiring, in a solemn case, assessment by the jury. Equally, too strong a focus on the individual charges is 'to risk compartmentalising the evidence rather than asking whether the evidence as a whole indicates a course of conduct.'[103] It is thus misleading to talk about a charge being corroborated. As the Appeal Court said in *CW*, 'what is being corroborated is the evidence of a witness in relation to a charge' (paragraph 34). Further:

> 'the search is not for corroboration of the individual elements of the crime spoken to by an individual witness, but whether the nature of the evidence spoken to by the other witness is indicative of that underlying unity of purpose behind the accused's acting which makes it appropriate to treat the several incidents as part of the one course of conduct.'[104]

19.75 Applying that broad principle, mutual corroboration can be found in the following situations:

- between an attempted crime and a completed crime;[105]
- between offences where force is used and where it is not: for a series of rapes (and, it is suggested, any other sexual offences based on the absence of consent), the course of conduct that needs to be demonstrated is simply non-consensual sexual intercourse with the requisite *mens rea*;[106]

101 Ibid.

102 *HMcA v HM Advocate* 2015 JC 27 at paras 9–11; *McMahon v HM Advocate* 1996 SLT 1139 at 1142E-F; *B v HM Advocate* 2009 JC 88 at paras 3–6; *MR v HM Advocate* 2013 JC 212 at paras 18–21; *Jamal v HM Advocate* 2019 JC 119 at para 21; and *Watson v HM Advocate* 2019 JC 187 at paras 15–19.

103 *TN v HM Advocate* 2018 SCCR 109 at para 12.

104 *CW v HM Advocate* 2016 JC 148 at para 34.

105 *PM v Jessop* 1989 SCCR 324 (there between sodomy and attempted sodomy); *MR v HM Advocate*, cited above (between rape and assault by lying on top of the complainer and placing his naked penis against her private parts).

106 *Kearney v HM Advocate* 2015 JC 259 at para 16.

- between different forms of penetration[107] and between penetrative and non-penetrative offences;[108]
- between offences where consent is a critical issue and offences where, because of the complainer's young age or the accused's position of trust, consent is irrelevant;[109]
- between offences where the accused is the actor and where he would be guilty art and part of offences committed by others at his instigation;[110]
- between different levels or types of sexual abuse (such as between incest and other offences against children);[111] and
- between offences occurring in different homes, where each are controlling, dysfunctional homes, and the complainers are vulnerable for living in them.[112]

19.76 Sexual offences and other offences: The doctrine does, though, have limits between sexual offences and other offences. Though the point was left open in *H v HM Advocate,*[113] the Full Bench in *Duthie* was clear that a physical assault which contained no sexual element could not corroborate a sexual assault or rape.[114] The Full Bench in *Duthie* was, however, prepared to accept that a combination of sexual and physical abuse by an accused within one family unit could, if the underlying similarities were present, afford mutual corroboration of a combination of sexual and physical abuse by the same accused in another family unit.[115] Thus, in a case involving different partners, one partner's testimony of sexual or physical assaults could be mutually corroborated by evidence of the same type of conduct coming from another partner.[116]

19.77 Different types of complainers: The doctrine can apply between child and adult complainers[117] and between complainers of different genders.[118] As with different crimes, the key point now is not that there might be dissimilarities between the types of complainers (the significance of which is for the jury to gauge); a judge only has to ask whether on no possible view of the evidence could it be said that the

107 *L v HM Advocate* [2016] HCJAC 120; and *TN v HM Advocate* 2018 SCCR 109.

108 *Watson v HM Advocate* 2019 JC 187.

109 *CW v HM Advocate* 2016 JC 148 at paras 27 and 28 (there between, on the one hand, indecent assault and sexual assault of one complainer and, on the other, sexual abuse of trust, contrary to s 42 of the Sexual Offences (Scotland) 2009 Act). See, too, *Edwards v HM Advocate* [2019] HCJAC 80 (between a charge of rape and charges of sexual intercourse and other sexual activity with older children).

110 *TN v HM Advocate* cited above.

111 *HM Advocate v M'Donald* 1928 JC 42.

112 See *TN*, cited above, at paras 14 and 15; and *L v HM Advocate* [2016] HCJAC 120 at para 8.

113 2015 SCCR 242.

114 At paras 21 and 22, following *MR* at para 17 and *McAskill v HM Advocate* 2016 SCCR 402 at paras 26–28.

115 See *Stalley v HM Advocate* 2022 JC 121 at para 31, which distils the relevant passages of *Duthie* paras 20–28.

116 See *Stalley* at para 32.

117 *B v HM Advocate* 2009 JC 88; *McCafferty v HM Advocate* 2020 SCCR 105.

118 *HM Advocate v BL* 2022 JC 176; *T (P) v HM Advocate* 2020 JC 205; *P v HM Advocate* 1991 SCCR 933 (quoted with apparent approval in *B v HM Advocate* 2009 JC 88).

respective accounts of different complainers constitute component parts of a single course of criminal conduct systematically pursued.[119]

19.78 **Different places:** Separate consideration of different places where the offences are alleged to have been committed rarely arises (and it might be thought to be at odds with the progressive extension of the extra-territorial jurisdiction to allow, for instance, the prosecution of UK nationals for sexual offences wherever in the world they are alleged to have committed them: see Chapter 1 at **1.25–1.46**). But it was a consideration in *HM Advocate v SM (no 2)*,[120] where the Appeal Court found that on no possible view could the doctrine apply to two episodes, one against a long-term partner who submitted to sexual intercourse while being held against her will, and the other the attack and rape of a stranger in a public place, when the episodes were separated by seven years, and the former took place in Scotland and the latter 350 miles away in Essex.

'Ricky Taylor' or single-complainer Moorov

19.79 On 22 March 2018, Ricky Taylor was convicted of one charge of coercing a person into being present during a sexual activity, contrary to section 5 of the Sexual Offences (Scotland) Act 2009. On four occasions, he had stood at his bedroom window, exposed his penis and masturbated in sight of his neighbour, SLD, as she smoked cigarettes at her back door. The fourth occasion was also witnessed by SLD's husband. There was no doubt that there was conventional corroboration for the fourth occasion: SLD's evidence was corroborated by what her husband had also seen. The issue was whether the other three incidents were corroborated. The High Court of Justiciary, overruling the Sheriff Appeal Court, found that they were.[121] Although the normal rule was that each incident in a single, composite charge required corroboration, where the incidents were a course of conduct systematically pursued (that is, a course of conduct in the *Moorov* sense), the corroboration could be by mutual corroboration. Mutual corroboration did not depend on whether the separate incidents were charged in separate charges or a single, composite charge.

19.80 Crucially, mutual corroboration did not require multiple complainers (it did not even require a complainer) and it could equally apply to a course of conduct against a single complainer. After all, the Court reasoned, a succession of criminal acts against a single complainer was as redolent (perhaps more so) of a single course of conduct persistently pursued as a succession of acts against different individuals.[122] The evidence of SLD's husband in respect of the last incident could corroborate the evidence of SLD on the first three incidents. It was evidence from a separate source which, taken with the evidence of SLD, enabled all four incidents to be corroborated

119 See, for instance, *L (B)* at para 11; *McCafferty* at paras 18 and 19.
120 2019 JC 183. The facts are more fully set out in an earlier appeal in the same case: [2019] HCJAC 39.
121 2019 JC 71.
122 At para 15. On this, see also *Wilson v HM Advocate* 2017 JC 64 discussed at paras 18 and 19 of *Taylor*.

on a *Moorov* basis. If he had been a complainer in the fourth incident, his evidence would have provided classic *Moorov* corroboration of the first three incidents; it made no difference that he was not a complainer but simply a witness.[123]

19.81 Despite the relatively few authorities since it was decided, *Ricky Taylor* corroboration has become a common form of corroboration. Like all corroboration, it is not limited to cases where the second source is another eyewitness. Its most common application is when a complainer speaks to a series of incidents and there are either admissions by the accused to one incident, or medical or scientific evidence of one incident, or evidence of distress after that incident. If the incidents are capable of being seen as forming a course of conduct systematically pursued by the accused, then the evidence supporting the complainer's account of one of those incidents can mutually corroborate her account of the other incidents. It is the second adminicle of evidence in relation to one of the incidents (the admission, the medical or scientific evidence, or the distress) that can mutually corroborate the other incidents in that course of conduct. It should be stressed that *Ricky Taylor* does not mean it is only necessary to corroborate one incident in the series of incidents.[124] *Ricky Taylor* is not an exception to mutual corroboration, but rather a form of it: the second adminicle of evidence must be capable of mutually corroborating each of the incidents in the course of conduct, not just capable of corroborating, in the conventional sense, one of the incidents.

19.82 Like mutual corroboration generally, *Ricky Taylor* corroboration has its limits. In *Faulkner v HM Advocate*[125] the Appeal Court emphasised (at paragraph 12):

> 'It is unnecessary for any part of a composite charge to be fully corroborated, in the sense of there being two witnesses speaking to that part. That was the case in *Taylor* but mutual corroboration can apply even if the complainer does not speak to part of a composite charge which is spoken to by another witness. However, in those circumstances what that other witness speaks to must be a crime. Mutuality in this context implies that two or more pieces of evidence rely on each other for corroboration. It is a two way street.'

19.83 We take three points from this passage. First, though it is said in respect of parts of composite charges, the same principle will apply to separate charges: as the Court said in *Taylor*, mutual corroboration does not depend on whether the separate incidents were charged in separate charges or a single, composite charge. Second, the passage that 'mutual corroboration can apply even if the complainer does not speak to part of a composite charge which is spoken to by another witness' derives from what was said at paragraph 16 of *Taylor*: that it cannot matter whether the corroborating evidence is given by another complainer or by another individual who observed and is able to speak to the relevant events. *Taylor* at paragraph 16 gives the example of a two-complainer case where the second complainer does

123 Para 20.

124 On this, see *Rysmanowski v HM Advocate* 2020 JC 84, discussed further at **19.84–19.87** below.

125 2024 SCCR 45.

not give evidence, but another witness speaks to the incident involving that second complainer. Third, the Court's desire to stress that what the second witness speaks to must be a crime applies generally to cases based on *Ricky Taylor* corroboration. The second source of evidence (the second witness, the admission, the medical or scientific evidence, the distress, etc) must speak to the fact that a crime has taken place. It is only if it does so that the evidence can be used to mutually corroborate the other incidents in a course of conduct.

Continuous criminal activity or a course of conduct

19.84 The post-*Taylor* authorities of *Wilson v HM Advocate*[126] and *Rysmanowski v HM Advocate*[127] have clarified the distinction between, on the one hand, a single episode of continuous criminal activity that might involve different elements and, on the other, a series of separate crimes that might amount to a course of criminal conduct, and how corroboration works for each.

19.85 Where there is a single episode of continuous criminal activity, it is not necessary for each of the elements of the libel to be corroborated (for instance, in an assault where a number of blows are inflicted, it is not necessary for each of the blows to be corroborated): *Campbell v Vannet*.[128]

19.86 It is different when the crimes are separate incidents. There, there must be corroboration of each crime in the series. This can be by conventional corroboration or by mutual corroboration (including *Ricky Taylor* corroboration) but whichever it is, each crime in the series requires to be corroborated.[129] *Rysmanowski* (disapproving of earlier dicta in *Stephen v HM Advocate*[130]) makes clear that these are the only two means of corroboration. There is no authority for the proposition that, when repeated crimes are libelled in a single charge, each element does not require corroboration, only the course of conduct.[131]

19.87 The difference between a single episode of continuous criminal activity and a series of distinct crimes forming a course of conduct is a question of fact and degree.[132] That is no less true in sexual offences cases. The Appeal Court in *Dalton v HM Advocate*[133] was prepared to countenance the possibility that repeated

126 2019 SCCR 273.

127 2020 JC 84.

128 1998 SCCR 207.

129 *Wilson* at para 37; *Rysmanowski* at paras 17–20. As the Court observed in *Wilson* (at para 37), this can include application of the principle in *Howden v HM Advocate* 1994 SCCR 19: that where one incident involving a complainer is proved by corroborated evidence to have been committed, then other incidents, which are themselves proved to have happened by corroborated evidence, will also be proved to have been perpetrated by the accused, if the evidence yields the inference that they must have been committed by the same person.

130 2007 JC 61.

131 At paras 17–21.

132 *Wilson* at para 37.

133 2015 SCCR 125 at para 42.

rapes over a short period of time might be considered to be part of one episode of repeated rape, just as in *Wilson* it was prepared to see a series of assaults during an abduction as a single episode of multiple assaults.[134] This, as always, will depend on the circumstances of the case. But the point is now settled that in a single episode of continuous criminal activity not all elements of the libel need be corroborated, whereas in a series of crimes amounting to a course of conduct each of the crimes in that series needs to be separately corroborated.

CORROBORATION: PROCEDURAL MATTERS

19.88 Three procedural matters can arise in sexual offences trials in respect of corroboration.

Submissions of no case to answer

19.89 The first relates to defence submissions that there is no case to answer. The test – and, as the Full Bench held in *Duthie v HM Advocate*,[135] the only test – is that laid down in section 97(2) of the Criminal Procedure (Scotland) Act 1995: whether the judge is satisfied that the evidence led by the prosecution is insufficient in law to justify the accused being convicted. It is for the accused to satisfy the judge on the absence of a sufficiency.[136] Where no issue of corroboration arises (that is, it is accepted that there is corroboration), it is only where there is no evidence from which a jury can infer that a fact in issue is proved that a no case to answer submission can be sustained.[137]

19.90 As discussed at **19.67** above, in the context of mutual corroboration the Full Bench in *Duthie* endorsed previous authority that a submission of no case to answer should only be sustained when 'on no possible view' could it be said that the individual incidents were component parts of a course of conduct persistently pursued by the accused.[138] The Full Bench also emphasised that this does not introduce any new or different element beyond the words of the statute. The court is not considering the acceptability of the testimony. It is simply asking whether there is no evidence which, if accepted, will entitle the court to proceed to conviction. The court must decide whether there is testimony relative to two or more incidents which, if accepted, contains the requisite similarities such as may demonstrate a course of conduct persistently pursued. If these similarities exist and one inference

134 At para 38.

135 2021 JC 207 at para 24.

136 Ibid.

137 See, for instance, *HM Advocate v I* 2022 SCCR 188 at para 9.

138 Para 25, confirming the earlier authorities on this point which date from *Reynolds v HM Advocate* 1995 JC 142.

is that there was a course of conduct, the submission of no case to answer must be repelled.[139]

Directing the jury on routes to verdict

19.91 The second procedural issue concerns the trial judge's direction to the jury on corroboration and possible routes to verdict. The Appeal Court in *Hogg v HM Advocate*[140] endorsed the view previously expressed in *Garland v HM Advocate*[141] that it is the responsibility of the trial judge to direct the jury on all reasonably available sources of corroboration, whether or not these are referred to or relied upon by the Crown or defence. The Court in *Hogg* went on to say that this would be so even if, by that time, it may be too late to seek the views of parties on the appropriateness of giving the direction.[142] It would appear to countenance the possibility that the trial judge can – without inviting submissions from the parties – set out a route to verdict that the Crown has not relied on, and that it would not be unfair for him to do so, even if that means the parties are deprived of the opportunity to comment on that route in their speeches.

19.92 However, the appeal in *Hogg* arose because the judge had discussed corroboration with the parties before their speeches. In that discussion, it was agreed that the only route to verdict was mutual corroboration. The parties addressed the jury on that basis. After those speeches, the trial judge directed the jury on an additional route to verdict he had identified that was based on conventional corroboration. The jury convicted.

19.93 The Appeal Court quashed the conviction, finding that what the trial judge had done was manifestly unfair and prejudicial to the defence. It observed that it was not mandatory or inevitable that a judge should discuss the issue of corroboration with parties before speeches. However, if the judge chooses to do so, fairness demands that, in that discussion, he should raise with parties any alternative approaches to corroboration which he considers to arise or upon which he intends to direct the jury (paragraph 23).

19.94 The ruling in *Hogg* does not therefore prevent a trial judge from directing the jury on further routes to verdict beyond any route identified by the Crown. Nor does it require the judge, if he has identified any such further route, to discuss it with the parties: all *Hogg* says is that it will be unfair to direct the jury on that route if that would be against any previous discussion the judge has had with

139 *Duthie* at para 26.
140 2024 JC 54 at para 21.
141 2021 JC 118 at para 20.
142 Also at para 21. This is by analogy to the duty to give a direction on any alternative verdicts, even where that has not been canvassed with parties: *Duncan v HM Advocate* 2019 JC 9, though it was also said in *Duncan* the need to direct on a matter not raised by the parties ought to be a rare event (para 28). See the discussion of *Duncan* and alternative verdicts in Chapter 2 at **2.131**.

the parties. It is suggested, however, that, if a judge does identify any additional route to verdict, the best and fairest course is to alert parties before their speeches. Indeed, it might be said that the best practice is for a discussion to take place between the judge and parties before speeches; certainly, nothing is ever lost by such a discussion.

Incompetent or inconsistent verdicts

19.95 The third procedural issue is what a trial judge should do when the jury returns a verdict which is incompatible with a direction on mutual corroboration: for instance, when they acquit on one charge and convict on another but the only route to verdict was mutual corroboration and thus they must convict on both charges or acquit on both.

19.96 It is incumbent on the trial judge to take action: the issue is whether the judge should direct that the verdict should be recorded as one of acquittal or should give further directions on mutual corroboration and ask the jury to retire for further consideration. In *SS v HM Advocate*,[143] the Appeal Court reviewed the previous authorities on the subject, which diverged on the correct course to take. The Appeal Court found that those authorities served to illustrate how difficult it was to lay down specific rules or guidance to cover the many different situations in which the jury's verdict might not conform to the directions given.[144] It did observe, however, that in a mutual-corroboration case there are two primary issues for the jury to determine: first, whether they find individual complainers credible and reliable; and second, whether, if so, the evidence justifies applying the doctrine of mutual corroboration.[145]

19.97 In *SS*, the appeal was allowed. There were three complainers in that case: K, L and D. Initially, the jury had acquitted of the charges involving K and L but convicted of the charges involving D. This was incompetent because the charges in respect of D depended on the doctrine of mutual corroboration. After a further direction from the trial judge, the jury then convicted on the charges involving K and D and again acquitted of the charge involving L. The Appeal Court found that the necessary implication of the jury's initial verdict was that they had considered D to be credible and reliable, but had not been able to reach such a conclusion for K and

143 2024 SCCR 37.

144 Para 16.

145 At para 23. On this, see also *T (P) v HM Advocate* 2020 JC 205, where the Court held that the jury are entitled, when assessing whether each complainer is credible and reliable, to take into account the evidence of the other complainer(s) (para 21). The Court observed (at para 22) that the jury require to determine whether they accept the complainers as credible and reliable. They also need to decide whether mutual corroboration is applicable. How a particular jury goes about these tasks is for the jury to determine. The Court also observed (again at para 22) that: 'there may be a degree of circularity, but it is none the worse for that. In some cases, the value of the other complainer's evidence in the assessment of credibility and reliability may be minimal. In others, where the similarities are great, it may be considerable.'

L. A correct application of the doctrine of mutual corroboration to that initial factual finding was an acquittal on all of the charges, and the verdict should have been recorded as such.[146] *SS* does not resolve what should happen in all circumstances in which the jury return an incompetent or inconsistent verdict, but it does clarify the approach which should be taken in many mutual corroboration cases.

146 *SS* at para 25.

PART IV

Sentencing in Sexual Offences Cases

Chapter 20

Sentencing

INTRODUCTION

20.01 This chapters covers sentencing in sexual offences cases and the various ancillary orders that the courts may – and in some cases must – make in such cases. We begin by setting out the general considerations that apply to sentencing (in sexual offences cases and otherwise), then the particular sentences that are available in such cases and finally the ancillary orders.

GENERAL CONSIDERATIONS

Sentencing guidelines

20.02 Sections 118(7) and 189(7) of the Criminal Procedure (Scotland) Act 1995 give the High Court and the Sheriff Appeal Court respectively, power to issue guideline decisions in relation to sentencing for any particular type of case. Section 197 provides that when passing sentence a court must have regard to any such relevant guideline decision. At present the only guideline decision which impacts on sentencing in relation to sexual offences is the case of *HM Advocate v Graham,*[1] which concerns making and distributing indecent images of children.

20.03 Section 6 of the Criminal Justice and Licensing (Scotland) Act 2010 provides that all courts must have regard to any sentencing guidelines published by the Scottish Sentencing Council which are applicable to the case before it when passing sentence for any offence. For the purposes of sentencing in relation to sexual offences, the guidelines which are currently in force are the principles and purposes of sentencing guideline, which applies to all sentences passed from 26 November 2018, the sentencing process guideline,[2] which has been in effect since 22 September

1 2011 JC 1.

2 The sentencing process guideline sets out a sequence of steps which a court should follow in order to reach a sentencing decision. One of its purposes in doing so is to promote a consistent approach to sentencing. However, it was made clear in *HM Advocate v GH* 2024 SLT 37 that this guideline does not impose a requirement on judges to set out in detail the method by which they arrived at the final sentence or require them to approach the issue of sentence by approaching the factors in question in a prescribed order. Sentencing remains an essentially holistic exercise.

2021 and the sentencing young people guideline which has been in effect since 26 January 2022.[3]

20.04 For the purposes of the sentencing young people guideline, a young person is someone who is under the age of 25 at the date of their plea of guilty or when a finding of guilt is made against them. It does not apply where the court is passing sentence on an older offender in respect of offences committed when he was under the age of 25.[4]

20.05 The Scottish Sentencing Council is in the process of developing various guidelines on sentencing in sexual offences, covering (at the time of writing) rape, rape of a young child, sexual assault, and indecent images of children. It is also working on a general guideline on domestic abuse. Once each guideline is in force, sentencers will require to apply it in determining the appropriate sentence for that offence or, if minded not to follow the guideline or to depart from it, to state the reasons for that decision.

English guidelines

20.06 The Sentencing Council for England and Wales produces what are called 'Definitive Guidelines' in relation to sentencing in respect of various different kinds of offending. It has available on its website guidelines in relation to each of the offences created by the Sexual Offences Act 2003. The Scottish courts have acknowledged the benefit of using guidelines prepared by the Sentencing Council as a useful cross-check for sentences in Scotland, especially where the offences are regulated by a UK statute and there are identical sentencing maxima.[5] The immediate point to note is that sexual offences are prosecuted in Scotland under a similar but different statutory regime. However even where the offences concerned are regulated by a UK statute it has always been emphasised that these guidelines should not be applied in Scotland in a rigid or mechanistic fashion, given the differences in sentencing purposes, practices and regimes between the two jurisdictions. In the case of *HM Advocate v G (M)*[6] (when considering a Crown appeal against sentence in respect of a charge of rape) the court expressly addressed the utility of the English sexual offence guideline and reinforced the need for caution by adopting what had been said in *HM Advocate v Milligan*:[7]

> 'We caution against too rigid an application of the English sentencing guidelines. They are not to be applied even in England in mechanistic

3 If the court decides not to follow an applicable guideline, or to depart from it, it must state the reasons for its decision – 2010 Act, s 6(2).

4 When an adult is being sentenced for crimes committed as a child, or as a young person, the individual's age at the time of offending is nevertheless a relevant factor in selecting the appropriate sentence. This is not a product of the guideline but a generally applied principle of sentencing – *HM Advocate v RM* 2024 JC 81.

5 *Sutherland v HM Advocate* 2016 SCCR 41.

6 [2023] HCJAC 3.

7 [2015] HCJAC 84.

fashion and it must be borne in mind that those guidelines in England are to be understood in a different sentencing regime from the Scottish sentencing regime … the Scottish approach to sentencing is rather less formulaic than the English sentencing guidelines.'

Despite these observations, there can be value in a cross-check with the Definitive Guidelines to determine whether any 'major disparity' in the sentencing range is disclosed.[8]

Victim impact statements

20.07 Section 14 of the Criminal Justice (Scotland) Act 2003 gave to some victims of criminal conduct a right to make a statement to the court setting out their own personal account of the impact which the crime had upon them. The right arises where proceedings are taken in respect of an offence in a prescribed court or class of court.[9] The policy objectives underpinning the legislation were to help victims feel that they have a more central role in the criminal justice process and to help inform the sentencing process.[10] The policy is reflected in section 14(5) of the 2003 Act which requires the prosecutor to lay before the court any victim impact statement which has been made when moving for sentence[11] and the court is required to have regard to so much of it as is relevant to the offence. The court may have regard to information within such a statement concerning harm to the victim caused by the offender's conduct even if this is not specified in the charge.[12] A particular benefit of the opportunity to provide a victim impact statement is that it avoids the need for a victim to explain the detailed effects and consequences of the offending in the setting of a courtroom (or commission hearing).

Discount of sentence

20.08 When an accused person's plea of guilty is accepted the provisions of section 196 of the 1995 Act may be engaged so as to permit the sentencer to grant a discount from the sentence which would otherwise have been imposed. This is intended to reflect the utilitarian value of the plea tendered and accepted. The case

8 *HM Advocate v AB* 2016 SCCR 47 at para 13, *HM Advocate v Docherty* [2024] HCJAC 36 at para 20.

9 The prescribed offences include any offence under the 2009 Act, the remaining sexual offences at common law, the offences in the Criminal Law (Consolidation) (Scotland) Act 1995 and any offence where there was a significant sexual aspect. The prescribed courts are all sheriff courts sitting in solemn jurisdiction and the High Court – Victim Statements (Prescribed Offences) (No.2) (Scotland) Order 2009 (SSI 2009/71) and Victim Statements (Prescribed Courts) (Scotland) Order 2009 (SSI 2009/134).

10 Paras 62 and 68 of the Criminal Justice (Scotland) Bill (SP Bill 50) Policy Memorandum.

11 Or after doing so but before sentence is imposed. In summary proceedings any statement made should be placed before the court when a plea of guilty is tendered or when the accused is convicted but before sentence is passed.

12 *HM Advocate v GH* [2023] HCJAC 45 at para 19.

of *Gemmell v HM Advocate*[13] provides general guidance as to the circumstances in which a discount of sentence may be available in both custodial and non-custodial disposals. It affirms that the questions of whether to grant a discount, and if so of how much, are for the discretion of the sentencer. Having emphasised that principle, the court in *Gemmell* also accepted that the approach by way of a sliding scale set out in *Spence v HM Advocate*[14] was sound. That approach has tended to be applied in practice with the result commonly being that a discount of one-third of the sentence will be allowed where the section 76 procedure allowing for a plea of guilty to be intimated in advance of service of the indictment is utilised. A discount of one-quarter is frequently afforded where a plea of guilty is tendered at a preliminary hearing or first diet (so long as that is the first of such hearings), a discount of one-fifth where a plea is tendered at a subsequent preliminary hearing and a discount in the region of one-tenth where a plea of guilty is tendered at the commencement of a trial diet.

THE PARTICULAR SENTENCES AVAILABLE

20.09 The penalties available on conviction for any offence under the 2009 Act are specified in Schedule 2. The full range of non-custodial sentences are available in respect of each offence and imprisonment (or detention) subject to the maximum specified is also available in respect of each offence. No minimum sentence is prescribed for any of the offences created by the Act.

20.10 It is beyond the scope of this work to attempt to identify the appropriate range or type of sentence which will fall to be imposed in respect of particular sexual offences. What follows is a discussion in relation to aspects of the more commonly encountered disposals in sexual offences cases. Certain decisions which provide general and high level guidance in relation to particular offences are also identified.

Non-custodial disposals

20.11 Perhaps the non-custodial disposal most likely to feature in sentencing for a sexual offence is a community payback order. This constitutes a flexible form of sentencing which can be moulded so as to provide a suitable element of punishment, rehabilitation and public protection. The provisions governing the imposition of a community payback order are set out between sections 227A and 227ZJ of the 1995 Act. If the court is considering disposing of the case by way of such an order it must, in most circumstances, first obtain a report from an officer of a local authority informing it about the offender and his circumstances.[15]

13 2012 SCCR 176.

14 2008 JC 174.

15 A report from a local authority officer in relation to the offender will be necessary before any community payback order may be imposed, unless the only requirement contained within the order is a level 1 unpaid work or other activity requirement – 1995 Act, s 227B(4) and (6).

20.12 If, after receiving that report, the court is inclined to make a community payback order, it may only do so having explained the purpose and effect of the requirements of the order, as well as the consequences of failing to abide by its terms, and having obtained from the offender confirmation that he both understands those matters and is willing to comply with the requirements to be imposed.[16]

20.13 A community payback order may be imposed under section 227A(1) as an alternative to a sentence of imprisonment, in which case any, or as many as may be appropriate, of the associated requirements listed in section 227A(2) may be imposed. These are:

- an offender supervision requirement;
- a compensation requirement;
- an unpaid work or other activity requirement;
- a programme requirement;
- a residence requirement;
- a mental health treatment requirement;
- a drug treatment requirement;
- an alcohol treatment requirement;
- a conduct requirement; and
- a restricted movement requirement.

20.14 A supervision requirement requires the offender to attend appointments with his responsible officer for a period of between six months and three years for the purpose of promoting his rehabilitation. This must be imposed as part of a community payback order where the offender is under 18 years of age at the time, or if the court imposes any of the other requirements, unless an unpaid work or other activity requirement alone is imposed.[17]

20.15 Even where the court decides to make only an unpaid work or other activity requirement, a local authority officer will be appointed who will have responsibility for making arrangements for the offender to comply with the order. The offender must comply with that officer's instructions. Any order for unpaid work or other activity must be for a minimum 20 hours and no more than 300. In any case, it will be for the responsible officer to determine the nature of the unpaid work to be undertaken and whether other activity as well as unpaid work must be undertaken. When the order is for no more than 100 hours it is known as a level 1 requirement and otherwise as a level 2 requirement. The work or other activity must be completed within three months in the case of a level 1 requirement or six months in the case of a level 2 requirement or, in either case, such longer period as the court may specify.

20.16 A community payback order may also be imposed under section 227A(4) where the court is disposing of an offence punishable by way of a fine, or decides not to impose a sentence of imprisonment or a community payback order as an

16 S 227B.
17 S 227G.

alternative to a sentence of imprisonment. In this event the court is restricted to imposing one or all of an offender supervision requirement, a level 1 unpaid work or other activity requirement and a conduct requirement.

20.17 The relevant provisions concerning the remaining requirements which may be imposed are set out between sections 227H and 227ZJ.

20.18 The opportunity to impose a restricted movement requirement as part of a community payback order has been available since 17 May 2022. Such a requirement may require the offender to be in a specified place at a specified time, or during specified periods, or not to be in a specified place or class of place at a specified time, or during specified periods. The period throughout which a restricted movement requirement has effect must be for not less than 14 days and not more than 12 months. When a restricted movement requirement is imposed the court may specify that compliance with the requirement will be electronically monitored, commonly known as 'tagging'. The detailed provisions covering the arrangements for electronic monitoring are set out in sections 8 to 11 of the Management of Offenders (Scotland) Act 2019. Given this power it would seem unlikely that a court would now wish to impose a restriction of liberty order under section 245A of the 1995 Act by way of disposal when sentencing in a sexual offences case.

Custodial sentences

20.19 The restrictions on the imposition of custodial sentences provided for by sections 204(2) and 207(3) of the 1995 Act apply when sentencing for sexual offences as they do for any other offence.[18]

Presumption against short sentences

20.20 Section 204(3A) of the 1995 Act provides that a court must not pass a sentence of imprisonment for a term of 12 months or less on a person unless it considers that no other method of dealing with the person is appropriate. If the court does decide to impose a sentence of imprisonment despite this presumption it requires to state its reasons for the opinion that no other method of dealing with the person is appropriate and record those reasons in the record of proceedings.

18 A person over the age of 21 who has not previously been sentenced to prison or detention may not be sentenced to a period of imprisonment unless the court considers that no other method of dealing with him is appropriate. A person under 21 may not be given a custodial sentence unless the court is satisfied that no other method of dealing with him is appropriate. In this case detention rather than imprisonment will be imposed. In either case the court requires to obtain a report from an officer of a local authority to assist it in determining whether any other sentence is appropriate.

Remit for sentence from the sheriff court

20.21 Where a case is prosecuted on indictment in the sheriff court section 195 of the 1995 Act allows the sheriff to remit the convicted person to the High Court for sentencing, if he or she considers their sentencing powers to be inadequate. Relatively few sexual offences cases are remitted; those that are tend to involve offenders with a substantial or serious record of previous sexual offending, or inchoate sexual offences whose circumstances suggest the offender presents a serious risk to the public, or both.

The form of sentence to be imposed

20.22 When passing sentence in sexual offences cases the court is regularly faced with having to select a sentence for multiple offences, involving either repeat offending against one complainer or against different complainers or both, in the context of a course of conduct, often over many years. In such cases the court may need to determine whether to impose concurrent, consecutive or *cumulo* sentences. It remains a matter of discretion for a sentencing judge to determine what form the sentences should take[19] but certain difficulties can be encountered. Making the sentences run consecutively might result in an excessive sentence, whereas ordering that the sentences should run concurrently might not reflect the overall criminality of the behaviour on the indictment. In such cases there is much to be said for the imposition of a *cumulo* sentence.[20]

20.23 The correct approach to follow in imposing a *cumulo* sentence in respect of multiple charges was set out in the case of *HM Advocate v Fergusson*[21] at paragraph 25, where the court explained that if a cumulative sentence is selected, the judge should explain what sentence would have been selected had the offence, or group of offences, stood alone and why a cumulative sentence of a lesser amount than the sum of the various sentences had been selected.[22]

Extended sentences

20.24 Section 210A of the 1995 Act permits the court to impose an extended sentence if it intends to impose a determinate sentence of imprisonment (or detention) of any length in relation to a sexual offence.[23] Before doing so it must obtain a report

19 *Nicholson v Lees* 1996 JC 173.

20 *HM Advocate v RM* 2024 JC 81at para 46.

21 [2024] HCJAC 22.

22 The overall sentence selected must take account of the totality principle, in other words the total headline sentence must be fair and proportionate (the Scottish Sentencing Council sentencing process guideline para 34).

23 The offences which may lead to the imposition of an extended sentence are specified in s 210A(10). A supervised release order in terms of s 209 of the 1995 Act may not be imposed in relation to a sexual offence.

from a relevant officer of a local authority about the offender and his circumstances. It would not be appropriate to set out publicly the nature of such reports, but they are more detailed reports than ordinary Criminal Justice Social Work Reports and focus on an assessment of risk using standardised risk assessment tools.[24]

20.25 An extended sentence may only be imposed if the court considers that the period of licence which the offender would otherwise be subject to would not be adequate to protect the public from serious harm from the offender. An extended sentence is the aggregate of the specified custodial term and a further extension period. Throughout that extension period the offender will be subject to licence conditions and liable to be recalled to prison to serve the remainder of the aggregate sentence should he fail to comply with any licence condition or otherwise fail to abide by the instructions of his supervising officer.

20.26 In relation to a sexual offence the extension period may not exceed a period of 10 years: section 210A(3)(a). If an extended sentence is imposed on conviction for a statutory offence the aggregate sentence must not exceed the maximum term of imprisonment provided for in relation to that offence: section 210A(5). Subject to this restriction, if an extended sentence is to be imposed in the sheriff court the sheriff may impose a custodial term of up to the maximum term which he or she may impose and an extension period of up to a further five years.[25]

20.27 It is important to understand the nature of an extended sentence, when it may be imposed and in what circumstances:

> 'An extended sentence has a considerable penal effect, given the power to revoke the licence and recall the offender to prison. Its purpose is to allow the court to make provision for public protection where that is necessary while not imposing a custodial sentence, which from other perspectives, might be disproportionate.'[26]

20.28 An extended sentence cannot be passed in order to ensure that the offender engages in post-release work and supervision simply because it would be in the public interest for him to do so.[27] Furthermore, it must be kept in mind that a sexual offender who is sentenced to a period of imprisonment of more than six months but less than four years, unlike other short-term prisoners, will be subject to the notification requirements of Part 2 of the Sexual Offences Act 2003 and remain subject to licence

24 While such reports generally do canvass the level of risk posed by the offender it is not an absolute requirement that they do so before an extended sentence may be passed, or that the report contains a recommendation for extended supervision. All that is strictly necessary is a report about the offender and his circumstances – *HM Advocate v McCarthy* [2021] HCJAC 46; *Spence and Steele v HM Advocate* [2024] HCJAC 11.

25 S 210A(6).

26 *S v HM Advocate* 2017 SCCR 129 at para 21.

27 *Kelly v HM Advocate* 2018 SCCR 104.

conditions until the expiry of the whole term imposed.[28] Before an extended sentence can be passed the court must take account of whatever licence period the offender will be subject to in light of the custodial sentence proposed and then determine whether that period will be sufficient to protect the public from a risk of serious harm. It is only if that licence period is insufficient that an extended sentence can be imposed. That is the level of risk which must be met before an extended sentence can be imposed. This is a particularly important consideration given the frequency with which social enquiry reports suggest the imposition of post-release supervision as part of the sentencing package.[29]

20.29 Five other considerations are important in relation to extended sentences. The decision to impose an extended sentence should not affect the length of the custodial term which the sentencing judge selects.[30] Second, the extension period cannot be discounted in light of a guilty plea since it is concerned only with public safety. If a sentence falls to be discounted then the length of the extension period should only be decided upon once the discounted custodial term has been determined.[31] Third, an extended sentence is not a sentence which is added on to a custodial sentence, nor is it an additional period of time tagged on to the end of the custodial sentence.[32] An extension period may be imposed as a cumulative sentence in respect of a number of charges but it is added to 'a' determinate sentence.[33] Fourth, while a prisoner serving an extended sentence with a custodial element of more than four years remains eligible for release on parole after serving at least half of that period, the automatic early release provisions do not apply.[34] Fifth, an extended sentence may only be imposed in respect of an offence which was committed after 30 September 1998, meaning it is not a competent sentence in older historical offences cases.[35]

28 Section 1 of the Prisoners and Criminal Proceedings (Scotland) Act 1993 provides that short-term prisoners, ie, those who are sentenced to a period of less than four years' imprisonment or detention, are entitled to be released unconditionally on serving one-half of that sentence. The amendments brought about by the Management of Offenders (Scotland) Act 2005 have the effect of imposing a period of post-release supervision on all qualifying sexual offenders which lasts throughout the entire period after release until expiry of the sentence.

29 In *Wood v HM Advocate* 2017 JC 185 at para 27 the court held that this test simply could not be met in the case of individuals who had been in possession of large numbers of category A indecent images of children.

30 *McGowan v HM Advocate* 2005 SCCR 497 at para 15.

31 *Jordan v HM Advocate* 2008 SCCR 618 at para 21.

32 *DS v HM Advocate* 2017 SCCR 129 at para 23.

33 *HM Advocate v Fergusson* [2024] HCJAC 22 at para 27.

34 Up until 1 February 2016 long-term prisoners, ie, those serving sentences of more than four years' imprisonment, were entitled to be released on licence after serving two-thirds of their sentence, unless earlier released on parole. Those sentenced after that date are only entitled to be released on licence when six months of their sentence is left to be served. A prisoner serving an extended sentence has no entitlement to be released prior to the expiry of the whole custodial element – Prisoners and Criminal Proceedings (Scotland) Act 1993, s 1(1A)(b)(ii).

35 1995 Act, s 210A(9), Crime and Disorder Act 1998 (Commencement No. 2 and Transitional Provisions) Order 1998/2327.

Orders for lifelong restriction

20.30 Section 210F of the 1995 Act provides for the imposition of a sentence of imprisonment or detention for an indeterminate period known as an order for lifelong restriction. This sentence is mandatory in relation to a defined sexual offence[36] where the court is satisfied, on the balance of probabilities, that the risk criteria specified in section 210E are met. The risk criteria are that:

> '… the nature of, or the circumstances of the commission of, the offence of which the convicted person has been found guilty either in themselves or as part of a pattern of behaviour are such as to demonstrate that there is a likelihood that he, if at liberty, will seriously endanger the lives, or physical or psychological well-being, of members of the public at large.'

20.31 This requires not only a serious risk by the offender but also that there is a link between the offence and that risk, or that the offence fits into a pattern of behaviour within the scope of the risk criteria. If there is no such link, the risk criteria cannot be satisfied, irrespective of the general level of risk posed by the offender in terms of the risk assessment report prepared on him.[37]

20.32 An order for lifelong restriction can only be made in the High Court. Where cases are prosecuted on indictment in the sheriff court the sheriff may remit the case to the High Court if it appears to him or her that the risk criteria may be met.[38]

20.33 The process for making an order for lifelong restriction begins with section 210B of the 1995 Act. That section provides that when considering sentence in a defined sexual case if the court considers that the risk criteria may be met, it must make a risk assessment order.[39] It is not possible to appeal a decision to make a risk assessment order. A risk assessment order results in a report being prepared on the offender by a psychiatrist or a psychologist accredited by the Risk Management Authority as to what risk the offender being at liberty presents to the safety of the public ('the assessor').

20.34 A risk assessment report is the most detailed and far-reaching report produced for the Scottish criminal courts. Section 210C(1) allows the assessor to take account of previous convictions of the convicted person (including in the rest of the UK and the EU), and any allegations that the person has engaged in criminal behaviour whether or not that behaviour has resulted in prosecution and acquittal. The assessor is required to assess risk as high, medium or low, having regard to

36 An offence listed in s 210A(10) of the 1995 Act.

37 *Kinloch v HM Advocate* 2016 JC 78 at paras 27 and 28; *McKinlay v Her Majesty's Advocate* [2019] HCJAC 15 at para 54.

38 S 195 of the 1995 Act.

39 The court may do so at its own instance or on the motion of the prosecutor if the prosecutor has given notice of his intention to make such a motion.

any standards and guidelines issued by the Risk Management Authority: section 210C(3).[40]

20.35 The practice generally followed is that, once the report has been prepared and sent to the court and defence, the defence will consider whether to instruct a second risk assessment report. This is an entitlement under section 210C(5) but carries the caveat that, once prepared, any such report must be submitted to the court and Crown. It is common, therefore, for the defence to instead instruct a second expert to examine the methodology used by the assessor and to identify any shortcomings in it (a so-called 'critique' of the original risk assessment report) and, on that basis, to decide whether to object to the content or findings of the original report, or to instruct a second report or both. Under section 210C(7), when there is a defence objection to the content or findings of the original report, this requires to be intimated to the court and Crown, stating the grounds of objection. When this happens the Crown and defence are entitled to produce and examine witnesses on both the original risk assessment report and any second risk assessment report instructed under subsection (5). This will generally involve the original assessor, any second assessor and any other defence-instructed expert giving evidence and being cross-examined.

20.36 Once the risk assessment report is available the court is required to take account of it, along with any other report, evidence or information available to it, and, if satisfied on a balance of probabilities that the risk criteria are met, it must then impose an order for lifelong restriction: section 210F(1).[41] In reaching that assessment, the court must consider the terms of the risk assessment report but is not bound by it. As the Court stated in *Ferguson*[42] (at paragraph 105):

> 'There is no indication that only those categorised as a 'high risk' should be made the subject of an OLR or that those thought by the risk assessor to be at 'low risk' should not be made so subject. This lack of instruction accords with the general principle that sentencing is for the judge, and not the risk assessor. In that context, the judge may disagree with the assessor's categorisation, having regard to his/her own knowledge and experience or because he/she does not consider that the risk assessor's conclusion is supported by his analysis of the facts.'

20.37 The Court went on to say (at paragraph 106) that an assessment that the offender is of high risk will, if the judge accepts it, be a strong indicator towards the necessity of an OLR, but not binding on the judge.[43]

40 A statutory body created by the Criminal Justice (Scotland) Act 2003 for this purpose and for the effective assessment and minimisation of the risk that offenders may pose to the pose to the public generally.

41 A detailed analysis of what considerations apply to the making of an order for lifelong restriction can be found in the case of *Ferguson v HM Advocate* 2014 SCCR 244.

42 Cited above.

43 See also *Laird v HM Advocate* 2015 SCCR 434 in which the court held that a judge is entitled to take the view that the criteria are met when the report has assessed the risk as medium.

20.38 There is a defence right of appeal against the making of an order (in the same way as any other sentence) and a limited right for the Crown to appeal against the refusal to make an order, on the sole ground that on a balance of probabilities the risk criteria are met (section 210F(3)).

20.39 Where an order for lifelong restriction is imposed, the court is obliged to identify the 'punishment part', being the period which must elapse before the offender is entitled to apply for release on parole. The punishment part falls to be calculated according to the somewhat complicated procedure set out in sections 2, 2A and 2B of the Prisoners and Criminal Proceedings (Scotland) Act 1993.

20.40 That procedure takes account of the different ways in which the public protection element of a custodial sentence is reflected as between a determinate period of imprisonment and an order for lifelong restriction and seeks to give effect to the manner in which the rules regarding early release apply. The statutory provisions as now framed were introduced by the Criminal Cases (Punishment and Review) (Scotland) Act 2012 and a helpful account of the evolution of the statutory provisions, as influenced by the developing case law in this area, is set out between paragraphs 9 and 30 of the Policy Memorandum relating to the preceding Bill.[44]

20.41 Where an order for lifelong restriction is imposed, the public protection element of the sentence is reflected in the fact that the offender will not be released until the Parole Board is satisfied that it is no longer necessary for the protection of the public that he should be confined. In an ordinary custodial sentence any element of public protection is simply an unspecified portion of the total sentence selected. The underlying purpose of the statutory provisions introduced in 2012 is to ensure that the court has a level of discretion available to it to specify that a prisoner who receives an order for lifelog restriction can become eligible to apply for parole at a point when the court considers that he will have served an appropriate period of imprisonment to satisfy the need for punishment of the offender.

20.42 This is achieved by following the distinct steps set out in sections 2A and 2B of the Prisoners and Criminal Proceedings (Scotland) Act 1993. Accordingly, when an order for lifelong restriction is to be imposed, the first step in determining the appropriate punishment part is to identify the period of imprisonment which would have been appropriate had the court not been inclined to make an order for lifelong restriction. In carrying out this exercise the court must 'strip out' (or ignore) any period in that notional sentence that would have been necessary for public protection. This is the effect of section 2A(1)(a) as read with section 2A(2)(a).

20.43 The next step is to identify the part of that adjusted notional period of imprisonment which would represent an appropriate period to satisfy the requirements of retribution and deterrence (section 2A(1)(b)). That exercise is achieved by applying section 2A(2)(b) along with section 2B(1). Doing so informs

44 Criminal Cases (Punishment and Review) (Scotland) Bill (SP Bill 5) as introduced in the Scottish Parliament on 30 November 2011.

the sentencer that the relevant period is one half of the adjusted period of the notional sentence of imprisonment as has been identified.

20.44 The court may specify a greater period than one half, if it is appropriate to do so taking account of the seriousness of the offence, or of the offence combined with other offences of which the prisoner is convicted on the same indictment or where the offence was committed when the prisoner was serving a period of imprisonment for another offence and any previous convictions which the prisoner may have – section 2B(1)(b), (2) and (5). This provides the court with a level of discretion, by permitting it to select a period falling within the range of one half of and the full amount of the part of the notional determinate sentence relating to punishment, to ensure that a prisoner serving an order for lifelong restriction does not become eligible for release prior to having served an appropriate period of imprisonment to satisfy the need for punishment.[45]

20.45 Once these two steps have been completed the final stage is to determine whether the figure for the punishment part identified at this stage falls to be discounted in terms of section 196 of the 1995 Act – section 2A(1)(c) as read with subsection (2)(c). Some sentencing statements issued by judges who impose orders for lifelong restriction appear to demonstrate that there is a level of variation in the stage at which the section 196 discount is afforded, with some judges taking it into account at the stage of identifying the adjusted notional period of imprisonment applicable to a determinate sentence, ie, before an appropriate period to satisfy the requirements of retribution and deterrence is selected. This would appear to be in direct conflict with the statutory provision which provides (in section 2A(2)(c)) that the assessment of any section 196 discount is inapplicable until the preceding steps have been completed.

20.46 The punishment part selected cannot exceed the maximum penalty for the offence of which the offender is convicted but there is nothing to prevent an order for lifelong restriction being imposed by way of sentence for a statutory offence which prescribes a particular maximum penalty.[46]

20.47 If an offender satisfies the criteria for a compulsion order under section 57A of the 1995 Act (an order for the detention and treatment of someone who has

45 Para 39 of the Policy Memorandum shows the effect of the legislation by giving the example of a case where the starting determinate sentence would have been 12 years, and the offender has pled guilty at an early stage:

> 'Using the Bill, the court would set the punishment part of the non-mandatory life sentence as follows. The starting notional determinate sentence would have been 12 years. The protection of the public element is 2 years. This leaves 10 years. The court therefore has discretion to set the punishment part at between 5 years and 10 years (this being between one half of and the full amount of the part of the notional determinate sentence relating to punishment (i.e. retribution and deterrence) and excludes the protection of the public element). Whatever the court decides, a sentence discount of 25% applies for an early guilty plea. This means a punishment part for offender A of between 3 years 9 months and 7 years 6 months can be set'.

46 *HM Advocate v Henderson* 2008 SLT 1077.

a mental disorder) and the court is satisfied that the risk criteria are also met it may either impose an order for lifelong restriction or a compulsion order.[47]

20.48 If considering the imposition of either an extended sentence or an order for lifelong restriction, the sentencer is required to make an assessment of the level of risk which the offender will likely pose at the point of release from custody. If the period of licence which is likely to be available at that point is thought to be inadequate to protect the public from serious harm then an extended sentence will be appropriate. If it is thought that at the expiry of the custodial element of a proposed extended sentence the offender will continue indefinitely to endanger the public seriously an order for lifelong restriction will be appropriate.[48]

The level of custodial sentence to be imposed

20.49 Once approved and published, the Scottish Sentencing Council's guideline on sentencing in sexual offences will provide guidance as to the nature of sentences which are appropriate in respect of particular offences and as to the range which may be appropriate for custodial sentences.

20.50 Many of the offences provided for by the Sexual Offences (Scotland) Act 2009 are likely to be of such seriousness as to warrant a custodial sentence. Possession of indecent images of children, at least where significant numbers of category A images are involved,[49] also falls into this category.

20.51 Beyond these statements it is very difficult to offer any even general guidance as to the sentence to be imposed in relation to specific offences. It would perhaps be uncontroversial to assert that a custodial sentence would be almost inevitable in any circumstances involving a contravention of sections 1 or 18 of the 2009 Act.[50] However every sentence requires to be individual to the circumstances of the case. As was made plain by the court in granting a Crown appeal against sentence in the case of *HM Advocate v TJ*,[51] there was no such thing as a generic serious rape by

47 1995 Act, s 210F.

48 *Miller v HM Advocate* [2024] HCJAC 3 at para 7.

49 In *Wood v HM Advocate* 2017 JC 185 at para 30, the Lord Justice General stated that a significant custodial disposal ought normally to be imposed for the possession of a significant amount of category A images and that in order to justify a community based disposal there would require to be some particular circumstance, such as a relatively fleeting possession, or particularly compelling personal circumstances, such as extreme old age.

50 In March 2017 a judge granted an absolute discharge to an offender who had pled guilty to the offence of rape of a girl under the age of 13 years, contrary to s 18 of the Act. The offender was 19 years old at the time and the victim was aged 12 years and 7 months. The circumstances as described appear to have been very unusual and included powerful evidence to the effect that the accused understood the victim to be 16 years old. The sexual intercourse took place in circumstances which the sentencing judge described as including the victim participating willingly – Scottish Legal News 17 March 2017.

51 2024 JC 1. The case involved a single charge of rape involving some use of force in the course of what was described as a sustained attack. The headline sentence of five years' imprisonment was held to be unduly lenient and was replaced by a sentence of nine years.

a generic first offender. In refusing a Crown appeal against sentence in the case of *HM Advocate v G (M)* the court observed that a sentence of four years' imprisonment for a contravention of section 1 of the 2009 Act was undoubtedly a lenient one.[52] One might perhaps conclude that this represents the lower, if not the lowest, end of the sentencing range for this offence in relation to an adult offender pleading not guilty and being convicted after trial.[53] By way of cross-check, four years' imprisonment is the lowest point in the England and Wales sentencing guideline range for such an offence.[54]

20.52 Some guidance in relation to sentencing for sexual offences committed whilst in a position of trust was offered in the case of *HM Advocate v Collins*, where the court conducted a review of some of the then relevant authorities.[55] The conclusions arrived at were:

- for sexual offences committed whilst in a position of trust or authority comprising historic charges of lewd and libidinous practices involving, for example, digital penetration or attempted sodomy, or offences involving indecent assault over a prolonged period of time, headline sentences of between four and nine years' imprisonment will be appropriate;
- for an offence involving the rape of a complainer or other penetrative sexual abuse of several complainers in respect of whom the offender was in a position of trust or authority, headline sentences in the region of eight to 10 years' imprisonment will be appropriate.

Aggravation under section 1 of the Abusive Behaviour and Sexual Harm (Scotland) Act 2016

20.53 Where an offence is libelled (or specified in a complaint) as being aggravated by involving abuse of the partner or ex-partner of the accused, the aggravation will be established where the accused person intends to cause that partner to suffer physical or psychological harm or, if committing an offence against that partner, that person is reckless as to whether physical or psychological harm is caused. For these purposes, partner means a spouse or civil partner, those living together as if spouses or civil partners, or those in an intimate personal relationship with each other. Evidence from a single source is sufficient to establish the aggravation. If established the court

52 2023 JC 68.

53 In the case *of HM Advocate v Shearer* 2003 SLT 1354, which concerned rape while the complainer was asleep or unconscious through alcohol (and which, prior to *Lord Advocate's Reference No 1 of 2001* 2002 SLT 466, would have been charged as clandestine injury, attracting a lower sentence), the court increased the sentence imposed from one of 18 months' imprisonment to one of three and a half years to reflect the fact that the offence was one of rape. As noted at para 19 of *HM Advocate v Cooperwhite* 2013 SCCR 461, that became the benchmark for sentences in rape cases of that kind, but that no longer reflects current sentencing practice for such cases, and no general distinction is drawn between sentencing for rape whilst the complainer is asleep or unconscious and other types of rape.

54 Rape – Sentencing (sentencingcouncil.org.uk).

55 2017 JC 99.

must take the aggravation into account in determining the appropriate sentence. The importance of this statutory aggravation was emphasised by the Lord Justice General in the case of *McGowan v HM Advocate*[56] where he stated that:

> 'No fixed percentage or other level of additional penalty is stipulated in respect of an abuse of partner aggravation of this nature, but its inclusion acknowledges the appropriate seriousness with which domestic offences are to be treated. It will no doubt depend on the circumstances of the cases, but it must be assumed that, although Parliament was content to leave the overall sentence to the discretion of the judge, it intended that the courts should normally add a significant penalty to that which would have attended a similar, but non partner abuse aggravated, crime.'

The subsequent case of *HM Advocate v AP*[57] can be seen to reinforce the need for an aggravation under the 2016 Act to be reflected in a significant additional penalty. In that case, which was a successful Crown appeal against an unduly lenient sentence, the court considered what might have been the appropriate sentences for each of two charges of rape perpetrated against a partner and an ex-partner, had it not been minded to impose a cumulo sentence. At paragraph 49 it observed that sentences of four and a half years on each charge would have been appropriate with an increase of about one year to reflect the statutory aggravation. Although it is clear that the court was not intending to set out general guidance, it is instructive to see that the additional penalty it had in mind was a little over 20% of the substantive sentence.

ANCILLARY ORDERS

Notification requirements

20.54 A person convicted of a sexual offence as listed in Schedule 3 to the Sexual Offences Act 2003 is known as a 'relevant offender' and becomes subject to the notification requirements specified in Part 2 of that Act. The period for which an individual will be required to comply with the notification requirements is identified by reference to the table set out in section 82 of the Act. Where either an order for lifelong restriction or a sentence of imprisonment for a term of 30 months or more has been imposed, the relevant offender will be liable to the notification requirements for an indefinite period. Where a sentence of imprisonment of between six and 30 months is imposed the period will be for 10 years, commencing from the date of sentencing. Where a sentence of imprisonment for a term of six months or less is imposed the period will be for seven years. If a community payback order including an offender supervision requirement is imposed the period will be the

56 [2024] HCJAC 20 at para 17.
57 [2024] HCJAC 31.

period specified for the supervision requirement. If any other disposal is ordered the offender will be subject to the notification requirements for a period of five years.[58]

20.55 Provisions concerning the review of any indefinite notification requirement are set out in sections 88A to 88H of the 2003 Act.

20.56 Where the offender is under the age of 18 years at the date of conviction the periods of 10 years, seven years and five years are subject to a deduction of one-half.[59] Where a relevant offender is under 16 years of age the court may direct that the notification obligations imposed on him are to be treated as obligations on the parent (or person having parental responsibilities) and the parent must ensure that the offender attends at the police station with him when notification is being given.[60]

20.57 An offender subject to the notification requirements must attend at a prescribed police station within three days of conviction (ignoring any period throughout which he was remanded in custody or serving a sentence of imprisonment) and provide information as to his date of birth, national insurance number, home address and whether he has any passports and if so, the relevant information concerning them. Any changes in any of this information must be notified within a period of three days of that change or of his release from custody.

20.58 If requested to do so when providing the required information, the offender must allow a police officer to take a photograph of any part of him and provide to that officer such relevant physical data as is considered appropriate. He must also allow samples of hair and finger or toe nails to be taken and to permit swabbing from an external part of his body along with a sample from inside his mouth by means of swabbing.[61]

20.59 A relevant offender is also required to provide notification should he intend to travel outside the United Kingdom. Not less than seven days before the date of his departure he must provide information as to the date on which he will leave the United Kingdom, the country to which he will travel and his point of arrival. In addition, where he holds such information, the offender must disclose his point of arrival in any additional country to which he intends to travel, the identity of any carrier that he intends to use for the purpose of departure from and return to the United Kingdom and of travelling to any other point of arrival, the dates on which he intends to be in each country to which he intends to travel, details of his accommodation arrangements and the date on which he intends to return to the United Kingdom along with his intended point of arrival.[62]

58 2003 Act, s 82. Different periods apply if a restriction order or other hospital order is imposed.
59 S 82(2).
60 2003 Act, s 89.
61 2003 Act, s 87(5A).
62 2003 Act, s 86, Sexual Offences Act 2003 (Travel Notification Requirements) (Scotland) Regulations SSI 2004/205.

Sexual Offences Act 2003 – Schedule 3 paragraph 60

20.60 As noted above, when a court is passing sentence in relation to a sexual offence specified in Schedule 3 to the 2003 Act, the notification requirements will be triggered, as will the opportunity to impose a sexual harm prevention order.[63] The effect of paragraph 60 of that schedule is that the same effect is brought about where sentence is to be passed in relation to an offence not listed but where the court determines that there was a significant sexual aspect to the offender's behaviour in committing the offence.

20.61 Whilst the question of whether or not the conduct concerned has a significant sexual aspect to it is primarily a matter for the judge of first instance to determine, in the case of *Hay v HM Advocate*[64] the Appeal Court set down guidance as to how this assessment should be carried out:

- The purpose of registration in terms of the notification requirements is not punitive but it does nonetheless create a grave stigma which places onerous restrictions and requirements on the offender's life (paragraph 35).
- Whether there is a significant sexual aspect to the offender's conduct is not necessarily to be determined exclusively by considering the acts libelled, it could be informed by a consideration of the whole circumstances surrounding the offence but any previous convictions cannot assist as they do not constitute behaviour in the context of paragraph 60 (paragraphs 49 and 51).
- Since the purpose of registration is to protect the public against the perceived danger, the question whether a sexual aspect of the accused's behaviour was significant should be assessed in that light. One way to approach that is to consider whether the sexual aspect is important enough to merit attention as indicating an underlying sexual disorder or deviance from which society is entitled to be protected (paragraph 52).
- Sentencers should consider the accused's behaviour in the context of the purpose and the effects of registration, keep a sense of proportion and use their common sense (paragraph 52).

20.62 In the same vein as the considerations discussed in *Hay,* the offender's motivation in engaging in his conduct can be a factor of importance.[65]

20.63 The question of whether paragraph 60 should be given effect to may often arise in circumstances where a charge of assault (other than indecent assault) or of breach of the peace has an apparently sexual element to it. An example of the latter circumstance can be seen in the case of *Buchan v Aziz,*[66] which concerned comments made by a taxi driver to two young women suggesting that he would take them home if they offered him sex. It was accepted that the evidence of the appellant's conduct was sufficient to constitute a breach of the peace (the main issue in the appeal being

63 See **20.76–20.79** below.

64 2014 JC 19.

65 *McHugh v Harvie* 2015 SCCR 430 at para 8.

66 2023 JC 51.

whether it constituted the offence of communicating indecently under section 7 of the 2009 Act). The court had no difficulty in holding that the appellant's conduct, if viewed as a breach of the peace, would have involved a significant sexual aspect. In delivering the opinion of the court at paragraph 26 the Lord Justice General stated:

> 'No doubt it is necessary for the sentencer to keep a sense of proportion and to use common sense when determining whether a significant sexual aspect is evident (*Hay v HM Advocate*). If the conduct indicates an underlying sexual disorder or deviance, that will be a strong indicator. Here, the respondent was carrying out his employment as a licensed taxi driver with responsibilities towards the persons whom he might encounter in his trade. Those persons, especially if they are vulnerable as a result of youth and alcohol, are entitled to be protected from predatory males seeking sexual favours in exchange for fares.'

20.64 Criminal conduct constituting the crime of assault or breach of the peace which appears to have some sexual connotations to it need not always satisfy the requirement of paragraph 60. The need for that aspect to be 'significant' is important, as can be seen from cases such as *Heatherall v McGowan*,[67] a case of breach of the peace involving the accused exposing himself to a young lady, and *Young v Brown*[68] and *Thomson v Dunn*,[69] both cases of assault involving uninvited kissing or touching of women.

20.65 In none of these cases was any perceived sexual element to the conduct sufficiently significant to meet the requirements of paragraph 60. In each case a relevant consideration was the offender's level of intoxication. This has sometimes led to the suggestion that drink-fuelled behaviour is to be seen as something distinct from sexual behaviour for the purposes of paragraph 60. However the notification requirements cannot be avoided just because the offender would not have behaved in the same way if sober or less intoxicated. Alcohol consumption may cause many forms of disinhibited conduct but disinhibited sexual behaviour is one such type. There may therefore be many circumstances in which it is obvious that an offender's conduct has a significant sexual aspect to it regardless of the issue of intoxication.[70] An example of such a case is *McGuire v Dunn*[71] in which an extremely drunk man was seen to be masturbating in public. In addressing the appellant's submission that the sexual aspect involved in his conduct was not 'significant' the Lord Justice Clerk sated:

> 'The behaviour in this case was, no doubt, caused partly by the disinhibiting effects of alcohol. This court is reasonably familiar with those effects in the context of cases which come before it. In this situation, however, as the Sheriff

67 2014 JC 8.
68 2014 JC 4.
69 2014 JC 16.
70 *Sutherland v HM Advocate* 2017 SCCR 268 at para 21.
71 [2012] HCJAC 86.

has observed, the type of behaviour under consideration is not of a type which is commonly, or indeed even occasionally, encountered in connection with intoxicated persons in city centre public streets. The fact that this is so points towards there being something beyond mere intoxication as a factor in the offence.'

20.66 Other conduct which may also require consideration to be given to whether the test in paragraph 60 of Schedule 3 is met can arise out of what is sometimes, but often misleadingly, called 'revenge porn'. Individuals who disclose intimate images on a private basis have little or no control of the image once it has been sent and are vulnerable to considerable embarrassment and upset if that anticipated privacy is not maintained. Media coverage has highlighted many examples of circumstances in which such unauthorised public disclosure has taken place by uploading or posting images onto one internet platform or another. Such unauthorised disclosure can involve criminal conduct which, depending on the circumstances, might be prosecuted as a contravention of section 6 of the 2009 Act, section 127 of the Communications Act 2003, section 2 of the Abusive and Sexual Harm (Scotland) Act 2016, or as a contravention of section 38 of the Criminal Justice and Licensing (Scotland) Act 2010.

20.67 A contravention of section 6 of the 2009 Act will lead to automatic application of the notification requirements, whereas a prosecution under any of the remaining provisions will do so only if paragraph 60 applies. This may be of particular importance in relation to prosecutions under section 2 of the Abusive and Sexual Harm (Scotland) Act 2016, since this is the statutory vehicle through which the Scottish Parliament sought to address public concern over 'revenge porn' and to make it clear that such non-consensual sharing or publishing of intimate images constituted a criminal offence (see Chapter 7: Further offences to protect those in intimate relationships).[72] The fact that Schedule 3 to the 2003 Act has not been amended so as to include contraventions of section 2 of this Act carries with it the recognition that not all cases of unauthorised sharing or publication of intimate images will require the application of the notification requirements.

20.68 As with any case in which this question arises, it will be for the sentencer to determine as a question of fact whether the conduct concerned has a significant sexual aspect to it applying the guidance given in *Hay v HM Advocate*. However, the context in which a person came into possession of an intimate image which is then shared or published and the reason for that disclosure can be important. The cases of *Sutherland v HM Advocate*[73] and *Sorrell v PF, Greenock*[74] may be instructive in this regard as both draw attention to the motivation which can lead to such conduct and to the distinction which exists between two different forms of public protection which can be engaged when considering criminal acts of this type. The first form is the protection to be afforded to an individual who has previously entrusted a partner

[72] Abusive Behaviour and Sexual Harm (Scotland) Bill Policy Memorandum paras 22–42.
[73] 2017 SCCR 268.
[74] [2020] SAC (Crim) 2.

or friend with an intimate image. Such a person is entitled to be protected from the deliberately caused distress which is often the motivation for subsequent unauthorised sharing.[75] That type of public protection is provided for by criminalising the conduct and the sanctions available, regardless of whether any sexual motivation is involved. The second type of public protection is that which is encompassed within registration, which is designed to enable monitoring of an individual who poses a continuing danger to others, or who displays an underlying sexual disorder or deviance from which society is entitled to be protected.[76] It follows that on conviction of an offence under section 2 of the Abusive and Sexual Harm (Scotland) Act 2016 it will be for the presiding sheriff or judge to determine whether a further element of public protection from the individual as a sex offender is necessary by considering whether the offence discloses a significant sexual aspect. It is implicit that it need not do so.

20.69 Where the Crown libels an offence that is not specified in Schedule 3 and intends, in the event of conviction, to contend that there is a significant sexual aspect to the offender's behaviour that fact should be narrated in the libel itself, together with the alleged facts and circumstances from which that aspect is to be inferred. If the Crown charges an offence of assault and in the event of conviction intends to contend that the assault was an indecent assault fair notice requires that the libel should specifically allege indecent assault. The sentencing judge may raise the question of whether paragraph 60 applies of his own volition.[77]

20.70 There is no statutory right of appeal against a determination under paragraph 60 but such cases have generally been appealed by way of a Bill of Suspension.

Lists of persons unsuitable to work with children or protected adults

20.71 Section 1 of the Protection of Vulnerable Groups (Scotland) Act 2007 requires the Scottish Minsters to keep lists of those individuals deemed unfit to work with children or vulnerable adults. Where a court convicts an individual of an offence listed in Schedules 1 or 2 to the Protection of Vulnerable Groups (Scotland) Act 2007 (Automatic Listing) (Specified Criteria) Order 2010 it must provide to the Scottish Ministers a statement of the offence of which the individual was convicted and a copy of the indictment, so that they may be included in whichever list the Ministers deem appropriate. The sexual offences which are included for these purposes are:

- rape;
- sodomy;
- a contravention of section 5(1) of the Criminal Law Consolidation (Scotland) Act 1995;

75 One of the requirements of the s 2 offence is that the disclosure is intended to cause the other person fear, alarm or distress.

76 *Sutherland* at paras 26–29.

77 *Hay* paras 41, 45 and 48. In *McHugh v Harvie* the matter was raised by the sheriff.

- a contravention of section 311(2)(a) of the Mental Health (Care and Treatment) (Scotland) Act 2003; and
- a contravention of any of sections 1, 2, 3, 18, 19 or 20 of the Sexual Offences (Scotland) Act 2009.[78]

Non-harassment orders

20.72 There are two types of non-harassment orders in the 1995 Act: general orders under section 234A and orders in domestic abuse cases under section 234AZA.

Orders under section 234A

20.73 Where a person is convicted of an offence involving misconduct towards another person, or is acquitted by reason of a special defence that he was not criminally responsible by reason of mental disorder, or where he was found unfit for trial in terms of section 53F of the 1995 Act, the prosecutor may apply to the court to make a non-harassment order against that person. Such an order may be made instead of, or in addition to, dealing with the person in any other way. The court will make such an order if satisfied on the balance of probabilities that it is appropriate to do so in order to protect the victim from harassment. A non-harassment order requires the person to refrain for such period as may be specified in the order from such conduct in relation to the victim as may be specified. Misconduct includes conduct that causes alarm or distress.[79]

Orders under section 234AZA (domestic abuse cases)

20.74 Where the offence of which the person is convicted is aggravated by involving abuse of that person's partner in terms of section 1 of the 2016 Act, the approach which the court must take is different. The court must consider the question of whether or not to impose a non-harassment order of its own volition, irrespective of any application by the Crown.[80] In such circumstances the court must then make a non-harassment order unless it is positively able to conclude that there is no need for the victim to be protected by such an order: section 234AZA(4) and (5). If the information before it is not sufficient to enable the court so to conclude the order must be made. Accordingly, a non-harassment order may be made even if the victim does not wish such protection.[81]

78 Automatic listing only applies in relation to convictions under ss 3 and 20 of the 2009 Act where the offence consists of a contravention of ss 3(1) and (2)(a) or 20(1) and (2)(a) – sexual assault by intentional or reckless sexual penetration of the victim's vagina, anus or mouth. The other types of sexual assault specified in each of ss 3 and 20 do not have the same effect by virtue of paras 8 and 11 of each of Schs 1 and 2 to the Order.

79 1995 Act, s 234A.

80 1995 Act, s 234AZA.

81 1995 Act, s 234AZA, *Finlay v PF, Perth* 2021 SLT (Sh Ct) 133 as approved by *HM Advocate v RM* [2023] HCJAC 43.

20.75 Section 234AZA(3) allows for the court, in addition to making a non-harassment order to protect the victim of domestic abuse, to extend the order to a child, if the court considers it appropriate for the child to be protected by the order. This power to extend the order applies when either: (a) the child usually resides with the victim, the convicted person or both; or (b) the offence is one under section 1(1) of the Domestic Abuse (Scotland) Act 2018 and one of the child aggravations in section 5(1) of the Act applies.[82] In *W (G) v HM Advocate*[83] an appeal concerning the making of NHOs for children, the Appeal Court found that there was a two-stage process for considering whether to make a non-harassment order in respect of a child: (i) the appropriateness test under subsection (3); and (ii) the general statutory test for making an order under subsections (4) and (5).

20.76 In addressing the appropriateness test under subsection (3), the Court found that when (b) applied, it was difficult to conceive of any circumstances in which an order would not be appropriate. For (a), it was less straightforward and depended on the circumstances of the case. It observed (at paragraph 23):

> 'Where such a child has witnessed, overheard or been a victim of domestic violence, it will only be rarely that the court should not have that child 'in mind' for the purposes of addressing the question posed in section 234AZA(4). Thereafter, issues such as the nature of the offence, the persistence of the offending, the offender's record, steps taken to address any issues the offender might have etc, will come into play when the statutory question is being considered, although there may well be some overlap between the two stages.'

The complainer's and any child's views

20.77 If the Crown seeks a non-harassment order under either of the provisions, it ought to move for the order at the time when it moves for sentence, though a motion may be made at any point until the convicted person is sentenced. If it seeks an order, the Crown will normally obtain the views of the complainer. The courts have not yet considered themselves under a duty to obtain the views of a complainer or child. In *Finlay*,[84] at paragraph 11 the Sheriff Appeal Court observed that section 234AZA does not make provision for the victim's views to be sought – the only criterion for making the order being one of necessity – though in considering that question of necessity, the victim's views may be relevant. The Court went on to state at paragraph 12 that, if a complainer's views on necessity are to be taken into account, it was incumbent on the parties to furnish the court with information as to what those

82 There are three: (i) if the convicted person, A, directs behaviour at a child or makes use of a child in directing behaviour at B (the victim); (ii) if a child sees or hears, or is present during, an incident of behaviour that A directs at B as part of a course of behaviour; (iii) if a reasonable person would consider the course of behaviour, or an incident of A's behaviour that forms part of the course of behaviour, to be likely to adversely affect a child usually residing with A or B (or both).

83 2022 JC 73.

84 See n 81 above.

views are. In *W (G)*, citing *Finlay* the Appeal Court found (at paragraph 26) that the statute does not require that the views of those who might be protected by an order should be sought and the Court 'did not think that necessary in any event'. *Finlay* and *W (G)* turned on an interpretation of section 234AZA. These cases leave open the separate questions of whether, and if so, to what extent, either Article 8 ECHR or the United Nations Convention on the Rights of the Child might require the views of a child to be obtained before any order is made.

Sexual harm prevention orders

20.78 Chapter 3 of the Abusive Behaviour and Sexual Harm (Scotland) Act 2016 provides for the imposition of a sexual harm prevention order (SHPO) on an offender who is convicted of an offence specified in Schedule 3 to the Sexual Offences Act 2003. It may also be made where the individual is acquitted by reason of a special defence that he was not criminally responsible by reason of mental disorder or where he was found unfit for trial in terms of section 53F of the 1995 Act.[85] Sexual harm prevention orders replaced, from 31 March 2023, sexual offences prevention orders, risk of sexual harm orders and foreign travel orders.

20.79 When passing sentence after conviction a sexual harm prevention order may be made in addition to dealing with the offender in any other way and either by the court at its own instance or on the motion of the prosecutor. Before the court can make such an order it requires to be satisfied that it is necessary to do so for the purpose of protecting the public or any particular members of the public from sexual harm from the person, or protecting children under 18 years of age or vulnerable adults generally or any particular children or vulnerable adults from sexual harm from the person outside the United Kingdom.[86]

20.80 The effect of an order can be to prohibit the offender from doing a particular thing or to require him to do a particular thing as specified in the order. The prohibition or requirement will apply throughout the United Kingdom or to particular specified localities for a fixed period of not less than five years.[87] A prohibition within a sexual harm prevention order may prohibit the offender from foreign travel to any country outside the United Kingdom. Any such order must be for a fixed period of not more than five years, but it may subsequently be extended.[88]

20.81 Sections 18 and 19 of the 2016 Act contain provisions concerning the application of the notification requirements to an offender made subject to a sexual harm prevention order.

85 A sexual harm prevention order can also be made by a sheriff on the application of the chief constable in respect of a qualifying offender, ie, a person to whom ss 13, 14 or 15 of the 2016 Act applies.

86 2016 Act, s 11.

87 2016 Act, s 16.

88 2016 Act, s 17.

Appendix 1: The High Court of Justiciary Commission Checklist

HMA v [ ]

PF REF: [ ]

VULNERABLE WITNESSES – EVIDENCE ON COMMISSION

Issues to be considered and ***questions to be answered*** in terms of HC Practice Notes No. 1 of 2017 and No. 1 of 2019 prior to preliminary hearing in cases where special measures are sought in the form of evidence on commission (including cases where it is proposed that a statement or recording will form evidence in chief).

IN ALL CASES

A	Has there been full disclosure?		
B	Has the court been provided with any relevant expert reports and sources of information germane to its consideration of the application?		

IN CASES WHERE IT IS PROPOSED THAT EVIDENCE IN CHIEF WILL TAKE THE FORM OF A STATEMENT AND/OR RECORDING OF AN INTERVIEW AND/OR TRANSCRIPT

Standard protocols govern the circumstances in which visually recorded prior statements may be made available to the defence

C	Where it is proposed to use an audio/ visual recording of JII as evidence in chief, has the Crown checked that the recording is of sufficient quality and is playable on court equipment?		

D	Has the Crown satisfied itself that the evidence in the recording and/or document is all relevant, admissible and in section 288C cases that its admission would not contravene section 274?		
E	Are the defence taking objection to any of the content of the recording/statement as a preliminary issue or otherwise?		
F	Have Crown and defence identified appropriate redactions to address the issues in paras D and E?		

IN ALL CASES

1	Is an interpreter required?		
2	Will the witness affirm or take the oath?		
3	What location for the commission will be the most suitable in the interests of the witness?		
4	What time for the commission is the most suitable in the interests of the witness?		
5	Does any special arrangement require to be made for communication between the accused and solicitor in viewing room and counsel/solicitor in the commission room? [*The standard protocol on communication is set out between Q 25 and Q 26 below*] If there are multiple accused, are any particular arrangements required for the accused to view by way of video link from the nearest court CCTV room?		
6	Should the judge and/or parties introduce themselves to the witness in advance and, if so how and when?		

7	What reasonable adjustments will be required to enable the effective participation of the witness?		
8	Will breaks be required? If the witness may require unscheduled breaks for a personal or medical reason which may be embarrassing to articulate, how is this to be communicated?		
9	What are the lines of enquiry to be pursued in chief and in cross-examination? Is there merit in the submission of written questions in advance of the Commission? [*See also Q 19 below]*		
10	Does the Crown have a section 275 application which may impact on the scope of questioning?		
11	Does the defence have a section 275 application which may impact on the scope of questioning?		
12	*i.* Is it anticipated that reference will be made to prior statements? *ii.* If so, what is the purpose? *iii.* What passages will be referred to? *iv.* Does any prior statement which may need to be put require redaction?		
13	Are any documents or label productions to be put to the witness?		
14	How is this to be managed and will any special equipment or assistance be required?		
15	Can the scope of any questioning be reduced which might shorten the length of the commission *i.* By further agreement of evidence. *ii.* By agreement between parties to avoid unnecessary questioning and duplication on the issues to be addressed?		

16	In cases of multiple accused, how will repetitious questioning be avoided?		
17	What are the specific communication needs of the witness?		
18	Are any communication aids required eg body maps?		
19	What is the appropriate form of questions which are to be asked? In cases of children under 12, and others for whom in terms of PN 1 of 2019 parties consider written questions are appropriate or likely to be required by the Court: Has a list of questions been prepared and intimated to the court: *i.* By the Crown, if the Crown envisages examining in chief? *ii.* By the defence?		
20	How long will the commission take? Please provide an accurate estimate expressed in minutes. *i.* Examination in chief *ii.* Cross examination		
21	What is the extent to which it will be necessary to "put the defence case" to the witness? (See R v Lubemba 2015 1 WLR 1579 and R v Barker 2011 Crim. LR 233)		
22	How is that to be done?		
23	Have parties agreed how this issue may be addressed in due course for the purposes of the jury?		
24	"Where a prior statement is to be used as part of the witness' evidence in chief, is the statement to be shown to the witness in advance of the commission and, if so, how, where and when?"		

<table>
<tr><td>25</td><td>If so, should there be any examination in chief of the witness (and, if so, to what extent)?</td><td></td><td></td></tr>
<tr><td></td><td colspan="3">DEFAULT ARRANGEMENTS FOR COMMISSION HEARINGS
• Pre-commission familiarisation will take place according to standard protocols operated by VIA.
• Wigs and gowns will not be worn.
• The accused will watch proceedings by way of a video link from the nearest court /CCTV room.
• There are standard protocols in place that communication will take place by ‘phone/text between the solicitor (sitting with the accused) and the counsel/solicitor advocate (sitting in the commission room). In many cases SLAB have granted sanction for two solicitors to be available to facilitate communication between the viewing room and the commission room.
• Standard protocols are in place for VIA to ensure that the witness and the accused will not come into contact with each other.</td></tr>
<tr><td>26</td><td colspan="3">If there is a particular issue which may require departure from these standard protocols, please set out the proposed variation and reasons for proposing it</td></tr>
<tr><td></td><td colspan="3">Standard protocols will apply to the arrangements for parties to view the recording after the Commission hearing.
At the preliminary hearing at which an application for commission is granted, the court will stipulate the arrangements.</td></tr>
</table>

Useful References/Links

http://www.theadvocatesgateway.org/

- 3. Planning to question someone with an autism spectrum disorder including Asperger syndrome – New!
- 4. Planning to question someone with a learning disability
- 5. Planning to question someone with ‘hidden’ disabilities: specific language impairment, dyslexia, dyspraxia, dyscalculia and AD(H)
- 6. Planning to question a child or young person
- 7. Additional factors concerning children under 7 (or functioning at a very young age)
- 12. General principles when questioning witnesses and defendants with mental disorder
- 14. Using communication aids in the criminal justice system
- 15. Witnesses and defendants with autism:memory and sensory issues

Special Measures Guidance – CPS, Bar Council and NSPCC

Appendix 2: Section 275 application form

FORM 21.5 **Form of application under section 275(1) of the Criminal Procedure (Scotland) Act 1995**

Rule 21.5

IN THE HIGH COURT OF JUSTICIARY

[or IN THE SHERIFF [or JUSTICE OF THE PEACE] [COURT]

AT (place)

APPLICATION UNDER SECTION 275(1) OF THE CRIMINAL PROCEDURE (SCOTLAND) ACT 1995

by

[A.B.] address

[or Prisoner in the Prison of (place)]

in

HER MAJESTY'S ADVOCATE [or THE PROCURATOR FISCAL, (place)]

Against

(Insert name(s) of accused)

TAKE NOTICE:

That [A.B.] makes an application to the court for the purposes of section 275(1) of the Criminal Procedure (Scotland) Act 1995 as follows:-

1. the following evidence is sought to be admitted or elicited:
2. the nature of the proposed questioning is as follows:
3. the issues to which the evidence is considered to be relevant are as follows:
4. the reasons why the evidence is considered to be relevant are as follows:
5. the inferences which the applicant proposes to submit to the court that it should draw from the evidence are as follows:

(signed)

Index

[*References are to paragraph number*]